The **BEST PLACES**
TO KISS
in the **NORTHWEST**

oft/21

The BEST PLACES

TO KISS

in the NORTHWEST

TERI CITTERMAN

EDITION 10

SASQUATCH BOOKS
SEATTLE

Printed in the United States of America
Published by Sasquatch Books
Distributed by PGW/Perseus

Tenth edition
15 14 13 12 11 10 09 08   9 8 7 6 5 4 3 2 1

ISBN-13: 978-1-57061-545-0
ISBN-10: 1-57061-545-4
ISSN: 1546-525X

Project editor: Rachelle Longé
Cover photograph: © Oliver Eltinger/Solus Photography/Veer.
Cover design: Rosebud Eustace
Interior design and composition: Scott Taylor/FILTER/Talent
Maps: Lisa Brower/GreenEye Design
Indexer: Michael Ferreira

Special Sales

Best Places guidebooks are available at special discounts on bulk purchases for corporate, club, or organization sales promotions, premiums, and gifts. For more information, contact your local bookseller or Special Sales, Best Places Guidebooks, 119 South Main Street, Suite 400, Seattle, Washington 98104, or 800/775-0817.

Sasquatch Books

119 South Main Street, Suite 400
Seattle, WA 98104
206/467-4300
www.sasquatchbooks.com
custserv@sasquatchbooks.com

Contents

British Columbia

Meet Our Writers

Teri Citterman is the editor of this tenth edition of *The Best Places to Kiss in the Northwest* and wrote the San Juans, Washington Wine Country, and Southern Gulf Island chapters. Teri won the Editor's Choice from the Napa Valley Wine Writers Symposium and author of the *Northwest Wine Journal*. A regular contributor to *Seattle Metropolitan* magazine, she writes a wine column for *Wine Press Northwest* and, as an extension of the column, blogs about life paired with wine in An Urban Sip (www.anurbansip.blogspot.com). Her articles have appeared in a variety of other outlets including *Puget Sound Business Journal*, *Portland Business Journal*, *Seattle* magazine, and the *Best Places* travel guidebooks. Though home is Seattle, Teri and her husband, Andreas, are avid travelers and enjoy sipping their way through the world.

Growing up in a suburb near Seattle, **Corey Anderson** often traveled on winter ski vacations to Whistler and spent many summer weekends exploring the Vancouver area, which made it a natural fit for her to take on those chapters. When not working at a marketing and public relations firm, Corey likes to take weekend trips with her husband, Josh, to uncover more great spots around the Pacific Northwest. Corey wrote the Vancouver, Lower Mainland British Columbia, and Puget Sound chapters.

Josh Anderson feels equally at home in his native New York City or on a secluded trail in the Central Cascades, his chapter in the book. He's a part-time screenwriter, and the acquisitions editor for a Seattle-area publishing company, living in Kirkland, Washington, with his wife, Corey, and their big slobbery dog, Brooklyn.

Kelly Burkett, a travel junkie who has lived on three continents and currently calls Seattle home, penned the section on the Olympic Peninsula. She relished touring the area with her Danish boyfriend, to whom she constantly brags about the unbeatable beauty of her home state.

Joanmarie Curran, who contributed to the North Cascades chapter, maintains a steady diet of reading, writing, and traveling. She is otherwise occupied with a medieval Tuscan farmhouse and Seattle real estate.

Originally a Seattleite, freelance writer **Ashley Gartland** now calls Portland home. For her chapters, she stepped outside her city limits to explore Southern Oregon and the Willamette Valley with her fiancé. Her articles appear in *Northwest Palate*, *Portland Monthly*, *Seattle Metropolitan*, and the *Oregonian*.

A Seattle resident for more than 20 years, **Ginny Morey** enjoys writing about restaurants, shopping, and travel ... almost as much as she enjoys going to restaurants, shopping, and traveling. This depth of knowledge made Ginny's job of writing the all-embracing Seattle chapter that much more fun.

Kate Pawlicki, contributer to the Oregon Coast chapter, began traveling up and down the West Coast at the age of three and still enjoys the journey. Her favorite quote comes from Helen Keller: "Life is either a daring adventure or nothing."

Andy Perdue is a third-generation Washington newspaperman who is founder and editor of *Wine Press Northwest*, a glossy consumer magazine that focuses on the wines of Washington, Oregon, British Columbia, and Idaho—which made it a natural that he cover the Okanagan Valley. He is the author of *The Northwest Wine Guide: A Buyer's Handbook* (Sasquatch Books, 2003). He lives in Richland, Washington, with his wife and daughter.

When writer **Amanda Weber-Welch** isn't cuddling up with her husband, Bill, at romantic venues around the Pacific Northwest, she is teaching at-risk high school students and parenting two lovely daughters. Writing the chapters on Portland, the Columbia Gorge, Mount Hood, Bend, and Victoria and Vancouver Island proved to be a wonderful exploration of her longtime stomping grounds.

About Best Places® Guidebooks

PEOPLE TRUST US. *Best Places®* guidebooks, which have been published continuously since 1975, represent one of the most respected regional travel series in the country. In 2004, we incorporated the *Best Places to Kiss* guidebooks into our publishing series, beginning with the eighth edition of *The Best Places to Kiss in the Northwest*, bringing our reputable stamp of high quality and research to this much-loved series. Our reviewers know their territory. They have your romantic interests at heart, and they strive to function as reliable guides for your amorous outings. The *Best Places to Kiss* guides describe the true strengths, foibles, and unique characteristics of each establishment listed. *The Best Places to Kiss in the Northwest* specifically seeks out and highlights the special parts of this region that harbor romance and splendor, from restaurants, inns, lodges, wineries, and bed-and-breakfasts to spectacular parks, pristine beaches, and romantic drives. In this edition, couples will find all the information they need: when to visit a place to find the most privacy, where to find the most intimate restaurants, which rooms to request (and which to avoid), and how to find each destination's most romantic activities.

NOTE: *The reviews in this edition are based on information available at press time and are subject to change. Romantic travelers are advised that places listed may have closed or changed management, and thus may no longer be recommended by this series. Your romantic feedback assists greatly in increasing our accuracy and our resources, and we welcome information conveyed by readers of this book. Feel free to write us at the following address: Sasquatch Books, 119 S Main St, Suite 400, Seattle, Washington, 98104. We can also be contacted via e-mail: BPFeedback@ sasquatchbooks.com.*

How to Use This Book

All evaluations in this book are based on numerous reports from local and traveling inspectors. Final judgments are made by the editors. **Every place featured in this book is recommended.**

Romantic Highlights

The Romantic Highlights section of each chapter provides a guide to the most romantic activities in the region. These pursuits are designed to be intimate and relaxing for couples, and might include strolling to a lighthouse, taking an easy guided kayaking tour, or enjoying an alfresco lunch. In Romantic Highlights, the establishments or attractions that appear in boldface are recommended as well.

Lip Ratings

The following is a brief explanation of the lip ratings awarded each location.

❤❤❤❤	Simply sublime
❤❤❤	Very desirable; many outstanding qualities
❤❤	Can provide a satisfying experience; some wonderful features
❤	Romantic possibilities with potential drawbacks
UNRATED	New or undergoing major changes

Price Range

Prices for lodgings are based on peak season rates for one night's lodging for double occupancy (otherwise there wouldn't be anyone to kiss!). Prices for restaurants are based primarily on dinner for two, including dessert, tax, and tip, but not alcohol. Peak season is typically Memorial Day to Labor Day; off-season rates vary, but can sometimes be significantly lower. Because prices and business hours change, it is always a good idea to call ahead to each place you plan to visit.

$$$$	Very expensive (more than $100 for dinner for two; more than $250 for one night's lodging for two)
$$$	Expensive (between $65 and $100 for dinner for two; between $150 and $250 for one night's lodging for two)
$$	Moderate (between $35 and $65 for dinner for two; between $85 and $150 for one night's lodging for two)
$	Inexpensive (less than $35 for dinner for two; less than $85 for one night's lodging for two)

Lodgings

Many romance-oriented lodgings require two-night minimum stays throughout the year (especially on weekends); during some holiday weekends or high-season periods, this requirement might be extended to three nights. *It is a good idea to call in advance to check the policy at your lodging of choice.* We have opted not to specify two-night minimum stays because the requirement is so common. In the spirit of romance, popular family lodgings are mostly not included; however, some accommodations included do allow children, particularly over age 12. Many have safeguards for your privacy, such as separate breakfast times (one seats children, the other is adults-only) or providing detached suites removed from other guests for those traveling with children. If having a kid-free environment is critical to your intimate weekend away, call ahead to find out an establishment's policy.

Addresses and Phone Numbers

Every attempt has been made to provide accurate information on an establishment's location and phone number, but it's always a good idea to call ahead and confirm. For establishments with two or more locations, we try to provide information on the original or most recommended branches.

Checks and Credit Cards

Many establishments that accept checks also require a major credit card for identification. Some places accept only local checks; this is noted in the reviews. Credit cards are abbreviated as follows: American Express (AE); Carte Blanche (CB); Diners Club (DC); Discover (DIS); Japanese credit card (JCB); MasterCard (MC); Visa (V).

Reservations

We used one of the following terms for our reservations policy: reservations required, reservations recommended, no reservations. "No reservations" means either reservations are not necessary or are not accepted.

Web Sites and E-mail Addresses

Web sites or e-mail addresses for establishments have been included where available and appropriate. Please note that the Web is a fluid and evolving medium, and that Web pages are often "under construction"—or, as with all time-sensitive information, may no longer be valid.

Accessibility

The icon ♿ appears after listings for establishments that have wheelchair-accessible facilities.

Indexes

In addition to the standard index of establishments and destinations, this book also features a wedding index. Organized by region, this index lists romantic restaurants and lodgings with facilities to accommodate wedding parties of at least 50 people. (Since one of the most auspicious times to kiss is the moment after you exchange wedding vows, we felt this was appropriate!)

♡ It All Begins with a Kiss

This is the tenth edition of *The Best Places to Kiss in the Northwest*, and we are proud to be providing better-than-ever coverage of the most romantic destinations in Washington, Oregon, and British Columbia with features such as the "Romantic Highlights" section, which appears in every chapter and details each region's most romantic activities. In this edition, we're emphasizing the region's romantic wineries and some wonderfully creative ideas on how to spend one, two, or three days kissing in any one of many destinations. As ever, our research is enthusiastic, our investigations thorough, and our criteria increasingly more restrictive. We gather numerous reports from local and traveling inspectors before recommending a place for romance. We highly value our mission as one of the few travel books to review romantic properties with a candid and critical eye, and we treasure the feedback from readers who report that our reviews offer a breath of amorous fresh air.

We admit a strong bias in our feelings about the Northwest. Without question, this area provides the best kissing territory anywhere in the continental United States and Canada, and we strive to recommend the most romantic times of year to visit particular regions. Ultimately, however, each season brings its own rewards, from the pink cherry blossoms of spring and warm, clear days of summer to the brilliant colors of crisp autumn or the dramatic storms of winter. Oh, and about the rain—it does. Enough said. Don't be one of those couples who wait until summer to travel and then decide not to go because it might be too crowded! The style and approach of the people in the Northwest are highly conducive to intimacy and affection. We are confident that, no matter when or where you travel, you will relish this glorious part of the world as much as we do.

Any travel guide that rates establishments is inherently subjective—and *Best Places to Kiss* is no exception. We rely on our professional experience, yes; we also rely on our reporters' instincts to evaluate the heartfelt, magnetic pull of each establishment or region. Whether or not we include places is determined by three main factors: setting, privacy, and ambience. Setting is quite straightforward, referring simply to location and view, but we feel the latter two categories deserve some clarification. In regard to privacy, our preference is for cottages and suites set away from main buildings: such locations allow couples to say or do what they please without fear of being overheard or disturbing others. However, many truly wonderful bed-and-breakfasts and hotels require sharing space; in these cases, we look for modern soundproofing techniques, as well as expert innkeepers who know how to provide guests with a sense of intimate seclusion. We also applaud the notion of private breakfasts, whether delivered straight to your suite or served at an intimate table for two in the dining room. (Here, as with all dining experiences, a warm and friendly greeting, knowledgeable and helpful service, and the ability of the staff to be nearly invisible when you lock eyes across the table is our ideal.)

Ambience is the final major criterion, and it includes a multitude of factors. Intimate environments require more than four-poster beds and lace pillows, or linen-covered tables set with silver and crystal. Ambience requires features that encourage intimacy and allow for uninterrupted affectionate discourse, and relates more to the degree of comfort and number of gracious appointments than to image and frills. We keep an eye out for details such as music, fresh flowers, and candles. Ambience is also created in part by innkeepers, and if you are traveling for a special romantic occasion, we highly recommend informing them in advance. With notice, the best innkeepers take extra care to ensure that an especially intimate ambience welcomes you and your loved one. They can also inform you of any "special occasion packages," which might include chilled champagne, breakfast in bed, and special touches during turndown service, such as dimmed lights and your beloved's favorite music playing in the background to set the right romantic mood.

If a place has all three factors going for it, inclusion is automatic. But if one or two of the criteria are weak or nonexistent, the other feature(s) have to be superior before the location will be included. For example, a place that offers a breathtakingly beautiful panoramic vista but is also inundated with tourists and children on field trips would not be featured. A fabulous bed-and-breakfast set in a less than desirable location might be included, however, if it boasts a wonderfully inviting and cozy interior that outweighs the drawback of the location. It goes without saying that we consider myriad other factors, including uniqueness, excellence of cooking, cleanliness, value, and professionalism of service. Luxuries such as complimentary champagne and handmade truffles, or extraordinary service, are noteworthy extras and frequently determine the difference between lip ratings of three-and-a-half and four. In the final evaluation, keep in mind that every place listed in this book is recommended. When you visit any of the places we include here, you should look forward to some degree of privacy, a beautiful setting, heart-stirring ambience, and access to highly romantic pursuits.

♡ Portland
& Environs

Portland & Environs

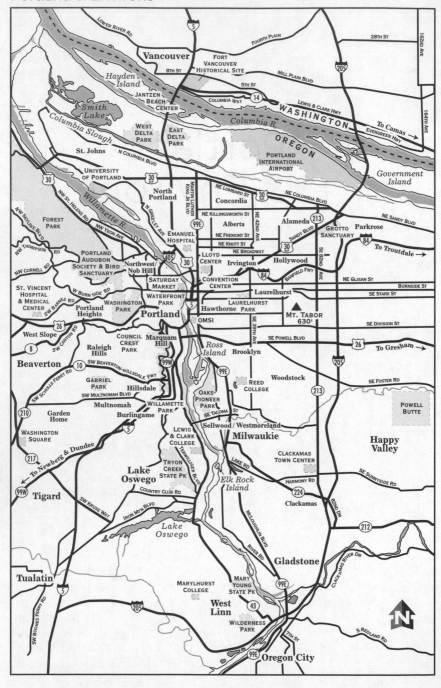

With a kiss let us set out for an unknown world.
—Alfred de Musset

♡ Portland
& Environs

Portland is one of the Northwest's true jewels, a friendly city that boasts sophisticated urban pleasures, lush parks and gardens, and a stunning natural setting on the Willamette River. Most getaways here will involve both outdoor and indoor excursions. The constantly evolving Pearl District and neighboring Northwest 23rd Street, as well as eastside gems along Hawthorne, Broadway, Alberta, and Mississippi streets, are home to hundreds of artists' lofts and galleries, cutting-edge restaurants, and excellent shopping. The city is gaining a strong reputation for its restaurants emphasizing local farm sources and for Oregon wines, highlighted in the growing number of wine bars scattered throughout the city. Meanwhile, the city's green space adds up to more than 37,000 stunning acres. Whether you explore the tiny 2-foot-long Mill Ends Park or the mammoth 5,000-acre Forest Park, the largest urban wilderness in the nation, you'll find lots of secluded spots for kissing.

For romantic travelers, there are plenty of great day trips from Portland, even if you're visiting for just a weekend. A short drive west puts you on the decidedly irresistible, rough-and-tumble Oregon Coast. Two volcanic mountains, Mount St. Helens and Mount Hood, are equally accessible day-trip destinations. The city itself is divided in two by the Willamette River (local pronunciation stresses the second syllable), which can be traversed via one of 10 bridges that provide gorgeous views and pleasant riverside walks along the westside Tom McCall Waterfront Park or across the river along the Eastbank Esplanade.

Portland's manageable size, along with its expertly executed urban plan, makes it easy to navigate. And, unless it's rush hour, crossing the city—diagonally from southeast to northwest, for instance—takes no longer than 15 minutes by car. Parking is rarely difficult. Couples who prefer two-wheel transport will find Portland refreshingly bike friendly. When it rains (a frequent occurrence from November through May), the two of you can take refuge from the wet weather in one of the cozy coffee shops, which seem to be on every corner, or in one of Portland's plentiful brewpubs. When the sunny summer months do arrive, the

3

city blossoms—literally. Flowering trees line the streets, and the roses—for which the city is famous—bloom in brilliant hues. Interstate 5 offers easy access to Portland from the north or south, and travelers approaching from the east can use Interstate 84.

Portland

Romantic Highlights

As home to three highly acclaimed rose gardens, Portland, affectionately named the City of Roses, is tailor-made for a romantic getaway. Shakespeare might have said that a city by any other name would be just as sweet, and we'd have to agree. With endless options for beautiful walks, cultural outings, and culinary adventures, everything to make your romantic sojourn complete is at your fingertips (see "Garden and Culinary Adventures").

Outdoor space may be the city's hallmark, but Portland's indoor romance abounds—especially if you spend an evening at the theater and share an intimate dinner afterward. The **Portland Center for the Performing Arts** (1111 SW Broadway; 503/248-4335; www.pcpa.com) hosts theater, opera, ballet, and symphony performances throughout the year. The nearby **Heathman Hotel** (see Romantic Lodgings) is a late-night romantic haven with live music and cozy fireside bliss. Art lovers can wander hand-in-hand through the **Portland Art Museum** (1219 SW Park Ave; 503/226-2811; www.portlandartmuseum.org) or tour downtown's public artwork (SW 5th and 6th aves) and explore contemporary works in the popular Pearl District galleries.

Spending a day near the river is always a treat. On weekends from March to Christmas, you can shop to your heart's content underneath the Burnside Bridge among the local artisans at the **Saturday Market** (108 W Burnside St; 503/222-6072; www.portlandsaturdaymarket.com). Afterward, walk south along the popular (and highly populated) **Tom McCall Waterfront Park** and stroll arm-in-arm past the shops and cafes along the **Riverplace Marina** boardwalk. In the evening, take a dinner cruise aboard the **Portland Spirit** (503/224-3900; www.portlandspirit.com) for breathtaking city views and tasty fare—just the recipe for romance.

Throughout Portland's vibrant downtown core and creative neighborhoods you'll discover many wonderful and unique nooks and crannies for shopping and exploring. You could spend an entire day inside **Powell's City of Books** (1005 W Burnside St; 503/228-4651; www.powells.com), one of the largest bookstores in the world. Get lost together in the stacks of this mazelike reader's mecca and whisper poetry into each other's ears. Across the river, the unpretentious shops along Hawthorne Boulevard reflect the street's laid-back reputation and make for great browsing. At **Escential Lotions & Oils** (3638 SE Hawthorne Blvd; 503/236-7976; www.escential.net) purchase a custom-blended massage lotion, shampoo, or bubble bath (try Portland Rain) to savor back at your room, or pamper your toes with essential-oil baths, massages, paraffin dips, and salt glows

Five Most-Kissable Portland Locations

1) The **Pittock Mansion** after a delicious picnic
2) The **Esplanade** along the Willamette River at sunset
3) The **waterfalls** across from Keller Auditorium
   (at SW 3rd Ave and Clay St)
4) Portland's **Classical Chinese Gardens**
5) A window seat at the **Portland City Grill** (111 SW 5th Ave;
   503/450-0030; www.portlandcitygrill.com), located
   on the 30th floor of the pink U.S. Bank Tower

at the incomparable **Barefoot Sage** (1844 SE Hawthorne Blvd; 503/239-7116; www.thebarefootsage.com). Hungry? Hawthorne offers eclectic dining delights. Whether you glide into **Pho Van** (3404 SE Hawthorne Blvd; 503/230-1474; www.phovanrestaurant.com) for delicious soup and other Vietnamese delicacies, soak in the upscale brewpub vibe at **Bridgeport Ale House** (3632 SE Hawthorne Blvd; 503/233-6540; wwwbridgeportbrew.com), pick up gourmet picnic supplies at **Pastaworks** (3735 SE Hawthorne Blvd; 503/232-1010; www.pastaworks.com), or sink into a savory brunch at **Bread and Ink Cafe** (3610 SE Hawthorne Blvd; 503/239-4756; www.breadandinkcafe.com), be sure to sneak in for a decadent, playful dessert at local **PIX Patisserie** (3731 SE Hawthorne Blvd; 503/236-4760; www.pixpatisserie.com).

Access and Information

Portland International Airport (PDX) (7000 NE Airport Wy; 503/460-4234; www.portlandairportpdx.com) is served by most major airlines, with excellent connections from points around the Pacific Northwest and beyond. Allow at least 30 minutes—more during rush hour—between the airport and town. All major car-rental companies operate from the airport. Taxis and shuttles are readily available; expect to pay at least $25 for the trip downtown. The most economical ride ($1.75) is via the Metropolitan Area Express (MAX) light-rail train. Catch MAX just outside the baggage claim; the ride to Pioneer Courthouse Square takes about 40 minutes.

Most drivers reach Portland via either Interstate 5, which runs north-south, or Interstate 84, which runs east-west and connects visitors to the beautiful Columbia River Gorge. Rush hours in Portland can mean gridlock, but if you arrive midday (after 9am, but before 3pm) or after 7pm, you should have smooth sailing into town. If you're traveling from Seattle, the drive takes approximately three hours. Amtrak (503/273-4866 or 800/USA-RAIL; www.amtrak.com) operates out of elegant, historical **Union Station** (800 NW 6th Ave), just north of downtown, with trains running daily from points north, east, and south. In the city, your best travel bets are via the bus or MAX light-rail train systems operated by **TriMet** (503/238-7433; www.trimet.org), which provides free service in the "Fareless Square," extending from points downtown to the eastside Convention Center. The **Portland Streetcar** (www. portlandstreetcar.org) is a fun way to travel from the South Park Blocks through the Pearl District to NW 23rd Avenue. In any case, it is easy to get to most Portland neighborhoods using public transportation, walking, or taking a cab—so dive in to the many corners of this city.

From May until August, the city celebrates the **Portland Rose Festival** with parades, concerts, and various other events. For information on area happenings, contact the **Portland Oregon Visitors Association** in Pioneer Square (701 SW 6th Ave; 503/275-8355 or 877/678-5263; www.pova.org).

Romantic Lodgings

Avalon Hotel and Spa / ❶❶❶❶

0455 SW Hamilton Ct, Portland; 503/802-5800 or 888/556-4402
If you're seeking a luxurious retreat, look no further than the elegant riverfront Avalon Hotel just south of downtown. The 99 stylish rooms are designed with your ultimate comfort in mind and combine Northwest casual with simple, Asian-influenced decor. Soft cotton sheets, goose-down duvets, cozy couches, marble baths, and warm tones create a pampering, sumptuous atmosphere. Eighteen rooms offer gas fireplaces and 78 offer balcony access (some are more private than others) with panoramic views of Mount Hood or the Willamette River. Enjoy room service or a meal at Aquariva (see Romantic Restaurants) and easy access to downtown with a scenic walk along the river path or a ride in the hotel's complimentary town car. Downstairs, the decadent Spa Chakra provides nurturing, but expensive, massages, facials, mud wraps, and other bodily pleasures using the exclusive Guerlain therapies. Guests may also access the hotel's extensive fitness club, offering Pilates and yoga classes. *$$$–$$$$; AE, DC, DIS, MC, V; checks OK; www. avalonhotelandspa.com.* &

The Benson Hotel / ❶❶❶

309 SW Broadway, Portland; 503/228-2000 or 888/523-6766
It's easy to get swept away by the grandeur of the Benson's massive lobby, where Austrian crystal chandeliers, Italian marble floors, stamped-tin ceiling, and rare imported Russian walnut wood paneling make it a sight to behold. This historic venue, the hotel of choice for a long line of presidents, movie stars, and big-time musicians, holds 287 tastefully, traditionally decorated rooms, many with city views. Luxurious bedding, plush robes, and turndown service are standard, with romance packages available. Truly special occasions call for a one-bedroom Penthouse Suite, particularly the number 4 Broadway Suite with its stunning views. Two notable restaurants within the Benson include El Gaucho (503/227-8794), known for serving some of the

city's finest steaks, and the romantic London Grill (call the main hotel number), where classic meals are served in an elegant, formal setting. The Palm Court Lounge also offers drinks, meals, and live jazz in the opulent hotel lobby. *$$$$; AE, DC, DIS, MC, V; checks OK; www.bensonhotel.com.* &

Blue Plum Inn / ⬢⬢⬣

2026 NE 15th Ave, Portland; 503/288-3848 or 877/288-3844
Like the City of Roses itself, the Blue Plum Inn is a beautifully cared for home that's so unpretentious and comfortable, you'll want to take up residence here. Hostess Suzanne Hansche and her husband, Jonathan, take great care with details that matter—abundant fresh flowers, home-baked treats, and delectable, hearty breakfasts. Each of three rooms has its own bath, beautiful thematic touches including murals painted by Myrna Anderson, and precious heirlooms. The private lower-level Hydrangea Suite includes a comfortable sitting room. Upstairs, the Tulip Room can optionally double in size with an adjoining living room to create a second suite. Shut the French doors and curl up with your other half to watch a movie or read before retiring to the queen bed with its intricate pink and green quilt. Special occasion? Your hosts will cheerfully accommodate requests for local wines, chilled champagne, or most anything else to make your occasion extra-special. *$$; MC, V; checks OK; www.bluepluminn.com.*

The Heathman Hotel / ⬢⬢⬢⬢

1001 SW Broadway, Portland; 503/241-4100 or 800/551-0011
Built in 1927, this 10-floor boutique gem is located in the heart of the Portland performing-arts scene. With its opulent Tea Court, secret passage to the Schnitzer Concert Hall, and original works of art displayed throughout the building, you are sure to feel inspired to artistic heights. Enjoy the services of the personal concierge assigned to you at check-in and the wonderful packages designed for a memorable interlude, most notably the Romeo and Juliet package with sparkling wine, rose petals, parking, and in-room continental breakfast. In your room, the Art Deco–inspired furniture, waffle-weave robes, French-press coffee, and loose-leaf tea—along with your choice of a European feather-top, pillow-top, or Tempur-Pedic bed—will transport you into pampered bliss. Before you snuggle into your room for the night, venture downstairs to the hotel's award-winning Heathman Restaurant (see Romantic Restaurants) for an amazing meal, live music in the Tea Court, a nearby performance, or a simple walk in the South Park Blocks. *$$$–$$$$; AE, DC, DIS, MC, V; checks OK; http://portland.heathmanhotel.com.* &

Hotel deLuxe / ⬢⬢⬢⬣

729 SW 15th Ave, Portland; 503/219-2094 or 866/895-2094
With potted palms, sand-colored brick, Big Band music, and dramatic curtains, the entrance to the Hotel deLuxe will transport you back in time. This

1912 historic landmark recently enjoyed an $11 million renovation and is now a fantastic space with 1940s Hollywood glamour, gorgeous Art Deco furniture and chandeliers, and plentiful marble flooring. All 130 rooms, expertly and luxuriously decorated in butter, mint, and olive hues, come with modern amenities like plasma TVs and iPod docks (with iPods available at the front desk). Rooms ending in 03 have panoramic city views, and our favorite is the delicious Deitrich Suite with its memorable round bed. Art on each floor follows the theme of a film director or movie genre. Visit the elegant lobby; intimate, curvaceous Driftwood Lounge; and delicious Gracie's Restaurant, which offers seasonally inspired cuisine and 24-hour room service. A final thrill? Check out creative romance packages like "All You Need is Love" or "Baby It's Cold Outside." *$$$–$$$$; AE, DC, DIS, MC, V; no checks; www. hoteldeluxeportland.com.* &

Hotel Vintage Plaza / ❂❂❂

422 SW Broadway, Portland; 503/228-1212 or 800/263-2305
Though located smack in the middle of downtown Portland, there's no place quite like Vintage Plaza to escape from it all. Everything about the hotel is cozy, beginning with the sumptuous, jewel-toned lobby and its rich marble fireplace, where guests are invited to nightly tastings of notable Northwest wines. Any one of the 107 guest rooms, named after local wineries, would be a good choice; the standouts, however, are spectacular. Snuggle under a twinkling sky in one of nine Starlight Rooms, featuring solarium-style privacy windows with electric blinds for nighttime stargazing. Or splurge on a Garden Spa room with a secluded outdoor Jacuzzi overlooking the city. For pampering ecstasy, add in-house spa services or the romance package: chilled champagne, rose petals scattered at turndown, and breakfast in bed. For a taste of fine Northern Italian cuisine, try adjacent Pazzo Ristorante (503/228-1515). *$$$; AE, DC, DIS, MC, V; no checks; www.vintageplaza.com.* &

Lion and the Rose Victorian Bed & Breakfast / ❂❂❁

1810 NE 15th Ave, Portland; 503/287-9245 or 800/955-1647
This historically designated 1906 Queen Anne mansion, located one block from busy NE Broadway, offers excellent access to shopping and dining in Portland's Irvington neighborhood. Each of the seven guest rooms meets a high standard of Victorian elegance, and the hosts let few details go untended, with candles, in-room beverages, and luxurious robes. The spacious Lavonna Room, boasting a marble shower and private bath, wins our hearts. Light, airy lavender and green decor immediately beckons, and the tower window reading nook is perfect for two (with or without a book of Shakespeare's sonnets). Joseph's Room, with its rich red and gold tones, fainting sofa, and lavish four-poster bed, distinctively sets the stage for romance. For its beautiful garden view and the home's only Jacuzzi tub, the first-floor Rose Room is another sweet retreat. Guests are greeted with afternoon tea, and the hearty

morning meal is served around a large formal table. *$$–$$$; AE, DIS, MC, V; checks OK; www.lionrose.com.*

Portland's White House / ●●●€

1914 NE 22nd Ave, Portland; 503/287-7131 or 800/272-7131
The oohs and aahs begin when you turn into the circular drive of this historic Greek Revival home with its lovingly manicured grounds near NE Broadway's shops and boutiques. Inside, the grand entrance hall's cascading staircase and hand-painted murals dazzle, and an inviting parlor features French doors and a grand piano. The formal dining room is exquisitely set with European linens and china, and owner, chef, and decorator Lanning Blanks pleases guests with his delightful breakfasts. The home and its adjacent Carriage House have been lovingly restored, and all eight guest rooms enjoy private baths. For the most romantic getaway, we recommend the private Chauffeur's Quarters with its four-poster king-size bed, beautiful views, double-headed shower, and Jacuzzi tub. Our next favorite is the richly decorated Canopy Room boasting a stunning jetted tub. With any room, Moonstruck chocolates assure a sweet arrival, and the sumptuous bedding guarantees a return visit. *$$–$$$; AE, DIS, MC, V; checks OK; www.portlandswhitehouse.com.*

Romantic Restaurants

Andina Restaurant / ●●●

1314 NW Glisan St, Portland; 503/228-9535
The inviting terra cotta–toned decor, warm lighting, lively Latin music, and delicious *nueva* Peruvian dishes at this popular spot in the Pearl District are guaranteed to put you into an exotic mood. Start with the tart Peruvian Pisco Sour or the traditional Mexican love potion Granada de Amor—Citroen vodka infused with pomegranate, lime, and Damiana—along with your choice of *cebiches de le casa* and other small plates. Entrées are creative, both in flavor and in presentation, but sure hits include the quinoa-encrusted scallops and the seasonal pork and lamb dishes. House-made desserts—like the quinoa-studded passion-fruit mousse cannoli paired with mango-lemongrass sorbet and caramel—will seduce you with an infusion of Peruvian flavors. *$$$; AE, DIS, MC, V; local checks only; lunch, dinner every day; full bar; reservations recommended; www.andinarestaurant.com.* &

Aquariva / ●●●

0470 SW Hamilton Ct, Portland; 503/802-5850
Whether sitting by the riverside window or in an intimately curtained raised dining area, the nighttime starlit-effect of pinpoint ceiling lights and abundant candles in this sleek, contemporary space will immediately transport the two of you to another world. Outdoor riverside seating, when weather permits, is another treat. Begin by sharing the current wine and cheese pairings (a great deal!) before selecting a delicious range of inventive *tapas* designed for tasting

Three Days of Romance

Day One: Portland is a walker's paradise, with many areas of the city easily accessible on foot or via public transit. Dive into the day by walking, shopping, and sightseeing in the trendy Pearl District and along Northwest 21st and 23rd avenues. After checking in to **Hotel deLuxe**, pack a light picnic lunch gathered from **Elephants Delicatessen** or **City Market NW**, and head up to your choice of gardens overlooking views of downtown all the way to Mount Hood (see "Garden and Culinary Adventures"). Splurge on a memorable meal at **Paley's Place** (see Romantic Restaurants) before strolling back to your abode for the evening.

Day Two: Begin with a delicious breakfast at the **Bijou Cafe** (132 SW 3rd Ave; 503/222-3187), then stroll the stalls at the city's long-standing **Saturday Market** (weekend mornings Mar–Christmas) along the Willamette River. Spend the afternoon on a sublime journey to the full-city block of the **Portland Classical Chinese Gardens** (see "Garden and Culinary Adventures"). For the evening, check into the **Heathman Hotel**, with its handsome accommodations (we recommend a seasonal romance package), chef Philippe Boulot's fabulous food, and the Tea Court's after-dinner coziness.

Day Three: Depart Portland's downtown core in favor of its atmospheric east side with a journey along Hawthorne Boulevard for people watching, shopping, and snacking. Slide into the comfy couches at the **Barefoot Sage** to enjoy a blissful foot treatment. Then hoof it up Hawthorne, peeking into shops along the way. An evening at the legendary **Genoa** will provide an amazing final culinary bite of Portland; however, **3 Doors Down Café** will also delight. Ending the evening with a decadent dessert at **PIX Patisserie** will surely lead to sweet dreams, or something sweeter, in your luxurious room at **Portland's White House**.

specifically with red or white wine selections. Ready for dessert? Try one of the mouthwatering gelatos with homemade cookies, or rich chocolate cake served with a glass of Alpenrose milk. An important bonus: complimentary valet parking is available . . . and necessary. *$$$; AE, DIS, MC, V; no checks; brunch Sat–Sun, lunch, dinner every day; full bar; reservations recommended; www.aquarivaportland.com.* &

Castagna / ✪✪✪❁

1752 SE Hawthorne Blvd, Portland; 503/231-7373
With impeccable service, delectable French and Italian–inspired dishes, and emphatically local produce and meats, Castagna is a food-lover's paradise.

Though simple, the space is elegant; ask for the back booth behind the bar for the most privacy. Prepare to be wooed by hand-built agnolotti pastas with nuanced fillings, sautéed sea scallops, and creative entrées, or simply select the reasonably priced three-course offering. Both the extensive wine list and seasonal cocktail specials are chosen with the experience of the diner in mind, as are the delicious desserts—frozen mascarpone cheesecake, chocolate *pot de crème*, or flavor-popping seasonal sorbets. *$$$; AE, DIS, MC, V; checks OK; dinner Wed–Sat; full bar; reservations recommended; www.castagna restaurant.com.* &

Ciao Vito / ❂❂❂

2203 NE Alberta St, Portland; 503/282-5522
Soaking in the atmosphere of this Alberta Street restaurant with its rich velvet curtains, crystal chandeliers, and candle-hued lighting is half the fun of a trip to Ciao Vito. Owner Vito DiLullo's Northern Italian food is supported by a strong Pacific Northwest seasonal influence in specialties ranging from pan-fried razor clams and in-house pastas to the legendary osso buco. Request West Booth 3 or the East Booth and toast to your love with a great selection of regional Italian and Oregon wines before perusing the creative dessert list. Gelato lovers will be seduced by offerings of tiramsu, seasonal fruits, and brown sugar pecan. *$$; MC, V; no checks; dinner every day; full bar; reservations recommended; www.ciaovito.net.* &

Fratelli / ❂❂❂

1230 NW Hoyt St, Portland; 503/241-8800
Whether you snuggle into the bar or enjoy a table in the simple, cavernous restaurant, Fratelli's ambience—a contrast between modern and rustic—pulls at the fringe of the well-heeled Pearl District: expanses of cement blend with Persian rugs; modern anemonelike lights float amid an elegant, oversize chandelier; and the simple wooden tables flaunt elegant candlesticks and formal linens. Not an authority on Italian vino? Never fear: servers expertly suggest pairings. Select from a creative range of antipasti; share delicious, seasonally inspired risotto or gnocchi; and settle into the bliss of a beautiful evening. *$$; AE, MC, V; no checks; dinner every day; full bar; reservations recommended; www.fratellicucina.com.* &

Genoa / ❂❂❂❂

2832 SE Belmont St, Portland; 503/238-1464
If you are looking for the ultimate dining experience, look no further than this nearly forty-year-old Portland institution. Unassuming on the outside, upon entering you are swept into the intimate, candlelit world of Genoa, where your server will expertly guide you through five courses, several amusebouche, and other-worldly desserts. Decisions are few, and all dishes are amazing, leaving plenty of time to gaze into each other's eyes while

Big City Vines

While Oregon wines are produced with grapes primarily grown outside of Portland, the city bustles with opportunities to play with blending, pairing, tasting, or simply sipping.

Urban Wineworks (407 NW 16th St; 503/226-9797; www.urbanwineworks.com; every day), the art-laden Portland home of Bishop Creek Cellars, offers creative pairing and blending classes in addition to tastings of Bishop Creek wines. Blend a custom wine made just for your tastes and take it home in an Italian glass carafe or bottled with your own label. Enjoy daily tastings and Friday-night "Bites and Flights" at **Urban Wineworks East** (1411 NE Broadway; 503/445-4747); check the Web site for events happening at all four locations.

If an intimate, other-worldly feel is what you seek, **Lupa** (3955 N Mississippi Ave; 503/287-5872; www.lupawine.com; every day) will delight you with wines from Missouri, Croatia, Israel, and Lebanon. A narrow path between a wall of wine bottles (cleverly tagged with one-word descriptions—smoky, velvety, opulent—to guide your choices) and the

you're carried through this meal. Select from the wonderful wine list or ask your server to pair your courses to perfection. Special occasion? Ask for the "engagement" number 7 corner table—and start celebrating. *$$$$; AE, DC, DIS, MC, V; checks OK; dinner Tues–Sun; full bar; reservations required; www. genoarestaurant.com.* &

The Heathman Restaurant and Bar / ❷❷❷❷

1001 SW Broadway, Portland; 503/241-4100
Executive chef Philippe Boulot oversees this sophisticated French-inspired, Northwest-influenced restaurant in the heart of downtown. Tuck into a private corner banquette table and select from an extensive, balanced wine list emphasizing French and Northwest wines. Appetizers including fresh oysters, rich sweetbreads, and decadent cheese selections are pleasing to the palette. Entrées offer delicious seasonal preparations of rabbit, quail, beef, and seafood. After your meal, retire to the overstuffed chairs and consistently stoked marble fireplace of the wood-paneled Tea Court to enjoy dessert and after-dinner apertifs with live jazz Wednesday through Saturday. A perfect place to enjoy a kiss! *$$$–$$$$; AE, DIS, DC, MC, V; no checks; breakfast, lunch, dinner every day; full bar; reservations recommended; www.heathman restaurantandbar.com.* &

warmly lit bar will lead you to a few tables where you can enjoy light dishes and purchase wines by the glass or by the bottle with reasonable $5–$10 corkage fees.

More retro-hip (and loud) is the Pearl District's **Vino Paradiso** (417 NW 10th St; 503/295-9536; www.vinoparadiso.com; dinner Tues–Sun) with all sorts of nooks and crannies to settle into, a terrific menu, and an assortment of wine prices and varietals, many available by the glass.

Back on the east side of the river, NE 28th Avenue is a street lined with several wine bar greats like **Noble Rot** (see Romantic Restaurants), and **Navarre** (10 NE 28th Ave; 503/232-3555; breakfast, lunch, dinner Thurs–Sun). **Wine Down on 28th** (126 NE 28th Ave; 503/236-9463; www.winedownpdx.com; dinner every day) offers guests excellent food, and live jazz or blues most evenings with plenty of candlelit places to hide. Snare the couches next to the gas fireplace, retreat into a curtained dining booth in back, or even snuggle up at a table by the front windows.

Farther east, newly established **Cru Wine Bar** (7907 SE Stark St, 503/262-0696; www.whynotwineoregon.com; open Tues–Sat) provides many kissable corners in which to wine the night away.

Higgins / ❶❶❶

1239 SW Broadway, Portland; 503/222-9070
Higgins is widely considered one of the city's finest restaurants: chef/owner Greg Higgins's passion for seasonal, local Northwest cuisine has earned him national praise, including a James Beard Foundation award in 2002. Soft lighting and a multi-tiered design turn a sizable space into a cozy one: although no table is secluded, the lowest level is quietest, as it escapes the clamor of the open kitchen. Seafood dishes shine, including the spicy red-wine cioppino with crab, prawns, mussels, and clams. Vegetarians will be thrilled with choices like risotto of Oregon truffles, leeks, and chèvre. Presentation is spectacular and so are the decadent desserts. *$$$; AE, DC, DIS, MC, V; checks OK; lunch Mon–Fri, dinner every day; full bar; reservations recommended; www.higgins.ypguides.net.* &

Il Piatto / ❶❶❶

2348 SE Ankeny St, Portland; 503/236-4997
Chef/owner Eugene Bingham has created one of southeast Portland's most charming (and hidden) restaurants tucked into a residential neighborhood. Lucky diners privy to its exact location will walk through velvet curtains to find a rich color scheme, rustic decor, chandeliers, and cozy booths or intimate tables separated by sheer curtains. The menu and wine list is Italian

through and through, with delectable pastas, risottos bursting with flavor, and signature dishes including pork saltimbocca. For an extra dose of romance, request booth C-8, "the proposal table." *$$–$$$; DIS, MC, V; checks OK; lunch Tues–Fri, dinner every day; full bar; reservations recommended; www. ilpiattopdx.com.* &

Lovely Hula Hands / ❶❶❶

4057 N Mississippi Ave, Portland; 503/445-9910
A two-story brick building on Mississippi Avenue is the newly renovated home of this sweet, dusty-rose-hued restaurant with soft vintage lighting and framed flower prints. Chef Troy MacLarty, formerly of Family Supper, has created a menu highlighting seasonal offerings with imaginative (and tasty) vegetable combinations. Cocktails are creative, like the Lovely Hula Hoop, or make a selection from the wine list—with wonderful choices from Oregon, Italian, and French wineries. While seating in the entire restaurant is rather cozy, the upstairs offers a livelier music-filled atmosphere and a window seat with a little more privacy. *$$$; MC, V; no checks; dinner Tues–Sun; full bar; no reservations; www.lovelyhulahands.com.*

Mint / ❶❶❶❶

816 N Russell St, Portland; 503/284-5518
Portland's long-reigning queen of cocktails and Mint owner, Lucy Brennan, masterfully mixes drinks (like Love on the Rocks and O Mojitos) as tempting as the flavorful, Latin-inspired dinner offerings. The not-to-be-missed tuna seviche, smoky sautéed mussels, and inventive main dishes will tempt your taste buds. Request a window nook or, better yet, cozy up cheek-to-cheek in the back corner; diffused lighting, rough brick, Oregon madrone branches, and black ceilings create low-lit opportunities to steal secret kisses. Finish a blissful evening with cinnamon-infused caramel-chocolate fondue and a Sweet Love concoction, one of many suggestively coined after-dinner drinks. Next door, the intimate 820 Lounge is another gem. *$$–$$$; AE, MC, V; no checks; dinner Mon–Sat; full bar; reservations recommended; www.mint and820.com.* &

Noble Rot / ❶❶❶

2724 SE Ankeny St, Portland; 503/233-1999
Always romantic, wine soars to new heights at this popular eastside wine bar/dinner destination. Walk between the bar and cozy booths into the distinct wine-cellar vibe of the back dining area. Oh, do we adore this little place! First, retail-priced wine selections mean that enjoying a bottle here—even with a corkage fee—is easy on the wallet. Second, inventive wine flights allow you to take a vineyard venture. Finally, the menu of delicious small plates lends itself to sharing a satisfying meal. Offerings change seasonally but usually include cheeses, savory terrines, salads, and creamy macaroni

Garden and Culinary Adventures

Portland offers countless paths for hiking and biking within city limits. With so many trails to choose from, couples often find themselves in the company of no one but each other—and what better opportunity to sneak a kiss? And no trip to Portland is complete without a wander through the **International Rose Test Gardens** (400 SW Kingston; 503/823-3636; www. rosegardenstore.org), located within Washington Park. If you visit during a summer weekend, chances are good there'll be at least one couple saying "I do" in this idyllic setting. For a more secluded garden stroll, head to the nearby serene **Japanese Gardens** (611 SW Kingston; 503/223-1321; www.japanesegarden.com) or **Hoyt Arboretum** (4000 SW Fairview Blvd; 503/865-8733; www.hoytarboretum.org) with its global collection of trees and plants. Set in the heart of Old Town, the **Portland Classical Chinese Garden** (NW 3rd and Everett; 503/228-8131; www.portlandchinesegarden. org) encloses a full city block that will sweep you both to another place and time. Don't miss the on-site tea house, **Tower of Cosmic Reflections** (503/224-8455), for delicate snacks and meditative teas.

If it's a beautiful day and nothing sounds better than a picnic, gather gourmet provisions at **City Market NW** (735 NW 21st Ave; 503/221-3007) or **Elephants Delicatessen** (115 NW 22nd Ave; 503/299-6304; www. elephantsdeli.com) and drive west (away from the river) on West Burnside Street, following signs to the **Pittock Mansion** (3229 NW Pittock Dr; 503/823-3624; www.pittockmansion.org), where you can spread out your picnic on the well-manicured grounds and enjoy the panoramic city view extending to Mount Hood. Walking tours of the 16,000-square foot landmark home are held in the afternoons. Another kiss-worthy destination in the West Hills is **Council Crest Park** (SW Council Crest Dr; 503/823-2223), a prime spot for gazing at the stars, the mountains, and each other.

and cheese. *$$; AE, MC, V; local checks only; dinner Mon–Sat; beer and wine; no reservations; www.noblerotpdx.com.* &

Paley's Place / ❂❂❂❂

1204 NW 21st Ave, Portland; 503/243-2403
Set in a lovingly renovated Nob Hill house, Paley's Place has been a popular destination for fine dining since chef Vitaly Paley and his wife, Kimberly, first opened this Northwest-sourced, French-influenced restaurant in 1995. Cream-colored walls, black wooden tables, and beautiful lighting make for a simple, intimate setting where attentive, but not intrusive, service is an art form. Begin your experience by sharing Paley's signature steamed mussels

or crab brioche with microgreens. Entrées change with the seasons and range from wild salmon to crispy veal sweetbreads and crawfish. The award-winning dessert menu offers both seasonal specialties and longtime favorites including a delirium-producing chocolate soufflé cake. *$$$–$$$$; AE, MC, V; local checks only; dinner every day; full bar; reservations recommended; www. paleysplace.net.*

Sapphire Hotel / ⬡⬡⬡⬡

5008 SE Hawthorne Blvd, Portland; 503/232-6333
The Sapphire Hotel—though now not, in fact, a hotel—creates the ambience of a historic hotel lobby with its dark red walls, gilded mirrors, whirling ceiling fans, plentiful candles, and jazz playing in the background. Explicitly inviting guests to "Eat, Drink, Kiss," owners Shannon Freeman and Carrie Engle deliver an intimate dining experience anywhere you sit, especially nestling into the front nooks. Inventive, delicious drinks, like Penthouse Suite, Going Up? and An Apricot Blonde, play up the hotel theme. Along with a short, well-picked wine list and very reasonably priced bottles, the flavorful menu items like sesame-crusted seared ahi and panzanella salad are another opportunity to share. *$–$$; AE, MC, V; checks OK; dinner every day; full bar; no reservations; www.thesapphirehotel.com.* &

3 Doors Down Café / ⬡⬡⬡⬡

1429 SE 37th St, Portland; 503/236-6886
Thanks to a spacious and atmospheric expansion, you may have an easier time getting a table at this popular, rustic Italian restaurant. Warm red, brown, and black tones accentuate unique wall cut-outs, best viewed with signature candlelit ambience. House-made, seasonal liquors and brandies, as well as a reasonably priced wine list with Northwest and global reach, are served from the beautiful bar. For all the atmosphere, the generously portioned food is what really shines here. Order the perennial favorite penne with creamy tomato-vodka sauce and spicy sausage or an expertly prepared seasonal dish. *$$–$$$; AE, MC, V; checks OK; dinner Tues–Sun; full bar; no reservations (call 1 hour in advance to get on the wait-list); www.3doorsdowncafe.com.* &

Toro Bravo / ⬡⬡⬡

120 NE Russell St, Portland; 503/281-4464
This Spanish-inspired *tapeo* restaurant located next to the Wonder Ballroom is blazing its own well-populated trail with an eclectic Mediterranean-influenced small-plates menu. Chef/owner John Gorham's locally sourced *tapas*, perfect for nibbling and pairing with a variety of Spanish and local wines, include marinated sheep's cheese, griddled bacon-wrapped dates, sautéed chard, and the sumptuous Paella Toro. Seasonal sweets, whether the apples baked to order, olive-oil cake, or *panna cotta*, are a smooth-talking finish to the evening. Overall, the atmosphere is convivially rowdy, but scoring

a spot in the cozy, aptly named "make-out room" will leave you both exclaiming, "Bravo!" *$$; AE, DIS, MC, V; no checks; dinner every day; full bar; no reservations; www.torobravopdx.com.* &

Veritable Quandary / ❂❂❂

1220 SW 1st Ave, Portland; 503/227-7342
Portland's bridges illuminate the nighttime sky and the mighty Willamette, providing an irresistible backdrop for kissing, and the VQ is the perfect locale. Enjoy an amorous alfresco meal surrounded by flowers and lush gardens on the intimate, fair-weather patio, or get closer in the gently lit dining room, the loft, or the private wine cellar, all insulated from the noisy bar. The extensive wine list offers modestly priced bottles and 30–40 glass selections. While the menu changes seasonally, it always includes the mouth-watering osso buco, house-made pastas, and creative meat preparations. Save room for VQ's famous, lighter-than-air chocolate soufflé (allow 20 minutes' preparation time). *$$–$$$; AE, DIS, MC, V; no checks; brunch Sat–Sun, lunch Mon–Fri, dinner every day; full bar; reservations recommended; www.veritablequandary.com.* &

Wild Abandon Restaurant and the Red Velvet Lounge / ❂❂❂

2411 SE Belmont St, Portland; 503/232-4458
The dramatic interior, friendly service, and varied menu offerings make for a decadent dining experience. Inside an unlikely corrugated metal building, the narrow dining area feels invitingly loungelike. Festive lighting illuminates tables and the back wall's dreamily painted fresco of indulgent Dionysian figures in repose. Any selection from the tempting dinner menu will be delicious, whether you keep it simple with pasta or a Red Velvet Burger, or splurge on the hearty Wild Cioppino Stew with scallops, prawns, clams, and other seafood delights. Wind up the evening with a glass or dish of sweetness before you head home for more wild abandon. *$$–$$$; AE, DC, DIS, MC, V; local checks only; brunch Sat–Sun, dinner Wed–Mon; full bar; reservations recommended; www.wildabandonrestaurant.com.* &

Columbia River Gorge & Mount Hood

Columbia River Gorge & Mount Hood

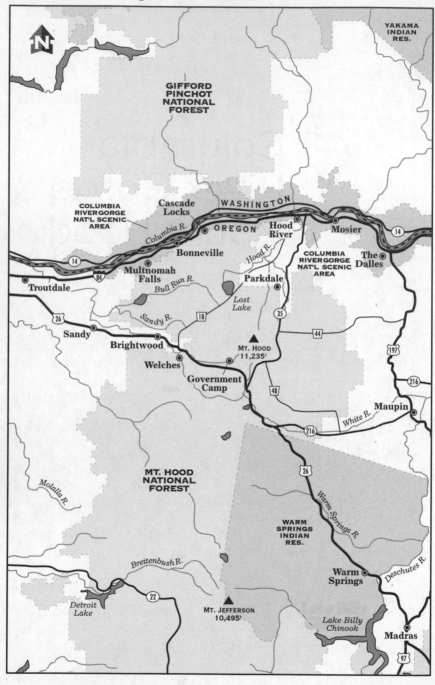

He who love touches walks not in darkness.

—Plato

♡ Columbia River Gorge & Mount Hood

The Columbia River Gorge offers some of the Northwest's greatest natural treasures in the beautiful chasm that separates part of Washington from Oregon. An obvious choice for adventures of all kinds—including amorous ones—the region stretches from The Dalles in the east to Troutdale in the west and encompasses both Oregon and Washington sites. Blessed with an abundance of panoramic vistas, wildflowers, magnificent waterfalls, quaint towns with charming country inns, and boundless opportunities for invigorating outdoor activities, the Columbia River Gorge offers an excellent setting for romance. Located less than an hour east of Portland, it can make a romantic day trip or inspire a weekend escape.

The sights in this historically rich area are best savored with a meandering drive along Oregon's Historic Columbia River Highway, a road built in 1915 specifically to display the gorge. Keep your eye out for the intricate stonework, arched bridges, viaducts, tunnels, and lookout points tailor-made for romantic discovery. Take the side trip to drive a stretch of this old highway from Troutdale to Multnomah Falls, Oregon's most popular (and most photographed) tourist attraction. Stunning waterfalls can be seen both from the road and from short hikes off the highway. Though less traveled, the Washington side of the gorge also has some luxurious lodging, dining, and scenic options. From Cascade Locks, cross the Bridge of the Gods to Washington to enjoy spa treatments at either Bonneville Hot Springs Resort & Spa or Skamania Lodge and to explore the many natural beauties of this side of the gorge.

Another popular destination on the Oregon side of the gorge is the town of Hood River, the area's main hub of activity. Known for its thousands of fruit trees—mostly apples, pears, and cherries—that blossom into abundance each year, Hood River is also the windsurfing capital of the Northwest. The town serves as an ideal base for starry-eyed couples exploring the area, with its plentiful eating establishments, wide array of lodging options, and easy access to Mount Hood, Oregon's highest peak.

On clear days, snowy Mount Hood seems just a few steps away from almost anywhere in central Oregon—and is easily accessible by car. As the seasons shift, so do the opportunities for romantic activities around the mountain. Summer offers the chance to backpack, golf, hike, climb, and share quiet days of fishing or dipping bare feet in the Salmon River. Winter provides ample opportunity for skiing or snuggling by a cozy fire. The mountain's crown jewel is Timberline Lodge, one of the only year-round ski resorts in the United States, and worth a snow-kissed visit at any time of year.

Columbia River Gorge

Romantic Highlights

Because there is so much to see and do on any given weekend in the Columbia River Gorge, one visit alone will not be enough. Spend a few days (or more) exploring in the summertime, when the wildflowers are in bloom, and then treat yourselves to another getaway in the fall to enjoy the leaves and the abundance of the harvest in the fruit- and wine-producing Hood River Valley.

If you're heading east on Interstate 84 from Portland, **Troutdale** (exit 17) is your first stop and an ideal entry point. Along with its core downtown shops, the main attraction in Troutdale, and one not to be missed by any pair of lovers, is **McMenamins Edgefield** (2126 SW Halsey, Troutdale; 503/669-8610 or 800/669-8610), a 38-acre estate run by local microbrew barons Mike and Brian McMenamin. Once a working farm and a poorhouse, Edgefield is now a haven for dining and drinking, massages, quirky artwork, gardens made for wandering, golf, cinema, and—frequently—weddings.

The second-largest city in the gorge is the very romantic **Hood River**, located off Interstate 84. Top-notch restaurants, plenty of lodgings tastefully tailored to lovers, and an adorable, very walkable downtown make it an irresistible place to spend time with your special someone. (The largest town, The Dalles, is an industrial area ill-suited to a romantic getaway.)

On Saturdays in summer, visit the **Hood River Saturday Market** (Cascade St between 5th and 7th aves; mid-May–mid-Oct) for fresh local produce, baked goods, and handcrafted gifts. And if you time it right, you can soak up more local culture at **Hood River's First Friday Art Walk,** held in downtown restaurants and shops on the first Friday night of the month from 5pm to 8pm between March and December. The wine industry in this part of the gorge has really taken off: many local wineries offer tastings and invite visitors to linger on their picturesque grounds for a picnic and a glass of wine (see "Columbia Gorge Wineries" for our favorite picks).

For a unique and romantic tour of the Hood River Valley fruit orchards, take the train. The **Mount Hood Railroad** (110 Railroad Ave; 541/386-3556 or

> ## Five Best Places to Sneak a Kiss in the Gorge and Mount Hood:
>
> 1) Timberline Lodge
> 2) Behind Oneonta Falls
> 3) The grounds of Cathedral Ridge
> 4) Crown Point
> 5) Columbia Gorge Hotel grounds

800/872-4661; www.mthoodrr.com) leaves from downtown Hood River and offers two- and four-hour excursions that stop in the tiny town of Parkdale, where you'll enjoy stunning views of Mount Hood. The brunch and dinner trains are even more romantic and offer four-course meals served in nicely restored 1940s dining cars. The Murder-Mystery dinner excursions offer a twist in the plot of your own romantic adventure.

Or take a leisurely drive on what's affectionately known as the **Fruit Loop** (541/386-7697; www.hoodriverfruitloop.com), a 35-mile route that leads you through the valley's orchards, forests, farmlands, and towns. Absorb the spectacular scenery and make a few stops along the way to sample, purchase, and sometimes harvest the local fruit and wine. Don't miss the view at Panorama Point, a half mile south of Hood River on Highway 35.

Access & Information

The Columbia River Gorge is most commonly approached from Portland via Interstate 84 east. Follow the freeway through the gorge to Hood River and The Dalles. Another more scenic option is to exit at Troutdale (exit 17) or Corbett (exit 22) and take the Historic Columbia River Highway. From Mount Hood, take Highway 35 north to Hood River. Travelers from Seattle should drive south on Interstate 5 to Portland, then east on I-84.

Visit in mid-April to experience the charming small-town atmosphere of the **Blossom Festival**, which celebrates the natural beauty of the area's orchards in spring, or in October for the bounty of the **Harvest Festival**. For tourist information, contact the **Columbia River Gorge Visitors Association** (2149 W Cascade Ave #106A, Hood River; 800/984-6743; www.crgva.org).

Romantic Lodgings

Bonneville Hot Springs Resort & Spa / ❂❂❂

1252 E Cascade Dr, North Bonneville; 866/459-1678
For a restorative splurge, escape to Washington's premier hot-springs resort and spa. One look at the three-story lobby, with its river-rock fireplace and floor-to-ceiling windows, and you'll know you're in for a treat. Inside, enjoy

one of 78 guest rooms, many with hot tubs containing the resort's healing mineral spring water. Outside, explore the beautifully landscaped grounds, with pools, hot tubs, saunas, hiking trails, and putt-putt golf. The real highlight is the range of more than 40 inspiring spa treatments, from mineral baths and body wraps to facials, massages, and reflexology. On-site wine tasting is available on weekends, and the resort's restaurant, Pacific Crest Dining Room (509/427-9711), serves healthful Northwest cuisine. *$$$$; AE, DIS, MC, V; checks OK; www.bonnevilleresort.com.* &

Carson Ridge Private Luxury Cabins / ●●●●

1261 Wind River Rd, Carson; 509/427-7777 or 877/816-7908
Enjoy rustic luxury in your own private cabin. Seven cabins grace the property of this bed-and-breakfast, where romance and comfort are in the details, like the lavender-oil bath salts, candles, Jacuzzi tubs, robes, fireplaces, leather chairs, log beds, private patios and porch swings, and gourmet breakfast served at tables for two. All cabins are tastefully furnished with natural themes; however, the Fishing Creel and Salmonberry rank among visitors' favorites. The Knotty Pine is a deluxe anniversary/honeymoon cabin with a kitchenette, sunken living room, and rock fireplace. Innkeepers Debbie and Jim Waters look for any opportunity to ensure that your stay is blissful and, for special events, add sparkling cider, a rose, truffles, and the option of breakfast delivered. An easy location from which to windsurf, raft, hike, or relax at one of several nearby spa locations—if you can pull yourself away from your cabin. *$$$; MC, V; checks OK; www.carsonridgecabins.com.*

Columbia Gorge Hotel / ●●●●

4000 Westcliff Dr, Hood River; 541/386-5566 or 800/345-1921
This beautiful 1920s Spanish-style villa overlooking the Columbia River boasts expertly groomed grounds, stone bridges crossing Phelps Creek, and the glorious 208-foot Wah Gwin Gwin Falls—all inspiring spots for kissing. Inside, find plenty more in the lavish, formal lobby and elegant restaurant, the Columbia Court Dining Room (see Romantic Restaurants), where you'll enjoy the wonderful seven-course World Famous Farm Breakfast (nonguests pay $60 for two). Request one of two Waterfall or four Fireplace rooms for added views and ambience. Nightly turndown service includes long-stemmed red roses and chocolates, and many romantic touches can be arranged to add to your experience—champagne, wine, cheese and fruit plates, pampering bath goodies, and spa services on-site. While summer is clearly a great time to visit for bocce ball or croquet for two on the manicured lawn, the hotel holds all-season appeal, particularly in winter with its elaborately lit grounds. If you can, schedule a visit for the hotel's Feast of Lights, when the dazzling twinkle lights are unveiled to officially begin the holiday festivities, followed by a five-course dinner. *$$$–$$$$; AE, DC, DIS, MC, V; checks OK; www. columbiagorgehotel.com.* &

Husum Highlands Bed & Breakfast / ◐◐◐

70 Postgren Rd, Husum; 509/493-4503 or 800/808-9812
When you're 7 miles off Highway 14 and winding your way up a gravel road, it's easy to wonder if you took a wrong turn—until you pull up to this beautiful, well-maintained home framed by what's easily the most stunning view of Mount Hood. The view alone makes a stay in this five-room bed-and-breakfast worthwhile, and—with hot tub, gazebo, and lingering spaces—there is plenty of opportunity and privacy to soak it up. Melanie's Suite offers the most privacy and best views both of Mount Hood and the manmade waterfall. In addition to preparing delicious breakfasts, owners Carol and Jerry Stockwell will also provide shuttle services for bike rides and picnic excursions, arrange in-house massages, and share great areas to recreate. Or, you can just stay put and blissfully snuggle up and enjoy the beauty right in front of you. *$$–$$$; MC, V; checks OK; www.husumhighlands.com.*

Inn at the Gorge / ◐◐◐◖

1113 Eugene St, Hood River; 541/386-4429
Near downtown, this sunny yellow Victorian exceeds our highest standards for romantic hideaways with its wraparound porch and beautiful gardens. All five rooms have tasteful, comfortable decor and private baths; however, the main floor Terrace Bedroom is a paradise for lovers. Its marble bathroom boasts a jetted tub for two, and the room itself offers a sumptuous bed facing a full wall of curtain-lined windows and two French double doors opening to a beautiful private garden, patio, and porch swing—undeniably the inn's best place to kiss. The spacious Rose and Cascade suites enjoy river-facing views and kitchenettes. Hosts Frank and Michelle Bouche pamper guests with additional services for special occasions. In the morning, breakfast will greet you on the front porch or in the dining room and—with local fruits, inventive main dishes, and a beautiful setting—is certain to inspire a return visit. *$$–$$$; MC, V; checks OK; www.innatthegorge.com.*

Lakecliff / ◐◐◐◖

3820 Westcliff Dr, Hood River; 541/386-7000
This historic 1908 summer home designed by Portland architect A. E. Doyle is a peaceful, woodsy retreat tucked off I-84 on 3 acres of prime Columbia riverfront property. A huge stone fireplace and luxurious couches beckon inside, and the back deck provides sublime surroundings for drinking wine, and watching wildlife and wild rides by the acrobatic windsurfers. Cheery colors, fresh flowers, and simple elegance grace four guest rooms, all with private baths. Most rooms in the house offer spectacular river views and fireplaces. Lilac, the largest room, offers the best views; however, its private bath is across the hall. Daffodil, also with river views, is another top choice. Celebrating a special occasion? Your hosts, Jim and Allyson Pate, aim to pamper and will happily arrange extra touches. After a delicious breakfast, stroll the

grounds or cuddle by the fire and savor every moment of this intimate riverside escape. *$$–$$$; MC, V; checks OK; www.lakecliffbnb.com.*

Mosier House Bed and Breakfast / ❂❂❹

704 3rd Ave, Mosier; 541/478-3640
Perched atop a knoll overlooking the Columbia River, this impeccably restored 1904 Queen Anne bed-and-breakfast is the only place to stay in Mosier, an ideal base for couples to enjoy the splendors of the gorge without the tourism (or hotel taxes) of Hood River. Five upstairs guest rooms, decorated with antique furniture and quilts, complement the architectural style. Because four rooms share baths, book the Master Bedroom, with its own entrance and porch overlooking the creek and a luxurious claw-foot tub beneath a well-placed skylight. Sweeping views from the river-facing Columbia Room make it our second favorite. Gracious innkeeper Cindy Hunter prepares a plentiful, delicious, and largely seasonal breakfast with specialties like eggs Florentine and blueberry pancakes. After breakfast, tap Cindy for her ideas on best places in the area to hike, bike, swim, and relax. For dinner, walk down the street to Good River (904 2nd Ave; 541/478-0199; www.good riverrestaurant.com), known for its great atmosphere and inventive meals. *$$; MC, V; checks OK; www.mosierhouse.com.*

Pheasant Valley Orchards / ❂❂❂

3890 Acree Dr, Hood River; 541/386-2803
Multitalented hosts Scott and Gail Hagee grow acres of organic pears and apples, produce hand-crafted (and good!) wine, and maintain one of the most pleasantly isolated, romantic B&B farmhouses in the Columbia River Gorge. All rooms offer pretty views of the orchards and Mount Hood. Our favorite place to snuggle is upstairs in the Comice Suite with its inviting king-size bed, private deck, raised Jacuzzi tub, and double-headed shower. Or stay in the cozy cottage affectionately known as "the coop," though this two-bedroom hideaway gives no hint of its former use as an authentic chicken coop and is perfect for those wanting a kitchen, grill, and private campfire under the stars. Wherever you choose to sleep, you'll wake to freshly brewed coffee and a sumptuous breakfast featuring orchard fruits. End your visit with a romantic stroll to the Pheasant Valley Winery tasting room. *$$; MC, V; checks OK; www.pheasantvalleyorchards.com.*

Sakura Ridge / ❂❂❂❂

5601 York Hill Dr, Hood River; 877/472-5872
Surrounded by organic cherry and pear orchards, beautifully tended gardens, fir trees, and eye-popping views of Mount Hood, this working farm and stunning home is carefully maintained by owners Deana and John Joyer. Soak in views of Mount Hood from four of the five guest rooms, common areas, or almost anywhere on the grounds. All rooms contain state-of-the-art

Waterfalls along the Columbia Gorge Historic Highway

Although most travelers approach the Columbia River Gorge via I-84 east, another more scenic option is to take exit 17 at Troutdale (or exit 22 at Corbett) to access one of the most romantic drives in the state: the Historic Columbia River Highway. And you'll see dramatic waterfalls all along the way. The recently restored **Vista House** (40700 E Historic Columbia River Hwy; 503/695-2230; mid-Apr–mid-Oct) at Crown Point should be your first stop. On a clear day, this octagonal stone structure, built atop a 733-foot cliff, is an exhilarating place to experience the beauty and expanse of the Columbia River Gorge. In summer, you can explore the historical displays and gift shop.

For a tour of waterfalls, continue heading east; you'll see **Latourelle Falls** as you cross a lovely bridge that arches over the water rushing to the Columbia. Next is **Bridal Veil Falls**, which, like the blushing bride for which it's named, hides from passing motorists. A steep two-thirds mile round-trip hike from the parking lot is worth the effort, especially with a kiss as your reward at the top. Next, you'll pass **Wahkeena Falls**, whose native name means "most beautiful."

While these waterfalls and the winding highway are indeed lovely, it's just a warm-up for what's to come: 620-foot **Multnomah Falls**, the nation's second-largest year-round waterfall. You can enjoy this gorgeous waterfall from a number of vistas depending upon your hiking interest and stamina; however, if possible, walk the paved path to at least the bridge spanning the waterfall for a memorable moment. After you've taken a few photos of each other before the falls and felt the mist refresh your faces, sit down to a rustic, romantic lunch of homemade soup and sandwiches inside the **Multnomah Falls Lodge** (53000 Historic Columbia River Hwy 30E, Bridal Veil; 503/695-2376; www.multnomahfallslodge.com).

A favorite among locals is the **Oneonta Gorge Trail**, accessed from the Horsetail Falls Trailhead parking area off the old scenic highway about 1.5 miles from I-5 at Ainsworth Park (exit 35). Oneonta Gorge Trail offers a beautiful hike that includes the opportunity to walk underneath a waterfall, a unique spot to sneak a smooch! Finally, **Horsetail Falls**, seen from the old highway, offers further evidence of the gorge's natural sources of inspiration.

amenities, quality bedding, Jacuzzi or old-fashioned-tub bathing, and windows or patios with beautiful vistas. The Orchard Room provides the greatest escape with an electric fireplace, a Japanese soaking tub, an eclectic mix of furnishings, and windows and a porch overlooking orchards and the mountain. Enjoy the best of all worlds here—comfort, beauty, privacy, and delicious foods. Extras include harvesting lessons and in-house massage. The journey to get here is well worth it; bring picnic supplies and snacks—once you arrive at Sakura Ridge, it is difficult to peel yourself away. *$$$; MC, V; checks OK; www.sakuraridge.com.*

Skamania Lodge / ✪✪✪❤

1131 SW Skamania Lodge Wy, Stevenson; 509/427-7700 or 800/221-7117
With beautiful river or forest views, spacious and comfortable rooms, and countless resort amenities, Skamania Lodge just might be the ultimate spa getaway. Guests enjoy access to the luxurious Waterleaf Spa and can use the pool, hot tub, and sauna to their heart's content. Pamper yourselves not only with the spa services but also with a phenomenal meal in the Pacific Crest Dining Room (509/427-7700), where the food actually eclipses the stunning river vistas. One of the lodge's many packages, the Ultimate Romance Getaway, includes dinner, hand-dipped strawberries and champagne served in-room, two plush terry-cloth robes, and a $180 allowance on-site at the Waterleaf Spa. For some of the best possible views of the gorge, request a river-view room, then lean back, relax, and soak in the experience. *$$$–$$$$; AE, DC, DIS, MC, V; no checks; www.skamania.com.* &

Villa Columbia / ✪✪✪

902 Oak St, Hood River; 541/386-6670 or 800/708-6217
A luxurious European-infused retreat has been created in this lovingly restored 1911 Craftsman bungalow. Hosts Boba and V. J. Jovanovich took great care to create private, comfortable surroundings in each of the five guest rooms, with added touches including rain showers, Jacuzzis, and electric fireplaces. For the view, the aptly named Columbia Suite can't be beat, and the Hood River Room opens onto the long main-level balcony. The atmosphere and architecture of the front room, balconies, and breakfast spaces invite you to sit and enjoy a cup of coffee, a glass of wine, or some of Boba's homemade cookies or fresh European-style breakfasts. A short walk down Oak Street, the central road through downtown, takes you to charming shops, restaurants, and parks, where you can gather goods before returning to your Hood River "villa." *$$–$$$; MC, V; checks OK; www.villacolumbia.com.* &

Romantic Restaurants

Abruzzo Italian Grill / ✪✪❤

1810 W Cascade St, Hood River; 541/386-7779
Effervescent host Glen Pearce and his top-notch team of chefs and servers will make you feel right at home at this wonderful Italian restaurant with excellent food available in a range of plate sizes. The place fills with locals and gets loud

at times, but it is easy to create your own romantic bubble within the good vibe. In warm weather, the outdoor patio offers more privacy. As with many local eateries, the menu changes every two weeks to reflect seasonal availability of local foods. Pearce also owns Panzanella Artisan Bakery and Italian Deli—a great stop for freshly baked bread and picnic-ready goodies. *$$; MC, V; local checks only; dinner Tues–Sat; full bar; no reservations.* &

Black Rabbit Restaurant / ⬡⬡⬡

2126 SW Halsey St, Troutdale; 503/492-3086
Located on McMenamins Edgefield's 25-acre colorful grounds, the Black Rabbit is the estate's most elegant dining option, softened with sconce lighting, white tablecloths, and private high-backed booths along the restaurant's perimeter. In summer, reserve a spot outside in the gorgeous New Orleans–style courtyard. Try the salmon tartare, creative salads, mahogany duck, potato-encrusted halibut, or lamb shanks braised in stout ale—and don't stop until you order the house-made apple pie à la mode topped with caramel sauce. While staying overnight is possible at Edgefield, we don't recommend the lodging option for romantic getaways. Luckily, you don't have to be an overnight guest to enjoy this intimate meal. *$$–$$$; AE, DIS, MC, V; no checks; breakfast, lunch, dinner every day; full bar; reservations recommended; www.mcmenamins.com.* &

Brian's Pourhouse / ⬡⬡⬡

606 Oak St, Hood River; 541/387-4344
Despite its first appearance, this restaurant happens to serve some of the most delicious, eclectic, and creative fare in the area. Here you can enjoy welcoming, attentive service and the relaxing surroundings of the dining room with white linens, abundant flowers, and plenty of window-side seating. Tables away from the door offer a more couple-friendly setting, or opt for the patio on warm summer nights. Options like sesame-crusted rare ahi tuna, wild salmon, and coconut green curry will entrance you, along with more traditional items and a large range of price options. Desserts are made in-house and are worth their own blissful visit. *$$–$$$; MC, V; checks OK; dinner every day; full bar; reservations recommended for parties of 6 or more; www.brianspourhouse.com.*

Celilo Restaurant / ⬡⬡⬡⬡

16 Oak St, Hood River; 541/386-5710
You and your sweetheart will settle right into this contemporary, elegant downtown dining spot. While Celilo is definitely a popular destination, table placement and acoustics allow for plenty of private conversation. Enjoy food adapted to the agricultural bounty of Hood River and environs with a range of creatively paired meat- and vegetable-based dishes and a knowledgeable waitstaff to offer suggestions. For starters, try the delicate uovo ravioli

appetizer (a single, large stuffed ravioli) and inventive cocktails, and peruse a wine list that highlights many locally produced bestsellers. Desserts, created in-house and perfect for sharing, include both perennial favorites—like the Wy'East Chocolate Volcano Cake and the Apple Tarte Tatin—as well as seasonal options. *$$$; AE, DC, DIS, MC, V; checks OK; lunch, dinner every day; full bar; reservations recommended; www.celilorestaurant.com.* &

Columbia River Court Dining Room / ⬡⬡⬡⬡

4000 Westcliff Dr (Columbia Gorge Hotel), Hood River;
541/386-5566 or 800/345-1921
A formal meal inside the Columbia Gorge Hotel (see Romantic Lodgings) is sure to sweep you off your feet, and the breathtaking views are the icing on the cake. Request a window table and spend a couple of hours enjoying the river, the food, and—most of all—your dining companion. The restaurant's focus is on local and international wines, seasonal fruits, vegetables, mushrooms, and fish, all prepared exquisitely and presented dramatically under silver domes. An attentive, professional waitstaff guides you through your dining experience from champagne-kissed sorbets to your final selections of nightcaps and sumptuous desserts. A walk through the hotel's serpentine, bench-strewn paths ends a memorable dining experience. *$$$–$$$$; AE, DC, DIS, MC, V; checks OK; breakfast, lunch, dinner every day; full bar; reservations recommended; www.columbiagorgehotel.com.* &

Sixth Street Bistro & Loft / ⬡⬡⬡

509 Cascade Ave, Hood River; 541/386-5737
Skip and Go Naked, a vodka, rum, and brandy concoction, will definitely set the pace for you at this "older sister" of nearby Celilo Restaurant that offers a more casual and lively atmosphere but still plenty of space to snuggle into your own conversation. The menu changes regularly and emphasizes sustainable and organic foods with a wide range of choices, from chipotle-lime chicken to oyster dishes to local favorites that include pad Thai, curries, teriyaki, and stir-fries. If you're looking for a pleasing standard, they've got a Damn Good Cheeseburger. Whatever you do, save space for house-made desserts—sure winners include crème brûlée and seasonal cobblers big enough to share. *$$–$$$; AE, DIS, MC, V; checks OK; lunch, dinner every day; full bar; reservations recommended; www.sixthstreetbistro.com.*

Stonehedge Gardens / ⬡⬡⬡

3405 Cascade Dr, Hood River; 541/386-3940
Travel a winding gravel road to one of Hood River's most notorious dinner destinations. Once you arrive, you'll see that this five-level garden is a stellar setting for the best alfresco dining spot in the gorge. In cooler months, snuggle near the crackling fire in the dark interior. Unfortunately, the service can be disorganized, and the food, while decent, moderately priced, and generously

portioned, is not terribly memorable. However, save room for the bread pudding for two, topped with crème brûlée and bourbon caramel sauce. North Oak Brasserie (113 3rd St, Hood River; 541/387-2310), run by the same owners, is an inviting spot for great Italian food. *$$–$$$; AE, DIS, MC, V; checks OK; dinner every day; full bar; reservations recommended; www.stone hedgegardens.com.*

Three Rivers / ◐◐◐

601 Oak St; Hood River; 541/386-8883
With four different indoor dining areas and outdoor seating surrounding most of this restored century-old house, tables with privacy and wonderful views abound. Gazing at views of the Wind, Columbia, and Hood rivers as well as downtown, diners are treated to amazing natural beauty with the evening sun reflecting on Washington Hills. Offering an excellent local wine list (only a few by the glass) and well-prepared food emphasizing wild, local, organic products—salmon, seasonal halibut, amazing locally foraged mushrooms—this place does it right. Servers are accomplished, offer good suggestions, and create an intimate dining experience, even in a crowded restaurant. *$$–$$$; AE, DC, DIS, MC, V; checks OK; lunch, dinner every day; full bar; reservations recommended; www.3riversgrill.com.* &

Mount Hood

Romantic Highlights

The snowy peak of Mount Hood beckons visitors year-round for beautiful scenery and recreation; as Oregon's highest peak (11,235 feet), this fabled mountain takes romance to new heights. The surrounding area offers a bounty for active nature lovers as well as for those simply seeking a quiet mountain retreat. With beautiful lakes, hiking and biking trails, and pristine ski slopes, there's never a shortage of ways to take in the fresh air and stunning surroundings. The popularity of this destination with climbers, backpackers, and snowboarders means that many of the accommodations are geared toward adventurers seeking a place to rest in between activity-filled days. Happily, more lodging options catering to romance seekers have opened up in the last few years.

Timberline is the main attraction at Mount Hood. This singular resort offers year-round skiing, fine dining, and accommodations in the impressive Timberline Lodge. Other towns that offer lodging close to the glacial peak include Welches, Brightwood, Parkdale, and Government Camp. Trust your instincts and avoid staying in Government Camp, the most commercial and least romantic of the towns. Just a few miles down the road, Welches offers several good restaurant options, an espresso shop, an information center, and the charming Wy'east Book Shoppe and Gallery (67195 E Hwy 26; 503/622-1623). Nearby Brightwood is home to three inns (see Romantic Lodgings) that will leave you swooning. Of course, the Mount Hood area is also reasonably accessible for a day trip from Hood River or Portland.

It is no surprise that winter is the busiest time on the mountain. Skiers often book their rooms months in advance and take advantage of the bargain-priced lift tickets offered by many of the lodgings. Whatever your level of expertise (or lack thereof), the five area ski resorts offer something for everyone—along with plenty of romantic opportunities to warm up with hot cocoa in front of the fireplace. While Cooper Spur and Summit are geared more toward families (and thus register lower on the romance meter), they do offer easier terrain for beginners. **Cooper Spur** (Hwy 35, 11000 Cloud Cap Rd; 541/352-6692; www.cooperspur. com), on the north side of Mount Hood, offers inexpensive day and night skiing. At an elevation of 7,300 feet, **Mount Hood Meadows** (2 miles north of Hwy 35 on Forest Rd 3555; 503/337-2222; www.skihood.com) is the largest and most popular area on the mountain.

In the town of Government Camp, **Mount Hood SkiBowl** (87000 E Hwy 26; 503/272-3206, or 503/222-2695 for recorded information; www.skibowl.com) offers the best place to ski under the stars, with 34 lighted runs. At 4,306 feet, **Summit** (Hwy 26, near rest area at east end of Government Camp; 503/272-0256; www.summitskiarea.com) is good for beginners. **Timberline** (4 miles north of Hwy 26, just east of Government Camp; 503/622-7979; www.timberlinelodge. com) is 6,000 feet, has six lifts, and offers year-round skiing.

For an easy—and romantic—way up the mountain any time of year, take Timberline's **Magic Mile Sky Ride,** a six-minute ride on an express chairlift to the 7,000-foot mark. Once you reach the top, hold each other tight and take in the magnificent view. When the snow melts in spring, hiking opportunities on the mountain abound with kiss-worthy trails accessible from the lodge and, in summer months, bursting with wildflowers. The **Magic Mile Interpretive Trail** returns to Timberline Lodge, and the **Timberline Trail** leads 4½ miles west from Timberline Lodge to flower-studded Paradise Park. Energetic twosomes can continue another 5½ miles to the sublimely beautiful mist of Ramona Falls.

Two of the area's lakes are prime destinations for romantic summer picnics. East of Government Camp on Highway 26 you'll find **Trillium Lake.** An easy walking trail circles the lake; wintertime explorers can tour it on cross-country skis or snowshoes. Farther toward Hood River is **Lost Lake** (541/386-6366 for driving directions), another paradise for couples. Trails are open for bikers and hikers, but watch where you step! Horseback riders frequent the trail as well. On a clear summer day, take advantage of the lake by renting a rowboat or canoe to soak up the sunshine, cast a line for trout and salmon, or serenade your sweetie. Campsites and cabins are available for rustic overnight stays.

Access and Information

From Portland, take U.S. Highway 26 to Mount Hood. From the north, Highway 35 from Hood River connects with Highway 26. In winter, traction devices are often required on Mount Hood. Call the **Oregon Department** of **Transportation** (503/588-2941 outside Oregon, or 800/977-6368 inside Oregon) to find out if roads are snowy or icy. The online **Travel Advisor** (www.tripcheck.com) has excellent, up-to-date information on road conditions. Also, an **Oregon Department of Transportation Winter Sno-Park Permit** is required if you plan to stop. Permits are sold at **Timberline Lodge** (see Romantic Lodgings), as well as at service stations, Department of Motor Vehicles offices, and sporting-goods stores in the gorge and on the mountain. In summer, you'll need a **Northwest Forest Pass** ($5 per day), which you can purchase at ranger stations and sporting-goods stores. The **Mount Hood Information Center** (65000 E Hwy 26, Welches; 503/622-4822 or 888/622-4822; www.mthood.info) provides tourist information, including hiking maps.

Romantic Lodgings

Brightwood Guest House / ●●●●

64725 E Barlow Trail Rd, Brightwood; 503/622-5783 or 888/503-5783
Prepare for absolute enchantment and relaxation at this beautiful creek-side guest house nestled in two secluded acres. Kissing opportunities are countless, including on a private deck with a koi pond, in a hammock by the creek, in the outdoor hot soaking tubs set next to a fireplace, in the well-tended gardens, and hidden in the meadows. The private guest house itself is not particularly large, but your hosts, Bonnie and Jeff Rames, have put great care into making it self-contained, with a fully equipped kitchen, comfortable nestling areas, and a sumptuous queen bed located up steep steps in a sleeping alcove. With some advance notice, your hosts will arrange on-site massages or almost any other romantic indulgence. Bonnie's cheerful morning knock at the time you request brings breakfast trays loaded with gourmet goodies. *$$; all credit cards via PayPal; checks OK; www.mounthoodbnb.com.*

Mt. Hood Bed and Breakfast / ●●●◖

8885 Cooper Spur Rd, Parkdale; 800/557-8885
Four wonderful and private cabins provide a sublime stay at the foothills of Mount Hood's north side. Owners Jackie and Mike Rice have surrounded the house (and breakfast area) with beautiful landscaping and flowers, creating a fantastic wedding setting. This 42-acre property—with its pond, gigantic wooden swing, and abundance of butterflies and other wild and domesticated animals—allows plenty of privacy for romantic moments. For a truly enchanted evening, book the 1904 Homestead Cabin with fireplace, old-fashioned tub, and well-placed windows providing views of sunflowers and Mount Hood aglow with the rising sun. Upon request, your hosts will draw baths, deliver rose petals or bouquets, and serve chilled champagne. In the morning, Jackie serves up a full country breakfast with home-grown fruit and delicious homemade jams. Linger all day long or enjoy nearby

Three Days of Romance

Day One: With picnic basket in hand, set off to the Columbia River Gorge with a meandering journey up the Historic Columbia Gorge Highway with its plentiful waterfalls and vistas. Upon reentering I-84, continue along the stunning Gorge to Hood River. At exit 62, you will see the striking Spanish-style building of the **Columbia Gorge Hotel** and its beautiful grounds. Check in and relax into all of the luxurious touches offered with spa treatments and a delicious dinner on-site at the elegant **Columbia River Court Dining Room**. After dinner, take a stroll, sit by the fire in the bar, or ask the bellman to show you the heavenly view from the tower. You really can't be off to a better start than this.

Day Two: After the seemingly never-ending World Famous Farm Breakfast downstairs at the Columbia Gorge Hotel, you'll likely need another walk or a quick nap before heading off to the adventures of the day. Take your time! Then, follow the **Hood River Fruit Loop** (Hwy 35 and Dee Hwy 281), a 35-mile meandering journey that highlights amazing views, fruit stands and orchards, as well as some wineries that invite you to taste and stay awhile. Be sure to stop at **Pheasant Valley Vineyards** (3890 Acree Dr, Hood River; 541/387-3040), the area's first organic orchard, with delicious wines and gracious hosts. You should also visit **The Gorge White House** (2265 Hwy 35, Hood River; 541/386-2828), a tasting room representing

Cooper Spur snow and hiking trails. *$$–$$$; MC, V; checks OK; www. mthoodbnb.com.*

Mt. Hood Hamlet Bed and Breakfast / ○○○◖

6741 Hwy 35, Mount Hood; 541/352-3547 or 800/407-0570
This New England–style Colonial overlooks the 9-acre farm where owner Paul Romans was raised, and magnificent Mount Hood appears close enough to touch. Paul and his wife, Diane, spoil guests every step of the way. Bask in the outdoor Jacuzzi tub (gazing at Mount Hood by day or stargazing by night) and pad up to your room in plush robes. With the heated deck, you'll stay cozy even when you emerge from the hot, bubbly water. Two of the largest rooms, Vista Ridge and Orchard, both boasting Jacuzzi tubs, are prime kissing quarters with a bonus tub view of Mount Hood in Vista Ridge. Wake up to astounding views of Mount Hood, lovely birdsong from the inn's gardens and orchards, and the scent of freshly brewed coffee and gourmet breakfast goodies, including veggie omelets, smoky sausage, scones, and jams made by your hosts. *$$; AE, DIS, MC, V; checks OK; www.mthoodhamlet.com.*

wines from most wineries in the area, and the picturesque **Cathedral Ridge** (4200 Post Canyon Dr, Hood River; 541/386-2882). With enough walking, you may have recovered from breakfast in time for a perfectly prepared dinner at **Celilo Restaurant** before eagerly returning to your room at **Sakura Ridge**. Enjoy the awe-inspiring views of Mount Hood and a taste of life in the orchards amid the star scape of Hood River.

Day Three: After breakfast and maybe a little harvesting at **Sakura Ridge**, you're off to Hood River for shopping and a quick stop at **South Bank Kitchen** (404 Oak St; 541/386-9876) or **Panzanella** (102 5th St; 541/386-2048) to gather the ingredients for a picturesque picnic. Head up and across the Columbia River for a day-long exploration of Washington's Columbia Gorge wineries. Start on the east end at **Maryhill Winery** (9774 Hwy 14, Goldendale; 877/627-9445) with its beautiful vistas and large range of wines. Share a glass and a picnic, and, frequently, enjoy the music on the expansive decks. Wineries are abundant, most notably **Cor Cellars** (151 Old Hwy 8; 509/365-2744) and **Syncline** (111 Balch Rd; 509/365-4361), both located in Lyle, Washington. Enjoy some of the art shops in White Salmon or continue to your final evening's destination at **Carson Ridge Cabins Bed and Breakfast** with dinner from the stunning vista of **Skamania Lodge's Pacific Crest Dining Room**. An evening enjoying the luxuries of your intimate cabin is the perfect way to conclude this Columbia River Gorge adventure.

Old Parkdale Inn / ❂❂❶

4932 Baseline Rd, Parkdale; 541/352-5551 or 877/687-4669
You don't have to be art lovers—lovers pure and simple will do—to enjoy this playful place. In-room kitchens, sitting areas, and the option to have a delicious breakfast delivered to your door begin a stay marked by privacy and relaxation. Mary and Steve Pellegrini have remodeled common areas to provide more light and conviviality, and the grounds offer many amenities including a fire pit, a hot tub, a gazebo area, and colorful gardens—complete with a pond and waterfall. Each of the three themed suites—Monet, Gauguin, and Georgia O'Keeffe—inspire different moods and have a private bath, distinctive decor, artwork, and quotes from the artist at the entrance. The O'Keefe suite is appealing for its Mount Hood view, the Monet for its garden-facing balcony. The tiny town of Parkdale makes a nice refuge, whether you're exploring wine country, enjoying valley fruit celebrations, or jumping into wintertime snow activities. *$$; MC, V; checks OK; www. hoodriverlodging.com.*

Columbia Gorge Wineries

The wine industry in the Columbia Gorge is booming, and beautiful tasting rooms and wineries exist on both sides of the Columbia River. Some of the best for romantic lingering include the following:

Oregon side

Many wineries offer free tastings and welcome you to relax—with a glass and a picnic on the grounds. The best in the area include **Cathedral Ridge Winery** (4200 Post Canyon Dr, Hood River; 541/386-2882 or 800/516-8710), **Pheasant Valley Winery** (3890 Acree Dr, Hood River; 541/387-3040), **Wy'East Vineyards Tasting Room** (3189 Hwy 35, Hood River; 541/386-8333), and, for a taste from several vineyards along with nice picnic tables, **The Gorge White House** (2265 Hwy 35, Hood River; 541/386-2828).

For delicious fruit wines and ports, **Hood River Vineyards** (4693 Westwood Dr, Hood River; 541/386-3772) can't be beat, and when downtown, enjoy the sophisticated tasting atmosphere at **Quenett Winery** (111 Oak St, Hood River; 541/386-2229) with its low lights and seating just made for gazing at each other.

The Resort at the Mountain / ○€

68010 E Fairway Ave, Welches; 503/622-3101 or 800/669-7666

The sublime setting of this 160-room Scottish-themed resort, nestled in 300 acres of evergreen woodland in the foothills of the Huckleberry Wilderness Area in the Mount Hood National Forest, makes up for the building's aesthetic shortcomings. The scenery is breathtaking in any season, but when the grounds are covered with snow it is nothing short of spectacular. The rooms may not be deluxe, but they're large and comfortable, and even the standard rooms come with a deck or patio (ask for one with a forest view). Each Fireside Studio offers a full kitchen and wood-burning fireplace glowing on a platform near the king-size bed. Before you arrive, pick up provisions—bottled water, fireplace logs, coffee, and popcorn are provided—so that once you settle in, your room can become your haven. When you're ready to venture out, the resort offers two restaurants, tennis and volleyball courts, a golf course, an outdoor heated pool, a Jacuzzi tub, a fitness center, and hiking trails. *$$–$$$; AE, DIS, MC, V; checks OK; www.theresort.com.* &

Salmon River Inn / ○○○€

20550 E Country Club Rd, Brightwood; 503/622-6212

At this riverside inn, lush, inspired gardens with artistic treasures create the perfect atmosphere for romance and relaxation. Artist/owner Tracy Mathey

Any of these excursions will be enhanced when you're stocked and ready with picnic provisions. Try **The Good Deli and Coffee House** (Mt. Hood Country Store, 6545 Cooper Spur Rd, Mount Hood; 541/325-6024) toward Mount Hood off Highway 35 and the Fruit Loop.

Washington side

See the Columbia Gorge from a different, and drier, perspective when traveling west along the gorge beginning in Goldendale. Visit **Maryhill Winery** (9774 Hwy 14, Goldendale; 877/627-9445), located beside the famous and fun-to-visit Maryhill Museum and the winery's amphitheater, which hosts great summertime concerts and smaller musical events on its picturesque decks. It will be difficult to pull yourself away, but other wineries await. **Cascade Cliffs Vineyard and Winery** (8866 Hwy 14, Wishram; 509/767-1100) and **Marshal's Winery** (150 Oak Creek Rd, Dallesport; 509/767-4633), as well as **Cor Cellars** (151 Old Hwy 8, Lyle; 509/365-2744) and **Syncline** (111 Balch Rd, Lyle; 509/365-4361), will tickle your taste buds and spur conversations—in between kisses. A little out of the way, but also fun to visit and enjoy the view, is **Wind River Cellars** (196 Spring Creek Rd, Husum; 509/493-2324).

designed a lovely space full of Northwest art that both integrates and plays with the natural beauty. For an additional fee you can feast on a seasonal gourmet breakfast at Tracy's Table, featuring a handmade table and stunning river views. Or, ask your hostess to pack a breakfast basket for you to enjoy in one of many scenic gardens or decks, a sure recipe for morning kisses. Upstairs, the inn offers two beautifully appointed guest rooms with Egyptian linens and feather bed toppers that beg you to dive right in. You will feel at home, whether in your own room, in the common areas, in the candlelit hot tub, or next to the cozy fire pit, all simply awaiting your arrival. *$$; MC, V; checks OK; www.salmonriverinn.com.*

Sandy Salmon Bed and Breakfast Lodge / ✪✪✪

61661 E Hwy 26, Sandy; 503/622-6699
The setting of this lodge above the confluence of the Sandy and Salmon rivers is genuinely awe inspiring, as are the lodge's dramatic touches, including an astounding Juniper-wood mantle, an indoor koi pond, river views, and art pieces. Common areas include a theater room, a gameroom complete with trophy heads on the wall above the custom pool table, and a three-tier deck with a fire pit. The plush rooms have Jacuzzi tubs, detailed themes, and bay windows or balconies. Both the pioneer-themed Barlow Trail room and the Fishing Hole room feature sinuously curved juniper beds and river-facing

private balconies. The premier room, Eagle's Nest, has a bay window looking out to the confluence. For a theme befitting your journey to Mount Hood and its rustic heritage, clearly the hosts have gone to great lengths to share such a vision in this stunning home, which is also complete with evening wine and desserts, and delicious breakfasts. *$$$; MC, V; checks OK; www. sandysalmon.com.*

Timberline Lodge / ❂❂❂

Timberline Ski Area, Timberline; 503/231-5400 or 800/547-1406
Driving up the wintertime road to Timberline Lodge at a 6,000-foot elevation, with its snow-covered trees and increasingly angelic views, is like climbing the stairway to heaven. This massive timber-and-stone lodge was built in just 15 months by President Franklin Roosevelt's 1930s Works Progress Administration program; well-preserved glass mosaics, stone chimneys, and handmade tapestries and fabrics display master craftsmanship. A recent upgrade to the 70 rustic guest rooms added premium featherbeds and duvets, linens, carpeting, and remodeled bathrooms, making the steep prices easier to justify. The renovated outdoor pool and spa are open year-round, though a private soak under the stars is most likely found midweek. Eight spacious Fireplace Rooms—with close-up Mount Hood or distant Mount Jefferson views—offer the most romantic potential. With rare year-round skiing, these accommodations are booked far in advance, so plan ahead and note that windows in lower-level rooms might be covered with wintertime snow. Northwest cuisine at the Cascade Dining Room (see Romantic Restaurants) is worth a splurge after a day of hiking or skiing—and kissing. *$$$–$$$$; AE, DIS, MC, V; checks OK; www.timberlinelodge.com.* &

Romantic Restaurants

Cascade Dining Room / ❂❂❂

Timberline Lodge, Timberline; 503/622-0700
With magical, historical surroundings, Timberline Lodge can be a thrill whether you're celebrating a special occasion or simply enjoying a refined meal on Oregon's highest peak. In the evening, the rustic, casual dining room takes on a soft glow with beautiful window views. For three decades, head chef Leif Eric Benson has prepared sophisticated, creative Northwest cuisine like grilled Alaskan king salmon or chanterelle-crusted rack of lamb to pair with this view. Complement your meal with a bottle from the extensive wine list, or select your own in a private trip to the wine cellar. Decadent housemade desserts like crème brûlée, chili-infused Molten Lava Cake, and fruit cobblers go perfectly with the beautiful sunset. *$$$–$$$$; AE, DC, DIS, MC, V; checks OK; breakfast, lunch, dinner every day; full bar; reservations recommended; www.timberlinelodge.com.* &

The Rendezvous Grill and Tap Room / ◐◐

67149 E Hwy 26, Welches; 503/622-6837
In the Mount Hood area, finding restaurants with romantic appeal can be a challenge. And though the Rendezvous may not be filled with doe-eyed couples, this unassuming spot with high ceilings, tables, and booths serves some of Mount Hood's best meals. Chef/co-owner Kathryn Bliss's emphasis is on seasonal, local produce, including chanterelle mushrooms and huckleberries. Pasta lovers will swoon for house specialty alder-smoked chicken rigatoni with toasted hazelnuts, dried cranberries, and fresh spinach. In the mood to splurge? Order the mouthwatering char-grilled New York steak with Oregon white-truffle butter. Sharing the chocolate pecan tart with chocolate mousse makes for nothing short of a heavenly finish. *$$–$$$; AE, DIS, MC, V; checks OK; lunch, dinner Wed–Sun (every day in summer); full bar; reservations recommended; www.rendezvousgrill.net.* &

♡ Willamette
Valley

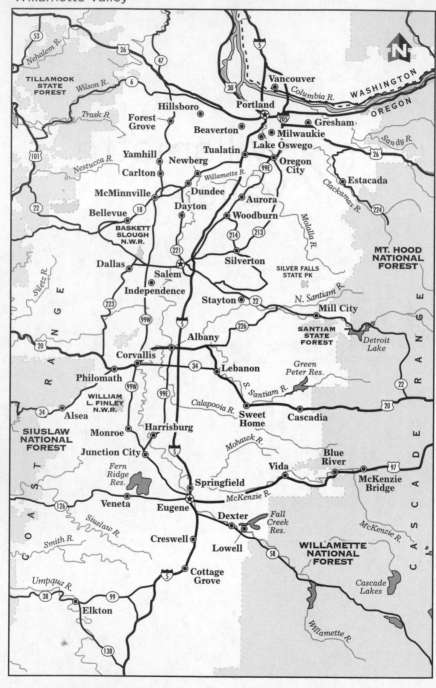

Where there is love there is life.

—Mahatma Gandhi

 # Willamette Valley

Although Portland is, geographically speaking, part of the Willamette Valley, the real romance begins when couples retreat to the valley's rural areas. Past the city's surrounding suburbs, rolling landscapes and groves of fruit, oak, and Douglas fir trees create picturesque scenery. Because of its mild climate—generous amounts of rain in winter and long, sunny summers—everything grows well in the Willamette Valley. Romance is in bloom year-round—especially in Yamhill County located southwest of Portland. Here, a string of tiny towns falls along Highway 99W, or "wine road," housing award-winning restaurants, peaceful B&Bs, and quaint city centers ideal for leisurely strolling. And for those who love wine—or simply the countryside and sweeping vineyard views—this region provides a bountiful wine-country experience.

Visitors may choose to stay in wine country at a growing number of elegant lodgings, or in nearby cities and towns with even more lodging and dining choices. Corvallis offers lovely B&Bs and a riverfront walkway; in Eugene, rose gardens, opera and symphony, and extensive riverside walking paths charm couples. Albany is known for antiquing, and Salem—the state's capital—has a rich history and a handful of pretty parks. Couples staying in larger towns will find themselves drawn to the country for day trips to enjoy the rural tranquility of the surrounding areas. You might cross the Willamette and its mellow tributaries by ferry or covered bridges, visit the dashing McKenzie River, enjoy the solitude of Finley National Wildlife Refuge in fall or winter, or find pleasure in the Heirloom Old Garden roses in summer.

Interstate 5 runs the length of the Willamette Valley and provides quick access to major cities. For slower-paced touring, take Highway 99W from the wine country at the valley's north end down to Eugene in the south—you'll pass through the wine-country hubs of Newberg, Dundee, and McMinnville along the way. Follow the blue signs that point out wineries for a pleasurable roadside stop.

Wine Country

Romantic Highlights

A 30-minute drive southwest from Portland brings you into the Willamette Valley, home of Oregon's most famous wine country. Framed by the gentle rise of the Coast Range in the west and the glacial peaks of the Cascades in the east, this lush terrain features rolling vineyard-covered hills and forested landscapes. The famous pinot noir grapes thrive in this region's mild climate, and today there are more than 200 wineries to visit. Guests will quickly find that, as with wine, some have more character than others.

Most of our favorite kissing destinations are in the North Willamette Valley (see Romantic Wineries), but adventurous couples might extend their tour to the wineries and vineyards that stretch south past Salem and Eugene. If no one wants to play designated driver, join a tour. Though organized tours are not exactly private affairs, they offer one great advantage—you can soak up scenery and sip wine while someone else does the driving. **Grape Escape Winery Tours** (503/283-3380; www.grapeescapetours.com) offers a variety of packages; **Wine Tours Northwest** (503/439-8687 or 800/359-1034; www.winetoursnorthwest. com) hosts two-person tours for a slightly higher fee. Or, float over wine country in a hot-air balloon with **Vista Balloon Adventures** (503/625-7385 or 800/622-2309; www.vistaballoon.com), which concludes with a champagne breakfast.

The Willamette Valley wine country is a lovely destination any time of the year. In spring, the trees are heavy with fragrant blossoms; summer is an ideal season for vineyard picnics. Fall ushers in golden landscapes and the wine crush. Winter brings rain, but there are plenty of cozy tasting rooms and restaurants to tuck into. Further acquaint yourselves with this region by contacting the **Oregon Wine Advisory Board** (www.oregonwine.org) or by picking up the complimentary *Guide to Willamette Valley Wineries*, available at visitor associations, hotels, and travel centers, and online (www.willamettewines.com).

If you tour the region by car on Highway 99W, you'll find that many of the wineries and tasting rooms are clustered around the small towns of Newberg, Dundee, Dayton, and McMinnville. Some wineries feature elegant, high-ceilinged tasting rooms, while others are housed in modest roadside buildings or barns. Oftentimes, fantastic wines make up for the sparse surroundings. Whichever wineries you visit, your entire winery-hopping tour will be an invigorating pleasure.

Each town has its own appeal. Stop in **Newberg** for picnic-ready goodies at the **French Bear** (107 S College St; 503/539-2609; www.thefrenchbear.com). Similar picnic provisions—and numerous tasting rooms—are found just miles away in Carlton. After visiting Carlton's plentiful tasting rooms, pop into the **Horse Radish Cheese and Wine Bar** (211 W Main St; 503/852-6616; www.thehorseradish. com) to sample artisan cheese flights and wine by the splash, glass, or bottle. If you arrive in Carlton in the evening, take a stroll along Main Street before dining at **Cuvée Restaurant** (see Romantic Restaurants).

Farther down wine road, you'll find old town **McMinnville**, where gracious tree-shaded streets house a number of wine bars, restaurants, and boutiques. Sample melt-in-your-mouth chocolates from local chocolatier **Honest Chocolates** (313 NE 3rd St; 503/474-9042; www.honestchocolates.com) or pop into McMenamins' **Hotel Oregon** (310 NE Evans St; 503/472-8427 or 888/472-8427; www.hoteloregon.com), where you can visit a rooftop bar, the casual ground-floor family pub, and a romantic wine cellar hidden away in the basement. Other stops include the towns of Gaston and Forest Grove. You can visit their wineries on your way into or out of Portland, since several highways link back to the city (and Interstate 5) from these northern areas.

Access & Information

Travelers from Seattle or Portland usually arrive in the wine country by car via Interstate 5. Out-of-towners can also fly into **Portland International Airport** (7000 NE Airport Wy; 503/460-4234 or 877/739-4636; www.flypdx.com), rent a car, and then proceed on to wine country. A popular and scenic alternate route from Portland to the northern Willamette Valley is via the old US Highway 99W, parallel to I-5 west of the Willamette River. Those who endure suburban traffic congestion in the early miles of the drive are rewarded when the route becomes more scenic. At the north end, where it's known as the "wine road," it passes through Newberg, Dundee, and McMinnville; blue signs point the way to wineries. All three towns make good headquarters for wine touring. McMinnville even has a helpful **Chamber of Commerce** (417 NW Adams St; 503/472-6196; www.mcminnville.org). For further information on the area, contact the **Chehalem Valley Chamber of Commerce** (415 E Sheridan, Newberg; 503/538-2014; www.newberg.org/web).

Be prepared for more traffic on summer and holiday weekends; on the other hand, one benefit of visiting during busy periods is that even the smaller wineries open their doors. Generally, driving conditions are fine—even in the winter.

Romantic Wineries

Anne Amie / ✪✪✪

6580 NE Mineral Springs Rd, Carlton; 503/864-2991
Named Anne Amie (pronounced on-ah-me) after the owner's two daughters, this hilltop winery and French-style chateau tasting room offer pastoral views and exquisite sunsets over the Coast Range. Purchase a bottle of wine and wedge of cheese from the tasting room, then spend the afternoon relaxing on the adjacent patio where a dozen lovely tables with shade umbrellas sit amid palm trees and flowering gardens. Savor the light breeze and sweeping views while finding romance over a glass of Pinot Noir or, for a lighter and whiter touch, try the Viognier. *10am–5pm every day; www.anneamie.com.* &

Willamette Valley Chocolatiers

Getting your chocolate fix is an easy task in Willamette Valley, where not one but four reputable chocolatiers have created a following. You'll find **Honest Chocolates** (313 NE 3rd St, McMinnville; 503/474-9042; www.honestchocolates.com) in McMinnville's quiet downtown; we positively swooned for their toffee bark.

Head to Eugene to sample treats from the remaining three artisans: **Euphoria**'s three locations each have their own appeal, but we prefer the original downtown store (6 W 17th Ave; 541/343-9223; www.euphoriachocolate.com); we recommend trying the Oreo dressed in a white-chocolate coat. At **Fenton & Lee** (35 E 8th Ave; 541/343-7629; www.fentonandlee.com), sample chocolate-dipped fruit. For a final thrill, find **KeKau**'s (541/338-7684; www.kekau.com) colorful, artistic chocolates—including their savory Habanero Tequila chocolate—at a number of local retailers like **Sweet Life Patisserie** (755 Monroe St; 541/683-5676; www.sweetlifedesserts.com) and **Marché Provisions** (296 E 5th Ave; 541/743-0660; www.marcheprovisions.com).

David Hill Winery / ✪✪✪✪

46350 NW David Hill Rd, Forest Grove; 503/992-8545 or 877/992-8545
After you've descended a dirt driveway, this pristine, beautifully restored 1883 farmhouse, surrounded by lush green lawns and brilliant flower gardens, is a refreshing sight. The bright, airy tasting room, located inside the historic home, is abundantly pleasant and charming. Plenty of tempting wine choices, including a delicious Pinot Noir and heavenly port, make up the winery's repertoire. For a truly sublime moment, step outside and share a kiss beneath the shady trees. It's a lovely spot for a private picnic, and it's no wonder that some couples choose to tie the knot here. *Noon–5pm every day; www.davidhillwinery.com.* &

Domaine Serene / ✪✪✪

6555 NE Hilltop Ln, Dayton; 503/864-4600 or 866/864-6555
The rules are strict at this regal Italian-style winery (no picnics and no opening of purchased bottles on-site), but the views are so breathtaking that visitors don't seem to mind. Before 3pm, guests may purchase a glass of the winery's award-winning Pinot Noir to enjoy on the outside patio where classical music is played. A handsome tasting room with marble floors, rich tapestries, high ceilings, and ornate chandeliers creates an opulent wine-tasting experience; the cozy fireplace provides a place to cuddle on a rainy day. *11am–4pm Wed–Sun; www.domaineserene.com.* &

Elk Cove Vineyards / ◗◗◗◗

27751 NW Olson Rd, Gaston; 503/985-7760 or 877/355-2683
Drive up the long, winding road and you will discover one of Oregon's most wildly romantic spots. Kissing is almost unavoidable here, whether you visit in summer when the vineyards are lush and green, or in fall when the landscape turns red and gold. In the tasting room, sip a single-vineyard Pinot Noir, a Pinot Gris, or an estate Riesling. A small, charming English garden courtyard adjoins the tasting room; from the patio, enjoy lovely views of vineyards enclosed by stately Douglas firs. This is a popular spot for weddings, but if you can get the lovely gazebo all to yourselves, it's also a perfect place to steal a smooch. *10am–5pm every day; www.elkcove.com.* ♿

Erath Vineyards / ◗◗◖

9409 NE Worden Hill Rd, Dundee; 503/538-3318 or 800/539-9463
You will want to drink in the sights, and the complimentary wine-tasting flight, at this scenic winery. The cozy tasting room, nestled in between vineyards high in the Dundee Hills, has stunning views in every direction. Sample the Pinot Noir, Pinot Blanc, Riesling, or Gewürztraminer. On slower days, the vine-covered terrace is yours alone. Tables here, and on the tent-covered patio around back, provide ideal spots for a picnic to go with your newly purchased wine; the tasting room sells a selection of gourmet goodies if you forget to bring your own. *11am–5pm every day; www.erath.com.* ♿

Rex Hill Vineyards / ◗◗

30835 N Hwy 99W, Newberg; 800/739-4455
Terraced lawns, divided by railroad ties and anchored by a forest of fir trees, provide a beautiful landscape for the prestigious Rex Hill winery, settled in acres of vineyards. While the grounds are ideal for picnics, and benches under a trellised walkway invite relaxation, there are few secluded spots for kissing. This is also an occasional tour destination, so crowds may detract from your experience. Once you taste the world-class Pinot Noir, however, you'll forget about these slight drawbacks. The tasting room welcomes visitors with a simple stone fireplace, antiques, and wine barrels displayed in the brick-lined cellar. *11am–5pm every day (10am–5pm summer weekends); www.rexhill.com.* ♿

Torii Mor Winery / ◗◗

18325 NE Fairview Dr, Dundee; 503/538-2279 or 800/839-5004
Dust off from the drive up the long gravel road that leads to this hidden hillside winery and enter its peaceful Japanese garden—complete with a small rock garden and grassy alcoves. Torii Mor's growing popularity means you'll likely share sipping space in the minimalist Japanese-style tasting room and garden with other oenophiles in search of remarkable Pinot Noirs. Enjoy

a tasting flight of the winery's high-end wines then steal a private moment while wandering through the adjacent vineyards. *11am–5pm every day; www. toriimorwinery.com.* ☆

Romantic Lodgings

Abbey Road Farm / ◑◐◖

10501 NE Abbey Rd, Carlton; 503/852-6278
Perched atop a hill overlooking acres of country landscapes, this working farm and bed-and-breakfast offers breathtaking views, as well as a spirit of adventure for guests: each of the five circular suites is located in a refurbished silo. These insulated spaces are the perfect secluded places for a peaceful country weekend. Modern amenities include Jacuzzi tubs, heated towel racks, Egyptian cotton sheets, in-room CD players, and a king-size bed in all but one room. In the fall, golden fields outside echo the Tuscan hues of the silo interiors. In spring, the farm's cherry orchard is in full bloom, providing a bud-covered walking path for twitterpated couples. Guests can pick fresh tomatoes and grapes from the spacious garden and enjoy an impromptu picnic here or on one of two decks overlooking the valley. *$$$; AE, MC, V; checks OK; www.abbeyroadfarm.com.*

Black Walnut Inn / ◑◐◑

9600 NE Worden Hill Rd, Dundee; 886/429-4114
Your anticipation will climb with the elevation as you drive the winding country road to this elegant inn. Sweeping vineyard views and a Tuscan-style courtyard—complete with a fountain and hanging flower baskets—welcome you into the lap of luxury. Of nine suites, the Vista is the most secluded. Located on the top floor of the adjacent Carriage House, this suite features rustic ambience, sunny hues, a private balcony, and a two-person soaking tub. Reserve the spacious Master Suite for a truly upscale stay. A king-size bed, two-person jetted tub, and two walls of windows offering views of nearby mountains and vineyards make it a popular pick for couples. *$$$–$$$$; AE, MC, V; no checks; www.blackwalnut-inn.com.* ☆

Brookside Inn / ◑◐◖

8243 NE Abbey Rd, Carlton; 503/852-4433
Thoreau might have traveled to this tranquil lakeside retreat to enjoy a quiet weekend in the woods. The surrounding property is the main draw with its private pond, burbling streams, and dozens of romantic wooded trails. The pond's tiny island is perfectly sized for a two-person picnic or an evening stargazing session. Afterward, retreat to the cozy outdoor fire pit or one of nine simple guest rooms. Of them, we recommend the Kittiwake room with its four-poster bed and silky winter-white linens, though its stark bathroom isn't exactly romance inspiring. The smaller, adjacent Mackintosh room

comes furnished with a lovely claw-foot tub and lodge-style furnishings. In the morning, nibble warm scones, fruit, yogurt, and homemade granola before the main country-style breakfast is served in the dining room overlooking a picturesque stream. *$$$–$$$$; AE, DC, MC, V; checks OK; www. brooksideinn-oregon.com.* &

The DreamGiver's Inn / ⚫⚫⚫

7150 NE Earlwood Rd, Newberg; 503/476-2211
Come for a breath of fresh air at this four-bedroom country-style inn. The inviting red house beckons with its wide porch, surrounding viewing gardens, manicured lawns, and acres of land for wooded wandering. Once inside, guests will also enjoy a cozy fireside lounge located next to each of four guest rooms. Of them, we found the Faith suite—often reserved by honeymooners—particularly lovely. Decorated in a warm yellow and black motif, this room boasts a four-poster bed, an in-suite bathroom, and an oversize window chair that overlooks valley views. The quaint Courage suite also charmed us with its gold and mauve hues, antique bed, and luxurious linens. Breakfasts are a decadent family-style affair and might feature sweet crème brûlée French toast, fresh fruit, yogurt, granola, sausage, coffee cake, and homemade muffins—all in one sitting. Afterward, retreat to your room and cuddle on your spacious window seat with a good book—or simply with each other. *$$$; AE, DIS, MC, V; checks OK; www.dreamgiversinn.com.*

Lions Gate Inn Bed and Breakfast / ⚫⚫❁

401 N Howard St, Newberg; 503/487-6559
Old-world elegance and modern-day amenities merge at this artistically renovated 1911 Craftsman-style bed-and-breakfast. Though the surroundings are not spectacular, the garden, complete with a patio and secluded hot tub, provide a charming outdoor retreat. Each of the four rooms is named for a season and comes with plush robes, silky bedding, and either a soaking tub or a rain-head shower. The Autumn Room casts a spell over us with its rich red and gold hues, a double-sided fireplace lending a cozy glow to the room, and a two-person soaking tub. The Summer Room—swathed in cool blue and chocolate tones—appeals to those who prefer a simple decor; it also boasts a dual-rain-head shower and a tiny fireplace. An upstairs sitting room can be used for in-house massages. Breakfasts in the elegant main dining room also cater to indulgences with seasonal spreads and fresh-baked croissants (one of innkeeper Lauren Wylie's specialties—the other being chocolate!). *$$$–$$$$; MC, V; checks OK; www.distinctivedestination.net.*

Mattey House / ⚫⚫❁

10221 NE Mattey Ln, McMinnville; 503/434-5058 or 877/434-5058
This stately 1892 Queen Anne Victorian, nestled between a vineyard and an orchard, is a delightful discovery. The charcoal-gray two-story home, with

stained-glass windows and an inviting wraparound porch, wows at the end of a dirt road. All four upstairs rooms are appointed with period antiques, patchwork quilts, and queen-size beds. We like the small Riesling Room—more specifically, its claw-foot tub with views overlooking the lawn and forest. The sunny Blanc de Blanc Room has a private bathroom in the hall, but is popular nonetheless. This being wine country, you might order a bottle to enjoy in your room, or sip a glass on the tiny patio overlooking the home's front entrance. The English proprietors dispel the poor reputation of British cooking with breakfast dishes like Dutch-apple pancakes, herb-baked eggs, and their famous scones. After breakfast, explore the secluded cedar grove, curl up on the porch swing, or kiss beneath the magnificent copper beech. *$$; AE, MC, V; checks OK; www.matteyhouse.com.*

Springbrook Hazelnut Farm Bed & Breakfast / ✪✪✪✪

30295 N Hwy 99 W, Newberg; 503/538-4606 or 800/793-8528
This vast property, surrounded by lush lawns, gardens, orchards, and a tiny, hidden swimming pool, makes this retreat feel like a secret garden hideaway. Though the rooms in the main house are no longer available, the Carriage House and the Rose Cottage offer some of the most secluded lodging in wine country. Similar in design, each elegant abode has Craftsman-style furnishings, lovely fir floors, large windows, and charming tiled kitchens with glass-front cabinets and big butcher-block tables. They also feature gas fireplaces, queen-size beds, and cream-colored walls with forest-green trim. Popular with honeymooners, the Carriage House offers the most space, but our favorite is the cozy Cottage, with its rose garden, terra cotta–tiled bathroom, and postage-stamp-size dining room overlooking a pond surrounded by irises and daffodils. Breakfast is supplied in the fridge so you needn't rush your morning; delicious treats include cinnamon rolls, ham and asparagus crepes, scones, and fresh fruit. For an incredibly romantic post-breakfast stroll, walk through the hazelnut orchard to the tasting room at Rex Hill Vineyards. Or, visit the historic barn on-site, which houses a one-man operated winery, J. K. Carriere Wines (503/554-0721; www.jkcarriere.com), and another amazing surprise (be sure to ask when you visit). *$$$; MC, V; checks OK; www.nutfarm.com.*

Wine Country Farm / ✪✪◖

6855 Breyman Orchards Rd, Dayton; 503/864-3446 or 800/261-3446
Relax on the porch of this renovated 1906 French stucco farmhouse and take in valley, mountain, and vineyard views. The real pleasures here involve unwinding in the shared hot tub or sauna, enjoying an on-site massage, and strolling through the 13-acre estate. Though rooms in the main house are available, their outdated interiors pale in comparison to the scenery. We recommend the three rooms located above the wine-tasting area, particularly the Sunset and Oregon rooms with king-size canopy beds, separate sitting areas, cozy fireplaces, and outdoor decks. Note that visitors will be sampling

wines in the tasting room below (weekends only Memorial Day to Labor Day). Couples can take advantage of the nearby horse stables by arranging a highly romantic private picnic: with advance notice, the proprietor will pack a gourmet lunch—complete with wine, silverware, and a big blanket—and take the two of you via horse-drawn buggy into nearby orchards, where you will be alone for as long as your hearts desire. *$$–$$$; MC, V; checks OK; www.winecountryfarm.com.* &

Youngberg Hill Vineyards & Inn / ❂❂❂❂

10660 SW Youngberg Hill Rd, McMinnville; 503/472-2727 or 888/657-8668
Climb a little closer to heaven at this magnificent hilltop bed-and-breakfast built in 1989 but with a turn-of-the-20th-century feel. A steep driveway winds past rolling fields, oak forests, and vineyards to this stunning inn. Choosing from among the three luxurious two-room suites and four delightful guest rooms (two with fireplaces) isn't easy; all feature elegant decor, private baths, inviting beds with down comforters, and outstanding views. Gleaming wooden antique-replica furnishings and carved headboards are set against walls of pleasing plum, sage, and buttercup-yellow. For the most space, try the Jackson Suite or the Martini Suite, both with king-size beds, French doors opening onto private decks, and luxurious baths. The Jackson has a double-headed shower; the Martini, a jetted tub. The front-facing Jura Suite has amazing views through the bay windows; the first-floor Gamay Room, despite its location near the front door, charms with its fireplace and private deck. In the morning, the airy dining room presents a perfect perch for watching the fog roll into the valley while you indulge in stuffed French toast, citrus salad, or salmon hash. *$$$–$$$$; MC, V; checks OK; www.youngberghill.com.*

Romantic Restaurants

Bistro Maison / ❂❂

729 NE 3rd St, McMinnville; 503/474-1888
Enjoy a romantic meal over candlelight in this cheery French bistro based on the ground floor of a historic bungalow in downtown McMinnville. If the weather is clear, opt for a private table for two on the charming outdoor patio. Chef Jean-Jacques and his wife, Deborah, have decorated the dining room with yellow French-country wallpaper and red leather-backed booths. There is a wine-tasting bar up front, as well as a comfortable waiting area at the top of the stairs. Start with an aperitif and sample the *moules* (mussels)—cooked in three different styles—served with *frites* and saffron aioli. Daily specials, alongside classics like confit de canard, coq au vin, and steak tartare, are mouthwatering fare. Save room and prep time (10–15 minutes) for the *moelleux au chocolat*—molten chocolate cake served warm. *$$–$$$; DIS, MC, V; local checks only; lunch, dinner Wed–Sun; full bar; reservations recommended; www.bistromaison.com.* &

Cuvée Restaurant / ◐◐◖

214 W Main St, Carlton; 503/852-6555
This charming French-influenced restaurant on Carlton's quaint Main Street is simply dressed with black wainscoting, cream walls, white tablecloths, and an artisan chandelier. Dinners here can be quiet, peaceful affairs or a touch crowded depending on the season. Service, however, is always amiable and the cuisine a delight for the senses. French transplant and head chef Gilbert Henry has an esteemed reputation for his pretty presentations and daily fish specials including a breadcrumb-coated salmon served atop silky potatoes beside crisp roasted vegetables. Heartier dishes like a fragrant lamb stew will also please palates. Try the prix-fixe dinner menu featuring an appetizer or dessert, salad, and entrée. Bon appétit! *$$$; AE, DIS, MC, V; checks OK; lunch Sat–Sun, dinner Wed–Sun; full bar; reservations recommended; www. cuveedining.com.* &

Joel Palmer House / ◐◐◐◐

600 Ferry St, Dayton; 503/864-2995
A romantic getaway in Oregon's wine country is simply not complete without an evening at the Joel Palmer House. Chef Jack Czarnecki is both world famous and a renowned authority on cooking with wild mushrooms; rare is the dish that emerges from his kitchen without some variety of fungi to tempt you. The backdrop for his culinary creations is one of Oregon's most famous historic homes, the restaurant's namesake, which is found on both state and national historic registries. Inside the 1849 Southern Revival–style house, Czarnecki serves Northwest-style cuisine featuring fresh, local produce and herbs from a charming on-site garden. Appetizers might include a wild mushroom soup or the house specialty, a three-mushroom tart. The rack of lamb comes with a rich hazelnut-pepper sauce and jalapeño cornbread, while an elk loin arrives alongside juniper red cabbage and black chanterelles. The wine cellar, which boasts more than 5,000 bottles and leans heavily toward Oregon Pinot Noir, is sure to have just the right something special to accompany a romantic meal. On warm twilight evenings, dine outside on the lovely patio. *$$$–$$$$; AE, DIS, MC, V; local checks only; dinner Tues–Sat; full bar; reservations recommended; www.joelpalmerhouse.com.* &

La Rambla / ◐◐◖

238 NE 3rd St, McMinnville; 503/435-2126
This dark, sexy Spanish restaurant in historic McMinnville is absolutely captivating. Exotic peacock fronds and a stuffed peacock frame the sleek bar while brocade curtains, high-backed leather chairs, and artisan pendant lights enhance the restaurant's upscale vibe. Within La Rambla's Northwest-inspired Spanish menu, paellas prove perfect for sharing, but make sure to sample the *tapas* portion of the menu as well. Great picks include a silky gazpacho, batter-fried green beans with garlic aioli, and baked goat cheese

with a smoky paprika-tomato sauce. Inventive cocktails and more than 250 wines of both Northwest and Spanish origin line the beverage menu; desserts include a baked Bartlett-pear tart and indulgent fried cinnamon doughnuts with warm chocolate sauce. This popular locale can get a bit loud with crowds; request the window seat for the most privacy. *$–$$; AE, DIS, MC, V; checks OK; lunch, dinner every day; full bar; reservations recommended; www. laramblaonthird.com.* &

The Painted Lady Restaurant / ●●●

201 S College, Newberg; 503/538-3850
The Painted Lady Restaurant is a magical place. The cozy dining room in this charming Victorian near downtown Newberg twinkles in evening candlelight. Chef Allen Routt's refined, modern American cuisine is highlighted in two tasting menus, both available with or without wines. Courses might include a refreshing heirloom-tomato-and-arugula salad with balsamic vinaigrette, pine nuts, and fresh mozzarella, followed by a bacon-and-cornbread-stuffed quail sauced with a blackberry demi-glace. The desserts, especially the s'mores chocolate lava cake, might be the best sweets you've eaten all year. *$$$$; AE, DIS, MC, V; no checks; dinner Wed–Sun; full bar; reservations recommended; www.thepaintedladyrestaurant.com.* &

Red Hills Provincial Dining / ●●●

276 N Hwy 99 W, Dundee; 503/538-8224
Located in a lovely 1912 Craftsman-style home, this restaurant offers a testament to the wonders of restoration. Two dining rooms, both appointed with linen-covered tables and fresh flowers, highlight the beauty and functionality of the home's original design features. Chocolate- and cream-colored walls add to the warm and inviting ambience. The location, above Highway 99, is not entirely scenic—but the drawback is slight given the surroundings. The simple European-country dinner menu changes often, and the choices are all intriguing, from sautéed chicken breast with fresh figs, walnuts, and pastis to grilled wild salmon with a ginger–Pinot Gris sauce. The kitchen pulls many ingredients from 12 raised-bed gardens as well as numerous fruit trees located on the property. Whether it's bread dusted with fresh rosemary, a crisp mesclun salad, or luscious desserts, the result is exquisite. Add to this an award-winning wine list with a huge worldwide selection, and you have a recipe for romance indeed. *$$$; AE, DIS, MC, V; no checks; dinner Tues–Sun; full bar; reservations recommended.*

Tina's Restaurant / ●●◖

760 Hwy 99 W, Dundee; 503/538-8880
Recommendations for this wine-country favorite come from miles around, though the dining room doesn't exactly inspire romance. White walls, simple tablecloths, and tea candles give off a ho-hum feel; fortunately, a cozy

fireplace, spot-on service, and a seasonally inspired menu improve Tina's image considerably. The menu is a parade of fresh, aptly paired ingredients, from the light green salad topped with crunchy hazelnuts to a brilliant roasted duck sauced with a sweet demi-glace and served over hearty greens. The accompanying sweet corn fritters and fresh grilled peaches prove that the cuisine—especially rich, addictive desserts made by Tina herself—are reason enough to dine here à deux. *$$–$$$; AE, DIS, MC, V; checks OK; lunch Tues–Fri, dinner every day; full bar; reservations recommended; www. tinasdundee.com.* ⅙

Salem & Historic Oregon

Romantic Highlights

History-rich Salem has appeal for romance seekers, particularly in the small, peaceful towns that fill the countryside surrounding downtown. True, there aren't many choices for romantic accommodations, but neither will you fight as many tourists for lodging. Summer is the busiest season in Salem, but still appealing: the abundant rose gardens are in bloom, and strawberries and marionberries are ripe for the picking at roadside stands. Outdoor activities—from hiking to concerts—beckon. Winter is rainy but provides the excuse to dine at popular restaurants and snuggle by the fire at a B&B. In any season, duck under a covered bridge for an atmospheric kiss; with nearly 50 covered bridges, Oregon is the roofed-span capital of the country.

Skip the State Capitol Building tour—it's a more appropriate destination for lobbyists than lovers. Instead, stroll the campus of neighboring **Willamette University** (900 State St; 503/370-6300; www.willamette.edu), the oldest university in the West (established in 1842); be sure to pop into **Hallie Ford Museum of Art** (700 State St; 503/370-6855; www.willamette.edu/museum_of_art) during your campus tour. Other historic buildings abound in Salem; you'll find several of them in **Historic Mission Mill Village** (1313 Mill St SE; 503/585-7012; www.mission mill.org). This impressive 42-acre cluster of restored buildings from the 1800s includes a woolen mill, a parsonage, a Presbyterian church, and several houses.

During warm-season visits, explore **Bush's Pasture Park** and the **Bush House Museum** (600 Mission St SE; 503/363-4714; www.salemart.org/bush; tours Tues–Sun, call for tour hours), with its conservatory, rose gardens, hiking paths, barn-turned-gallery, and—for one weekend in July—the Salem Art Festival (www. salemart.org). Bring a picnic or head downtown to the **Arbor Café** (380 High St NE; 503/588-2353) or **Wild Pear** (372 State St; 503/378-7515) for a light lunch.

The *Queen Mary* it's not, but the rail of the stern-wheeler **Willamette Queen** (503/371-1103; www.willamettequeen.com) has its own vintage charm as a kissing venue; both short excursions and brunch, lunch, and dinner cruises are available year-round. South of town, the views are just as romantic as the wine at

Willamette Valley Vineyards (8800 Enchanted Way SE, Turner; 503/588-9463 or 800/344-9463; www.wvv.com), which towers above the valley.

Nearby, the area abounds with several other respected wineries including **Eola Hills Winery** (501 South Pacific Highway 99W, Rickreall; 503/623-2405 or 800/291-6730; www.eolahillswinery.com), **Stangeland** (8500 Hopewell Rd NW, Salem; 503/581-0355 or 800/301-9482; www.stangelandwinery.com), **Witness Tree** (7111 Spring Valley Rd NW, Salem; 503/585-7874 or 888/478-8766; www.witnesstreevineyard.com), **Cristom** (6905 Spring Valley Rd NW, Salem; 503/375-3068; www.cristomwines.com), and **Bethel Heights** (6060 Bethel Heights Rd NW, Salem; 503/581-2262; www.bethelheights.com). Call ahead as tasting-room days and hours vary. Cross the river on the charming, four-car **Wheatland Ferry** (503/588-7979; www.wheatlandferry.com)—river crossings for passengers are free (cars cost a dollar and change)—and disembark on the other side for bird watching, wildlife sightings, and scenic, flat walking paths at **Willamette Mission State Park** (www.oregonstateparks.org/park_139.php).

Head west on Hwy 22 toward **Independence** and follow the Buena Vista Road to the tiny **Buena Vista Ferry** (503/588-7979; 7am–5pm Wed–Fri, 9am–7pm Sat–Sun, mid-Apr–Oct). If you're not in a hurry, be sure to take this charming ride into the farm and wine country west of the river. (If you're driving from Interstate 5, take exit 242 and follow signs west about 5 miles to the ferry.) If you're used to riding the huge car ferries on Puget Sound, you'll love this altogether more leisurely ferry experience.

Albany is the next big town to the south on I-5. Stroll the 50-block Monteith Historic District to see everything from colorful Queen Anne houses to Craftsman bungalows built between 1849 and 1915; or experience the romance of covered bridges on a drive to Scio, northeast of Albany. For either excursion, contact the Albany Visitors Center for maps (see Access & Information). Then, head to First Avenue and the side streets to browse antique shops, making your first stop something sweet at **Boccherini's Coffee and Tea House** (208 1st Ave SW; 541/926-6703). Bring along a blanket and picnic, and check out one of the many outdoor summer concerts at **Monteith Riverpark** (Water Ave and Washington St; 541/917-7772; www.riverrhythms.org).

For a beautiful drive south, follow the river road to **Corvallis** and stop immediately when you get to town to take a romantic stroll in downtown's immaculate **Riverfront Park**. This beautiful, paved pedestrian esplanade runs for several blocks along the Willamette River and includes a lovely fountain, stone benches, hanging flower baskets, and sculptures by Northwest artists. It's the perfect spot for a romantic picnic or a quick smooch. Afterward, stop for a well-earned espresso at **The Beanery** (500 SW 2nd St; 541/753-7442). For a quieter experience, wander the walkway at dusk before popping into **Big River Restaurant and Bar** (101 NW Jackson St; 541/757-0694) for a nightcap of decadent desserts, seductive libations, and live music.

Though tiny, **Silverton** just east of Salem should not to be ignored by the romantically inclined. Stroll its historic downtown, festooned with hanging

Riverfront Walkways

There are few things more romantic than wandering hand-in-hand along a tree-lined riverbank with your special someone. Fortunately, the Willamette Valley offers plenty of waterfront wandering. Here, our three favorites:

Corvallis's **Riverfront Park** boasts a meticulously cared-for esplanade that runs for several blocks along the Willamette River. If you time your visit right, you can enjoy fresh produce and baked goods from the local Saturday Farmers Market (1st Ave and Jackson St; Apr–Nov) before or after your leisurely stroll.

Eugene's riverside bike and pedestrian trails span many miles, but the most romantic walk begins at **Autzen Foot Bridge** (unless it's game day at Autzen Stadium, an event certain to beget crowds). Follow the path toward the town's simple duck pond; hang a left at the next footbridge, and follow the signs to **Owen Rose Garden**, where 400 varieties of roses produce a stunning, fragrant garden come spring and summer. Soak up the natural beauty then follow the looped trail back to your starting point.

Salem's **Riverfront Park** is located on 23 acres next to downtown Salem and boasts a paved riverside path along the banks of the Willamette River, perfect for couples to explore. Along your walk, make time to ride the nostalgic 42-horse hand-carved **Salem Carousel**.

baskets overflowing with flowers in summer, and browse the shops; then pamper yourselves with lunch or afternoon tea at **Oregon Tea Garden** (305 Oak St; 503/873-1230; www.oregonteagarden.com), before embarking on the scenic country road to the **Oregon Garden** (879 W Main St; 503/874-8100 or 877/674-2733; www.oregongarden.org). Wander through more than 20 specialty gardens featuring waterfalls, quiet ponds, fountains, 400-year-old trees, and beautiful vistas. For an equally stunning outdoor experience, head southeast of town to the lush **Silver Falls State Park** (off Hwy 214, 26 miles east of Salem; 503/873-8681; www.oregonstateparks.org/park_211.php); there's not a more dramatic place to kiss than behind 177-foot South Falls. Iris farmers cultivate acres of fields around Silverton, creating a brilliant palette in late May; that's also the time to wander **Cooley's Iris Display Gardens** (11553 Silverton Rd NE; 503/873-5463; www.cooleysgardens.com). North of Silverton in Aurora, browse antique shops, many of which are housed in preserved 19th-century buildings. You can also learn about historic Aurora at the **Old Aurora Colony Museum** on the corner of 2nd and Liberty streets (503/678-5754; www.auroracolonymuseum.com).

Access & Information

The town of Salem makes a centralized base for exploring the historic (and romantic) charms of the mid-Willamette Valley. Most travelers arrive by car via Interstate 5; a more leisurely route is the scenic old US Highway 99W, parallel to I-5 west of the Willamette. Travelers from farther afield can fly into Portland or Eugene before starting their driving tour. Another romantic option is to take the train (800/USA-RAIL; www.amtrak.com) from Seattle or Portland; both **Amtrak's Coast Starlight** route and **Amtrak's Cascades** route stop in Salem, Albany, and Eugene.

For invaluable information and guides for wine touring; call the **Oregon Wine Advisory Board** or visit their Web site (503/228-8336; www.oregon wine.org). You can also get travel tips from the **Salem Convention and Visitors Association** (503/581-4325 or 800/874-7012; www.travelsalem.com). **The Albany Visitors Association** (250 Broadalbin SW, #110; 541/928-0911 or 800/526-2256; www.albanyvisitors.com) is another excellent resource—request their map of covered bridges in the area. Those traveling to Corvallis can check in with its **Convention and Visitors Bureau** (553 NW Harrison Blvd; 541/757-1544 or 800/334-8118; visitcorvallis.com).

Romantic Lodgings

Hanson Country Inn / ◐◐◖

795 SW Hanson St, Corvallis; 541/752-2919
It's only a short drive from the Corvallis city center, but you'll feel you've entered rural Willamette Valley when you arrive at Hanson Country Inn. It's no wonder the inn, with its surrounding lawn, garden, and gazebo, is a favorite among local brides. This wood-and-brick 1928 farmhouse was once the centerpiece of a prosperous poultry ranch; it's now on the Benton County Historical Register. Downstairs, you can enjoy a book or a kiss by the living room fireplace, in the light-washed sunroom, or in the cozy library where tunes drift from an old-fashioned radio. Three large guest suites upstairs (two with their own sitting rooms and decks, and all with private baths) feature beautiful wallpaper and fine linens. For the utmost privacy, take the charmingly decorated two-bedroom cottage tucked in the trees behind the main house. Cottage guests enjoy the complimentary breakfast (as do in-house guests) but may also want to bring fresh groceries and stay in for dinner; with a living area, a fully equipped kitchen, a private bath, and two bedrooms (one with a queen-size bed, one with a double), you'll have everything you need for a cozy weekend à deux. *$$; AE, DIS, MC, V; checks OK; www.hcinn.com.*

Harrison House Bed & Breakfast / ◐◐

2310 NW Harrison Blvd, Corvallis; 541/752-6248 or 800/233-6248
Set in a quaint neighborhood just blocks from downtown, Harrison House boasts a country ambience and a close-in location perfect for exploring the

city's restaurants and public parks. Here each of four rooms (all with private baths) provide vintage charm, but we recommend the private backyard Cottage Suite with its queen-size bed, full bath, kitchenette, and French doors that open to a semiprivate patio overlooking a peaceful garden. This historic Dutch Colonial–style bed-and-breakfast has flourished under the direction of new owners Hilarie Phelps and Allen Goodman, who stock the sunroom with complimentary local wines for afternoon sipping and provide truffles in guest rooms upon arrival. These one-time restaurateurs have also garnered a reputation for their exquisite breakfast spreads that feature fresh, seasonal fruit from the Corvallis farmers market and—if you are lucky in love—Goodman's marvelous hazelnut-crusted French toast. *$$; AE, DIS, MC, V; checks OK; www.corvallis-lodging.com.*

Water Street Inn / ◑◑

421 N Water St, Silverton; 503/873-3344 or 866/873-3344
After a day of waterfall watching at Silver Falls State Park or strolling in the Oregon Garden, collapse into luxury at the Water Street Inn, the most luxurious accommodations for miles around. Originally built as the Wolford Hotel in 1890, it now operates as a handsome bed-and-breakfast. Each of the five guest rooms is elegantly and individually appointed with period-style furniture, heavy cut-velvet drapes, and thick comforters. Each has a TV/VCR and private bath with shower, and all but Room 2 have queen-size beds. We also recommend spacious Room 4's double shower and feather bed, or Room 5's fireplace and jetted tub for two. Guests gather in the formal dining room each morning to enjoy a full and tasty homemade family-style breakfast. Be sure and linger over the savory Grand Marnier French toast served with yogurt and fresh fruit—assuredly, a romantic way to start the day. *$$–$$$; AE, MC, V; checks OK; www.thewaterstreetinn.com.*

Romantic Restaurants

Iovino's / ◑◑

136 SW Washington Ave, Corvallis; 541/738-9015
Work up an appetite for your romantic dinner with a leisurely stroll along Corvallis's riverfront walkway, making sure to end your walk at the newly relocated Iovino's for a taste of big-city atmosphere and flavorful nouvelle-Italian cuisine. In its new space on the bottom floor of Corvallis's first high-rise condominium, Iovino's has embraced a swanky, stylish ambience—but gets a bit loud at times. For a quieter meal, dine under cherry-colored umbrellas on the outside riverfront patio when the weather allows. Start with crostini with soft goat cheese, artichoke hearts, fresh tomato salsa, and basil chiffonade or an insalata mista in a citrus-balsamic vinaigrette. The menu is full of surprises—all of them good. Consider butternut squash–gorgonzola ravioli tossed in a sweet marsala-reduction sauce, and a hearty bistecca steak

drizzled with aged balsamic vinegar and crowned with gorgonzola butter. *$$; AE, MC, V; lunch Mon–Sat, dinner every day; full bar; reservations recommended.* &

J. James Restaurant / ◐◐

325 High St SE, Salem; 503/362-0888
Couples who find good food more important than an intimate dining atmosphere will appreciate chef/owner Jeff James's restaurant, on the fringe of downtown Salem. A Salem native, James uses the region's seasonal ingredients in simple yet creative dishes, including starters such as Dungeness crab cakes, baked sartu, and a caramelized-onion cheese spread served with grilled garlic crostini and green apples. The entrée selections include a mix of meat and seafood dishes, such as grilled pork loin marinated in molasses and parmesan-griddled rockfish. The large dining room is softened by white linens and floor-to-ceiling windows; service is crisp and professional. Bring healthy appetites and enjoy what this restaurant does best—delicious meals and desserts that are worth the indulgence. *$$; AE, MC, V; local checks only; lunch Tues–Fri, dinner Tues–Sat; full bar; reservations recommended; www.jjamesrestaurant.com.* &

Le Bistro / ◐◐

150 SW Madison Ave, Corvallis; 541/754-6680
Easily the top recommendation from locals, Le Bistro is a quietly elegant French restaurant, and its recent renovation adds warmth to the historic building. Here, Chef Iain Duncan keeps the focus on the food and often heightens the dining experience by hand delivering his esteemed dishes to privileged tables. The delightful menu might feature country-style farmer's pâté and escargot paired with garlic, almonds, Pernod, and parsley butter as starters, and coq au vin or pan-seared filet mignon as main courses. Dessert choices include chocolate mousse, bananas Foster, and chocolate fondue made with Spanish dark chocolate and served alongside fresh seasonal fruit and fluffy angel food cake. *$$–$$$; AE, DIS, MC, V; local checks only; dinner Tues–Sun; full bar; reservations recommended; www.lebistrocorvallis.com.*

Morton's Bistro Northwest / ◐◐◐

1128 Edgewater St NW, Salem; 503/585-1113
If you are looking for exquisite food in an intimate setting, make your way to Morton's. Tucked below the road off a busy highway in West Salem, the dining room's low ceiling, dark wood beams, and soft lighting add up to romantic ambience. It can be noisy, but in a way that creates intimacy. No one will overhear your sweet nothings above the lively hubbub of conversation surrounding you. National magazines have singled out the restaurant's food—elaborately prepared Northwest cuisine with an international influence—as among the best in Oregon. A grill-roasted rack of lamb

marinated in Pinot Noir with sage and rosemary might be accompanied by a pesto-stuffed risotto cake; a bistro chicken roast marries with mushrooms, capers, tomatoes, and summer greens. Give serious consideration to the mixed grill and the cioppino. Service is expert and pleasant, and there's a good selection of reasonably priced Northwest wines. *$$–$$$; MC, V; checks OK; dinner Tues–Sat; full bar; reservations recommended; www.mortons bistronw.com.* &

Silver Grille Café & Wines / ❂❂❂

206 E Main St, Silverton; 503/873-4035
The Silver Grille, with its tiny, softly lit dining room and deep red walls, embraces you warmly from the moment you walk in the door. And once you taste the food, you'll be hooked. The menu changes seasonally, with specials written on a chalkboard, and features the bounty of Willamette Valley farms and fields. Winning entrées might include a grilled chicken Alfredo tossed with spinach, dried sour cherries, and filberts or a pair of roasted Oregon quail with a cognac-porcini reduction and wild-grain pilaf. Start with a salad of local organic greens or a smoky corn chowder, and end your meal with a flourless chocolate torte drizzled with local berry *coulis.* A Northwest wine list complements the esteemed cuisine. *$$; DIS, MC, V; checks OK; dinner Wed–Sun; full bar; reservations recommended; www.silvergrille.com.* &

Sybaris / ❂❂❂

442 1st Ave W, Albany; 541/928-8157
In ancient Greece, the city of Sybaris was synonymous with luxury and pleasure. So it is with this elegant restaurant on Albany's historic First Avenue. Sybaris is charming and boasts exposed brick and large windows, high ceilings, and an English-style wood-burning fireplace. Back in the kitchen, chef/owner Matt Bennett and his wife, Janel, create rotating menus that reflect a fearless and playful approach to food. Inventive options might include a "build-it-yourself little shrimp salad" with radishes, chopped herbs, hard-boiled eggs, and lemony mayo, or seared venison loin with homemade honey bacon, grilled asparagus, cracked pepper–cheese bread pudding and balsamic caramelized onions. Bennett relies on local farms for many of his ingredients and plans his monthly menus according to what's in season. The generous entrée portions may lead you to pass on dessert—which would be a shame, for you'd miss the Sybaris chocolate-hazelnut cake, a dense, flourless, decadent work of art filled with a cache of crème brûlée. The wine list is short but well matched to the menu. Monteith Riverpark is just across the street; extend the evening's pleasure with a starlit stroll by the river. *$$–$$$; AE, MC, V; checks OK; dinner Tues–Sat; full bar; reservations recommended; www. sybarisbistro.com.* &

Eugene Area

Romantic Highlights

Portland's laid-back sister lies to the south end of the Willamette Valley where the Cascade and Coast Range foothills both draw close to enclose the town in a green embrace. In the spring and fall, the changing seasons inspire natural beauty in local parks, making it a particularly romantic time to visit. Summertime is of the quieter sort as the town's local college population empties out, giving guests free reign to soak up Eugene's small-town ambience.

Eugene has long been known as an outdoor enthusiasts' playground; for lovebirds, this translates into many spaces boasting the kind of natural beauty most suitable for romance. The high point within Eugene's city limits is **Skinner's Butte**—known by locals as the nearest Blueberry Hill. A road leads to the top of the butte; visit at sunset to catch the town sheathed in a pink, golden haze. Look to the east to the snow-covered Three Sisters mountains and to the south to the city lights stretching out toward forested Spencer's Butte—another worthy vantage point most often shared with only a few birds and squirrels, and perhaps a hiker or two.

At the base of Skinner's Butte is the esteemed **Owen Rose Garden** (end of N Jefferson St, at Willamette River), home to Charisma, French Perfume, Golden Slippers, and 400 varieties of roses in all. In summer, there isn't a sweeter-smelling spot in town to wander hand-in-hand (or if the time is right, pose a query on bended knee in the enchanting garden gazebo). Riverside trails sprawl from the garden's entrance, offering prime opportunities to meander along the banks of the pristine Willamette River.

In spring, idyllic **Hendricks Park** (Summit Ave and Skyline Dr) is Romance Central. Ten acres of dazzling rhododendrons and azaleas burst into bloom from late April to early June under a tall stand of Douglas fir, inspiring many an impromptu kiss; in between plantings green lawns and benches beg to be graced with a picnic spread. Many places in town provide picnic provisions, including the aptly named **Marché Provisions** (296 E 5th Ave; 541/743-0660), offering house-made pâtés, mousses, cheeses, cured meats, and wines perfect for a Francophile's fantasy; and the nearby **Humble Bagel** (2435 Hilyard St; 541/484-4497) with fresh-baked muffins perfectly sized for a two-person picnic brunch.

Take a leisurely stroll through the broad lawns and historic buildings of the **University of Oregon** campus (13th Ave and University St) to bring a touch of nostalgia to your visit. Sneak a kiss at the waterfall fountain behind the science complex, or linger in the **Jordan Schnitzer Museum of Art** (1430 Johnson Ln; 541/346-3027; uoma.uoregon.edu) before enjoying a glass of wine and lunch à deux at the museum's French-inspired **Marché Museum Café** (1430 Johnson Ln; 541/346-6440).

There's no shortage of intriguing art galleries, trendy brewpubs, fabulous bakeries, and hip coffeehouses in Eugene, including **Perugino** (767 Willamette

St; 541/687-9102), an authentic Italian coffeehouse, wine bar, and gallery. Sit at the intimate table by the window and share a frothy cappuccino and decadent European pastry while taking in Eugene's downtown scene. Enjoy a drink and live music at **Luna** (30 E Broadway; 541/434-5862; www.lunajazz.com), a stylish bar located next to the restaurant **Adam's Place** (see Romantic Restaurants), where live music is performed every night, with the best shows reserved for weekends.

Eugene has not one but three serious chocolatiers: **Euphoria** (6 W 17th Ave; 541/343-9223; www.euphoriachocolate.com), **Fenton & Lee** (35 E 8th Ave; 541/343-7629; www.fentonandlee.com), and **KeKau** (541/338-7684; www.kekau.com), which has a new retail shop due to open this year. From April through the second week in November, spend a morning at **Saturday Market** (8th Ave and Oak St; 541/686-8885; www.eugenesaturdaymarket.org), perusing the local artisan booths while enjoying live music, colorful personalities, and a slice of classic cheesecake from the **Dana's Cheesecake** booth.

To explore outside the city limits, head west on Highway 126 to Veneta for a bite at **Our Daily Bread Restaurant** (88170 Territorial Rd; 541/935-4921; www.ourdailybreadrestaurant.com), a bakery and restaurant housed in a former church (hence the biblical name). Take Territorial Highway west a short distance to visit **Secret House Vineyards** (88324 Vineyard Ln; 541/935-3774 or 800/497-1574); once you're finished here, head south and watch for blue signs leading to five more excellent wineries: Italian-inspired **Silvan Ridge–Hinman Vineyards** (27012 Briggs Hill Rd; 541/345-1945; www.silvanridge.com); **King Estate Winery** (80854 Territorial Rd; 541/942-9874 or 800/884-4441; www.kingestate.com), with a palatial hilltop home and spacious dining and tasting room; **Iris Hill Winery** (82110 Territorial Rd; 541/345-1617; www.iris-hill.com); **Sweet Cheeks Winery** (26961 Briggs Hill Rd; 541/349-9463 or 877-309-9463; www.sweetcheekswinery.com); and the woodsy, intimate **Chateau Lorane** (27415 Siuslaw River Rd; 541/942-8028; www.chateaulorane.com). All are open weekends; some are open weekdays, as well.

The wild McKenzie River lies to the east of Eugene; follow it along Highway 126 past small mountain towns, boat launches, and riverside parks and picnic sites. A detour up Highway 242 (open summer and fall only) is especially appealing in autumn, when the vine maples turn gold and crimson and the hiking trails and picnic sites are yours alone. Post picnic, stop in at **Belknap Resort and Hot Springs** (541/822-3512; www.belknaphotsprings.com), where an outdoor swimming pool full of hot mineral water awaits. (Privacy is often lacking, but there's no rule against kissing in the pool!) The pool is relaxing in any season, but pure magic when snow is falling. Cross the river on a footbridge to stroll the adjacent extensive formal gardens in the woods.

Couples who enjoy music festivals and fairs will find much to consider when planning a trip to Eugene. (If you prefer to avoid crowds, steer clear during the most popular summer events.) What, for example, could be more romantic than a full orchestra and chorus engaged in the perfect harmony of a Bach oratorio? The second weekend in July, the world-class **Oregon Bach Festival** (541/682-5000 or 800/457-1486; www.oregonbachfestival.com) concludes its two-week run at the Hult Center for the Performing Arts and smaller concert venues around town. Bond over a truly alternative experience at the **Oregon Country Fair** (541/343-4298; www.oregoncountryfair.org), a wild and wacky three-day celebration held on a wooded retreat west of town. There's food, art, music, men dressed like flamingos parading on stilts, and women wearing a smile and little else—call it a throwback, but we prefer to think of it as the town's best showcase of hippie-style love.

Access & Information

Commuter airlines US Airways Express, Horizon Air, Delta Connection, United Express, and Allegiant Air serve the **Eugene Airport** (north of town, off Hwy 99; 541/682-5544; www.eugeneairport.com). Car rentals are available at the airport and in town. Most travelers arrive by car via Interstate 5; it's less than two hours from Portland to Eugene. More leisurely north-south travelers prefer the scenic, older US Highway 99W, parallel to I-5 west of the Willamette River. Winter driving is generally easy, but if you're worried about road conditions contact the **Oregon Department of Transportation** (503/588-2941 or 800/977-6368; www.tripcheck.com). For old-fashioned travel, **Amtrak's Coast Starlight** and **Cascades** routes (800/USA-RAIL; www.amtrak.com) from Seattle and Portland stop in Salem, Albany, and Eugene.

Romantic Wineries

Iris Hill Winery / ◐◑

82110 Territorial Rd, Eugene; 541/895-9877
A warm, Italian-style tasting room and patio preside over 44 acres of vineyards at this hilltop winery. Select a glass of Pinot Noir, Pinot Gris, or Chardonnay from the offerings before entering the trellised patio for peaceful, private outdoor sipping. Springtime visitors will be delighted with sweeping countryside views, particularly in May when the hillside meadows and woodland edges surrounding the vineyard display the vibrant hues of blue, purple, violet, and lavender that inspired the winery's poetic name. *Noon–5pm Thurs–Sun; www.iris-hill.com.* ♿

King Estate Winery / ◐◑◐◖

80854 Territorial Rd, Eugene; 541/942-9874
Situated just a short drive away from Eugene through rolling countryside, this established winery offers spectacular views and award-winning wines. Steal a moment while wandering through the barrel room, or in warmer weather, sip a glass of signature Chardonnay on one of three secluded patios (our favorite is hidden away in the pear orchard). Enjoy the winery's spacious tasting room and a restaurant that serves lunch and dinner daily. Ingredients for its farm-fresh cuisine hail from the estate's organic farm. Highlights include a plentiful artisan cheese plate adorned with sweet wine grapes; a light baby Belgian

endive salad served with candied walnuts, Oregon blue cheese, and a delicate orange champagne vinaigrette; and roasted chicken served over wild mushrooms, baby Yukon potatoes, and sautéed greens. Or, come for an indulgent dessert of cinnamon crème brûlée or an apricot *tartine* as the sun descends behind the surrounding hills of this spectacular hilltop winery. *11am–8pm every day; www.kingestate.com.* ♿

Romantic Lodgings

Campbell House Inn / ⬤⬤⬤♿

252 Pearl St, Eugene; 541/343-1119 or 800/264-2519
From the gorgeous guest rooms to the lavish landscaping to the tables for two in the breakfast and dining rooms, the Campbell House is designed for romance. Built in 1892 and lovingly restored as a grand bed-and-breakfast, the house is set on an acre of beautiful grounds with a secluded yet convenient location two blocks from Eugene's bustling Fifth Street Public Market. Elegant, ornate rooms have both old-world charm (four-poster beds, high ceilings, dormer windows) and modern amenities (tastefully hidden TV/VCRs, wireless Internet, air conditioning). Throughout the main house, unusually shaped rooms with dormer ceilings are charming, but some create almost too-cozy quarters. For a more spacious, private stay, request one of the five suites in the Carriage House—rooms feature sitting areas, jetted tubs, and wet bars. Or retreat instead to the Celeste Cottage, a separate guest house located next door and available as a one- or two-bedroom option, complete with gas fireplace and wet bar. Complimentary tea, coffee, and wine are served in the Victorian parlor each evening. A full breakfast is served in the main house overlooking the grounds, and for guests not wanting to venture into town, dinner is offered at the Dining Room at the Campbell House. *$$–$$$$; AE, DC, DIS, MC, V; no checks; www.campbellhouse.com.* ♿

C'est La Vie Inn / ⬤⬤♿

1006 Taylor St, Eugene; 541/302-3014 or 866/302-3014
As Eugene's newest—and most vibrantly colored—bed-and-breakfast, C'est La Vie Inn sits in a quiet residential neighborhood minutes from downtown. Built as a private residence in 1891, this lovingly restored home offers a magical retreat surrounded by stunning gardens. Enter through the charming blue and gold fence, modeled after the original home's front gate, into a world of whimsy and old-world elegance. Rooms are appointed with silky window treatments and stylish antiques, and a few of the inn's 35 fanciful clocks are displayed in each room. We were especially fond of the soft blue hues and claw-foot soaking tub in the Matisse Room, and the separate Casablanca Suite, which occupies the entire floor of the inn's adjacent carriage house. Roman-style columns and an in-room Jacuzzi tub add luxurious touches. *$$–$$$; AE, MC, V; checks OK; www.cestlavieinn.com.*

Eagle Rock Lodge / ♥♥❦

49198 McKenzie Hwy, Vida; 541/822-3630 or 888/773-4333
It's a trek to get to this riverside lodge located along the McKenzie River some 40 miles from Eugene, but it's worth it. The eight rooms each present unique appeal, whether it's with a Jacuzzi tub for two, a handsome fireplace and sitting area, or a river view. Wake up to views of the lush McKenzie River from the three-room Riverview Suite, which has multiple sitting areas, a carved four-poster queen-size bed, and a cozy woodstove. Or, seek even more spacious lodging in the Fireplace Suite situated just off the backyard deck. This large suite has a cabin feel with a queen-size bed, rustic decor, and a stately fireplace. Feast on elegantly presented three-course breakfasts that might include fruit, a homemade cinnamon-roll ring, and a main course of house-made sausage patties, vegetable frittata, roasted potatoes, and fresh tomatoes. Note that nearby eateries don't compare to the cuisine served here—or anywhere in Eugene. Each room comes equipped with a microwave and mini fridge, and owners Randy and Debbie Dersham keep the common room stocked with chocolates, cookies, and wine. *$$–$$$; MC, V; checks OK; www.eaglerocklodging.com.* &

Excelsior Inn / ♥♥♥

754 E 13th Ave, Eugene; 800/321-6963
Located just around the corner from the University of Oregon campus, this 14-room inn originally served as a sorority house until 1972 when it reopened as the Excelsior Café. In this elegantly appointed retreat, the rooms—each named for a famous composer—are as private and lavish as can be. With its in-room fireplace and deep whirlpool tub, the Tchaikovsky Room caught our eye, as did the Bach Room, which is the largest and often used as a honeymoon suite. All of the rooms reveal an old-world charm with comforts of the modern sort. Common gathering spaces are sparse, but guests can descend into the adjacent Excelsior Inn Ristorante Italiano (see Romantic Restaurants) for a glass of wine or ambience-rich dining. Breakfasts feature fresh, local ingredients and are served each morning in the restaurant. *$$–$$$$; AE, DC, DIS, MC, V; no checks; www.excelsiorinn.com.* &

Romantic Restaurants

Adam's Place / ♥♥♥

30 E Broadway, Eugene; 541/344-6948
Whether you're here to pop the question or to celebrate the anniversary of your first kiss, Adam's Place is *the* place for special occasions. From the elegant interior to the highly professional service to the inventive entrées perfectly arranged on the plate, Adam's manages to be both sophisticated and warmly unpretentious. Chef/owner Adam Bernstein, a third-generation

restaurateur who trained at the Culinary Institute of America, specializes in Northwest cuisine with European and Asian influences. Start with a classic Cambozola fondue appetizer—all the better for its sharing potential—or a light artisan goat cheese and strawberry salad. Parade through the entrée menu with a Moroccan-style halibut or a French boned breast of chicken à la Forrestier. In true Eugene spirit, a creative vegetarian trio plate is available. Desserts are indulgent, and the wine list would please the most discriminating oenophile. End the evening with brandy and live jazz (often best on weekend evenings) at the adjacent Luna. *$$–$$$; AE, MC, V; dinner Tues–Sat; full bar; reservations recommended; www.adamsplacerestaurant.com.* &

Café Lucky Noodle / ◐◐

207 E 5th Ave, Eugene; 541/484-4777
The sister restaurant to Eugene's popular Ring of Fire, Café Lucky Noodle is the place to go when one of you is craving Thai and the other wants Italian. It sounds like an unlikely marriage between two cuisines, but the offerings here prove that opposites really do attract. The menu at this swanky downtown locale floats freely between Italian- and Thai-influenced dishes with entrées of a rosemary-infused roasted-chicken lasagne and Ring of Fire's signature pad Thai (called the Lucky Noodle here). The artistic, energetic space can get loud and is often packed with local fans; request an intimate corner booth and use crowds as an excuse to cozy up or steal a kiss over dinner. For dessert, indulge in a traditional Italian gelato to go and wander through the quaint (often deserted) downtown. *$$; AE, MC, V; no checks; breakfast, lunch, dinner every day; full bar; www.luckynoodle.com.* &

Café Soriah / ◐◐

384 W 13th Ave, Eugene; 541/342-4410
Wedged between a dress shop and an auto-repair business on a busy street outside downtown, Café Soriah is a diamond in the rough. Enjoy a glass of wine at the dimly lit bar before entering the pretty, well-appointed dining room, airy and smart with original art and fine woodworking. In spring and summer, step outside for a dinner à deux in the secluded, leafy walled terrace. Chef/owner Ibrahim Hamide focuses the menu on Mediterranean and Middle Eastern cuisine. For starters, nibble on tender souvlaki, baba ghanouj, stuffed grape leaves, or frog legs provençal, but save your appetite for the entrées. Divine dishes arrive with excellent flavor, including a lime-glazed flank steak layered over rice-and-black-bean salad. Expertly sauced pastas are also awe-inspiring, but for a truly extravagant main course, order the Steak Diane—a butterfly tenderloin sautéed in a Burgundy brown sauce with mushrooms, scallions, Dijon, and garlic—prepared tableside by Hamide himself. *$$; AE, MC, V; checks OK; lunch Mon–Fri, dinner every day; full bar; reservations recommended; www.soriah.com.* &

Best Place to Smooch over Something Sweet

Eugene might be rumored to be a tofu-loving hippie town, but don't let that fool you: these people love their desserts. **Sweet Life Patisserie** (755 Monroe St; 541/683-5676; www.sweetlifedesserts.com) is the local favorite for its European ambience and an array of goodies to satiate sweet tooths. Sisters Catherine and Cheryl Reinhart started baking treats in their home garage before turning it into a cozy bakery. Today, they serve up all types of made-from-scratch goods for breakfast, snacks, and dessert. We recommend the latter, especially a slice of Cloud Nine Cake or Triple Chocolate Obsession. Other favorite dessert choices include the tiny, romantic **Savoy Truffle** (460 Willamette St; 541/343-1586) and **Prince Pucklers** (1605 E 19th Ave; 541/344-4418)—an old-fashioned ice cream shop that offers little atmosphere but serves phenomenal ice cream in seasonal flavors.

Chanterelle / ◗◗◗

207 E 5th St, Suite 109, Eugene; 541/484-4065
Walk into Chanterelle, and you might think you've been transported to an intimate French *auberge*: a warm welcome from the dining-room captain, white table linens, and the heady fragrance of Gruyère-topped French onion soup and escargots bubbling in red wine all greet you at once. The muted lighting and clean interior keeps diners focused on one another—and on the distinguished cuisine. Chef John-Patrick creates a fine dining experience with a French-informed menu, featuring such items as richly sauced tournedos of beef and a classic *zwiebelsteak*. All come with salad and choice of potatoes or spaetzle. You'll also find a respectable wine list and extraordinary desserts. Or consider a nightcap and tête-à-tête in Chanterelle's adjacent, intimate lounge. *$$$; AE, DC, MC, V; dinner Tues–Sat; full bar; reservations recommended; www.chanterellerestauranteugene.net.* &

Excelsior Inn Ristorante Italiano / ◗◗◖

754 E 13th Ave, Eugene; 541/342-6963 or 800/321-6963
Pick your pleasure: a glass of wine and hand-holding across an intimate table at an airy, European-style bar, or snuggling by the fire in the embrace of a formal dining room. The Excelsior offers both—and a sky-lit indoor terrace and walled outdoor courtyard, too. Owner/executive chef Maurizio Paparo has brought his Italian background to both the menu and the interior of this elegant establishment. Try the crispy Oregon rainbow trout sauced with a

prosecco-pomegranate glaze, *spaghetti allo scoglio*, or *gnocchi pomodoro fresco* for an authentic Italian experience. Celebrations call for one of pastry chef Milka Babich's outstanding desserts, particularly her Italian almond *torta* with raspberry sauce. The 200-plus-bottle wine list is extensive. *$$$; AE, DC, DIS, MC, V; no checks; breakfast, dinner every day, lunch Mon–Fri, brunch Sun; full bar; reservations recommended; www.excelsiorinn.com.* ♿

Marché / ⬡⬡⬡

296 E 5th Ave, Eugene; 541/342-3612
Lovers with refined palates will appreciate the well-crafted combinations of fresh and often organically grown local foodstuffs at the heart of Marché's meals. This sophisticated restaurant on the ground floor of the Fifth Street Public Market celebrates the seasonal Northwest bounty with menus that change daily and entrées prepared with a French sensibility. In fall, pork chops from local farms may come with an autumn fruit-and-onion confit, and the sage-infused roasted leg of venison is accompanied by sweet-potato purée, baked apple, and huckleberry sauce. Come summer, Oregon albacore is seared rare and served with smoked-tomato *coulis* and fried squash blossom. Lunch is lighter, with the addition of a few *pizzettas* from a wood-fired oven (picture pancetta, delicata squash, sage, and Romano cheese) and sandwiches such as portobello mushroom with sun-dried-tomato relish and smoked mozzarella on homemade flatbread. The wine list and dessert menu reflect the same regional leanings and attention to detail. The interior—elegantly hip with dark, gleaming wood and wry artwork—sets the stage for an enjoyable and tasty evening with your sweetheart. *$$$–$$$$; AE, DC, DIS, MC, V; checks OK; lunch, dinner every day, brunch Sun; full bar; reservations recommended; www.marcherestaurant.com.* ♿

Red Agave / ⬡⬡⬡

454 Willamette St, Eugene; 541/683-2206
Consistently voted one of the city's best ethnic restaurants by *Eugene Weekly*, Red Agave offers a distinctive blend of flavorful Nuevo Latino cuisine. Although it has a quasi-high-energy atmosphere, its subtly sexy Latin influence recommends it for romance. (For a quieter experience, arrive either at opening or later in the evening.) Inside, the high ceilings and glowing red lanterns make the open floor plan and airy dining room feel lively and vibrant. Ask to be seated in a tucked-away corner for more intimacy. Small starter plates are perfect for sharing; begin with a spinach salad with grilled pears and juicy bacon or a duo of prawns perched atop local merguez sausage and a bed of unbelievably creamy polenta. Proceed with spicy entrées like Hawaiian sea bass sautéed with garlic, mild guajillo chile, and lime, or prettily presented chicken enchiladas with green mole, addictive ancho chile–pepper sauce, and *queso barra*. A rotating selection of desserts ranges from spiced Mexican

chocolate cheesecake with warm caramel–arbol chile sauce to an aged Manchego cheese plate served with quince paste, cayenne, toasted almonds, and baguette. *$$$; AE, DIS, MC, V; checks OK; dinner Mon–Sat; full bar; reservations recommended.* &

♡ Oregon
Coast

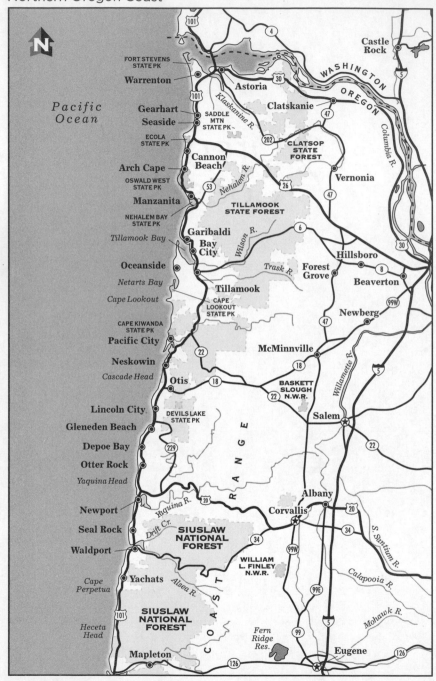

Until then, mio dolce amor, a thousand kisses; but
give me none in return, for they set my blood on fire.
—Napoleon Bonaparte

 Oregon Coast

The stunning scenery is nonstop along the two-lane highway of Oregon's 101, which follows the entire Oregon Coast, stretching about 400 miles from Astoria south into California. Winding along, you never know what you'll see around the next curve, but be assured, it will be spectacular. There are plenty of pull-off points, parks, trails, coves, and inlets where you can stop and take in the view—or steal a kiss—in the presence of a magnificent sunset. Charming shops, small restaurants, and an endless choice of romantic hotels and inns dot the quaint, rural surroundings. You can eat, drink, and lodge very well along the Oregon Coast—before, during, and after ocean gazing.

Constant changes in the weather enhance the boundless drama of the area. At times the mixture of fog and sea mist settles like a gauzy veil over the region. At other times, dramatic tempests brew on the horizon. Yet even on the calmest summer days, the siren song of the waves breaking over beaches, headlands, and rocks is simply spellbinding. Time shared on the Oregon Coast can rekindle your relationship with the world—and with each other. The two of you can hike through coastal rain forest, beach comb for agates, explore tide pools, fly kites, whale watch, or build a toasty bonfire.

On the northern coast, romance is easy to find in cultured little towns like Cannon Beach, while the central coast offers both the sophisticated pleasures of boutiques and fine dining and the charm of working harbors where fresh seafood abounds. Farther south, the remote terrain feels wild and unsettled—the perfect setting for romance-infused exploration. Driving the entire coast would take the better part of a day, even without stops. So you're better off choosing a part of the region and really getting acquainted with it. If, however, you have the time, a few days spent meandering from one port to the next would certainly make for a memorable journey.

Northern Coast

Romantic Highlights

Couples seeking romance while sipping their way down the coast will find a plethora of wine shops along the way. In **Astoria,** a picturesque town set on the mouth of the Columbia River characterized by a working waterfront, begin with **The Cellar on 10th** (1004 Marine Dr; 503/325-6600). This huge wine shop often earns national awards and offers weekly wine tastings.

For an excellent introduction to the waterfront, cuddle up with your favorite travel companion on the **Riverfront Trolley** (503/325-8790; every day in summer, Fri–Sun during the rest of the year). Jump on at marked stops all along the riverfront. The 4-mile journey along the river, over old railway lines, takes in the recently expanded Columbia River Maritime Museum, historic buildings, working boat crews, and, of course, beautiful views. Once you've enjoyed the scenery up close, get a bird's-eye view by climbing the spiraling staircase of the **Astoria Column** (1 Coxcomb Hill; 503/325-2963; 8am–dusk). A tribute to the Lewis and Clark Expedition, this 125-foot-tall structure has been inspiring lofty kisses since 1926. During the day, enjoy sweeping views of the surrounding rivers, mountains, and ocean, along with the 4-mile-long Astoria-Megler Bridge, which connects Oregon and Washington. At night, be sure to catch the lighted column twinkling in all its luminous glory high above the town.

Speaking of twinkling, Astoria is known for its stars, and we mean the Hollywood kind. With a long list of movies filmed here, Astoria fascinates film fans. It was at a restaurant at West Mooring Basin that Arnold Schwarzenegger traded passionate kisses with costar Penelope Ann Miller in *Kindergarten Cop.* As local lore has it, boat owners helped set the mood by leaving their lights on during the nighttime filming. The stone and marble building that houses the **Columbia River Day Spa** (1215 Duane St; 503/325-7721) is the sort of grand landmark that keeps Hollywood coming. You'll want to indulge in the spa's Couples Package, which includes a warm-up in the sauna, side-by-side Swedish massages, and a hot soak in the Japanese geisha tub.

Seaside, 20 miles south of Astoria, hasn't always been known as a romantic destination; but that's all changing. You can now find a slice of sophistication downtown at **The Wine Haus** (1111 N Roosevelt St, Ste 200; 503/738-0201), which features small-production wines and a tasting bar. In addition, **Yummy Wine Bar & Bistro** (see Romantic Restaurants) is *the* place to see and be seen while sipping in Seaside. With the flood of families flocking to Seaside by the thousands during the summer months, you can still find several secret places to kiss on the beaches at the north and south ends of town. Stop first at the **French Hen Wine & Cheese Co.** (see Romantic Restaurants), adjacent to **McKeown's** restaurant, and put together the perfect picnic lunch to take along to the vast, romantic beaches. In the off-season, you might even find yourselves alone on Seaside's famous **Prom,** the 1½-mile-long cement trail that meanders along the beachfront. Stay away from the video arcades and the kid-lined streets of the town center and you may find Seaside to be a place of unexpected fun and romance.

Cannon Beach, just a few miles south of Seaside, is a decidedly quieter and a more sophisticated destination (though the new savvy wine bars in Seaside may start to challenge Cannon Beach in its draw for chic visitors). With more than 7 miles of solid sand and rolling waves, this town beckons dreamers and lovers alike to roll up their jeans, hold hands, and stroll at the edge of the churning surf. Start your day with a walk down the beach to the base of the freestanding monolith, **Haystack Rock,** the third largest of its kind in the world and a true natural wonder, followed by brunch at **Gower Street Bistro** (1116 S Hemlock St; 503/436-2729), a European-style charcuterie serving brunch seven days a week during the summer. Back in town, wander Hemlock Street's art galleries and boutiques, and drop in on a glassblowing demonstration at **Icefire Glassworks** (corner of Hemlock and Gower sts; 503/436-2359), where visitors can watch artists from a special viewing area. After lunch, grab an ice cream cone from **Osburn's Ice Creamery** (240 N Hemlock St; 503/436-2578), then sit side-by-side on the sprawling front porch and watch the world go by. Wine aficionados should not miss a visit to **The Wine Shack** (124 Hemlock St; 503/436-1100 or 800/787-1765), named one of the top 50 wine shops in the United States by *GQ* magazine.

Between Cannon Beach and **Arch Cape** there are several parks and viewpoints, including **Hug Point** (8 miles south of Cannon Beach; 800/551-6949), but the really spectacular part starts with the tunnel just south of Arch Cape. As the highway passes over the lower slopes of Neahkahnie Mountain, several turnouts provide opportunities to steal a kiss amid amazing views of the coast both north and south. Another romantic highlight nearby is the **Arcadia Beach State Park** with picnic tables and beach access. A trail leads to a scenic beach in a beautiful little cove—the perfect spot for a cozy picnic lunch.

For something decidedly chic, make your next stop **Vino Manzanita** (387-D Laneda Ave; 503/368-8466), an intimate wine bar located in the quaint beach community of **Manzanita,** settled between the Pacific Ocean and the base of Neahkahnie Mountain. Before you leave, stop next door at the superb bakery, **Bread & Ocean** (387 Laneda Ave; 503/368-5823), for a whole-wheat cinnamon roll or savory fig and brie roll. **Wheeler** is a good starting point for indulging your beach fix with a day of kayaking. Calm waters make this a relaxing trip even for beginners, and the folks at the **Wheeler Marina** (278 Marine Dr; 503/368-6055) will make sure you paddle away with all the information you need.

If you prefer to pander to your palate, head inland to the **Nehalem Bay Winery,** just a mile up Highway 53 from the Highway 101 junction. This historic winery has been in business for 30 years and is nestled in a lush, green valley that resembles parts of France or Germany's Black Forest. With picnic tables overlooking the dairy farms and the coastal range, nearby boutiques, antique shops, and forested state parks, the Nehalem Bay area is a romantic spot that should not be missed. Wherever you decide to stay, be sure and find a front-row seat in the evening—your hotel deck, the beach, a park bench—to watch the spectacular

Three Days of Romance in Cannon Beach

Day One: Start the day by beachcombing near Haystack Rock at low tide (find sand dollars and view amazing tide pools) and walk hand-in-hand down the beach to breakfast at **Gower Street Bistro** (1116 S Hemlock St, Cannon Beach; 503/436-2729) for out-of-this world French toast and crab eggs Benedict. Stroll back to town along Hemlock, stopping in the numerous small boutiques, art galleries, and tastefully designed mini malls. Stop in for a bowl of creamy clam chowder at **JP's** (240 N Hemlock St, Cannon Beach; 503/436-0908), then find a quiet bench in front of the library to people watch before heading back to your room for a leisurely afternoon retreat. When you're ready to face the world again, pack an early-dinner picnic and take off for a hike at **Ecola State Park**, where you can trek the 6-mile Tillamook Head Trail (located off Hwy 101 north of downtown Cannon Beach), which runs from Cannon Beach to Seaside—the very same one Lewis and Clark followed. Or watch surfers from vantage points along the trail. Plan it so you make it back just in time to watch the sunset while sipping champagne on the deck of your room at the **Stephanie Inn** (see Romantic Lodgings).

Day Two: Head to Gearhart and start the morning with a scone and coffee from **Pacific Way Bakery and Café** (601 Pacific Way, Gearhart;

sunsets that have earned the Oregon Coast its nickname, Sunset Empire. On a clear evening, as the sun descends to the sea, you'll watch its rays infuse the lavender-blue dusk with brilliant shades of golden amber and blaze red before they disappear completely and the sky changes to cobalt and then, finally, inky black.

Access & Information

Driving is your best bet to and from the northern Oregon Coast. From Seattle, take Interstate 5 to Longview, Washington, cross the interstate bridge, and follow Highway 30 west to Astoria. From downtown Portland, take Highway 26 west (the road traverses the Coast Range mountains and can be dangerous in winter) to its intersection with Highway 101 at the Cannon Beach Junction. Highway 6 from Portland isn't quite as direct a route to the north coast, but it's also popular. Highway 101 (also known as the Coast Highway) is the only road along Oregon's coast. The **State Welcome Center** (111 W Marine Dr, Astoria; 503/325-6311 or 800/875-6807) and the **Seaside Visitors Bureau** (7 N Roosevelt Dr, Seaside; 503/738-3097 or 888/306-2326) are good starting points. The **Oregon Coast Visitors Association** (888/628-2101; visittheoregoncoast.com) also offers helpful information.

503/738-0245). Spend the day golfing at **Gearhart Golf Links** (1157 N Marion, Gearhart; 503/738-3538), a classic links-style 18-hole course open to the public. Or, if you're the spa type, pass on golf and head back to Cannon Beach for some rest and relaxation. Try the Wild about Seaweed package at the **Cannon Beach Spa** (232 N Spruce St, Cannon Beach; 503/436-8772 or 888/577-8772). Pick up a bottle or two of wine from **The Wine Shack** (124 Hemlock St, Cannon Beach; 503/436-1100 or 800/787-1765) on your way back to the Stephanie Inn—because you never know when that moment will strike. Then, dine at **Bistro** (263 N Hemlock St, Cannon Beach; 503/436-2661), an intimate setting featuring classic Northwest cuisine.

Day Three: Get an early start and rent beach bikes from **Mike's Bikes** (248 N Spruce St; 503/436-1266) and cruise up and down the beach and around town. Work up a sweat before brunching at the **Lazy Susan Café** (126 N Hemlock St, Cannon Beach; 503/436-2816). For some, nothing says romance like bird-watching, so head back out on your bikes to Chapman Point at the north end of Cannon Beach for some gazing at our fine feathered friends. Save your appetite for dinner at **Newmans at 988**, where you'll nuzzle at a quiet corner table and feast on foie-gras pasta with black truffles, lobster ravioli, and spectacular local wines.

Romantic Lodgings

Arch Cape House / ✿✿✿

31970 E Ocean Ln, Arch Cape; 503/436-2800 or 800/436-2848
Like a picture from a fairy tale, this wood-shingled chateau is reminiscent of an old-world castle. Located just a few miles south of Cannon Beach, the Arch Cape House emanates romance and charm. The inn's seven guest rooms are bona fide masterpieces, each enjoying unique themes, views of the ocean across Highway 101, fireplaces, and private bathrooms. Our favorite is the Provence Room, with its cathedral ceiling, authentic French linens, terracotta floors, and French doors that lead to a private patio. A wood-accented tiled Jacuzzi is an added luxury here. Breakfast is an all-out affair and owner Barbara Dau is known for her fabulous cooking, though she can be a bit rigid. Nonetheless, after her delicious multicourse breakfast, you will not think again about food until dinnertime. *$$$; AE, DIS, MC, V; checks OK; www.st-bernards.com.* &

Astoria Inn Bed and Breakfast / ✿✿❦

3391 Irving Ave, Astoria; 503/325-8153 or 800/718-8153
Perched above the city and just minutes from downtown, the Astoria Inn enjoys expansive views of the Columbia River and good old-fashioned peace and quiet—with lots of places and time for kissing. All four guest rooms are cozy retreats with private baths. Three rooms are located on the second floor and share a small common area. Our favorite is Cape Virginia, with its dark green walls and a whimsical canopy bed; a claw-foot tub and pedestal sink embellish the modest bathroom. The fourth room is situated off the dining room, and talkative breakfast guests may impede sleep or other activities. Breakfast is a not-to-be-missed event and may include warm Dutch pastries, French toast, or homemade quiche. *$; DIS, MC, V; checks OK; www.astoria innbb.com.*

Cannon Beach Property Management, Inc. / ✿✿✿

3188 S Hemlock, Tolovana Park; 503/436-2021 or 877/386-3402
Whether you're looking for quaint and quiet, an ocean view, or an ocean-front home-away-from-home, owner Tami Florer can help choose the perfect romantic retreat from their selection of spotless properties. The homes range from charming bungalows to newly renovated houses to condominiums with designer decor, updated kitchens and baths, and spectacular ocean views. The Rose Cottage is a romantic two-bedroom close to town and the beach; Aldoren's Wind 'N Tide is a two-story oceanfront bungalow—a spacious deck provides a great place to watch the sunset over a meal you've lovingly prepared for your sweetheart. Inquire about pets. *$$–$$$; DIS, MC, V; checks OK; www.cpbm.com.*

Clementine's Bed and Breakfast / ✿✿❦

847 Exchange St, Astoria; 503/325-2005 or 800/521-6801
With its baby grand piano, crystal chandeliers, and collection of vintage glass-ware, this 120-year-old Italianate Victorian sits on the edge of downtown. Five rooms feature private baths, antique wrought-iron beds, warm floral decor, and wireless Internet. For romance, book an upstairs room with a private balcony and a captivating river vista; the spacious Clementine's Suite, done up in shades of apricot and green with a separate sitting area and gas fireplace, is our favorite. Innkeepers Judith and Cliff Taylor possess a wealth of knowledge about Astoria and the surrounding region, and Judith serves one of Astoria's finest breakfasts. *$$; AE, DIS, MC, V; checks OK; www. clementines-bb.com.* &

Eagle's View Bed and Breakfast / ✿✿❦

37975 Brooten Rd, Pacific City; 503/965-7600 or 888/846-3292
A stay at Eagle's View is hands-down the best kissing bargain along the Oregon Coast. Set inland, about 70 miles south of Cannon Beach, and surrounded

by 4 acres of gently rolling countryside, the house commands sweeping views of Nestucca Bay. Rooms are comfortably appointed with goose-down comforters, European armoires, and plenty of sunshine. The Garden Room downstairs offers a private entrance and a whirlpool tub. Rooms called Love Spoken Here and Whimsy boast whirlpool tubs and incredible views. Dine in the privacy of your room or join others downstairs in the Great Room for fresh fruit, homemade pastries, and famous German pancakes or Nestucca Eggs. *$$; DC, DIS, MC, V; checks OK; www.eaglesviewbb.com.* &

Gilbert Inn / ●●●

341 Beach Dr, Seaside; 503/738-9770 or 800/410-9770
Although Seaside's popular beachfront is just a block away, inside this picturesque yellow Victorian, Seaside's crowds simply fade into oblivion. Fluffy down comforters and armfuls of pillows embellish the antique beds in every room, and even the smallest of the inn's 10 guest rooms offers comfort and charm. The best getaway of all is the Turret Room, a circular wall of windows with loads of sunlight and an inviting four-poster cherry-wood bed. The newer wing offers cheerful suites with wicker furniture, country fabrics, and private bathrooms. All rooms are equipped with DVD players and wireless Internet. Raspberry French toast or blueberry pancakes might be featured in the generous morning meal. *$$; AE, DIS, MC, V; checks OK; www.gilbertinn.com.*

Hotel Elliott / ●●●(

357 12th St, Astoria; 503/325-2222 or 877/378-1924
The Hotel Elliott, a luxurious boutique hotel, is located in the revitalized downtown Liberty District, an exciting culinary and arts scene with coastal recreation just minutes away. Each of the restored 32 rooms has Egyptian cotton sheets, a featherbed, and sumptuous terry robes. A spa tub, heated-stone bathroom floor, marble vanity, and spun-glass sink add to the undeniably luxurious setting. For the ultimate indulgence, the top-floor Presidential Suite wins our most enthusiastic nod: lounge on the rooftop terrace and gaze at the stars or snuggle under the covers in front of the fireplace. In the morning, enjoy the complimentary continental breakfast or, better yet, stay in bed and have the Schooner Twelfth Street Bistro (360 12th St; 503/325-7882) deliver breakfast to you. *$$$–$$$$; AE, DC, DIS, MC, V; checks OK; www.hotelelliott.com.* &

Inn at Cannon Beach / ●●●

3215 S Hemlock St, Cannon Beach; 503/436-9085 or 800/321-6304
While the Inn at Cannon Beach does not have ocean views, it offers amenities you don't often find in a coastal setting: lush green lawns, a koi pond, and gardens. Four rustic natural-wood bungalows, each with private deck and porch, house the rooms and are tucked among the trees—creating a

surprisingly secluded feel. Inside the bungalows, casual but chic furnishings in natural tones and nature themes suggest simple sophistication. All rooms have fireplaces, kitchenettes, and wireless connectivity; 11 rooms offer corner Jacuzzis for two. The newspaper is delivered to your door, you can check out DVDs at the front desk, and the staff is gracious and very accommodating. Breakfast is buffet-style in the great room that otherwise acts as a gathering place and art gallery. You may encounter families with young children, so if you are looking for ultimate intimacy, enjoy your meal in your room. The ocean is just a 3-minute walk from your door, though you will have to take the passing shuttle (or drive) to downtown Cannon Beach. *$$$; AE, DC, DIS, MC, V; checks OK; www.innatcannonbeach.com.* &

The Inn at Manzanita / ❂❂❆

67 Laneda Ave, Manzanita; 503/368-6754
Just 200 feet from Manzanita's 7-mile stretch of beach, this contemporary Northwest-style inn offers 14 rooms including a penthouse suite for luxurious comfort. Guest rooms in the main building suggest a hybrid of sunny log cabin and comfortable hotel room, with private decks that afford partial views of the ocean through the treetops. Romantic frills include two-person Jacuzzi tubs, gas fireplaces, wet bars, and firm, cozy beds with down comforters. Rooms in the North Building, a stunning two-level cottage, feature captain's beds tucked into snug, sunlit nooks separated from the living area by curtains. Considering the reasonable prices, this could easily become a favorite coastal getaway. *$$–$$$; MC, V; checks OK; www.innatmanzanita.com.*

Ocean Lodge / ❂❂❂❆

2864 S Pacific St, Cannon Beach; 503/436-2241 or 888/777-4047
The *Oregonian* calls Ocean Lodge the best coast home-away-from-home, and we couldn't agree more. The lodge combines rustic elegance—think open-beamed ceilings and massive stone hearths—with the nostalgic style of an old-time beach resort. The result is truly delightful. Reclaimed hardwood floors from an old warehouse and thick beam stairs that were once local gymnasium bleachers add timeless warmth. The decor, in neutral and dark tones, is tasteful and understated. In-room amenities include corner Jacuzzi tubs and fireplaces, and 33 of the main lodge's 37 rooms have oceanfront views. While most of the rooms are similar, units 207 and 309 feature vaulted ceilings and bigger oceanfront decks. Bungalows across the street lack the views, but they make up for it in cozy privacy and also come with Jacuzzis and king-size beds. Service is first-rate, as are the locally baked breakfast goodies. *$$$–$$$$; AE, DC, DIS, MC, V; checks OK; www. theoceanlodge.com.* &

Rosebriar Hotel / ◐◐◖

636 14th St, Astoria; 503/325-7427 or 800/487-0224
Tucked in a residential neighborhood only blocks from the waterfront, this magnificent, restored 1902 Neoclassical home retains much of its original charm. Inside, you'll find a fir-paneled front desk and a cozy parlor with overstuffed floral couches, elegant window treatments, and a fireplace with a wooden mantel. Our top vote for romance goes to the Captain's Suite with its private staircase leading to the third floor. The room offers panoramic views of the Columbia River, Astoria Bridge, and spectacular sunsets; a breakfast nook and sitting room with a fireplace; a large master bedroom; and a spacious bathroom with a soaking tub. Adjacent to the hotel and its courtyard, the 1885 carriage house offers the most privacy, as well as a kitchenette, a fireplace, a jetted tub, and stained-glass windows. In the morning, the seductive smells of homemade goodies float overhead. *$$–$$$; AE, DC, DIS, MC, V; checks OK; www.rosebriar.net.*

Rose River Inn Bed & Breakfast / ◐◐◖

1510 Franklin Ave, Astoria; 503/325-7175 or 888/876-0028
Located three short blocks from the historical downtown and four blocks from the Columbia River, the Rose River Inn is a favorite for weddings, anniversaries, and getaways of all kinds. Lush gardens teeming with flowering shrubs, evergreens, and climbing rosebushes embellish this circa-1912 lodging, which best exemplifies American four-square architecture. Our pick for the most romantic room is the Rose Room, complete with fireplace and canopied queen-size bed. If it's a chilly evening, curl up with a warm beverage in the glow of the parlor fireplace. For added warmth, the River Suite is a great romantic bet, with its claw-foot tub and authentic Finlandia dry sauna. The Romantic Getaway package, features a dozen roses, chocolate strawberries, and your choice of champagne, wine, or sparkling cider awaiting you in your room. *$$–$$$; DIS, MC, V; checks OK; www.roseriverinn.com.* &

Sandlake Country Inn / ◐◐◐◐

8505 Galloway Rd, Cloverdale; 503/965-6745
This secret hideaway boasts no ocean views, but instead offers acres of privacy tucked into gardens of roses, just a mile from the ocean. Bountiful flower gardens fill the front yard of this 115-year-old old farmhouse, hidden on a quiet country road off the Three Capes Scenic Loop, about 10 minutes north of Haystack Rock. The inn's countrified, farmlike surroundings only hint at the elegance and luxury that await you in the three private suites and creek-side cottage. The spacious four-room Starlight Suite occupies the entire second floor. This romantic hideaway features a half-canopy queen bed and a large private deck overlooking the gardens. A double-sided fireplace warms the master bedroom and extra sitting room, and the suite boasts a

luxury bathroom with a double whirlpool tub. In the morning, a decadent four-course breakfast is delivered to your room. *$$; DIS, MC, V; checks OK; www.sandlakecountryinn.com.* &

Stephanie Inn / ❂❂❂❂

2740 S Pacific St, Cannon Beach; 503/436-2221 or 800/633-3466
The Stephanie Inn exemplifies classic luxury on the edge of the shore. The surf practically laps at the foundations of this New England–style inn, where a fire is always glowing in the river-rock hearth of the front parlor, and overstuffed sofas, impressive wood detailing, and hardwood floors create an inviting and elegant ambience. The inn offers 46 rooms and the adjacent Carriage House contains four more. Rooms are spacious yet cozy with plush terry-cloth robes and four-poster beds made up with beautiful floral linens, and nearly every room has a private deck, gas fireplace, and corner Jacuzzi or whirlpool tub in its spacious bathroom. A complimentary breakfast buffet is served in the inn's mountain-view dining room. During spring and summer the Romantic Beach Bonfire Package includes wood and a starter log and your choice of champagne, wine, or cider, along with turndown service and a scattering of rose petals on the bed and a bubble bath awaiting in the Jacuzzi for two. *$$$$; AE, DC, DIS, MC, V; checks OK; www.stephanie-inn.com.*

Romantic Restaurants

Baked Alaska / ❂❂

1 12th St, Astoria; 503/325-7414
It's hard to believe that this charming little waterfront restaurant, located at the foot of 12th Street on a dock over the Columbia River, grew out of a mobile soup wagon in Alaska. Back in the '80s, owners Chris and Jennifer Holen coined the phrase "Have soup, will travel" and took their wagon on the road all over the 49th state. The pair retired the wagon and created a romantic little spot in Astoria. Signature dishes include Broiled Pacific Sea Scallops over fresh black pepper linguini tossed with Fuji apples, fennel, and ginger in a light champagne sauce; and Campfire Salmon, prepared in an Alaskan Amber barbecue marinade and flambéed campfire-style. Another favorite is the Thundermuck Tuna, which includes a coffee-dusted albacore tuna seared rare, with a honey-sesame sauce, balsamic reduction, and pickled ginger. To make dining that much sweeter, every seat in the place comes with a view of the Columbia River. *$$; AE, DC, DIS, MC, V; no checks; lunch, dinner every day; full bar; no reservations; www.bakedak.com.* &

Bistro / ❂❂❂

263 N Hemlock St, Cannon Beach; 503/436-2661
Candlelight creates the glow of this Tudor-style cottage, nestled within a cluster of small shops off the main thoroughfare in Cannon Beach. Past the

bustling bar area, you'll find a snug dining room handsomely appointed with French-country decor, dark wood, and blue tablecloths. Signature dishes include Seafood Stew, chock-full of fresh seafood and bathed in a tomato, fennel, garlic, and herb broth topped with rouille; and crab cakes with an oriental flare: spiced with ginger and garlic, finished with a rice-wine-and-butter sauce. Bistro is slightly noisier than most places we recommend for amorous encounters, but tables are sufficiently spaced to ensure the privacy for a kiss or two. *$$$; MC, V; local checks only; dinner every day (Thurs–Mon Nov–Mar); full bar; reservations recommended.* &

Gunderson's Cannery Café / ●●

1 6th St, Astoria; 503/325-8642
If you're looking for a dining room with a view, you'd have a hard time finding a better one than this. Perched over the river, this cozy and intimate cafe offers front-row viewing for spectacular sunsets. Everything on the menu is made daily from scratch; fish is fresh and caught locally. Signature entrées include a slightly altered interpretation of the traditional Scandinavian Laksloda, thinly sliced potatoes layered with salmon then baked and topped with lemon-dill cream sauce. There's also a filbert-crusted salmon, or red meat eaters might prefer a blackened rib eye or teriyaki-glazed flank steak. The full-service bar showcases the best regional wines. Once you're sated, wander down to the end of the 6th Street Pier or out to the riverfront-viewing tower for even better panoramas. *$$; DC, DIS, MC, V; checks OK; breakfast Tues–Sun, lunch, dinner every day; full bar; reservations recommended; www. cannerycafe.com.*

JP's / ●●●

240 N Hemlock St, Cannon Beach; 503/436-0908
Large and lofty, with sky-high ceilings, fine art, and mahogany tables, this European-style restaurant is an intimate gem with just 10 tables. Even the bathrooms—works of art in purple and orange—win raves. Chef Bill Pappas calls his award-winning fare of seafood, poultry, pasta, or beef *à la minute,* which means "as fresh as possible." While that may also mean waiting just a bit longer for your food, it's definitely worth it. The crab cakes are moist and surprisingly creamy, yet still crisp on the outside. The clam chowder is thick and smooth, flavored with a touch of salmon, and topped with hazelnuts. The award-winning wine list offers a nicely balanced selection of Oregon wines, an outstanding array of Washington vintages, and some unusual bottles that might spice up a romantic dinner. The chef's favorites include Oregon's Chateau Lorane Baco Noir and Beran Pinot Noir. *$$; MC, V; local checks only; lunch, dinner Mon–Sat; beer and wine; reservations recommended.* &

McKeown's and French Hen Wine & Cheese Co. / ◗◖

714 Broadway, Seaside; 503/738-5232
Charming and comfortable with a European style, McKeown's offers a generous menu of breakfast, lunch, and dinner items served in a courtyard setting. The breakfast menu includes complimentary fresh-baked scones, served with house favorites, such as eggs Benedict, farmers omelet, and frittatas. Lunch offers a satiating selection of home-style cooking, including fresh ground-beef burgers on homemade buns and giant hand-dipped onion rings. For dinner, slow-roasted prime rib, fresh wild salmon, or pasta are all served with family-style salad and hot bread. Adding to the Continental feel is the adjoining wine-and-cheese shop, featuring Pacific Northwest wine and daily wine tastings. As an alternative to dining in, cozy up to the intimate bar and sample the top-notch wine flights, while the personable staff puts together the perfect picnic to go. *$$; MC, V; no checks; breakfast, lunch, dinner every day; beer and wine; reservations recommended; www.mckeownsrestaurant.com.* &

Newmans at 988 / ◗◗◖

988 S Hemlock St, Cannon Beach; 503/436-1151
Nestled in a turn-of-the-century yellow farmhouse, Newmans at 988 is a food and wine lover's dream. With menu offerings that include foie gras, pasta with black truffles, fresh fish in a caviar butter sauce, and heavenly chocolate mousse, Newmans is a must-eat experience. Chef John Newman, formerly known for his eight-year tenure as the executive chef for the Stephanie Inn, and his wife, Sandy, brought their dream of a French Italian restaurant to life in 2006. Newmans has only 10 tables and offers a charmingly modest dining atmosphere. Request a corner table in the smaller side of the house for the most privacy. The lighting is dim enough to sneak a kiss across the table in between courses. The wine list is extensive and includes a vast selection of regional Pinot Noirs and internationally recognized wines, which Chef Newman thoughtfully pairs with his five-course prix-fixe menu that changes nightly. *$$$; MC, V; no checks; dinner 5:30pm–9pm every day in summer (not open Mondays in winter); beer and wine; reservations recommended; www. newmansat988.com.*

Roseanna's Cafe / ◗◖

1490 Pacific St, Oceanside; 503/842-7351
Roseanna's is Oceanside's only oceanfront restaurant. In fact, except for the little coffee shop down the road, it's the only restaurant in town, period. But even if there were a number of dining establishments to choose from, we would still recommend eating here. While the atmosphere is easygoing, the kitchen takes its job seriously, producing delicious and healthy made-from-scratch lunches and dinners. Views of the ocean and Three Arch Rocks offshore help make meals memorable, and the food is simply a delight. The menu highlights regional cuisine and fresh seafood; expect salads chock-full

of crisp, fresh vegetables, and a variety of satisfying, creative pasta dishes. In the evening, nature prepares another treat to enhance your meal: an ambrosial sunset for two. *$$; MC, V; local checks only; lunch, dinner every day; beer and wine (limited cocktails); no reservations.* &

Yummy Wine Bar & Bistro / ❂❂❂

831 Broadway, Seaside; 503/738-3100
This smart new wine bar and bistro calls itself "a magnet for the grooviest people in town." Located on Broadway in the heart of downtown Seaside, Yummy offers an affordable assortment of seasonal food and wine meant for pairing and sharing. The friendly and relaxed atmosphere is the perfect spot to mix and mingle amid a sophisticated crowd or nuzzle in a cozy corner, while sipping your way through the featured wine flight (three 2-ounce pours). Not much of a wine aficionado? Don't let that stop you from dropping by to enjoy a small plate or hot *panini* or to take in the art installations that change seasonally along with the wines. You can also purchase retail wines by the bottle or case. *$$; AE, DC, DIS, MC, V; no checks; dinner Thurs–Mon; beer and wine; no reservations; www.yummywinebarbistro.com.*

Central Coast

Romantic Highlights

Wine, cheese, and fine foods are all the rage along the central coast, starting with the **Flying Dutchman Winery** (915 1st St, Otter Rock; 541/765-2553), a working winery perched high on a cliff above the ocean. The tasting room (open every day) features handcrafted wines. About 8 miles to the south is the neighborhood of Nye Beach in **Newport**, home of the **Blu Cork Wine Bar** (613 SW 3rd St; 541/265-2257) and the **Village Market & Deli** (741 NW 3rd St; 541/574-9393), where you can pick up high-end cheeses, homemade chicken pâté, delicious chutneys, a bottle of wine, and some fresh-baked bread to make an exceptional lunch with a beautiful partial view of the ocean in this charming section of Newport.

In **Newport**, start your day with fresh goodies from **Panini Bakery** (232 NW Coast St; 541/265-5033), then make your way to the **Yaquina Head Lighthouse** (follow the signs off Hwy 101 in Newport; 541/574-3100), which some consider one of the most beautiful lighthouses in the country. The stately structure stands at the tip of a coastal headland jutting far out into the Pacific. Beyond the lighthouse there's a hillside of wildflowers and sea grass (did someone say picnic?). Hike the nature trails that lead to magical views or wander down to **Cobble Beach**, made of basalt rock, where you'll find tidal pools, harbor seals, and maybe, if you visit during migration times (Mar–May and Dec–early Feb), a gray whale or two. For more marine life, visit the **Oregon Coast Aquarium** (2820 SE Ferry Slip Rd; 541/867-3474). Tucked into the woods on Yaquina Bay, this surprisingly romantic aquarium houses the largest walk-through seabird aviary in North America.

There are also lots of romantic outdoor activities available on the coast. Rent a kayak for two at the **Embarcadero Resort** (1000 SE Bay Blvd, Newport; 541/265-8521) and paddle about Yaquina Bay, where you'll pass sea lions, seabirds, and sailboats; fly a kite; beach comb for agates; or simply stroll the miles upon miles of sand. You'll discover plenty of vantage points from which to observe the astounding mixture of rock, sand, and surf so common to this stretch of coast. **Fogarty Creek State Park** (on Hwy 101, 1 mile north of Depoe Bay; $6 day-use parking fee) may not look like much at first—signs from the highway lead to a rather unattractive parking area with a few picnic tables scattered about. But once you take the pedestrian underpass to the other side of the highway, you're in for a treat. This small stretch of beach is an ideal setting for picnics and whale watching. Snuggle together while you take in the dramatic display of waves and mist as the turbulent surf breaks against the rugged rock formations, or, if the sea is in a more tranquil mood, explore marine life in the peaceful tide pools.

Other destinations along the central part of the coast include **Depoe Bay**, a colorful little town with a stretch of shops set right on the water's edge; it's Oregon's prime spot for whale watching. **Yachats** is an artsy community harbored in the Siuslaw National Forest, and one of the few places where the coastal mountain range actually merges with the shoreline. Cape Perpetua offers 2,700 acres of scenic area, and the **Devils Churn** is accessible via an exciting descent down a steep flight of wooden stairs that leads to a rocky, narrow channel. At the exchange of tides, the movement of water through this natural cut into the land is simply electrifying. Make a stop at the **Cape Perpetua Interpretive Center** (2400 Hwy 101, Yachats; 541/547-3289; May–Sept) and stock up on hiking maps for a diverse range of trails. A tour map is also available for those who want to see the area by car; the drive is fantastic. There's a $3 day-use fee per vehicle for each location.

Lincoln City is a bit commercial though the Historic Taft District offers the romantic beachfront accommodations of the **Looking Glass Inn** (861 SW 51st Ave; 800/843-4940) and the **Inn at Spanish Head** (see Romantic Lodgings). Find your inner artist at **The Jennifer L. Sears Glass Studio** (4821 SW Hwy 101; 541/996-2569) where you can blow your own glass float, and then reflect on your creations at **Rejuvenation Massage and Spa** (4783 SW Hwy 101; 541/994-1819). For couples who find romance in a day of shopping together, Lincoln City's **outlet stores** (1500 SE East Devils Lake Rd; 541/996-5000) offer everything from designer sunglasses to upscale clothing—all at Oregon's sales tax–free prices.

Access & Information

US Highway 101 follows the Pacific coastline from Washington to Southern California and links most of the towns along the central Oregon Coast. Highway 101 parallels Interstate 5 and can be accessed via any number of secondary roads throughout the state. From I-5, travelers heading toward the central coast can take Highway 99W to Highway 18 or, from the Corvallis area, Highway 20 or 34. For more information, call the **Newport Chamber of Commerce** (555 SW Coast Hwy; 541/265-8801 or 800/262-7844;

The Most Romantic Beaches on the Oregon Coast

Cannon Beach

The seemingly endless 7-mile-stretch of walkable beach is perfect for romantic encounters. Pretend to study the tide pools at **Haystack Rock** while nuzzling with your honey. Or pack along a picnic from **Seasons Café & Deli** (255 N Hemlock St; 503/436-1159) or **The Wine Shack** (124 Hemlock St; 503/436-1000) and find your own hidden sand dune from which to watch the sunset.

Lincoln City

The beaches here are great for tide-pool searching, whale watching, wind surfing, and kite flying together. Evening walks along the beach are especially romantic. Pick up a tide-table booklet from the local newspaper or a nature guide from **Bob's Beach Books** (1747 NW Hwy 10; 541/994-4467) so you can take advantage of walking out as far as you can go when the ocean tide is out.

Rockaway Beach

With 7 miles of open beach, Rockaway has a romantic, small-town feel. This is one beach without the tourist distractions that clutter other beaches. The **Ocean Rogue Inn** (19130 Alder St; 503/355-2093) offers spectacular views of the famous Twin Rocks from its beachfront location.

Bandon Beach

This quaint seacoast town with numerous 19th-century buildings full of small craft shops, art galleries, restaurants, and bakeries is full of romance. If riding horseback along a pristine beach at sunset is your idea of romantic bliss, the **Bandon Beach Riding Stables** (54629 Beach Loop Rd; 541/347-3423) is your place.

www.newportchamber.org) or the **Lincoln City Visitor & Convention Bureau** (801 SW Hwy 101; 541/994-8378; www.oregoncoast.org). The **Oregon Coast Visitors Association** (888/628-2101; www.visittheoregoncoast.com) is also a good place to start for general information.

Romantic Lodgings

Channel House / ✿✿✿

35 Ellingson St, Depoe Bay; 541/765-2140 or 800/447-2140
Perched high on the rocky cliffs of Depoe Bay, this towering, yet unexceptional, building reveals little about the magic found inside. The interior of this cozy getaway features a nautical theme, from the whales etched into the glass

entrance doors to guest rooms with names like Channel Watch, the Bridge, and Crow's Nest. Most of the 17 units are suites and nearly all feature views of waves crashing against the coastline. The larger, more desirable oceanfront rooms and suites have their own private decks, where you can lie back in a steaming hot tub for two and watch the evening sun disappear into the sea. Most popular and romantic is the Admiral Suite, a top-floor corner affording spectacular views that make you feel at times that you're actually floating at sea. The suite features a queen-size bed, gas fireplace, and whirlpool on the deck. Each room comes equipped with a pair of binoculars for whale watching, and several units offer the additional convenience of full kitchens and small kitchenettes. In the morning, head downstairs to the ocean-view dining room for a buffet of fresh fruit and pastries. *$$$–$$$$; AE, DIS, MC, V; checks OK; www.channelhouse.com.*

Cliff House / ❂❂❂

1450 SW Adahi Rd, Waldport; 541/563-2506
Overlooking the Pacific Ocean and Alsea Bay on the central Oregon Coast, this bed-and-breakfast is full of personality, from its bright blue exterior to the eclectic decor of intriguing heirlooms and knickknacks. All four guest rooms are plush, with chandeliers and exquisite American antiques. Enjoy coffee or tea, delivered to your room upon request, on the private balcony of the Morning Star Room, or stargaze through skylights above the king-size bed. A panoramic view and a private entrance make the Alsea Room a good choice as well. Our favorite for romance is the supremely private Suite: furnishings in this room include a four-poster mahogany king-size bed, an English settee, and matching antique English chairs. A private balcony with sweeping ocean views and a wood-burning stove add that much-needed coziness. Soak your cares away in the large Jacuzzi tub in the fully mirrored bathroom, or try out the two-headed shower for some good, clean fun. After your rich and satisfying morning meal, be sure to take advantage of the large shared deck, which has an excellent view of the ocean to the north, west, and east. In the center of the glassed-in deck you'll find a massive hot tub with massaging jets that move up and down your spine—a terrific way to begin your day on the Oregon Coast. *$$$–$$$$; MC, V; checks OK; www.cliffhouseoregon.com.*

Fairhaven Vacation Rentals / ❂❂❂❂

1109 SW Fall St, Newport; 541/574-0951 or 888/523-4179
This collection of homes offers all the creature comforts with an elegant and sophisticated flair. After spending a few nights in any one of these houses—three Victorians, one Cape Cod—it's a safe bet that kissing couples won't want to go home. Set in the charming Nye Beach neighborhood, these elegantly appointed houses are two blocks from the beach, shops, and cafes, and just across the street from the Newport Performing Arts Center. Inside, the homes' layouts are open and airy, featuring slate accents, designer decor,

fireplaces, window seats, full kitchens, washer/dryers, and views of the town and the ocean. Each has a private garden, hot tub, and barbecue. A couple looking for the perfect place to make memories could hardly ask for more. There's a three-night minimum stay during holidays and special events. If you must bring along friends or family, the houses offer sleeping accommodations for six to nine, and each has two full bathrooms. While the houses are a bit large for two, this is as classy as it gets for privacy and upscale living. *$$$; MC, V; checks OK; www.fairhavenvacationrentals.com.*

Heceta Head Lighthouse Bed & Breakfast / ❂❂❂

92072 Hwy 101 S, Yachats; 866/547-3696
There is something eerily romantic about foghorns and lighthouses, and you can experience it firsthand at the Heceta Head Lighthouse. This Queen Anne–style house turned bed-and-breakfast was once the lighthouse keeper's home. Located at the foot of the lighthouse, today it welcomes travelers to what may be one of the most ruggedly romantic settings ever. Set on the cliff with dramatic views of the ocean and beach, the bed-and-breakfast features six rooms decorated in turn-of-the-20th-century style. The Mariner's Rooms I and II both offer spectacular, up-close views of the ocean and have private bathrooms with marble showers. Travelers with romance in mind will find the Queen Anne Room the most inspiring, offering an elegant four-poster queen-size bed with Austrian sheers, a chaise lounge, forest and garden views, and terry-cloth bathrobes for the walk across the hall to the European-style bath. Soak in a porcelain claw-foot tub and gaze at the beach below. *$$–$$$; MC, V; checks OK; www.hecetalighthouse.com.*

Inn at Spanish Head / ❂❂❂

4009 SW Highway 101, Lincoln City; 541/996-2161 or 800/452-8127
If a room with an ocean view, a private deck, and dinner in a penthouse restaurant isn't romantic enough, why not throw in a personalized beach-art message drawn in the sand in front of your window for an over-the-top romantic experience? Rooms in this cliff-side hotel offer spectacular views and are well appointed with comfortable new decor. Ground-floor rooms next to the beach come with fully stocked kitchenettes and glassware, making a shared bottle of bubbly on your own private balcony a must. At the inn's Fathoms restaurant (see Romantic Restaurants), you can choose from a vast selection of wines to accompany your meal, or try the Inn at Spanish Head's own private-label Sauvignon Blanc. The staff here works hard to deliver a unique visit for each guest—from the beach art and easy beach access, to the official whale watching designation and recommendations for best tide pools, to the prime beach spots to explore during your stay. *$$–$$$; AE, DIS, MC, V; www.spanishhead.com.*

Ocean House Bed and Breakfast / ✿✿✿✿

4920 NW Woody Wy, Newport; 866/495-3888
This charming and sophisticated wood-shingled two-story Cape Cod has garnered rave reviews from many honeymooners. New owners and innkeepers Charmaine and Lex Humphrey have created a place to make memories. Guests choose from a variety of spacious and romantic accommodations (all of which are TV and telephone free), from the 2,000-square-foot penthouse, to the cottage, to one of the lovely guest rooms. We recommend any of the second-floor rooms, each featuring sweeping views, gas fireplaces, lovely sitting areas, and Jacuzzi tubs for two. The cottage, a small house with a private entrance, has country charm with hardwood floors, a king-size wrought-iron bed with patchwork quilt, wood ceilings, a stone fireplace, a west-facing wall of windows, and a Jacuzzi tub. If you are looking for space, the penthouse is quite enormous, with vaulted ceilings, a full kitchen and dining room, two bathrooms, and an upstairs loft. Enjoy the gardens, Asian in design, featuring pebble paths, birdhouses, and benches for quiet musings à deux; a private staircase winds down to Agate Beach. The satisfying breakfast might include bacon-potato frittata, smoked salmon quiche, and Oregon hazelnut–stuffed French toast. *$$$–$$$$; AE, DIS, MC, V; www.oceanhouse.com.* &

SeaQuest Inn Bed and Breakfast / ✿✿✿✿

95354 Hwy 101 S, Yachats; 541/547-3782 or 800/341-4878
A mere 50 feet from the ocean, this contemporary 7,000-square-foot wood home exemplifies Oregon Coast architecture at its best. The Martinique Suite occupies its own wing of the house and features a king-size bed, a private entrance, a fireplace, a large jetted tub, oversize furniture, and spectacular ocean views from 40 feet of glass spanning ceiling to floor. The six other beautifully designed guest rooms feature bright linens, thick down comforters on queen-size beds, private entrances, and tantalizing views. Shutters open from the bedrooms onto spacious Jacuzzi soaking tubs in the tiled bathrooms. Eclectic framed artwork covers just about every inch of wall space, while corners and sitting areas overflow with knickknacks and trinkets. A room off the common area called General Mess is generously filled with beach toys, boots, and jackets for guests to use. Upstairs, a crackling fire warms the shared dining/living room, where three walls of windows showcase the fantastic ocean view. This comfortable room is where you'll enjoy the buffet-style breakfast of homemade granola and jams, fresh fruit, a variety of baked breads, coffee cake, and delicious croissants stuffed with eggs, cheese, and mushrooms. *$$$–$$$$; AE, MC, V; checks OK; www.seaquestinn.com.*

Whale Cove Inn / ◐◑◐◑◖

2345 S Hwy 101, Depoe Bay; 541/765-4300 or 800/628-3409
New to the neighborhood, the Whale Cove Inn opened in early 2008 and embodies luxury. Operated by the owners of the Channel House B&B, the Whale Cove Inn is smaller, with only eight rooms, but each room has expansive views and space. Looking over Whale Cove and the Pacific Ocean, each room features a king-size bed, high-definition television with satellite in both the living room and the bedroom, a private deck with Jacuzzi, and a large bath with an enormous walk-in tiled shower. If more space is what you need, splurge on the immense Presidential Suite, which sleeps three couples. Breakfast is served in the dining area on the main floor. *$$$$; AE, DIS, MC, V; checks OK; www.whalecoveinn.net.*

Romantic Restaurants

April's at Nye Beach / ◐◑◐

749 NW 3rd St, Newport; 541/265-6855
Imaginative Mediterranean-inspired cuisine shines at this little cafe in Nye Beach. It's small and stylish with just 12 tables, meaning intimacy is never a problem, though privacy can be. The seafood is particularly noteworthy, and the menu features a daily fresh sheet at market prices. Preparations include grilled wild salmon topped with saffron aioli and surrounded by Manila clam broth, tomatoes, and fresh herbs; halibut coated with *romescu* sauce; and fish and shellfish rolled into cannelloni tubes redolent of lemon, dill, and tarragon. A Portuguese-style clam dish is another favorite and is served with grilled *linguiça* sausage, zesty tomato herb broth, and crispy polenta. The wine list includes an array of choices by the glass and by the bottle. *$$; DIS, MC, V; checks OK; dinner Wed–Sun (closed Jan); beer and wine; reservations recommended.*

Bay House / ◐◑◐◑◖

5911 SW Hwy 101, Lincoln City; 541/996-3222
Just about every table in the Bay House is blessed with its share of lovely scenery through large picture windows. The interior is elegant and modern, and with the current proprietor's philosophy on excellent service, the Bay House has stood the test of time for more than three decades. The menu lists an enterprising assortment of Northwest creations made from local fish and meats, as well as an extensive wine list featuring more than 30 wines by the glass. Signature dishes include pan-seared Maine scallops with Tuscan white-bean stew, seared oxtail, sautéed Black Trumpet mushrooms, smoked Manchego foam, and crispy shallots. Equally wonderful are the desserts—like Blis Maple Syrup Crème Brûlée. It's big and blissful enough to share. *$$$; AE, DIS, MC, V; checks OK; dinner every day (Wed–Sun in winter); full bar; reservations recommended; www.thebayhouse.org.* &

Fathoms Restaurant & Bar / ◐◐

4009 SW Hwy 101 (Inn at Spanish Head), Lincoln City; 541/994-1601
Perched atop the Inn at Spanish Head Resort Hotel, Fathoms's view of the coastline, the ocean, and the beach below is simply breathtaking. The main dining room tends to draw families and large parties, so we recommend a more intimate affair in the stylishly appointed lounge. Enjoy light fare and drinks, or order your meal to be enjoyed from the plump chairs by the fireplace. The dining room serves Northwest fresh salmon, Dungeness crab, and thick, juicy steaks; the Sunday champagne brunch is wonderful. *$$; AE, DC, DIS, MC, V; checks OK; breakfast, lunch, dinner every day; full bar; reservations recommended; www.spanishhead.com.*

Quimby's / ◐◐

740 W Olive St, Newport; 541/265-9919 or 866/784-6297
The ambience at Quimby's is casual, comfortable, and relaxed, and features consistently good Pacific Northwest fare. For lunch, sandwiches range from the standards to the Floppy Sloppy Super Grilled Ham-and-Cheese Thingy. For dinner, the food is a bit more elegant. The Seafood Stew—fresh salmon, halibut, and prawns in an herb-infused broth of tomatoes, onions, saffron, shrimp stock, and Oregon Riesling—is absolutely delicious and comes in huge portions. Equally good are the chef's famous crab cakes and crispy oyster sauté. Outside of seafood, entrées include osso buco or Chef's Chicken Marsala served with shitake, chanterelle, oyster, and field mushrooms. *$$; AE, DC, DIS, MC, V; local checks only; breakfast, lunch, dinner every day; full bar; reservations recommended; www.quimbysrestaurant.com.* &

Saffron Salmons / ◐◐◖

859 SW Bay Blvd, Newport; 541/265-8921
With an eye toward catering to couples, owners Michael and Stacy Waliser offer a menu of fresh foods, locally obtained and prepared in the Northwest tradition. Saffron Salmons has firmly established a stellar reputation for fine regional dining: with excellent food, a waterfront setting, and contemporary decor, this cozy place fills every one of the 13 tables most nights. The signature Saffron Salmon is pan-seared local Chinook salmon served with saffron crème sauce, risotto cake, basil chiffonade, and roasted tomato confit. Also popular with regulars are the clam chowder, crab cakes, and rack of lamb; the crème brûlée has been called the best in town. Wines come from Northwest vineyards; beer is from the Rogue Ale Brewery. Even the art coloring the saffron walls comes from nearby Bay Street Gallery. *$$–$$$ AE, MC, V; local checks only; lunch, dinner Thurs–Tues; beer and wine; reservations recommended; www.saffronsalmon.com.* &

Village Market & Deli / ●●

741 NW 3rd St, Newport; 541/574-9393

What this little eatery lacks in intimacy it more than makes up for in scene. Set in the lovely nook of Newport that is Nye Beach, the Village Market & Deli has that upscale deli-slash-European-sidewalk-cafe feel—indoors and out. Most of the handful of tables are positioned for a view of the quaint neighborhood and are set amid the shelves of gourmet market fare and wine; one of the two bars is situated along the window for outstanding ocean views. The deli opened as a place for a light lunch and has nurtured a big enough fan base to warrant opening for dinner, though the lunch and dinner menus are the same. The menu features sandwiches, soups, salads, and wine sides (small plates), with specialties along the lines of roasted red potato soup, Tuscan turkey, or the Forrester ham sandwich. Wine sides include pâté or meat and cheese plates. The Market & Deli stays open late on weekends for those who are looking to enjoy a nice glass of wine on into the night. *$$; AE, DIS, MC, V; local checks only; lunch, dinner Wed–Sun; beer and wine; reservations recommended.*

Southern Coast

Romantic Highlights

Heading south on Highway 101 takes you through more rural and sparsely populated coastal towns, perfect for the two of you to retreat into solitude and explore some of the best beaches in Oregon. There are fewer crowds, little traffic, and rarely a line for anything. Of course, that means fewer restaurant and lodging choices—and fewer amenities when you do find a place to stay. The fact is there is nothing very romantic about many of the communities straddling the southern portion of Highway 101—but if you venture a few miles east or west, you might easily find yourselves someplace unexpectedly charming.

Florence is just such a hidden gem; on the outskirts it offers little beyond an overabundance of gas stations and mini-marts, but the historic Old Town, situated along the Siuslaw River, is an absolute delight. Here, in the quaint surroundings of old, wooden two-story buildings, you can park the car and wander about the gift, candy, and coffee shops to your heart's content. You can find a few good "kissing chairs" at **Lovejoy's** (195 Nopal St; 541/902-0502), a traditional English tea and delicacies haven in Old Town. Florence is also home to the **Oregon Dunes National Recreational Area**, stretching 38,000 acres and 42 miles from Florence to Coos Bay. Unless you consider noise and grit romantic, pass on the dune buggies for rent and hike the nature trails, which take you to Sahara-sized dunes, coastal rain forests, ocean overlooks, beaches, and wetlands. Because of the diversity of the landscape, what you will find in some parts of the dunes you will not find in others, but tundra swans, great blue herons, bald eagles, snowy plovers, osprey, hummingbirds, and great egrets, among other birds, have all been spotted here. Keep your eyes out also for the berries—strawberries, huckleberries, salmonberries, and blackberries, to name a few. Northwest Forest Passes ($5) are required and may be purchased at any Forest Service office or at the **Oregon Dunes Visitor Center** (855 Highway Ave, Reedsport; 541/271-3611).

You can also explore the dunes mounted on a horse from **C&M Stables** (90241 Hwy 101, Florence; 541/997-7540; www.oregonhorsebackriding.com), which is open year-round and guides guests on rides through the forest and by the sea. The Dune Trail Ride winds through scenic dunes and beaches, while a Coast Range Ride will fill a half or a full day and will take you from ocean vistas to evergreen forests. The most romantic ride is the Sunset Ride, which includes an optional barbecue dinner.

The trio of state parks south of Coos Bay known collectively as **Charleston State Parks** (watch for signs to the parks; they're 12 miles due west of Hwy 101) are well worth the detour from the main road. Though the parks are separated from one another by only a few miles, each one has distinctive terrain. The northernmost park is **Sunset Bay** (541/888-3778), where majestic cliffs and thick forest flank a small, calm ocean inlet. A bit farther south, **Shore Acres** (541/888-3732; $3 day-use fee) is home to the remains of an old estate sprawled out on a cliff soaring high above the coast. Intriguing paths ramble over rock-strewn beaches gouged with caves and granite fissures where the water releases its energy in spraying foam and crashing waves. This park is renowned for its extensive botanical gardens, which are maintained to resemble their original glory. Numerous lookouts offer bird's-eye views. The most informal park is **Cape Arago** (541/888-3778), an outstanding picnic spot high above the shoreline, with a northern view of the coast. It is best known for the sea lions and harbor seals that can be seen romping in the surf or napping on the rocks below. Bring along your binoculars for optimal viewing of these friendly creatures. The town of Charleston is south of Coos Bay, on a small peninsula 30 miles due west of Highway 101.

Like Florence, the sea-coast town of **Bandon** has a charm of its own. The Old Town district is the city center for art galleries, boutiques, and gift shops. It's also home to three world-class golf courses including **Pacific Dunes, Bandon Trails**, and **Bandon Dunes Golf Resort** (541/347-4380 or 888/345-6008), voted one of America's 100 Greatest by *Golf Digest*. Bandon beaches are just as spectacular and interesting as the more popular sites farther north, with a multitude of haystack rocks that rise in tiers out of the ocean. **Face Rock Wayside** (turn off Hwy 101 at signs for Beach Loop Dr and follow this until you reach the Wayside) offers unparalleled views and stupendous scenery. Get lunch to go at **Bandon Baking Co. & Deli** (160 2nd St; 541/347-9440), a local favorite for deli sandwiches, baked goodies, and gourmet coffee, then find a secluded spot on the grassy bluff and take in the magical 180-degree view of crashing surf, dramatic rock formations, and awesome expanse of sandy beach below. We can almost guarantee that lunch will be followed by a kiss.

Southern Oregon Coast

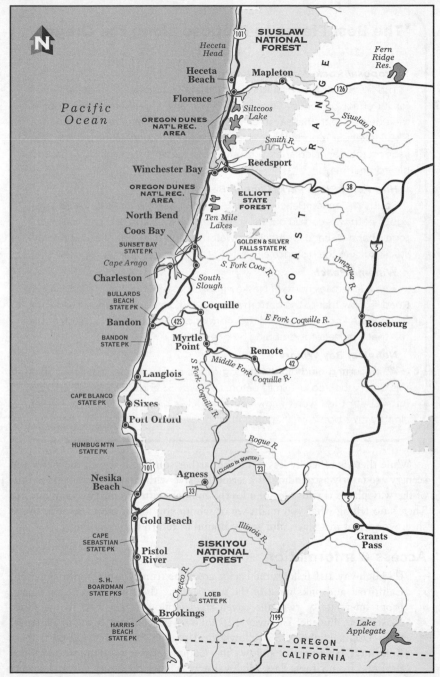

Pacific
Ocean

SIUSLAW
NATIONAL
FOREST

*Heceta
Head*

101

*Fern
Ridge
Res.*

**Heceta
Beach**

Mapleton

Florence

126

*Siltcoos
Lake*

Siuslaw R.

OREGON DUNES
NAT'L REC.
AREA

Smith R.

R A N G E

Winchester Bay

Reedsport

OREGON DUNES
NAT'L REC.
AREA

38

ELLIOTT
STATE
FOREST

North Bend

*Ten Mile
Lakes*

Coos Bay

GOLDEN & SILVER
FALLS STATE PK

SUNSET BAY
STATE PK

S. Fork Coos R.

Umpqua R.

5

Cape Arago

Charleston

*South
Slough*

C O A S T

BULLARDS
BEACH
STATE PK

Coquille

E Fork Coquille R.

Roseburg

Bandon

425

BANDON
STATE PK

**Myrtle
Point**

Remote

S Fork Coquille R.

42

Middle Fork Coquille R.

Langlois

CAPE BLANCO
STATE PK

Sixes

Port Orford

Rogue R.

HUMBUG MTN
STATE PK

101

**Nesika
Beach**

Agness

(CLOSED IN WINTER)

23

33

Gold Beach

Illinois R.

**Grants
Pass**

CAPE
SEBASTIAN
STATE PK

**Pistol
River**

SISKIYOU
NATIONAL
FOREST

5

S. H.
BOARDMAN
STATE PKS

Chetco R.

LOEB
STATE PK

Brookings

199

*Lake
Applegate*

HARRIS
BEACH
STATE PK

OREGON

CALIFORNIA

The Best Places to Propose along the Oregon Coast

Proposal Rock, Neskowin Beach

The history of Proposal Rock is long and romantic; it's a place known for its effect on lovers. Over the years, many a gentleman has popped the question with this haystack-shaped behemoth as a backdrop. A local B&B innkeeper reports that many of those same couples return year after year on their anniversaries, presumably to relive the memory of that first big commitment.

Hug Point State Park, Cannon Beach

South of Cannon Beach lies the Hug Point State Recreation Area. Long ago, a path was carved out for stagecoach travel, and you can walk it still today, hand-in-hand. Sea caves, a waterfall, and the sight of beautiful Haystack Rock in the distance all set the stage for a wedding proposal.

Winema Beach

Just a few miles north of Neskowin, an unassuming sign marks Winema Road. Follow that to the bottom and you'll find a tract of sandy beach that few people know about. The rock formations include a flat stretch at the top that's perfect for dropping on one knee.

Nehelem Bay Winery

After getting giddy in the tasting room, picnic on the lush grounds of this winery located just 1 mile before Highway 53 ends at Highway 101. Your future betrothed won't know you've snuck a ring into the picnic basket, along with a bottle of champagne.

While there is officially less to do the farther south you travel, the views and scenery are utterly astounding. If a leisurely drive with chance encounters at out-of-the-way places is your idea of a lovely, romantic afternoon, then continue on. There's no telling what you might see or whom you might meet. Be open to the sheer wonder of this place, and you're bound to return home smiling.

Access & Information

US Highway 101 follows the Pacific coastline from Washington to Southern California and links most of the towns along the southern Oregon Coast. From Interstate 5, two-lane paved roads follow rivers west to the south coast; from Eugene, Highway 126 follows the Siuslaw River to Florence; from Drain, Highway 38 follows the Umpqua River to Reedsport; from Roseburg, Highway 42 follows the Coquille River to Bandon and Coos Bay; and from Grants Pass, Highway 199 follows the Smith River, then cuts through the redwoods and dips into Northern California near the Oregon border and Brookings. All of these routes are scenic. For information, call the **Bay Area Chamber of Commerce** (50 Central Ave, Coos Bay; 541/269-0215 or 800/824-8486; www.oregonsbayareachamber.com) or the **Brookings-Harbor Chamber of Commerce** (16330 Lower Harbor Rd, Brookings; 800/535-9469; www.brookingsor.com). The **Oregon Coast Visitors Association** (888/628-2101; www.visittheoregoncoast.com) is also a good place to start for general information.

Romantic Lodgings

Coast House / ❂ ❂ ❂ ❂

Off Coastal Hwy 101, Florence; 541/997-7888
If it's privacy you're after, you'll find it in abundance at this tranquil retreat located 10 miles north of Florence. A short lantern-lit pathway meanders through a grove of evergreens to this round cedar-shake home set high on a towering cliff overlooking the blue waters of the Pacific. An expansive deck, complete with outdoor shower and wooden chairs, offers a stunning view. (Please note that the deck sits very high and is not fenced.) Inside, throw rugs cover hardwood floors and an antique woodstove supplies cozy warmth. Floor-to-ceiling windows in the comfortable living room allow a view of the ocean through lofty pines. Ladders lead to two sleeping lofts, where you can stargaze through windows and skylights. In the bathroom, a claw-foot tub sits next to windows looking out on the ocean. Stock up on provisions in Florence before you arrive, because the only staples you'll find here are coffee, tea, and a complimentary bottle of wine (a nice romantic touch). The house is equipped with a full kitchen, a microwave oven, and a stereo with a collection of CDs; there is no TV or telephone. *$$$; no credit cards; checks OK; www.coasthouseflorence.com.*

The Edwin K Bed and Breakfast / ❂ ❂ ❂

1155 Bay St, Florence; 541/997-8360 or 800/833-9465
Beautifully tended flower gardens surround this white Craftsman-style home located at the edge of Old Town and across the street from the Siuslaw River. (Unfortunately, the inn's river views are obstructed by a building and a large parking lot.) Built in 1914, the home has been lovingly refurbished to provide thoroughly comfortable accommodations. The six guest rooms are named after seasons and times of the year. We prefer the four very spacious rooms upstairs, all of which are appointed with stained- and leaded-glass windows, period antiques, modern fabrics and linens, and tiled bathrooms with large tubs or showers. Do note that the lovely Winter Room—with its blue and silver theme, queen-size four-poster bed, and open floor plan—has only a screen separating the toilet from the room (not exactly private). Some of the rooms have patios that overlook a rock waterfall at the back of the house. When you

awaken, follow your nose to the wood-paneled Victorian dining room for a formal five-course breakfast served on fine china at one large table. Complimentary sherry, tea, and cookies can be enjoyed each afternoon. *$$–$$$; DIS, MC, V; checks OK; www.edwink.com.*

Lighthouse Bed and Breakfast / 🟢🟢

650 Jetty Rd SW, Bandon; 541/347-9316
If you do nothing else here but cuddle up and take in the stunning views, your stay will be memorable. This spacious, warm contemporary house is oriented toward the mouth of the Coquille River, which means guests get front-row seats for the lighthouse, the river, and the ocean. At any given moment you might spy windsurfers, seals, or seabirds—or maybe even a migrating whale. All five rooms are spacious, with private baths and homey decor. Our favorite is the Gray Whale Room with a California king bed and whirlpool tub for two overlooking the spectacular view of the Pacific Ocean, river, and Bandon Lighthouse. Breakfast specialties include three-cheese quiche, fruit platters, croissants, homemade muffins, and French toast. *$$; MC, V; checks OK; www.lighthouselodging.com.*

Rogue River Lodge / 🟢🟢🟢

94966 North Bank Rogue River Rd, Gold Beach;
541/247-9070 or 800/924-4481
Tucked away in the trees (but with lots of sun shining through), the Rogue River Lodge is a charming blend of Northwest architecture with Japanese detail. The six spacious, comfortable suites and two guest rooms are situated on a bluff overlooking the Rogue River; some have Jacuzzis on private decks. Constructed from Port Orford cedar, each room has that aromatic, calming scent. We like the Falcon's Lair or Solitude suites, both with king-size beds and enough privacy to skinny dip in the hot tub. With its adults-only policy, solitude and romance abound. Spread a blanket on one of the many private grassy nooks and read, write, or be creative. An expanded continental breakfast is served in the dining room, and guests can enjoy breakfast on the wraparound deck, at the hidden table in the trees, or seated in the chairs on the plateau closest to the river—or any one of the very intimate settings. *$$$–$$$$; AE, V, MC; checks OK; closed Nov–Apr; www.rogueriverlodge.com.*

Tu Tu' Tun Lodge / 🟢🟢🟢🟢

96550 N Bank Rogue, Gold Beach; 541/247-6664 or 800/864-6357
Tu Tu' Tun (meaning "people by the river") is nestled in the heart of a quiet forested valley, next to the winding Rogue River 7 miles from Gold Beach. Be prepared for enchantment at this renowned Northwest retreat: ivy cloaks the wood pillars of the cedar lodge, colorful flower boxes line the stairs, and manicured grounds include a heated outdoor lap pool and stone terrace. The lodge's 16 attractive rooms, two suites, and two separate homes are all

decorated with a distinctive Northwest style. Unique art pieces and sumptuous linens and fabrics, along with open-beamed ceilings, set the stage for romance. Some units offer slate fireplaces; others have sliding doors that open onto private balconies or patios where guests can relish river views from a "moon soaker" tub. There's also a Look Good–Feel Good Basket full of complimentary toiletries in each room in case you've forgotten anything. During high season (May–Oct) fresh flower bouquets adorn each room, and nightly turndown service includes homemade fudge. Guests also enjoy a complimentary refreshment bar—homemade goodies and snacks—every afternoon on the herb terrace overlooking the river. For added indulgence, book a couples massage at Tututni Waters Cabana sitting on the edge of river. For an extra charge, breakfast, hors d'oeuvres, and dinner are served in a comfortable common lodge, warmed on cool evenings by a crackling fire in an immense river-rock fireplace. All meals are served family-style at several round eight-person tables, or you can request a candlelit dinner for two served in the privacy of your room. *$$$; MC, V; checks OK; www.tututun.com.*

Romantic Restaurants

Spinner's Seafood, Steak & Chop House / ◎◎

29430 Ellensburg Ave, Gold Beach; 541/247-5160
As the restaurant's name suggests, the menu here offers something for everyone, but the sweeping views of the water should especially delight romancing couples. Most tables overlook the ocean, and the sunset panoramas are impressive. You might begin with a wild-mushroom napoleon bathed in an herb-cognac sauce, then move on to a charbroiled whiskey steak, cedar-planked salmon garnished with a Pinot Noir reduction, lamb chops marinated in garlic and herbs, or one of a slew of chicken preparations (for example, sautéed breast of chicken with hazelnut-butter sauce) or pasta plates (maybe pasta Marsala with jumbo prawns, oyster mushrooms, sea scallops, and pea pods in a creamy Asiago cheese sauce). *$$; AE, MC, V; checks OK; dinner every day (closed Jan 2–Feb 13); full bar; reservations recommended.* &

Wild Rose Bistro / ◎◎

130 Chicago Ave SE, Bandon; 541/347-4428
This is the kind of place that's custom-made for couples looking for a quiet place to enjoy tasty food with a healthy twist. Located in Old Town, it specializes in fresh seasonal food, with an emphasis on all things organic. Vegetables often come straight from the bistro garden, and seafood specials are made fresh from the catch at the local docks. There's an impressive selection of vegetarian dishes, and locals rave about the chocolate torte. The restaurant is small and simple, though it's not without a certain friendly charm; linens cover the tables at night, but there's no stuffy formality. Special requests are happily accommodated whenever possible. *$$; AE, DIS, MC, V; checks OK; dinner Thurs–Mon; full bar; reservations recommended.*

♡ Southern Oregon

Southern Oregon

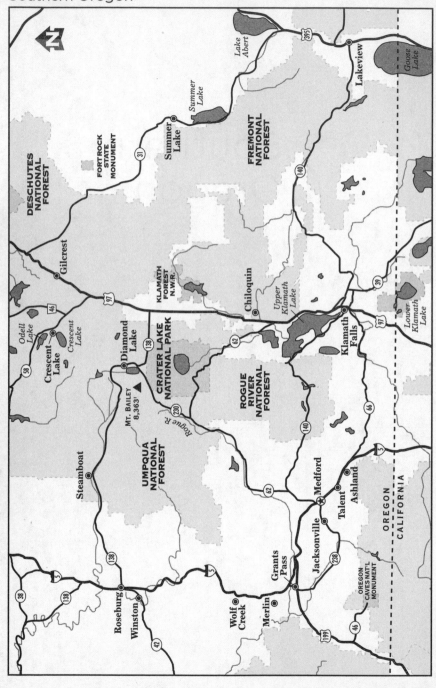

How did it happen that their lips came together?
How does it happen that birds sing, that snow melts,
that the rose unfolds, that the dawn whitens behind
the stark shape of trees on the quivering summit of
the hill? A kiss, and all was said.

—Victor Hugo

 Southern Oregon

Southern Oregon's rolling hills, majestic mountains, rapid rivers, and sweeping valleys make it an ideal destination for couples any time of year but none so much as in fall. The crisp air ushers in golden landscapes splashed with bright red and orange hues; the weather is pleasant but not too hot—especially compared with the summer season when temperatures often soar to triple digits. Cheery spring is also a good time to visit, as it brings early blossoms. Winter can be snowy in the high country but milder and rainy in the valley.

Whatever the season, Southern Oregon's tiny towns, each with a distinctive character, make for pleasurable destinations and welcome visitors with open arms. Ashland's adorable downtown boasts cozy storefronts and a handful of restaurants. Nearby Medford is Southern Oregon's biggest city and retail hub, but probably not the most idyllic destination for lovers: think of Medford for shopping, golfing, antiquing, and stopping in Harry and David's flagship store.

Quaint Jacksonville, while a bit off the beaten path, deserves at least a day's visit. Known for hosting the annual Britt Music Festival, the town also charms with its historical downtown and a number of independent stores you'll adore for their window-shopping potential during a hand-in-hand stroll. Beyond the cities, a short drive in almost any direction delivers visitors to the countryside, where wineries, fruit orchards, farms, and pastoral landscapes abound. Make sure to spend an afternoon touring the wineries and tasting rooms in Applegate Valley wine country.

Ashland & Rogue Valley

Romantic Highlights

Ashland is the teeming cultural center of Southern Oregon; shops, cafes, hotels, and reputable restaurants line its bustling downtown streets. The downtown caters to art-loving couples, while nearby country and mountainous landscapes will please those looking for a rural escape. Ashland's famous Oregon Shakespeare Festival, which runs mid-February through October, draws theater fans from all over the world, creating crowds as well as a fun-loving spirit. The plentiful festival-season attractions may tempt you to plan a packed itinerary, but be sure to leave plenty of time for leisurely wandering in this lovely town.

During the bustling summer festival season, you'll be hard pressed to find quiet, romantic dining spots. Everyone wants to eat before the show, so theater-goers pack restaurants between 5pm and 7:30pm. If you have an open agenda, book a reservation for later in the evening. Or, beat crowds by enjoying, instead, a substantial outdoor picnic. Pick up gourmet takeout foods from **Market of Choice** (1475 Siskiyou Blvd; 541/488-2773), or visit **Allyson's Kitchen** (115 E Main St; 541/482-2884), a gourmet kitchen store with a deli that will supply made-to-order sandwiches for lovebirds. You can place an order to go at **Ashland Bakery Café** (38 E Main St; 541/482-2117), a local institution since 1983 that serves fresh, simple food and elegant desserts. Or, for more sweets, walk over to **Mix Sweet Shop** (57 N Main St; 541/488-9885), a sassy shop serving truffles, gelato, tarts, cupcakes, and more to satisfy your sweet hankerings.

Ashland is filled with romantic possibilities, but what could be more enchanting than snuggling together at dusk in an outdoor Elizabethan theater, listening to poetry written by England's leading authority on love? At the **Oregon Shakespeare Festival** (541/482-4331 or 800/219-8161; www.osfashland.org), you can see a variety of the Bard's works in several different theaters (both indoor and out) throughout downtown Ashland. And since not all performances are Shakespearean, you can find other kinds of shows to enjoy as well. Season after season, the costumes are spectacular, the sets imaginative, and the acting superb. Be sure to arrive early to catch the lively "Green Show," a 30–45-minute music-and-dance presentation that precedes every outdoor performance.

Outdoor adventurers or simply those who love natural scenery and frequent wildlife sightings will enjoy a stroll in **Lithia Park**. This national historic landmark begins in the heart of Ashland's theater district and extends southward. With nearly 100 acres of forest, lawns, ponds, and flower gardens, this lovely playground holds plenty of hidden spaces for intimate moments. Stroll beneath the ponderosa pines or share a kiss on one of the small bridges crossing the burbling creek. Rhododendrons, dogwood trees, azaleas, and forget-me-nots fill the park with blooms each spring; fall brings striking displays of colorful foliage. Picnic tables are sprinkled liberally throughout the park. Immaculate paved walkways eventually turn into trails as you wind your way upward to a panoramic view of Ashland and the valley beyond.

Ashland is crowned by the 7,500-foot summit of **Mount Ashland** (541/482-2897; www.mtashland.com). In winter, Nordic buffs hit the more than 100 miles of cross-country ski trails that snake their way through forests, open fields, and crystal-clear mountain lakes, while alpine skiers schuss their way down terrain ranging from easy cruisers to steep chutes. In spring and summer, the steep trails are both challenging and beautiful, and reward your toil with spectacular views. Starting in late December, the mountain also offers twilight downhill skiing.

For sheer indulgence after a day of activity, consider a couple's massage or body treatment at the recently expanded **Blue Giraffe Day Spa** (51 Water St; 541/488-3335; www.bluegiraffespa.com). This stylish two-story spa, set on the banks of Ashland Creek, also offers facials, wraps, aromatherapy sessions, and hydrotherapy treatments, as well as a full complement of hair and nail services. End with a soak in the tumbled-marble tub, big enough for two.

Southern Oregon is famous for its whitewater adventures, and a number of licensed guides offer trips. For a particularly romantic river tour, **Kokopelli Kayak** (2475 Siskiyou Blvd; 541/201-7694; www.kokopellikayak.com) offers a custom trip for two. Your guide will lead you down the Klamath River, where you'll paddle through the scenic quiet of forest and meadow, home to blue herons, deer, otters, and all sorts of creatures great and small. You'll be served a light lunch with wine off river, and then delivered back to your hotel doorstep.

From Ashland, retreat to nearby **Jacksonville** for at least one day, if not more. The town, designated a National Historic Landmark, has preserved its 1800s gold-rush roots. Tour Jacksonville aboard an old-fashioned trolley or take a self-guided walking tour with a map available from the **Visitor Information Center** (185 N Oregon St; 541/899-8118; www.jacksonvilleoregon.org); it features more than 100 historical buildings and landmarks. Make sure to stroll the downtown streets where old-fashioned brick and wooden buildings house antique shops, art galleries, boutiques, and gourmet food shops.

Nestled in the foothills of the Siskiyou Mountains, Jacksonville's scenic setting is naturally romantic. Within minutes outside of town, farms, orchards, and wineries create pastoral landscapes and an ideal midday drive. Follow the trail from one vineyard to the next, stopping at our favorite two (see Romantic Wineries) along the way. In recent years, the area has welcomed new wineries and tasting rooms; oenophiles should reserve part of their time in Jacksonville for wine touring.

Cap off your Jacksonville visit with an evening at the **Britt Music Festival** (800/882-7488; www.brittfest.org; June–Sept), held at an outdoor concert venue set amid pine and madrona trees on the hillside estate of 19th-century photographer Peter Britt. The festival lineup includes world-class artists in jazz, blues, folk, classical, country, and pop music, as well as comedians and other international performers. For the full Britt Fest experience, hail the vintage trolley (yes, like a taxi) anywhere along its route, and take a lift to the festival grounds with gourmet fare at the ready; picnic baskets, wine, and beer (no hard alcohol) are permitted (as are blankets and chairs with legs of 4 inches or less in height). Or you can purchase food, wine, beer, ice cream, espresso, and popcorn from the on-site concessionaires. With the stars overhead and great music on the stage, love is definitely in the air.

Access & Information

The primary access to Ashland is via Interstate 5. Visitors traveling from the east can connect with Highways 62, 66, or 140, all of which meet up with I-5; from the west, take Highway 199, which also connects with the interstate. From Ashland, Jacksonville is only a short drive along Hwy 99. For more information about the area, contact the **Ashland Chamber of Commerce** (110 E Main St; 541/482-3486; www.ashlandchamber.com) or the **Jacksonville Chamber of Commerce** (185 N Oregon St; 541/899-8118; www.jackson villeoregon.org).

Romantic Wineries

Schmidt Family Vineyards / ○○●

320 Kubli Rd, Grants Pass; 541/846-9985
There's no shortage of private spaces at this vineyard and tasting room. A spacious backyard garden provides plenty of private places to steal a kiss; a small patio with fire pit and a shimmering lake lined with pairs of Adirondack chairs invite couples to enjoy afternoon picnics and sip in spaces made for two. In colder weather, cuddle by the hearth of a stately fireplace inside the tasting room—housed in a high-ceilinged, remodeled train turn house—and enjoy a glass of Merlot, Cabernet Sauvignon, Syrah, or the winery's signature blend, Soulea. *Noon–5pm every day; www.sfvineyards.com.* &

Valley View Winery / ○○

1000 Upper Applegate Rd, Jacksonville; 541/899-8468 or 800/781-9463
The region's premier and most established winery, Valley View is surrounded by lush hills and vineyards. In the center of this gorgeous landscape sits a spacious, simply decorated tasting room, with attention focused on the vineyard's Anna Maria labeled wines. Take a glass of Anna Maria Chardonnay, Viognier, or Rosato and enjoy it on the outside wine pavilion. The grounds are open and vast; come expecting a wide selection of wines to taste but few private spaces to enjoy them in. *11am–5pm every day; www.valleyview winery.com.* &

Romantic Lodgings

Ashland Creek Inn / ○○○●

70 Water St, Ashland; 541/482-3315
This vine-covered inn boasts one of the finest bed-and-breakfast experiences in town. The 10 suites have all been designed in international themes from

exotic to elegant, furnished with antiques and fine art, and given private entrances and kitchens. The Matsu suite is a Japanese-themed space with a king-size bed, antique tansu, Asian artwork, and views of the inn's koi pond. For something truly exotic, we like the Marrakech, with its vaulted-ceiling king bedroom, Moroccan antiques, and oversize deck. Breakfasts here are a three-course gourmet affair with fresh smoothies, seasonal fruit dishes, and frittatas or French toast with praline syrup. *$$$$; MC, V; checks OK; www. ashlandcreekinn.com.* &

Ashland Springs Hotel / ❷❷

212 E Main St, Ashland; 541/488-1700 or 888/795-4545
Old Hollywood glamour abounds at this historic hotel. Built in 1925, it was once considered the most luxurious hotel between San Francisco and Portland. Today, the boutique hotel's old-style architecture—ornate chandeliers and tiny rooms with the tall, original 1920s windows—is enhanced with a pretty naturalist theme. A shell, bird, and floral motif decorates guest rooms and the comfortable lobby, where weary travelers can settle into cozy sofas and watch Ashland's bustling Main Street through the windows. More private places to relax are the elegant mezzanine and the shaded outdoor patio located off the hotel's second floor. Guests can also dine at the hotel's adjacent restaurant, Lark, which offers farm-to-table comfort cuisine in an inviting setting. *$$–$$$; AE, DIS, MC, V: checks OK; www.ashlandsprings hotel.com.* &

Bybee's Historic Inn / ❷❷❷

883 Old Stage Rd, Central Point; 541/899-0106 or 877/292-3374
Built in 1857 by one of Jackson County's most influential and wealthiest residents, William Bybee, this classic revival Victorian home sits on 3½ idyllic acres outside of Jacksonville. Luxurious renovations have achieved a perfect blend of history and romance inside this historic landmark. Start your day with coffee in the exquisite sitting room, which boasts the home's original ornate plaster ceiling and Italian-marble fireplace. Furnishings are accurate to the period, but not so elegant that you don't feel comfortable curling up contentedly with your sweetie. The four guest rooms achieve this same balance of glamour and ease. Our favorites are the Elizabethan Room on the ground floor, which has plush, felt-lined walls, a jetted tub, and a candlelit fireplace, and the Renaissance Room upstairs, which has a lighted canopy over the bed and is decorated in gentle pastel shades. Seasonal breakfasts might feature roasted-vegetable egg crepes with fig drizzle, lemon ricotta crepes with raspberry sauce, and homemade pastries. *$$–$$$; MC, V; local checks only; www. bybeeshistoricinn.com.* &

Coolidge House / ⬡⬡⬢

137 N Main St, Ashland; 541/482-4721 or 800/655-5522
This finely restored Victorian makes a good first impression with manicured shrubs and gardens adorning the front yard and flower baskets lining the porch. The interior confirms it. Of the six guest rooms, four are in the main house and two are in the Carriage House. Rooms in the main house vary in size, but all have private baths and are furnished with gorgeous antiques. We especially love the regal Parlor Room, with its hardwood floors, fabulous window seat, luxurious furnishings, and spacious bathroom with Jacuzzi tub for two. The Carriage House rooms have the advantage of being larger, and are ideal for couples seeking a quiet, private getaway. Full gourmet breakfasts are offered each morning. Depending on the season, you can enjoy your morning meal in the dining room, on the flower-trimmed brick patio behind the house, or on the second-story balcony at charming white iron tables for two. *$$–$$$; MC, V: checks OK; www.coolidgehouse.com.*

Country Willows Bed and Breakfast Inn / ⬡⬡⬡⬡

1313 Clay St, Ashland; 541/488-1590 or 800/945-5697
This nine-room estate, located just outside downtown Ashland, is a marvelous kissing destination. At the end of a gravel road rests a quaint country-style home. Huge willows, a groomed lawn, lovely gardens, and a duck pond beautify the property, which lies at the foot of wooded hills and boasts a heated pool and hot tub. Four rooms are located on the second floor of the farmhouse, where an expansive deck with willow furniture provides a place to appreciate the surrounding scenery. Lodged in an adjacent barn, the aptly named Barn Suites offer the ultimate retreat. Our favorite is the luxurious Pine Ridge Suite, a stunning, spacious room with a fireplace, high open-beam ceilings, skylights, a small kitchen, and a dazzling slate bathroom with a double open shower and Jacuzzi tub for two. The Northwest-style decor—a peeled-log king-size bed frame, pine furnishings, and coordinating pine-tree wallpaper and linens—creates an overall effect that is simply glorious and entirely tasteful. Sunrise is accompanied by freshly brewed coffee and a farm-fresh breakfast of homemade granola, fruit parfaits, and frittatas. *$$–$$$$; AE, DIS, MC, V; checks OK; www.countrywillowsinn.com.* &

A Cowslip's Belle Bed & Breakfast / ⬡⬡⬡

159 N Main St, Ashland; 541/488-2901 or 800/888-6819
Located blocks from downtown Ashland, this 1913 bungalow houses a delightful mix of rooms. The adjacent carriage-house accommodations, each with a private entrance, down comforters, and soft linens, are ideal. The upper Daffydown Dilly suite is the most spacious and features a handmade twisted-juniper bed, a triple-sided fireplace, a Jacuzzi tub, and mountain views. The lower Daffydown Dilly suite (they can be reserved together or separately) features a king-size bed, fireplace, Jacuzzi tub for two, and full

kitchen. Cuckoo-Bud has a magnificent four-poster bent-willow canopied bed entwined with carved roses, an antique stained-glass window, and upholstered floral-chintz walls. Outside, a shady lawn and koi pond enhance this lodging's appeal. Breakfast may include a vegetable frittata or Dutch-apple French toast. Indulge! *$$$; MC, V; checks OK; only long-term stays Nov–Feb; www.cowslip.com.* ♿

Elan Guest Suites / ◐◑◕

245 W Main St, Jacksonville; 541/899-8000 or 877/789-1952
With sleek, stylish decor—not a bit like a country-cozy B&B—the Elan is best suited for couples looking for modern romance. After arriving and chatting up the fashionable host, Cherie Reneau (who also owns the downstairs art gallery), expect the utmost in privacy. Choosing one of the inn's three suites is difficult at best. The Luna Vista suite is the most spacious and luxurious, with two balconies, cream-colored walls, and thick velvet curtains that shield the room from passersby. The Milan suite gives off a masculine feel with vibrant green hues; the Portofino suite boasts a sultry style with burnt-orange accents. Each suite comes with a full kitchen, a TV, a queen-size bed, ceiling speakers, and a separate living room—perfect for an evening in. *$$$–$$$; MC, V; no checks; www.elanguestsuites.com.*

Flery Manor Bed & Breakfast / ◐◑◕

2000 Jumpoff Joe Creek Rd, Grants Pass; 541/476-3591
Those seeking opulence in a country setting will adore this large blue house a few miles north of Grants Pass. Nestled on 7 acres of mountainside, the inn features an ornate two-story common room with arched windows, antiques, lavish window treatments, and plush carpeting. Ponds, waterfalls, walking paths, streams, and spectacular views enhance the grounds. Each of the five guest rooms is richly appointed with lace and satin accents, fluffy pillows, framed artwork, and antiques. A private garden entrance leads to the Vintage Suite, which features a king-size canopied feather bed, a fireplace, and a two-person Jacuzzi. In the Moonlight Suite, fine European linens top the king-size bed and French doors open onto a private balcony ideal for watching the sunset. The suite's spa is also spectacular with its pink double Jacuzzi tub surrounded by flickering candles. If a creative moment strikes the two of you, guests have access to a private, serene art studio equipped with materials from canvas and paints to clay and sculpture. In the evening, enjoy the turndown service of homemade chocolate truffles and flowers on pillows. With morning comes a three-course breakfast in the formal dining room featuring the signature dish "eggs on a cloud"—eggs baked on mounds of bread, served with hollandaise sauce and poached salmon. Note: This B&B is about a 45-minute drive from Ashland, with easy highway access. *$$–$$$; MC, V; checks OK; www.flerymanor.com.*

Jacksonville Inn / ●●●

175 E California St, Jacksonville; 541/899-1900 or 800/321-9344
This landmark brick hotel is located in the heart of downtown Jacksonville. Built in 1861 and lovingly restored over the years, the inn mixes old and new to create comfortably elegant lodgings. The eight rooms upstairs have exposed-brick walls, private baths, handsome antique armoires, oak furnishings, comfortable beds, and an elaborate Victorian style. The inn also rents out four private guest cottages, approximately a block away, providing the optimum option for romance. A white picket fence surrounds these side-by-side cottages while gardens line the walkways. Three have a modern style, with vaulted ceilings, large jetted tubs with steam showers, and double-sided gas fireplaces. The fourth cottage is a wonderful hideaway, with country-Victorian furnishings, a lace-canopied bed, a gas fireplace, a kitchenette, and a steam shower with jetted tub. Cottage guests can have a full breakfast delivered or venture to the inn's famous Victorian dining room. *$$$–$$$$; AE, DC, DIS, V; checks OK; www.jacksonvilleinn.com.* &

A Midsummer's Dream / ●●●

496 Beach St, Ashland; 541/552-0605 or 877/376-8800
This blue Victorian B&B set on a quiet Ashland street takes the Shakespeare theme to a tastefully elegant place. Each of the five suites is named for a Shakespearean character and features a king-size bed, fireplace, and two-person tub. For the utmost privacy, choose the Romeo Suite in the backyard cottage, complete with a canopied bed and corner spa tub. The Othello Room, with four-poster bed and see-through fireplace (viewed from the tub and the room), is also a romance-enhancing pick. A gourmet breakfast, complimentary in-room snack baskets, and port served in the game room are part of this dreamy package. *$$$; AE, DIS, MC, V; checks OK; www.amidsummer.com.* &

Morical House Garden Inn / ●●●

668 N Main St, Ashland; 541/482-2254
This Eastlake-style Victorian farmhouse is a study in Eastern elegance. The five guest rooms in the main house feature finely crafted Asian furniture, luxurious linens, down comforters, orchids, plush bathrobes and slippers, and custom organic soaps. A backyard-garden carriage house offers luxury suites, each setting the tone for a romantic interlude. Suites 6, 7, and 9 include king-size beds, vaulted ceilings, cozy window seats, fireplaces, kitchenettes, separate showers, and Jacuzzi tubs. Suite 8, at the top of a private staircase, has a wet bar, king-size bed, and double shower. Guests awaken to a three-course gourmet organic breakfast including such delectables as mandarin-orange spritzers, mocha-pear coffee cake, and poached eggs over a bed of orzo, arugula, shitakes, prosciutto, and chives. *$$–$$$; AE, MC, V; checks OK; closed Jan–Feb; www.garden-inn.com.* &

Mt. Ashland Inn / ●●●●(

550 Mt Ashland Rd, Ashland; 541/482-8707 or 800/830-8707

Sheltered by pine trees near the summit of Mount Ashland, this handcrafted cedar inn provides an extraordinarily romantic Northwest alpine-lodge experience. Arrive early enough to take a stroll through the woods, then take a dip in the outdoor hot tub with views of Mounts Shasta and McLoughlin before settling in for a gloriously private night in one of five serene guest rooms. In the second-story Mt. McLoughlin Suite, you'll feel like you're in your very own cabin, with exposed-log walls and a rose-marble gas fireplace near the foot of the king-size bed. A lovely rectangular window above the bed perfectly frames Mount McLoughlin, while Mount Shasta rises off to the south. However, even the delightful Mt. McLoughlin Suite can be topped—journey upward to the third-floor Sky Lakes Suite, where the bathroom centerpiece is a small river-rock waterfall that sends water cascading into a two-person Jacuzzi tub. A skylight, walk-in double-headed shower, king-size bed, river-rock fireplace, microwave, refrigerator, and wet bar leave nothing to be desired. Days here begin with a full breakfast that may include chilled mango and kiwi soup or spiced cran-apple pears, followed by an entrée such as toasted almond–cheese French toast. Amenities also include a Finnish cedar sauna and large outdoor spa. Consider bringing a takeout supper from town, as there are no dinner dining options near the inn—plus, once you check in, you'll never want to leave. *$$$; DIS, MC, V; no checks; www. mtashlandinn.com.*

The Peerless Hotel / ●●●●(

243 4th St, Ashland; 541/488-1082 or 800/460-8758

A bold name like "Peerless" sets up lofty expectations in a traveler's mind. Happily, this inn lives up to its name by offering a memorable, unique-to-Ashland experience. Outside, colorful flower boxes and an old Coca-Cola sign painted on an outer wall adorn this turn-of-the-20th-century brick building; inside, a polished interior delights guests. All six grand guest rooms are decorated with large murals or intricate stencil work and feature towering 12-foot ceilings, original woodwork, rich colors, and glistening hardwood floors warmed with Oriental rugs. Although each room is different, a flamboyant and stylish Victorian theme prevails throughout, accomplished with antiques, queen-size beds, and sumptuous furnishings and linens. Suite 3 has his-and-her claw-foot tubs and a spacious sitting area adjacent to the bedroom. French-influenced Room 5 has a two-person Jacuzzi tub positioned beneath a skylight. And Suite 7 features a four-poster mahogany bed, two-person shower, and jetted tub for two. This elegant, sunlight-filled suite is painted a calming green, complemented by hardwood floors and white shutters. A private patio adds an extra-special touch. Turndown service is provided in the evening, but otherwise, once you check in, you are left alone—perfect for those with romance on their minds. Enjoy dinner at the Peerless Restaurant (see

Romantic Restaurants) next door before settling in for the night. *$$$; AE, DIS, MC, V; checks OK; limited availability in Jan; www.peerlesshotel.com.* ⅍

Touvelle House / ❻❻❻

455 N Oregon St, Jacksonville; 541/899-8938 or 800/846-8422
Built in 1916, this lovely, well-preserved house sits just outside the charming town of Jacksonville. You'll find many of the home's original features intact, including built-in hutches, push-button light switches, and the wonderful wraparound porch. Some guest rooms boast the delicate floral motifs of the Victorian era; however, of the six rooms, we like the Garden Suite for its abundance of natural light and the third-floor Crater Lake Room for its coziness and view of Mount McLoughlin. Two gigantic oak trees shade the entire home, making some rooms a bit on the dark side (often a bonus come summer). The lovely grounds are highlighted by a private pool—a welcome refreshment at the end of a hot summer day. *$$–$$$; DIS, MC, V; checks OK, closed Jan; www.touvellehouse.com.*

Weasku Inn / ❻❻❶

5560 Rogue River Hwy, Grants Pass; 541/471-8000 or 800/4-WEASKU
This old Hollywood retreat rests off the beaten path—and therein lies the draw for romance-minded couples. The remodeled rooms of this rustic inn come equipped with lodge-style furnishings, queen- or king-size beds, and fireplaces. Though the five rooms located in the main lodge are lovely, we recommend the private cabin suites that come with cozy beds, fireplaces, and private decks. Stay in cabin 42 or 43 for greater romantic potential; both spacious cabins boast king-size beds, river-rock fireplaces, private decks with distant river views, full-size Jacuzzi tubs, and wet bars. Wooded grounds and riverside paths create places for stolen moments. Note that local eateries are few; the lodge provides wine, cheese, and cookies for snacking, but bring your own dinner and cozy into your cabin for the evening. *$$$–$$$$; AE, DIS, MC, V; no checks; www.weasku.com.* ⅍

Winchester Inn / ❻❻❻

35 S 2nd St, Ashland; 541/488-1113 or 800/972-4991
This charming 1886 Victorian house is located just one block from downtown Ashland but feels a world away. Manicured gardens and a quaint country porch frame this lodging; inside, old-world elegance welcomes guests. When we visited, an ongoing redesign promised more modern decor and amenities in each of the 19 guest rooms. Of them, we recommend the new Fordyce Suite, appointed with rich tapestries, antique furniture, a king-size bed, a gas fireplace, and a two-person jetted tub. We were also drawn to the Barbara Howard Suite (named for a relative of the owner), located in the adjacent Heritage House, featuring a king-size bed, separate living room with gas fireplace, and spacious bathroom with a two-person jetted tub and

shower. In the morning, make your way to the dining room and enjoy a full breakfast, including buttermilk pancakes with seasonal fruit or decadent poached eggs over croissants. *$$$–$$$$; AE, DIS, MC, V; checks OK; www. winchesterinn.com.* ⅙

Romantic Restaurants

Amuse Restaurant / ❷❷❷❹

15 N 1st St, Ashland; 541/488-9000
With its polished-concrete floor, velvet drapes, and handblown lamps, this sophisticated little place is at once intimate and elegant. The heavenly menu is best described as French with a Northwest twist. The dining experience begins with the traditional French amuse-bouche, a savory treat designed as a prelude to the meal. Entrée offerings change almost daily but might include dishes like Parisian gnocchi with zucchini, olives, tomatoes, basil, and brown butter, or a black-truffle roasted game hen with fingerling potatoes, pole beans, and tarragon jus. Follow the main course with a rich dessert like a caramel *pot de crème.* In the summer, dine alfresco on the restaurant's airy patio. Chances are good you'll leave here primed for a kiss. *$$$; AE, DIS, MC, V; local checks only; dinner Tues–Sun (Wed–Sun in winter); beer and wine; reservations recommended; www.amuserestaurant.com.* ⅙

Chateaulin Restaurant / ❷❷❷❹

50 E Main St, Ashland; 541/482-2264
Conveniently located in the heart of Ashland's theater district, this French-country restaurant is one of the best places to enjoy a romantic meal. Inside, subtle lighting is augmented by flickering candlelight, exposed-brick walls exude rustic charm, and rosy stained-glass windows frame the bar area. Lace window treatments and dark woodwork create a rich ambience. The seating is perhaps too intimate, particularly during festival season. For a bit more space, try reserving one of the window tables. Fresh seafood and dishes prepared with local produce and meats are the specialties here. Desserts border on euphoric, especially the chocolate-mousse cake. *$$$–$$$$; AE, DIS, MC, V; local checks only; dinner every day (Jun–Oct), Wed–Sun (Nov–Apr), Tues–Sun (Apr–May); full bar; reservations recommended; www.chateaulin.com.*

Gogi's Restaurant / ❷❷❹

235 W Main St, Jacksonville; 541/899-8699
This cozy restaurant tucked off Jacksonville's busy Main Street has flourished under new owners; brothers Gabriel and Jonah Murphy entice lovers of both romance and fine cuisine. The stylish interior, done in warm colors, rich wood, and cheerful works of art, exudes quiet elegance. The well-stocked bar is the source of tasty mixed drinks and a thorough wine list, which includes selections from local wineries and more worldly varietals. Chef

A Foodie's Dream

Those who love to eat will find their place in Southern Oregon. Take your sweetie on a tour of the region's finest food purveyors and artisans with a stop at each of these gourmand gathering spots.

Lillie Belle Farms (211 N Front St, Central Point; 541/664-2815 or 888/899-2022): The recently relocated Lillie Belle Farms specializes in chocolate delights including cayenne or salted-lavender caramels and a sweet selection of bonbons and buttercreams. Visit their tasting room to sample before you purchase.

Pennington Farms and Bakery (11115 Williams Hwy, Grants Pass; 541/846-0550): For old-school-style baked goods and fresh berries, visit this 90-acre farm in the heart of Applegate Valley. Inside their rustically renovated barn, sample a selection of made-from-scratch goods (including an olallieberry mini-slab pie) while picking up a few of their amazing jams, conserves, apple butters, and syrups to take home.

Rising Sun Farms (5126 S Pacific Hwy, Phoenix; 800/888-0795): Set on a 28-acre farm overlooking the Siskiyou Mountains, this quaint little shop off Highway 99W boasts a wide selection of gourmet goodies—and its own wine bar. Let the staff pour you a glass of their favorite wine before you sample the treats on hand. Then enjoy some of their famous cheeses before heading to the outdoor patio to take in the scenery.

Rogue Valley Cheeses (311 N Front St, Central Point; 541/665-1155 or 866/665-1155): If cheese is your first love, you'll be in heaven at Southern Oregon's most famous creamery. Wander the adjacent gourmet food shop to sample their award-winning varieties, including blue cheese, which won top honors at the esteemed London World Cheese Awards in 2003. This is the perfect place to put together a picnic to share later in the afternoon.

Gabriel demonstrates his skills in the kitchen with excellent and eclectic fine-dining fare—crafted with French technique and influenced in Northwest style. The butter-lettuce salad with Dungeness crab, avocado, apples, and creamy chèvre-lemon vinaigrette is a medley of wonderful flavors. A three-pepper-encrusted local filet mignon—served with a potato croquette, roasted root vegetables, and cognac reduction—is inspiring. Desserts, such as a flourless chocolate-espresso torte, are indulgent. For gourmet meals to go, lighter but equally tasty fare is available in Gogi's Britt Boxes. Order these by 2pm to ensure that you'll dine like a gourmand at your Britt Festival show. *$$$; DIS, MC, V; local checks only; brunch Sun, dinner Wed–Sun; full bar; reservations recommended; www.gogis.net.* &

Il Giardino Cucina Italiana / ❶❷❸

5 Granite St, Ashland; 541/488-0816
You and your beloved are in for a cozy Italian treat at Il Giardino. This family-run restaurant is both casual and personable, and though linen-covered tables are close to their neighbors, the ambience has charm nonetheless. Just off the dining room, a garden patio allows alfresco dining beneath wisteria vines and hanging baskets of flowers. No matter where you sit, be aware that the restaurant is usually too noisy and bustling for intimate conversation. However, the authentic Italian cuisine—prepared with the utmost care and expertise—makes crowds bearable. Try the *crostini del giorno* or sample from the pasta menu. Every single pasta dish is delicious. We recommend the linguine with clams in a light white-wine sauce, or the capellini with tomato sauce and basil. Even the classic spaghetti bolognese is a masterpiece. Now that's amore. *$$; AE, MC, V; local checks only; dinner Tues–Sun; full bar; reservations recommended.* &

Monet / ❶❷❸

36 S 2nd St, Ashland; 541/482-1339
Named after the famous French Impressionist, this restaurant is as pretty as a picture. The culinary masterpieces from French-born chef Pierre Verger include smoked salmon wrapped around a delicate avocado mousse; comforting *soupe a l'oignon*, or French onion soup; and *coquilles St. Jacques aux poireaux et anise*, bay scallops sautéed with leeks, mushrooms, and fennel then flambéed with Pernod and finished with a creamy sauce. Outside, a delightful garden, filled with plants resembling those in Monet's garden, is a perfect spot for summer dining. The pale pinks and greens of the artist's palette saturate the interior; replicas of Monet's paintings adorn the walls. Fresh flowers, floral tablecloths, and comfortable, elegant chairs complement each table. The dining room is perhaps a little cozy—but all is forgiven once the meal begins. *$$–$$$; MC, V; local checks only; dinner Tues–Sat; full bar; reservations recommended; www.restaurantmonet.com.* &

New Sammy's Cowboy Bistro / ❶❷

2210 S Pacific Hwy, Talent; 541/535-2779
From the outside, this bistro looks like nothing so much as a rundown roadside shack. Be sure to visit, however, as you won't want to miss what's inside. Attractive country wallpaper, pastel accents, and candles on the tables make for a dining room reminiscent of a quaint little dollhouse. The kitchen emphasizes fresh, organic, regional ingredients, and the food ranks among the best in the Northwest. The French-influenced menu usually lists a handful of entrées, such as a duck-leg confit and grilled duck breast served with cauliflower, braised beans, fingerling potatoes, and a balsamic vinegar sauce. The wine list includes more than 3,000 choices from Oregon, California, and

France. A recent expansion added a wine bar and three dining tables for a total of nine; be sure to make dinner reservations to get a taste of this place. *$$$$; MC, V; checks OK; lunch, dinner Wed–Sun; beer and wine; reservations required for dinner.* &

The Peerless Restaurant / ○○◖

265 Fourth St, Ashland; 541/488-6067
At first glance, this restaurant located next door to the Peerless Hotel appears too vast a dining room to encourage an intimate dining experience—until you note the dim lighting and tucked-away tabletops for two. Cuisine reflects the flavors of the season; sample a smoked-salmon pâté or fish-cake appetizer served with Meyer-lemon coleslaw to start. From the entrées, stray toward the seafood specials as new chef Mark Carter has a way with fish preparations. Heartier dishes might include a New York strip steak grilled with paprika oil and served with an olive tapenade and ricotta whipped potatoes, or duck confit and corn crepes served with sweet jalapeño chutney. Make sure to sample from the award-winning wine list and indulge in dessert before departing this peerless locale. *$$$; AE, DIS, MC, V; checks OK; dinner every day (June–Oct), Tues–Sun (Nov–May), limited hours in Jan; full bar; reservations recommended; www.peerlessrestaurant.com.* &

Winchester Inn Restaurant / ○○○

35 S 2nd St, Ashland; 541/488-1115 or 800/972-4991
The main floor of a renovated Queen Anne Victorian house is the setting for this winningly romantic restaurant. Tables are placed casually throughout the two front rooms; windows look out onto tiered gardens where you can also dine. The mood is cordial and relaxed but the true draw here is the updated, innovative menu from new chef Shane Hardin, who sends masterpiece after culinary masterpiece out of his esteemed kitchen. A strawberry *caprese* with fresh buffalo mozzarella, balsamic cinnamon reduction, and a fried basil leaf gives a new twist to a reputable starter. Entrées like a chef's risotto with creamy havarti and crisp asparagus, and pork loin rubbed with achiote accompanied by dark mountain spaetzle and a mango-chocolate mojo are dangerously delicious. Service is prompt and professional. For dessert, sample the apricot-croissant Grand Marnier bread pudding—it will be love at first bite. After you're pleasantly full, retire upstairs to a room in the Winchester Inn (see Romantic Lodgings) for the night. *$$$–$$$$; AE, DIS, MC, V; checks OK; www.winchesterinn.com.*

Crater Lake

Romantic Highlights

This region is famous worldwide for its extraordinarily beautiful lake. It's hard to wrap your mind around the dimensions of this volcanic formation, cut into the earth thousands of years ago by natural forces so grand, they make the Mount St. Helens eruption seem about as big as a firecracker on the Fourth of July. At 1,943 feet deep, Crater Lake is the deepest lake in the United States, and the seventh deepest in the world. A towering border of golden, rocky earth encompasses this inconceivably blue body of water. You can revel in the views as the two of you drive around the entire perimeter (except in the winter and early spring), take a two-hour boat ride from Cleetwood Cove to Wizard Island, or hike down to the lake and embrace amid scenery that will take your breath away. Alas, caravans of summer tourists can also take your breath away and steal away some otherwise prime kissing opportunities. Snow lasts nine months of the year, and cross-country trails will delight skiers and snowshoers of all abilities.

Access & Information

Crater Lake is off Highway 62, 80 miles northeast of Medford and 60 miles northwest of Klamath Falls. It is about a two-hour drive from either Ashland or Bend. The lake is accessible from Bend via Highway 97 or Roseburg via Highway 138 (Diamond Lake). For information on activities at Crater Lake, including ranger-led walks and boat tours, call the **Steel Visitor's Center** (541/594-3100), or, during the summer months, the **Sinnott Memorial Center** at Rim Visitor's Center (541/594-3090).

Romantic Lodgings

Steamboat Inn / ❀❀

42705 N Umpqua Hwy (Hwy 138), Steamboat; 800/840-8825
It may feel like you're in the middle of nowhere, but the Steamboat Inn is approximately halfway between Interstate 5 and Crater Lake, in the heart of the Umpqua National Forest. Its remote location along the rushing North Umpqua River is the best reason to stay at this rustic lodge. Hiking to a dozen different waterfalls, wading in the river, and fly-fishing top the list of potential activities. Accommodations come in a variety of shapes and sizes. The five Hideaway Cottages, set in forested surroundings, are spacious and private. Each one features comfortable furnishings, knotty-pine walls, a white-tiled soaking tub, a wood-burning fireplace, a small kitchenette, and a spacious bedroom and living room. The only thing they lack is a river view. That feature is available in each of two luxurious River Suites, free-standing cottage-style private structures that feature king-size beds, soaking tubs, fireplaces, and private decks overlooking the river. Eight small

Activities for Adventurous Couples

Southern Oregon's scenic countryside and proximity to rivers, lakes, and open landscapes offer plenty of excursions for couples who love to be outdoors together. Here, our top five sites to visit:

Crater Lake The famous Crater Lake National Park has been called one of America's crown jewels. Visit this deep, strikingly blue lake, surrounded by nearly 2,000-foot-high cliffs, for cross-country skiing, snowshoeing, camping, boat touring, and hiking.

Diamond Lake This sparkling lake rests near the peaks of Mounts Thielsen and Bailey in the Cascade Range, and is both a summer and winter destination. In summer, visit for trout fishing, cycling, swimming, camping, and horseback riding; in winter, take in the winter white by snow-mobiling, sledding, and cross-country skiing together.

Rogue River National Forest In this scenic setting, the U.S. Forest Service operates hike-in campgrounds, cabin and fire-lookout rentals, and lakeshore areas for picnicking, swimming, and boating. The lake extends to the California border and a hiking trail follows the 18-mile shoreline.

Table Rock Ten miles east of Medford, couples will delight in a hike to Upper and Lower Table Rocks—two giant buttes all the more perfect for the hiking opportunity they afford. The trail to Lower Table Rock is a mere 2 miles to the top; the steeper 1-mile-long trail leads to Upper Table Rock. Complete the climb to enjoy views of the Rogue River and the Siskyou Mountains. Hint: Visit in spring to catch the wildflower displays that grow on the rocks.

Umpqua National Forest Take Highway 138 along the river to view dozens of picturesque waterfalls and some of the most ancient old-growth Douglas fir trees in the world. Couples who enjoy casting together can spend an afternoon fly-fishing for steelhead trout along the North Umpqua. Other couples might just sit beside the water and enjoy each other's company.

pine-paneled Streamside Cabins are also available and share a pleasant veranda that overlooks the river. These sparse but clean cabins serve as a reminder that many guests come here more to fish than to kiss. The rusticity is part of the fun, and the secluded setting lets you get away from it all. *$$$–$$$$; MC, V; checks OK; open Mar–Dec, closed Jan–Feb (call for seasonal closures); www.thesteamboatinn.com.* &

Union Creek Resort / ◆€

56484 Hwy 62, Prospect; 541/560-3565 or 866/560-3565
If you're looking for something off the beaten path, the affordable Union Creek Resort might be for you. Located 23 miles west of Crater Lake, the resort offers 23 cabins on 12 acres surrounded by the Rogue River National Forest and is just minutes from horseback riding, snowmobile trails, pristine hiking trails, cross-country skiing, fishing, and absolute solitude. Cabins are simple and somewhat dated, but this is in keeping with the rustic setting—once a favorite of Zane Grey, Jack London, and Herbert Hoover. "Sleeping" cabins are equipped with microwaves, coffeemakers, and bedding; "housekeeping" cabins come with fully equipped kitchens. There's a country store, ice cream shop, and cafe just a romantic stroll away. *$–$$; AE, DC, DIS, MC, V; no checks; www.unioncreekoregon.com.*

♡ Central
Oregon

Central Oregon

John Day R.

OCHOCO NATIONAL FOREST

20

97

197

CROOKED RIVER NAT'L GRASSLAND

SMITH ROCK STATE PK

126

Redmond

DESCHUTES NATIONAL FOREST

26

White R.

Deschutes R.

Warm Springs

WARM SPRINGS INDIAN RES.

97

Bend

Sunriver

NEWBERRY NAT'L VOLCANIC MONUMENT

Gilcrest

Camp Sherman

Sisters

372

42

45

MT. BACHELOR 9,085'

46

Odell Lake

Crescent Lake

MT. HOOD NATIONAL FOREST

20

242

126

WILLAMETTE NATIONAL FOREST

Westfir

58

CASCADE RANGE

Molalla R.

22

S. Santiam R.

Mohawk R.

Salem

5

99

Eugene

5

18

20

99

Fern Ridge Res.

Siuslaw R.

126

38

138

"Where should one use perfume?" a young woman
asked. *"Wherever one wants to be kissed,"* I said.
—Coco Chanel

Central Oregon

Surrounded by the rugged peaks of Mounts Jefferson, Washington, and Bachelor, this land of high mountain lakes, pine forests, sagebrush, and tumbling streams beckons lovers of the outdoors—and just plain lovers—to play year-round. Set just west of the true center of the state, the Central Cascade region of Oregon remains one of the rare places in the United States that has pockets of cities amid long stretches of wilderness.

The terrain is varied and dramatic, with the mountain landscape changing abruptly from lush alpine to high desert just east of the Cascade Range. Here, at 4,000 feet, canyons and rivers carve paths through dry expanses brightened by the red bark of the ponderosa pine, berried junipers, manzanita, and sage.

The cities here, however, offer couples many recreational, dining, and romantic opportunities. With at least two quite romantic destinations—the city of Bend and the neighboring small town of Sisters—this region merits more than just one visit. Even the journey, along quiet country roads through mountains, valley, and a dramatically changing climate, is a destination in itself.

Central Oregon draws visitors during all four seasons. Humidity is low, nights are cool, and temperatures are reasonably mild, with the average July high peaking at 83 degrees F and January lows at 20 degrees F. Winters bring abundant snow and cold temperatures, perfect for downhill or cross-country skiing, snowmobiling, skating, snowshoeing, or simply cuddling up by a warm fire. Summers are pleasantly mild in the higher regions, warmer in the lower elevations, and ideal for fishing, hiking, biking, boating, or enjoying a romantic picnic by a hidden lake. For those who like their outdoor adventure on the quiet side, there are shops to browse, county fairs to visit, outdoor concerts and summer fests to attend—each with its own possibilities for romance. The highways in and around the Cascades, many closed from late fall through early spring, showcase dramatic views of volcanic cones, lava flows, basalt cliffs, waterfalls, and twisting gorges.

Bend & Mount Bachelor

Romantic Highlights

Blessed with scenic beauty and a mild climate, and cultivating a personality that can be both sophisticated and simple, Bend offers the sort of setting that can make even routine things seem romantic. Fifty years ago, this small city in the heart of Oregon was barely known beyond its borders. That all changed in 1957, when nearby Mount Bachelor, then called Bachelor Butte, opened as a ski resort. Today, with a population of more than 75,000, innumerable parks (including 11-acre Drake Park, with its picturesque Mirror Pond), as well as hiking trails, golf courses, and the state's largest ski resort, opportunities for leisure and play abound. Add incredible natural beauty to the mix, and romance is inevitable.

Downtown **Bend** offers just enough urban variety and bustle to keep life interesting, but without the hectic pace of larger cities. Ponder the possibilities of the day at one of many local bakeries and coffeehouses; browse unique clothing, outdoors, and home-decorating stores; splurge for the one-hour Yin-Yang couple's massage at **Jinsei Spa** (118 NW Newport Ave; 541/383-8282; www.jinseispa. com); or select from a large number of world-class dining establishments (see Romantic Restaurants).

Of course, winter offers all sorts of snow-filled adventures from downhill or cross-country skiing to snowshoeing. A number of local companies provide both rentals and tours; **Wanderlust Tours** (541/389-8359; www.wanderlusttours.com) offers Moonlight Snowshoeing at select times throughout the winter. The same company also provides summertime moonlight canoe trips on the Cascade Lakes (see "Stargazing"). And gazing at the sunset in Bend in any season is essential to a romantic rendezvous. Watch twilight fall from the sloping lawns of Drake Park, in the heart of downtown Bend on the Deschutes River, or snuggle as you view the changing sky from atop Pilot Butte, on the east side of town on Highway 20 (the turn is well-signed) or **Mount Bachelor's** (541/382-2442; www.mtbachelor.com) heights in any season (see "Three Days of Romance").

Mount Bachelor Ski Area (on Century Dr, 22 miles southwest of Bend; 541/382-7888 for ski report or 800/829-2442; www.mtbachelor.com) is one of the biggest in the Northwest, with 7 high-speed lifts (10 lifts in all) feeding skiers onto 3,100 vertical feet of groomed and dry-powder runs. The tubing park has a surface lift and five groomed runs. When you and your ski bunny have worked up your appetites, the **Skier's Palate** (located at midmountain in the Pine Marten Lodge) serves excellent lunches; **Scapolo's** (on the lodge's lower level) features hearty Italian cuisine. Skiing closes on Memorial Day, but the slopes reopen July 1 for summer sightseeing. During the high season, Mount Bachelor offers a ski school, racing, a day care, rentals, and an entire Nordic program and trails.

If you and yours are charmed by towns small and decidedly Western, plan to spend a few hours wandering the streets of **Sisters**. Located 20 miles west of Bend on Highway 20, Sisters is named for the three mountain peaks—Faith,

Stargazing

Nothing beats the open sky of the high desert, and the Bend area offers many opportunities for moon and stargazing. If you visit Bend during the summer, check the calendar for a full moon, then sign on with **Wanderlust Tours** (541/389-8359; www.wanderlusttours.com) for a very romantic moonlight Cascade Lakes canoe trip led by a naturalist, who will point out all the geographic wonders of the area as you paddle your canoe across still waters beneath a nighttime summer sky. In wintertime, the snow brings additional delights with the company's Moonlight Snowshoe Tours including a naturalist guide, instruction, and hot drink up in the powder of the High Cascades, or their Bonfire in the Snow, offered on select winter weekends, New Year's Eve, and Valentine's Day. Snowshoe through the forest toward the soft fire glow awaiting you at a hand-carved snow amphitheater. Upon arrival, enjoy hot drinks, desserts, and snuggling beneath the winter sky. You won't have the lake or mountain to yourselves; there will be others—also romantics at heart, no doubt—along on the tour, but the memories are for you to share all alone.

For a view of the stars like you've never seen before (except, perhaps, in each other's eyes), head to the **Pine Mountain Observatory** (from Bend, take Hwy 20 east toward Burns, turn right [south] on a washboard dirt road just beyond the abandoned Millican gas station, and continue about 8 miles to the top; 541/382-8331; Fri–Sat evenings late May–late Sept). The observatory offers three telescopes—15, 24, and 32 inches in diameter, respectively—providing views of sunspots and sun flares, the discs and rings of planets, distant galaxies, and the star clouds of the Milky Way. Focus on your favorite constellation, then let your sweetheart make a wish. Come to the observatory prepared: Once you leave Bend, there are no stores or gas stations. Be sure you have enough fuel for the return trip, and bring along bottled water and some warm clothing; after all, you may want to linger up here among the heavens.

Finally, the **Sunriver Resort** also offers amazing views of the stars from 4- to 20-inch telescopes at its **Sunriver Nature Center and Observatory** (541/598-4406; www.sunrivernaturecenter.org; 9–11pm Tues–Sun summer), including occasional summertime Dinner Under the Stars events or the annual Mount Bachelor Star Party (www.mbsp.org).

Hope, and Charity—that dominate the horizon. Surrounded by mountains, trout streams, and pine and cedar forests, Sisters is perfect for both lovers of nature and those whose idea of a perfect afternoon outing is browsing small shops filled with antiques, art, and souvenirs while enjoying a good old-fashioned ice cream cone. One word of warning: Sisters in the summer is not the place for solitude, especially during the second weekend in June or the second weekend in July, when the rodeo and outdoor quilt show, respectively, draw crowds. Privacy, however, is only a short drive away (take Highway 20 west from Sisters 10 miles and look for Road 14) with a trip to the peaceful and fish-filled Metolius River and nearby **Wizard Falls Fish Hatchery**.

Access and Information

Access to Bend or Sisters from the Salem region is via Interstate 5 to Highway 20, which runs over the Santiam Pass. From Eugene, take Highway 126 to access Highway 20. From Southern Oregon, reach the region from Highway 97 (via Highway 62 if you're coming from I-5). From Portland and the north take Highway 26 from I-5. During the winter months, traction devices and good snow tires are musts. For snow and road conditions, call the **Oregon Department of Transportation** (800/977-ODOT; www.oregon.gov/ODOT). For more information about Bend, call the **Central Oregon Visitors Association** (800/800-8334; www.visitcentraloregon.com). For information on Sisters, call the **Sisters Area Chamber of Commerce** (541/549-0251; www.sisterschamber.com).

Romantic Lodgings

Blue Spruce Bed & Breakfast / ❂❂❰

444 S Spruce St, Sisters; 541/549-9644 or 888/328-9644
This farmhouse-style inn nestled in a grove of evergreens offers rustic comfort with a dash of luxury. Sit on the expansive back porch, dip your feet in the small creek, or enjoy the tearoom and nearby fire pit, surrounded by wildlife and beautiful garden views. Four generously sized guest rooms are decorated with hunting, logging, fishing, or western themes that include delightful mouse-hole nightlights with miniature scenes replicating each guest room. Each room has a comfortable sitting area, king-size bed, private bath with two-person spa, waterfall-head shower, and towel warmer. Lasso up some fun in the delightfully decorated Ponderosa room or relax "among the trees" (log furniture and accents) in the Cascade room, both with garden views. For breakfast, hosts Sandy Affonso and daughter Lizzie serve lemon-ricotta pancakes, gingerbread waffles, or eggs Benedict family-style at an enormous round table. *$$$; AE, DIS, MC, V; checks OK; www.blue-spruce.biz.*

Cricketwood Country Bed & Breakfast / ❂❂❂

63520 Cricketwood Rd, Bend; 877/330-0747
If you're looking for an intimate, affordable escape, you'll find it here. Set on 10 country acres, the inn is just 5 miles from Bend—but the two of you might feel you're in another world. Three guest rooms have garden themes: the Secret Garden Suite features a double Jacuzzi, a massage table and oil,

candles, and even some romantic (naughty but nice!) games. Recently completed, the separate Champagne Chalet provides even more seclusion with a double-sided fireplace, fireside hydrotherapy tub for two, massage table, and fully equipped kitchen. (Note, however, that there is no breakfast service in the chalet.) In addition to delivering complimentary champagne or cider and bedtime cookies to your door, innkeepers Jim and Tracy Duncan have mastered the art of providing superb service—welcoming, without being constantly present. Breakfasts are ordered from a large menu and include such delights as crème brûlée–baked French toast or made-to-order omelets. After you've fed the ducks or taken a countryside walk, continue to enjoy the backyard scenery—from the hot tub. *$$; AE, DIS, MC, V; checks OK; www. cricketwood.com.*

FivePine Lodge / ✪✪✪✪

1021 Desperado Trail, Sisters; 541/549-5200 or 866/974-5900
At this luxurious retreat, the sustainably built cabins, lodge, and conference center sit surrounded by pine trees and a meandering stream. Owners Zoe and Bill Willitts have spent 12 years envisioning and building a space for couples to reconnect. All rooms feature private patios or decks, stone fireplaces, and delicious king-size beds. Each of the five Romance Cabin suites also boasts a soaking tub with a natural water feature and a large double-headed walk-in shower. Access to the Sisters Athletic Club, a healthy breakfast, an evening wine reception, and use of the center's cruiser bikes are all included with your stay. Be sure to book the best amenity of all: a spa service at the Shibui Spa (541/549-6164; www.shibuispa.com). The Sisters' Movie House and the seasonally focused Pleiades restaurant are also located on-site. *$$$; AE, DIS, MC, V; checks OK; www.fivepinelodge.com.* &

Lara House Lodge / ✪✪✪✪

640 NW Congress St, Bend; 541/388-4064 or 800/766-4064
This beautifully remodeled 1910 Craftsman on a quiet residential corner near downtown Bend features a light-filled sunroom, garden deck, and large front porch framing views of tranquil Drake Park and Mirror Pond. All six guest rooms are luxurious, with sumptuous king- or queen-size beds and private baths, some with old-fashioned tubs, some with Jacuzzis. For the utmost in intimacy, we favor the third-floor Summit Suite, tucked under the eaves with a king-size bed, a cozy living room, and original artwork. A nightly turndown service with chocolates and spa-quality bath products will remind you that you are somewhere special. In the afternoon, enjoy delicious food and wine selections in the Great Room. In the morning, feast on a generous gourmet breakfast featuring house-made pastries, seasonal fruit, crepes, quiches, or chili-cheese puffs; genuine smiles from the innkeepers are always present. *$$$–$$$$; AE, DC, DIS, MC, V; no checks; www.larahouse.com.*

Three Days of Romance

Day One: Begin a summer day in Bend with a trip to its most famous and stunningly beautiful peak, Mount Bachelor. Athletic couples can hike to the top or, between Independence Day and Labor Day, romantics can hop on the Pine Marten Lift for a relaxing ride to the midmountain lodge, where **Scapolos Italian Bistro** (541/382-2442; www.mtbachelor.com), over a mile in the air, offers lunch with front-row seats to the breathtaking mountain scenery (sunset dinners, too, on the weekends). After your mountain adventure, return to Bend to enjoy an afternoon exploring lovely **Drake Park** with its beautiful Mirror Pond. At the end of the park along nearby Brooks Street, you'll discover a variety of wine shops and tasting bars; the **Bendistillery** (860 NW Brooks St; 541/388-6868; www.bendistillery.com) even offers artesian gin and vodka tastings (see "Central Oregon Wines"). Or, enjoy a coffee-laced snuggle on the ski-lift swing that overlooks the lake and the Deschutes River at **Balay** (961 NW Brooks St; 541/389-6464) before a sumptuous dinner at **Ariana**. End your evening at **River Ridge at Mt. Bachelor Village Resort**, where your suite with a hot tub on the deck overlooking the Deschutes River will lull you into romantic bliss. Or, if the moon is full, enjoy **Wanderlust**'s moonlight canoe ride or their wintertime snowshoe tours (see "Stargazing").

Day Two: After a delicious breakfast of gourmet eggs Benedict at the **Victorian Cafe** (1404 NW Galveston Ave; 541/382-6411), stop to grab

McMenamins Old St. Francis School Hotel / ✪✪✪

700 NW Bond St, Bend; 541/382-5174
Yet another fabulous remake by the McMenamin brothers—this time a Catholic school cum hotel reopened in 2005. Many rooms have artistic and unique touches, but we favor Father Dominic O'Connor's room with its rustic king bed, wood panels, and spacious two-person shower or, best of all, the Hoaglands room with a king bed, a couch, side-by-side old-fashioned tubs, bath salts, and two showers. A Turkish-style soaking pool and movie theater are free to guests, and the on-site restaurant offers room service for no additional charge. What you get is a rejuvenating retreat without ever leaving the premises. *$$–$$$; AE, DIS, MC, V; no checks; www.mcmenamins.com.* ᶘ

Metolius River Resort / ✪✪✪✦

25551 SW Forest Service Rd #1419, Camp Sherman;
541/595-6281 or 800/818-7688
Not to be confused with the lower-priced, well-worn, and well-loved Metolius River Lodges across the bridge, this 11-cabin resort on the west

picnic supplies at **Devore's Good Food Store and Wine Shop** (1124 NW Newport Ave; 541/389-6588) or **Newport Market** (1121 NW Newport Ave; 541/382-3940) across the street. Then, head out for a meandering drive along the **Cascade Lakes National Scenic Byway** past pristine lakes, forests of ponderosa pine, the Deschutes River, basalt lava flows, and awe-inspiring views of some of the area's biggest mountains. There are plenty of lounge- and swim-inducing lake beaches, or if you prefer a more active search for romance, take one of the fabulous hikes that begin right from the road. When you return to town, check in to the **Lara House Lodge** and enjoy wine tasting paired with cheeses and conversation. Take the scenic route through Drake Park up to **The Blacksmith** for an expertly prepared meal featuring Cascade natural beef. The stroll back through the park, whether at twilight or by moonlight, will be lovely.

Day Three: After breakfast at Lara House, head to neighboring Sisters for luxurious pampering at the newly completed **FivePine Lodge** with its Romance Cabins and on-site Shibui Spa. Put yourselves in the literal lap of luxury and enjoy a couple's massage or any number of delicious packages, and—following this afternoon of delight—enjoy a meal at **Pleiades** on-site or venture a short way down the road to **Jen's Garden** for their prix-fixe Southern French–inspired meals. An evening enjoying the luxuries of your room is the perfect way to conclude this central Oregon adventure.

bank of the river offers the height of rustic romance. Trimmed in woodshake and featuring river-rock fireplaces, most of the cabins have river views, master bedrooms and lofts, furnished kitchens, and French doors leading to large, river-facing decks. In this setting tucked snugly within the Deschutes National Forest, you'll awaken to sweet birdsong and the rushing river. You'll then wind down in the evening to the evocative chirping of crickets and frogs. Whether you choose to snuggle inside by the fire or to sit out on the deck, take a peaceful stroll through the woods or cast your fishing line, time spent here can't help but be romantic. Because the cabins are privately owned, interiors, while all nice, are individually decorated; bring food from town and enjoy. *$$$; MC, V; checks OK; closed first 2 weeks in Dec; www.metoliusriverresort.com.*

Pine Ridge Inn / ✪✪✪✿

1200 SW Century Dr, Bend; 541/389-6137 or 800/600-4095
Set on a bluff above the Deschutes River, this charming luxury inn caters to romantics by offering the ultimate in personal attention and privacy. All

20 guest rooms have well-stocked baths or Jacuzzi tubs and evening turn-down service. Suites are spacious with living rooms, gas fireplaces, two-person Jacuzzi tubs, and private porches. For an indulgence, the 900-square-foot Hyde Suite takes the cake: with a luxurious king bedroom, a living/dining room, a two-person Jacuzzi, an adjoining powder room, two decks, and expansive river views, this is the best place to kiss in the inn. In the evening, wine and cheese are served in the communal fireside parlor; in the morning, a delicious complimentary breakfast is set out (including a hot entrée, fruit, and cereals). Inn guests may choose to use the exercise facilities and outdoor pool at the nearby athletic club. Celebrating? Check out the moderately priced romance packages and be greeted with chilled champagne and homemade desserts. *$$$; AE, DC, DIS, MC, V; checks OK; www.pineridgeinn.com.* &

River Ridge at Mount Bachelor Village Resort / ❂❂❂❂

19717 Mount Bachelor Dr, Bend; 541/389-5900 or 800/452-9846
Tucked in the heart of Mount Bachelor Village Resort, River Ridge offers tastefully finished, contemporary suites. The spacious river-facing one-bedroom (or more) suites are the crème de la crème, each featuring a full kitchen, hot tub on the deck, Jacuzzi tub in the bathroom, and gas fireplace—with serene views of the forest or river. The price is steep but well worth it for your romantic getaway. River Ridge is set within a larger resort with people visiting for a variety of occasions, but once enclosed in your suite you'll notice nothing but idyllic isolation. The luxurious decor and spectacular view—not to mention melodious sounds of the river—will make you feel as if you're the only two in the whole wide world. The resort also offers access to many more amenities, including the 2-mile nature trail—perfect for a romantic meander—and athletic club and swimming pool, both open year-round. *$$–$$$; AE, DC, DIS, MC, V; checks OK; www.mtbachelorvillage.com.* &

Sunriver Resort's River Lodges / ❂❂❂❂

17600 Center Dr, Bend; 541/593-1000 or 800/547-3922
Encompassing a stunning 3,200 riverside acres, this self-sufficient community's reputation is built around its three championship golf courses; the surrounding mountains, Deschutes River, and resort itself offer endless recreational opportunities including tennis, biking, swimming, horseback riding, cross-country skiing, and whitewater rafting for you and your athletic honey. Unlike many resorts, Sunriver is well spread out, so you can find many private spaces, even in high season. For an idyllic romantic retreat, reserve a room at the luxurious River Lodges; each comes furnished with a fireplace, soaking tub, and private deck with mountain views. Indulgences include spa treatments, couple's and in-room massages, or a privately catered dinner for two. At the Lodge nearby, enjoy the Meadows restaurant for lunch, dinner,

and Sunday brunch, or, for a really romantic and memorable meal, travel up the road to the Grille at Crosswater (541/593-3400), open only to Sunriver guests. *$$$$; AE, DIS, MC, V; checks OK; www.sunriverresort.com.* &

Romantic Restaurants

Ariana / ●●●●

1304 NW Galveston St, Bend; 541/330-5539
It doesn't get much better than this family-run, candlelit bungalow. With a seasonal Mediterranean menu pulling the best from Italian, French, and Spanish cuisines, a talented husband-and-wife chef team, and impeccable service, you are sure to find yourselves sharing tastes of handmade cannelloni, spice-rubbed quail, jumbo diver scallops, and many other offerings. Bonus: a great, reasonably priced international and local wine selection. Summertime meals on the back deck are wonderful, and for true romantic bliss in winter request a seat by the fireplace and enjoy this favorite spot among the locals. *$$$; AE, MC, V; no checks; lunch Tues–Fri, dinner Tues–Sat; full bar; reservations recommended; www.arianarestaurantbend.com.* &

The Blacksmith / ●●●◑

211 NW Greenwood Ave, Bend; 541/318-0588
The Blacksmith—with its award-winning "new ranch cuisine," elegance, and fabulous service—concocts delicious fish and chicken plates. But the real stars here are the creatively prepared steaks, including the Border tenderloin with wild mushroom enchiladas and a verde sauce; the infamous Blacksmith cheese steak, a flank with truffle-scented potato sauce and shaved Tumalo Farms Pondhopper cheese; or the marinated Rancher's rib eye. A prix-fixe, chef-guided six-course journey is also available for those ready for a true culinary tour. Regardless, the chance to snuggle up with a crème brûlée and a nightcap will prove a blissful conclusion to an intimate dining experience. *$$$; AE, DC, DIS, MC, V; dinner every day; full bar; reservations recommended; www.bendblacksmith.com.* &

Bluefish Bistro / ●●●

718 NW Franklin Ave, Bend; 541/330-0663
Set right on the edge of Drake Park, this intimate restaurant offers diners a sophisticated Euro-Asian experience. With expertly and creatively prepared fish, fowl, meat, and vegetarian dishes, the Bluefish offers entrées like pan-seared scallops in a yam and goat-cheese puree, seasonal risotto and pasta, and pork tenderloin with saffron-risotto cakes. With a wonderful selection of local wines and house-made desserts, as well as quick access to the park for an after-dinner stroll, this bistro stands out for both its cuisine and elegant atmosphere. *$$$; AE, DIS, MC, V; local checks only; dinner Tues–Sun; full bar; reservations recommended; www.bluefishbend.com.* &

Cork / ✿✿✿

150 NW Oregon Ave, Bend; 541/382-6881
With a cozy, candlelit bar, high-backed booths, and contemporary decor, this restaurant invites its diners to settle in for conversation and "American eclectic" cuisine including lamb shank, prawns and crab, spicy puttanesca, or cioppino. A signature dish is the Black Sesame Pesto-kissed Scallops, which will surely make you swoon. Both the restaurant and wine bar offer an extensive wine list, many served by the glass. To end your meal, you and your sweetheart will relish the French-press coffees and homemade desserts. *$$$; AE, DC, MC, V; no checks; dinner Tues–Sat; beer and wine; reservations recommended; www.corkbend.com.* &

Jen's Garden / ✿✿✿✿

403 E Hood Ave, Sisters; 541/549-2699
In Sisters, enjoy a delicious prix-fixe five-course (or à la carte) dinner at this French Provincial–inspired restaurant. The menu, to the delight of locals, regularly changes with the seasons and with the creative urges of chef/owners T. R. and Jennifer McCrystal and their able staff. Relish the intimate interior, the impeccable service, and the opportunity to indulge in a wine flight prepared specifically for the selected menu, which may include hazelnut-encrusted halibut, mango and sausage–stuffed chicken breast, or Guittard chocolate torte. The wine and food go hand-in-hand, as will you and your love, as you savor the last morsels of this scrumptious meal. *$$$; MC, V; local checks only; dinner Tues–Sun; beer and wine; reservations recommended; www.intimatecottagecuisine.com.*

Merenda / ✿✿✿

900 NW Wall St, Bend; 541/330-2304
With exposed brick walls, high ceilings, and rich gold and red tones throughout, Merenda is where urban trendy meets old-world charm in downtown Bend. During packed, noisy happy-hour and weekend nights, head upstairs to the quieter fireplace room, or grab a window seat or booth. You'll soon be so enchanted by the extensive wine list and excellent French- and Mediterranean-inspired cuisine (and each other, of course!) that you'll forget about the bustle below. Wine flights, hors d'oeuvres, and entrées from the wood-fired oven are superb. Save room for dessert: beignets dipped in chocolate, caramel, and whipped cream will leave a sweet taste on your lips until your next kiss. *$$; AE, DC, DIS, MC, V; checks OK; lunch, dinner every day; full bar; reservations recommended; www.merendarestaurant.com.* &

Scanlon's / ✿✿✿

61615 Athletic Club Dr, Bend; 541/382-8769
It's true that Scanlon's shares a building with an athletic club—but don't let that scare you away. Offering consistently exceptional Northwest and

Central Oregon Wines

While the high desert is not necessarily a wine-grape-growing mecca, central Oregon is filled with wine aficionados; therefore, wine-tasting opportunities abound. In downtown Bend, Brooks Street overlooking Drake Park is home to several tasting options, including **Volcano Vineyards** (930 NW Brooks St; 541/617-1102; www.volcanovineyards.com), the **Wine Shop and Tasting Bar** (924 NW Brooks St; 541/389-2884; www.thewine shopbend.com), and the **Bendistillery** (860 NW Brooks St; 541/388-6868; www.bendistillery.com) with its artesian Cascade Mountain Gin and Crater Lake Vodka. All of these shops invite tasters to linger and to bring or purchase picnic items. Or, an easy walk lands you at **Maragas Winery Tasting Room** (643 NW Colorado Ave; 541/330-0919). You and your love can sit at a patio table and sample one of the winery's delicious signature varietals, such as Legal Zin, Pinot Riche, and Kool Kat Muscat. After enjoying the clever beatnik labels (penned by owner Doug Maragas's mother in the 1950s), you may feel inspired to stop by their red-barn winery located on Highway 97 outside of Madras (15523 SW Hwy 97, Culver; 541/546-5464). Here at the winery, enjoy a chat with the entertaining owner and take in views of the mountains and the recently planted pinot gris vineyard.

When in Sisters, don't miss the wine flights and events at **Cork Cellars Wine Bar and Bottle Shop** (161A Elm St; 541/549-2675; www.corkcellars. com). Small, delicious plates and a comfortable couch will allow you to take your time and sip a few eclectic wines. And **Jen's Garden** offers a wine flight specially paired to their five-course dinners (see Romantic Restaurants).

Mediterranean cuisine and attentive yet unobtrusive service, Scanlon's is wonderful for either a casual lunch or an extravagant dinner. The restaurant's Hood River cherry wood–fired oven turns out freshly baked breads and pizzas, and adds delectable smokiness to many signature dishes. The entrée menu, which changes twice a year, reflects a variety of influences, from Asian to European; the dessert menu will tempt you with house-made specialties like sweet-tart Key lime or decadent peanut butter pies. Bonus: If you have children, babysitting and children's meals are complimentary at the athletic club's childcare center—so the two of you can linger awhile. *$$; AE, DC, DIS, MC, V; checks OK; lunch, dinner every day; full bar; reservations recommended; www.athleticclubofbend.com.* &

Staccato at the Firehall / ✪✪✪❶

5 NW Minnesota Ave, Bend; 541/312-3100
While you're locked in each other's gaze and surrounded by exposed brick, black leather, and burnished copper, you might just forget that this restaurant is really hopping! Servers are knowledgeable, attentive, and unobtrusive, careful to give you a leisurely, intimate dining experience, especially in the Fireside room. Italian specialties, each expertly prepared, include calamari, clams and mussels, wood-fired pizzas, lamb *sous vide*, cioppino, and inventive pasta dishes. Along with creative cocktails, Staccato's wine list maintains a fittingly heavy Italian and local focus. Desserts—whether cannoli, profiteroles, croissant bread pudding, or the decadent chocolate bar with pistachio ice cream—allow you to savor even more of Staccato. *$$–$$$; AE, DC, DIS, MC, V; checks OK; lunch, dinner every day, brunch Sun; full bar; reservations recommended; www.staccatosfirehall.com.* &

28 / ✪✪✪

920 NW Bond, Bend; 541/ 385-0828
Romance abounds in this trendy urban "scene." As you peer in through the main window, the place seems aglow with a colorful wall of radiant, back-lit liquor bottles behind the long, sexy bar made from one large curve of lighted orange glass. Known for its cocktails, 28's popular drinks include the Galvanizer, a blend of orange and pear vodkas with fresh-squeezed lime, and the Electra, a cherry-lime infusion that glows blue. Cherry-wood tables speckle the restaurant and dim, flickering candles add to the mood. The small-plate menu includes the signature 28 flatbread with your choice of three toppings, and the entrée menu features specialties such as BBQ shrimp in a Worcestershire-cream reduction and whipped mashed potatoes. Finish the evening with the pure decadence of Godiva chocolate panna cotta or white chocolate pecan bread pudding. *$–$$; MC, V; no checks; dinner Tues–Sat; full bar; reservations recommended; www.myspace.com/28bend.*

♡ Seattle & Environs

Seattle

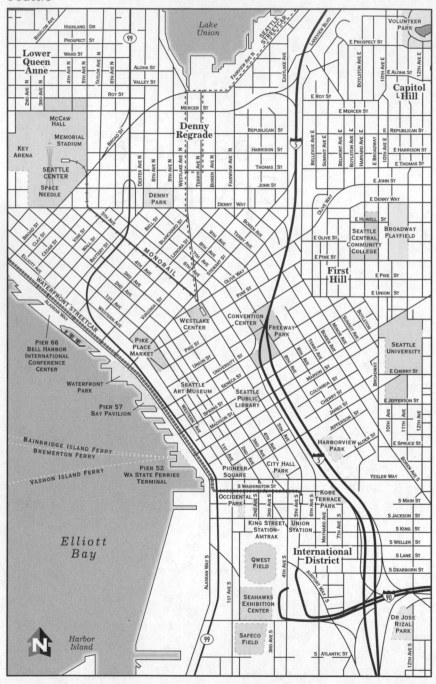

Love builds bridges where there are none.
—R. H. Delaney

 # Seattle & Environs

Seattle's awe-inspiring natural beauty attracts visitors and new residents in droves, and most of them fall in love with its eccentricities and charms, even as they bemoan persistent gray skies and congested highways. Traffic and precipitation aside, few cities offer so many different, equally appealing vistas. Verdant hills rise above numerous glistening waterways, and mountains, snow-dusted for much of the year, lie all around: the Olympic Mountains to the west, accenting spectacular sunsets; the jagged Cascade Range to the east; the majestic, often mist-shrouded Mount Rainier to the south; and Mount Baker in the northern distance.

Major corporations such as Microsoft, Amazon.com, Nordstrom, Starbucks, Boeing, Costco, Paccar, T-Mobile, and Safeco are some of the region's biggest employers, drawing talent from around the world: they have given—and continue to give—Seattle its reputation for prosperity and innovation. Also known for a lively arts scene, Seattle offers culture hounds cutting-edge visual arts exhibitions, theater, opera, touring Broadway shows, symphony and chamber orchestras, and music and comedy clubs. Acclaimed restaurants boast chefs who capitalize on the seasonal bounty offered by the Northwest's ocean waters and microclimates, making Seattle a bona fide foodie's town. Stereotypes of coffee addicts and micro-brew aficionados are virtually passé: increasingly, Washington is on the map for its exploding wine industry. Though the overwhelming majority of the state's grapes are grown east of the Cascades, Seattle and the Eastside—Woodinville in particular—are home to dozens of award-winning wineries.

Despite its growing urbanity, Seattle clings to small-city roots and the linger-ing shadow of a pioneering spirit. People here may seem a bit reserved at the outset, but scratch the surface and their warmth shines through. Older neighbor-hoods are fiercely individualistic, each priding itself on the unique history, busi-nesses, and people that define it. Across floating bridges to the east, the rapidly expanding Eastside has towns and cities that boast their own distinct charac-ters, from upscale, old-money Mercer Island; to commerce-driven Bellevue (the fourth-largest city in the state); to the lakefront resort town of Kirkland, which draws day-trippers year-round. A short ferry ride from Seattle's waterfront puts you on woodsy Bainbridge Island: enjoy its quaint downtown, or simply pass through on the way to the magnificent Olympic Peninsula, with its rugged coastlines and forests primeval. If you prefer urban excursions, Portland is a three-hour drive south, and Vancouver, British Columbia, is a 2½ hour drive north, but it's relaxing—and romantic—to avoid hitting the highway entirely by taking the Amtrak train to either destination.

What unites residents of this metropolitan area is the tendency to be environmentally "green" and to possess a great passion for the outdoors (after all, this is the home of REI). Easy access to urban, state, and national parks abounds, with no shortage of adventure. From biking, hiking, running, and in-line skating to boating, windsurfing, snowboarding, and skiing, outdoor recreation is a serious year-round pursuit in Seattle, making it one of the "fittest cities" in the country according to several polls. Any season is an excellent time to visit, from blossom-filled spring and sunny summer (when gardens and plantings flourish) to crisp, colorful autumn and chilly winter, ideal for snuggling by a roaring fire.

In short, for people who call this region home (or for those just paying a visit), there are enough kissing destinations to fill a lifetime of romance.

Seattle

Romantic Highlights

For an authentic Seattle experience, there is no better place to start than the beloved **Pike Place Market** (Pike St and 1st Ave), which celebrated its 100th anniversary in 2007 with great fanfare. This is the most densely romance-packed part of the city, so a smooch beneath the neon Public Market sign is de rigueur—despite the crowds.

Fresh seafood, colorful regional produce, gorgeous floral bouquets, and locally made arts and crafts are the highlights of the market's bounty. You can't miss **Pike Place Fish Market** (86 Pike Pl; 206/682-7181; www.pikeplacefish.com), home to the famous "flying" fish, which is situated right behind Rachel, the iconic bronze piggybank who welcomes all visitors with a smile. Right down the stairs from the market's entrance is one of the city's most kiss-worthy restaurants, **Il Bistro** (see Romantic Restaurants). If you snack your way through the market, don't miss **Beecher's Handmade Cheese** (1600 Pike Pl; 206/956-1964) for their transcendent macaroni and cheese, and **Daily Dozen Doughnut Company** (93 Pike St; 206/467-7769), for fresh, hot minidoughnuts. Movie buffs should lunch at **Athenian Inn** (1517 Pike Pl; 206/624-7166): the diner-ish fare isn't particularly remarkable (except for the seafood bisque), but this is where Tom Hanks and Rob Reiner, sitting at the counter, opined about relationships in one of the great romantic comedies, *Sleepless in Seattle*.

Veer slightly off the beaten path and explore charming Post Alley, where you'll find gems like **Rose's Chocolate Treasures** (1906 Post Alley; 206/441-2936; www.roseschocolatetreasures.com), the **Perennial Tea Room** (1910 Post Alley; 206/448-4054; www.perennialtearoom.com), stocked with teas and paraphernalia, and **The Tasting Room** (1924 Post Alley; 206/770-9463; www.winesof washington.com), a rustic-elegant shop and bar where you can sample offerings from six Washington wineries. Particularly beloved in the summertime for its shaded terrace, **The Pink Door** (see Romantic Restaurants) feels like a secret club, easy enough to spot because of its—you guessed it—pink entrance. Another wildly popular eatery is **Steelhead Diner** (95 Pine St; 206/625-0129; www.steelheaddiner. com), offering sophisticated comfort food, and the semi-subterranean **94 Stewart** (94 Stewart St; 206/441-5505; www.94stewart.com), which has an extraordinary, award-winning wine list.

If you're in the neighborhood and in the mood for French, arguably the most romantic of all cuisines, head for **Maximilien-in-the-Market** (81 Pike St, #A; 206/682-7270; www.maximilienrestaurant.com) or **Place Pigalle** (see Romantic Restaurants), both of which have wonderful water views, especially at sunset. **Campagne** and **Café Campagne** (see Romantic Restaurants) may lack views but the food is marvelous. **Le Pichet** (1933 1st Ave; 206/256-1499; www.lepichet seattle.com) and **Entre Nous** (216 Stewart St; 206/905-1633; www.entrenous seattle.com) offer casual, bistro-style ambience.

For more market information, pick up a map and self-guided-tour pamphlet at the information booth (corner of 1st Ave and Pike St; 206/682-7453), and while you're there check out what's offered at **Ticket/Ticket** (206/682-7453, ext. 226), the place to get half-price tickets for same-day showings (or day before for matinee performances). Lovers who love food should consider a Pike Place Market tour with **Savor Seattle Food Tours** (800/838-3006; www.savorseattletours.com), a fine introduction to Seattle's thriving culinary scene.

Charming boutiques and restaurants of all descriptions abound along First Avenue. Head north into Belltown, window-shopping your way to such perennial favorites as **Flying Fish** (2234 1st Ave; 206/728-8595; www.flyingfishrestaurant. com) or **Macrina Bakery & Cafe** (2408 1st Ave; 206/448-4032; www.macrina bakery.com). Walk south from the market along First and you'll find more shops and wonderful restaurants, including one of Seattle's most acclaimed, **Union** (1400 1st Ave; 206/838-8000; www.unionseattle.com), with daily changing menus and a 200-bottle cellar. Carry on and you'll end up in the neighborhood where Seattle history began, **Pioneer Square**. The area around Occidental Square can feel a bit dicey, but **Pioneer Place Park** (1st Ave and James St), home to a Tlingit totem pole and ornate iron pergola, is a great place for a smooch. Directly behind the park is the historic **Underground Tour** (608 1st Ave; 206/682-4646; www.undergroundtour.com): a little cheesy, but smooching in a darkened subterranean corner is as easy as stealing candy from a baby. A must-see for book lovers is the multilevel, brick-walled **Elliott Bay Book Company** (101 S Main St; 206/624-6600; www.elliottbaybook.com), a legendary independent bookstore

Kissing by the Water

We admit that the phrase "romantic walks on the beach" is a personals-ad cliché, but there's something undeniably transporting about the sound of waves lapping against shore or hull. A ferry ride makes a delightful (and affordable) focus to a romantic afternoon—especially if you leave the car behind. Among the numerous **Washington State Ferries** (www.wsdot. wa.gov/ferries) routes, the return sailing from Bremerton is the most scenic, combining breathtaking views of both Mount Rainier (weather allowing) and the downtown skyline. For a shorter jaunt, take the 12-minute trip from **Pier 55** (1101 Alaskan Wy) downtown to West Seattle's **Seacrest Park** (1660 Harbor Ave SW) on the **Elliott Bay Water Taxi** (206/553-3000; http://transit.metrokc.gov/tops/oto/water_taxi.html). Operating seasonally (usually May–Oct), the ride is $3 each way, and there's also a free shuttle (Metro DART Rte 773; http://transit.metrokc.gov/tops/bus/route_maps/m773_0.html) that runs between Seacrest Park and Alki Point, Admiral District, and the West Seattle junction.

The popular **Carkeek Park** (950 NW Carkeek Pk Rd; 206/684-0877; www.seattle.gov/parks) in northwest Seattle has a sweeping lawn, picnic areas, hiking trails, and a lovely stretch of waterfront with views of Puget Sound and the Olympic Mountains, but the best thing about this location is locking lips on the pedestrian bridge (that connects the parking lot and the sandy beach) while a train thunders past beneath your feet.

with a cafe, distinguished author readings, 150,000 volumes, and plenty of nooks and crannies.

The pan-Asian **International District** is a bustling mélange of cultures, its nebulous parameters extending roughly between Yesler Way to the north and South Dearborn Street to the south, and 4th Avenue to the west and 12th Avenue to the east. Colorful, exotic, crammed with history, and sometimes a little seamy, romantic destinations do exist here: we particularly adore the inexpensive, excellent Vietnamese food and cocktails at **The Tamarind Tree** (1036 S Jackson St; 206/860-1404; www.tamarindtreerestaurant.com), a surprisingly gorgeous dining room tucked into the unassuming Asian Plaza.

Heading back into the downtown area, the **Seattle Art Museum** (1300 1st Ave; 206/654-3100; www.seattleartmuseum.org), reopened in May 2007 after an expansion integrating old and new architecture, actually makes a fine place to steal a kiss: on quiet days it's not unusual to find yourselves alone in a gallery. Also on the premises, **TASTE Restaurant** (206/903-5921), while a bit bright and modern for serious smooching, offers excellent cocktails and menus. At SAM's **Olympic Sculpture Park** (2901 Western Ave; 206/654-3100; www.seattleartmuseum.org),

It's always time for a kiss when you're standing on the sundial at the apex of **Gas Works Park** (2101 N Northlake Wy; 206/684-4075; www. seattle.gov/parks), with its view of Lake Union and downtown, but for another angle on the city, drive out to the **Elliott Bay Marina** (2601 W Marina Pl; 206/285-4817; www.elliottbaymarina.net) in Magnolia. In what remains a well-kept secret, the marina is obliged to provide free shuttle-boat service upon request—daily during daylight hours—between Pier G and an observation platform atop the 2,700-foot-long breakwater sheltering the marina. This is a great spot for smooching with an unimpeded view of the Seattle waterfront, even better when combined with a cocktail or meal at **Palisade** (2601 W Marina Pl; 206/285-1000; www. palisaderestaurant.com), an elegant restaurant with a Northwest-meets-Polynesian menu.

Another clandestine spot is the **Waterfall Garden Park** (219 2nd Ave S; 206/624-6096), a serene, landscaped garden oasis tucked into Pioneer Square, dotted with bistro tables and chairs, where the roar of the 22-foot-high waterfall tumbling over boulders all but drowns out the noise of city streets. Hemmed in by walls, the park feels quite secluded, but for the greatest possible privacy avoid weekday lunchtimes. Before heading to the park, stop by **Salumi** (309 3rd Ave S; 206/621-8772; www.salumi curedmeats.com) to pick up a sandwich: opened by Armandino Batali, celebrity chef Mario's father, it's a shrine for charcuterie-loving foodies.

where admission is free year-round, **TASTE Café** (206/332-1376) has bites just as delectable as its big sister eatery. There's also a **TASTE Café** (206/654-1382) at the **Seattle Asian Art Museum** (1400 E Prospect St; 206/654-3100; www. seattleartmuseum.org) in Volunteer Park on Capitol Hill—not as convenient for out-of-town visitors, but the setting is serene and conducive to a little discreet romancing.

The downtown retail core offers blocks of upscale shopping, including **Macy's** (1601 3rd Ave; 206/506-6000) and the flagship **Nordstrom** (500 Pine St; 206/628-2111). **Pacific Place** is home to **Tiffany & Co** (600 Pine St, Ste 100; 206/264-1400), in case you're in search of a bit of flash. Cultural pastimes abound in Seattle, from the symphony to theater to opera to a range of concerts in virtually every genre. While it can be tricky to indulge in a proper kiss during most performances, art can inspire you to greater heights. The city's most renowned height is the **Space Needle** (206/905-2100; www.spaceneedle.com) at Seattle Center, easily reached from downtown's Westlake Center via the **Monorail**. The elevator line to the top can be long and the ticket price dear, but the spectacular view, particularly on a clear day, is well worth the investment. If you dine at **SkyCity at the Needle** (see Romantic Restaurants), the ride up and down is free. If you want a bird's-eye view from a clandestine, off-the-beaten-path locale, head for **Top of the Hilton** (1301 6th Ave; 206/695-6015; www.hilton.com).

For a taste of the Seattleite's Seattle, go to the neighborhoods. Up the hill from Seattle Center, the top of **Queen Anne** offers one of the most popular views of downtown from **Kerry Park** (211 W Highland Dr), as well as an enticing strip of shops and eateries. However, the must-kiss spot is inside the Latin-flavored **El Diablo Coffee Co** (1811 Queen Anne Ave N, Ste 101; 206/285-0693; www. eldiablocoffee.com), which has a "love grotto" labeled Besame Mucho. What are you waiting for, an engraved invitation?

Capitol Hill is vibrant and youthful, with hipster bars and edgy shops lining Pike and Pine streets. For a little extra romantic inspiration, check out the grown-up toy store, **Babeland** (707 E Pike St; 206/328-2914; www.babeland.com). Excellent restaurants are plentiful and include the bustling **Osteria La Spiga** (1429 12th Ave; 206/323-8881; www.laspiga.com), the sister bistro to Le Pichet dubbed **Café Presse** (1117 12th Ave; 206/709-7674; www.cafepresseseattle.com), and gastropub **Quinn's** (1001 E Pike St; 325-7711; www.quinnspubseattle.com), the laid-back little sib to Belltown's **Restaurant Zoë** (2137 2nd Ave; 206/256-2060; www.restaurantzoe.com).

What the **University District** may lack in fine wining and dining, it makes up for in other ways. On the grounds of the University of Washington, the **Burke Museum** (17th Ave NE and NE 45th St; 206/543-7907; www.washington.edu/ burkemuseum) features a wonderful collection of Northwest Coast Indian art and artifacts, and the **Henry Art Gallery** (4100 15th Ave NE; 206/543-2280; www.henryart.org) focuses on mid-19th- to 21st-century works. Strolling the university grounds is particularly inspiring when cherry blossoms are in bloom on the Quad, but for near-year-round horticultural pleasures, visit Madison Valley's **Washington Park Arboretum** (2300 Arboretum Dr E; 206/543-8800; every day until dusk). Hold hands as you wander through this sylvan realm of 5,500 different kinds of plants, and, for a small fee, enter the Japanese Garden (closed Dec–Feb). If all that vegetation whets your appetite, one of the city's best gourmet vegetarian restaurants is nearby. **Café Flora** (2901 E Madison St; 206/325-9100; www.cafeflora.com) doesn't stint on romance and elegance, nor does **Carmelita** (7314 Greenwood Ave N; 206/706-7703; www.carmelita.net), our other favorite vegetarian oasis, in the northerly neighborhood of Greenwood.

Fremont has dubbed itself "the center of the universe." Although some of its überfunky charm has been sacrificed to the march of progress (condos and office buildings), it still has plenty to offer in the form of offbeat public art, such as the **Fremont Troll** (N 36th St at Troll Ave N, under the Aurora Bridge), **Statue of Lenin** (N 36th St and Evanston Ave N), and **Waiting for the Interurban** statue (N 34th St and Fremont Ave N), all picture-perfect spots for locking lips. There are good bars and restaurants, including **35th Street Bistro** (709 N 35th St; 206/547-9850; www.35bistro.com), chic boutiques and retro-vintage shops, and the year-round **Fremont Sunday Market** (N 34th St between Evanston and Phinney aves;

206/781-6776; www.fremontmarket.com), a Euro-style street market with up to 150 crafts vendors and secondhand-wares dealers. Around the corner is the site of the summertime **Fremont Outdoor Cinema** (N 35th St and Phinney Ave N; www. fremontoutdoormovies.com) that screens at least a dozen flicks every season.

Also held every Sunday is the **Ballard Farmers Market** (Ballard Ave between 20th and 22nd aves NW; 206/781-6776; www.fremontmarket.com/ballard): it's fun to wander up and down the stalls, ending at **Portalis Wine Shop & Wine Bar** (5205 Ballard Ave NW; 206/783-2007; www.portaliswines.com), **diVino Wine Bar** (5310 Ballard Ave NW; 206/297-0143; www.divinoseattle.com), **Volterra** (see Romantic Restaurants), or **Bal-Mar** (5449 Ballard Ave NW; 206/297-0500; www.thebalmar.com), a chic two-story watering hole and eatery with plenty of cozy seating. Venture out of Old Ballard and head west to the busy **Hiram M. Chittenden Locks** (3015 NW 54th St; 206/783-7059): not only can you watch vessels travel between Puget Sound and Lake Union, but there's also a fish-ladder viewing window; lovely, picnic-worthy grounds; and a botanical garden. Travel farther along the water and you'll come to **Ray's Boathouse and Café** (6049 Seaview Ave NW; restaurant 206/789-3770, cafe 206/782-0094; www.rays.com), a Seattle favorite for waterside dining, and, past the Shilshole Bay Marina, **Golden Gardens Park** (8498 Seaview Pl NW; 206/684-4075; www.seattle.gov/parks), one of the city's most popular beaches.

Home to another popular beachfront, **West Seattle** is a world unto itself. The largest Seattle neighborhood, this is where local history began, when settlers landed at Alki Point in 1851 near a spot marked by the **Alki Point lighthouse** (3201 Alki Ave SW; 206/217-6203). Dotted with bars and restaurants, Alki Beach is a great promenade for a warm-weather stroll, and the long-respected **Salty's on Alki** (1936 Harbor Ave SW; 206/937-1600; www.saltys.com) combines fine seafood-centric dining and a terrific wine program with one of the best all-encompassing views of the downtown skyline that anyone can hope for. Running north-south along the top of West Seattle, California Avenue is the focus of this large neighborhood's commerce. We like the area around the intersection of California Avenue SW and SW Alaska Street (known as the Junction), with its concentration of shops and restaurants, also home to the **West Seattle Farmers Market** on Sundays in warm months. Don't miss **Bakery Nouveau** (4737 California Ave SW; 206/923-0534; www.bakerynouveau.com), whose breads, chocolates, and pastries merit a trip to West Seattle on their own. Turn off California Avenue onto Fauntleroy Way SW and follow it to the end past lush **Lincoln Park** (8011 Fauntleroy Wy SW; 206/684-4075; www.seattle.gov/parks) to reach the ferry dock for Southworth and **Vashon Island**. You'll need wheeled transport (car or bicycles) to explore Vashon, a destination that makes for a fun day away.

Locals regard **Washington State Ferries** (206/464-6400 or 800/843-3779; www.wsdot.wa.gov/ferries), the largest fleet of passenger and automobile ferries in the United States, as a necessity, but they're also fitting for romance, whether you're off to explore islands or peninsulas, or simply taking a ride for its own sake. The vessels themselves are functional, not fancy, but step out on deck, day or night, and you'll be treated to views that inspire snuggling, from the stunning Seattle waterfront and skyline to moonlight sparkling on inky waters.

Access & Information

Interstate 5 is the primary north-south arterial in Seattle, and, as anyone who has spent time here knows, it's frequently clogged with traffic from Tacoma to Everett. Surveys rank Seattle among the top ten least drivable metropolitan areas in the country (with no improvement in sight). Two east-west arterials, Highway 520 (north of downtown) and Interstate 90 (south of downtown) connect to the Eastside over Lake Washington, and these, too, are often bumper-to-bumper, as is the major north-south highway on the Eastside, Interstate 405. Downtown Seattle is divided into avenues that run north-south (First Avenue is nearest the waterfront) and streets that run east-west, an important distinction to remember. Driving downtown can be daunting for the uninitiated, further complicated by one-way streets and steep hills: a good map can help with the former but won't indicate the latter. Though parking is fairly plentiful, lots and garages can be expensive if you don't take advantage of early-bird specials. Before parking anywhere on the street, read all signage carefully: you may be lucky enough to snag a free spot, but otherwise parking is $1.50 per hour with a two-hour limit between 8am and 6pm, with some exceptions. Generally, street parking is free from 6pm to 8am, all day Sunday, and most Federal holidays. Coin meters are gradually being replaced by parking stations that accept coins, credit cards, and debit cards and print a timed sticker that you affix to the interior of your curbside window.

Getting downtown from **Seattle-Tacoma International Airport** (17801 Pacific Hwy S, SeaTac; 206/431-4444; www.portseattle.org/seatac) is a 35-minute straight shot north on I-5, provided you don't hit traffic (peak rush hours are Mon–Fri 7–9:30am and 3:30–7pm). **Gray Line of Seattle** (206/626-6088; www.graylineseattle.com), in addition to offering sightseeing tours, runs airport passengers to and from major downtown hotels for $10.25 one way, $17 round-trip. **Shuttle Express** (425/981-7000; www.shuttleexpress. com) is a good option for those staying outside the downtown core, but taxis are often not much more expensive. From the airport (STITA cabs exclusively; STILA limousines are only about $10 more), the cost starts at about $35–$40 to downtown, and by law, taxis to the airport from downtown must charge a flat rate of $28, plus fuel surcharges.

Amtrak (303 S Jackson St; 206/382-4126 or 800/USA-RAIL; www.amtrak. com) trains arrive at and depart from King Street Station. Seattle is a stop on Amtrak's Coast Starlight route; the Portland-to-Seattle segment, much of which runs along the shores of Puget Sound, is especially scenic and rather romantic, though be warned: delays and cancellations are not unknown.

The city's **Metro Transit** (206/553-3000; transit.metrokc.gov) serves Seattle and the Eastside and connects with buses from greater Puget Sound to the north and south. Metro buses are free until 7pm in the downtown core (between the waterfront and I-5, and Jackson and Bell sts). The charming vintage Waterfront Streetcar Line has been temporarily suspended, replaced by Metro Route 99 buses (painted to look like the green streetcars), and the South Lake Union line of the **Seattle Streetcar** (www.seattlestreetcar.com) went into operation in December 2007. For aboveground transport, ride the space-age **Monorail**, which takes only 90 seconds to glide between downtown's Westlake Center (Pine St and 4th Ave, 3rd floor) and Seattle Center.

The **Citywide Concierge Center**, part of the Seattle Convention and Visitors Bureau (Washington State Convention and Trade Center, Pike St between 7th and 8th aves; 206/461-5840; www.visitseattle.org), is an excellent source for information and maps.

Romantic Lodgings

Alexis Hotel / ❂❂❂

1007 1st Ave, Seattle; 206/624-4844 or 800/426-7033
With the Seattle Art Museum, Benaroya Hall, numerous galleries, and Safeco and Qwest fields not far away, this historic hotel offers many fitting packages, including the Seahawks-focused Art of Football, and The Art of Doing Nothing, involving in-room movies, popcorn, and a copy of the book of the same name. Etherea Salon.Spa is the on-site destination for pampering, but in-room spa services are also possible. Literary mavens should consider the Author's Suite, featuring a jetted tub, an antique writing desk, and a fireplace flanked by bookshelves filled with the works of celebrated writers: no Reader's Digest Condensed Books here. Guests can dine at the Library Bistro (206/624-3646; www.librarybistro.com), offering breakfast, brunch, and lunch only; or the Bookstore Bar (206/382-1506), a publike space featuring a range of 60-odd scotches and an extensive bar menu. Guests gather in the lobby for daily wine tastings. *$$$–$$$$; AE, DC, DIS, JCB, MC, V; checks OK; www.alexishotel.com.* ♿

Arctic Club Hotel / ❂❂❂

700 3rd Ave, Seattle; 206/340-0340 or 800/323-7500
Opened in 2008, a century after the fraternal Arctic Club was founded by adventurers who struck it rich in the Klondike gold rush, this boutique hotel combines 21st-century amenities with early-20th-century architecture and flavor. Built in 1917 and listed on the National Register of Historic Places, the landmark still boasts the original Alaskan marble–lined foyer and stairways, the grand Northern Lights Dome Room, and 27 signature walrus heads, but has added 120 guest rooms, 32 with jetted baths and 8 with rooftop terraces, plus a restaurant, lounge, and lobby bar. Spacious and masculine, all rooms have such a period feel that you might imagine the likes of detective novelist Dashiell Hammett scribbling out hard-boiled pulp fiction while seated at the

dark-wood writing desk. Situated between the downtown business core and Qwest and Safeco fields, this atmospheric hotel makes a fine spot to create a little Seattle history of your own. *$$$–$$$$; AE, DC, DIS, MC, V; no checks; www.arcticclubhotel.com.* &

Chambered Nautilus Bed and Breakfast Inn / ◐◐❨

5005 22nd Ave NE, Seattle; 206/522-2536
Named one of the Top Ten Urban B&Bs in 2007 by *USA Today*, this spot is ideal for people who want a full-on cozy-inn experience close to the city center. Still, with restaurants and upscale shopping at University Village and movie theaters and museums on the University of Washington campus all reasonably nearby, guests can find plenty to do without ever venturing downtown. The inn offers six guest rooms in the main house—a 1915 Georgian Colonial—and four suites (with private entries and kitchenettes) in an adjacent building across lush gardens surrounded by trees. The most kissably romantic guest room is the Crow's Nest Chamber, with an antique claw-foot tub, a dormer window seat, and a gas fireplace. (All have private baths.) Breakfast is a three-course affair, and with any luck their famous stuffed French toast will be on the menu. *$$–$$$; AE, MC, V; checks OK; www. chamberednautilus.com.*

The Edgewater / ◐◐❨

2411 Alaskan Wy, Pier 67, Seattle; 206/728-7000 or 800/624-0670
In 1964, the Beatles famously dangled fishing poles out the window of Seattle's only waterfront hotel. (Fab Four fans should request the music-and-memorabilia-filled Room 272, also fun for anglophiles.) Not all of the 241 rooms have water views, so request one that looks out on the Olympic Mountains and shimmering Elliott Bay. We especially like the private balconies of the luxe Fourth Floor Executive and Waterfront Junior suites. Decor is national-parks-lodge-style with a designer-fairy-tale twist: river-rock fireplaces, log beds, and antler occasional tables lend a woodsy flavor, and in the common areas you almost expect the faux-tree support columns to magically spring to life. The Northwest-meets-pan-Asian Six Seven restaurant does wonders with seafood, and its dim, comfortable bar, often lively, is a magnet for locals and hotel guests alike. (Did we mention that Led Zeppelin and the Stones stayed here?) *$$$–$$$$; AE, DC, DIS, MC, V; checks OK; www. edgewaterhotel.com.*

11th Avenue Inn / ◐◐❨

121 11th Ave E, Seattle; 206/720-7161 or 800/720-7161
Befitting this stately 1906 home, furnishings are vintage or antique without being fussy. Persian rugs lie atop honey-gold hardwood floors, and tastefully plush linens cozy up to carved headboards, some delightfully elaborate. Guest rooms are named for gemstones. We like the peekaboo skyline view

from the Topaz Room, the rosy glow of the Garnet Room (which has a tub instead of just a shower, as does the Amethyst Room), but the spacious Opal Room—with its daybed and diamond-shaped window in the bathroom—is the most appealing. (Only the Ruby and Emerald share a bath.) Breakfasts in the grand dining room are lavish and might feature cinnamon-bread French toast one morning, spinach and feta omelets topped with pesto cream the next. For other meals there are dozens of restaurants of all descriptions and price ranges within easy walking distance, and in this densely populated neighborhood, the free, on-site parking is a real boon. *$$–$$$; AE, MC, V; no checks; www.11thavenueinn.com.*

Fairmont Olympic Hotel / ✪✪✪✪

411 University St, Seattle; 206/621-1700 or 800/441-1414
A grande dame of Seattle lodging, the Olympic opened to great fanfare in 1924 and has been a favorite ever since, garnering its 23rd consecutive AAA Five Diamond designation in 2007. Following a 2005 renovation, the lobby is more sumptuous than ever. All 450 rooms and suites combine old-world elegance with modern conveniences, but what sets this hotel apart is the exacting and exemplary staff. Despite a very central location near most of Seattle's major attractions, the Olympic is a world unto itself: there's a top-notch fitness center (with 42-foot indoor pool), 24-hour room service, and a range of dining and drinking options, from a piano bar (The Terrace) to the oak-paneled Shuckers, to the grand chandeliered Georgian (see Romantic Restaurants), serving dinner and afternoon tea. The Do Not Disturb package is a recipe for romance, including champagne and chocolate-dipped strawberries, a four-course tasting menu in the Georgian, breakfast in bed, late checkout, and storage of all intrusive electronic devices. *$$$$; AE, DC, DIS, JCB, MC, V; checks OK; www.fairmont.com/seattle.* ♿

Four Seasons Hotel / ✪✪✪✪

99 Union St, Seattle; 800/819-5053
One of the most contemporary in design among all Four Seasons properties, this five-star hotel is Seattle's most desirable new destination (opened in 2008), and the location could hardly be better. Drawing you in, a grand lobby leads to the spacious restaurant, raw bar, and lounge, and there's also a spa, with services available to guests and residents (luxury condominiums occupy floors 11–21). Sheltered by the building on three sides, the pool deck, with whirlpool and cozy fire pit, faces Elliott Bay and the Olympics. Clean lines and a light color palette in guest accommodations serve to accent the spectacular views that lie beyond floor-to-ceiling windows. All 145 rooms (13 of them suites) feature sinfully comfortable beds and two-person bathtubs, so you can enjoy a soak with your dearest. (If that weren't entertainment enough, televisions are embedded in the bathroom mirrors!) The

Presidential Suite has one of the best vistas two people in love could hope for. *$$$$; AE, DC, DIS, JCB, MC, V; checks OK; www.fourseasons.com.* &

Greenlake Guesthouse / ❷❷❷

7630 E Greenlake Dr N, Seattle; 206/729-8700 or 866/355-8700
Situated beside one of the city's most popular destinations, the four tastefully appointed guest rooms in this 1920 Craftsman differ slightly in character and amenities. Cozily romantic without being fussy, Parkview, our favorite, has a picture window facing the lake. The largest of the rooms, it features a sitting area with a daybed and jetted tub for two with a separate shower. Though it can be hard to leave your oh-so-comfortable bed in the morning, the full gourmet breakfast (including freshly baked pastries and favorites like Swedish pancakes and omelets) served in the communal dining room isn't to be missed—nor is a Green Lake stroll: it's one of the must-do Seattle pastimes. *$$–$$$; DIS, MC, V; no checks; www.greenlakeguesthouse.com.*

Hill House Bed and Breakfast / ❷❷❸

1113 E John St, Seattle; 206/323-4455 or 866/417-4455
Located within strolling distance of Volunteer Park and numerous restaurants, this beautifully renovated 1903 Victorian home houses five guest rooms, two of which make perfect secluded getaways: Bordeaux and Madras, the two spacious garden suites, feature handsome, mostly understated decor; fluffy down comforters; pressed bed linens; sofas; private, period-tiled bathrooms; and separate entrances. (Two of the three other rooms, Rose and Celadon, share a bath.) One of three common areas, the back porch provides a relaxing spot to bask on a warm summer's day. Served on a lace-topped table in the bright dining room, breakfast begins with fresh fruit and includes hot dishes like smoked-salmon omelets, eggs Florentine, and French toast. Off-street parking is a welcome amenity on crowded Capitol Hill. *$$–$$$; AE, DC, DIS, MC, V; no checks; www.seatttlehillhouse.com.*

Hotel Andra / ❷❷❷❸

2000 4th Ave, Seattle; 206/448-8600 or 877/448-8600
Simultaneously minimalist and urbane, warm and sexy, this Scandinavian-inspired hotel displays elemental neutrals (mustard, taupe, slate, olive, brushed stainless steel, and dark wood) accented by brighter colors and splashy geometric prints—think Ikea, but upscale. Andra's guests so love the luxe Italian bed linens that the hotel has made them available for purchase. Not all of the 119 rooms and suites are created equal, though: boasting a two-person Jacuzzi with a city view, the bathroom alone makes the Monarch Suite a picture-perfect splurge for any special occasion, but some rooms are a bit dreary. Book the Romantik package and you'll find chilled champagne and gourmet organic chocolates awaiting your arrival. Located right downstairs are two of our favorite Seattle restaurants—Tom Douglas's homage

to Greek cuisine, Lola (206/441-1430), whose sleek little bar connects to the hotel's lobby, and Mauro Golmarvi's Assaggio Ristorante (see Romantic Restaurants), a beloved Italian destination. Looking for a little retail therapy? The downtown shopping core is just a couple of blocks away. $$$–$$$$; AE, DIS, MC, V; no checks; www.hotelandra.com. ￡

Hotel Deca / ❍❍❍

4507 Brooklyn Ave NE, Seattle; 206/634-2000 or 800/899-0251
Located conveniently near downtown, this Art Deco–era hotel is a good choice for a getaway—minus hefty downtown price tags. A $2 million renovation was completed in January 2007. Still, the smallest of the refurbished 158 guest rooms are small indeed, so we suggest upgrading to a Junior Suite, or, for supreme luxury, splurge for the 16th-floor Presidential Suite: it boasts contemporary furnishings, a wet bar and kitchen, and a 1,000-square-foot patio with extraordinary views of downtown, Lake Washington, and Mount Rainier. Deca offers seductive package deals, too, like the Deca Romantik, with champagne and box of inspiring treats. Immediate surroundings offer little nightlife, but travel west on 45th Street for great dining options, including Joule (1913 N 45th St; 206/632-1913; www.joulerestaurant.com) and award-winning chef Maria Hines's delightful Tilth (1411 N 45th St; 206/633-0801; www.tilthrestaurant.com). The hotel provides free shuttle service within a 4-mile radius, depending upon availability. $$–$$$; AE, DC, DIS, MC, V; checks OK; www.hoteldeca.com.

Hotel Max / ❍❍❍

620 Stewart St, Seattle; 206/728-6299 or 866/833-6299
Contemporary art and music lovers should consider Hotel Max, a hipper-than-thou hostelry that showcases local and nationally known artists with more than 350 original paintings and photographs displayed throughout the premises. Sporting monochromatic backgrounds punched up with tangerine and tomato, the 163 guest rooms are more cool than posh, but all offer plush robes and a pillow menu. The fifth floor is dedicated to Seattle grunge: the Rock This Way package includes a room, two passes to Experience Music Project, and a CD to keep. The Hubba-Hubba Hanky Panky Romance package comes with a bottle of Washington wine and Seattle Chocolates. You're in the thick of it as far as shopping, theaters, and restaurants go, and the hotel's Red Fin (206/441-4340; www.redfinsushi.com) is a stylishly appointed Asian-fusion restaurant with memorable sushi, cocktail, and sake menus. $$$–$$$$; AE, DC, DIS, JCB, MC, V; no checks; www.hotelmaxseattle.com. ￡

Hotel Monaco / ❍❍❍

1101 4th Ave, Seattle; 206/621-1770 or 800/945-2240
No one can accuse Hotel Monaco of having a bland, cookie-cutter personality: its vibrant decor is opulent yet whimsical—sort of Louis XIV meets

The Court Jester (the 1955 Danny Kaye classic) with a soupçon of Salvador Dali. Standing in the plush lobby, you're James Bond on the way to the baccarat table in a Monte Carlo casino. We're perfectly happy with the Monte Carlo Suite, or the Mediterranean or Majestic suites, which have two-person jetted tubs. In keeping with the Euro-hip theme, L'Occitane toiletries are in each of the 189 rooms, along with animal-print bathrobes. The hotel is pet friendly; you can even ask to have a goldfish delivered to your room for company. By all means sup at Sazerac (206/624-7755; www.sazeracrestaurant. com) for a little boisterous southern comfort (we love the flash-fried catfish with lemon whipped potatoes) or a single-barrel bourbon. *$$$$; AE, DC, DIS, JCB, MC, V; no checks; www.monaco-seattle.com.*

Hotel 1000 / ✪✪✪✪

1000 1st Ave, Seattle; 206/957-1000
The beauty of this luxe boutique hotel is that it appeals equally to hi-tech aficionados and true romantics. Dark wood and rich, earthy hues impart a serene, Zen-inspired aesthetic, and in each room rotating selections of art and music on a 40-inch high-def LCD television let you tailor the mood. Light and temperature control is at your fingertips and, registering body heat, infrared sensors ensure you won't be interrupted by housekeeping as you laze between smooth damask sheets. Witty and diverting volumes, like *Schott's Original Miscellany*, grace the bedside table. Bathing is a particular delight: featured in most rooms, big-enough-for-two tubs fill from the ceiling so there's no hardware to impede relaxation. (From Grand Luxe Room 1402, for example, it's possible to bask with a breathtaking view.) If you can't tear yourselves away from the in-room amenities for dinner at the sexy BOKA Kitchen + Bar downstairs (see Romantic Restaurants), there's room service—prompt and always gracious. *$$$–$$$$; AE, DC, DIS, MC, V; checks OK; www.hotel 1000seattle.com.* &

Hotel Vintage Park / ✪✪✪

1100 5th Ave, Seattle; 206/624-8000 or 800/853-3914
Paying homage to the exploding Washington wine industry, this European-style hostelry appeals to dedicated oenophiles and wine dabblers alike. Dubbed one of the world's 100 sexiest hotels (by Sexy, Inc. in 2005), the Vintage Park is located near shopping and numerous attractions. All 126 rooms are elegantly appointed in neutral tones, with sumptuous linens and accents in tapestry, velvet, and leather; but arguably the most kissable is the Chateau Ste. Michelle Suite, with a four-poster bed, Jacuzzi for two, and cozy fireplace. The chef concierge organizes the daily wine receptions (often with winemakers in attendance—Vintage Park has more than a hundred winery partners) and plans unforgettable wine-country adventures. Pooch friendly, the hotel arranges dog-sitting services and offers grape-shaped doggie treats during the whine—ahem, wine—hour. Humans, however, prefer the rustic Italian fare

served at Tulio Ristorante (206/624-5500; www.tulio.com), one of Seattle's most respected restaurants and a wonderful setting for a romantic meal. *$$$; AE, DC, DIS, JCB, MC, V; no checks; www.hotelvintagepark.com.*

The Inn at El Gaucho / ❂❂❂

2505 1st Ave, Seattle; 206/728-1133 or 866/354-2824
Glorious things often come in small packages (diamonds, for instance!). With only 18 junior suites, this hotel above Seattle's swankest steakhouse is the very definition of *boutique*. Book the Romance Package or create your own: except for corner units, the masculine, Tuscan-toned rooms aren't expansive, but they *are* richly appointed, with leather furnishings, luxurious linens, exceptionally comfortable beds, the coziest of robes, Riedel stemware, and plasma TVs. Request either room 8 or 9 if you'd like an Elliott Bay view. The inn is ideally situated for an exploration of Belltown and the Pike Place Market, but there's really no need to leave the premises, what with El Gaucho (see Romantic Restaurants), the Pampas Room (90 Wall St; 206/728-1337), and the Big Picture (an intimate cinema that serves cocktails but is not connected to the inn or restaurants) just steps from your door. *$$$; AE, DC, DIS, MC, V; checks OK; http://inn.elgaucho.com.*

Inn at the Market / ❂❂❂

86 Pine St, Seattle; 206/443-3600 or 800/446-4484
For both tourists and locals desiring a quintessentially Seattle weekend getaway, this perennially popular setting can't be beat. Among the 70 guest rooms, those above the fifth floor have views, and those facing west boast tall windows that open to usher in the breeze and market bustle, but the best special-occasion choice is the elegant and understated Parlor Suite, with king-size bed, sitting room, wet bar, and microwave. Atop the seasonal rooftop terrace (one of the city's best-kept secrets), guests are invited to bring breakfast pastries or a picnic: after all, some of the finest, freshest foodstuffs available can be procured just steps from the hotel's front door. Sip glasses of bubbly and steal a kiss or three with the Olympic Mountains and sparkling Elliott Bay as a cinematic backdrop. You needn't travel far for a romantic repast, either. Two of our favorites, Campagne and Café Campagne (see Romantic Restaurants) are right next door. *$$$–$$$$; AE, DC, DIS, JCB, MC, V; checks OK; www.innatthemarket.com.*

Olympic View Bed and Breakfast / ❂❂❂❰

2705 SW 164th Pl, Seattle; 206/243-6900
Although the Olympic View Bed and Breakfast is technically located within Seattle city limits, romantics looking for a quick getaway from their hectic city lives will feel worlds away. Once you see the B&B's stunning views of the Puget Sound and the Olympics, you'll find it hard to believe the house is only 10 minutes west of Sea-Tac Airport. And for couples seeking seclusion,

the house is occupied by only one party at a time, which means a soak in the deck's hot tub is a totally private affair. The fully equipped kitchen inside and barbeque outside encourage guests to bring along groceries for lunch and dinner (breakfast is provided). Plan to cook a romantic meal and sit out on the patio in one of the Seattle area's most beautiful natural settings. The closest town is Burien, which isn't all that appealing, but who'd ever want to leave such a gorgeous hideaway anyhow? *$$$; MC, V; checks OK; www. olympicviewbb.com.*

Pan Pacific Hotel / ●●●

2125 Terry Ave, Seattle; 206/264-8111 or 877/324-4856
The only Washington hotel named to Condé Nast Traveler's Hot List Hotels 2007, this luxurious boutique property of 160 rooms is characterized by serene, Japanese-influenced design and exemplary, personalized service. In each corner king room, a soaking tub—sadly, tight quarters for two—is separated from the bedroom with a sliding shoji screen, so guests can bathe with a view through expansive windows. We're unapologetically enamored with the spacious 14th-floor Denny Suite, a bona fide splurge. From here you can gaze at one of the most captivating vistas offered by any Seattle hotel: to the west are the Space Needle and (sometimes) breathtaking sunsets over the Olympic Range, and, to the north, Lake Union and a snow-capped Mount Baker. (Plan ahead and book the Fourth of July for front-row seats to both of Seattle's spectacular fireworks displays.) There's a full-service spa, a fitness center, a Whole Foods market (206/621-9700), and an outpost of a favorite Seattle pizzeria, Tutta Bella (206/624-4422; www.tuttabella.com), sharing the premises. *$$$$; AE, DC, DIS, JCB, MC, V; no checks; http://seattle. panpacific.com.*

Salisbury House / ●●◖

750 16th Ave E, Seattle; 206/328-8682
This stately 1904 prairie-style home offers a peaceful retreat on a tree-lined street, even though it's only a block off bustling 15th Avenue. Each of the second-floor guest rooms is a corner room with private bath, sharing a sun porch with a refrigerator. On the lower level is the generous Salisbury Suite, larger than many apartments and the only option with cable television and VCR. It also has a 6-foot whirlpool bath, but if agitation isn't essential, the Lavender Room has a 6-foot-long claw-foot soaking tub. For an extra charge, the Romance Package includes chocolates and a dozen roses. Served in the formal dining room overlooking the lush garden, family-style breakfasts are meatless affairs, but it's hard to miss bacon when there's orange croissant French toast on offer. *$$–$$$; AE, MC, V; checks OK; www. salisburyhouse.com.*

Sorrento Hotel / ✿✿✿

900 Madison St, Seattle; 206/622-6400 or 800/426-1265
Grand architecture is in short supply in Seattle, which is why we so love the Italianate elegance of the century-old Sorrento. Surrounded as it is by the medical facilities on First Hill (referred to as Pill Hill by locals) it's hard to appreciate the glorious, embracing exterior, but inside, the richly appointed decor more than compensates. As long as you're content to bask in the romantic ambience of the Hunt Club (see Romantic Restaurants) or the octagonal Fireside Room—one of Seattle's most desirable destinations for afternoon tea, live piano music, and evening cocktails—a standard guest room will suffice, but for ultimate kissability, only a suite will do. We prefer a Corner King or the Music Suite, filled with memorabilia (including a signed guitar from legendary rock band The Who) sure to delight avid music lovers. The Penthouse is the crème de la crème of opulence. With an outdoor-view terrace, a fireplace, a baby grand piano, and a two-person fill-from-the-ceiling jetted tub, you'll never want to leave. Be sure to request a lift in the hotel's courtesy car, a genuine, retrofitted London Black Cab. *$$$$; AE, DC, DIS, JCB, MC, V; checks OK; www.hotelsorrento.com.*

W Seattle Hotel / ✿✿✿

1112 4th Ave, Seattle; 206/624-6000 or 877/W-HOTELS
By mid-2010 there will be nearly three dozen W Hotels open worldwide, so this chain's popularity shows no sign of abating. Keep in mind, however, this is a hotel aimed at the young (or, at least, the young at heart). A hip, urban soundtrack pulses throughout the modern premises and lighting is shadowy and dim. Rooms are plentiful (426 to be exact), but request a higher floor to ensure a city view. That said, with the comfort of your Heavenly Bed, topped with goose-down duvets and smooth white linens, you're not likely to spend much time gazing out the window. Adjacent to the hotel's Earth & Ocean (206/624-6060) restaurant, the bar proffers sexy cocktails to pair with Sexy Fries. If you want more than the standard chocolate-and-champagne package, on-staff Passioneers will arrange romance enhancements, from in-room massages to dinner for two by candlelight. *$$$$; AE, DC, DIS, JCB, MC, V; checks OK; www.whotels.com.*

Romantic Restaurants

Andaluca / ✿✿✿

407 Olive Wy (Mayflower Park Hotel), Seattle; 206/382-6999
If some restaurants seem too cavernous for romance and others a bit cramped, this richly hued jewel box is just right, even for a first date. Andaluca has plenty of booths that are cozily intimate even when fellow diners raise the volume level. The seasonal Mediterranean menu's focus stays mainly on Spain, but Italian and French influences are present, including a wine list that

Where to Get a Really Good Drink

Some evenings seem better suited for sipping than noshing. While elaborate specialty drink menus are increasingly commonplace, a handful of bars stand out from the crowd for their classic, beautifully crafted cocktails, a seductive atmosphere, or both. Make a beeline for **Zig Zag Cafe** (1501 Western Ave, #202, Pike Place Market; 206/625-1146; www.zigzagseattle.com), where legendary, award-winning bartender Murray "Murr the Blur" Stenson holds court. Next to the 5th Avenue Theatre, **Vessel** (1312 5th Ave, Downtown; 206/652-5222; www.vesselseattle.com) has a mod two-story vibe, a list of historic drinks, and an array of house-made bitters, skillfully employed. Attached to Le Gourmand, the postage-stamp-size **Sambar** (see Romantic Restaurants) boasts house-infused spirits, select rums, and a cozy warm-weather patio. Little sister to John Sundstrom's delightful **Lark** (see Romantic Restaurants) next door, **Licorous** (928 12th Ave, Capitol Hill; 206/325-6047; www.licorous.com) is a destination in its own right, pairing bites and small plates with inventive concoctions. The bar at **Canlis Restaurant** (see Romantic Restaurants) offers live piano music, flawless service, a breathtaking view, and top-notch cocktails, all at a fraction of the price of an evening spent in the dining room. Known for its Really Big 'Tinis, some refined, some downright wacky, **Tini Bigs** (100 Denny Wy, Queen Anne; 206/284-0931; www.tinibigs.com) is a sexy joint tailor-made for sitting close and canoodling with your date.

also offers sherries and plenty of domestic bottles. The must-order dish is the signature Cabrales-blue-cheese-crusted beef tenderloin (with grilled pears, Marsala demi-glace, and Idiazabal mashed potatoes); paella comes a close second. Take time to wander through the lobby to Oliver's Lounge (206/623-8700; www.mayflowerpark.com) for a prize-winning martini. This elegant, high-ceilinged showcase of a bar makes a wonderful spot to sit hand-in-hand, sipping a pre- or postdinner libation. *$$$; AE, DC, DIS, MC, V; local checks only; breakfast, dinner every day, lunch Mon–Fri; full bar; reservations recommended; www.andaluca.com.* &

Assaggio Ristorante / ○○○◐

2010 4th Ave, Seattle; 206/441-1399
From the moment you set foot in the door you feel the amore, the welcoming tone set by executive chef and owner Mauro Golmarvi. More often than not, he's at the entrance, hailing guests with infectious gusto. High walls are graced by stunning, subtly toned reproductions of works by painters Michelangelo and Fra Lippo Lippi. Tables are positioned close together, and when

the restaurant's full—which it usually is—the atmosphere is boisterous, so unless you luck into a booth this may not be the best choice for intimate conversation or a first date. Is the cuisine cutting edge? Nah. This is comfort food, Italian-style. Preparations are simple and simply perfect for sharing, from the *caprese* salad and *insalata di Stefano* (with apples, fennel, pecorino, and truffle oil) to classic fettuccine bolognese and veal piccata. The wine list reaches beyond Tuscany to feature bottles from more obscure Italian regions. *$$–$$$; AE, DC, DIS, MC, V; no checks; lunch Mon–Fri, dinner Mon–Sat; full bar; reservations recommended; www.assaggioseattle.com.* &

Barolo Ristorante / ○○○(

1940 Westlake Ave, Seattle; 206/770-9000
My, what a stunning room. Modern curves and tall windows are softened by gauzy curtains, twinkling chandeliers reflected in oversize mirrors, and dripping candles that lend an almost medieval quality to the ambience. They're open for lunch and offer a terrific happy hour, but after dark is when Barolo really shines. To optimize kissing potential, either head to the far end of the bar or request a rounded, soft-to-the-touch booth. It's hardly surprising that the wine list is heavily Italian and predominantly red, but there's also a fine grappa collection. We love the gnocchi, but few plates can rival the *tortelloni alla Piemontese*, filled with porcini mushrooms and topped with creamy truffle-leek sauce. And not like we're encouraging anything indecorous, but the *gabinetti* are among the sexiest in town. For a more traditional Italian atmosphere, visit Barolo's older sister, Mamma Melina (4759 Roosevelt Wy NE; 206/632-2271; www.mammamelina.com). *$$–$$$; AE, DIS, MC, V; no checks; lunch Mon–Fri, dinner every day; full bar; reservations recommended; www.baroloseattle.com.* &

Beàto / ○○(

3247 California Ave SW, West Seattle; 206/923-1333
West Seattle boasts many laudable restaurants, some with spectacular views, but intimacy-inspiring dining is in short supply. Beàto (pronounced "bay-AH-tow," meaning "blessed" in Italian) is an elegant room with dark wood, sunny walls, and a six-seat wine bar—though we're more comfortable at banquette tables. Theirs is an extraordinarily comprehensive Italian wine list, with selections from all 20 regions. The assortment of cheeses and meats on the *piatti misto* is a fine place to start, and bread is from Bakery Nouveau (see Romantic Highlights). Oxtail ragù, with house-made fettuccine and truffle oil, is a must-order signature dish. Sample chocolate ravioli for dessert, if for the novelty alone. *$$; AE, MC, V; no checks; dinner Tues–Sun; beer and wine; reservations recommended; www.beatoseattle.com.* &

Bleu Bistro / ●●◖
Chez Gaudy / ●●

202 Broadway E, Seattle; 206/329-3087
1802 Bellevue Ave, Seattle; 206/329-4047
Though it sees its share of "Bleu-curious" one-time visitors, Bleu Bistro is predominantly a scenester date spot. Its slightly dive-y appearance is part teenage rec room, part adults-only fun house, and there's a party-ready soundtrack to match. Things are G-rated early in the evening, but later on, the cubby-hole tables, tucked around corners and concealed behind velvet drapes, become settings for pettings (ranging from fairly innocuous entanglements to second base and beyond). Sister venue Chez Gaudy, notoriously difficult to locate, has minimal signage and an off-street screen-door entrance. Like Bleu, the layout is labyrinthine. Tiny tables are squeezed into nooks so cozy it's almost impossible to avoid holding hands and playing footsie. On Tuesday *tapas* nights business is brisk, bolstered by bargain-priced bottles of wine. Menus at both locations feature long lists of eccentric cocktails and Italian-ish, mostly vegetarian dishes. *$$ (Bleu Bistro), $$ (Chez Gaudy); AE, DIS, MC, V; no checks; lunch, dinner Wed–Sun (Bleu Bistro), dinner Tues–Sun (Chez Gaudy); full bar; reservations recommended.*

BOKA Kitchen + Bar / ●●●◖

1010 1st Ave (Hotel 1000), Seattle; 206/957-1000
If Hollywood producers wanted to cast a restaurant with irresistible sex appeal and an ingenue's blush of youth, BOKA wouldn't even have to audition. Lounge and dining room curve together seamlessly, with rich textures and backlit walls that rotate through a spectrum of soothing hues, bathing guests in every most flattering light. Happily, food and drink measure up to the trendy trappings. The wine list is expertly honed, and signature cocktails are fun and flirty, particularly the aptly named Fresh, made with gin, cucumber, mint, lime, and soda. BOKA's laurels justifiably rest on its sharable "urban bites" and small plates, from truffle fries to short-rib sliders on biscuits, panko-crusted mac 'n' cheese to the house signature Dungeness crab mini-cornbread cupcakes topped with crème fraîche frosting—a sweet-savory flavor sensation that could masquerade as dessert. *$$$; AE, DC, DIS, MC, V; checks OK; lunch Mon–Fri, dinner every day, brunch Sat–Sun; full bar; reservations recommended; www.bokaseattle.com.* &

Campagne / ●●●
Café Campagne / ●●◖

86 Pine St (Inn at the Market), Seattle; 206/728-2800
1600 Post Alley, Seattle; 206/728-2233
Established in 1985, Campagne is a quietly romantic room that offers French-country ambience without clobbering you with quaintness, and the winning

details, from fresh flowers and candles to servers de-crumbing crisp linens between courses, are present and accounted for. It's long been a favorite with locals, tourists, and visiting film stars, and the sheltered courtyard is one of the city's best locales for alfresco dining. Looking over Post Alley, the bar is a civilized perch for the hip and trendy to see and be seen. It's also a wonderful place to linger with a date, sharing a bottle of Bordeaux over a lamb burger and steak *frites*. Café Campagne is the casual younger sister, a great launching pad for a weekend market crawl. Wood banquettes and vintage French posters lend an authentic Parisian flavor, as do the *croque monsieur* and eye-rollingly satisfying *oeufs en meurette*, and they also do a classic *cassoulet* in cool months, for you to eat in or take home. For lovers of French wines, the respective lists read like a gripping novel: we love that the cafe loves rosés and offers all glass wines by the taste, too. *$$$ (Campagne), $$ (Café Campagne); AE, DC, MC, V; no checks; dinner every day (Campagne), lunch Mon–Fri, dinner every day, brunch Sat–Sun (Café Campagne); full bar; reservations recommended; www.campagnerestaurant.com.*

Canlis Restaurant / ❂❂❂❂

2576 Aurora Ave N, Seattle; 206/283-3313
How do we love thee? Let us count the ways. A Seattle institution since 1950, Canlis is recognized as exceptional on all levels, from location and architecture to menu, service, and the world-class 15,000-bottle cellar that has garnered the Wine Spectator Grand Award every year for a decade. Linger over the signature Canlis Salad and Peter Canlis Prawns, Wagyu tenderloin and Muscovy duck breast. Finishing with Grand Marnier soufflé is de rigueur. The kitchen is happy to honor special requests, from nostalgic recipes to vegan tasting menus. Indubitably one of the most romantic nooks in all of Seattle, the Cache is an upstairs corner space for two that comes with a chaise, a telescope, a sound system, its own server, and panoramic views of Lake Union and the Cascades. Naturally, the full-on Canlis experience doesn't come cheap, so if dinner isn't in the cards, soak in the ambience from the lounge over drinks and appetizers while enjoying the live piano music. *$$$$; AE, DC, DIS, MC, V; checks OK; dinner Mon–Sat; full bar; reservations required; www.canlis.com.* &

Chez Shea and Shea's Lounge / ❂❂❂❂

94 Pike St, Ste 34, Seattle; 206/467-9990
One of Seattle's sweetest date destinations, Chez Shea, tucked above Pike Place Market, utterly lacks street presence, which is part of its charm: you feel like you're in on a best-kept secret. Tables are topped with crisp linens, fresh flowers, and candles, and if you're lucky you'll be seated at a cushioned banquette beneath one of the large, semi-circular windows. Order à la carte from the seasonal, French-inspired menu, which might feature mushroom-leek tart, beet carpaccio, sweetbreads, Sonoma foie gras, or pan-seared Arctic

char, or go all out on an eight-course tasting menu with paired wines. A more relaxing choice for a first date might be the adjacent Shea's Lounge, featuring a short-but-sweet bar menu and three-course prix-fixe dinner, not to mention tasty and tasteful cocktails. *$$–$$$; AE, MC, V; no checks; dinner Tues–Sun; full bar; reservations recommended; www.chezshea.com.*

Crush / ✪✪✪

2319 E Madison St, Seattle; 206/302-7874
What better stratagem than to bring a first—or seventh—date to an establishment called Crush? Chef/owner Jason Wilson and his wife, Nicole, gave this 100-plus-year-old Tudor house a crisp, contemporary conversion, and the vibe is youthful and hip. Romantics take note: Crush is crushingly popular, so for a quieter experience we suggest avoiding weekends. Surprisingly comfortable, the restaurant's modern, molded chairs don't exactly facilitate canoodling, but the lighting is flattering, and it's easy to steal a kiss on the warm-weather patio or in the cheek-by-jowl bar. Order an expertly crafted cocktail, particularly anything involving house-infused pear vodka—it'll buy some time to peruse the lengthy global wine list. And then there's the menu, a seasonally rotating, locally and artisanally inspired odyssey that garnered Wilson a Best New Chef Award from *Food & Wine* in 2006. *$$$; AE, DIS, MC, V; no checks; dinner Tues–Sat; full bar; reservations recommended; www. crushonmadison.com.* ⅋

Dahlia Lounge / ✪✪✪

2001 4th Ave, Seattle; 206/682-4142
The most romantic of Tom Douglas's restaurant quintet (which includes Etta's Seafood, Palace Kitchen, Lola, and Serious Pie), Dahlia has crimson walls, cozy booths, Chinese lanterns, and some of the most polished servers in Seattle. Booths are preferable, most secluded if you're seated at the north end of the dining room. The Northwest Asian–inspired menu changes daily, but seafood is always a good bet, such as wild Alaskan salmon or Dungeness crab cakes, a signature. As far as sweets go, we'd come here for the half-dozen mini sugar-cinnamon doughnuts alone, served hot in a paper bag with jam and vanilla mascarpone on the side, but one of the most famous desserts in the city is Tom Douglas's coconut cream pie. Rich yet light, it's ideal for sharing, and if you want to take one home, stop into Dahlia Bakery next door (206/441-4540). *$$$; AE, DC, DIS, MC, V; no checks; lunch Mon–Fri, dinner every day; full bar; reservations recommended; www.tomdouglas.com.* ⅋

El Gaucho / ✪✪✪✪

2505 1st Ave, Seattle; 206/728-1337
Look up *swank* in the dictionary and the name El Gaucho should be there in boldface type. Hearkening back to a bygone era, it's precisely the sort of place befitting Sinatra and his cronies, commanding the room in exquisitely

tailored haberdashery. Renowned for exemplary service, a world-class wine program, and tableside preparation of dishes like chateaubriand and bananas Foster, this windowless, bilevel steak house can get a bit loud, but not so much as to compromise your evening—particularly from the sensuous comfort of a mink-lined banquette. All this luxury doesn't come cheap, unless you sup exclusively on sides (modestly priced, except for the criminally rich lobster mashed potatoes). If there's live jazz and dancing in the Pampas Room (90 Wall St; 206/728-1337) downstairs, make a complete night of it, especially if you've procured a room at the boutique inn upstairs (see Romantic Lodgings). *$$$–$$$$; AE, DC, DIS, MC, V; checks OK; dinner every day; full bar; reservations recommended; www.elgaucho.com.* &

Fu Kun Wu @ Thaiku / ❂❂❂

5410 Ballard Ave NW, Seattle; 206/706-7807
Popular for its consistently tasty noodle and rice dishes, the dim, exotic Thaiku (www.thaiku.com; lunch, dinner every day) is also home to a deliciously clandestine destination for romance: decorated like an old Chinese apothecary, the bar, Fu Kun Wu, has its own all-but-invisible entrance off 22nd Avenue. You can order plates from Thaiku's menu, but we like to show up during happy hour for reduced-price drinks and appetizers. *Giow tawt*, deep-fried crab and cream cheese wontons, are so good you'll need two orders, and *mieng kahm* wraps aren't to be missed. Some specialty cocktails are laced with the herb *yohimbe*, reputed to be an aphrodisiac so powerful only one per customer is permitted. Downstairs is the private-parties-only Opium Den (once an actual opium den), but even a brief glance into its dim recesses can spark the illicit imagination. *$–$$; AE, DIS, MC, V; no checks; dinner every day; full bar; no reservations; www.fukunwu.com.* &

The Georgian / ❂❂❂❂

411 University St (Fairmont Olympic Hotel), Seattle; 206/621-7889
Sometimes the recipe for romance calls for charming and cozy, but on very special occasions, no less than the grandest, most deliciously decadent dining room in Seattle will do. Sparkling chandeliers. Potted palms. Soaring windows. Sumptuous textiles. Throw on a tiara or double-breasted jacket with gold epaulets and—voilà!—you're transformed into visiting royalty. Tables are strategically arranged to minimize eavesdropping on the sort of intimate conversations that can arise between courses of heirloom tomato consommé, wild sockeye salmon with lobster whipped potatoes, and the Georgian black-and white-chocolate soufflé, a dessert as nattily appointed as the tuxedoed maître d'hôtel. Live jazz on Friday and Saturday nights is a nice, contemporary touch. *$$$–$$$$; AE, DC, DIS, MC, V; checks OK; breakfast, lunch, dinner every day; full bar; reservations recommended; www.fairmont. com/seattle.* &

The Hunt Club and Fireside Room / ✪✪✪

900 Madison St (The Sorrento Hotel), Seattle; 206/343-6156
In 2007, the Hunt Club's decor was updated. A partition between the Honduran mahogany dining room and bar was eliminated, windows were enlarged, and most booths—once prime kissing locales—were removed. While still dark, handsome, and elegant, the intimacy quotient has been somewhat compromised, but thankfully the legendary, octagonal Fireside Room remains one of the most sumptuous places to nuzzle over a coffee nudge, settled into a leather loveseat. Though the dinner menu is less game-heavy than the restaurant's name implies, we enjoy the pan-seared pheasant and Sonoma duck confit when they're on the menu, and Alaskan halibut with saffron-fennel sauce is another favorite entrée. If you really want to pull out all the stops, book the Penthouse Suite, hire a piano player, and enjoy a candlelit dinner on the private terrace. *$$$–$$$$; AE, DC, DIS, MC, V; checks OK; breakfast, dinner every day, lunch Mon–Fri, brunch Sat–Sun; full bar; reservations recommended; www.hotelsorrento.com.* &

Ibiza Dinner Club / ✪✪✪✪

528 2nd Ave, Seattle; 206/381-9090
When it comes to dress-up destinations, Seattle lags behind many (okay, *most*) major cities, but Ibiza provides an excellent reason to dust off those Jimmy Choos. Decor is retro-glam South Beach or Hollywood, with moody lighting, oversize mirrors, white banquettes, dramatic columns, and floor-to-ceiling gauze: tell Mr. DeMille Ibiza's ready for her close-up. On the Spanish-Latin menu, we focus on small plates like the Ibiza tortilla, *croquetas* (fritters filled with serrano ham and Manchego cheese), and seviche martini. Speaking of drinks, cocktails are tantalizing: ever tried Sex on a Mexican Beach? After 9pm, restaurant becomes nightclub, with hip DJs and weekend bouncers, so dine early (or early in the week) for a more conversation-friendly milieu. If you *really* want to impress, reserve the VIP room upstairs and recline on a pillow-laden sofa in semiseclusion. *$$–$$$; AE, MC, V; no checks; dinner Tues–Sat; full bar; reservations recommended; www.ibizadinnerclub.com.*

Il Bistro / ✪✪✪✪

93A Pike St, Seattle; 206/682-3049
There's hardly a more evocative, Euro-atmospheric destination in Seattle, especially on a rainy night, streetlamps glinting off slick cobblestones. (Picture the scene in stark cinematic black and white, Humphrey Bogart sheltering a woman with his overcoat until they step inside, immediately bathed in the golden glow of the lively bar.) In the dining room, arched doorways and ceilings soften the high contrast of creamy walls and dark wood, and candles illuminate diners' faces as they lean close over crisp white napery and sparkling stemware. We favor affordable pastas—such as rigatoni bolognese, pear-gorgonzola ravioli, or lasagne—over the considerably pricier rack

Seattle's Most Enchanting Evening Out

"Love. Chaos. Dinner." That's what **Teatro ZinZanni** promises . . . and delivers. Going strong since 1998 (with a brief hiatus) and staging up to four different productions a year, this isn't grandma's dinner theater in Boca Raton. Inside the lavishly appointed, Belgian-made *Spiegeltent* ("mirror tent"), seated at tables and nestled in booths, guests act as participants throughout the three-hour cabaret extravaganza, engaged and mesmerized by a dozen or so expert performers (musicians, singers, dancers, acrobats, clowns, jugglers, magicians, comedians—whatever the theme requires), whose myriad talents include serving the five-course gourmet meal (designed by Seattle's favorite chef, Tom Douglas). Paired wine flights are optional, and there's a full bar, specialty cocktail menu, and wine list by bottle or glass. The mistress of ceremonies is Madame ZinZanni, a role that in the past has been filled by the likes of disco-diva Thelma Houston, Ann Wilson (of the band Heart), Sally Kellerman ("Hot Lips Houlihan" in Robert Altman's *M*A*S*H*), and Tony award–winning French actress Liliane Montevecchi. Following dessert, audience members are encouraged to kiss a pair of lips "other than the ones you came with," ending the night on a doubly sweet note. Whether you're on a first date or celebrating a milestone anniversary, a trip to ZinZanni is sure to be unforgettable. *222 Mercer St at 3rd Ave N, Queen Anne; 206/802-0015; http://dreams.zinzanni.org; Wed–Sat 6:30pm, Sun 5:30pm; reservations recommended.*

of lamb. With advance notice, staff members are happy to rise to a special occasion, but steer clear of weekends if you're looking for the most intimate rendezvous possible. *$$$; AE, DC, DIS, MC, V; no checks; dinner every day; full bar; reservations recommended; www.ilbistro.net.*

Il Terrazzo Carmine / ❂❂❤

411 1st Ave S, Seattle; 206/467-7797
Restaurants come and go, but few have the consistency and staying power of Il Terrazzo, which has enjoyed a loyal following since opening in 1984. Though ensconced inside an office building, the bar and airy dining room feel far removed from their surroundings, with the namesake terrace making a delightful—if somewhat noisy—urban refuge in warm weather (especially following an afternoon game at nearby Safeco Field). Roasted rack of lamb, sweetbreads, veal, and pork chops are standouts among meat offerings on the predominantly traditional Northern Italian menu, and popular pastas include *linguine alla vongole* and pennette with smoked salmon, peas, and

cream. Over the years, owner Carmine Smeraldo has honed his 300-plus bottle wine list to a shapely work of art. *$$$; AE, DIS, MC, V; no checks; lunch Mon–Fri, dinner Mon–Sat; full bar; reservations recommended; www. ilterrazzocarmine.com.* &

Lark / ⬢⬢❰

926 12th Ave, Seattle; 206/323-5275
Opened to immediate acclaim by chef John Sundstrom, Kelly Rowan, and J. M. Enos, Lark possesses rustic-elegant charm, but the real thrill is less in the surroundings and more on the plate. Sundstrom works with local farmers, fishers, and foragers to provide the best bounty of every season: designed for sharing, his small-plates menu offers delights that illustrate, bite after ethereal bite, why he was named 2007's Best Chef in the Northwest by the James Beard Foundation. If there's a wait—and there often is—head next door to Licorous (206/325-6947; www.licorous.com), Lark's sexy sibling lounge offering inventive, tasty snacks and tastier cocktails, the best of which feature house-infused spirits. There's a chance you'll get so comfortable you'll save Lark for another time. *$$–$$$; MC, V; local checks only; dinner Tues–Sun; full bar; no reservations; www.larkseattle.com.* &

Le Gourmand and Sambar / ⬢⬢⬢❰

425 NW Market St, Seattle; 206/784-3463
From a decidedly unassuming exterior, you step into the twinkling candlelight of a country garden–inspired dining room, the surrounding neighborhood completely screened from view. Some consider the decor more shabby-chic fusty than romantic, but nobody's here for the ambience. The attraction is gastronomic—the freshest of Northwest ingredients, many of them foraged, prepared with near-impeccable French technique. Passionate chef/owner Bruce Naftaly, who keeps his own kitchen garden, is a king of rich sauces and deep flavors. Highlights include rabbit liver pâté, intricately poached salmon, sheep's milk cheese blintzes, and nettle soup. Sara Naftaly makes the irresistible sweets, from crème brûlée to profiteroles. Ideal for a post-meal *digestif* or a visit all on its own, Sambar (206/781-4883; closed Sun), the hip, tiny adjoining lounge, offers a kiss-friendly summertime patio and meticulously crafted cocktails and snacks, including *frites* that even the snootiest Belgian would inhale. *$$$ (Le Gourmand), $$ (Sambar); AE, MC, V; checks OK; dinner Wed–Sat (Le Gourmand), dinner Mon–Sat (Sambar); full bar; reservations recommended.*

Matt's in the Market / ⬢⬢

94 Pike St, Ste 32, Seattle; 206/467-7909
An expansion completed in summer 2007 means that getting a table here is slightly—only *slightly*, mind you—less difficult than it used to be. Decor isn't inherently smooch-inspiring but the location is: from the second story in

the Corner Market Building, broad demilune windows look down upon the market's entrance and out to Elliott Bay, and after dusk, the room is bathed in the crimson glow of the Public Market sign. The rotating lunch and dinner menus at Matt's take advantage of the freshest that fishers, farmers, and foragers can provide, so it's hard to go wrong, but the kitchen truly excels with seafood. Finish with *tarte Tatin*, if it's available. Due to its popularity, this isn't the place to dine if you're in a hurry. *$$$; MC, V; no checks; lunch, dinner Mon–Sat; full bar, reservations recommended; www.mattsinthemarket.com.*

Mona's Bistro and Lounge / ❍❍❍

6421 Latona Ave NE, Seattle; 206/526-1188
Appealing to a wide age range, Mona's—named for the world's most famous painting—is casually sophisticated yet isn't afraid to let her naughty-girl side show, a high ceiling setting off walls of dusky periwinkle and claret that lend a slightly bordello-ish flavor to the ambience. Fittingly, the bar dominates the room: Mona's mixologists craft beautifully balanced and very grown-up cocktails. (Try the El Floridita, our favorite.) Cuisine is Mediterranean Italian, with a rotating menu of dishes too tasty not to share. Music, however, is the romantic icing on the cake: Wednesday through Saturday evenings, Mona's swaps her restaurant mantle for club attire, with alternating nights of a DJ setting the mood with ultralounge beats and live jazz combos that draw a more seasoned crowd. *$$–$$$; AE, DC, DIS, MC, V; no checks; dinner every day, brunch Sun; full bar; reservations recommended; www.monas seattle.com.* ⅙

Oliver's Twist / ❍❍❶

6822 Greenwood Ave N, Seattle; 206/706-6673
Consider yourself . . . at home! With clever food, cleverer cocktails, smooth service, and a comfortably chic environment, this neighborhood haunt is one of our favorites for late afternoon or later evening. The lighting is dim—one might say Dickensian—with flickering candles standing in for hissing gas lamps. There are no entrées on the menu (and no gruel), just small plates, but, oh, what glorious snacks they are! We always ask for more, particularly of the blue-cheese-and-bacon-stuffed dates, garlic truffled popcorn, and mini-grilled-cheese sandwich with frothy tomato "cappuccino." They offer several beers (only one from Blighty) and a pleasing wine list, but we love the drinks, especially those named for Fagin and the Artful Dodger. Cozy back tables are prime kissing territory. *$$; AE, MC, V; no checks; dinner every day; full bar; no reservations; www.oliverstwistseattle.com.* ⅙

The Pink Door / ❍❍❍

1919 Post Alley, Seattle; 206/443-3241
Depending upon when you go, a visit to this enduringly popular Italian-American restaurant can feel more like you've stumbled into a Fellini film

than a meal. In the evenings, cabaret-style entertainment can include a trapeze artist suspended from the dim and slightly gothic dining room's 20-foot ceiling, a tarot card reader, a tap-dancing saxophonist, and burlesque shows staged in the crowded bar. On warm afternoons, a meal under the arbor on the deck is a quintessential Seattle experience. Some people come for the ambience, but with a talented chef in the kitchen, the cuisine—drawing on the bounty of the region—can be regarded as the Main Event. *$$–$$$; AE, DIS, MC, V; no checks; lunch Mon–Sat, dinner every day; full bar; reservations recommended; www.thepinkdoor.net.*

Place Pigalle / ✪✪✪

81 Pike St, Seattle; 206/624-1756
More than a quarter century ago, a dive bar beneath a former bordello was transformed into this atmospheric French-inspired cafe, and it has lost none of its charm to the passage of time. It boasts creamy walls, a black-and-white floor, candles on tables, a tiny bar specializing in unusual spirits, a picture-postcard view of Elliott Bay, and Edith Piaf's music playing in the background. (Wooden bistro chairs, best for petite derrières, are the only compromise to comfort.) The wine list offers modestly priced domestic and European bottles, and the menu spotlights classic preparations of rabbit, lamb, duck, and the house signature Mussels Pigalle, flavored with bacon. What makes this meal even more intimate? Patrons are asked to turn off their cell phones. *La vie* is, indeed, *rose. $$–$$$; AE, DC, DIS, MC, V; no checks; lunch, dinner Mon–Sat; full bar; reservations recommended; www.placepigalle-seattle.com.*

Ponti Seafood Grill / ✪✪✪

3014 3rd Ave N, Seattle; 206/284-3000
The Fremont Bridge may not possess the charm of the Rialto in Venice, but the Mediterranean villa–inspired Ponti, surrounded by lush greenery, has offered a sedate, secluded setting for wining and dining since 1989. Northwest and Asian flavors predominate and—no surprise—seafood of all descriptions is outstanding. We'd walk a mile for the Dungeness crab spring rolls or a plate of the creamy, complex Thai curry penne with shrimp, scallops, and tomato-ginger chutney. While away a cold, rainy evening beside the bar's fireplace, but when weather permits, the sheltered, heated loggia is ringside seating for watching boats passing to and fro between the Hiram M. Chittenden Locks and Lake Union. For a lavish private dinner, reserve the canal-side Buena Vista room. *$$$; AE, JCB, MC, V; no checks; dinner every day; full bar; reservations recommended; www.pontiseafoodgrill.com.* &

Purple Café and Wine Bar / ✪✪✪

1225 4th Ave, Seattle; 206/829-2280
With a two-story, 5,000-bottle wine "tower" centerpiece, Purple's a grand, splashy affair that would be right at home in New York, L.A., or Vegas. Jaw

dropping, yet they're all about approachability: servers are warm, and there's always someone to consult about the global, 300-label, 70-glass wine list. If the food menu seems daunting, simplify matters by ordering prix fixe (including starter, main course, and dessert, with optional 3-ounce wine pairings). Otherwise, you can't go wrong with baked Brie, lobster mac-and-cheese, stuffed pork tenderloin, and the Syrah brownie. The noise level runs high and the temperature's often chilly, but these aren't deal breakers when you're snuggling on a leather loveseat in the mezzanine Tasting Bar. *$$; AE, DIS, MC, V; no checks; lunch, dinner every day; full bar; reservations recommended; www.thepurplecafe.com.* &

Queen City Grill / ❍❍❍

2201 1st Ave, Seattle; 206/443-0975
Having forged the way for the culinary gentrification of Belltown, this casually elegant dining room appeals largely to a clientele who remember when Belltown wasn't a place to hang out after dark. Parchment-hued walls set off arched windows and dark wood, and sconces and large cylindrical pendants suspended over the bar cast a flattering tangerine glow. Booths are deep enough for six and tall enough to feel like private nooks for a little intimacy, and in summer we like to relax on the sidewalk patio. Their reputation has been built on seafood (simply prepared wild salmon and Dungeness crab cakes are favorites), but local organic produce and grilled meats shine. Though their impressive cellar has garnered the Wine Spectator Award of Excellence, the list offers many bottles priced around $20. *$$$; AE, DC, DIS, MC, V; no checks; dinner every day; full bar; reservations recommended; www.queencitygrill.com.* &

Rover's / ❍❍❍

2808 E Madison St, Seattle; 206/325-7442
Open in its notably secluded location since 1987, Rover's offers tasting-menu-proportioned, almost-too-pretty-to-eat plates that are flawlessly balanced interplays of flavor and texture. Celebrated chef Thierry Rautureau's energy is unflagging and his skills at helming a first-class French restaurant seem, like the fine wines in his prodigious cellar, only to improve with time. We especially love ahi tuna tartare with minced-cucumber salad and white sturgeon caviar; chilled heirloom-tomato soup with basil oil, toasted brioche, and herbed goat cheese; and salmon tournedos with chanterelles, smoked bacon, and sage butter. Cast convention to the wind: instead of a traditional dessert, finish with Hudson Valley foie gras and Sauternes. Sequestered nooks are in short supply, but the table nearest the wine sideboard affords a soupçon of privacy. Service is gracious, unpretentious, and invisible when the occasion warrants it, and Rautureau always comes out to visit with his guests. All this luxury comes at a price, but dining at Rover's is extraordinary and

memorable, worth every penny. *$$$$; AE, MC, V; no checks; lunch Fri, dinner Tues–Sat; full bar; reservations required; www.rovers-seattle.com.* &

SkyCity at the Needle / ⬢⬢⬢

400 Broad St, Seattle; 206/905-2100 or 800/937-9582
What you've heard is true. It's expensive for what you get. But on a clear, moonlit evening (and there are plenty of them every year), there's no better dinner-with-a-view than from this rotating landmark. The inner row of tables is elevated, so there isn't really a bad seat, but it's best to sit nearest the windows, side-by-side so you can steal kisses between courses. Best bets are dishes featuring salmon, halibut, regionally harvested mushrooms, and local berries. Don't expect to come for drinks and dessert only, as there's a per-person minimum charge for food. Remember, however, the ticket price is included: during a two-hour meal you'll get to see the entire Seattle panorama twice. *$$$–$$$$; AE, DC, DIS, JCB, MC, V; no checks; lunch Mon–Fri, dinner every day, brunch Sat–Sun; full bar; reservations recommended; www. spaceneedle.com/restaurant.* &

Sostanza Trattoria / ⬢⬢◖

1927 43rd Ave E, Seattle; 206/324-9701
Among early Baroque painters, few are more darkly sensual than Michelangelo Merisi da Caravaggio. Reproductions of his works adorn this two-story neighborhood favorite—not that diners need additional inspiration, what with the warm, Tuscan-villa tones, cozy fireplace, and enduringly popular central and Northern Italian menu. We like to keep it simple: carpaccio and Belgian endive salad (with crispy pancetta, radicchio, and creamy gorgonzola dressing); *linguine alla vongole* (or any of the lovely, toothsome pastas), veal saltimbocco; and—what else?—tiramisu. It's lovely to be here on a sunny summer evening, taking in the water view from the sidewalk patio (assuming you can snag a coveted table), but the romance quotient is intensified on stormy winter nights when the roaring fire is at its most welcoming. *$$–$$$; AE, DC, MC, V; local checks only; dinner Mon–Sat; full bar; reservations recommended; www.sostanzaseattle.com.* &

Stumbling Goat Bistro / ⬢⬢⬢

6722 Greenwood Ave N, Seattle; 206/784-3535
Despite an unromantic name and unassuming location, this is a wonderful dinner-date destination. Not too casual, not too dressy, not too large, not too small, the dark wood, moody retro lighting, and crimson accents may seem best suited to chilly weather, but don't miss what the kitchen creates from the bounty of summer. In the cozy, sexy Enchantresse Lounge, romance is always on the menu. (No, really! They serve a cocktail called Romance, that's "just like love . . . a little bitter, a little sweet.") With dinner, choose the Mollydooker Shiraz, Carnival of Love, to cement the mood. The very

seasonal menu changes often, but in the past we've raved over crispy duck leg with mushrooms, a spectacular cheese plate, and any salad featuring beets. And for dessert? Share the 4-inch-round Lovers' Cheesecake, naturally. *$$; MC, V; local checks only; dinner Tues–Sun; full bar; reservations recommended; www.stumblinggoatbistro.com.* &

Tango Restaurant & Lounge / ◐◐◐◖

1100 Pike St, Seattle; 206/583-0382
El tango is a passionate dance born in the brothels of Buenos Aires, and sensuality is often in the air inside this dim, high-ceilinged space, particularly when you and your date are concealed in a tall-backed booth. The Latin-inspired menu offers hot and cold *tapas, ensaladas* and *sopas,* cheese, seafood, paella, meats, and seviches. Set the mood with a plate of Cheap Dates (dates wrapped in bacon, grilled eggplant, and red onion). *Queso Azul (Valdeon* blue-cheese soufflé with seasonal fruit compote and port wine syrup) would also make a fine dessert, but Tango is known for El Diablo—bittersweet chocolate, cayenne, spicy almonds, burnt meringue, and tequila caramel sauce, a hot, sexy sweet once featured on the Food Network television show *Sugar Rush. $$–$$$; AE, MC, V; no checks; dinner every day; full bar; reservations recommended; www.tangorestaurant.com.*

Veil / ◐◐◐

555 Aloha St, Seattle; 206/216-0600
Concealed behind an inconspicuous facade, the winter white Veil is modern, urban, and beautifully lit, ringed and bisected by gauzy curtains that effectively erase the outside world. As the name might suggest, it would make a fitting backdrop for a marriage proposal. Equally dreamy is the dim, pink-blushed lounge, with its cocktails both inventive and classic. Still, noise levels can be high, tables are close together, and the Progressive American menu is slightly less magical than the ambience: some items delight, others puzzle (e.g., peanut butter is better in the signature ice cream than paired with foie gras and jelly), but most significantly, portions are petite. Veil is a beautiful place to wear an underused chic ensemble, perhaps not the best destination for hearty appetites. *$$$; AE, MC, V; no checks; dinner Tues–Sun; full bar; reservations recommended; www.veilrestaurant.com.* &

Via Tribunali / ◐◐◐◖

913 E Pike St, Seattle; 206/322-9234
317 W Galer, Seattle; 206/264-7768
Pizza may be a staple, but rarely are pizzerias . . . sexy. Enter Via Tribunali: with properties as hot as their wood-burning brick ovens, each is appealing in slightly different ways. The Capitol Hill original is reminiscent of a medieval chapel, ultradark and a little goth, with stained glass and pillar candles glowing above tall, secluded booths. The Queen Anne outpost may be brighter, but

there's a tiny mezzanine that's perfect for smooching with a view of the action below. Most ingredients are imported from Italy, reinforcing Tribunali's certified authentic Neapolitan status. Menus are written entirely in Italian, and the hand-tossed pizzas—such as the margherita, funghi, and rich lasagne—are brought to the table unsliced, meant to be eaten with knife and fork. Feeding each other bites? Now, that's amore. *$$; AE, MC, V; no checks; dinner every day (Capitol Hill), dinner Tues–Sun (Queen Anne); full bar; no reservations; www.viatribunali.com.* &

Volterra / ●●❶

5411 Ballard Ave NW, Seattle; 206/789-5100
Chef/owner Don Curtiss and his wife, Michelle Quisenberry, named their labor of love for the Tuscan hill town where they tied the knot, and Curtiss's deliciously contemporary Italian interpretations have made it a popular destination since day one (despite notoriously vexing neighborhood parking). Enduring favorites include prosciutto, fava bean, and cauliflower tart, and *pappardelle* with wild boar ragù. We like to finish with the chestnut *panna cotta* and house-made *limoncello*, in that order. You're better off avoiding weekends if you want a chance to snuggle up at a banquette table, or come in for brunch before wandering through the year-round Ballard Sunday Market. There's also a street-side patio open during warm weather. *$$$; AE, DIS, MC, V; no checks; dinner every day, brunch Sat–Sun; full bar; reservations recommended; www.volterrarestaurant.com.* &

Wild Ginger / ●●●

1401 3rd Ave, Seattle; 206/623-4450
Internationally recognized, Wild Ginger is a Seattle icon serving exquisite preparations and consistent pan-Asian cuisine. For intimate seating, request a high-back wooden booth lining the walls. If wine is in order, Wild Ginger boasts one of the most robust lists in the city. Pair a bottle with a signature dish (and there are plenty of greats to choose from): fragrant duck with steamed buns and plum sauce, seven-flavor beef, or black pepper scallops. For smaller appetites, choose from their infamous satays. The restaurant's bar is one of the darkest corners in the city, serving a variety of specialty cocktails, including the thick and creamy mango daiquiri. If you're looking for entertainment with a romantic backdrop, Triple Door (216 Union St, Seattle; 206/838-4333; www.tripledoor.com) is housed beneath Wild Ginger in the restored Embassy Theater. The Musicquarium is a no-cover lounge with a 1,900-gallon aquarium and a private hideaway that's perfect for a little nuzzling. The 300-seat Mainstage has the feel of a mid-20th-century supper club and the musical lineup is impressive. *$$–$$$; AE, DC, DIS, JCB, MC, V; no checks; lunch Mon–Sat, dinner every day; full bar; reservations recommended; www.wildginger.net.* &

Eastside

Romantic Highlights

When it comes to romance in the Seattle area, it used to be that east was east and west was best. Those who lived east of Lake Washington, in suburbs like Bellevue, Woodinville, Kirkland, and Redmond, had to brave traffic on Interstate 90 and State Route 520 to seek out cultural and dining diversions in Seattle. Times have changed: Seattle residents no longer turn up their noses at the idea of heading over to the booming Eastside for fun, whether it's dining out with friends; shopping in downtown Bellevue, Kirkland, or Redmond; or overnighting in a romantic hotel or lodge, like the luxurious destination **Salish Lodge & Spa** next to the 268-foot Snoqualmie Falls (see Romantic Lodgings).

One of the biggest tourist draws on the Eastside—just as it is in Eastern Washington—is wine. Annual weekend events like Passport to Woodinville, Washington Wine Highway, and St. Nicholas Days are sellouts, drawing visitors to **Woodinville** in droves to sample the wares at the more than 40 wineries that have set up shop in this once-sleepy burg. (In 2000 there were but a handful of wineries in Woodinville.) Some wineries are open daily, some on Saturdays or Sundays, and some only for special events, so it's advised to contact wineries directly before dropping in. For an excellent resource, visit www.woodinvillewinecountry.com. Large operations such as **Chateau Ste. Michelle** (14111 NE 145th St; 425/488-3300; www.chateaustemichelle.com) and **Columbia Winery** (14030 NE 145th St; 425/488-2776; www.columbiawinery.com), the oldest premium winery in the state, are open every day and have wonderful tasting rooms and gift shops. The grounds of Ste. Michelle are lush, perfect for an impromptu picnic, and their amphitheater is home to a popular outdoor summer concert series. It would be a mistake to miss some of the area's fine, smaller wineries, but in case your top choices aren't open for tastings, the **Purple Café** (14459 Woodinville-Redmond Rd; 425/483-7129; www.thepurplecafe.com) is nearby: it's a great spot for local and global wine sipping and a light nosh. As a palate cleanser, pop into **Redhook Brewery** (14300 NE 145th St, Woodinville; 425/483-3232; www.redhook.com), sample their signature beers, and enjoy lunch on the patio or in the handsome pub, Forecasters. **Willows Lodge and Spa** (see Romantic Lodgings) is *the* place for an overnight stay in Woodinville.

On the scenic shores of Lake Washington, **Kirkland** feels like a resort town, a little quaint and a lot upscale. Art lovers should pay a visit to the gallery in the historic brick **Kirkland Arts Center** (620 Market St; 425/822-7161; www. kirklandartscenter.org) or any of the numerous other downtown galleries, or try the **Kirkland Art Walk**, held the second Thursday of every month. **Argosy Cruises** (206/623-4252; www.argosycruises.com) offers Lake Washington tours, a fine opportunity for a kiss on the water, particularly in the summer. You'll get to enjoy priceless views of Mount Rainier and the downtown skyline, and take a gander at Bill Gates's compound to see what $54 million will buy you. After disembarking, head to the seafood-centric favorite **Third Floor Fish Cafe** (205 Lake St S; 425/822-3553; www.fishcafe.com) overlooking the marina.

Bellevue continues to grow with amazing speed, with high-rise office buildings, hotels, and condominiums giving this city—the state's fourth largest—a dramatic skyline of its own. Shopping and dining your way through **Bellevue Square** and **Lincoln Square** (at the intersection of Bellevue Wy and NE 8th St) can occupy hours on end, but if you're in the mood for fine dining with a spectacular view—a rare thing on this side of Lake Washington—head to **Daniel's Broiler** (10500 NE 8th St, 21st Floor; 425/462-4662; www.schwartzbrothers. com). There you'll find terrific steaks, a piano bar, and the **Vintage Lounge**, a clubby, plushly furnished room that always offers 30 wines by the glass rated 90 and above by *Wine Spectator*.

Banish thoughts of clogged streets and exhaust fumes by visiting the **Bellevue Botanical Garden** (12001 Main St; 425/452-2750; www.bellevuebotanical.org), a serene haven with walking trails and a 19-acre nature preserve. Quiet paths lead past an alpine rock garden, filled with mountain hemlock and tiny wildflowers, to the exquisite Yao Garden. Dahlias and fuchsias abound during the summer, and Garden d'Lights is a wintertime display of colorful lights used to create botanical wonders. Walk for an hour or so and it's easier to justify a trip to **Fran's Chocolates** (10036 Main St; 425/453-1698; www.franschocolates.com) for some of their famously delicious salt caramels.

Known around the world as the home of Microsoft, even **Redmond** boasts its own first-rate shops and restaurants at **Redmond Town Center** (16495 NE 74th St; 425/867-0808; www.redmondtowncenter.com), including **The Big Picture** (7411 166th Ave NE; 425/556-0566; www.thebigpicture.net), a grown-up's cinema with a full bar, cushy seats, and billiards room dubbed the Q Club. For wholesome, outdoorsy activities, or just a cozy picnic à deux, head to the 640-acre **Marymoor Park** (6046 W Lake Sammamish Pkwy NE; 206/205-3661; www.metrokc.gov/ parks), offering running trails, tennis courts, horse paths, a velodrome, a climbing wall, and summertime festivals and concerts.

Access & Information

From Interstate 5, there are two east-west arterials connecting to the Eastside communities via floating bridges: Interstate 90 (south of downtown Seattle) and Highway 520 (north of downtown). The major Eastside north-south highway is Interstate 405. Located northeast of Seattle, Woodinville is accessed by either I-405 or State Route 522. For more information, contact the **Woodinville Chamber of Commerce** (425/481-8300; www.woodinville chamber.org). For information on Kirkland, contact the **Kirkland Chamber of Commerce** (425/822-7066; www.kirklandchamber.org), and for Bellevue, contact the **Bellevue Chamber of Commerce** (425/454-2464; www.bellevue chamber.org).

Romantic Lodgings

Bellevue Club Hotel / ✪✪✪✪

11200 SE 6th St, Bellevue; 425/454-4424 or 800/579-1110
Attached to the Eastside's most exclusive health club, this elegant and understated 67-room boutique hotel is a reminder that exercise isn't the only thing that gets the heart pumping. All guest rooms offer opulent bathrooms and luxuriously dressed beds. Ground floor Club Rooms offer handsome private patios. At 1,900 square feet, the Rainier Suite seems excessive for two, but both the Wilburton and Fountain suites have jetted tubs and sitting rooms with fireplaces. For a "spa-stravaganza," book the Spa Romance package that comes with champagne, chocolate-covered strawberries, two 50-minute massages, and more. (Guests have full access to all club facilities, from tennis courts to swimming pools.) World-class shopping is minutes away and Bellevue's dining and nightlife options are expanding rapidly; but if you want to retreat from the outside world, the property's exclusive Polaris (425/637-4608) restaurant offers all meals and a notable wine list to boot. *$$$–$$$$; AE, DC, MC, V; checks OK; www.bellevueclub.com.* &

The Heathman Hotel / ✪✪✪

220 Kirkland Ave, Kirkland; 425/284-5800 or 800/551-0011
The sister property of a long-cherished destination in Portland, this second Heathman is pure Northwest contemporary, understated and elegant, with neutral tones and natural elements. Of the 91 guest rooms, 15 are suites, 5 have fireplaces. (The Terrace Suite has a hot tub on its private deck.) The Heathman's Art of Sleep menu makes comfort a priority, offering three types of beds (Tempur-Pedic, European pillow top, or feather bed) and six different pillows, and the Romance Package includes champagne and chocolate-covered strawberries, plus restaurant and spa credits. Trellis (see Romantic Restaurants) provides first-rate dining, and Penterra Spa (425/284-5855; www.penterraspa.com) is perfect for paired pampering—massages in the double treatment room followed by a candlelit session in side-by-side soaking tubs strewn with rose petals. The hotel's motto is "Where service is still an art," and it shows: guests are assigned their own concierge to see that each stay is memorable. *$$$–$$$$; AE, DC, DIS, MC, V; www.heathman kirkland.com.* &

Salish Lodge & Spa / ✪✪✪✪

6501 Railroad Ave SE, Snoqualmie; 425/888-2556 or 800/826-6124
More than 1.5 million tourists, locals, and inveterate *Twin Peaks* fans flock to Snoqualmie Falls annually. Most wander through the lodge's common areas, but guest wings are accessible only via key cards, so you can feel free to travel between room and spa in your robe. Be sure to include heated-river-rock massages in a couple's treatment room as part of your stay. If you'd rather

Three Days of Wining and Dining

Day One: The first day of your odyssey is spent exploring downtown. Drop off luggage at **Hotel Vintage Park** and head to **Pike Place Market** for a quick, light breakfast at **The Crumpet Shop** (1503 1st Ave; 206/682-1598). Open since 1976, they offer this savory, perforated British snack with a wide variety of toppings, and the scones are also delicious. Wander through the shops and stalls at the market—depending upon the time of year, you can buy a vibrant bouquet of fresh flowers for as little as ten dollars, an accessory to enhance any ensemble. For lunch, sojourn in France at **Café Campagne**, and then return to the Hotel Vintage Park for some downtime before dinner downstairs at **Tulio Ristorante** (1100 5th Ave; 206/624-5500; www.tulio.com), an Italian favorite. The hotel's own wine expert, known as the chef concierge, is happy to answer any questions about area wines and wineries.

Day Two: Only minutes away, a delicious breakfast awaits at **Crave** (1621 12th Ave; 206/388-0526; www.cravefood.com), a cozy Capitol Hill favorite. Fortified with apple Dutch babies and pomegranate champagne mimosas, head to Broadway for a stroll, trying out your fancy footwork on the numerous sidewalk-imbedded bronze dance steps. After getting the circulation moving, it's time to hop in the car and cross Interstate 90, bound for **Issaquah** and **Coho Café** (6130 E Lake Sammamish Pkwy SE; 425/391-4040), whose salmon burger is a house favorite. From there, it'll only take about 20 minutes to get to **Salish Lodge & Spa**, perched beside **Snoqualmie Falls**, one of the region's most popular scenic attractions.

be in the great outdoors, adventures abound. When you're ready for meals, the Attic Bistro is cozy and casual, but a candlelit dinner in the Dining Room (see Romantic Restaurants) is a must. Choicest guest rooms overlook the river (none actually face the falls): on a clear night, part the drapes to enjoy the moon glow, open a window to hear the rushing water (most dramatic in early spring with the melting of mountain snows), light a crackling fire, and settle into the two-person pipeless Sanijet bath with built-in mood lighting, flutes of champagne in hand. *$$$–$$$$; AE, DC, DIS, MC, V; checks OK; www.salishlodge.com.* &

Willows Lodge / ✪✪✪✪

14580 NE 145th St, Woodinville; 425/424-3900 or 877/424-3930
One of the best escapes around, in 2007 alone, this award-winning property was named by *Travel + Leisure* magazine to position 12 of the Top 100 Hotels in the Continental U.S. and Canada, as well as one of its Top 50

Schedule hot-stone massages or unwind by soaking in the state-of-the-art tub in your guest room before dinner at **The Dining Room**, which, in addition to its remarkable menu, offers more than 1,700 bottles in the Wine Loft Collection.

Day Three: It's painful to abandon the comforts of Salish, but depart you must. Drive northwest toward **Redmond** and **Pomegranate Bistro** (18005 NE 68th St, Ste A150; 425/881-3250; www.pomegranatebistro. com): their weekend brunch is marvelous, but failing that, the Grab-N-Go espresso counter opens at 7am every day, proffering fresh baked goods, made on the premises. Fortification is essential, because your next stop is **Woodinville wine country**. Many wineries are open by appointment, only on Saturday and/or Sunday afternoons, or not at all, so it's crucial to firm up plans in advance. **Chateau Ste. Michelle** (14111 NE 145th St; 425/415-3300; www.ste-michelle.com) and **Columbia Winery** (14030 NE 145h St; 425/488-2776; www.columbiawinery.com) are open daily, but we suggest also checking out **DiStefano Winery** (12280 Woodinville Dr SE; 425/487-1648; www.distefanowinery.com), **Matthews Estate** (16116 140th Pl NE; 425/487-9810; www.matthewscellars.com), or **JM Cellars** (14404 137th Pl NE; 425/485-6508; www.jmcellars.com), whose signature blend is Tre Fanciulli. If you'd rather make just one stop to taste several Washington vintages, head to **Purple Café and Wine Bar** (14459 Woodinville-Redmond Rd, 425/483-7129; www.thepurplecafe.com) before checking into your plush room at **Willows Lodge**. The culmination of your three unforgettable days is dinner at the world-class **Herbfarm Restaurant**.

Romantic Getaways. Located in the heart of Woodinville wine country, Willows Lodge shares the same property as both the acclaimed Herbfarm Restaurant and the Barking Frog (see Romantic Restaurants). All 84 guest rooms epitomize modern, rustic elegance and, above all, comfort. We love the stone fireplaces, Egyptian cotton linens, garden-view patios and balconies, walk-in showers, and soaking tubs for two, some jetted. The latter nicely complements a spa visit for a hot-stone scrub, detoxifying wrap, or facial. For unparalleled romance, the Do Not Disturb Package features in-tub dining, strawberries with whipped cream and chocolate fondue, champagne, a mood-setting CD, and more. Alas, you can't stay forever but you can! $$$–$$$$; AE, DC, DIS, MC, V; checks OK; www.willowslodge.com. &

Woodmark Hotel / ●●●

1200 Carillon Pt, Kirkland; 425/822-3700 or 800/822-3700
There's plenty of opportunity for intimacy and romance at the Woodmark, particularly if you avoid wedding crowds (it's a very popular knot-tying site), unwind at the serene full-service day spa (remodeled in 2008), and book a room facing the Seattle skyline and Olympic Mountains. All 100 guest-room baths have been upgraded with limestone tile and soaking tub with rain shower (at the minimum), but we like the jetted tubs in the secluded corner Executive Suites. Carillon Point is home to several eateries, including Yarrow Bay Grill (see Romantic Restaurants), but with a new wine-centric restaurant on the hotel's premises (not named as of this writing) as well as the Library Bar (for proper afternoon tea as well as bar fare), there's little need to step off the property. Be sure to ask about a complimentary lake cruise aboard the hotel's 1956 Chris-Craft, and don't miss Raid the Pantry, a complimentary snack buffet laid out in the restaurant nightly at 11:30. *$$$–$$$$; AE, DC, JCB, MC, V; checks OK; www.thewoodmark.com.*

Romantic Restaurants

Barking Frog / ●●◐

14580 NE 145th St, Woodinville; 425/424-2999
Sometimes overshadowed by the Herbfarm Restaurant (see Romantic Restaurants) next door, Barking Frog marries rich, Northwest-centric decor and a Woodinville-centric wine list with a remarkable menu. Attached to the award-winning Willows Lodge (see Romantic Lodgings), this excellent restaurant merits a visit even if you're not staying overnight. The seasonal menus may appear daring at first glance, but the kitchen essentially produces Euro-influenced Northwest comfort food, from starters of Grand Marnier prawns, lobster bisque, and Hudson Valley foie gras (served, for example, with a mini cinnamon waffle and huckleberry flan) to entrées such as black cod, pumpkin agnolotti, and elk tenderloin with lentils and brussels sprouts. The warm, wood-lined interior seems more suited to colder months, especially when we sit near the roaring circular fireplace, so we suggest a courtyard table on warm summer evenings. *$$$; AE, DC, DIS, MC, V; checks OK; breakfast, dinner every day, lunch Mon–Fri, brunch Sat–Sun; full bar; reservations recommended; www.willowslodge.com.* &

Cafe Juanita / ●●●◐

9702 NE 120th Pl, Kirkland; 425/823-1505
Sparely decorated in neutral tones, this L-shaped dining room is a serene oasis backed by trees and Juanita Creek, though we prefer the corner table opposite the stone fireplace (by the parking lot), a near-perfect kissing location after dark. For her Northern Italian–inspired menus, chef/owner Holly Smith draws substantially on regional, sustainable, organic products, though

the focus sometimes falls on imported treasures, such as Piemontese white truffles. Sweetbreads, foie gras, fresh pastas, and rabbit are outstanding, and every plate is a work of art, from breads and crackers to beautifully arranged desserts. Service is polished and friendly, never intrusive, and we encourage consulting the sommelier about wine: there are 150 Italian reds alone to choose from (though if you're in the mood to splurge, make it a Sassicaia). *$$$; AE, MC, V; local checks only; dinner every day; full bar; reservations recommended; www.cafejuanita.com.* &

The Dining Room / ❂❂❂❂

6501 Railroad Ave SE (Salish Lodge & Spa), Snoqualmie; 425/888-2556 or 800/826-6124
Though it's ensconced in the award-winning Salish Lodge & Spa (see Romantic Lodgings), it would be a mistake to overlook the Dining Room as a romantic dinner-only destination. Ambience is rustic yet intrinsically elegant: you can't beat a candlelit window table above Snoqualmie Falls on a clear night, but entwining fingers next to the original 1916 stone fireplace comes close. If it's a special occasion, say so when you request Table 5: you might arrive to find the table garnished with red rose petals. Chef Roy Breiman's menus are extraordinary, each plate a perfectly composed work of art worthy of the world's grandest restaurants. He derives inspiration from the natural surroundings, including river rocks that he hand selects, halves, polishes, heats to 500 degrees, and uses to cook fresh fish morsels, table-side. The Dining Room also serves wonderful breakfasts, especially popular on weekends. *$$$–$$$$; AE, DC, DIS, MC, V; checks OK; breakfast every day, dinner Tues–Sat; full bar; reservations recommended; www.salishlodge.com.* &

The Herbfarm Restaurant / ❂❂❂❂

14590 NE 145th St, Woodinville; 425/485-5300
Theatrically over-the-top, the resplendent European country house atmosphere of this food fanatic's mecca is so fairy-tale fabulous we wouldn't be surprised to see Cinderella pull up in her transformed-gourd carriage. Seasonally themed nine-course tasting menus are always paired with five or six wines from the award-winning cellar (Northwest-focused, 4,000 selections, with a staggering Madeira collection). Unless you specify otherwise, there's a chance you'll be seated at the communal table—entertaining, but not as conducive to romance as a table for two. A classical guitarist performs throughout the five-hour culinary odyssey, and owners Ron Zimmerman and Carrie Van Dyck talk about the evening's offerings between courses. Service is polished and almost psychically attentive: whenever you leave the table a fresh napkin is placed at your seat. Make a special evening transcendent and unforgettable by reserving either the Herb Garden or Orchard House, the Herbfarm's ultraromantic suites at Willows Lodge (see Romantic Lodgings)

next door. *$$$$; AE, MC, V; checks OK; dinner Thurs–Sun; full bar; reservations required; www.theherbfarm.com.* &

Sea Star Restaurant and Raw Bar / ◑◑

205 108th Ave NE, Bellevue; 425/456-0010
Dining options in Bellevue have greatly expanded since chef/owner John Howie opened Sea Star in 2002, but they still offer the most seductive array of bivalve aphrodisiacs for miles. Though comfortable, the dining room is a bit spacious for intimacy, and there's no inspiring view from the office-building setting. The wine program has garnered numerous accolades, and the kitchen expertly prepares top sirloin and chicken breasts, but underwater fare is the focus. Howie is an expert in the technique of plank cooking (having demonstrated his method on *The Martha Stewart Show*), so it's hard to go wrong with anything—king salmon, halibut, trout, swordfish, sturgeon, scallops, and more—grilled or roasted atop cedar or apple wood. For afters, don't miss the signature banana spring-roll sundae. *$$$; AE, DC, MC, V; checks OK; lunch Mon–Fri, dinner every day; full bar; reservations recommended; www. seastarrestaurant.com.* &

Trellis / ◑◑◖

220 Kirkland Ave (the Heathman Hotel), Kirkland; 425/284-5900
"Farm to table" is an increasingly popular concept, but few chefs embrace it as whole-heartedly as Brian Scheehser, who sustainably farms 3 acres and "puts up" all manner of lush produce so that Trellis guests can enjoy the fruits of his labors year-round. If a booth isn't available in the casually elegant dining room, sit in the sleek bar (sipping cucumber Cosmos and pineapple-sage Mojitos) or on the heated patio, weather allowing. It's hard to play favorites with Scheehser's best-of-the-season dishes, but at breakfast, look for housemade corned-beef hash with poached eggs and hollandaise, and at lunch, wild salmon niçoise salad. For dinner try Sonoma duck with braised endive, grilled pears, and figs. If the evening goes spectacularly well, book a room upstairs. *$$$; AE, DC, DIS, MC, V; no checks; breakfast, dinner every day, lunch Mon– Fri; full bar; reservations recommended; www.trellisrestaurant.net.* &

Yarrow Bay Grill / ◑◑

1270 Carillon Pt, Kirkland; 425/889-9052
At this Eastside mainstay, all windows and the deck look out over the marina of Lake Washington, and the menu, presided over by executive chef Vicky McCaffree since 1991, continues to delight. There are numerous booths (though one nearest the fireplace offers the most seclusion), but the decor feels just a tad "last century." Entrée prices, however, are very much *this* century, so we sometimes go for starters or the Nosh & Nibble section of the menu, saving room for dessert. Classic profiteroles are divine, but we also like having house-made crepes delivered to the table for self-assembly. Directly

downstairs is the Beach Café (425/889-0303; www.ybbeachcafe.com; lunch, dinner every day), a casual eatery with a popular happy hour and one of the best patios on the Eastside. *$$$; AE, DC, DIS, JCB, MC, V; no checks; dinner every day; full bar; reservations recommended; www.ybgrill.com.* ⅋

Bainbridge Island & Kitsap Peninsula

Romantic Highlights

Bainbridge Island's charming downtown and beautiful parks and gardens, a short ferry jaunt from Seattle, make it ideally suited for a romantic getaway. If you continue to the Highway 305 bridge over Agate Passage you'll reach the Kitsap Peninsula, which brings you to quaint, Scandinavian Poulsbo and picturesque communities set along scenic Hood Canal (actually a 60-plus-mile-long fjord), such as Seabeck and Port Gamble. Take the Bremerton ferry to or from downtown for wonderful views of Seattle's waterfront and Mount Rainier, weather allowing. The naval port city of Bremerton isn't renowned for its romantic charms, but there are certain surprises tucked away, such as the Italian-themed restaurant La Fermata (2204 E 11th St; 360/373-5927), a great spot for holding hands.

Bainbridge Island can easily be enjoyed in a day, as long as you don't try to do too much. If you go on a Sunday, street parking near Seattle's Colman Dock (Pier 52) is free, so just walk onto the ferry and spend the day wandering around downtown Bainbridge. Stop by **Blackbird Bakery** (210 Winslow Wy E; 206/780-1322) for tea and pastries, then continue on to **Eagle Harbor Book Company** (157 Winslow Wy E; 206/842-5332; www.eagleharborbooks.booksense.com), an independent bookstore selling both new and used volumes, or browse through the gallery at **Bainbridge Arts & Crafts** (151 Winslow Wy E; 206/842-3132; www.bainbridgeartsandcrafts.org). Stop for an expertly poured pint on the cozy deck of **The Harbour Public House** (231 Parfitt Wy SW; 206/842-0969; www. harbourpub.com), but if you're looking for a fancier meal than their excellent fish-and-chips, visit **Madoka** (241 Winslow Wy W; 206/842-2448; www.madoka onbainbridge.com), offering Northwest-meets-Pacific-Rim cuisine in elegant surroundings, including a second-story loft lounge. Also inviting (and for adults only) is **The Living Room** (123 Bjune Dr SE; 206/855-0959; www.thelivingroomon bainbridge.com), a plushly furnished, eclectic wine bar, one of the few nice spots serving food after 10pm.

If you'd rather dine alfresco, consider bringing a picnic from home or picking up goodies at **Town & Country Market** (343 Winslow Wy E; 206/842-3848; www.townandcountrymarkets.com), or take-away pasta dishes from **Mon Elisa's** (450 Winslow Wy E; 206/780-3233; www.monaspasta.com), and head for **Fay Bainbridge State Park** (from downtown Bainbridge, take SR 305 north to the turnoff at Day Rd E and follow signs; 15446 Sunrise Dr NE; 206/842-3931; www.parks.wa.gov), with picnic shelters and a lovely beach for a stroll. **Fort Ward State Park** (2241 Pleasant Beach Dr NE; 206/842-4041; www.parks.wa.gov) is a scenic, back-roads drive, so bring a good map. For a little less rusticity, you can spend a romantic afternoon at **Bloedel Reserve** (7571 NE Dolphin Dr; 206/842-7631; www.bloedelreserve.org; Wed–Sun, by reservation only), wandering 150 acres of gorgeous Northwest landscape, including a Japanese garden, reflecting pond, and bird refuge. **Bainbridge Island Vineyards and Winery** (8989 Day Rd E; 206/842-9463; www.bainbridgevineyards.com; Fri–Sun) is fun for oenophiles: all of their fruit is island grown, including the berries used in their strawberry and raspberry wines.

Poulsbo lies north of Bainbridge over Agate Pass Bridge. Skip the too-touristy shops and make for **Sluy's Poulsbo Bakery** (18924 Front St NE; 360/779-2798) to share a life-preserver-sized Viking doughnut or cream-cheese cinnamon roll. If chocolate's more your bag, duck into **Boehm's Chocolates** (18864 Front St NE; 360/697-3318), then work off the sugar rush by renting a kayak from **Olympic Outdoor Center** (18971 Front St NE; 360/697-6095; www.olympicoutdoorcenter. com). **MorMor Bistro & Bar** (see Romantic Restaurants) is your best bet for a sophisticated lunch or dinner.

North of town lies **Kitsap Memorial State Park** (from Poulsbo, head north on Hwy 3; look for signs to the park 4 miles south of the Hood Canal Bridge), which offers sweeping views of Hood Canal from its 1,797-foot stretch of shoreline. Near **Hansville** to the east are two more charming beaches: **Point No Point** boasts a beautiful lighthouse, but even more appealing—despite the discouraging name—is **Foulweather Bluff** (follow the road from Hansville to the west). Look for the Nature Conservancy sign on the south side of the road and follow a short trail to the secluded beach, suitable for a picnic or snuggle.

Visiting the town of **Port Gamble** (near the Hood Canal Bridge) is like taking a step back in time, complete with a picturesque church and general store. Built in the mid-19th century, it was modeled on a New England village and features lovely Victorian architecture and the **Port Gamble Historic Museum** (32400 Rainier Ave; 360/297-8074), a period gem that illustrates the community's social and industrial heritage. Stop by the **Tea Room at Port Gamble** (32279 Rainier Ave NE; 360/297-4225; www.tearoomatportgamble.com) for a proper cream tea or selection of truffles from their Candy Shoppe.

To visit a seaside town at the opposite end of the peninsula, head south past Bremerton to **Port Orchard**, which has a boardwalk and the long-standing **Port Orchard Farmers Market** (1 block from Bay St at Marina Park, 360/377-3173; www.pofarmersmarket.org; late Apr–Oct), one of the oldest and largest in Western Washington. This is only a minor detour if you're on your way to **Alderbrook Resort & Spa** (see Romantic Lodgings). Though it's not, strictly speaking, on the Kitsap Peninsula, Alderbrook's location at the south end of the Hood Canal is scenic and serene, one of the most romantic overnight destinations a couple can hope for.

Access & Information

Washington State Ferries (206/464-6400 or 800/843-3779; www.wsdot. wa.gov/ferries) run regularly between downtown Seattle and Bainbridge Island. This is the most popular jumping-off point to get to the **Olympic Peninsula** (via the Hood Canal Bridge), home to the Northwest's largest national park and some of Washington's most spectacular scenery. The **Bainbridge Chamber of Commerce** (590 Winslow Wy E; 206/842-3700; www. bainbridgechamber.com) provides excellent visitor information. It's good to remember that this ferry route is at its busiest during the summer months, on weekends, and during Monday-through-Friday rush hours: leave the car (and its associated frustrations) behind and you can easily explore downtown Bainbridge on foot.

Some choose to drive around Puget Sound and cross the Tacoma Narrows Bridge to reach the Kitsap Peninsula, but ferry travel is quicker, providing nicer views and considerably greater romance potential. Sailings to Bremerton depart from downtown Seattle; ferries to Southworth (near Port Orchard) depart from Fauntleroy in West Seattle; or head to Edmonds, north of downtown Seattle, to catch a ferry to Kingston, another Kitsap Peninsula port. For more information, contact the **Kitsap Peninsula Visitor and Convention Bureau** (360/297-8200; www.visitkitsap.com).

Romantic Lodgings

Alderbrook Resort & Spa / ❂❂❂

7101 E SR 106, Union; 360/898-2200 or 800/622-9370
There has been some manner of vacation getaway on this property since 1913, but a $13 million transformation, completed in 2004, made Alderbrook the destination it is today. With a modern Craftsman aesthetic inspired by the natural surroundings, the dramatic main structure has 77 richly appointed guest rooms. There's a spacious dining room and bar, but room service paired with a DVD borrowed from the resort's collection makes a cozy alternative. Guests are given preferred tee times at Alderbrook Golf Club, unlimited use of the pool, hot tub, steam room and sauna; and the spa offers a full menu of treatments. For a little more seclusion, there are 16 semidetached cottages; all but 1 have two bedrooms. Our hands-down favorite is number 1, which faces the Olympic Mountains: at high tide, the waters of Hood Canal lap under its sheltered patio. Bask beside the fireplace, bathe in the soaking tub, play a board game in the den, or prepare dinner and cocktails in the full kitchen. There's no need to leave the cottage at all, but on clear nights, we can't resist venturing out to the sweeping lawn, where we settle into Adirondack chairs, hold hands, and gaze up in wonderment at the glimmering Milky Way. *$$$–$$$$; AE, CB, DC, MC, V; checks OK; www.alderbrookresort.com.* &

The Eagle Harbor Inn / ●●◖

291 Madison Ave S, Bainbridge Island; 206/842-1446
Sited near the marina and town center, this urban inn blends convenience with cozy sophistication in its five suites and quartet of fully appointed townhomes, with a garden courtyard common area and direct, keyless access. Though the building also includes privately owned condos, there's no reception area: you may never see an actual employee, which makes for an unusually anonymous stay. We like the vaulted ceiling and soaking tub in the soothing Rockaway Beach room, but if more space is required, the Vineyard Suite offers a view of Eagle Harbor and beyond. Aside from fresh coffee in the entryway of the main building each morning, no food or drink is provided, so if you're not self-catering (in a townhome kitchen), consider your stay a golden opportunity to explore the restaurants of downtown Bainbridge. *$$$–$$$$; AE, DIS, MC, V; no checks; www.theeagleharborinn.com.* &

Illahee Manor / ●●●●

6680 Illahee Rd NE, Bremerton; 360/698-7555 or 800/693-6680
Built in 1926 by Russian immigrants on a bluff overlooking Puget Sound, this castlelike manor house sports old-world grandeur with expansive common areas and a bona fide veranda. If it's a weekend of isolation you seek, the safari-themed, vaulted-ceiling Penthouse Suite has its own entrance, a spacious Jacuzzi, and a full kitchen, but we're fond of the cozy Library: the smallest room, it features a private spa across the hall with sauna, Jacuzzi, and immense shower with skylights. There are also two separate properties, the Beach House and the Cottage—which welcome children—but these more rustic accommodations are larger than needed for a cozy retreat. Be sure to tour the lovely gardens, with their rockeries, ponds, fruit trees, and bird-watching opportunities. Served in the conservatory, the gourmet three-course breakfast will keep you going until well past lunchtime. *$$–$$$; AE, DC, DIS, MC, V; checks OK; www.illaheemanor.com.* &

Morgan Hill Retreat / ●●●◖

1921 NE Sawdust Hill Rd, Poulsbo; 360/598-4930 or 800/598-3926
Located only about an hour's traveling time from downtown Seattle, this magical B&B feels worlds away. Proprietress Marcia Breece offers three rooms, two with private entrances. Upstairs, the aerielike Hideaway is a complete apartment, featuring a living room, kitchen, bedroom, and lovely bath. The ground-level Sunflower Suite offers a luxurious king bed and large jetted tub and spacious shower. (In-room massages can be scheduled.) Mountain views are spectacular and the grounds feature a labyrinth and the summertime aroma of 200 lavender plants. (However, Breece uses fragrance-free organic cleansers and detergents throughout the property's interior.) Fauna is integral to the Morgan Hill experience: in addition to llamas, geese, ducks,

chickens, sheep, and Howard the bichon frisé, look for wading birds noshing at the trout pond. It's delightful to relax on the wraparound porch on a sunny morning, dining on pecan pancakes and fresh poached eggs. *$$–$$$; MC, V; no checks; www.morganhillretreat.com.* &

Selah Inn Bed & Breakfast / ❶❶❶

130 NE Dulalip Landing, Belfair; 360/275-0916 or 877/232-7941
For an entrancing Hood Canal escape, any one of the seven guest suites at Selah Inn fits the bill beautifully. Inside the main house—which also includes a library, a sunroom, a dining room, and an inviting living room with massive stone fireplace—request the King Suite, with its cozy sitting area, large Jacuzzi, fireplace, and luxurious canopied bed looking out to the private deck. The Canal House includes the Beach Suite, one of our favorite waterside escapes on the entire peninsula: it has an incredible view, in addition to a fireplace, deck, and step-up jetted tub—the perfect unwinding spot after clamming or beachcombing. (Incidentally, all guest accommodations feature extra soundproofing for privacy.) Gourmet breakfasts are included, but consider booking dinner, too. You can enjoy elegant multicourse meals featuring fresh local seafood and produce as long as the minimum of four reservations is met. *$$–$$$; MC, V; checks OK; www.selahinn.com.* &

Willcox House / ❶❶❶❶

2390 Tekiu Rd NW; Seabeck; 360/830-4492 or 800/725-9477
The drive to Willcox House takes you past towering evergreens and rolling countryside, and the location—on a forested bluff with superb views of Hood Canal and the Olympic Mountains—is sublime. The structure's vintage grandeur belongs to a bygone era, the romantic heyday of 1930s Hollywood. (One of the five guest rooms is named after former guest Clark Gable.) Julian's Room has a masculine decor and two-person Jacuzzi, and spacious Constance's Room is made cozy by a fireplace. The property may be showing its age, but there's much to distract: depending upon the season, you can curl up beside a roaring fire in the library or on a chaise in the garden, shoot some pool or stroll the palatial grounds. Breakfast and dinner are served daily, but the four-course Saturday dinners are the most lavish. There is also a dock for guests who arrive by boat or seaplane. *$$$; DIS, MC, V; checks OK; www. willcoxhouse.com.* &

Romantic Restaurants

Cafe Nola / ❶❶❶

101 Winslow Wy E, Bainbridge Island; 206/842-3822
A prime Bainbridge spot for a "nice meal out," this cheerful, elegant bistro is a fixture for locals and a fun destination for visitors. Sit at a private booth, if possible—barring that, the seductive bar or the patio, weather allowing,

are also conducive to conversation. At brunch, our favorite is eggs Benedict with Dungeness crab, a fine mate for the lemony hollandaise. At dinner, look for the double pork chop with chipotle smashed sweet potatoes or rosemary-crusted halibut, but be sure to save room for dessert, like white chocolate–caramel bread pudding. On the downside, service can be uneven, so arrive with perhaps a little extra patience. *$$; AE, MC, V; checks OK; lunch Mon–Fri, dinner every day, brunch Sat–Sun; full bar; reservations recommended; www.cafenola.com.* &

The Four Swallows / ❂❂❂❂

481 Madison Ave N, Bainbridge Island; 206/842-3397
Those who call Bainbridge Island home would probably prefer to keep this sophisticated, easy-going 1889 farmhouse-turned-restaurant to themselves. However, take the ferry from downtown Seattle, and Four Swallows is but a 5-minute drive or 15-minute walk from the dock. The interior is richly appointed with plenty of secluded nooks, particularly the tall, dark wood booths, petite lamps casting a golden glow, and tables narrow enough to lean across for a lingering lip-lock. The wine list offers outstanding choices to complement the rotating menu: Italian inspiration is married with the freshest of local and regional ingredients, resulting in elegant comfort food. Crab cakes come with piquant lemon aioli and crispy shoestring fries, and the secret ingredient in the mussels is smoked paprika. For dessert, we look for *panna cotta* with seasonal berries. *$$; MC, V; local checks only; dinner Tues–Sat; beer and wine; reservations recommended; www.fourswallows.com.* &

Molly Ward Gardens / ❂❂❂

27462 Big Valley Rd NE, Poulsbo; 360/779-4471
Sometimes treasures are elusive, and such is the case with this picturesque retreat housed in a converted barn and named for the late family pooch; it's a little tricky to locate unless you're actively looking. The dining room is fairy-tale magical, particularly after dark, when antique lighting and candles cast a warm glow over white linens. Proprietors Sam and Lynn Ward maintain gorgeous organic gardens, perfect for a pre- or post-prandial stroll. Carefully selected and simply prepared dishes are devised from the bounty of their land and what's market fresh. Spaghetti squash may be topped with a creamy gorgonzola sauce, Copper River salmon may be accompanied by fruit chutney, and desserts are a must. It's also a popular setting for weddings, from rehearsal dinners to garden ceremonies. *$$–$$$; AE, MC, V; no checks; lunch Wed–Sat, dinner Tues–Sun, brunch Sun; reservations recommended; www. mollywardgardens.com.* &

MorMor Bistro & Bar / ◆◆◖

18820 Front St, Poulsbo; 360/697-3449
This comfortable, sophisticated restaurant is an urban oasis in quaint, Scandinavian-styled Poulsbo, with several tucked-away tables that feel secluded even on busy nights, and an intimate bar serving delectable cocktails and handcrafted beers. Inspired by their grandmothers' cooking, owners John and Laura Nesby named their restaurant for the Norwegian word meaning "mother's mother." A broad wine list emphasizes Northwest bottles, and the creative menu changes nightly, depending upon availability from the Poulsbo Farmers Market and other local vendors, but expect to find the likes of slow-braised pork osso buco, Oregon-raised beef, wild Alaskan salmon, fresh pastas, sandwiches, appetizers and salads, a large selection of small plates, and brunch items on weekends. The Nesbys also host popular wine dinners and classes spotlighting different regions and themes, joined by guest winemakers, farmers, and other industry experts. *$$; AE, MC, V; local checks only; lunch, dinner every day; full bar; reservations recommended; www. mormorbistro.com.* &

♡ Puget
Sound

Puget Sound

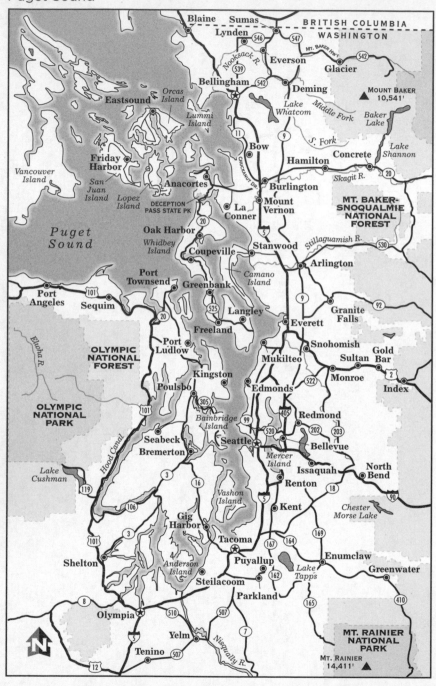

Never a lip is curved in pain
that can't be kissed into smile again.

—Brete Harte

 # Puget Sound

With the enormous Cascade Mountain Range to the east and the majestic Olympic Mountains to the west, the Puget Sound region abounds in dazzling views no matter which way you turn. Add to this the beauty and mystique of the Sound itself and lovers have a multitude of options for romantic trips in the region.

The long, spectacular summer days and easy access to both the islands and Skagit Valley make the Puget Sound an immensely popular locale for weekend getaways. Winter, of course, brings rain to the entire region, although Whidbey Island tends to get less because of the famous Olympic "rain shadow." Among locals, complaining about the rain during the winter months is as much a regular pastime as rooting for the Seahawks or Mariners. But even those who carp are forced to admit that the year-round moderate temperatures and crystal-clear summers help make this region special, even on days intruded upon by a spate of stormy weather. And, of course, the inclement weather allows the spring to reap its rich rewards, when the meadows flourish with blossoms as bright and varied as a box of crayons.

Interstate 5 is the main thoroughfare from Olympia, at the southern edge of Puget Sound, to Bellingham at the northern end, which isn't too far from the border to British Columbia. Driving north from Seattle, the interstate takes you to the Skagit Valley, home to the famous and much-visited tulip fields, and waterfront towns like Anacortes and La Conner. Farther north is Bellingham, with its parks, sparkling lakes, and restored historic districts. But Puget Sound is best explored by getting away from the freeways and heading for the back roads—drives that are endlessly rewarding in water views, forests, and bucolic scenes that seem straight from a storybook.

Access & Information

For those coming by airplane and arriving at **Seattle-Tacoma International Airport** (17801 Pacific Hwy S, SeaTac; 206/433-5388), you'll want to rent a car to properly enjoy the region. Most of the large car-rental agencies have outposts at Sea-Tac.

For those traveling between Portland, Seattle, Bellingham, and Vancouver, BC, **Amtrak** (206/382-4125; www.amtrak.com) provides an alternative to the drive, and train travel is certainly romantic in its own right.

For access to Whidbey Island, take the **Washington State Ferries** (206/464-6400; www.wsdot.wa.gov/ferries) from Mukilteo to Clinton, which takes approximately 20 minutes. From Clinton, drive north on SR 525 and Langley Road to Langley, about 10 minutes north.

For access to Vashon Island, depart from downtown Seattle (this ferry allows for foot traffic only), West Seattle (Fauntleroy ferry), or Tacoma (Point Defiance ferry). Contact Washington State Ferries for details.

Whidbey Island

Romantic Highlights

With 148 miles of gorgeous coastline promising romantic solitude, Whidbey Island is one of the most naturally passion-inspiring places in the entire country. Less than an hour from Seattle via ferry ride, because of its location, even when it's raining in the big city Whidbey tends to stay dry.

Perched on a bluff above the water's edge, the small, sophisticated town of **Langley** enjoys breathtaking views of Mount Baker, the Cascades, and Saratoga Passage. The First Street shops and galleries are designed for hand-in-hand strolling and browsing. Take in work from more than 40 local artists at **The Artists' Galley Cooperative** (314 1st St; 360/221-7675) or check out the supplies at **Chef's Pantry** (112½ Anthes Ave; 360/221-2060). Then, pick up lunch provisions at **Langley's Star Store** (201 1st St; 360/221-5222) and have a picnic along the beach at **Seawall Park** (1st St). For an after-lunch pick-me-up, order a tasty java drink at the **Useless Bay Coffee Company** (121 2nd St; 360/221-4515). While the summer months are Whidbey's busiest, a visit during **Langley's Mystery Weekend** (www.visitlangley.com), held once a year in February or March, is a fine reason to also take advantage of some B&Bs' low-season rates.

Traveling north on Whidbey Island, stop in **Greenbank** on a spring day to stroll through **Meerkerk Rhododendron Gardens** (3531 Meekerk Ln; 360/678-1912), a large, wooded preserve that will delight green thumbs. Then, try a slice of the famous loganberry pie at **Whidbey Pies Café** (Hwy 525 at Wonn Rd). This was once the site of the world's largest loganberry farm.

From Greenbank, drive farther north to Coupeville. Once you're in town, drive past the commercial part of Main Street until you find the small selection of turn-of-the-20th-century harbor-style storefronts, selling antiques and trinkets. Coupeville is a Mecca for artists of all colors: visual, performing, and culinary. The shorelines, forests, prairies, and waters of central Whidbey prove to be inspiration for the many residents whose paintings, photographs, pottery, baskets, jewelry, and woodcarvings are featured around town in galleries and studios. The food artistry should not be overlooked—cafés, chocolate shops, and restaurants each highlight a unique creativity in the dishes, drinks, and desserts they offer.

And, no trip to Whidbey is complete without venturing north for the exhilarating views of the treacherous gorge of **Deception Pass**. Words can't describe the heart-stopping sensation of driving across the narrow bridge that spans the chasm; all the more reason to cling to your companion.

Access & Information

From Seattle, take Interstate 5 north about 17 miles, then take State Route 525 north another 9 miles to Mukilteo; driving time is about 40 minutes. Take the **Washington State Ferries** (206/464-6400 or 800/843-3779; www. wsdot.wa.gov/ferries) from Mukilteo to Clinton; crossing time is approximately 20 minutes and reservations are not accepted for this route. From Clinton, drive north on State Route 525 and Langley Road to Langley, about 10 minutes north.

From farther afield, fly into **Seattle-Tacoma International Airport** (17801 Pacific Hwy S; 206/433-5388)—14 miles south of Seattle and 20 miles north of Tacoma—from where you'll have easy access to Interstate 5. You'll need a car to best explore the region; most car-rental agencies have outlets at Sea-Tac Airport.

Romantic Lodgings

Chauntecleer House, Dove House, and Potting Shed Cottages / ✿✿✿✿

5081 Saratoga Rd, Langley; 360/221-5494
Sitting on a bluff overlooking Saratoga Passage, and surrounded by 6 acres of spectacular, bejeweled gardens, these unique cottages are among the most enchanting in the area. In fact, it's hard to imagine a setting more exquisite than the Chauntecleer House. With its full kitchen, wood-burning fireplace, private hot tub tucked away in a secret garden, and panoramic views, extending one's stay becomes all too tempting. While the Dove House lacks the same awe-inspiring vistas, an intimate loft bedroom, terra-cotta floors, and stained-glass windows evoke a rustic, cozy charm that will leave couples questioning why they'd ever want to venture outside at all. And the smaller garden-style Potting Shed will appeal to couples with whimsical tastes, or to those eager to soak in its two-person jetted tub. Even the fussiest romantics will have trouble finding fault with any of these Whidbey Island gems. *$$$$; no credit cards; checks OK; closed Dec–Jan; www.dovehouse.com.*

Three Days of Puget Sound Romance

Day One: Begin the day in Mount Vernon with a late-morning and afternoon wine tour. Hire a driver for the day from **Triangle Vans Charter** (360/293-4496) or **Valley Taxi Plus** (360/336-3283), snuggle in the back seat as you admire the bucolic scenery passing by, and worry about little more than which wines to purchase at each stop. Start at **Carpenter Creek Winery** (20376 E Hickox Rd, Mount Vernon; 360/848-6673) and make sure to stop at **Valley Vineyard and Orchard** (16163 SR 536, Mount Vernon; 206/321-9424; call for appointment), where you can sample the Red Barn Cider brewed from juicy Jonagold apples grown on-site. Next, enjoy lunch at **The Farmhouse Restaurant** (13724 La Conner Whitney Rd, Mount Vernon; 360/466-4411), where a diner-style menu provides many tempting options.

In the mood for more sipping? Then head to the tasting room at **Pasek Cellars Winery** (18729 Fir Island Rd, Mount Vernon; 360/336-6877) or, since you're heading to La Conner anyway, end your tour at **Hellam's Vineyard** (Limedock Bldg, 109 N 1st St #101, La Conner; 360/466-1758), where you can pick up a few bottles to enjoy another day. Take an afternoon stroll along the water in La Conner, stopping to seek out treasures in the many antique shops that dot First and Morris streets. For dinner, dine on tasty Spanish and Mediterranean cuisine at **The Dulce Plate** (508 Morris St; 360/466-1630), and then head to **The Heron Inn** (117 Maple Ave; 360/466-4626) for the evening where you'll thank yourselves for having booked the Romantic Suite.

Cliff House and Seacliff Cottage / ◆◆◆◆

727 Windmill Dr, Freeland; 360/331-1566 or 800/297-4118
Privacy abounds at the Cliff House, an architectural masterpiece and lavish retreat secluded on more than 14 forested acres. The house's centerpiece—a 30-foot glass-enclosed atrium, coupled with open wood-beamed ceilings and floor-to-ceiling windows, all contribute to the property's majestic tranquility, which is immediately present upon stepping through the front door. Two upstairs bedrooms, a sunken living room with fireplace, and a full gourmet kitchen complete this secluded retreat. The only decision you'll need to make is whether to gaze out at Admiralty Inlet from your king-size feather bed, from a softly swaying hammock, or from the spacious hot tub. The Cottage, tucked away from the Cliff House and beneath the towering trees, is another cozy lodging option and the perfect private hideaway. Just before dusk, be sure to pay a visit to the tree house on the grounds—it's a perfect vantage point to catch the sunset as it dips below the horizon. A continental

Day Two: Start with a sweet treat and espresso at the famous **Calico Cupboard Café and Bakery** (720 S 1st St, La Conner; 360/466-4451), then head to nearby **Anacortes**, where you'll board a ferry for an eight-minute ride to quiet and pastoral **Guemes Island** and witness small-town island life at its best. Grab lunch at the island's only retailer, **Anderson's General Store** (7885 Guemes Island Rd; 360/293-4548), whose motto is, "If we don't have it, we'll explain how you can get along without it." From Guemes Island, take the ferry back to the mainland and drive up Highway 20 toward Whidbey Island and the infamous **Deception Pass Bridge**. Hold on to each other tight while walking across the towering bridge for a heart-pounding thrill. Next, continue to **Coupeville** on Whidbey Island and have dinner at **Christopher's** (105 NW Coveland St; 360/678-5480), before retiring for the night at **The Blue Goose Inn** (702 N Main St; 360/678-4284).

Day Three: In the morning, explore Coupeville's historic waterfront district before heading to **Langley** for a casual day of strolling. Don't miss **Whidbey Island Antiques** (113 Anthes Ave; 360/221-2393) and **Moonraker Books** (209 1st St; 360/221-2393). Grab a picnic from the **Star Store Grocery** (201 1st St; 360/221-5222), then find a perfect bench from among the many choices and partake in your goodies while admiring the view. In the early evening, have dinner at the delightful **Prima Bistro** (201½ 1st St; 360/221-4060) before heading to the ferry for your return trip home. If you can, stay another night at the Blue Goose Inn or at one of the lovely inns in Langley.

breakfast is included with your stay. *$$$–$$$$; no credit cards; checks OK; www.cliffhouse.net.*

The Cottage at Home by the Sea / ❂❂❂

2388 E Sunlight Beach Rd, Clinton; 360/321-2964
Showcasing views of Admiralty Inlet and the Olympic Mountains, and positioned to lay witness to spectacular sunsets, the Cottage at Home by the Sea is a sublime place to escape from the stress and obligations of everyday life. Instead of exploring the island, guests may while away an afternoon lounging in the seaside Adirondack chairs, sipping wine, and reconnecting with each other in one of the area's most relaxing settings. Inside the suite, a quaint yet fully equipped kitchen, wood-burning stove, and king-size feather bed in the master bedroom leave little to be desired for even the most discriminating couple. Nature lovers, take note: The beachfront location is also a birder's paradise. In fact, the Audubon Society declared the area one of the island's

most amazing places for bird-watching. *$$$; MC, V; checks OK; www.home bytheseacottages.com.*

Country Cottage of Langley / ❂❂❂

215 6th St, Langley; 360/221-8709 or 800/713-3860
Any of these six darling cottages will offer enough serenity, privacy, and charm to play the perfect backdrop to an intimate weekend retreat on Whidbey Island. Perched on a bluff overlooking the town of Langley, the cottages delight guests with stunning views of Puget Sound and the Cascade Mountains from each room's luxurious feather bed. Every cottage has its own distinctive theme, such as the nautical motif of the aptly named Captain's Cove. But, with a wraparound porch and a two-person jetted tub, the spacious Cabernet Cottage is particularly appealing. In the morning, fresh fruit, pastries, and main dishes—such as savory strata or quiche—are set in a basket outside your door, to be enjoyed at your leisure. *$$–$$$; AE, MC, V; checks OK; www.acountrycottage.com.*

Eagles Nest Inn / ❂❂❂

4680 Saratoga Rd, Langley; 360/221-5331
Just a mile from downtown Langley, the four suites at the Eagles Nest Inn and the surrounding grounds transport guests into a state of instant bliss. Three of the four suites showcase jaw-dropping views of Saratoga Passage and Mount Baker, and all share access to an outdoor spa and library lounge (complete with a constantly replenished jar of complimentary freshly baked cookies). Although each suite offers its own particular charms, we prefer the Eagles Nest Room on the top floor with a spectacular 360-degree view. Nature lovers will delight in the verdant grounds surrounding the inn, teeming with birds, chipmunks, quail, rabbits, and even bald eagles. Those in the mood for adventure can continue searching for wildlife on nearly 400 acres of public trails abutting the inn. *$$–$$$; MC, V; local checks only; www. eaglesnestinn.com.*

Garden Path Suites / ❂❂❂

111 1st St, Langley; 360/221-5121
Located just a few steps from Langley's bustling First Street, these suites are ideal for couples preferring to stay in the heart of the quaint village. Cloaked in wisteria, and heavenly with nature's scents in springtime, a brick garden path leads away from the busy shopping street to the front door of this inn. Once inside, you'll find skylights brightening the stately living room, which is filled with impressive antiques, colorful artwork, and artistic touches. Each of the two suites includes all of the amenities needed for a romantic getaway, but the Sea Suite is more spacious and luxurious, with views of Langley and the Saratoga Passage, and a Jacuzzi tub. You won't regret having chosen this inn, which offers the perfect combination of garden hideaway and village convenience. *$$–$$$; MC, V; checks OK; www.gardenpathsuites.com.*

Guest House Log Cottages / ❂❂❂

24371 SR 525, Greenbank; 360/678-3115
Surrounded by acres of meadows and forest, the Guest House Log Cottages are set in a pastoral wonderland, perfect for those seeking woodsy seclusion robust with rustic charms. Five quaint cottages and one spectacular lodge are spread out across the property, affording the level of privacy hoped for in a romantic retreat. Inside, the cabins all feature old-fashioned country touches like patchwork quilts and rustic oak furniture, while also offering several appealing amenities, including Jacuzzi tubs, fireplaces, and kitchens. Serious romantics should consider splurging on the larger and more luxurious lodge. With soaring cathedral ceilings and floor-to-ceiling windows overlooking the grounds, the grand log house sets the stage as an exquisite backdrop for a special occasion. A heated swimming pool (open seasonally) and an outdoor hot tub are also available for guests to enjoy. *$$$–$$$$; DIS, MC, V; checks OK; www.guesthouselogcottages.com.*

The Inn at Langley / ❂❂❂❸

400 1st St, Langley; 360/221-3033
Often dubbed the crown jewel of Whidbey Island accommodations, the Inn at Langley lives up to its sterling reputation, truly making it one of the area's most spectacular places to kiss. Each of the 26 guest rooms and cottages is decorated in clean, simple lines and in neutral hues of beige, grey, and white, allowing the splendid 180-degree water views to take a starring role. The inn is situated on a bluff overlooking Saratoga Passage, so early risers will delight in sitting on their large, private decks and catching the sun as it peeks over the Cascades. Each room's giant two-person spa tub is precisely placed so guests can enjoy both the spectacular vistas and the fireplace. Although excellent dining options abound in town, guests should not pass up eating on-site at the Chef's Kitchen, which consistently serves some of the most inventive and delicious dinners in the area. Also on-site: Spa Essencia (360/221-0991), where you can (and should) splurge on a spa treatment for two. *$$$$; AE, DIS, MC, V; no checks; www.innatlangley.com.*

Island Tyme Bed and Breakfast / ❂❂❸

4940 Bayview Rd, Langley; 360/221-5078
Sit back and relax; you're now operating on island "tyme." Just 2 miles from Langley but tucked away on 20 acres of forested land, this multicolored Victorian-style inn encourages a slower, simpler pace—one that is sure to rejuvenate and uplift even the most harried of souls. Of the five delightful guest rooms, we favor either the Heirloom Suite, with its wood-burning fireplace and two-person jetted tub, or the Masterpiece, which houses a luxe king-size bed and several antiques and collectibles. By day, couples will delight in strolling hand-in-hand around the property's bucolic surroundings, perhaps stopping to enjoy a picnic in the meadow or visiting with the three

resident goats. Couples with doggy companions, take note: Well-behaved canines are welcome guests in the pet-friendly Keepsake Room. *$$; DIS, MC, V; no checks; www.bbonline.com/wa/island.*

Saratoga Inn / ❂❂❂

201 Cascade Ave, Langley; 360/221-5801
Although this lovely inn has its gorgeous views of Saratoga Passage marred at times by heavy summer traffic, it is nonetheless a cozy escape. With its wood-shingle exterior and long wraparound porch, the inn looks like a slice of New England set in the heart of Whidbey. Choose from among 15 cozy rooms, all with fireplaces, or the splurge-worthy Carriage House suite, which boasts a spacious marble bathroom and an enormous deck. Rooms on the top floor, with cathedral ceilings, are particularly appealing, but the traffic noise may bother light sleepers. In the afternoon, head downstairs to the common area to sit by the crackling fire and enjoy the complimentary afternoon tea and hors d'oeuvres. Or, if the weather is pleasant, the front porch's rocking chairs are a prime spot to sit side-by-side and enjoy the beautiful surroundings. *$$$–$$$$; AE, DC, DIS, MC, V; no checks; www.saratogainnwhidbey island.com.*

Woodland Retreat Bed and Breakfast / ❂❂❂❂

4925 Crawford Rd, Langley; 866/265-4106
Serenity abounds at this immaculate escape in a quiet and woodsy setting just five minutes from Langley's downtown area. Both guest rooms are sizable and decorated with refined yet comfortable and understated touches—perfect for couples who dislike the cluttered kitsch and fussy floral decor often associated with bed-and-breakfasts. And, with a selection of board games, newspapers, and DVDs, it would be easy to spend an entire weekend inside, hugging and cuddling—and competing. In fact, with luxurious beds dressed in down and Egyptian cotton, just getting out of bed may seem a chore. It would be a shame, though, to miss the breakfast, which is something of local yore. Every morning, guests choose from several tantalizing homemade breakfast items, including chocolate and hazelnut crepes, quiche prepared with fresh herbs, and piping hot breakfast *panini* stuffed with eggs, bacon, and melted mozzarella. *$$; MC, V; no checks; www.wrbb.us.*

Romantic Restaurants

Café Langley / ❂❂❂

113 1st St, Langley; 360/221-3090
On the surface, Café Langley appears more casual than romantic, but this spot has been a date-night legacy for years. Yes, the dining room is small, but under a glow of candlelight, the space feels intimate and charming. The kitchen uses locally grown, seasonal ingredients, and the menu showcases

creative takes on Mediterranean cuisine, like an inspired version of the classic hummus and warm pita. Signature dishes include pan-roasted leg of lamb served with brandy-cherry demi-glace. Reservations are a must on weekends, as locals and visitors alike will be clamoring for a table. *$$; AE, MC, V; checks OK; lunch, dinner every day (closed Tues in winter); beer and wine; reservations recommended; www.cafelangley.com.*

Prima Bistro / ◐◐◐

201½ 1st St, Langley; 360/221-4060
Prima combines classic French bistro style with fresh, local ingredients in a warm, fun atmosphere—making it an exciting addition to the Langley dining scene. The Salad Niçoise with slices of rare ahi tuna is an exceptionally rendered version of a classic, and prawns sautéed in white truffle oil, honey, and Marcona almonds are nothing short of sublime. The owners share their passion for wine during Prima's special wine dinners, which highlight the products of different vineyards around the world. When the weather cooperates, this is also a wonderful spot for lunch on the deck. *$$; MC, V; checks OK; lunch, dinner Tues–Sun; full bar; reservations recommended; www.primabistro.biz.*

Trattoria Giuseppe / ◐◐◐

4141 E Hwy 525, Clinton; 360/341-3454
Are you in Little Italy or on Whidbey Island? Follow the wafting scent of garlic to this unlikely locale (in an otherwise unspectacular shopping plaza) for fantastic, authentic Italian food and heartwarming ambience. Despite the cramped tables, cathedral ceilings, stucco walls, and softly lit chandeliers set the perfectly rustic atmosphere. Guests enjoy well-crafted, hearty meals like Linguine alla Romana or Chicken Parmigiana. Saturday nights feature a jazz pianist to accompany your meal. Make sure to save your appetite for dessert: the rare joy of lovingly crafted cannoli—pastry shells filled with ricotta, chocolate shavings, and almonds—should not be missed. *$$; AE, DC, DIS, MC, V; local checks only; dinner every day; full bar; reservations recommended; www.trattoriagiuseppe.com.*

Skagit Valley

Romantic Highlights

In the shadow of grand Mount Baker, and renowned for the endless rows of colorful tulips reigning across the region during springtime, Skagit Valley is a wonderful choice for a quiet getaway during any season. The charming towns of La Conner, Mount Vernon, and Anacortes all offer enchanting places to kiss, as does Camano Island, a bit farther afoot.

La Conner is a Victorian waterfront town filled with antique stores, art galleries, and three museums. Because La Conner is situated right on the Swinomish Channel, you're ensured a fantastic view no matter where you go. One unique stroll to take is the **La Conner Sculpture Walk** (starts outside the Chamber of Commerce; 413 Morris St), featuring 20 pieces of original art. Dine at **Seeds—A Bistro & Bar** (623 Morris St; 360/466-3280), or pick up sandwiches at **La Conner Fruit and Produce Market** (116 S 1st St; 360/466-3018) and find a seat at whichever scenic spot strikes your fancy.

Instead of rushing through Anacortes, known as the gateway to the San Juan Islands, take in the scenery of spectacular **Washington Park** (less than a mile west of the ferry terminal). Summer (May–Sept) is the perfect time for nature-loving couples to charter a boat from **Mystic Sea Charters** (800/308-9387) for a whale-watching trip. If you're lucky, you'll see a pod of orcas, along with eagles, sea lions, porpoises, and seals.

A trip to Camano Island (not technically part of the Skagit Valley), which does not require ferry travel, is a great option for a Friday or Saturday evening of wine tasting at **Great Blue Heron Wine Cellars**, located in **Brindle's Marketplace** (848 N Sunrise Blvd, Building C; 360/722-7482).

Access & Information

North of Seattle, Interstate 5 carries you to exits for Camano Island and La Conner, and then on to the tulip town of Mount Vernon, located just off the interstate. Camano Island can be reached directly by car: take I-5 exit 212 and follow the main thoroughfare through Stanwood. There are several ways to get to La Conner, but taking back-country roads is by far the most romantic: take I-5 exit 221, drive east on Fir Island Road, and follow the signs. The countryside is ideal for bicyclists, so do bring your bikes if you're so inclined; however, it's best to leave them at home during the annual **Tulip Festival** in April (360/428-5959; www.tulipfestival.org), when crowds descend. For more information about the area, contact the **La Conner Chamber of Commerce** (360/466-4778 or 888/642-9284; www.laconnerchamber.com).

Romantic Lodgings

Alice Bay Bed & Breakfast / ◐◐◐

11794 Scott Rd, Samish Island, Bow; 360/766-6396
Burgeoning naturalists who make the trip to Alice Bay Bed & Breakfast— located outside of La Conner on quiet Samish Island—may just proclaim it their personal wonderland by the end of their stay. Alice Bay is home to a great blue heron rookery, but couples strolling along the private beach may be lucky enough to also spot the area's resident bald eagles, hawks, and falcons. As for the guest quarters, which are separated from the owners' house by a breezeway, the modest but comfortable setup includes a queen bed, a serene view of the bay, and thick, cozy robes—to keep you warm on the journey to

The Five Most Romantic Shops in the Puget Sound

Angel Place Chocolate Bar (138 2nd St, Langley; 360/221-2728): Luscious melted-chocolate drinks.

Escape Bath, Candles & Gifts (710 S 1st St, La Conner): Featuring Thymes, Crabtree, Camille, and Provence products.

Island Thyme (17233 Vashon Hwy SW, Vashon Island; 206/463-4438): Specialty gifts and embellishments for home and garden.

Whimsey Gallery (1200 10th St, Bellingham; 360/733-5568): Eclectic collection of jewelry from more than 50 different artists.

Barker Road Collection (2225 N 30th St, Tacoma; 253/572-9686): Creative high-end wares from around the world.

the outdoor hot tub. As you are the only guests on the premises, a sumptuous breakfast is delivered to your door at the time you specify. Do your best to wake up with a healthy appetite for signature Alice Bay French Toast or a Grand Dutch Baby. Due to popular demand, the *Alice Bay Cookbook* of favorite recipes was compiled to include these two specialties. *$$$; AE, DIS, MC, V; checks OK; www.alicebay.com.*

Autumn Leaves Bed and Breakfast / ❍❍❋

2301 21st St, Anacortes; 360/293-4920
Most folks pass through Anacortes only briefly on their way to the San Juan Islands, but this bed-and-breakfast just may give romantic travelers a reason to stop and discover the unknown charms. Decorated throughout with exquisite antiques, Autumn Leaves combines elegant Victorian touches with modern amenities. Each of the three rooms boasts a two-person jetted tub, and gas fireplaces create a distinctive atmosphere with all the creature comforts desired in a romantic getaway. With views of Mount Baker in the distance, the King Louis Room, accented in rich ruby tones, is our favorite. The delicious breakfast, served in the dining room, is a highlight, featuring delightful dishes like French toast, lemon crepes, and frittatas. *$$$; MC, V; checks OK; www.autumn-leaves.com.*

Blue Moon Beach House / ❍❍❋

3267 Shoreline Dr, Camano Island; 360/387-6666
Although the funky blue exterior may put off some visitors, the Blue Moon Beach House's well-appointed suites and waterfront location on peaceful Camano Island make the inn an excellent choice for couples seeking a romantic retreat on the water. With no ferry lines to contend with, a reasonable drive from either Seattle or Vancouver gets you to the doorstep in no time.

The guesthouse practically sits on top of Puget Sound, affording each of the three suites spectacular views. If you're lucky enough to nab the two-story Moonlight Suite, set aside ample time to soak in the gorgeous wood-fired hot tub out on the private deck. Or, on stormy days, get cozy by the gas fireplace. The Sea Star Room also has a king-size comfort-top bed and its own deck with sweeping views of the Sound. The Blue Moon Room is an adequate, but distant third, option. By day, rent one of the available kayaks to explore the surrounding waters or take a rejuvenating walk along pebbled Tyee Beach. *$$–$$$; MC, V; local checks only; www.bluemoonbeachhouse.com.*

Camano Island Inn / ✪✪✪

1054 SW Camano Dr, Camano Island; 360/387-0783
Each of the six guest rooms is truly a room with a view at this hidden gem accessible by car from Seattle. From your cozy bed or private waterfront deck you can gaze at the Olympics and keep your eye out for eagles, seals, and even orcas. Room 1 is impressive with a large jetted tub and king-size canopy bed. Rooms 2 and 4 offer outdoor jetted tubs on the deck. The 1904 house includes a welcoming sitting room with a river-rock fireplace. After a tasty breakfast, get closer to the abounding wildlife (and each other) with a walk along the pebble beach. *$$$; AE, DIS, MC, V; checks OK; www. camanoislandinn.com.* &

The Heron Inn and Watergrass Day Spa / ✪✪✪

117 Maple Ave, La Conner; 360/466-4626
Home to the Watergrass Day Spa—with a cozy champagne and wine bar adjacent to the lobby and within strolling distance of La Conner's downtown—relaxation is not hard to come by at the stylish 11-room Heron Inn. So long as a view of the parking lot won't spoil your mood, opt for the most luxuriously appointed Romantic Suite, which features vaulted ceilings, a queen sleigh bed, a fireplace, and a two-person jetted tub. Or, for views of the inn's gardens and the Cascades in the distance, choose Room 32. With common outdoor decks perfect for gazing at Skagit Valley's bucolic beauty, a 56-jet therapeutic garden hot tub, and a spa that specializes in luxurious, organic treatments, the Heron Inn seems tailored to a proposal, honeymoon, or anniversary getaway. *$$–$$$; AE, DIS, MC, V; checks OK; www. theheron.com.*

La Conner Channel Lodge / ✪✪

205 N 1st St, La Conner; 360/466-1500
Although this large establishment has some of the uninspired trappings of standard hotels—such as long, drab hallways—Northwest charm is still prevalent at the La Conner Channel Lodge, particularly in the guest rooms. Most feature views of the Swinomish Channel and gas fireplaces; couples who can splurge on a King Parlor room will truly enjoy kiss-worthy amenities such as

a private deck overlooking the water, Jacuzzi tub, and sumptuous king bed. Although this might not be an establishment in which you'll want to hole up for days, its location within a block of La Conner's eminently strollable main street makes the lodge a geographically desirable option. $$$–$$$$; AE, DIS, MC, V; checks OK; www.laconnerlodging.com.

Samish Point by the Bay / ✪✪✪✪

4465 Samish Point Rd, Bow; 360/766-6610
This Cape Cod–style cottage, secluded on breathtaking Samish Point, provides the ultimate in privacy for a weekend of reflection with the one you love. Surrounded by cedar, fir, and maple trees, and a pear, apple, and plum orchard, the house accommodates up to six, but the natural inclination for couples is to keep this gem all to themselves. Right outside, a hot tub beckons on the wooden deck, and a little farther afoot, acres of walking trails and a driftwood beach are intriguing options for exploring the area's ample beauty. Inside the cozy retreat, a bright living room boasts a river-rock fireplace, and the designer kitchen will be stocked with continental breakfast fixings when you arrive. Bring your favorite food and drink and plan to settle in for a while—a hasty departure from this kind of romantic solitude seems downright silly. $$$; AE, MC, V; checks OK; www.samishpoint.com.

Skagit Bay Hideaway / ✪✪✪✪

17430 Goldenview Ave, La Conner; 360/466-2262
At this magnificent getaway overlooking Skagit Bay, every detail seems to have been carefully chosen to maximize romance. The two suites both feature exquisite water views, fireplaces, and private rooftop decks with two-person jetted spa tubs to be enjoyed at a couple's leisure. One of the most divine features is each suite's impressive bathroom, which showcases an Italian-tiled double-headed shower with multiple jets that emerge from the walls to massage you from all directions. And, while the other suite may be occupied during your stay, the decks are staggered, so you'll most likely never see your neighbors. The suites are nearly identical, so take whichever one is available. Seamlessly integrated into the natural beauty of the surroundings, this hideaway is a rare gem indeed. $$$$; AE, MC, V; no checks; www.skagitbay.com.

The Wild Iris Inn / ✪✪✪

121 Maple Ave, La Conner; 360/466-1400
This 16-room boutique hotel oozes country refinement and bills itself as an "alternative to 'cookie-cutter' hotels and 'touchy-feely' bed-and-breakfasts." For couples looking for something in between those two extremes, the uncluttered elegance displayed throughout the inn certainly makes the Wild Iris an attractive choice. The deluxe king suites are best for a romantic weekend getaway, with two-person jetted tubs, fireplaces, and private decks or balconies.

And, for those who take special delight in outdoor spas, the three king suites have hot tubs on their private decks. No matter which room type you choose, a luxurious king-size bed topped by an impossibly fluffy comforter awaits your slumber. While the front of the two-story Victorian-style inn overlooks a parking lot, it's a minor quibble, because the thoughtful amenities, attentive staff, and lavish complimentary breakfast make the Wild Iris one of Skagit Valley's most distinctive and attractive establishments. *$$–$$$; AE, MC, V; checks OK; www.wildiris.com.* &

Romantic Restaurants

Kerstin's / ❂❂❂

505 S 1st St, La Conner; 360/466-9111
To enjoy the most spectacular views of the Swinomish Channel, ask to sit upstairs at this elegant establishment, or if the weather permits, opt for a table on the tiny, charming deck. While the warm feelings may well up in this sumptuous atmosphere, those planning to sit on the deck should bring along a shawl or jacket to temper the cool breeze. With the restaurant's extensive wine list and a menu that takes advantage of the valley's seasonal bounty, diners can choose from local seafood like Samish Bay oysters or wild salmon in a lime-butter sauce. Meat and pasta options are also available. *$$$; AE, MC, V; local checks only; dinner every day; full bar; reservations recommended.*

Nell Thorn Restaurant and Pub / ❂❂❂

205 E Washington St, La Conner; 360/466-4261
The mostly organic, seasonal menu at Nell Thorn is "inspired to nourish," and the creatively delicious cuisine succeeds time and again in achieving that goal. While locals know of Nell Thorn for its sensational homemade bread, the restaurant is also an ideal place to head for an unforgettable romantic meal in La Conner. Soft lights illuminate the wood-beamed ceiling in the upstairs dining room, and tables cloaked in white linen and awash in candlelight set an intimate atmosphere. Choosing an entrée from the numerous delectable options may be difficult, but favorites here include classics from the sea and land, like pan-seared halibut and New York steak. For a less expensive, more casual meal, try the pub downstairs. *$$; AE, DIS, MC, V; local checks only; lunch Thur–Sun (summer), Sat–Sun (winter), dinner Tues–Sun; full bar; reservations recommended; www.nellthorn.com.*

The Oyster Bar on Chuckanut Drive / ❂❂❂

2578 Chuckanut Dr, Bow; 360/766-6185
This small and elegant setting, known as much for its award-winning wine cellar as the oysters in its name, is the most formal of the restaurants located along the breathtakingly beautiful Chuckanut Drive. Children under 11 are not allowed, which ensures that the quiet, romantic atmosphere created by

the surrounding water and cedars is uncompromised. Oenophiles travel great distances to the tiny cedar dining room to partake in the impressive wine list (practically as long as a novella), pairing bottles with the restaurant's freshly caught and deliciously rendered seafood and shellfish. House specialties include oysters pan-fried in panko and Dungeness crab and shrimp cakes. *$$$; AE, MC, V; local checks only; lunch, dinner every day; beer and wine; reservations recommended; www.theoysterbaronchuckanutdrive.com.*

Rhododendron Café / ◕◕

5521 Chuckanut Dr, Bow; 360/766-6667
This casual favorite is a lovely stop for hungry couples enjoying the many splendors of Chuckanut Drive. Each month the tiny, cheery restaurant embarks on an "Ethnic Odyssey," choosing a different region or country's cuisine on which to base its inventive daily specials. Meanwhile, the regular menu features a variety of dishes, with pan-fried Samish oysters, savory pasta entrées, and homemade soups and chowders—reliably delicious. After a day of taking in Chuckanut Drive's bounding bluffs, a visit to the Rhododendron is sure to bring you back to earth . . . gently. *$$$; AE, DIS, MC, V; checks OK; breakfast Sat–Sun, lunch, dinner Wed–Sun (closed Dec–Jan); beer and wine; reservations recommended for parties of 5 or more; www.rhodycafe.com.*

Star Bar / ◕◕◕

416½ Commercial Ave, Anacortes; 360/299-2120
For warm elegance in the Skagit Bay region minus the stodgy, old-fashioned menu found at many of the area's white table–clothed establishments, Star Bar provides a setting without peer. For lighter dining, the restaurant offers a selection of creative, scrumptious *tapas*. If you do opt for entrées, dishes like the braised short rib and coriander crusted yellowfin tuna are hard to pass up, and the chocolate-banana *pot de crème* makes for a sensuous conclusion to your meal. The restaurant's lounge, especially the outdoor patio, is geared toward more casual seating and dining options. *$$$; AE, MC, V; checks OK; dinner Tues–Sat; full bar; reservations recommended; www. starbaranacortes.com.*

Bellingham

Romantic Highlights

Bellingham seemingly has it all with an abundance of natural beauty, its endlessly charming historic Fairhaven district, and a wide variety of accommodations and restaurants. The area's rugged splendor is apparent even before you reach the city, particularly for travelers lucky enough to arrive from Bow on **Chuckanut Drive** (Hwy 11; from Bellingham, follow 12th St south out of town; from I-5 northbound, take exit 231). The dramatic stretch of road abuts cliffs that plunge deep into the water. Along Chuckanut Drive, about 7 miles south of Bellingham, make sure to stop at **Larrabee State Park** (360/902-8844; www.parks.wa.gov). Avid hikers will find spectacular vistas and privacy by following the trailhead directly across the road from the park with signs for **Fragrance Lake**. Climb about a mile straight uphill to the viewpoint, and you'll be rewarded for your hard work.

For a different kind of seclusion, quiet **Lummi Island** (www.lummi-island.com) is located off Gooseberry Point northwest of Bellingham. Lummi is serviced by the tiny **Whatcom Chief ferry** (360/676-6876; www.co.whatcom.wa.us/publicworks), which leaves Gooseberry Point one to three times per hour from about 6am until midnight. It's easy to find (follow signs to Lummi Island from I-5, north of Bellingham), cheap (about $10 for two people in a car), and quick (six-minute crossing). From Lummi Island, the ferry-return schedule is similar to the departure schedule. If famished when visiting the island, check out the **Beach Store Café** (2200 N Nugent Rd; 360/758-2233), where pizza and clam chowder are served up.

Within Bellingham, the Fairhaven district is a charming area by day for strolling, and a cosmopolitan nightspot for rock and rolling. Try award-winning soups, huge sandwiches, and tasty desserts at **Colophon Café** (1208 11th St; 360/647-0092). **The Old Fairhaven Winery and Boutique** (1106 Harris Ave, Ste 104; 360/738-9463) offers wine tasting right in town. On Saturdays from April through Christmas, the **Bellingham Farmers Market** (inside the Depot Market Square) offers fresh produce and unique crafts—perfect for a leisurely walk. Finally, **Quel Fromage** (1200 Old Fairhaven Pkwy, Ste 101; 360/671-0203) is as much a cheese museum as a cheese shop, serving more than 100 artisan cheeses and many other goodies to pair with your selections; decadent epicureans should not pass up a stop here.

Access & Information

Driving north from Seattle, Interstate 5 leads you right to Bellingham. Fly into **Seattle-Tacoma International Airport** (17801 Pacific Hwy S, SeaTac; 206/433-5388)—14 miles south of Seattle and 20 miles north of Tacoma—from where you'll have easy access to I-5. You'll need a car to best explore the region; most car-rental agencies have outlets at Sea-Tac Airport. **Amtrak** (401 Harris Ave, Bellingham; 360/734-8851 or 800/USA-RAIL; www.amtrak.com) provides a link to Portland, Seattle, or Vancouver, BC. You can arrange with several area lodgings to pick you up at the depot in the historic district of Fairhaven. For more information, contact the **Fairhaven Association** (360/738-1574; www.fairhaven.com).

The **Mount Baker Highway** (Hwy 542) starts right near Bellingham, parallels the sparkling Nooksack River, and passes through little towns like Deming and Glacier to reach two of the state's loveliest sights: 10,778-foot Mount Baker and 9,127-foot Mount Shuksan. Skiers and snowboarders from all over the world journey to the **Mount Baker Ski Area** (360/734-6771; www.mtbaker.us), 56 miles east of Bellingham. The mountain never lacks for snow—it's a glacier—but it's not always a skier's paradise and conditions vary. When the snow falls, Baker is a famously popular destination, offering the kind of steep terrain that satisfies avid boarders. Call ahead to get conditions if you're planning a ski getaway; in summer, you can enjoy beautiful vistas and exhilarating day hikes.

Romantic Lodgings

Chrysalis Inn and Spa / ◉◉◉◉

804 10th St, Bellingham; 360/756-1005
See "The Chrysalis Inn and Spa" on page 204. *$$$–$$$$; AE, DC, DIS, MC, V; checks OK; www.thechrysalisinn.com.*

Fairhaven Village Inn / ◉◉◉

1200 10th St, Bellingham; 360/733-1311
From the outside, the Fairhaven Village Inn looks more like a giant old-western saloon than a kiss-worthy accommodation option. But, despite the old-time appearance, couples in-the-know will love both the inn's prime location in the heart of charming Fairhaven and the luxurious amenities offered in each of the 22 guest rooms, including down comforters and lush robes. In our opinion, the spacious suites are only worth the splurge if a jetted tub and extra-large quarters are paramount to your enjoyment. Otherwise, the less expensive guest rooms should please even the most discriminating duos. If your day out and about is going to include a detour back to the inn, try to time it with the appearance of fresh-baked cookies each day at about 3pm. And for those who want peace and quiet, note that train noise can be an occasional annoyance, but it's a small price to pay to stay at the otherwise ideally situated inn. *$$$; AE, MC, V; no checks; www.fairhavenvillageinn.com.*

Hotel Bellwether / ◉◉◉◉

1 Bellwether Wy, Bellingham; 360/392-3100
You crave mountain vistas, but your loved one longs for a getaway on the water? No compromise is necessary at Hotel Bellwether, which showcases breathtaking views of the Cascade Mountains in a peaceful Bellingham Bay setting. In fact, guests arriving by boat can moor their vessels at the hotel's private dock. Inside, the 66 guest rooms are handsomely appointed and exceptionally comfortable, with imported Italian furniture, down pillows and comforters, and jetted bathtubs. The hotel's most luxurious guest quarters—the free-standing, three-story Lighthouse Suite—is a 900-square-foot condominium chock-full of high-end amenities. One night here does come at cruise-ship costs, but for a special occasion, the exceptional setting just might be worth the splurge. In fact, we can hardly imagine a more picture-perfect spot for a marriage proposal than the Lighthouse balcony at sunset. *$$$–$$$$; AE, DC, DIS, MC, V; local checks only; www.hotel bellwether.com.* &

The Chrysalis Inn and Spa

The **Chrysalis Inn and Spa** (see Romantic Lodgings) deserves special mention here because, frankly, there just aren't enough lips in our rating system to do it justice. A spectacular waterfront locale within close proximity to the Historic Fairhaven District and all its charms, the Chrysalis Inn and Spa provides a picture-perfect setting for a luxurious romantic retreat. Designed in a simple and uncluttered contemporary Northwest style, the handsome decor is impressive throughout, starting with the soaring heights of the post-and-beam foyer that's sure to take your breath away upon entering. Whether you're scouting the perfect place to pop the question or an ideal stop on a fantasy Puget Sound honeymoon, you needn't look further than the Chrysalis, which truly caters to couples.

The on-site spa is by far the most luxuriously equipped in the region and is just as extraordinary as spas typically found in five-star resort properties around the world. Unique treatments include the Lomi Lomi massage, which uses ancient Hawaiian techniques; the exfoliating French Body Polish; and energy healing, which promises to increase one's physical, mental, and emotional well-being. For the ultimate in pampering, the Chrysalis Package is a five-hour extravaganza including a Raining Water massage and scalp treatment, facial, manicure, pedicure, spa cuisine meal, and special gift. Or, if you so desire, create a custom couple's

Semiahmoo Resort / ❂❂❂

9565 Semiahmoo Pkwy, Blaine; 360/318-2000 or 800/770-7992
This sprawling 198-room resort set north of Bellingham on the sparkling bay waters beside Washington's Canadian border boasts two of the state's most acclaimed public golf courses and numerous other amenities that will appeal to even those couples with no intentions of hitting the links. The 4,000-square-foot spa includes 10 treatment rooms (one is a couple's Swedish-massage room) and offers a multitude of luxurious face and body services. Many of the comfortable (but not exceptionally special) guest rooms feature amenities like wood-burning fireplaces and balconies, which encourage cozying up to the one you love. While romance can surely abound in this beautiful setting, the resort is very family friendly, so don't expect a subdued, adults-only atmosphere in the pool or Jacuzzi area. *$$$–$$$$; AE, DIS, MC, V; checks OK; www.semiahmoo.com.* &

package and spend the day being pampered together.

As for the guest quarters, the standard ("deluxe") rooms at the Chrysalis Inn are on par with, or better than, the top-shelf options at most other hotels in the region. Each one of the inn's 43 guest rooms includes a water view, a cozy window seat for quiet contemplation, a fireplace, a two-person bathtub, cable TV and DVD player, aromatherapy amenities, and luxurious linens. The next step up is a Luxury King Suite, which showcases a living room with a wet bar, a two-person jetted tub, and a two-person shower. At the highest end, the Luxury Corner Suite also features a two-person jetted tub cradled in a bay window overlooking the magnificent views. These rooms are the real deal for romance, but they come at a steep price. And, lest we forget to warn you, once you get comfortable in your suite at the Chrysalis, you may never want to leave.

The Fino Wine Bar downstairs gives couples yet another reason to stay on Chrysalis's premises. It offers up sophisticated meal options, such as pan-seared scallops with Brie whipped potatoes and red-onion confit, sumptuous desserts, and a fantastic wine selection.

Any requests to up the romantic quotient a bit more, like wine and a cheese plate, or truffles and champagne? Just say the word and the helpful and skillful Chrysalis staff will see to it that they magically appear in your room—a gesture that earns a big kiss of approval.

The Willows Inn / ❶❷❸

2579 W Shore Dr, Lummi Island; 360/758-2620
Located on petite Lummi Island, the northernmost San Juan island, and accessible from the mainland by a six-minute ferry ride, this secluded getaway offers sparkling views of the Strait of Georgia and the forested hills of nearby Orcas Island. Although there are five guest rooms in the main building, we recommend staying in either the separate guest house or the cottage, which both provide ample privacy. The two-bedroom guest house features a double walk-in steam shower, gas fireplace, and private deck with a barbeque. Our favorite, the cottage, is both cozy and serene, with a covered deck on which to sit and gaze out at its own secret garden and phenomenal views of Rosario Strait. The owners also started nearby Nettles Farm and are devotees of the Slow Food movement. So, in the house's dining room, guests are treated to sumptuous organic meals made with the freshest seasonal ingredients from local sources. Highlights include savory breakfasts (included with the cost of the room) with fresh eggs unlike any you've ever tasted. Delicious! *$$$–$$$$; AE, DIS, MC, V; checks OK; seasonal closures; www.willows-inn.com.*

Romantic Restaurants

Flats Tapas Bar / ◗◗◗

1307 11th St, Bellingham; 360/738-6001
The exposed-brick walls, warm lighting, and inventive *tapas* all create a fun, laid-back antidote to the stuffiness of a more typical upscale fish-and-steakhouse restaurant. Located in the Fairhaven district, this charming establishment instead offers up uniquely rendered small plates (that aren't all that small) like Macarrones, a grown-up mac 'n' cheese served with mascarpone and white truffle oil, and scintillating stuffed piquillo peppers topped with garlic yogurt and a balsamic glaze. Each month, the restaurant hosts a wine-and-*tapas*-pairing dinner, a special treat if you're in town. *$$; MC, V; local checks only; lunch, dinner every day; beer and wine; no reservations; www.flatstapas.com.*

Harborside Bistro / ◗◗◗

1 Bellwether Wy (Hotel Bellwether), Bellingham; 360/392-3200
Time your meal to catch the sunset over Bellingham Bay at this intimate bistro located inside Hotel Bellwether (see Romantic Lodgings). Decorated in elegant dark woods and crimson, the gracious dining room sets a romantic mood with its white linens, soft lighting, and elegant European antiques. The surf-and-turf menu changes seasonally, save for a few favorites, such as the divine coconut-lime seafood chowder. Linger over a pre- or post-dinner drink at the Sunset Lounge. In the winter, cozy up on the leather couch in front of the fireplace; in the summer, enjoy the impressive view—and a kiss—in the outside seating area. *$$$; AE, DIS, MC, V; local checks only; breakfast, lunch, dinner every day; full bar; reservations recommended; www.harborsidebistro.com.*

Mannino's Restaurant / ◗◗◗

1007 Harris Ave, Bellingham; 360/671-7955
After moving in 2003 from downtown to a splendid Fairhaven district location, this family-run Italian restaurant opened under a new name with a radically different menu. The outcry among regulars devoted to the old Mannino's was such that the owners changed their minds and reopened under the familiar name once again. The devotion to the restaurant is still well deserved, as the traditional Italian pasta dishes are exceptional. We recommend a seat on the heated outdoor deck, or, if it isn't occupied by another amorous couple, the tiny "proposal balcony," a private area for two that looks like something out of a romantic movie. *$$$; AE, DC, DIS, MC, V; local checks only; lunch, dinner every day; full bar; reservations recommended.* &

Milano's Restaurant and Deli / ♨♨

9990 Mt Baker Hwy, Glacier; 360/599-2863
Located between Bellingham and Mount Baker, this unassuming Italian restaurant might not appear deserving of a stop. But visiting gourmands in-the-know and locals flock here for Milano's exceptional cuisine, particularly the freshly made pasta with creative fillings and sauces. House specialties include Seafood Linguine, tossed with fresh mussels, calamari, clams, and prawns; and Pasta Toscana, a spinach-and-fusilli dish topped with gorgonzola cheese. Be sure to finish off with one of the pastry chef's excellent desserts: the tiramisu and polenta dolce, a tender cornmeal pound cake, are two of the tempting options. *$$; MC, V; local checks only; lunch, dinner every day; beer and wine; no reservations; www.milanorestaurant.us.* &

South Sound

Romantic Highlights

The often-unheralded South Sound, with its breathtaking mountain and water views, serene public gardens, and impressive arts scene, is a more whimsical destination than its reputation would suggest. Sunny Vashon Island may seem to be the most romantic area in the region, but both Gig Harbor and Tacoma boast their own unique charms. Always in Seattle's emerald shadow, Tacoma is finally gaining appreciation for its burgeoning cultural scene—which includes many impressive museums and theaters.

Vashon Island is an excellent place to explore on two wheels, so consider renting a bike from **Vashon Island Bicycles** (9925 SW 178th St; 206/463-6225). Or, if you'd rather take in views from the water, rent a boat from **Vashon Island Kayak** (Jensen Point Boathouse; 206/463-9257). After working up an appetite, stop by **Express Cuisine** (17629 Vashon Hwy SW; 206/463-6626) for some gourmet takeout and claim a picnic table near the lighthouse at **Paul Robinson Park** (east end of SW Point Robinson Rd on next-door Maury Island). A visit to the Vashon location of Seattle's favorite **Macrina Bakery & Cafe** (19603 Vashon Hwy SW; 206/567-4133) is a must.

Back on the mainland of **Tacoma**, there are several fun options for day activities. While a day among tigers, elephants, and polar bears may not scream "blissful date," a few hours at the charming **Point Defiance Zoo** (5400 N Pearl St; 253/591-5337) is a must for animal lovers. For a more traditionally romantic outing, there's the **W. W. Seymour Botanical Conservatory** (316 S G St in Wright Park, Tacoma; 253/591-5330; www.metroparkstacoma.org), which boasts more than 550 distinct kinds of plant growth. In the evening, **Bacchante Wine and Essentials** (606 N Prospect St Tacoma; 253/573-9463) is a great place to enjoy a glass of wine, or pick up a bottle to bring back to your hotel for later in the evening.

In **Gig Harbor**, spend a couple of hours, or an entire day, at the **Purdy Spit**, an aptly named mile-long stretch perfect for beachcombing, swimming, sunbathing, or windsurfing. And, a visit to the town wouldn't be complete without enjoying a piece of the famous blueberry pie at **Le Bistro** (4120 Harborview Dr; 253/851-1033).

Access & Information

The two largest South Sound cities, Tacoma and Olympia, are most easily accessed via Interstate 5, the multilane highway that runs north/south through Western Washington. Several exits off I-5 easily direct travelers to the main areas and attractions in both cities. Vashon Island is accessible only by ferry, from three docks: downtown Seattle (foot traffic only), West Seattle (Fauntleroy ferry), or Tacoma (Point Defiance ferry). Contact **Washington State Ferries** (206/464-6400 or 800/843-3779; www.wsdot.wa.gov/ferries) for details. You can reach Gig Harbor via Highway 16 across the Tacoma Narrows Bridge, which requires a $3 toll to cross. Boating remains an important part of Gig Harbor's identity; good anchorage and various moorage docks are here if you travel via watercraft. Be aware the traffic on both I-5 and Highway 16 can be challenging and unpredictable during rush hour—and even on weekends.

Romantic Lodgings

Aloha Beachside Bed and Breakfast / ❂❂❂

8318 SR 302, Gig Harbor; 888/256-4222
If you can't plan a romantic getaway in Hawaii anytime soon, don't despair: the spirit and hospitality of the islands is alive and well at Aloha Beachside Bed and Breakfast. Perched just above Puget Sound, the inn reveals gorgeous views everywhere you turn, and ambitious couples may choose to start their morning with a leisurely stroll along the beach to catch a glimpse of the area's resident bald eagle. The property's carefully manicured rose and dahlia gardens, pretty gazebo, and trout pond all serve as quiet spots to meander with your loved one. The Honeymoon Suite is an obvious romantic choice; with a gas fireplace, shower for two, and bathtub overlooking the bay, it won't take long for all of life's stresses to fade away. The room's picture window is especially enchanting; turn out the lights, snuggle close, and watch the moon rise over the water. In the morning, the inn's scrumptious, tropically themed breakfast is exceptional. *$$–$$$; AE, DIS, MC, V; checks OK; www.aloha beachsidebb.com.*

Artists Studio Loft Bed and Breakfast / ❂❂❂

16529 91st Ave SW, Vashon Island; 206/463-2583
Nestled among 5 acres of meadows and flower gardens, this B&B is an enchanted wonderland of vine-draped arbors, winding paths, and blooming

trees—a pastoral paradise in which lovers immediately forget all of the day-to-day pressures that can damper romance. The two guest rooms in the main house exude warm ambience, but the cottages are a better choice for couples seeking privacy. With a large Jacuzzi tub, a walk-in shower for two, a private porch, and rustic, well-appointed decor, the River Birch Cottage may be the most romantic of all. For duos desiring to reconnect with nature and each other, a tempting option is to soak in the covered outdoor hot tub, which is surrounded by the lush gardens that make this property so alluring. *$$–$$$; AE, DIS, MC, V; checks OK; www.vashonbedandbreakfast.com.*

Betty Macdonald Farm / ◑◑

12000 99th Ave SW, Vashon Island; 206/567-4227 or 888/328-6753
This B&B is tucked among 6 acres of 350-year-old trees and has sweeping views of Puget Sound and Mount Rainier, so it's not difficult to imagine that its namesake and former resident found the spectacular setting an inspiring spot to write many of her books, including the children's beloved Mrs. Piggle-Wiggle series. The furnishings are aged and amenities a bit dated, so if you are looking for true elegance you might search elsewhere, though lodging options on Vashon are limited. What you will certainly find are wonderful views and lush gardens full of Asian pear trees, raspberries, and walnuts. Nearby trails lead through lush wooded areas to the beach below, and you will pass several splendid sitting areas along the way. The spacious All Cedar Loft provides the best view, which can be enjoyed from the room's private deck. The Cottage has a six-foot-long, claw-foot tub flanked by windows on all sides, through which you can peer into the orchids and across the vast Puget Sound to Mount Rainier. Both accommodations are rustic and filled with mixture of Oriental rugs, eclectic antiques, and books galore. They also both have self-catering kitchens and are stocked with makings for a continental breakfast. *$$–$$$; no credit cards; checks OK; www.bettymacdonaldfarm.com.*

Chinaberry Hill / ◑◑◑◐

302 Tacoma Ave N, Tacoma; 253/272-1282
This 1889 Victorian home is on the National Historic Register but in no way shows its age to visitors, except for its ample old-world charm. Situated on a quiet residential street, this beautifully maintained home with verdant gardens may cause guests to forget that they're merely blocks from the Stadium District's interesting shops, museums, and waterfront. Each guest room is thoughtfully appointed with antique furnishings, a plush queen bed, and either a claw-foot tub or a Jacuzzi. Most romantic is the Pantages Suite, with its remarkable view of Commencement Bay, vaulted ceilings, and luxurious four-poster bed. Another thoughtful perk is the guest kitchen, which is always stocked with water, sodas, popcorn, gourmet hot chocolate, and delicious cookies. *$$$; AE, MC, V; no checks; www.chinaberryhill.com.*

DeVoe Mansion Bed and Breakfast / ❍❍❍

208 E 133rd St, Tacoma; 253/539-3991
This historic Victorian inn was once home to a pioneer of the suffrage movement. Today, DeVoe Mansion is a wonderful choice for couples seeking to connect in a distinguished, old-fashioned setting, whether they're celebrating an occasion or looking for a short getaway. The common rooms and guest quarters are all thoughtfully decorated with elegant antique furnishings—in fact, if you're so inclined, go ahead and treat your sweetheart and fellow guests to a tune on the 1860s rosewood square grand piano. Three of the four rooms have large soaking tubs, but do note that only two of the rooms have in-suite bathrooms. Choose the most romantic option, Emma's room, and you'll have both, along with an antique-oak queen sleigh bed. The inn's irresistible breakfast, which may include Parmesan eggs or green-chili potato tarts, is a delight unto itself. *$$; MC, V; no checks; www.devoe mansion.com.*

Thornewood Castle Inn and Gardens / ❍❍❍❍

8601 N Thorne Ln, Lakewood; 253/584-4393
In the late 1800s, a prominent banker bought a Gothic Tudor home in England, which he dismantled, shipped, and rebuilt in Lakewood for his bride, Anna Thorne. More than 100 years later, guests can witness firsthand the fruits of Thorne's grand gesture. This "house that love built" thankfully has no trouble living up to its grandiose name. Nestled in a gated community on the banks of American Lake, the home is entered through the heavy wooden front door to the grand living room, where soft music, fluffy couches, and a crackling fire greet guests. Each ornately decorated room comes furnished with a fireplace, exquisite linens, terry-cloth robes, and a lovely view. For the ultimate splurge, request the spacious Grandview Room, but prepare to pay for the privilege of having your own large private deck and Jacuzzi tub overlooking the beautiful sunken garden. The inn was the setting for the Stephen King–scripted television miniseries *Rose Red*. *$$$$; AE, DIS, MC, V; checks OK; www.thornewoodcastle.com.*

The Villa Bed and Breakfast / ❍❍❍❍

705 N 5th St, Tacoma; 253/572-1157
When jet-setting off to the Old World for a quick getaway isn't in the cards, a visit to this Italian-style villa in Tacoma's Stadium District is a wonderfully appealing alternative. Each of the five guest rooms is named after a different city in Italy, and each is painted in different warm hues, like buttery yellow or cantaloupe, creating a soft, yet refined, atmosphere that is instantly inviting. The spacious apple green Sorrento Room is the most romantic option, with its large private veranda (which includes a hammock), 9-foot-tall four-poster king bed, and two-person shower. Couples seeking a less-expensive

option will enjoy the Caserta Room, which features a two-person Jacuzzi tub overlooking the villa's gardens. *$$–$$$; AE, MC, V; checks OK; www. villabb.com.* &

Romantic Restaurants

Anthony's Homeport / ●●❶

8827 Harborview Dr N, Gig Harbor; 253/853-6353
Who says a restaurant has to be one-of-a-kind to be truly romantic? Sure, you may have eaten at one of Anthony's many other Northwest locations, but the restaurant chain's stellar reputation is certainly well deserved. What's more, this particular location perfectly channels Gig Harbor's natural beauty with large picture windows showcasing jaw-dropping Mount Rainier and water views. Dine outside for more kiss-worthy views during the drier months, and partake in reliable favorites like Alder-Planked Salmon, Fishermen's Cioppino, or Alaska Weathervane Scallops. *$$–$$$; AE, MC, V; no checks; lunch Fri–Sat, dinner every day; full bar; reservations recommended; www.anthonys.com.*

Cliff House / ●●●

6300 Marine View Dr, Tacoma; 253/927-0400
Views of Mount Rainier, Puget Sound, and the Tacoma skyline abound at the Cliff House, which is not quite a hot spot, but more of an institution. The elegant restaurant, sitting high above Commencement Bay, prides itself on preparing local produce, seafood, and meats. Reliably delicious options include the Golden Pork Loin or Stuffed Tiger Prawns. Downstairs, Guido's offers a more casual and (much) less-expensive dining option. *$$$; AE, DC, DIS, MC, V; no checks; dinner Tues–Sun; full bar; reservations recommended; www.cliffhouserestaurant.com.*

El Gaucho / ●●●❶

2119 Pacific Ave, Tacoma; 253/272-1510
Descend into El Gaucho's main dining room, take a seat, steal a kiss under the soft lighting, and get ready to enjoy some of the most finely prepared food in the region. Carnivores will revel in the many choice cuts of 28-Day Dry-Aged Angus Beef. Table-side preparations of both Caesar salad and chateaubriand, a sophisticated wine list, and an impressive selection of 27 different martinis set El Gaucho apart from many of the other establishments in Tacoma's rejuvenated downtown area. *$$$; AE, MC, V; no checks; dinner every day; full bar; reservations recommended; www.elgaucho.com.*

The Green Turtle / ●●●

2905 Harborview Dr, Gig Harbor; 253/851-3167
Proclaimed by some to have the best views in Gig Harbor, particularly on clear days when Mount Rainier dazzles in the distance, the Green Turtle is

a favorite with locals and visitors alike. On a sunny day, sit on the deck to enjoy views of the harbor. Seafood lovers will delight in the deliciously rendered fish and shellfish options, while those with a hankering for meat will be equally satisfied. Whatever you do, remember to save room for one of the Green Turtle's amazing desserts. *$$; AE, DIS, MC, V; checks OK; lunch Tues–Fri, dinner Tues–Sat; beer and wine; reservations recommended; www. thegreenturtle.com.*

Il Fiasco / ❂❂❂❂

2717 6th Ave, Tacoma; 253/272-6688
Whisk away the one you love to enjoy a traditional Italian meal at this delightful restaurant, worthy of any celebration. Called "upscale but down-to-earth" by the *Tacoma News Tribune*, shades of straw and claret provide the wonderful backdrop for the romance of Tuscany. Order one of the pasta specialties, like the Ravioli al Fungi or Linguini alla Cioppino, or one of the decadent entrées, which include such unusual specialties as braised wild boar. For a true splurge, you can't go wrong with an Italian wine off the high-end Captain's List. And, yes, if you're wondering about the name, Il Fiasco is in on the joke, promising that your meal will never be a fiasco. The unusual name instead comes from the straw basket that is wrapped around many bottles of Chianti. *$$$; AE, DIS, MC, V; checks OK; lunch Mon–Fri, dinner every day; full bar; reservations recommended; www.ilfiasco.com.*

Over the Moon Café / ❂❂❂

709 Opera Alley, Court C, Tacoma; 253/284-3722
Tucked away on a slim city street in Tacoma's historic Opera Alley, Over the Moon Café serves reliably satisfying fare, including wild salmon, certified Black Angus steaks, and a respectable wine list. We love the relaxed mood, as romance sometimes comes most easily in a more relaxed environment like this. Try the pasta primavera with fresh tomatoes, shiitake mushrooms, broccoli, and basil. Like many other choices here, the ingredients truly sing, as dishes are rarely doused in heavy sauces. During dessert, amorous couples may even find themselves reading poetry to each other from the tiny books thoughtfully placed on every table. *$$–$$$; AE, DIS, MC, V; local checks OK; lunch, dinner Tues–Fri; beer and wine; reservations recommended; www. overthemooncafe.net.*

Portofino / ❂❂

101 Division St NW, Olympia; 360/352-2803
It's easy to overlook this small restaurant located next to an unattractive office building, but you'd be wise to seek it out. Set in an 1890s farmhouse, Portofino offers a quiet, elegant alternative to the staggering number of chain restaurants in the area. The menu consists of inventive, skillfully prepared Pacific Northwest fare. Be sure to consider the savory crab cakes, made from

shrimp and crab shucked on the spot. To up the romance quotient, choose a bottle from the extensive wine list. In the warmer months, a glass-enclosed porch lets you enjoy the sunshine while you dine. *$$; no credit cards; checks OK; dinner every day; beer and wine; reservations recommended.*

♥ The San Juan Islands

The San Juan Islands

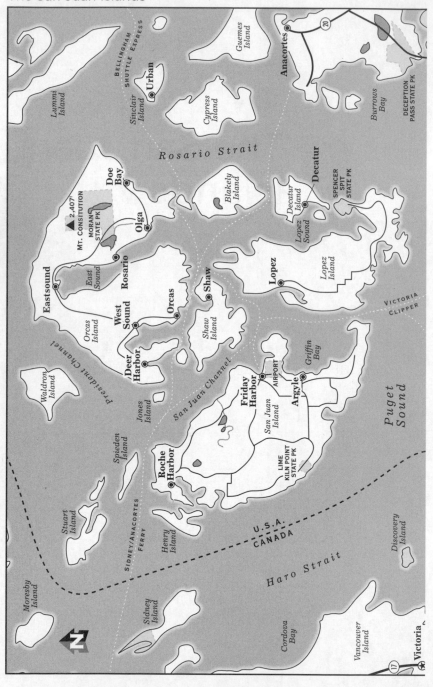

The sound of a kiss is not so loud as that of a
cannon, but its echo lasts a great deal longer.
—Oliver Wendell Holmes

♡ The San Juan Islands

Entering the San Juan Islands—whether by boat, ferry, or seaplane—is a breath-taking experience. There are hundreds of these islands; 172 have names, 60 are populated, and 4 have major ferry services. The trio of main islands—Lopez, Orcas, and San Juan—is the biggest draw for romance-seeking couples in search of an island retreat complete with lodging, eateries, and scenic parks. Best of all, the islands are frequently sunny since they lie in the rain shadow of the Olympic Mountains. Most receive just half the rainfall of nearby Seattle. But be forewarned: these islands are about as far north as you can go in the continental United States, and any flush on your cheeks will more likely be from the brisk air than from a heat wave. There will be lots of incentive to snuggle, however.

Each island harbors a distinct personality. Many tourists opt for the convenience of a more-populated island, while those with access to a boat might enjoy a rustic holiday on a lesser-known island. Picking a season for visiting is also difficult. Although summers are the most beautiful, these sparsely populated islands are positively overrun, causing three-hour waits (or longer) at the Anacortes ferry terminal. Fortunately, the fall, winter, and spring seasons are equally beautiful in different ways. Off-season rates are more reasonable, and diminished crowds mean you'll be better able to relax into the unhurried pace of island life.

The easiest way to reach the San Juans is via the Washington State Ferries (206/464-6400 or 800/843-3779 in WA only; www.wsdot.wa.gov/ferries), which run year-round from Anacortes. Located a little more than an hour and a half north of Seattle, Anacortes is itself on the island of Fidalgo. Though most travelers rush through on their way to catch their ferry, this town is on its way to becoming a destination in its own right.

San Juan Island

Romantic Highlights

Known as the hub of this island chain, San Juan Island is a northern vacation paradise. It is the largest and most developed of the San Juans and the most westerly destination in the Strait of Juan de Fuca. Visitors can even look across the water and see the mountains on Vancouver Island and the lights of Victoria twinkling in the distance. With restaurants, bed-and-breakfasts, hotels, and enough shoreline to wow nature lovers, San Juan offers vacations for all tastes. Driving through the island yields an ever-unfolding scenic masterpiece, and, on foot, you can also explore the island's numerous parks. Be sure to spend time browsing the shops and galleries in lively Friday Harbor, the island's main town.

If you prefer kissing alfresco to the tune of birdsong, this island offers excellent opportunities to do so. **American and English Camps** (360/378-2240; www.nps. gov/sajh) provide couples with an abundance of options, from adventuresome to leisurely. Choose a strenuous hike toward higher elevations or leisurely strolls through wildflower fields or along a deserted beach. These mid-19th-century sites were established when ownership of the island was under dispute. (The Americans and British in fact shared joint occupation until 1872, when the dispute was settled in the United States's favor.) The American Camp, at the south end of the island, showcases open, windy prairie and beach, ranking it among the most glorious seaside spots in all the islands. Travel along the shoreline or wander through sand dunes and sea grass; plentiful opportunities exist for a private moment within secluded, sheltered coves along the path. You'll be mesmerized by the views of both the Olympic and Cascade mountains in this spectacular park. Toward the island's northwest end, the English Camp is set in wooded seclusion. For a little activity, climb the uphill trail from English Camp to Young Hill. You'll hike through tree-canopied pathways and madrone forests to reach the majestic, windswept top. There are plenty of nice spots up here to catch your breath (and then lose it again to the panoramic view—or a kiss). Give yourselves at least an hour for this round-trip excursion and bring along a picnic because once you're atop Young Hill, you won't want to leave. If this lovely hike leaves you craving natural landscapes, explore beautiful **San Juan Country Park** (50 San Juan Park Dr; 360/378-2992) on the island's west side.

Another popular outdoor activity is whale watching. For a close-up look at the island's wildlife, nothing beats a boat. Take a nautical journey with **Western Prince Whale & Wildlife Tours** (1 block from ferry landing; 360/378-5315 or 800/757-6722; www.orcawhalewatch.com) or with **Victoria San Juan Cruises** (360/738-8099 or 800/443-4552; www.whaletour.com; prices start at $49 per person). This is the chance of a lifetime to come face-to-face with harbor seals, bald eagles, or a pod of orcas, among other magnificent creatures. There are many other whale-watching companies based on San Juan Island; look for the flyers posted all over the ferry landing. We suggest calling around to get the price and experience you're looking for (and dress warmly to fend off the ocean air). Kayaking couples should also follow this advice, as there are plenty of outfitters to choose from. Truly adventurous individuals who find a plunge into cold water the ultimate vacation experience may want to take advantage of the diving in the archipelago—some claim it's the best cold-water diving in the world. **Island Dive & Watersports** (2A Spring St Landing, Friday Harbor; 360/378-2772; www.divesanjuan.com) offers rentals, charters, and classes.

If the thought of getting on a boat makes you woozy, you can also whale watch from terra firma at the nation's first official whale-watching park: **Lime Kiln Point State Park** on the island's west side. Several whale pods make regular trips past the park; if whales fail to materialize, you'll likely see a bald eagle or, if you time your visit right, a sensational sunset with the snowcapped Olympic Mountains in the distance. Note that folks flock here in the summer, so bring your binoculars and patience; in the off-season, you and the seagulls might have the place to yourselves.

If you leave your car at home—a great option in summer when the ferries are crowded—you can navigate the island by scooter or bicycle; rent scooters at **Susie's Mopeds** (up the hill from the ferry dock; 360/378-5244 or 800/532-0087; www.susiesmopeds.com) or bikes at **Island Bicycles** (380 Argyle Ave; 360/378-4941; www.islandbicycles.com). Roads are steep and winding and without much of a shoulder, so ride with caution. There are plenty of lodging options on the island, but if you're planning a week or extended stay, look into renting a house on the island through **Windermere Vacation Rentals** (360/378-3601 or 800/391-8190; www.windermerevacationrentals.com). Prices drop, often dramatically, in low-season months.

For a lovely and fragrant picnic spot, visit **Pelindaba Lavender Farm** (off Wold Rd; 360/378-4248 or 866/819-1911; www.pelindaba.com; every day May–Sept). The farm's downtown product gallery, cafe, and meeting place is one block from the ferry in Friday Harbor (150 1st St; 360/378-4248) and is open every day year-round. If wine tasting is on your agenda, visit **San Juan Vineyards** (3136 Roche Harbor Rd; 360/378-9463; www.sanjuanvineyards.com; call ahead for hours); the tasting room is housed in a renovated turn-of-the-20th-century schoolhouse. At **Westcott Bay Sea Farms** (904 Westcott Dr; 360/378-2489; www.westcottbay.com) off Roche Harbor Road you can help yourself to fresh oysters at bargain prices.

Access & Information

The most popular way to reach San Juan Island is via the **Washington State Ferries** (206/464-6400, or 800/843-3779 in WA only; www.wsdot.wa.gov/ferries), which run year-round from Anacortes. From Seattle, Anacortes is approximately an hour and a half north by car. To avoid long ferry lines in summer, leave your car behind; many B&B owners will gladly pick up guests at the ferry dock with prior notification. (For more on Anacortes, see the Skagit Valley section of the Puget Sound chapter.) Companies such as Kenmore Air provide an exciting, if more expensive, alternative way to reach the islands—via seaplane. No matter how you get there, these peaceful islands will blow you away with their striking natural beauty and atmosphere. Another option in summer for those willing to go without a car is the passenger-only **Victoria Clipper** (2701 Alaskan Wy, Pier 69, Seattle; 206/448-5000; www.victoriaclipper.com), which travels from downtown Seattle to San Juan Island.

Kenmore Air (425/486-1257 or 800/543-9595; www.kenmoreair.com) schedules multiple floatplane flights per day during peak season; there are fewer flights in the off-season. Round-trip flights leave from downtown Seattle at Lake Union and from north Lake Washington. A shuttle is available from Sea-Tac Airport to Lake Union. Luggage is limited by weight. **San Juan Airlines** (800/874-4434; www.sanjuanairlines.com) flies from Anacortes to San Juan Island; the flight takes approximately 15 minutes. Either air service will be met by the rental-car operator on the island, **M&W** (360/378-2886 or 800/323-6037). More information is available from the **San Juan Island Chamber of Commerce** (135 Spring St, Friday Harbor; 360/378-5240; www.sanjuanisland.org). Some restaurants and lodgings have seasonal closures, so check with the San Juan Island's Visitors Bureau (888/468-3701; www.guidetosanjuans.com) before making your travel arrangements. The bureau can also provide recommendations for campgrounds and outdoor activities.

Romantic Lodgings

Elements San Juan Islands Hotel and Spa / ❍❍❸

410 Spring St, Friday Harbor; 360/378-4000 or 800/793-4756
Your first reaction to seeing this converted motor inn might be, "Romance, what romance?" But step inside and *cozy* immediately comes to mind. The spare, clean lines of the modern architecture are refreshing; it doesn't take long before relaxation, a prelude to snuggling, takes over. Every room is a "place" in nature: Earth, Sky, Water, Sun, and Wind, of which the first three are perfect for couples. We recommend Sky Places, which features a signature king-size bed. Earth has two queen beds (the second is for the luggage, silly!) with industrial-grid headboards. Rooms have coffeemakers, mini fridges, and microwaves for the nights you don't order room service from Steps Wine Bar & Café (see Romantic Restaurants). Step outside to ride the hotel's beach-cruiser bikes or to take a lap around the island's only heated indoor pool. Its Lavendera Day Spa, located next door, features couple's massages, body wraps, and other luxurious treatments you can both enjoy. *$$–$$$; MC, V; no checks; www.hotelelements.com.* &

Friday Harbor House / ❍❍❍❸

130 West St, Friday Harbor; 360/378-8455 or 866/722-7356
The stunning views from this inn-on-a-bluff will leave you breathless aside from the sweet nothings you might whisper. Below, the village buzzes with

art lovers and antique shoppers. The water sparkles, and Mount Constitution on Orcas Island beckons to be conquered. Each simple, elegant guest room offers a different view. The jetted soaking tub brings the water indoors; the soft glow from the fireplace is reminiscent of the light from the setting sun. Craftsman-style furnishings and subdued colors combine for a comfortable and fresh ambience. There is a telephone with a data port and a television, but one foot in the door and the rest of the world disappears as you melt into each other's arms. The view from Harbor House Restaurant is complemented by the tasty menu, which changes seasonally. *$$$–$$$$; AE, DIS, MC, V; checks OK; www.fridayharborhouse.com.* ♿

Friday's Historic Inn / ◐◐◐

35 1st St, Friday Harbor; 360/378-5848 or 800/352-2632
No matter the weather, it's always suite season at this boutique hotel. Begin your getaway with one of the special add-ons, which include champagne and gourmet chocolates, while you enjoy views of the water from the Bainbridge, Marrowstone, or San Juan suites. The Marrowstone has an outdoor hot tub in a private courtyard. The San Juan's two-person jetted tub is inside. Both have double-headed showers, luxurious robes après-bath, and king-size beds. The intimate Orcas Suite has a partial view of the harbor and a two-person jetted tub just steps away from the king-size bed. Charming and comfortable furnishings are inviting and inspire a desire to curl up close. Break away in time for the homemade continental breakfast, including fresh-baked scones, seasonal fruits, cereal, and locally roasted coffee. *$$–$$$; MC, V; checks OK; www.birdrockhotel.com.* ♿

Harrison House Suites / ◐◐◖

235 C St, Friday Harbor; 360/378 3587 or 800/407-7933
The five suites in this sweet bed-and-breakfast each have their own distinct character, while featuring the same amenities: gas fireplaces, private decks, hot tubs, and fully stocked kitchens. The Orcas Suite, affectionately nick-named the "honeymoon suite," has water, sunrise, and sunset views. The Roche Harbor Cottage, a separate building with a private entrance, has a full kitchen and private hot tub. Its front deck overlooks the wildflower garden. Complimentary bicycles are ready for a romantic ride and kayaks are set to sail for a sunset cruise. A four-course gourmet breakfast is served in the Garden Café or delivered at a prearranged time. *$$$$; MC, V; checks OK; www.harrisonhousesuites.com.*

Highland Inn Bed & Breakfast / ◐◐◐◐

West side of San Juan Island; 360/378-9450 or 888/400-9850
Drive along the private road to this secluded inn and know you're in for a special getaway. Subscribing to the highest standards and regarded as the Four Seasons of the San Juans, the privacy of the two suites provides all

the space for relaxation that you need. Helen King, former owner of the renowned Babbling Brook Inn in Santa Cruz, California, built the inn of her dreams on this spectacular hillside. The suites are located at opposite ends of the house, joined by a sprawling 88-foot-long veranda on the outside and an elegant living room on the inside. Cuddle up together on the hammock or on the swing. That is, if you can manage to break away from the graceful peace of your suite. At your request, the bountiful breakfast can be served in your suite to ensure a lovely, lazy morning together. *$$$$; AE, DIS, MC, V; checks OK; www.highlandinn.com.*

Hillside House Bed and Breakfast / ◐◐◖

365 Carter Ave, Friday Harbor; 360/378-4730 or 800/232-4730
Attractive landscaping and an inviting hammock welcome guests who wander up the path to this bed-and-breakfast, located in a residential neighborhood. All guest rooms have private bathrooms (either in the room or across the hall—robes provided), plush linens, down featherbeds, and individualized decor to suit most every taste. For a truly romantic getaway, reserve the Eagle's Nest Suite. This third-floor loft has a private stairway from the common area, cathedral ceilings, a king-size bed, a sumptuous leather love seat, and a jetted tub for two. If you visit when cherries are on the trees, you can look forward to a fresh-baked pie in the afternoon. Pick blackberries in season and they'll appear at breakfast, in the form of pancakes and syrup. Year-round, guests love the lavender-pecan pancakes. *$$–$$$; AE, DIS, MC, V; checks OK; www.hillsidehouse.com.*

Lonesome Cove Resort / ◐◐◖

416 Lonesome Cove Rd, Friday Harbor; 360/378-4477
Drive down the long, wooded gravel road and into the dreamy, sepia-colored past to secluded Lonesome Cove Resort, located on the northernmost part of the island. Six cabins with vintage Lincoln Log charm skirt a private pebbled beach, their decks and living rooms looking out across the channel to Spieden Island. On a hill above the cabins you can sit (and kiss!) in solitude on a wooden bench beside a trout-stocked pond. Inside the cozy cabins, huge stone fireplaces, exposed log walls, and full kitchens will help you relax in unfussy comfort. For those arriving by water, a 100-foot private dock with power and water is available May through October. Be sure and stock up in Friday Harbor or Roche Harbor. Once you've settled in, you won't want to leave. *$$; MC, V; checks OK; 3-night minimum stay in summer; www.lonesomecove.com.*

Roche Harbor Resort / ◐◐◐

Roche Harbor; 360/378-2155 or 800/451-8910
This scenic, historic harbor and marina, protected by a tiny barrier island, is a yachting and tourist playground. Wander the winding brick pathways

Spring in the San Juans

Romance will blossom along with the splendid scenery on a spring trip to the San Juan Islands. During this calmer season, fewer crowds mean couples will likely have beaches and popular tourist spots all to themselves. Nothing inspires a kiss like a walk along the beach at sunrise or sunset—especially when you are the only people on the sandy stretch.

Other popular venues—like ambience-rich waterside eateries and romantic lodgings—will not feel as crowded and overwhelming as they can during high tourist season (summer). As for the weather, it will often delight as the islands receive an average of 247 days of sun a year. The temperatures may not be as warm as they are come summer, but colder days bring an excuse to snuggle beside the fire for an afternoon.

An additional spring bonus: off-season rates. You may not necessarily associate *bargain* with *romance*, but maybe that extra bit of money could go toward a little something special—perhaps a bottle of champagne to an outdoor porch or hot tub would be an ideal way to inspire a kiss?

through the resort's crisp white and dark green New England–style buildings, gazebos, and rose gardens. The McMillin suites are the most romantic accommodations overlooking the harbor with incredible water and sunset views. The suites boast high ceilings, polished wood floors, and leather wingback chairs facing gas fireplaces. Bedrooms feature king-size four-poster beds; bathrooms include heated floors, double sinks, and claw-foot soaking tubs with separate showers. The suites are expensive, but Roche Harbor is a popular site for marriage ceremonies, and the resort offers the only acceptable on-site lodgings for the wedding night. There are three restaurants on-site: the formal McMillin's Dining Room with spectacular harbor views and an upscale menu; the casual lower-level Madrona Grill, which has waterfront patio dining in summer; and the Lime Kiln Café on the pier, with standard breakfast and lunch options. The Afterglow Spa features luxurious treatments and packages, including couple's massage and a signature caviar facial. Pampering at its finest. $$$$; AE, MC, V; checks OK; www.rocheharbor.com. &

Trumpeter Inn Bed & Breakfast / ✿✿✿

318 Trumpeter Wy, Friday Harbor; 360/378-3884 or 800/826-7926
Set on an emerald-green lawn and surrounded by meadows, this bucolic spot allows for quiet romantic moments in a calm country atmosphere, nationally recognized for its exceptional birding. The rooms boast private baths, fluffy down comforters, pretty linens, views of the garden or meadow, and slippers and plush robes. Bay Laurel and Rosemary both have gas fireplaces and

private decks. Your hosts will happily arrange individual or couple's massages in the massage room, painted in deep, soothing plum and forest colors. They also offer full concierge services, including packing a picnic lunch to enjoy by the pond or elsewhere on the island. Enjoy an exquisite breakfast, ranging from baked apple pancakes, chocolate-hazelnut waffles, blueberry scones, cinnamon rolls, spiral-cut ham, and vegetable frittatas. The grounds include cobblestone paths with rose-blooming trellis and arbor, and a cement-brick patio covered with flowering pots. Soak in the private outdoor hot tub, surrounded by lush plantings and twinkling lights. Just be sure to turn off the jets for a moment, so you can listen to the night sounds and gaze at the stars. *$$$; AE, DIS, MC, V; checks OK; www.trumpeterinn.com.* &

Tucker House / ●●❬

260 B St, Friday Harbor; 360/378-2783 or 800/965-0123
The seven rooms, one suite, and two cottages comprising Tucker House's property are each named after a quilt-block design and painted in soft colors. The Four Winds Suite is the sweetest of all and features angled attic ceilings, a king-size bed with down comforter behind French doors, a sitting room with a cozy leather couch, a spacious bath with a two-person Jacuzzi tub and separate shower, and a private balcony. Among the cottages (where your pets can stay, too), the Goose in the Pond is our favorite and features a queen-size bed, a kitchenette, a woodstove, vaulted sky-lit ceilings, and a private entrance and patio. Enjoy a four-course gourmet breakfast at the Garden Café (located down the path to the adjoining Harrison House property) or have it delivered to your cottage or suite. A lazy afternoon is a perfect time to schedule an in-room massage. Bicycles and kayaks are complimentary to guests. *$$–$$$; MC, V; checks OK; www.tuckerhouse.com.*

Romantic Restaurants

Backdoor Kitchen / ●●❬

400b A St, Friday Harbor; 360/378-9540
A restaurant named Backdoor Kitchen, in what appears to be an industrial site, surrounded by bamboo and stone sculptures: it doesn't make sense but it works. In fact, it's a perfectly tranquil setting for this well-kept island secret. International food made from locally grown ingredients and a robust selection of wine are standard, though there isn't anything unusual about them. Feed each other lamb sausage and feta cheese wrapped in grape leaves, and share an order of Westcott Bay oysters (topped with breadcrumbs) and clams (cooked in coconut-milk broth). Summer dinner offerings include Mediterranean lamb sirloin, Indian thali platter, and fresh Alaskan halibut. In addition to the wine, order from the list of 10 specialty cocktails. You'll leave shaken and stirred. *$$$; MC, V; checks OK; dinner Thurs–Sun; full bar; reservations recommended; www.backdoorkitchen.com.* &

Duck Soup Inn / ●●●◐

50 Duck Soup Ln, Friday Harbor; 360/378-4878
Duck Soup Inn is the restaurant of choice for island-going lovebirds. Tucked into the woods, the arbor-fronted, shingled cottage overlooks a tranquil pond. The wood-paneled dining room with stone fireplace, wooden booths, and high windows is filled with works by local artists; open-air seating allows for nature's canvas. House specialties comprise the menu, and many of the fresh herbs and edible flowers are grown by chef/owner Gretchen Allison. Apple wood–smoked Westcott Bay oysters appear frequently as starters, and for good reason. Chile rellenos with Jack and goat cheeses and lavender-thyme-crusted free-range chicken breast with blueberry-habanero chutney are favorites for dinner. The wine list is extensive and is easily accessible to nonconnoisseurs, with descriptions such as tropical, fat, buttery, round, polished, sensual, big, spicy, and muscular. So many wines for so many occasions; it's easy to find just the right drink to pair with the evening. *$$; MC, V; no checks; dinner Wed–Sun Apr–Oct (closed Nov–Mar); full bar; reservations recommended; www.ducksoupinn.com.* ઼

The Place Bar & Grill / ●◐

1 Spring St, Friday Harbor; 360/378-8707
You can cruise in here for a quick bite before you catch your ferry, but why not stay awhile? A far better plan is to enjoy a quiet dinner at this waterfront eatery. The three walls of windows at this restaurant perched on pilings—the oldest building still standing on the island—give diners excellent views of the ferry terminal and marina. Comfortable chairs complement tables set with fresh flowers and thick linen tablecloths and napkins, and light wood paneling softens the room. A recent remodel and new gas stove in the dining room add ambience. Chef/owner Steven Anderson features a rotating menu of Northwest cuisine, focusing on local and regional fish and shellfish, from British Columbia king salmon to Westcott Bay oysters. Giant Alaskan weathervane scallops might arrive in a pool of ginger-lime beurre blanc; black bean ravioli could come topped with tequila shrimp. A full-service bar blends in nicely with the decor and offers plentiful options for romantic libations. To finish, try the warm chocolate pudding with toffee sauce or a simple ice cream sundae dressed with homemade chocolate–Grand Marnier sauce. *$$; MC, V; local checks only; dinner Tues–Sat (closed January; call for seasonal closures); full bar; reservations recommended; www.theplacesanjuan.com.* ઼

Steps Wine Bar & Cafe / ●●●

140A 1st St, Friday Harbor; 360/370-5959
The rich earth tones, wood accents, and soft lighting are a sophisticated surprise in this wine bar tucked into a walkway mere steps from the harbor. The menu is equally cosmopolitan, featuring Szechuan braised pork, goat cheese rellenos, unagi oshizushi, and ratatouille terrine. It is the wine,

however, that is most impressive, with a unique selection from around the globe complementing Northwest varietals. At any given time, there are 60 wines offered by the glass. Opt for a seat in the loft, where intimate conversations blossom despite the long counters. September through May, wine dinners help chase the cool-weather blues away; summer brings special events such as the Tomato Dinner, featuring island-grown tomatoes in five courses. $$$; MC, V; checks OK; dinner Wed–Mon; wine; reservations recommended; www.stepswinebarandcafe.com. &

Orcas Island

Romantic Highlights

Those lucky in love will appreciate horseshoe-shaped Orcas Island's breathtaking rural scenery, enchanting mountain wilderness, and several relaxed communities. Eastsound resides in the north-central part of the island and is the largest town. Visit for an intimate dinner, groceries or gas, or boutique shopping.

Artists have long been drawn to the San Juans because the islands' natural beauty provides immediate inspiration. For an artistic excursion on Orcas, tour the artists' studios scattered around the island. Open since 1959, **Crow Valley Pottery and Gallery** (on Horseshoe Hwy to Eastsound from Orcas, just before golf course; 360/376-4260; www.crowvalley.com) is housed in a cozy log cabin overflowing with artwork such as pottery, paintings, jewelry, and sculpture. The selection makes it easy to find a unique souvenir of your island excursion. In summer and fall, at the **Saturday Farmers Market** (10am–3pm May–Oct), you can meet artisans and browse their wares while stocking up on fresh provisions.

Behold Mount Constitution at the incredible **Moran State Park** (800/233-0321), the island's most dramatic viewpoints to steal a kiss. From the top of Mount Constitution—at 2,409 feet, the highest elevation on the San Juans—the surrounding views stretch to unbelievable distances. It's a pleasant hike (or an easy drive) to the summit, where a historic stone lookout tower rises well above the treetops. On a clear day, you can see Mount Baker, Mount Rainier, the Olympics, the Cascades, and the Gulf Islands, not to mention the entire San Juan archipelago and the coastal towns across the water. Tourists flock to this popular spot, so come for the view and then turn around and head to the turnout for Cascade Falls where a short, easy hike leads to a fern-lined stream and cascading waterfall. This scene provides a great photo opportunity—and a great setting for a more private kiss. Moran State Park is 14 miles northeast of the ferry landing and 5 miles from Eastsound. Once you enter the park, look for the 6-mile road to Mount Constitution, clearly marked on the left.

Before you arrive, a bit of history: The man responsible for Moran State Park was former Seattle mayor and shipbuilding tycoon Robert Moran. His former mansion is now the focal point of **Rosario Resort & Spa** (see Romantic Lodgings), just west of the park. Even if you don't stay here, you may want to visit for a meal

Best Excuse to Cuddle Close

The historic Moran Mansion at **Rosario Resort & Spa** (see Romantic Lodgings) gives visitors perhaps the best excuse to cuddle on the islands: it's rumored to be haunted. Seattle mayor and shipbuilder Robert Moran built the home between 1906 and 1909 but eventually sold it to a man named Donald Rheem, who shared the space with his flamboyant wife, Alice.

Alice was the town outcast who rode a Harley Davidson and played cards at the corner store wearing only her red nightgown. Some say she died of alcoholism, others say she committed suicide. Either way, locals have claimed to have spotted her ghost since the tragic day.

Today, the house is open to the public for self-guided tours. It is filled with original furnishings, photos from the early 1900s, and an extensive display of the ships built by the Moran Brothers Company in Seattle. But for some, the property has another draw as well: they come looking for the ghost driving her motorcycle and wandering the halls, acting just as the rumors describe.

or to tour the **Moran Museum,** which takes up the second floor of the mansion. You can walk through rooms originally used by Moran family members and imagine what it must have been like to live here in simpler days. On your way to the park, stop in Eastsound for provisions at **Roses** (382 Prune Alley; 360/376-5805 store, 360/376-4292 restaurant), located in the old firehouse in town. Come for gourmet cheeses, fresh breads, Northwest wines, and delicious bakery goods. Or do as the locals do and dine on fresh, organic, free-range delectable local foods in the old fire-truck bay.

Like its neighboring islands, Orcas offers ample opportunities to find romance on the open water. Rent a two-person kayak and paddle through the blue waters around the forested island. Eagles and seabirds swoop across the water's surface, and otters and seals dart below. Few dates can compare with watching the world from this vantage point. And, if serious kayaking alone sounds too strenuous an activity for a relaxing trip, custom kayak tours are also available. There are several kayaking outfitters, but we like **Shearwater Adventures** (360/376-4699; www.shearwaterkayaks.com). Prices start at $59 per person; opt for a sunset or moonlight tour to experience the pristine sea at its most beautiful times.

Another popular option is to cruise on an engine-propelled boat for a whale-watching excursion. Your best chances of spotting these stunning creatures are May through September, with June and July being particularly good whale-watching months. The tours on Orcas Island have a naturalist bent, so even if you don't cross paths with a pod of orcas gliding through the water, you'll get an expert tour of this region and likely meet plenty of porpoises, seals, and bald eagles. **Deer Harbor Charters** (360/376-5989 or 800/544-5758; www.deerharbor charters.com) leaves from Deer Harbor or Rosario Resort; **Orcas Island Eclipse Charters** (360/376-6566 or 800/376-6566; www.orcasislandwhales.com) departs from the Orcas Ferry Landing. Prices start at about $62 per person; call for reservations and seasonal closures.

Access & Information

The most popular way to reach Orcas Island is via the **Washington State Ferries** (206/464-6400, or 800/843-3779 in WA only; www.wsdot.wa.gov/ ferries), which run year-round from Anacortes. From Seattle, Anacortes is approximately an hour and a half north by car. To avoid long ferry lines in summer, leave your car behind; many B&B owners will gladly pick up guests at the ferry dock with prior notification.

Kenmore Air (425/486-1257 or 800/543-9595; www.kenmoreair.com) schedules multiple flights each day during peak season; there are fewer in the off-season. Round-trip flights start at about $208 per person and leave from downtown Seattle at Lake Union and from north Lake Washington. A shuttle is available from Sea-Tac Airport to Lake Union. Luggage is limited by weight. **San Juan Airlines** (206/768-1945 or 800/874-4434; www.san juanairlines.com) also flies into the airport on Orcas Island.

More information is available from the **Orcas Island Chamber of Commerce** (221 A St, Orcas Island; 360/376-2273; www.orcasislandchamber.com).

Romantic Lodgings

The Anchorage Inn / ❂❂❂❆

249 Bronson Wy, Eastsound; 360/376-8282
Situated on 16 acres of wooded beachfront land, the Anchorage Inn is far removed from civilization. The three suites, designed for maximum privacy (all entrances are from different directions), boast simple but comfortable decor with hardwood floors, queen-size beds, gas fireplaces, and kitchenettes. Enjoy your private deck, which looks through the trees to the water and the distant lights of Eastsound. A short walk from your suite is the two-person hot tub set beneath magnificent fir trees. The lighted path marks the way to its waterfront location (and alerts fellow guests that it's occupied, thus ensuring your privacy while you soak). Another nearby path leads to a secluded pebbled beach. Continental breakfast provisions and a selection of snacks are stocked in the kitchens. A tasty dish that's easy to heat (such as crab quiche or baked oatmeal) is delivered to your door in the evening so you can pop it in the microwave at your convenience in the morning. Bring grill-worthy goodies and make your honey's favorite meal on the gas grill in the gazebo. For romantics who prefer quiet, privacy, and plush simplicity, this inn will provide a wonderful refuge. *$$–$$$; DIS, MC, V; checks OK; www.anchorageonorcas.com.*

Bayside Cottages / ⬡⬡⬡

65 Willis Ln, Olga; 360/376-4330
This waterfront hideaway offers several accommodation options, but the most romantic by far are the two adorable cottages on a hillside that slopes down to the water. The Lummi Cottage feels more like a getaway in the woods, with a classic Northwest frontal view of fir trees framing the water. Cypress Cottage is closer to the water, with a bigger deck and more expansive water views. Both have polished wood floors, queen-size beds tucked into alcoves, cozy sitting areas with wood-burning stoves, and kitchens. Best of all, the outdoor garden with wooden table is yours alone to enjoy. Bring your own provisions, as breakfast is not included with your stay. *$$$; MC, V; checks OK; www.orcas1.com.*

Cabins on the Point / ⬡⬡⬡⬡

2101 Deer Harbor Rd, Eastsound; 360/376-4114
The Cape Cod cottages perched on the point are favorites among couples. Kayak to Skull Island or take a quick dip in the chilly water. Then, indulge in a long soak in the waterfront hot tub. For ultimate romance, book the Heather Cottage, a cozy, renovated century-old cabin on the bluff with the nicest sleeping nook we've ever seen. The queen-size bed is tucked into a windowed alcove overlooking the water, making it look as if the fiery sunset is lingering right over the tips of your toes. The smaller, charming Primrose Cottage lies beneath the fir trees farther back from the water, and Willows Cottage is located near the owner's house overlooking the flower garden (and driveway, making it slightly less private). Meals are not included in your stay, so bring your own groceries or journey 15 minutes to Eastsound. Elopement and engagement packages are a popular specialty. *$$$; no credit cards; checks OK; 3-night minimum stay in summer; www.cabinsonthepoint.com.*

Inn at Ship Bay / ⬡⬡⬡

326 Olga Rd, Orcas Island; 360/376-5886 or 877/276-7296
With an unobstructed backdrop of Ship Bay, this inn provides wonderful inspiration for sharing a kiss. The furnishings are comfortable, plush, and waiting for you to sink into them. Each of the 11 rooms has a view of the East Sound, private bath, television, fireplace, and balcony. The nine staterooms have king-size beds and love seats for cuddling. We recommend the suite with separate living and sleeping areas, an oversize tub under a skylight, and a double bathroom. Built in 2000, the inn has a room specially designed for mobility-impaired guests; it comes complete with wide doorways, a low bed for easier access, and a private handicap-accessible bathroom. In the morning, a continental breakfast is served. In the evening, enjoy fine dining at the Inn at Ship Bay Restaurant (see Romantic Restaurants). *$$$-$$$$; MC, V; local checks only; www.innatshipbay.com.* ♿

Inn on Orcas Island / ❍❍❍❍

114 Channel Rd, Deer Harbor; 360/376-5227 or 888/886-1661
Expect pure opulence at this luxury inn, which includes such amenities as 300-thread-count sheets and heated floors. The two beautifully decorated king suites feature slate-tiled fireplaces and jetted tubs in the spacious bathrooms. The Harvest Suite, located upstairs, is the only room without a deck but nonetheless is our favorite with its grand wrought-iron bed. Of the smaller rooms, we like the aptly named Love Nest. Book the completely private and wonderfully personal Waterside Cottage, adjacent to the main house. The jetted tub with a double-headed shower is a great place to start some clean fun. Then move to the cozy sofa in front of the slate fireplace or outside to the private porch. Breakfast can be delivered to the Waterside Cottage or Carriage House. Guests can bike island roads or indulge in "paddlin' Madeline"—that is, taking Madeline the canoe out on the water. On your way back from water's edge, sit a while at the bench anchored by two sculptures—*the* best place on the island to kiss. *$$$$; AE, MC, V; checks OK; www.theinnonorcasisland.com.*

Orcas Hotel / ❍❍

8 Orcas Hill Rd, Orcas Island; 360/376-4300 or 888/672-2792
The stately Orcas Hotel is easy to spot on approach to the ferry landing. This striking Victorian inn is trimmed by a white picket fence and a flowering English garden. In terms of kiss-inspiring accommodations, we recommend the two rather luxurious rooms, the Blue Heron and the Killebrew Lake; each has a private balcony, whirlpool tub in the bathroom, and charming stained-glass windows. (Note that during high season, their high price tag is not exactly a bargain compared with other island accommodations that offer equal privacy and style.) Breakfast presents several options: grab a complimentary scone and coffee at the bakery downstairs or pay for a meal in Octavia's Bistro (open Sundays only in winter). Since this hotel is located right at the ferry dock, expect heavy tourist and car traffic during the summer. And when there is a delay in boarding the ferry, the downstairs public rooms can get crowded with curious travelers. *$$$; AE, MC, V; no checks; www.orcashotel.com.*

Otter's Pond Bed and Breakfast of Orcas Island / ❍❍❍

100 Tomihi Dr, Eastsound; 360/376-8844 or 888/893-9680
Bird-friendly—both for lovebirds and for the feathered variety. Serene views take center stage; and just off the huge deck overlooking the pond sits the hot tub, housed in a pretty Japanese-style cottage complete with shoji screens for privacy. Of the five guest rooms—all with private baths and plush robes—our favorites are the Goldfinch and the Swan. The Goldfinch has a private entrance off the front porch, a king-size bed, a gas fireplace, generous skylights, and views of the front garden. Upstairs, the light, airy Swan Room

has a pond view, a king-size bed, elegant country furnishings, and an extra-long claw-foot tub and double shower. Mornings are busy times here with all the early birds, so come prepared with earplugs. An elegant five-course breakfast will keep you singing all day. *$$$; DIS, MC, V; no checks; www. otterspond.com.*

Rosario Resort & Spa / ❂❂❶

1400 Rosario Rd, Eastsound; 360/376-2222 or 800/562-8820
This gorgeous historic Orcas Island landmark is no secret, but with all of its private nooks and crannies, you're sure to find a perfect place to kiss. The most noteworthy part of the resort is the historic Moran mansion, a sparkling white home with groomed lawns and a luxurious interior, though most of the guest rooms are not nearly as romantic as the setting and grounds. If you're willing to pay a lot for luxury, reserve one of the cottages: the Cliffhouse, located on a short cliff directly over the bay, features a gas fireplace, a king-size four-poster bed, a private deck, and an extra-long jetted tub with windows overlooking the bay; the Roundhouse, formerly the playhouse for the Moran children, is now a quaint circular cottage on a little point, featuring a separate living room and panoramic views. Rosario is extremely popular in the summertime and securing a reservation can be difficult, so plan your getaway early. Once you arrive, treat each other to a spa service or check out the Mansion Dining Room (see Romantic Restaurants), Moran Lounge, Mansion Pool Bar & Grill, or Cascade Bay Grill. You might also hit up the gift shops, kayaking concession, and dive shop. *$$$–$$$$; AE, DC, DIS, MC, V; checks OK; www.rosarioresort.com.* ⅃

Spring Bay Inn / ❂❂❂❂

464 Spring Bay Trail, Olga; 360/376-5531
Spring Bay Inn continues to live up to its stellar reputation for romance and relaxation; so much so, we have a difficult time doing it justice. Rain or shine, a guided kayaking adventure along pristine coastline is offered every day. If weather is uncooperative, enjoy a nature walk through the inn's 57 acres and the adjoining Obstruction Pass State Park. Fuel up—Spring Bay offers *two* fresh-made breakfasts—a continental is offered outside your room at 7:30am; after the paddle, a full brunch is served in the common area. The lodge-style inn has a 14-foot-high exposed-beam ceiling, two river-rock fireplaces, and expansive windows overlooking a glorious scene of fir trees, the bay, a small marsh, and a trail leading to the pebbled beach—where a large hot tub awaits. Upstairs, of the four generous guest rooms, the two larger rooms have private decks—excellent for stargazing and the requisite kissing. The main-floor Ranger Suite is the grandest of all with a private entrance, high ceilings, a glass solarium, a wood-burning fireplace, a queen-size bed, and a small private courtyard with soaking tub. *$$$$; DIS, MC, V; checks OK; call for seasonal restrictions; www.springbayinn.com.*

Turtleback Farm Inn / ❂❂❂

1981 Crow Valley Rd, Eastsound; 360/376-4914 or 800/376-4914
At dawn, the colors of the countryside come alive. The inn overlooks 80 acres of hills, pastures, ponds, and orchards in the breathtaking Crow Valley. There are rooms in two locations: seven in the beautifully renovated, turn-of-the-century farmhouse, and four in the separate two-story Orchard House. The rooms in the farmhouse, all of which have private baths, range from charming to more charming. The Valley View Room is the most luxurious. Fluffy comforters full of Turtleback Farm's own cozy lamb's wool endow every room with elegant simplicity. Six of the seven baths are outfitted with porcelain and silver antique claw-foot tubs, separate showers, and pedestal sinks—tubs and sinks rescued, after years of romantic service, from the Savoy and Empress hotels. In the separate Orchard House, rooms have similar spacious, elegant bathrooms; taupe walls; polished floors; throw rugs; gas fireplaces; king-size beds; and private decks overlooking the orchard. Although newer, the house doesn't seem to have much soundproofing; we recommend the two top rooms for this reason. The innkeeper, who has published a cookbook, serves a dazzling breakfast, which can be delivered to your room. *$$$; DIS, MC, V; checks OK; www.turtlebackinn.com.*

Romantic Restaurants

Bilbo's Festivo / ❂

310 A St, Eastsound; 360/376-4728
This popular spot—in a small house with generous garden courtyards, mud walls, Mexican tiles, a fireplace, and Navajo and Chimayo weavings—offers a festive atmosphere with a good deal of charm. On the outdoor deck, carved wooden benches surround a blazing fire; a foliage-covered lattice conceals the patio from the road. Inside, the stone fireplace and soft lighting provide some romance—although the noisy bustle of the large groups and families who frequent this spot do not. The food is light and mildly spicy, with generous portions. If you order seafood, you'll find it to be remarkably fresh. A word to the wise: This is a local favorite, so on busy weekends, call ahead or be prepared to wait. In summer, lunch is served taqueria-style, grilled to order, outdoors. *$; MC, V; local checks only; lunch every day (June–Sept), weekends only (Apr–May), dinner every day; full bar; reservations recommended.*

Cafe Olga / ❂

Olga Road (11 Point Lawrence Rd), Olga; 360/376-5098
Want to experience island dining the way islanders do? Travel a few miles south of Mount Constitution to this charming, remodeled 1936 strawberry-packing-plant-turned-rustic-cafe, art gallery, and gift boutique. The atmosphere is laid-back and casual, and the food is tasty and eclectic. Everything is made from scratch, using local ingredients. Arrive early if you want one of

the popular cinnamon rolls (make that two!) or a slice of the blackberry pie. Dining at this leisurely pace, you'll have plenty of time for each other. If you have to wait for a table (which is often the case), browsing in the art gallery is a nice way to pass the time. $–$$; MC, V; *local checks only; breakfast, lunch every day, dinner Fri–Mon in summer (closed mid-Dec–Valentine's Day); beer and wine; reservations recommended.* &

Christina's / UNRATED

310 Main St, Eastsound; 360/376-4904
Serving as an island destination for 28 years, this heavenly little spot enjoys a terrific perch above Eastsound and offers fantastic views of the mountains surrounding the inlets. On pretty summer evenings, linger on the open deck at sunset with a glass of wine (from the unique selection). At press time Christina's had been sold to new owner Maureen Mullen, who plans on updating the menu and interior décor. $$$; AE, DC, MC, V; *checks OK; dinner every day (call for seasonal hours); full bar; reservations recommended; www.christinas.net.*

Inn at Ship Bay Restaurant / ❶❶❶

326 Olga Rd, Orcas Island; 360/376-5886 or 877/276-7296
The wine selection and water views make this a truly wonderful place to dine. The seasonal menu offers fresh, mostly local ingredients, and all the food is created in-house. House bread is made using a sourdough starter that is more than 100 years old; the thought of bread baking from the same equipment our ancestors used has a certain romantic flair. The menu is divine, with first courses such as roasted asparagus salad with sweet onion, and arugula and blood orange salad. Entrées include seared and roasted duck with a tart cherry sauce, bouillabaisse with finfish and shellfish, scallops, and shrimp. House-made ice creams, orange-and-rosemary crème brûlée, and warm flourless chocolate cake gracefully finish the meal. Head to a room at the Inn at Ship Bay (see Romantic Lodgings) to end the evening right. $$$; MC, V; *local checks only; dinner Tues–Sat; full bar; reservations recommended; www.innatshipbay.com.*

Rosario's Mansion Dining Room / ❶❶❶

1400 Rosario Rd (Rosario Resort & Spa), Rosario; 360/376-2152
Quiet music, attentive service, and crisp white table linens are the perfect backdrop to gourmet Northwest-inspired food. Take a moment between courses to appreciate the view out the large windows looking over Cascade Bay (where resident otters occasionally play) and the mouth of East Sound. Executive chef Steve Lutz creates Northwest island cuisine with fresh seafood and quality meats. Menu specialties include fresh Alaskan halibut and Misty Isle filet mignon. Don't miss the desserts. Be sure to arrive well before your reservation for an intimate cocktail in a polished-leather club chair in the

Moran Lounge. Attire is "marina casual." *$$$$; AE, DC, DIS, MC, V; checks OK; breakfast, dinner every day; full bar; reservations recommended; www. rosarioresort.com.*

Lopez Island

Romantic Highlights

The most famous feature of Lopez Island is not its million-dollar waterfront homes, its pastoral farmlands, or even its close proximity to miles upon miles of idyllic bike paths. It's the local islanders' happy, slow-motion wave—administered to everyone they pass—that earned the island the nickname the "Friendly Isle." But, even with such a welcoming spirit, Lopez is still somewhat of a hidden gem. Miles of rolling farmland, gentle inclines, and a tendency toward quiet make this an idyllic spot to retreat from the rest of the world and focus on each other.

Lopez is also famous for having some of the best and easiest bicycling in all the islands; the mostly level 30-mile circuit is suitable for just about anyone who can balance on two wheels. If you don't bring a bike, rent one from **Lopez Bicycle Works** (2847 Fisherman Bay Rd; 360/468-2847; www.lopezbicycleworks.com). Many bed-and-breakfasts are just a few miles' ride from the ferry terminal. Lopez Village, 4 miles south of the ferry dock on the west shore near Fisherman's Bay, is the center of island activity. From May through October, you can also rent kayaks from **Lopez Island Sea Kayak** (360/468-2847; www.lopezkayaks.com).

Like its neighboring islands, Lopez offers great opportunity for wildlife sightings—particularly for bird lovers. Visit the protected tide flats of Fisherman's Bay and narrow Fisherman Spit, accessible from **Bayshore Drive** (park at Otis Perkins Park), where you might spot horned grebes, double-crested cormorants, ducks, plovers, and yellowlegs, among many others. A paved road running down the middle of the spit makes walking and watching easy; keep your eyes open here for brants, snow buntings, and Lapland longspurs. There's beach access at Otis Perkins Park, and you can also dip your feet in the water and explore at Agate County Park. Be sure to bring along a picnic so you can spend all afternoon out. Pick up fixings in town at the **Lopez Village Market**. Organic goods are available at **Blossom Organic Grocery** (Lopez Village; 360/468-2204) across the street, or, if you'd prefer a ready-made picnic, locals will point you in the direction of **Vita's Wildly Delicious** (77 Village Rd, Lopez Village; 360/468-4268), a Mediterranean-style takeout. For baked goods of all sorts, visit **Holly B's Bakery** (Lopez Village; 360/468-2133; www.hollybsbakery.com; Apr–Nov) for "world famous" cinnamon rolls and coconut macaroons. If it's already lunchtime, eat at **Vortex Juice Bar and Café** (135A Lopez Rd; 360/468-4740) in the village.

From Lopez, it's a quick ferry ride over to **Shaw Island** for a day trip. Shaw is the smallest, least populated, and least developed of the ferry-served islands, making it an utterly tranquil place to slow down and relax. The best way to enjoy Shaw is to pack up a picnic, hop on your bikes, and ride along the rural country roads to your own secluded stretch of shoreline or private meadow. The sunsets here are magnificent. With no distractions save an occasional sighting of a deer or a blue heron, and the continuous chirping of the birds, your day exploring Shaw Island will leave you content and bliss-filled. (Note: Your only options for an overnight stay on Shaw are a few state campsites).

The simplistic life also exists back on Lopez Island, especially in the village. Split a delicious cone, float, or malt at **Lopez Island Creamery's Parlor and Café** (3185 Fisherman Bay Rd, Lopez Island; 360/468-2051; www.lopezisland creamery.com). Flavors can include "luscious lemon," "decidedly chocolate," and "just peachy." Stroll hand-in-hand at the Lopez Village Saturday **farmers market** (360/468-4748; 10am–2pm Sat, summer only) and pick up handmade scented soaps or local berry jam for souvenirs. At **Lopez Vineyard & Winery** (724 Fisherman Bay Rd; 360/468-3644; www.lopezislandvineyards.com; call for hours), head to the tasting room to sip Madeleine Angevine, a Cabernet-Merlot blend, or a rich blackberry dessert wine; then stop by the gift shop and pick up a bottle to take home.

Access & Information

The most popular way to reach Lopez Island is via the **Washington State Ferries** (206/464-6400, or 800/843-3779 in WA only; www.wsdot.wa.gov/ ferries), which run year-round from Anacortes. From Seattle, Anacortes is approximately an hour and a half north by car. To avoid long ferry lines in summer, leave your car behind; with its flat farmland and mild hills, Lopez is the best place in the San Juan Islands for biking. **Kenmore Air** (425/486-1257 or 800/543-9595; www.kenmoreair.com) offers floatplane flights during peak season. Round-trip flights start at about $208 per person and leave from downtown Seattle at Lake Union and from north Lake Washington. A shuttle is available from Sea-Tac Airport to Lake Union. **San Juan Airlines** (800/874-4434; www.sanjuanairlines.com) also flies to Lopez.

More information is available from the **Lopez Island Chamber of Commerce** (16 Old Post Rd #A, Lopez Island; 360/468-4664 or 877/433-2789; www.lopezisland.com). Contact them in advance for a map of the island, or you can easily find one when you arrive at area lodgings.

Romantic Lodgings

Blue Fjord Cabins / ✪✪❢

862 Elliott Rd, Lopez Island; 360/468-2749 or 888/633-0401
Sequestered beneath groves of cedar and fir trees, these cabins provide a total escape from everything but each other. Both chalet-style cabins are simply decorated and feature skylights and open-beam ceilings. The Norway cabin, hidden among the cedars, is best for couples who enjoy long, leisurely mornings. The Sweden Cabin catches the morning light—perfect for early risers looking to explore. Each cabin has a voluptuous queen-size bed with

Top Three Sunset Kayak Cruises

Join Friday Harbor's **Discovery Sea Kayaks** (866/461-2559; www. discoveryseakayak.com) for a quiet, scenic trip along the west side of San Juan Island in the Haro Strait. Take in the surrounding mountains and sweeping views of the Canadian Gulf Islands from your sea-level seat. If you're lucky, you'll spot a pod of whales gliding past as the sun goes down: the route follows the foraging path of the southern-resident orca whale pods. Trips start at $69 a person.

The popular **Lopez Island Sea Kayak** (360/468-2847; www.lopez kayaks.com; May–Oct) has been offering this relaxed sunset tour for many years. Expect to see spectacular colors reflecting off the water as well as eagles, seals, otters, and the occasional whale. Note: This trip is recommended for first-time kayakers. Trips start at $35 a person.

Orcas Island's Shearwater Adventures (360/376-4699; www.shear waterkayaks.com; June–Sept) recently celebrated its 25th year of service, so be assured you'll get nothing short of professional guides and tours from this outfitter. Its sunset trips from the island are still popular after all these years. Cross the President's Channel during the calmest hours of the day, while the sun sets over the Canadian Gulf Islands. Prices start at $59 per person. (Ask also about the less-frequent Moonlight Kayaking tours for a truly magical experience.)

featherbed and duvet, a fully equipped kitchen, a TV, a secluded deck with forest views, and utter privacy. Seashells mark the beginning of a five-minute nature-trail walk to a "minifjord" in Jasper Bay. Savor the stillness as you snuggle in the private gazebo on the beach, by far the best place to kiss, with its stunning view of Mount Baker. Catch a glimpse of your only other neighbors: bald eagles, blue herons, and sea otters. Since this isn't a bed-and-breakfast, stock up in Lopez Village before arriving. *$$; no credit cards; checks OK; www.bluefjord.com.*

Edenwild Inn / ✪✪✪

132 Lopez Rd, Lopez Island; 360/468-3238 or 800/606-0662
The Edenwild Inn is tailor-made for couples seeking a romantic island get-away. This modern Victorian inn is located in the center of Lopez Village—which means an easy walk to shops and restaurants, though the surrounding lawns, herb garden, wraparound clematis-draped porch, and an arbor with antique white roses and wisteria will make you feel as though you're in the country. The rooms are beautifully appointed with antiques, artwork, and beveled-glass windows. Some include fireplaces and water views. The

Sunset and Village suites are particularly charming, with gorgeous sunset and water views, king-size Victorian sleigh beds, and comfortable sitting areas. The casual self-serve breakfast, available throughout the morning, includes freshly brewed coffee, breads, fresh fruits, yogurts, cereals, and breakfast meats. Two-person tables in the dining room let you enjoy breakfast à deux. *$$$; MC, V; checks OK; www.edenwildinn.com.* &

Lopez Farm Cottages and Tent Camping / ❂❂❂❅

555 Fisherman Bay Rd, Lopez Island; 360/468-3555 or 800/440-3556
Dim the lights, prop the pillows, and enjoy the crackling fire with no distractions. Each of these five cottages on this 20-acre farm offers a private oasis. Every cottage has unique character along with hardwood floors, fireplace, kitchenette, queen-size bed (in cottages 2–5), double-headed shower, high ceiling with fan, and plenty of natural light. We recommend Cottage 1, which features a king-size bed, large tiled bathroom, and private outdoor jetted tub. Other cottages share a jetted hot tub hidden in a cedar grove. A breakfast basket is delivered the evening before, so there's no hurry to wake up. (Note that if you prefer to camp, the private sites—with available showers—are among the most romantic we've seen; reserve Camp Nest or sites A, B, or C.) *$$–$$$; MC, V; no checks; www.lopezfarmcottages.com.*

MacKaye Harbor Inn / ❂❂❅

949 MacKaye Harbor Rd, Lopez Island; 360/468-2253 or 888/314-6140
This gracious sea captain's house, built in 1927, sits above a sandy, shell-strewn beach, perfect for sunset strolls or pushing off in a kayak. Each of the four cozy guest rooms and private baths offer full or partial water views. We recommend the Harbor Suite with gorgeous views from the private, covered deck. It also features a fireplace and queen-size bed. The innkeepers have gone to great lengths to create lots of intimate nooks and crannies. Enjoy the romantic Selah House, adjacent to the main house with wicker chairs on the porch and table and chairs for two on the beach. Rent a two-person kayak on-site and paddle off to sea. Complimentary mountain bikes are also available, and after your hard work, enjoy port and chocolates in the evening. Morning breakfast is served in the dining room and offers organic fruit, granola, yogurt, and baked goods. *$$–$$$; MC, V; checks OK; www. mackayeharborinn.com.*

Romantic Restaurants

The Bay Cafe / ❂❂❂

9 Old Post Rd, Lopez Village; 360/468-3700
Spending an evening at the twinkling Bay Cafe is part of any complete trip to this serene isle. Its close-to-the-beach location is spacious and full of windows; the spectacular, sweeping sunset view of Fisherman Bay and beyond

could alone draw fans. It's a come-as-you-are kind of place—and people do just that. The oft-changing menu features nightly seafood specials and could include starters of sweet-corn-and-white-cheddar griddle cakes or roasted garlic–pine nut hummus, entrées such as a chicken breast roulade, and seafood or vegetarian *tapas*. Savor your meal, but save room for dessert. Afterward, stroll down to the beach and kiss under the light of the moon. *$$; AE, DIS, MC, V; checks OK; dinner every day (Thurs–Sat in winter; call for hours); full bar; reservations recommended; www.bay-cafe.com.*

Vita's Wildly Delicious / ⬡⬡

77 Village Rd, Lopez Island; 360/468-4268
Only a few chairs and picnic tables are available here, as the specialty is takeout. Choose from "little plates of food from which you are welcome to assemble a delightful meal of your own design." The portions are perfect for a romantic picnic on the beach or a dream dinner in front of your fireplace. There is also a good wine selection, if your destination is the privacy of your suite. The gourmet offerings are updated frequently, but you'll always find tasty bites that go well on toast points, such as curried shrimp spread, and more robust meat and vegetarian items. *$–$$; AE, MC, V; checks OK; lunch, dinner Tues–Sat; 10am–5pm; wine only; no reservations; vitas@rockisland.com.*

♡ Olympic Peninsula & Long Beach

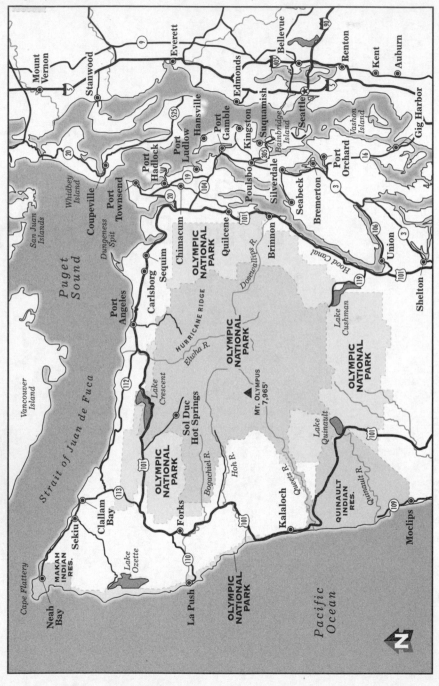

Kissing is a means of getting two people so close together that they can't see anything wrong with each other.

—Rene Yasenek

Olympic Peninsula & Long Beach

There's nothing quite like this unique part of the world, renowned for its rugged beauty. Nowhere else on earth can you experience puzzlelike shorelines, alpine meadows bookended by glaciers, and dense rainforest valleys within a few short hours of each other.

The vast and immensely varied wonders of the Olympic Peninsula are wildly romantic. To say this area will make you feel exalted is an understatement; it is an absolute must-see for anyone venturing to the Northwest. Whether your idea of romance is a breathtaking mountaintop vista, the ethereal magic of a rain forest, a jazz concert and dinner at an elegant Italian trattoria, a sparkling lake surrounded by pristine forest, or a dip in the Pacific Ocean, you'll find it here. At the top of Hurricane Ridge at the northern edge of Olympic National Park, snowcapped peaks extend up to seemingly forever; in the forested territory below, old-growth evergreens reach heavenward to mesmerizing heights. Deeper into the woods to the west, the Hoh Rain Forest is a mystical Eden draped in moss and shadows. Farther out, the powerful Pacific Ocean explodes against the western shore of the peninsula. If you are in search of more tranquil scenery, visit Lake Crescent and Lake Quinault, sparkling blue jewels amid the mountains and trees. For small-town pleasures, Port Townsend offers an impressive array of cultural events, restaurants, and historic architecture.

The rugged geography and remote location of the peninsula mean it's far less crowded than other scenic destinations in the Northwest. If you're hoping to leave the world behind, you'll delight in the splendid isolation of the area, and it would be hard to find any place in Olympic National Park that does not inspire a truly romantic adventure.

Some of the wettest areas in the world are to be found here, though surprisingly just a few miles away are the exceptionally sunny lavender fields of Sequim, located

241

where the Olympic Mountains create a rain shadow. Here romance will likely involve curling up beside a fireplace or under the covers with a cup of hot cocoa after an invigorating hike or a visit to the windswept beaches of the Pacific.

The southern coast of Washington is also a romantic draw. Of the many destinations here, Long Beach Peninsula offers the most alluring escapes for travelers in search of romance. Forested hillsides, beautiful and isolated beaches, and wildlife refuges share space along this magnificent stretch of coastline.

Crowds flock to the Long Beach Peninsula in July and August, but fortunately, numerous accommodations make it possible to find a private romantic spot even during the high tourist season—you just have to make your reservations well in advance. Those seeking total privacy or making a last-minute getaway, particularly on the coast, will have better luck visiting during the fall or winter, when romantic solitude is easy to come by.

Port Townsend

Romantic Highlights

Port Townsend, a small town at the northeast corner of the Olympic Peninsula, is easily accessible compared with the rest of this expansive tract of land. Originally settled in the 1800s, the town's authentic and lovingly restored period architecture is its trademark. Beautifully cared-for Victorian Painted Ladies are perched on a bluff overlooking the waterfront. Nearby parks—and a quaint main street lined with boutiques, antiques shops, and restaurants—project an aura of charm and tranquility. A favorite weekend getaway for Seattleites escaping hectic urban life, Port Townsend is sweet and slow-paced all year long.

Stroll along the main thoroughfare downtown, aptly named **Water Street** (and declared a National Historic District), and take in the beautifully restored buildings, the peekaboo views of the Sound and the islands, and the eclectic medley of antiques stores, art galleries, and gift and craft shops. Indulge in an ice cream or a hot chocolate (depending on the weather) at one of the many cafes that dot the street, then visit the harbor, stopping at the edge to savor the sweeping views. If it's a gray day, take in a movie at the beautifully restored **Rose Theatre** (235 Taylor St; 360/385-1089).

Chetzemoka Park, an ocean-flanked patch of land at the corner of Jackson and Blaine streets, makes an ideal spot for a romantic picnic for two. Wander through scattered pines along a cliff with an eagle's-eye view of Admiralty Inlet and Whidbey Island. Take the arbor walk to the gazebo overlooking the water or follow the paths past the gardens and waterfall.

Fort Worden State Park (200 Battery Wy; 360/385-4730) is another great destination. Miles of hiking trails are scattered throughout the 433-acre waterside park, and the turn-of-the-20th-century officers' quarters date back to a time when this area was part of the defense system protecting Puget Sound. Fly a kite in the vast field, go for a leisurely stroll along the beach, explore the deserted concrete bunkers on the hillside above, or head down to the lighthouse at the water's edge.

Port Townsend has earned a reputation as the hub of cultural activity on the Olympic Peninsula, and diverse events are scheduled from spring through fall. Contact **Centrum** (360/385-3102 or 800/733-3608; www.centrum.org) for details about the many activities taking place both in Port Townsend and in the surrounding area.

Access & Information

To get there, you could drive around Puget Sound from Seattle to reach Port Townsend, but the more popular route is via a 35-minute ferry ride from Seattle to Bainbridge Island on **Washington State Ferries** (206/464-6400, or 800/843-3779 in WA only; www.wsdot.wa.gov/ferries), followed by a drive across the Agate Pass Bridge, north up the Kitsap Peninsula, and then over the Hood Canal Bridge. Beyond the bridge, head north to Port Townsend. For general information about local events, contact the **Port Townsend Chamber of Commerce Visitor Information Center** (2437 E Sims Wy, Port Townsend; 360/385-2722 or 888/365-6978; www.ptchamber.org).

Romantic Lodgings

Bay Cottage / ◐◐

4346 S Discovery Rd, Port Townsend; 360/385-2035
If you're looking for a homey escape with access to a private sandy beach, this is the place. These two cabins, located about 6 miles from Port Townsend on a bluff at Discovery Bay, are casual, inviting, and charming. The cabins, built in the 1930s, have low ceilings and are slightly weathered, but you'll be comfortable here amid the handsome, country style furniture and the sumptuous feather beds. Brass bed frames, claw-foot tubs, and private decks lined with clematis vines add to the charm. The surrounding rose gardens are fragrant, and the views of Discovery Bay and the Olympics are stunning. Both cabins feature full kitchens stocked with snacks and beverages. Meals are up to you, so bring along all the necessities for a light breakfast and perhaps a picnic lunch on the beach (picnic baskets provided) to take advantage of this premium location. *$$; MC, V; checks OK; www.baycottagegetaway.com; just south of Port Townsend.*

Big Red Barn / ◐◐◖

309 V St, Port Townsend; 360/301-1271
This 113-year-old barn transformed into an unusual romantic getaway is just a few houses down from Fort Worden State Park. The completely restored, cozy interior offers not only abundant privacy but also a gas fireplace, luxurious bed, TV/VCR, stereo, microwave, toaster, and refrigerator, all in a rustic, uncluttered setting. The fantastic bathroom features a Jacuzzi tub for two

Grape Finds

Unbeknownst to most travelers to the region, the Olympic Peninsula boasts several wineries within an hour's drive. Starting in Port Townsend and spreading west through Port Angeles, most of the wineries that call the peninsula home produce less than 2,000 cases per year. The small-scale, limited production ensures that such wines are almost impossible to find outside the communities in which they're created, making for a charming and sentimental treat.

There's one winery that stands out from the rest. Over the years, Don and Vicki Corson of **Camaraderie Cellars** (334 Benson Rd; 360/417-3564; www.camaraderiecellars.com) in Port Angeles have strived not only to produce high-quality wines that routinely take top merits at international competitions but also to create what they call a "little piece of Eden" on their grounds.

The result is a delight for the senses, particularly the eyes and taste buds. The Corsons understand the beauty of the winery is in the nature; they merely (successfully) try to enhance it with whimsical and perfectly imperfect touches, like the table made out of a tree trunk and an irregularly shaped piece of marble.

On a warm day, bring a light snack of grapes and crackers, buy a bottle of Trinquer ("to toast" in French), and bask outside in the sun. On a cooler

overlooking a meadow, adjustable lighting, white tiles, fluffy towels, candles, bath salts, and fresh flowers. A breakfast basket of muffins, bagels or English muffins, fruit, coffee, and tea is set up prior to your arrival, allowing for maximum privacy and flexibility when you start your day. A porch with Adirondack chairs invites you to linger outside and listen to the waterfall while you decide whether to stroll over to Fort Worden, down to the lighthouse, or along the beach into downtown Port Townsend. *$$; MC, V; checks OK; www.bigredbarngetaway.com.*

Chevy Chase Beach Cabins / ✪✪

3710 S Discovery Rd, Port Townsend; 360/385-1270
If your idea of romance includes candlelit dinners, long walks on the beach, and evenings by the fire, then this is the place for you. Located on 7 acres overlooking Discovery Bay and the Olympic Mountains, this casually comfortable resort includes seven cabins (two are beachfront), a heated pool (June–Sept), a tennis court, shuffleboard and croquet courts, and a rope swing, with an 18-hole golf course next door. Of course, there's also the beach, a perfect place for strolling, napping in the sun, or building a campfire and snuggling with

day, sit on one of the plush couches near the fireplace in the large tasting room, and cuddle up with your sweetie and a cozy red.

In addition to Camaraderie Cellars, check out the other Port Angeles vintners, perhaps during one of three annual winery tours: toast St. Valentine during the Red Wine & Chocolates event in February, taste the year's new vintages at the Spring Barrel Tasting over Memorial Day weekend, and celebrate the harvest with the Passport Wine Tour in November.

Wineries on the Olympic Peninsula include **Harbinger Winery** (2358 Hwy 101 W, Port Angeles; 360/452-4262 or 888/900-3015; www. harbingerwinery.com), **Black Diamond Winery** (2976 Black Diamond Rd, Port Angeles; 360/457-0748; www.blackdiamondwinery.com), and **Olympic Cellars** (255410 Hwy 101, Port Angeles; 360/452-0160; www. olympiccellars.com). Farther east in Sequim, there's **Lost Mountain Winery** (3174 Lost Mountain Rd; 360/683-5229 or 888/683-5229; www.lost mountain.com) and in Port Townsend, **Sorensen Cellars** (274 S Otto St; 360/379-6416; www.sorensencellars.com) and **FairWinds Winery** (1984 Hastings Ave W; 360/385-6899; www.fairwindswinery.com).

Regardless of your wine preferences, you're sure to find something to strike your fancy, especially when set against such a dramatically beautiful backdrop as the Olympic Peninsula.

your sweetie after cooking the clams you dug earlier in the day. Our favorite accommodation is Cabin 4, perched on a cliff with sweeping views and a private cantilevered deck. Note: Breakfast is not provided. *$$–$$$$; MC, V; checks OK; www.chevychasebeachcabins.com.*

Holly Hill House / ♥️🌙

611 Polk St, Port Townsend; 360/385-5619 or 800/435-1454
This Victorian bed-and-breakfast, located in the heart of the Port Townsend Historic District, is a peaceful setting for lovers. Surrounded by rose gardens and ancient holly trees, this home boasts a main-floor parlor filled with antiques and warmed by a glowing fireplace. Upstairs, three guest rooms are done up in handsome Victorian appointments; in the Carriage House behind the main house, two additional rooms complete the inn's offerings. Tea or lemonade and other treats are served each afternoon on the back patio, where flowerpots and wonderful gardens abound. Be sure to take a look at the Camperdown elm off to one side of the yard; this unique tree actually grows upside down and produces enough lush foliage to create a private little alcove that's perfect for shady summer smooching. *$$–$$$; MC, V; checks OK; www.hollyhillhouse.com.*

The Honey Moon Cabin on Marrowstone Island / ✪✪✪

1460 East Marrowstone Rd, Nordland; 509/662-0849 or 509/630-2119
Secluded in 6 acres of woods and connected to the mainland by a small bridge, this inn, located 20 minutes from Port Townsend, is a spectacular romantic destination. The woods are filled with paths to explore, and a short walk reveals a rocky beach with remarkable views of the Olympics and Puget Sound. The cabin itself is essentially one large room, filled with lovely furnishings and cozy comfort. Almost as big as the main room, the bathroom has a glass-block shower and giant Jacuzzi tub. Outside, the wraparound deck is perfect for barbecuing and enjoying the surrounding tranquility. The cabin features a kitchen stocked with all the breakfast fixings you'll need, plus extra goodies like a complimentary bottle of wine, champagne, and chocolates. *$$$; no credit cards; checks OK; www.olympicgetaway.com.*

The James House / ✪✪✪

1238 Washington St, Port Townsend; 360/385-1238 or 800/385-1238
This striking Queen Anne home is as Victorian as it gets in Port Townsend. And, since it's set right on the bluff overlooking town and Puget Sound, the view is totally unobstructed. Most of the 12 guest rooms have impressive water views, and all have private baths. The elegant Bridal Suite, with its unsurpassed water and mountain views, soft lighting, wood-burning fireplace, and complimentary champagne, is the most grand. Freshly baked cookies in the afternoon and complimentary sherry are nice extras, but the real treat is the full breakfast, which may include fresh scones, baked pear with walnut-fruit filling, and a tasty egg dish. Next door, a modest, more contemporary brick house holds another romantic lodging called A Bungalow on the Bluff, managed by the James House. To be perfectly honest, kissing here is inevitable. *$$; AE, DIS, MC, V; checks OK; www.jameshouse.com.*

Morgan Hill View Loft / ✪✪✪✪

606 Roosevelt St, Port Townsend; 360/385-2536 or 800/490-9070
This romantic perch overlooking Puget Sound is an elegant getaway with unfussy and immensely soothing atmosphere. The panoramic view of the water is unbeatable, and when the windows are open, you'll hear foghorns and seals. The sloped-ceiling sitting room has an inviting pillow-covered window seat/day bed, a TV/VCR, a sound system, and a kitchenette with a fully stocked breakfast that encourages you to start your day privately and at your leisure. Ask the owner for directions to the romantic and little-known bluff perched on the edge of the sea, or rent the two available mopeds and follow her "Kissing Tour" map for fun and adventure. *$$–$$$; no credit cards; checks OK; www.morganhillgetaways.com.*

Old Consulate Inn—F. W. Hastings House / ❂❂❦

313 Walker St, Port Townsend; 360/385-6753 or 800/300-6753
If pampering yourselves with modern comforts in the atmosphere of a
bygone era is a combination that appeals, this inn is the place for you. This
red Victorian inn boasts elegant period antiques and eight private rooms,
each with its own bath and charming amenities like cozy alcoves, turret
lookouts, canopied king-size beds, and expansive views of the waterfront.
Especially alluring are the Master Anniversary and Tower Honeymoon
suites. Tea or lemonade and cookies are served in the afternoon in the spacious floral dining room with water views, and liqueurs and desserts await
in the evening. Enjoy a romantic soak in the glassed-in outdoor hot tub, set
in a gazebo overlooking the bay. In the morning, perk up with the inn's own
blend of coffee along with a three-course breakfast served banquet-style,
including fresh fruits, hot breads, gourmet egg dishes, and granola. *$$–$$$;
MC, V; checks OK; www.oldconsulateinn.com.*

Ravenscroft Inn Bed and Breakfast / ❂❂❂❦

533 Quincy St, Port Townsend; 360/385-2784 or 800/782-2691
The stately Southern architecture of Ravenscroft sets it apart from the
other—mostly Victorian—bed-and-breakfasts found in the historic district
of Port Townsend. Furnishings are casual and traditional, and each of the
eight delightful guest rooms has an immaculate, attractive bath, unlimited
privacy, and room to spare. Decorated in a whimsical nautical theme with a
gas fireplace, a Victorian claw-foot soaking tub, and a fabulous 6-foot window seat overlooking Admiralty Inlet, the Admiralty Suite is a particularly
romantic splurge. The Rainier Suite at the very top of the house is another
choice room. Breakfast may include such delectable treats as frappés, Egg
Blossoms, or pumpkin-apple waffles with pecan caramel sauce; fresh baked
cookies, tea, spiced cider, and cocoa are available each afternoon. *$$–$$$;
MC, V; checks OK; www.ravenscroftinn.com.*

Romantic Restaurants

Castle Key Restaurant and Lounge / ❂❂

*7th and Sheridan sts (Manresa Castle), Port Townsend;
360/385-5750 or 800/732-1281*
Roosting on a hill overlooking town, the impressive Manresa Castle, in
which this kiss-worthy restaurant and lounge reside, was built in 1892 to
resemble a Prussian castle. The cocktail lounge is an irresistible setting for
a romantic interlude, and next to it, the dining room has tall, lace-covered
windows, soft lighting, and handsome wood furniture. The Swiss-German
chef has put together an inventive international menu, including bacon-
wrapped filet mignon and curry chicken Casimir. Sunday brunch makes for
an exceptionally elegant start to the day. *$$–$$$; AE, DC, DIS, MC, V; checks*

OK; brunch Sun, dinner Tues–Sat; full bar; reservations recommended; www. manresacastle.com.

Fins Coastal Cuisine / ◐◖

1019 Water St, Port Townsend; 360/379-3474
Located on the second floor of a mall, this eatery has a spare and somewhat sterile interior but boasts a charming terrace overlooking the water and islands beyond. With its intriguing menu, friendly staff, and second-to-none view, this is a delightful place for lunch on a sunny day. At dinner, the ambience remains fairly informal, but at a candlelit table overlooking the water, with fine food and wine—and the right companion, of course—you are sure to enjoy a casually romantic evening. *$$; AE, DIS, MC, V; checks OK; lunch, dinner every day; full bar; reservations recommended; www.finscoastalcuisine. com/fins.*

Fountain Café / ◐◖

920 Washington St, Port Townsend; 360/385-1364
Come to this coffeehouse-esque establishment to romance your taste buds, not your honey. Although the food is undeniably creative and delicious, the tiny, dimly lit dining room is usually packed with people, and the closely arranged tables don't afford much privacy. It's worth a visit, however, with its jovial, attentive staff, and you can't go wrong with seafood here—it is always fresh. Try the Penn Cove mussels steamed with saffron, fresh herbs, and tomato, then move on to the smoked salmon topped with a cream sauce and a hint of scotch, garnished with caviar and served with fettuccine. *$$; MC, V; checks OK; breakfast Sat–Sun, lunch, dinner every day; beer and wine; no reservations.*

Lanza's Ristorante / ◐◑

1020 Lawrence St, Port Townsend; 360/379-1900
With subdued lighting and cozy booths, this Italian restaurant is intimate and romantic. Painted gray with one wall of exposed brick, the interior is reminiscent of a New Orleans jazz club. Live music Friday and Saturday nights reinforces this impression, but the music is soothing rather than raucous. Lanza's is known for its pasta; we recommend the pollo bolognese with chicken, prosciutto, and provolone in a Marsala cream sauce, or the Seafood Lorraine. *$; MC, V; checks OK; dinner Tues–Sat; beer and wine; reservations recommended.*

T's Restaurant / ◐◑◐◖

2320 Washington St, Port Townsend; 360/385-0700
This local favorite has relaxed elegance, Mediterranean ambience, and outstanding food. Tawny stucco walls; soft lighting; a crackling fire; and tables and booths set with crisp white linens, olive oil, and flowers help set

the mood for a memorable evening. Signature specials include apple-wood bacon-wrapped king salmon and rack of lamb served with horseradish and new potatoes. The refined setting, distinctive and well-executed menu, top-quality service, and flawless presentations make this a perfect choice for a special night out. *$$–$$$; AE, MC, V; checks OK; dinner Wed–Mon; beer and wine; reservations recommended; www.ts-restaurant.com.*

The Wild Coho / ○○○◖

1044 Lawrence St, Port Townsend; 360/379-1030
This bright little gem located a few blocks above Port Townsend's downtown creates a romantic atmosphere through careful attention to detail—such as candlelight on every table—and a warm and intimate setting. The award-winning chef is a pioneer of the farm-to-table concept and takes his food and ingredients very seriously. Whether you order the crab cakes, the polenta soufflé with mushrooms, or the salmon in sweet potato crust served with green onion butter and tomato relish, you're sure to have an unbelievable meal and a romantic evening. *$$$; MC, V; checks OK; dinner Tues–Sat; full bar; reservations recommended; www.thewildcoho.com.*

Olympic National Park, Port Angeles & Lake Crescent

Romantic Highlights

An outdoor enthusiast's mecca, this breathtaking region is the epitome of natural beauty—yet it's also close enough to civilization to ensure your outdoor activities are balanced by indoor luxuries, such as decadent dinners and lavender-infused bubble baths. Whether you want to be swept off your feet by mountain vistas or savor lakeshore views; whether you want adventurous hikes or boutique wineries, this area has it all.

Port Angeles may not have overtly romantic charm, but its prime location at the entrance of the Olympic National Park and on the Strait of Juan de Fuca is undeniable. Check out **Webster's Woods Art Park** at the Port Angeles Fine Arts Center (1203 E Lauridsen Blvd; 360/417-4590 or 360/457-3532)—the moniker "sculpture garden" just doesn't do it justice. It's more like a display without walls, a 5-acre museum of second-growth forest set atop a bluff overlooking the Strait of Juan de Fuca. More than 100 interesting (and at times, bizarre) sculptures and site works exist throughout the grounds and make for a whimsical and enchanting woodsy stroll—remember to look up and down if you want to catch everything there is to see.

Sequim, just east of Port Angeles in the rain shadow of the Olympic Mountains, gets more sunshine than anywhere else in the region, making it an ideal destination for a sunny escape. Visit the **Cutting Garden** (303 Dahlia Llama Ln;

360/681-3099), a lavender farm and you-cut flower garden filled with hundreds of floral varieties, or walk along the **Dungeness Spit**, the longest natural sand spit in the United States and a refuge for birds.

Twenty miles west of Port Angeles, enveloped by mountains and sky, the sparkling blue jewel of **Lake Crescent** is Olympic National Park's deepest lake. The drive around the lake is a monumental treat (unless you're prone to car sickness—there are lots of curves). Access to the lake is limited to just a few areas: the small East Beach, which is usually crowded on summer days; some boat launches; and the shore fronting the **Lake Crescent Lodge** (see Romantic Lodgings).

The spectacular **Olympic National Park** (visitor center is at 600 E Park Ave, Port Angeles; 360/565-3130; www.olympic.national-park.com) is perhaps the biggest romantic draw on the peninsula. Nearly a mile up at 5,200 feet, the park's **Hurricane Ridge** is a must-see for any visitor to the region. After stopping at the visitor center to check road conditions and pick up a park map and seasonal newspaper, drive the 17-mile-long Hurricane Ridge Road as it snakes up the side of the Olympic Mountains. If it's warm, hike out on one of the trails and enjoy a sunny picnic in a wildflower-filled meadow. Or, in winter, take a free guided snowshoe tour. Be sure to walk the short paved loop trail to savor the view of Vancouver Island and the Strait of Juan de Fuca.

Average temperatures on the Olympic Peninsula range from 45 degrees F in January to 72 degrees F in August. Rainfall averages 2 to 3 inches per month, less in Sequim, and more—up to 121 inches annually—in Forks. The Olympic Peninsula's rainy winter weather may be nature's way of keeping visitors from overwhelming this exquisite area, so be a good sport and bring some rain gear.

Access & Information

Visitors coming from Seattle will find it easiest to reach this part of the peninsula by taking the 35-minute car ferry from Seattle to Bainbridge Island on **Washington State Ferries** (206/464-6400, or 800/843-3779 in WA only; www.wsdot.wa.gov/ferries). From there, cross the Agate Pass Bridge and drive north up the Kitsap Peninsula and over the Hood Canal Bridge. Beyond the bridge, two-lane Highway 101 makes a big loop around Olympic National Park and passes through Sequim, Port Angeles, and Lake Crescent. Another option is to arrive in Port Angeles by boat from Victoria, British Columbia, with the **MV Coho**, operated by **Black Ball Transportation** (360/457-4491; twice daily Feb–Dec, one trip daily in Jan), or via the much-quicker **Victoria Clipper** (360/452-8088 or 800/633-1589; www.victoriaclipper.com), a foot-passenger ferry that runs two times daily in summer, and once daily in fall and winter. In summer, **Royal Victoria Tours** (888/381-1800; www.royaltours.ca) offers guided bus trips to Victoria and Butchart Gardens. Small planes land at airports in Bremerton, Jefferson County, Shelton, Sequim, and Port Angeles. The largest airline serving the peninsula is **Horizon Air** (800/547-9308; www.horizonair.com), which lands at Fairchild International Airport in Port Angeles. For information on visiting the area, contact the **North**

Olympic Peninsula Visitor & Convention Bureau (338 W First St, Ste 104, Port Angeles; 360/452-8552 or 800/942-4042; www.northwestsecretplaces. com/vcb) in Port Angeles.

Romantic Lodgings

A Hidden Haven / ❍❍◖

1428 Dan Kelly Rd, Port Angeles; 360/452-2719 or 877/418-0938
In this idyllic setting just outside Port Angeles, you'll feel as though you're a million miles away from it all. In reality, you're very close to Port Angeles, Lake Crescent, and Olympic National Park, making it a wonderful point of departure for exploring the area. Two room options cater specifically to romance. Our favorite is the Garden Suite, which features a sitting room with a vaulted ceiling and tall windows overlooking a pond, skylights, a big-screen television, and a Jacuzzi tub for two. If you plan a longer stay, ask about the five cottages; each offers a Jacuzzi, private deck, kitchen, living room, TV, fireplace, gas grill, and washer/dryer. The Sweet Heart Cottage, with its elegant decor, rich furnishings, and heart-shaped whirlpool tub, is another excellent romantic choice. The pond draws all kinds of wildlife and makes for excellent bird-watching. A hearty breakfast brought to your room will get your day off to a delicious start. *$$$; MC, V; no checks; www.ahidden haven.com.*

BJ's Garden Gate / ❍

397 Monterra Dr, Port Angeles; 360/452-2322 or 800/880-1332
Aside from being a charming and personable innkeeper, owner B. J. Paton is also a master gardener whose waterfront grounds perched on a cliff top over the Strait of Juan de Fuca have been featured in *Country Garden* magazine. Indoors, B. J. and her husband, Frank, have created a quiet, old-fashioned Victorian sanctuary with old-world Europe in mind. The five rooms, all with fireplaces, have names like Victoria's Repose (our favorite), Marie Antoinette's Boudoir, and Ludwig's Chamber—with antiques and wall hangings to match. Given its location on a steep bluff, the B&B does not allow children; they cater strictly to couples who want "away time." *$$$; MC, V; checks OK; www.bjgarden.com.*

Colette's Bed and Breakfast / ❍❍❍◖

339 Finn Hall Rd, Port Angeles; 360/457-9197 or 877/457-9777
In French the name Colette means "victorious people," which precisely describes the owners of this immaculate and well-groomed inn. Lynda and Peter Clark have unquestionably succeeded in their quest to create a utopian oceanfront hideaway. Prepare to indulge in one of five deluxe rooms offering water views, two-person spa tubs, king-size beds (choose your own bedding when you reserve online), fireplaces, luxurious robes, private entrances, and

Festive Best Bets

There are several charming annual festivals throughout the region. While such events are typically packed with people and not terribly intimate, they can also be a delightful way to spend several hours and get a feel for the local flavor. (Keep in mind, however, that you'll experience crowds—especially on the weekends—so make sure you reserve your accommodations and dining well in advance.) Some our favorites:

Juan de Fuca Festival of the Arts
Memorial Day weekend in Port Angeles

This four-day festival features more than 100 performances of music, dance, and theater from around the world, including musical workshops, a street fair, public art, and special activities for children. *360/457-5411; www.nwperformingarts.com.*

Olympic Music Festival
Every Saturday and Sunday from June to early September in Quilcene

Arguably the Northwest's most beloved event, the Olympic Music Festival pairs beautiful chamber music with bucolic scenery. A turn-of-the-20th-century dairy farm nestled on 55 acres of farmland is transformed into a pastoral concert arena. World-renowned musicians trade their tuxedos for blue jeans, sit on hay bales, and play for the picnickers on the lawn just outside the barn. *206/527-8839; www.olympicmusicfestival.org.*

Celebrate Lavender Festival
Mid-July in Sequim

This celebration of the senses includes tours of the many lavender farms in the Sequim-Dungeness Valley, the lavender capital of North America. See how lavender is grown and used in gardening, decor, and cooking. Workshops, demonstrations, food, crafts, and lavender products are available at the farms and at the street fair in downtown Sequim. *360/681-3035 or 877/681-3035; www.lavenderfestival.com.*

SandSations Sand Castle Building Contest
Late July in Long Beach

Every year, amateurs and professionals alike descend upon the beach to vie in this anticipated event. While you may not want to spend the whole

thoughtful details such as in-ceiling speakers and soft lighting to help set an intimate mood. The beautiful landscaping and lush, manicured foliage not only provide a gorgeous setting but also enhance guest privacy and create several ideal spots in which to steal a kiss. *$$$–$$$$; MC, V; checks OK; www.colettes.com.*

weekend here as crowds and kids are abundant, it makes for a very amusing and relaxing way to spend a few hours, especially if the tide stays low and the sun stays out. *www.funbeach.com/events/sandsations.*

Jazz & Oysters
Mid-August in Long Beach

The name says it all. But this outing has more than just great musical entertainment and scrumptious barbecued oysters; it also features a beer and wine garden, fruit and cheese nibbles, and delicious desserts from the peninsula's most renowned restaurants. An all-day pass is $18. *800/451-2542; www.watermusicfestival.com/pages/jazzoys.html*

Washington State International Kite Festival
Third full week of August in Long Beach

This week-long extravaganza attracts kite fliers from all around the world, lighting the skies with color, highflying action, and choreographed movement. Events throughout the week include both friendly and fierce competitions, races, and theme days. Booths and concessions dot the 26-mile beach and offer lemonade and other treats. *360/642-4020; www.kitefestival.com.*

Wooden Boat Festival
Early September in Port Townsend

Every year, this festival showcases all kinds of wooden boats, and the maritime skills and culture that have made them such a big part of Port Townsend's Victorian seaport heritage. The festival offers workshops, exhibits, tours, and activities all around the town. The sight of the harbor filled with so many beautiful sailing vessels is worth the trip alone. *360/385-3628; www.woodenboat.org.*

Dungeness Crab & Seafood Festival
Second full weekend in October in Port Angeles

This celebration of the region's diverse bounty features a traditional Dungeness crab feed and the freshest Northwest seafood, with wine tasting, a beer garden, a demonstration kitchen, entertainment, a craft and food fair, and more. No experience or boat necessary. *360/452-6300; www.crabfestival.org.*

Domaine Madeleine / ✿✿❧

146 Wildflower Ln, Port Angeles; 360/457-4174 or 888/811-8376
There are two reasons to stay here: the unrivaled views and the equally spectacular breakfasts. Boasting the best scenery of any B&B on the peninsula, this inn perched on a bluff overlooking the Strait of Juan de Fuca affords

views of Victoria and the San Juan Islands, Olympic Mountains, and perhaps even whales and other wildlife. The abundant beauty outdoors is on par with what's indoors, and romance thrives here. The four suites all have private entrances and sweet touches, such as a cake made in celebration of your anniversary. Save room for breakfast, an ornate five-course culinary treat that is as pretty as it is delicious. *$$$–$$$$; AE, MC, V; checks OK; www. domainemadeleine.com.*

Lake Crescent Lodge / ✿✿❤

416 Lake Crescent Rd, Port Angeles; 360/928-3211
Lake Crescent Lodge rests on the bank of its namesake, and from your rustic cabin you can view this glassy stretch of water as it curves around forested mountains that ascend magnificently in the distance. By far the most romantic accommodations are the Roosevelt Fireplace Cottages. In warm weather, grab your honey and a bottle of wine and watch a beautiful sunset on the peninsula from your Adirondack chairs placed at the water's edge. In cooler months, build a fire in the wood-burning fireplace and savor the splendid view. If a Roosevelt Cottage is not available, consider a Singer Tavern Cottage; these cottages don't afford as much privacy but are still more romantic than the motel-like units on the lodge's second floor. *$$–$$$; AE, DC, DIS, MC, V; no checks; Roosevelt Cottages available weekends only Nov–Apr; www.lakecrescentlodge.com.*

Lost Mountain Lodge / ✿✿✿✿

303 Sunny View Dr, Sequim; 360/683-2431 or 888/683-2431
This soothing lodge on 6 acres of sunny meadows is the very definition of easygoing romance. Its unfussy decor, vaulted ceilings, and airy spaces are delightfully refreshing and immediately calming; stepping into its spaces creates an *aah* feeling. Built for romance, every suite has a wood-burning fireplace and king-size bed, as well as a private bathroom stocked with tea lights, lavender bath salts, and French toiletries. (Our favorite is the new Hideaway on Quail Lake, the largest, most luxurious, and most private suite.) The owners are gracious hosts who delight in providing thoughtful treats throughout your stay, including resort-quality robe and slippers and decadent crab dip and cider delivered to your room shortly after your arrival. *$$$–$$$$; MC, V; checks OK; www.lostmountainlodge.com.*

Romantic Restaurants

Alder Wood Bistro / ✿✿

139 W Alder St, Sequim; 360/683-4321
Although the atmosphere is too cafe-ish and the music too raucous to be called truly romantic, what this quaint bistro lacks in ambience it makes up for with unbelievable food. The chef exclusively uses local ingredients and

purchases products from purveyors who practice sustainable methods, so the specials change wildly depending on what's in season. The result is a menu that boasts fresh, homegrown flavors enhanced by culinary creativity. For starters try the prosciutto-wrapped figs, then indulge in an entrée such as the grilled lamb with *muhammara*—but make sure to save your appetite for the equally scrumptious desserts. With such epicurean treats, it's no wonder everyone raves about this organic oasis. *$$; AE, MC, V; local checks only; lunch, dinner Tues–Sat; beer and wine; reservations recommended; www.alder woodbistro.com.*

Bella Italia / ●●(

118 E 1st St, Port Angeles; 360/457-5442
An excellent romantic choice, Bella Italia is painted in Tuscan colors and has an inviting bar, a bustling dining room, and a charismatic staff. A winner of *Wine Spectator*'s "best wine list" award, the restaurant offers you a choice of more than 450 wines. Reasonably priced classics—chicken saltimbocca, pizza, pasta, steak, duck, tiramisu—and a menu of daily specials featuring the catch-of-the-day make this a tasty option after cleaning up from a day of hiking. Settle into one of the candlelit booths, soak up the convivial atmosphere, and savor the fine flavors. *$$; AE, DIS, MC, V; local checks only; dinner every day; beer and wine; reservations recommended; www.bellaitaliapa.com.*

Cedar Creek / ●●

665 N 5th Ave, Sequim; 360/683-3983
Cedar Creek evokes different moods depending on where you sit. Outside, the deck is light and casual, while the tables in the yard are infinitely more romantic. Inside, the white booths with ivy delicately crawling up the walls give a rustic feel, while a more formal dining room across the way with dark wood paneling and rich wall tapestries creates a stately atmosphere. Regardless of where you sit, the Italian cuisine is good but generic. Elevating its stature, however, is the impressive and selective wine list, premium liquors, and abundant after-dinner cordials. With good food and better ambience, Cedar Creek will create the backdrop for a romantic meal. *$$; AE, DIS, MC, V; checks OK; lunch, dinner every day; full bar; reservations recommended; www.cedarcreekcuisine.com.*

C'est Si Bon / ●●(

23 Cedar Park Dr, Port Angeles; 360/452-8888
The bright exterior may be slightly garish, but inside, everything is wonderfully elegant. The crystal chandelier hanging from the vaulted ceiling, upholstered chairs providing comfortable seating, and silk flower arrangements on every table all lend a sophisticated air. The French chef prepares each entrée personally, so busy weekend nights can bring lengthy waits, although fans say it's worth it. Try the Cornish game hen with mushroom stuffing and brown

sauce or the filet mignon with crabmeat and cream sauce. Service can be slightly intrusive, especially if you are enjoying a quiet tête-à-tête. Still, overall, the name says it all. *$$$; AE, DIS, MC, V; checks OK; dinner Tues–Sun; full bar; reservations recommended; www.cestsibon-frenchcuisine.com.*

Michael's Divine Dining / ❂❂❂

117 B 1st St, Port Angeles; 360/417-6929
With big booths, intimate lighting, and fresh Northwest-Mediterranean fusion fare, this restaurant lives up to its lofty name. A seafood and steakhouse, Michael's also serves pizza and decadent pastas in healthy portions that can easily be shared. The extensive wine list features global favorites as well as local highlights. Start with the crab, artichoke, and spinach dip made with local Dungeness crab, and split the chicken gnocchi for an entrée. If possible, call ahead to reserve one of the booths; they're much more intimate than the tables in the middle of the floor. *$$$; AE, DIS, MC, V; checks OK; lunch Mon–Sat, dinner every day; full bar; reservations recommended; www. michaelsdining.com.*

Toga's / ❂❂

122 W Lauridsen Blvd, Port Angeles; 360/452-1952
This family-managed establishment boasts the most creative menu in town, which offsets the intimacy lacking in the decor. European sauces and techniques are combined with fresh local ingredients to produce inventive dishes, such as crab-stuffed prawns topped with Jarlsberg and Gruyère cheeses. For the house specialty, called Jägerstein, the waitstaff brings to your table an extremely hot stone on which you prepare your meat or seafood. The concept is similar to fondue, except you use the stone to cook the food instead of a pot of hot liquid. *$$$; AE, DIS, MC, V; checks OK; dinner Tues–Sat (call for seasonal closures); beer and wine; reservations recommended.*

Hoh Rain Forest, Western Beaches & Lake Quinault

Romantic Highlights

Wild coastal beaches, ethereal rainforests dense with ancient trees, and glacier-carved lakes top the list of natural wonders found in this unique, remote part of the world. Although the area gets plenty of visitors in the summer, many claim they love it best in fall and winter, when the crowds thin to a trickle and whoever's left can claim the glorious landscapes. The weather can be fierce, but with the right person along, retreating to the coziness of your room after a day of braving the elements can be downright heavenly.

The **Hoh Rain Forest** (visitor center on Hwy 101 south of Forks; 360/374-6925) demonstrates what Mother Nature can do with an abundance of moisture to thrive on (150 inches of rain annually). Every inch of the forest, including decaying trees, is covered with moss, lichens, mushrooms, ferns, and sorrel. You will also see some of the largest spruce, fir, and cedar trees in the world. Some are 300 feet tall and 23 feet around. Silence surrounds you as all traces of sky disappear under the canopy of moss-covered trees. On a rare sunny day, streams of light penetrate the thick foliage in a golden, misty haze. Don't miss the chance to share a kiss behind the curtains of moss.

Carved from a glacier, **Lake Quinault** (off Hwy 101), surrounded by cathedral-like firs, offers an abundance of romantic options. Rent a canoe, rowboat, or sea cycle at **Lake Quinault Lodge** (see Romantic Lodgings). If you're staying there, ask the lodge to prepare a picnic basket for you, and head off in search of a secluded inlet. Or put together a picnic at the mercantile across the street from the lodge and hike in the rain forest. As the southwest gateway to Olympic National Park, the Quinault Valley is the ideal point of departure for hikes up to scenic alpine meadows, small lakes, and ice-carved peaks; less-athletic types will be glad to know that there are several easy trails. If a hike sounds too ambitious, drive around the lake, which takes about an hour and a half and offers magnificent bird's-eye views, as well as glimpses of the biggest trees in the Northwest.

The western beaches are among the most humbling sites in the world—there's nothing like coming to the edge of a continent and experiencing the raw power of the ocean. **Rialto Beach,** off Mora Road near La Push, boasts some of the most awesome views of the Pacific Coast. The main attraction here—aside from the dramatic sea stacks—is Hole-in-the-Wall, a tunnel-like structure 3 miles from the beach (6 miles round-trip) formed by centuries of wave erosion. Rialto Beach is great on a warm summer day but even better during the heavy winter storms. **Ruby Beach** (off Hwy 101 north of Kalaloch), named for the rosy sand that contains tiny garnets, is accessible via a well-maintained trail, making it ideal for long, meandering walks. For a more rugged experience, head to **Third Beach** (Hwy 101 to La Push), a surf-pounded beach where hidden caves and rock formations await exploration. A three-quarter-mile walk on a forest path leads to the beach. Be very careful of the tides, as you could get trapped around a point or headland during an incoming tide.

Access & Information

Lake Quinault is best accessed by car; the drive from Port Angeles takes a little over three hours. At the inland apex of the Quinault Indian Reservation, the lake is usually the first or the last stop on Highway 101's scenic loop around the peninsula's Olympic National Park and Forest.

Romantic Lodgings

Kalaloch Lodge / ◐◑

157151 Hwy 101, Forks; 360/962-2271
The Pacific Ocean is in Kalaloch's front yard and is the primary reason to come here. During low tide, take a long, sandy hike along the shore; at high tide, you will hear the roar of the ocean surf. The main lodge has nine adequate rooms and a mediocre ocean-side restaurant. Farther down is a motel unit with less-than-romantic rooms stacked tightly together. On a bluff overlooking the ocean are the primo accommodations—20 cabins with views of the magnificent seascape. An additional 24 cabins are available, set back from the bluff and view. The interior decor in all the rooms is less than inspiring, but you'll likely be spending most of your time outdoors anyway. In the evening, light a fire after dinner, turn the lights down low, and cuddle the night away. *$$–$$$; AE, MC, V; checks OK; www.visitkalaloch.com.*

Lake Quinault Lodge / ◐◖

345 S Shore Rd, Quinault; 360/288-2900 or 800/562-6672
One of the first things you'll notice at the Lake Quinault Lodge is a lack of modern conveniences—but we consider that a splendid thing. There's no better place to get "unplugged" than in this cedar-shingled lodge where you won't find an abundance of telephones, televisions, or radios; in fact, it's doubtful your cell phone will even work. Instead, enjoy the natural wonders of the area—and your sweetheart—by hiking or taking a lake cruise just before sunset. Note the area's stormy weather and keep in mind that the lodge experiences about 40 power outages a year—undeniably romantic, but also, at times, inconvenient. *$$–$$$; AE, DC, MC, V; checks OK; www. visitlakequinault.com.*

Lake Quinault Resort / ◐◖

314 N Shore Rd, Amanda Park; 360/288-2362 or 800/650-2362
With nine rooms and two cabins along 600 feet of Lake Quinault, the resort is a pleasant option for those who want a quieter and more secluded alternative to the massive and bustling lodge across the lake. Five of the rooms offer full kitchens, while all share a wide deck overflowing with flower-filled planters, wisteria, and Adirondack chairs. On the grounds, there are many secluded outdoor spots—the gazebo just above the beach is especially inviting—from which to sit and savor the view. *$$–$$$; AE, DIS, MC, V; checks OK; www. lakequinault.com.*

Miller Tree Inn / ◐

654 E Division St, Forks; 360/374-6806
Romantic accommodations are hard to come by in this area, but this pretty white house located in Forks offers comfortable options—and allows kids

Three Days of Romance

Day One: Start your getaway in the charming Victorian–seaport town of **Port Townsend**. Stroll along the main thoroughfare downtown and take in the beautifully restored buildings, the peekaboo views of Puget Sound and the islands, and the eclectic medley of antiques stores, art galleries, and gift and craft shops. Indulge in an ice cream or a hot chocolate (depending on the weather) at one of the many cafes that dot the street, then visit the harbor, stopping at the edge to savor the sweeping views. Dine at the **Wild Coho**, popularly cited as the best restaurant on the peninsula (reservations are a must), and stay at the **James House**, perched atop a hill overlooking the Sound.

Day Two: After eating a sumptuous breakfast at the James House, drive to **Hurricane Ridge** in the **Olympic National Park**, a must-see drive up to an elevation of 5,200 feet. On a clear day, the views of the park's jagged peaks are breathtaking. If it's warm, hike one of the trails and enjoy a picnic in a wildflower-filled meadow. In winter, take a free guided snowshoe tour. **Camaraderie Cellars** in Port Angeles is a beautiful place to spend a relaxing late afternoon after a hike before eating at **Michael's Divine Dining**. If you can get a private cabin at the **Lake Crescent Lodge**, be sure to leave dinner early enough to catch an unbelievable sunset from the lakeshore.

Day Three: No Olympic Peninsula trip is complete without experiencing the **Hoh Rain Forest** and western beaches—there's just nothing like coming to the edge of a continent. Two short trails provide a good look into this enchanting natural wonder: the **Hall of Mosses Trail** (¾ mile) and the **Spruce Nature Trail** (1¼ miles). If you have the time and inclination, drive west to **Ruby Beach** or **Third Beach** on the western shore. The former is accessible via a well-maintained trail and is graced with majestic sea stacks jutting up from the ocean. The latter is more rugged and is filled with hidden caves and rock formations that await exploration. Either spot is ideal for a picnic before you head back to civilization. To continue your outdoor experience, consider staying at one of the nearby lodges; for luxurious pampering after a long day, drive back to Port Angeles or Sequim. Dine on Northwest, Italian-influenced cuisine at **Bella Italia** and then end the evening with a wonderfully luxurious stay at **Lost Mountain Lodge**.

and pets. The two deluxe suites at the back of the house are the most romantic rooms by far. Very private and quiet, each of these contemporary suites offers views of the surrounding farmlands, a king-size bed, a gas fireplace, a Jacuzzi tub for two, a TV/VCR, and a love seat. An abundant breakfast is served in the morning; the gingerbread pancakes are amazing. With the Hoh Rain Forest 45 minutes away and the Olympic beaches only 20, this is a snug retreat from which to explore this rugged region. *$$–$$$; DIS, MC, V; checks OK; www.millertreeinn.com.*

Romantic Restaurants

Lake Quinault Lodge / 🌑🌑

345 S Shore Rd, Lake Quinault; 360/288-2900 or 800/562-6672
The most romantic spot in this vast restaurant is a seat by the grand stone fireplace in the main lodge. Have a predinner drink and request a table by the window to better savor the view, especially at dusk when the lights begin to sparkle around the edge of the lake. Dining at this restaurant, one of the best bets in the area, gives you a chance to visit the historic lodge (see Romantic Lodgings) if you are staying elsewhere. If you come in the evening, ask about taking a predinner boat ride. *$$–$$$; AE, MC, V; checks OK; breakfast, lunch, dinner every day; full bar; reservations recommended; www. visitlakequinault.com.*

River's Edge / 🌑🌑

41 Main St, La Push; 360/374-5777
Perched on the banks of the Hoh River right where it opens into the Pacific Ocean, this eatery boasts a gorgeous location in an old boat-launch building, complete with high ceilings, soaring windows, exposed beams, and sepia-toned photos of the Quileute tribe. The menu is simple, and note that no alcohol is served, although you can bring your own beer or wine (no corkage fee). Though very informal and not especially romantic in the traditional sense, this is a great choice in an area with few dining options, and a surprisingly hip, cosmopolitan find on the edge of the continent. *$$; MC, V; local checks only; breakfast, lunch, dinner every day; no alcohol; no reservations.*

Long Beach Peninsula

Romantic Highlights

The Long Beach Peninsula is a marvelous coastal destination, with 28 miles of accessible sand beaches (making it the longest natural beach in the United States), a number of beautiful parks and gardens, and some of the most intimate small-town restaurants in the Northwest. During the summer, however, crowds can seem overwhelming—especially if it's a quiet retreat you're seeking. In July or August, the key to a successful intimate getaway is finding an idyllic spot and staying put. Fortunately, you'll find plenty of extremely romantic lodging options, some of which are even quickly becoming Washington's most sought-after sites for tying the knot. Another alternative is to visit during the quiet winter season and cozy up before a fire and a picture window to watch the fury of the storms along the coast. Above all, it's the natural beauty of the remote areas here that will inspire kisses.

A crown jewel among coastal Northwest parks, **Leadbetter Point State Park** is set at the northern end of the Long Beach Peninsula (3 miles north of Oysterville, on Stackpole Rd). The route to the park involves a peaceful drive through a canopy of leafy trees—a nice lead-up to the park itself. The two of you can wander hand-in-hand all day without running into another soul, so bring a picnic and a warm blanket and enjoy the vast expanse of sand flanked by stretches of dune grass, lupine, and wild strawberry. Your only neighbors will be the great blue herons, brown pelicans, bald eagles, and seals who call the place home. Keep in mind that the park's beach trails, while a great place to bird-watch in the spring and fall, flood with deep water during the rainy season (Oct–May).

On the drive back from the park, stop in **Oysterville**, a picture-postcard of a tiny 19th-century sea town, listed as a Historic District on the National Register of Historic Places. **Oysterville Sea Farms** (1st and Clark; 360/665-6585 or 800/272-6237) is the only industry here and sells the marvelous fresh oysters promised by the town's name—along with other goodies such as rich chocolate fudge.

On the southern end of the peninsula, explore the 3-mile scenic loop that begins at the town of **Ilwaco**. (In Ilwaco, you'll see signs for the loop.) From the parking lot for the **North Head Lighthouse**, a short walk along a pretty wooded trail ends in an astounding view of both the Pacific Ocean and the entire Long Beach Peninsula. Be it high noon or sunset, views from this vantage point—with the picturesque, century-old lighthouse in the background—are sure to inspire a kiss. For a small fee, you can climb to the top of the lighthouse and take a short tour. Continue driving south along the loop, pass through an entrance to the U.S. Coast Guard Station, and look for the path that leads to Cape Disappointment Lighthouse. The hike up is a bit steep, but you'll be glad you made the effort when you take in the view from this historic lighthouse, which has been guiding sailors into the Columbia River's entrance since 1856. Other highlights along the loop include **Cape Disappointment State Park** (formerly Fort Canby State Park), with 16 miles of hiking trails (2½ miles south of Ilwaco off Hwy 101; 360/642-3078) and Waikiki Beach, the only swim-safe beach on the Peninsula; the **Ilwaco Heritage Museum** (115 SE Lake St; 360/642-3446); and the **Lewis and Clark Interpretive Center** (high on the cliffs of Cape Disappointment State Park, 360/642-3029), which also offers a wonderful view of the Columbia River.

The colorful little towns lining the Pacific Highway—Ilwaco, Seaview, Long Beach, and Ocean Park—offer lots of opportunities for exploration (those seeking privacy should steer clear during summer). The **Saturday market** at the Port of Ilwaco (May–Oct) is an excellent place to browse for locally made crafts and edible treats. **Seaview** offers some lovely spots for an intimate lunch (see Romantic Restaurants), and since it seems that all roads in town lead to the beach, you will undoubtedly find yourselves drawn west to stroll the dunes afterward. You can also check out the arts scene; **Campiche Studios** (101 Pacific Ave S; 360/642-2264)

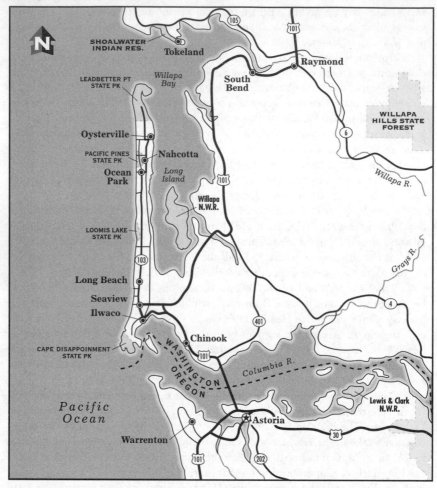

features watercolors, sculptures, and photography. **Long Beach**, the center of peninsula tourist activity, has crowded gift shops, amusement arcades, and a beach boardwalk for an old-time beach-holiday experience.

Access & Information

Most travelers exploring the Long Beach Peninsula by car approach from Interstate 5. Between the major cities of Portland and Seattle, you'll find Vancouver, Washington, just north of the Columbia River. Longview is a half-hour's drive farther north, where Highway 4 turns west to the coast. Other major highways that provide access to the region include US Highway 101 (to the south this runs to Astoria, Oregon; to the north, it connects via

Highway 4 to I-5). Unless you find festivals particularly romantic, you might want to work around the region's busiest weekends, such as the International Kite Festival in Long Beach (Aug), and the Northwest Garlic Festival in Ocean Park (June). On the other hand, Jazz and Oysters in Oysterville (Aug) and February's peninsula-wide Old Fashioned Valentine's Day events sound potentially romantic to us. Contact the **Long Beach Peninsula Visitors Bureau** (intersection of Hwy 101 and Hwy 103; 800/451-2452; www.funbeach.com).

Romantic Lodgings

Boreas Bed & Breakfast Inn / ❂❂❂

607 N Ocean Beach Blvd, Long Beach; 360/642-8069 or 888/642-8069
Romance is infused in every detail of this delightful inn, from fresh flower bouquets in every room, luxurious bedding and robes, and a lavish breakfast served at 9:30am, considerably later than most B&Bs. All five guest rooms have ocean views and private bathrooms—our favorites are the Garden Suite, with French doors opening onto a private deck and views of the dunes, and the Pacifica and Stargazer suites, with simply spectacular views of the ocean. The owners delight in being co-conspirators and have helped plan many romantic surprises for their guests; they claim, in fact, to have had engagements in every spot on the property. Whether you're looking to pop the question or simply to get away for a weekend sans kids, you'll have your pick of places to kiss at Boreas. *$$$; AE, DC, MC, V; checks OK; www.boreasinn.com.*

Caswell's on the Bay Bed & Breakfast Inn / ❂❂❂

25204 Sandridge Rd, Ocean Park; 360/665-6535 or 888/553-2319
This Victorian-style house, on 5 acres at the edge of Willapa Bay, has a top-notch, well-deserved reputation for romance. Surrounded by flower gardens and water views, the house is close to attractions but well-removed from traffic and noise. It's bright and airy inside, with high ceilings and excellent soundproofing. The five guest rooms all have private baths and pleasant sitting areas; two offer beautiful bay views, and the other three overlook the garden. Hand-carved antique furniture and down comforters, deluxe sheets and towels, and custom Caswell soaps and lotions all add to the feeling that you're making a luxurious getaway. This is one of the most sought-after coastal wedding sites in the Northwest, so reserve early. The white gazebo by the water is an excellent little spot for a lot of kissing. *$$–$$$; AE, MC, V; checks OK; www.caswellsinn.com.*

China Beach Retreat / ❂❂❂

222 Robert Gray Dr, Ilwaco; 360/642-5660 or 800/INN-1896
This retreat at the corner of the Pacific Ocean and the Columbia River has been known as China Beach since the late 19th century, when Chinese immigrants drawn to jobs at the nearby salmon canneries flocked to the area. Here

you'll find a spacious, renovated wooden-house-turned-romantic-getaway that sits on the last mile of the Lewis and Clark trail and offers a quiet escape. Under the same ownership as the historic Shelburne Inn nearby, the house includes many luxurious, thoughtful touches, such as the addition of Victorian stained-glass panels that cast romantic light in the rooms. There are three guest rooms and the new Audubon Cottage to choose from, all with private spa tubs, tiled showers, and queen-size beds raised on wooden dais to enjoy beautiful views of Baker's Bay while snuggling under the covers. Breakfast is provided at the Shelburne Inn, five minutes up the road by car—although the owners have been known to send their wild mushroom frittatas to your room at China Beach upon request. *$$$; AE, MC, V; checks OK; www. chinabeachretreat.com.*

The Shelburne Inn / ✪✪✪❁

4415 Pacific Way S, Seaview; 360/642-2442 or 800/INN-1896
One of the Northwest's premier country inns, the Shelburne Inn is a wonderfully romantic retreat. Inside, the ambience is so memorable that the setting—right on busy Highway 103—is the first thing you'll forget. The 15 small, elegant rooms and two luxury suites all feature private baths, beautiful antiques, down comforters, lace pillows, and handmade quilts, and many have a balcony or deck. Most rooms have queen beds; some face the garden, while others offer less inspiring street views. No matter which room you book, expect fresh flowers and freshly baked cookies awaiting you upon arrival. The highly romantic suites downstairs, furnished with remarkable antiques, are simply spectacular; guests may choose the luxurious option of having breakfast delivered to their room in the morning, instead of dining family-style in the lobby. *$$–$$$; AE, MC, V; checks OK; www.the shelburneinn.com.*

Romantic Restaurants

The 42nd Street Café / ✪✪❁

4201 Pacific Way, Seaview; 360/642-2323
This local favorite may not look like much from the outside, but inside, tables adorned with flowers and colorful linens arranged around the country kitchen–style dining room make for a charming ambience. Lace half curtains shield the view of the busy highway outside and the service is cheerful and efficient. Its unusual offerings, such as chèvre fondue with apples, fried green tomatoes with cumin-orange mayonnaise, and halibut and shrimp cake with parsley-caper mayonnaise, are simply delicious. *$$; AE, MC, V; checks OK; breakfast, lunch, dinner every day; beer and wine; reservations recommended; www.42ndstreetcafe.com.*

The Sanctuary / ●●●

794 Hwy 101, Chinook; 360/777-8380
This 92-year-old former church retains the hushed, echoing atmosphere one might expect from such reverent beginnings. Original stained-glass windows, angel sconces, a pump organ, and leaded-glass door insets are admired from the wooden pews, where diners sit at tables covered with white linens. The food here is—pardon the pun—divine, from the fresh local seafood to the Scandinavian specialties. Try the *Köttbullar* (Swedish meatballs) for starters and the chicken roulade or rack of lamb for your entrée. Save room for the famous lemon cream sherbet or *Krumkake*—wafflelike cones filled with whipped cream and topped with berry sauce. Note: Dinner hours change seasonally, so it's best to call ahead. *$$–$$$; AE, DIS, MC, V; checks OK; dinner Thur–Sun; full bar; reservations recommended; www.sanctuary restaurant.com.*

The Shoalwater / ●●●●
The Heron and Beaver Pub / ●●●

4415 Pacific Way (The Shelburne Inn), Seaview; 360/642-4142
Everything from the imaginative and wide-ranging menu at this warm, country-Victorian dining room is utterly fresh, delicious, and beautifully presented. Mouthwatering crab and shrimp cakes are kissed with sesame oil and ginger, and roasted herb-encrusted duck breast is served with a cranberry and truffle butter. The wine list here is so extensive that some bottles have to be stored off site, and the array of delicious desserts will tempt you to indulgence. The decor charms, with leaded and stained-glass windows, high ceilings, soft candlelight, and crisp white linens on well-spaced antique tables. Reserve well in advance for the Shoalwater's popular wintertime winemakers dinner series, featuring seven-course meals designed around wines from a visiting winemaker. The Heron and Beaver Pub, this destination's more casual sister, shares the same kitchen. This tiny establishment re-creates that old-world magic of an English pub with a wide selection of excellent beers. Some tasty items off the Shoalwater's menu are served here, including delicious Cajun-style blackened Willapa Bay oysters; other fare includes classic comfort food with a twist, like the wild mushroom–goat cheese lasagne. *$$$ (Shoalwater); $$ (Heron and Beaver Pub); AE, DC, MC, V; checks OK; lunch, dinner every day, brunch Sun; full bar; reservations recommended; www. shoalwater.com.*

♡ North
Cascades

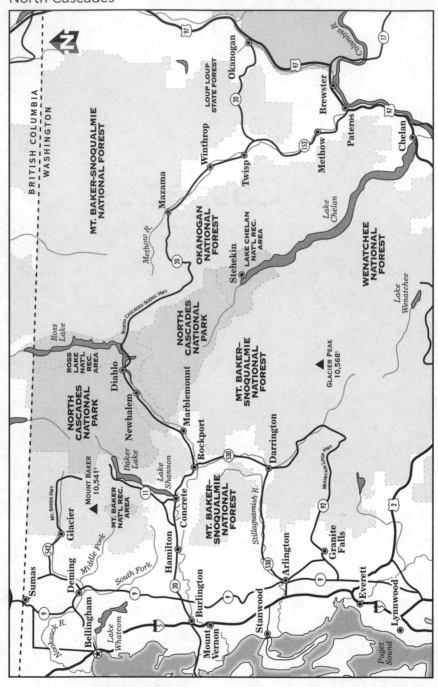

Doubt thou the stars are fire; / Doubt that the sun doth move; / Doubt truth to be a liar; / But never doubt I love.

—William Shakespeare

# North Cascades

This expansive region in northwest Washington is simply and breathtakingly magnificent. The Cascades rank among the world's greatest mountain ranges, extending from Canada's Fraser River south into Oregon. The vast North Cascades National Park, part of the Cascade Range, is composed of 505,000 acres of untamed, unspoiled, and nearly impenetrable majestic grandeur, offering some 318 glaciers, rugged clusters of 8,000-foot ice-capped peaks, wildflower-dotted alpine meadows, dense stands of virgin Douglas fir and western red cedar forests, and brilliant jade-blue lakes. Travel through this region is by car or on foot; there are no access routes for plane or train. To access the North Cascades, set squarely in the northwest part of the state, you have two road options: the North Cascades Scenic Highway (Hwy 20) and the Cascades Loop. Highway 20, the most northerly east-west route, leads through stunning mountain passes, winds into the expansiveness of the Methow River Valley (pronounced "MET-how") east of the Cascades, and turns south toward pristine Lake Chelan. The other popular route is the Cascade Loop, which incorporates a network of roads encircling the region. This area encompasses three national parks that allow access into the more hidden wilderness. A 386-mile trail system, mostly in high-elevation backcountry, takes you into breathtaking alpine scenery with more than 200 designated backcountry campsites. All of this grandeur and wild, elusive beauty draws hikers, backpackers, and mountaineers from around the world. The many trailheads along Highway 20 open to endless and diverse views of glacier-sculpted valleys, cascading waterfalls in subalpine stillness, and hidden lakes surrounded by lush woodlands. Couples less inclined to outdoor adventures can experience an equally stirring thrill by absorbing the scenic overlooks at the high-elevation mountain passes.

The drive from Seattle along Highway 20 is approximately two hours of stirring vistas and mountain passes, which lands you in the towns of Mazama, Winthrop, and Twisp in the Methow Valley, a wide open grassy meadowland with dramatic ridges fringed with evergreens. The great outdoors is the key ingredient here, whether you are hiking, camping, mountain biking, fishing, boating, hot-air ballooning, downhill or cross-country skiing, or simply savoring the ambience from a private retreat.

South of the Methow Valley, Lake Chelan lies nestled in North America's deepest gorge, 55 miles long and less than 2 miles wide in the Lake Chelan Valley, approximately an hour-and-a-half drive south of Winthrop. A vacation getaway for the past century, it offers a blend of quaint, small-town community; every imaginable waterfront activity; and an emerging, sophisticated wine-growing region and clientele. The pristine lake, sandy beaches, and 300-plus sunny days a year are compelling features that have contributed to its current and proposed resort and golf developments.

At Lake Chelan's southern tip, the popular resort communities of Manson and Chelan balance bustling vacation activities with relaxing hideaways and in-town explorations of galleries and specialty shops. At the lake's northern tip, the limited local roads do not connect the tiny but beautiful town of Stehekan to the outside world; access to this remote and tranquil setting is by ferry or floatplane.

Methow Valley

Romantic Highlights

One of the Northwest's most famous routes, the **North Cascades Scenic Highway** (Hwy 20) cuts through the mountains to reach the Methow Valley. As you drive along this stretch of highway, you'll see an extraordinary array of landscapes, from rolling farmland to dramatic evergreen ridges, rugged mountain passes and glaciers to alpine meadows, thundering waterfalls to brilliantly colored lakes. Stop for a quiet, hand-in-hand stroll at **Cascade Farms**, nestled against the tree line of the Cascade foothills. A small shop in a perennial garden offers organic products, excellent homemade ice cream, and, weather permitting, pick-your-own blueberries. Or stretch your legs at the pretty riverside park across the road. Farther along the road, stop in the Newhalem powerhouse, where you'll find the **North Cascades Visitor Center** (502 Newhalem St, Newhalem; 206/386-4495; www.marblemount.com), a good place to pick up maps and brochures. Behind the powerhouse, a short hike leads to a beautiful, out-of-the-way waterfall, perfect for sneaking a kiss before returning to the car.

Along the route are a number of scenic overlooks, perfectly timed, it would seem, to allow for hand-holding in silent awe and wonder. The massive granite walls of **Liberty Bell Mountain** (7,600 feet) seem to make passage impossible until the road turns to clamber up its face. The off-road viewpoint of **Washington Pass** is magnificent and worth a stop for a quick kiss. Looking down on the road 700 feet below is like being in your own Ansel Adams photograph. Pack a picnic lunch and take any number of short hikes from trail heads along the highway. The best months for hiking are July and August as the meadows are resplendent

Three Days of Romance in the Methow Valley

Day One: Sun Mountain Lodge is the perfect place for a three-night stay. Spend the first day and night exploring the outdoors (the activities center is able to satisfy any interest) and pampering yourselves with a Double Decadence spa treatment. Enjoy dinner and an evening walk before retiring to watch the valley sky from your deck.

Day Two: After breakfast at Sun Mountain Lodge, head out to the **Freestone Inn**, your base camp for the day. Across the parking lot, rent bikes at **Jack's Hut** and explore Lost River Road, which meanders beside the river with little scenic nooks along the way. Stop by the **Mazama Store**, where you will find picnic-perfect food to go. Trade the bikes for the car and bring your picnic up to **Slates Peak** overlooking the majesty of alpine meadows and have a top-of-the-world kiss. Returning to Winthrop, stop in at **Lost River Winery** tasting room for a few sips of Merlot and Cabernet Sauvignon. Then ease into the evening with a hand-in-hand stroll along the picturesque main street of Winthrop. Later dine at the **Freestone Inn**. Top it off with a walk around the lake listening to night sounds and sweet nothings then head back to Sun Mountain Lodge to settle into your lavishly cozy room.

Day Three: Rouse yourself early enough to take a **Morning Glory Balloon** flight. Later, do a little window-shopping in Winthrop and arrive for dinner at **Arrowleaf Bistro**. The menu is small and inventive, emphasizing fresh and local fare, with care given to complement wines from Lost River Winery.

with wildflowers. The overlooks above **Ross and Diablo lakes** are stunning with distinctive color (Ross is teal, Diablo is jade); the color is caused by fine stone particles suspended in the water that reflect the forest and the sky.

Arriving into the wide-open **Methow River Valley**, the outdoor recreational opportunities abound. Summers offer fishing, horseback riding, and mountain biking; winter is a paradise for **cross-country skiers** of all levels. The **Methow Valley Sports Trails Association** (509/996-3287 or 800/682-5787; www.mvsta. com) maintains approximately 100 miles of trails, consisting of four linked sections. (In the summer, the trails are primarily used by mountain bikers.) For those seeking more adrenalin surges, there is the opportunity for **heli-skiing**. Founded in 1988, **North Cascade Heli-Skiing** (509/996-3272 or 800/494-4354; www.heli-ski.com) operates from the **Freestone Inn** in Mazama (see Romantic Lodgings). For couples yearning for untouched powder runs, you'll find 1,500 to 4,000 vertical feet and altitudes to 9,000 feet. For a little less active (but no less inspiring) romance, **hot-air ballooning** is a spectacular, dreamy outing. Centered in Winthrop, tours operate year-round champagne flights and generally travel south over the Methow Valley.

Each town in the Methow Valley has its own unique romantic appeal. As you head east on Highway 20, **Mazama** is the first tiny town you'll encounter. The **Mazama Store** (50 Lost River Rd; 509/996-2855; www.methow.com/mazama store) remains the only store in town and is a good place to stop for picnic supplies while out on a bike ride or before heading toward **Okanagan National Forest**. Bring your own bikes or rent them from Jack's Hut, adjacent to the Freestone Inn. You'll need a sturdy four-wheel-drive car or SUV to continue the trip up to **Harts Pass** and the ascent to **Slates Peak**. This will take several hours round-trip as you ascend more than 19 miles on a single-lane gravel (at best) road, with hairpin turns, no guard rails, and 1,000-foot sheer drop-offs. Arriving at 7,440 feet, well above the tree line, you will reach the highest drivable point in the state. A short walk up the drive leads to the fire lookout tower, built in the 1930s, where you will be rewarded with an extraordinary alpine vista that spreads out into infinity; you will tumble into each other's arms from the sheer exuberance of it all. Outdoor opportunities abound, from partaking in strenuous backpacking adventures to relaxing to the sounds of annual music festivals. The classical outdoors music festival series, the **Methow Music Festival** (509/996-6000; www.methowmusic festival.org), or the annual **Winthrop Rhythm and Blues Festival** (877/996-9283; www.winthropbluesfestival.com) are great choices.

Winthrop was founded during the lure of gold mining. Promised riches failed to materialize and the town fell on hard times and nearly disappeared. When the North Cascades Highway was nearing completion in 1972, the business community restored the Western theme to the town and focused on the region's spectacular appeal as a scenic and recreational destination. Although popular with tourists, especially in the summer, there are plenty of open spaces that allow for quiet time together. Cozy strolls along the main street are relaxing, with plenty of eclectic diversions along the way. A gem of a discovery is the **Trails End Bookstore** (231 Riverside Ave; 509/996-2345; trailsendbookstore@mymethow.com). After you've browsed through the carefully selected titles, stop in the "castle" built by one of the Winthrop founders, Guy Waring. The castle is a log cabin, which is now the centerpiece of the **Shafer Historical Museum** (285 Castle Ave, Winthrop; 509/996-2712). It features original and reproduction installations of a late-19th-century frontier town, including stables, smithy, printing shop, schoolhouse, and cabin. After traipsing through, make your way to the **Winthrop Brewing Company** (155 Riverside Ave; 509/996-3183; www.webspinnings.com/winthrop), located in an old schoolhouse—a great place to relax together with a beer in hand.

Driving 8 miles south of Winthrop will get you to **Twisp**, a little river town that has survived several reincarnations since its boom-town days of gold and silver mining in the early 1900s. With a history in farming and ranching, Twisp has redefined itself as a growing artist community and a regional center for art events. The **Confluence Gallery and Art Center** (104 Glover St; 509/997-2787; www.confluencegallery.com) offers exhibits, gift shop, classes, and events. The

Ghosts in this Town?

Barron is an old, abandoned mining ghost town. For history buffs or those who enjoy the romantic appeal of unfinished stories, visiting Barron is an intriguing albeit challenging outing. If you are staying at the Sun Mountain Lodge, talk with Margrit, the concierge, who was the sole occupant some years ago. Or look for Sally Portman's *The Smiling Country: A History of Methow Valley*. **Trail's End Bookstore** (509/995-2345) in Winthrop may also have a copy.

Drive as far as Harts Pass along the Methow Valley Road and you will come to a fork in the gravel road. You can continue to ascend to Slates Peak, or turn off onto the Pacific Crest Trail . . . or drive straight down a slope, if your car is very sturdy (otherwise, walking might be a better idea) until you come to a locked gate, which precludes further driving. At this point you must walk. Turn left and trek into Barron. Though ghost towns are not for everyone, this is a unique hike for more athletically inclined couples—with a bent toward piquing their imaginations.

Methow Valley Farmers Market (near the community center) is open every Saturday, mid-April through mid-October, with fresh seasonal produce, herbs, homemade products, and local artisan wares. The **Merc Playhouse** (101 Glover St; 509/997-7529; www.mercplayhouse.com) offers summer theater performances in the historic landmark Twisp Mercantile Building, built in 1926 after the fire that burnt most of the town. For those seeking outdoor fun, **Osprey River Adventures** (509/997-4116 or 800/997-4116; www.methow.com/osprey) provides both ends of the spectrum in river rafting: originating in Twisp, the river runs range from smooth, lazy floats to whitewater rushes.

Access & Information

The North Cascades Scenic Highway (Highway 20) is accessed at Sedro Wooley, exit 230 on Interstate 5, about 65 miles north of Seattle. It traverses the mountain range to Twisp, east of the Cascades. From there, the Twisp-to-Chelan leg goes south along Highway 153 and US Highway 97. Snow closes the North Cascades Highway from approximately mid-November to mid-April. In winter, visitors from the Puget Sound area can reach the Methow Valley by crossing the Cascades via the longer southerly routes of US Highway 2 or Interstate 90. This route takes in Leavenworth and Wenatchee and heads north to Lake Chelan, Winthrop, and Highway 20. It is accessed from Interstate 90 at Cle Elum by taking Highway 970 to US Highway 97 north, which joins US Highway 2 just east of Leavenworth. This entire series of connecting roads is known as the 400-mile Cascade Loop. Brochures are available from the **Cascade Loop Association** (509/662-3888; www. cascadeloop.com). The 70-mile stretch between Mazama and Marbelmont on the North Cascades Scenic Highway (Hwy 20) does not have any services, so remember to check the gas tank.

For information about hiking and camping in this area, contact the **North Cascades National Park Headquarters** (2105 Hwy 20, Sedro Wooley, WA, 98284-9394; 360/856-5700; www.nps.gov/noca).

Methow Valley Central Reservations (14F Horizon Flat Rd, Winthrop; 509/996-2148 or 800/422-3048; www.methowreservations.com) books lodging for the entire valley and sells tickets to major events. The **Winthrop Chamber of Commerce Information Center** (220 Hwy 20; 509/996-2125 or 888/463-8469; www.winthropwashington.com) can provide additional information about everything from llama packing to snowmobile renting. Twisp also has its own **Visitor Information Center** (509/997-2926; www. twispinfo.com).

Romantic Lodgings

Freestone Inn and Early Winters Cabins / ❂❂❂

31 Early Winters Drive, Mazama; 509/996-3906 or 800/639-3809
This Northwest lodge, in the fullest and most gracious use of the word, is lovely: comfortable with rugged refinement. A two-story log structure overlooking Freestone Lake offers guests trout fishing in summer and ice skating in winter. An enormous stone fireplace in the Great Room divides the sitting room from the dining room (see Romantic Restaurants). Remote and romantic, this is a blend of rustic country with warm, welcoming furnishings. All guest rooms and suites have lake views and feature king-size beds, wrought-iron or pine furniture, cozy gas fireplaces, and private patios or decks. The Early Winter Cabins are set on Early Winters Creek adjacent to the lodge and are extremely private. Cabin sizes vary from studio to two bedrooms, and the decor has a simpler country feel. Jack's Hut (509/996-2752) across the parking lot can arrange everything from horseback riding and fly-fishing to mountain biking, hiking, and whitewater rafting. *$$$; AE, MC, V; checks OK; www.freestoneinn.com.*

Mazama Country Inn / ❂❂

42 Lost River Rd, Mazama; 509/996-2681 or 800/843-7951
Cozy, comfortable charm, hospitable owners, and lots of quiet places to nestle make it easy to slow down and focus attention on one another at the Mazama Country Inn. This 18-room inn offers simple, home-style rooms and amenities. Intentionally quiet, there are no telephones or TVs in the rooms. The interiors are wood trimmed and airy, with country-rustic charm. The newest rooms have king-size beds, gas fireplaces, and jetted tubs. This secluded getaway focuses on outdoor activities as hundreds of acres unfold outside

the front door, encouraging biking, cross-country skiing, and snow shoeing. A small shop on the property rents outdoor equipment. A pool, sauna, and outdoor hot tub are perfect for easing sore muscles while the light dims on the day. Family-style dining is encouraged in the excellent restaurant, and both guests and locals are invited to gather around the Russian stone fireplace in the evening for drinks and hors d'oevres. *$$; MC, V; checks OK; www. mazamacountryinn.com.*

River's Edge Resort / ❷❷

115 Riverside Ave, Winthrop; 509/996-8000 or 800/937-6621
These simple, light, and airy cabins are located on the north end of town on the Chewuch River. Cozy and quiet, they still are within easy walking distance to Winthrop restaurants and shops. Furnishings are simple and comfortable and thoughtfully designed. Ten cabins (ranging in size from one to three bedrooms) sit nestled among the trees and feature private riverside decks with hot tubs, propane fireplaces, and full kitchens. Buy some gastronomic goodies and a great bottle of local wine, and plan to stay in for a romantic dinner, stargazing from your hot tub while listening to rustling river sounds. *$$–$$$; AE, MC, V; checks OK; www.riversedgewinthrop.com.*

Sun Mountain Lodge / ❷❷❷❷

604 Patterson Lake Rd, Winthrop; 509/996-2211 or 800/572-0493
In all its details Sun Mountain Lodge combines privacy and tranquility with excellent service and amenities. This mountaintop resort is perched atop 3,000 acres of awe-inspiring pristine wilderness overlooking a mountain lake and the Methow Valley. The massive timber and stone exterior is perfectly complemented by stone floors, gorgeous wood trim, and rock fireplaces inside. Made by local artisans, the wrought-iron fixtures, hand-painted duvet covers, and cherry and maple furniture in the 97 guest rooms are a sensual treat. The views of open rolling hills are mesmerizing from nearly every room. Night skies are black velvet, so lush it almost makes you swoon. The most luxurious and private rooms are the elegantly understated Mount Robinson rooms, featuring fireplaces, king-size beds, whirlpool tubs, thoughtfully appointed sitting rooms, and private patios and decks with spectacular views. The Patterson Lake cabins are a mile or so down the road, surrounded by cottonwood trees and rebuilt within the last several years; these are popular with families during holidays but wonderfully private for couples at other times. Centered in the midst of a 44-mile cross-country ski trail system, Sun Mountain Lodge offers an exhaustive list of activities or simple, restorative serenity. A massage is a special treat at the Double Decadent Spa, and the lodge's restaurant offers a full wall of windows overlooking the valley (see Romantic Restaurants). Do reserve early for summer or ski-season stays and look for off-season packages. *$$$–$$$$; AE, DC, MC, V; checks OK; www. sunmountainlodge.com.* &

Romantic Restaurants

Arrowleaf Bistro / ◐◐

253 Riverside Ave, Winthrop; 509/996-3919
Opened in 2007 by new owners Jon Brown and Joanne Uehara, this small, charming establishment located on the main street in Winthrop is housed in a white bungalow with a welcoming front porch, period detail, and inviting corner nooks. The cozy interior invites whispered intimacies; it's just private enough to forget there is anyone else in the room. The menu is inspired by the local countryside, using seasonal organic ingredients and often paired with local wines from Lost River Winery. Both visitors and locals have enthusiastically embraced the interesting dishes and welcoming atmosphere. *$$; AE, MC, V; local checks only; lunch July–Aug, dinner every day (open Thurs–Tues summer, Fri–Tues winter); beer and wine; reservations recommended.*

Freestone Inn / ◐◐◐

31 Early Winters Drive, Mazama; 509/996-3906 or 800/639-3809
Separated from the Freestone Inn (see Romantic Lodgings) by a magnificent floor-to-ceiling river-rock fireplace, the dining room offers classic romance by candlelight. Cozy tables line the windows overlooking Freestone Lake, or in cooler months are tucked in by the dramatic stone fireplace. A simple, elegant menu coupled with a simple, elegant presentation . . . undoubtedly a winning combination. Chef Brian and staff successfully and consistently create offerings that proudly support local Northwest farmers and showcase unique flavors, often paired with Washington wines. Indulge in the nightly chocolate surprise for dessert. At press time the restaurant was scheduled to be closed for renovations and expected to reopen in late summer 2008. *$$$; AE, MC, V; checks OK; breakfast, lunch, dinner every day; full bar; reservations recommended; www.freestoneinn.com.*

Sun Mountain Lodge / ◐◐◐◐

604 Patterson Lake Rd, Winthrop; 509/996-4707 or 800/572-0493
The views here are hypnotic, and couples seem to float right through the floor-to-ceiling windows in the dining room. All of the tables and booths are intimate, so it's easy to feel suspended over the vistas within your own private world. Executive chef Patrick Miller consistently offers superb Northwest seasonal cuisine featuring fresh local ingredients, herbs and vegetables grown on the Sun Mountain farm, and Washington State organic Angus beef. The service is professional, gracious, and considerate. The lodge's wonderful wine cellar houses a 6,000-bottle collection; though primarily Northwest labels, there's a fine selection of European and South American wines. The cellar makes for a dramatic setting for small private parties, and you can bet those stone walls have witnessed more than a few marriage proposals. *$$$$; AE, DC, MC, V; checks OK; breakfast, lunch, dinner every day; full bar; dinner reservations recommended; www.sunmountainlodge.com.* &

Wolf Creek Bar and Grill / ❶❶❶

604 Patterson Lake Rd, Winthrop; 509/966-4707 or 800/572-0493
A casual alternative, the Wolf Creek Bar and Grill sits adjacent to the dining room at the Sun Mountain Lodge. The environment is lighter and a bit more open than the lodge's main restaurant; the same spectacular views abound, though, with the option of deck seating and outdoor grilling. Think of it as an expansive tree house for grown-ups. The fare is lighter than what's served in the dining room, but equally well prepared and presented. *$$–$$$; AE, DC, MC, V; checks OK; lunch, dinner every day; full bar; dinner reservations recommended; www.sunmountainlodge.com.* &

Lake Chelan

Romantic Highlights

The glacially carved Chelan Valley lies south of the Methow Valley; its center-piece is the pristine, crystal-clear **Lake Chelan**, which snakes its way through deep canyons, forested mountainsides, and hillsides laden with orchards and vineyards where the Cascade Mountains meet the Eastern Washington desert. At the southern end of the lake, the waterfront resort towns of **Chelan** and **Manson** offer specialty shops, boutiques, restaurants, and galleries with a small-town-Americana feel. Lovers and old-timers share an equal interest in the warm summer nights and bountiful harvest festivities. Add to this a nearly endless array of ways to play in the water: parasailing, jet skiing, swimming, fishing, boating, and water sliding to name a few. When you tire of putting sunscreen on each other's backs, don a shirt and attend one of the many music events in Chelan. The **Riverwalk Park and Pavilion** hosts a year-round program of musical concerts ranging from classical to blues, as well as numerous special events. It is a great place for picnics and a morning jog. The **Lake Chelan Chamber of Commerce and Visitor Information Center** (102 E Johnson St, Chelan; 800/424-3526; www.lakechelan.com) provides a schedule of the extensive range of programming in this destination community. For those romantics with a taste for nostalgia, the **Ruby Theatre** (135 E Woodin Ave, Chelan; 509/682-5016; www.rubytheatre.com) in Chelan, which opened in 1914 and is on the National Register of Historic Places, is one of the oldest continuously running movie theaters in the Northwest.

"Uplake" you will find the idyllic remote community of **Stehekin**, located at the northern tip of Lake Chelan. No trip to Lake Chelan is complete without a visit here, and for many couples, it has become an annual pilgrimage. There are no roads to Stehekin; most visitors come by private or chartered boats or by riding one of the daily **Lady of the Lake** passenger ferries (see Access & Information).Couples seeking privacy are more than rewarded in Stehekin; overnight stays are a must for the romantically inclined. Once the day-trippers are gone, you will be swept away by the uninterrupted peacefulness and unspoiled natural environment. There are no phones in Stehekin and your cell phone will not work here. Internet is available and the approximately 70 permanent residents rely on it.

Once at the landing, the central resources for all happenings are here: a modern lodge, waterfront bed-and-breakfast, private homes, rustic cabins, and a historic ranch provide accommodations for amorous explorers. A restaurant, bakery, and gift shop contribute to the unique culture of this remote village. Newly renovated in 2007, **Stehekin Landing Resort** (509/682-4494; www.stehekinlanding.com) is a National Park Services concession facility that is privately owned by members of the Courtney family, and it is the only facility open all year long (though the restaurant is closed in winter). A full range of recreational activities are available. The information network is quite centralized; a five-minute walk up from the boat landing will bring you to the **Courtney Log Office**, where you can make reservations for **Cascade Corrals** (www.cascadecorrals.com), which offers horseback base-camp hikes throughout the valley. The very informative and succinct Cascade Corrals Web site will also link you to **Stehekin Outfitters** for river rafting and kayaking.

The Log Office also distributes the *Stehekin Guidebook*, makes reservations for overnight stays in rustic tent cabins at the **Stehekin Valley Ranch** (800/536-0745 or 509/682-4677), also owned by the Courtney family, and is the place to get on the list for the popular dinner at the ranch if you are not a guest in one of their cabins. In Stehekin, restaurant options are two in summer and early fall and none in the winter or spring. There are limited offerings in the landing store, so plan on bringing your favorite indulgences and make reservations in a cabin with a kitchenette. The most romantic getaway and idyllic honeymoon for nature-minded couples is the **Silver Bay Inn Resort** (see Romantic Lodgings).

A trip to **Rainbow Falls** and a stop at the **Stehekin Pastry Company**, housed in a picture-perfect cabin, is an irresistible combination. This beautiful 312-foot waterfall is just up the road from the landing. Late spring is the best time to see the falls, after the winter thaw when the water flows like liquid thunder.

A good resource for accommodations is the **Lake Chelan Chamber of Commerce** Web site (www.cometothelake.com or www.lakechelanrentals.com). The newest lodging option, which opened in spring 2008, is the conversion of the old waterfront Caravel Resort into Washington State's first condo-hotel, the **GrandView** (322 W Woodin Ave, Chelan; 800/962-8723; www.grandviewonthelake.com). It's designed with a full array of amenities for the urban visitor who wants to keep connected to all the comforts of home.

Lake Chelan Valley, renowned for its apples, is quickly growing into an exciting **wine-growing region**. Thanks to nutrient-rich soil resulting from 30,000 years of glaciations, cool nights and warm summer days, clean air, and the benefits of the lake, hundreds of acres are under cultivation, producing many varieties of grapes. Wine enthusiasts can visit a dozen or so boutique wineries nestled in the rolling hills that cradle the clear waters of the lake. This young, vibrant wine scene is rapidly gaining recognition and has a well-organized association and Web site (www.lakechelanwinevalley.com).

Access & Information

Highway 20 and Highway 153 link to alternative Highway 97 south to reach Chelan and Manson. From Seattle, take Highway 2 to Wenatchee and head north on alternative Highway 97. To reach Stehekin at the northern tip of the lake, board the **Lady of the Lake** (888/401-2224; www.ladyofthelake.com), which offers year-round round-trip scenic cruises from Chelan. A more thrilling arrival is to come by **Chelan Airways** (509/682-5065 or 509/682-5555; www.chelanairways.com) and enjoy the pleasure of a bird's-eye view from a classic seaplane. They also specialize in extended scenic flights over the North Cascades Glaciers, a photographer's paradise. A few hardy souls arrive on foot over one of the hiking trails in and out of the valley. For those more active couples, the **Stehekin Valley** is in the heart of the **Cascade Mountains** and is part of the **North Cascades National Park**, providing some of the best backpacking and hiking in the country.

Romantic Lodgings

Campbell's Resort / ⬢⬢

104 W Woodin Ave, Chelan; 509/682-2561 or 800/553-8225
Centrally located in Chelan, Campbell's has been a family-vacation destination for more than 100 years—and yet the resort is surprisingly full of opportunities to get close to one another. The beach is long enough (over 1,200 feet) for you to find some solitude, and the 8 acres of landscaped grounds allow for strolling in between kayaking and swimming. The facility's recent complete renovation adds an upscale sophistication to its longtime emphasis on down-home comfort and customer service. All rooms feature lovely lake views, private balconies or patios, king-size beds, kitchenettes, and Internet service. Lodge 1's top-floor guest rooms are impressively quiet, with fireplaces, soaking tubs, original artwork, and full kitchens. Across the street at the RiverRoom Spa (509/682-2561, ext 2007), overlooking the water, you can choose from a full range of feel-good pamperings in a wonderfully relaxing setting. Stroll down the street for dinner or choose one of the resort's two dining options: the Campbell House Café features a comprehensive local and regional wine list to accompany the fresh takes on classic comfort foods; the second-floor Veranda offers outdoor pub fare with a full bar and an impressive list of single-malt offerings—a relaxing way to watch the night wind down. *$$–$$$; MC, V; checks OK; www.campbellsresort.com.* ♿

Silver Bay Resort Inn / ⬢⬢⬢

10 Silver Bay Rd, Stehekin; 800/555-7781
Steeped in serenity and with spectacular lake and mountain views, these waterfront cabins offer unequaled peace and privacy. Two lakeside cabins are tucked around the peninsula and screened by stands of trees and expansive lawns, providing the most secluded settings. Once you settle into the

Our Favorite Wineries in Chelan

Chelan's wine industry is rapidly growing, and new wineries spring up each year. Pick up a tour map at any one of the wineries to ensure you taste all that this valley has to offer. Or let someone else create your tour by hiring **Lakeside Limousine Tours** (319 Orchard View Dr, Chelan; 509/470-0333; www.chelanlimo.com). They're happy to plan a half-day excursion and can make arrangements for special occasions.

Here are our top choices worthy of a visit:

Tsillan Cellars (3875 Highway 97A, Chelan; 509/682-9463) is the romantic vision of Italophile owner Bob Jankelson. The exquisitely executed tasting room is replete with sensory opportunities in a gorgeous setting (a glass of the Bellissima Rossa is reason enough to stay the afternoon). Enjoy a pizza fresh from the wood-fired *forno* and served on the lake-view terrace overlooking the vineyards. Linger long into the evening while local musicians perform against the amphitheatre backdrop of three waterfalls. *Every day; www.tsillancellarswines.com.*

Vin du Lac Winery (105 Highway 150, Chelan; 509/682-2882 or 800/455-9463) is housed in a yellow country cottage in the midst of an orchard. The vineyards slope to the tasting room with peekaboo lake views filtering through the branches above the perennial-garden wine patio. Owners Larry Lehmbecker and Michaela Markusson have created a kind of outdoor living room—an intimate and comfy spot to slow down and watch the sun set. The small menu offers French bistro fare, perfect in its simplicity. *Every day; www.vindulac.com.*

The Winemaker's Grill at **Wapato Point Cellars** (200 Quetilquasoon Rd, Manson; 509/687-4000) emphasizes food and wine pairings in the tasting room and adjacent restaurant. The Kludt family opened one of the first wineries in Chelan; their philosophy is that the wine-tasting experience lies within the context provided by first-class food. The Winemaker's Grill is open for dinner with classic entrées, private tables, continental decor, and pleasant piano accompaniment. For a mid-day wine tasting, **Lake Chelan Winery** (3519 SR 150, Chelan; 509/687-9463; www.lake chelanwinery.com)—owned by the same family—is up the road a few miles. *Every day; www.wapatopointcellars.com.*

cabins, with their country antiques and comfy decor, the five-day minimum stay during summer seems a natural requirement. Hammocks sway and deck chairs perch upon sandy beaches in this landscape. Complimentary canoes, rowboats, and bicycles are available for you to explore the lake and countryside before you return to skinny dip under shooting stars. The cabins come with full kitchens and woodstoves, so come prepared to make your own feasts and stargaze from the wraparound cedar decks. Updated bathrooms with soaking tubs and Internet access are modern amenities that add to the simple splendor. *$$–$$$; MC, V; checks OK; closed mid-Oct–early May; www.silverbayinn.com.*

Romantic Restaurants

Capers / ✪✪✪

127 E Johnson Ave, Chelan; 509/682-1611
Comfortable, understated continental decor is the backdrop for an extensive classic menu with innovative flair. Rich sauces, delicate herbs, and delightful spices hint at chef Hendrika Isensee's European heritage. Everything from eclectic game to more classic entrées is flawlessly paired with an award-winning wine portfolio. The winemakers dinners are reason enough to plan an off-season trip to Chelan for a menu coupled exclusively with local wines. *$$–$$$; MC, V; checks OK; dinner Wed–Sun; wine only; reservations recommended; www.capersfinedining.com.*

CRS Winery and Bistro / ✪✪

137 E Woodin Ave, Chelan; 509/682-3704
Located on the main street of Chelan, this tasting room and bistro invites you into an attentive wine tasting (the Viognier is a crisp, clean midafternoon treat) accompanied by a savory Mediterranean menu and seasonal entertainment. The bistro has an intimate ambience with few tables and walls adorned with vintage photos. The side dishes are particularly inventive and savory, and the chocolate desserts (like the six-layer semisweet chocolate decadence cake) defy adjectives. Listen to the lake settle into the evening as you take an after-dinner stroll back to your room, and you'll be lulled into a return visit. *$$–$$$; MC, V; checks OK; dinner Wed–Sat 5:30pm–9pm (tasting room opens at noon); wine only; reservations recommended; www.crsandidgewines.com.*

♡ Central
Cascades

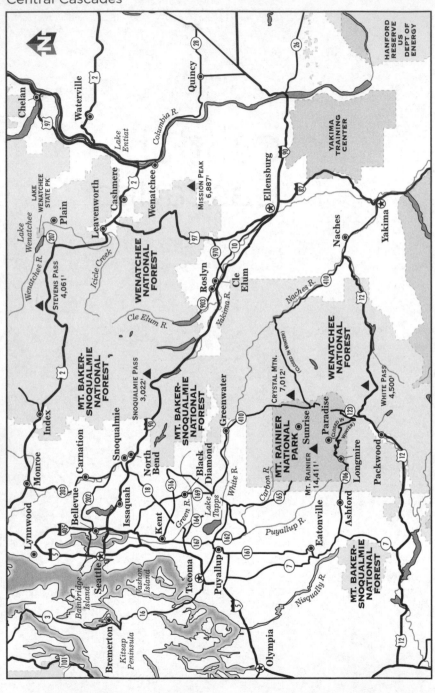

For it was not into my ear you whispered but into
my heart. It was not my lips you kissed, but my soul.
—Judy Garland

Central Cascades

The Central Cascades offer the ultimate in dramatic visages and varied outdoor diversions. With so many ways to explore the natural beauty of the area, it's hard to recommend just one. For the adventurous, possible daytime activities include hiking, whitewater rafting, horseback riding, golfing, bird-watching, cross-country skiing, and snowshoeing. Though a visit to this region can be enjoyed in just a few days, you may decide on a longer stay: the brand of accommodation and cuisine is generally simpler and more rustic in this region, but there are plenty of exceptions worthy of high lip ratings.

The main thoroughfare here is Interstate 90, or US Highways 2 and 12, which pass directly through the Central Cascades and serve as the main arteries between the eastern and western portions of Washington.

Make sure to spend some time in and around the village of Leavenworth, where the charming (or corny, depending on your taste) Bavarian-themed buildings only scratch the surface of what the area has to offer. Several restaurant and lodging options rise above the theme park–like atmosphere, boasting cosmopolitan offerings and plenty of style. Leavenworth is also a great home base for trips to the pristine Alpine Lakes Wilderness Area, with its sapphire-hued lakes, and the Wenatchee National Forest, featuring more than 2,600 miles of trails winding through some of the Cascades' most breathtaking scenery.

This area also includes the defining geographical feature of the entire region—Mount Rainier. Picnicking among wildflowers on one of Rainier's meadows makes for a sublime outdoor experience. And the view from Paradise, one of the mountain's most popular summer destinations, simply must be seen to be believed. From Puget Sound, the mountain is an easy day trip, but, if you have time to spare, make an entire weekend of your visit and choose from a number of deluxe inns or cabins in nearby Ashford.

Leavenworth & Lake Wenatchee

Romantic Highlights

Even before the Bavarian Village theme was contrived as a way to save **Leavenworth** from economic troubles, its obvious resemblance to a town in the Swiss Alps must have been apparent. At a time when the sagging logging industry had threatened its vitality, the town decided to take advantage of this. This presents a conundrum for amorous couples. On one hand, the pervasive Bavarian motif gets old very quickly. On the other hand, eschewing the entire town would be to leave behind some of the most kiss-worthy luxury accommodations in the entire Northwest, and nearly infinite nearby natural beauty.

During the winter, take a break from the touristy downtown area and rent cross-country skis or snowshoes from **Leavenworth Mountain Sports** (220 Hwy 2; 509/548-7864). Then, take Highway 2 to Chumstick Parkway and head 5 miles on Eagle Creek Parkway to **Eagle Creek** (www.leavenworth.org/trails/xski/eagle creek.html), where you can set out on the gorgeous, ungroomed trails. Note: Be sure to visit the Web site above for specific instructions; if you take a wrong turn, you could wind up in a snowmobile-only area. On essentially the same terrain, **The Eagle Creek Ranch** (end of Eagle Creek Rd; 509/548-7798) hosts guided horseback trail rides from April through October.

A walk through downtown Leavenworth can be a tad stifling in summer heat with hordes of visitors, but in wintertime, you'll have a little more room to stroll hand-in-hand. The Bavarian theme is thoroughly more charming with snow on the ground, appearing like a gingerbread village come to life. Stop by **A Book for All Seasons** (703 Hwy 2; 509/548-1451) to browse, or visit the **Fudge Hut** (933 Front St; 509/548-0466) to pick up some sweets for later, or **Leavenworth Chocolates** (222 8th St; 509/548-4300), where you can espy the chocolatiers crafting their goods. Complete your round of purchases fittingly at **Bavarian Soap & Candle Company** (217 8th St; 509/548-9000), to pick up some romantic accessories.

Nearby Lake Wenatchee is much more of a family destination, particularly in summertime, but still boasts kissable views and plenty of rustic fun.

Access & Information

Highway 2 heads east-west across Washington from Interstate 5 at Everett to Spokane. The highway winds its way up to Stevens Pass along the Skykomish River. Stevens Pass itself (exit 194 off Hwy 2; 206/812-4510; www.stevenspass.com) is a popular destination with Seattle-area skiers, offering downhill and cross-country (the Nordic center is located 5 miles east of the summit). Day lodges at the summit house have half a dozen casual eateries. From the pass, Highway 2 descends to the turnoff for Lake Wenatchee (at Cole's Corner, about mile marker 85, turn onto Hwy 207) and leads directly to Leavenworth.

Highway 2 is part of one of the Northwest's most beautiful drives, the 400-mile Cascade Loop. This route takes in Leavenworth and Wenatchee, and heads north to Lake Chelan, Winthrop, and the North Cascades Scenic Highway (see the North Cascades chapter). The route can be accessed from Interstate 90 at Cle Elum by taking Highway 970 to US Highway 97 north, which joins US Highway 2 just east of Leavenworth. A brochure is available from the **Cascade Loop Association** (509/662-3888; www.cascadeloop.com).

For more information on Leavenworth, along with helpful maps, check with the **Leavenworth Chamber of Commerce** (220 9th St; 509/548-5807; www.leavenworth.org). Excellent hiking information is available from the **Leavenworth Ranger Station**, just off Highway 2 (600 Sherbourne St, eastern edge of town; 509/548-6977).

Romantic Lodgings

Abendblume Pension / ✪✪✪✪

12570 Ranger Rd, Leavenworth; 509/548-4059
Styled after an Austrian chalet, the Abendblume Pension offers many layers of luxury and endless opportunities for quality time away with the one you love. Hand-carved, arched double doors open to reveal a gorgeous limestone foyer. All seven of the guest rooms at this European-style inn have their own sumptuous touches, including down comforters, tiled bathrooms, and fireplaces. Soft lounging robes are provided, and in-room massages for two can be arranged upon request. The top floor Tannenbaum Suite offers both a gas and wood fireplace, a two-person jetted tub, and a king bed. But, the most romantic choices are the Dornröschen and Almrosen rooms, which also have two-person jetted tubs, along with marble showers with two shower heads and four body sprayers, balconies, and wood-burning fireplaces. Special requests, such as chocolates or champagne ahead of your arrival, are yours for the asking. *$$–$$$; AE, DIS, MC, V; checks OK; www.abendblume.com.*

All Seasons River Inn / ✪✪✪✪

8751 Icicle Rd, Leavenworth; 509/548-1425
Sitting on a bluff overlooking the Wenatchee River, this modern two-story cedar house's plain exterior belies the country-style comforts inside. When the weather permits, the deck is a great location for couples to crack open a bottle of wine, sit back, and enjoy the inn's sublimely peaceful location. With views of the river; gas fireplaces; thick, luxurious bedding; and Jacuzzi tubs standard, any of the six guest rooms will provide the ideal setting in which to recharge your batteries, and your love life. Several of the rooms have private decks or balconies as well. The sizable Evergreen Suite is the best choice for couples seeking the most romance-minded amenities, such as a king bed, gas fireplace (Oct–May), jetted tub for two, and peaceful river views. *$$$; MC, V; checks OK; www.allseasonsriverinn.com.*

Bavarian Lodge / ✿✿✿

810 Hwy 2, Leavenworth; 509/548-7878
The Bavarian theme at this establishment is actually fairly understated and tastefully executed compared to the corny faux-European touches that may seem a bit overdone at other spots in town. The guest rooms are pleasantly decorated, with pale wooden furniture and butter yellow walls, and contain every amenity you'll need for your romance to bloom. But, since the lodge is large and caters to families as well, you won't feel the sense of seclusion you might have elsewhere. If you hole up in a Turret Suite, there's nothing in the world to complain about. Snuggle up next to the fireplace, or take a dip in the large, spectacularly romantic in-room hot tub. Breakfast, too, eschews a completely Bavarian affair and includes bagels, eggs, and the chance to make your own delicious waffles. *$$–$$$$; AE, DIS, MC, V; checks OK; www. bavarianlodge.com.*

Enchanted River Inn / ✿✿✿

9700 E Leavenworth Rd, Leavenworth; 509/548-9797
Located on a bank only 30 feet from the Wenatchee River, this three-guest-room establishment is a short 15-minute walk from downtown Leavenworth but feels utterly removed from its busy streets. You'll start your day with a full (read: full!) breakfast, which includes such delights as sorbet, a freshly baked cinnamon roll, and an entrée such as a Leavenworth Breakfast Burrito or Dijon Sunrise. Each of the suites has a pillow-top king bed, a two-person jetted tub, and a stunning vantage point of the river. Our favorite is the Sojourner Suite, with its added privacy on the lower level and its wall of windows affording serene views of the enchanting local landscape. But stargazers may prefer the Starlight Suite: the king-size bed is a dreamy place to snuggle up to your sweetheart and gaze at the stars through 12-foot-wide skylights. *$$$$; AE, MC, V; checks OK; www.enchantedriverinn.com.*

Hotel Pension Anna / ✿✿❁

926 Commercial St, Leavenworth; 509/548-6273
Designed to give guests the feeling they're in the picturesque Tyrolean Alps of Austria, no detail at Hotel Pension Anna betrays that mindset. Each of the 16 guest rooms includes imported Austrian and German furniture and decor. The truly special option here is the Chapel Suite (called the Alte Kapelle), which is located adjacent to the main house in a renovated church, giving you and your loved one privacy you might lack elsewhere on the property. Standard rooms are comfortable, with stately armoires and thick pillows and comforters, but couples looking for some of the more modern amenities might be better served elsewhere. A delicious European breakfast starts each morning off right. *$$–$$$$; AE, DIS, MC, V; checks OK; www. pensionanna.com.* &

Top Five Romantic Hikes around Leavenworth and Lake Wenatchee

Waterfront Park Hike (easy, 1 hour): Winding trails along the Wenatchee River, inlets for swimming, and excellent bird-watching.

Icicle Gorge Hike (easy, 2 hours): Gentle loop, no significant climbing, gorgeous bridge over rushing waters about halfway through.

Eight-mile Lake Hike (moderate, 4 hours): Bearable uphill hike for those in average to good shape, but the view from the lake at the top is worth the effort.

Penstock Trail (easy, 2 hours): Old pipeline hike; view raging waters in the spring and early summer.

Merritt Lake Hike (moderately difficult, 4 hours): Steep trail to an alpine lake flanked by lofty mountains.

Visit www.leavenworth.org/trails/hiking/index.html for directions to these and other hikes.

Mountain Home Lodge / ✿✿✿❦

8201 Mountain Home Rd, Leavenworth; 509/548-7077 or 800/414-2378
This wonderful lodge is located a mile above Leavenworth in a breathtaking mountaintop setting. Winter visitors will be picked up in a heated snowcat from the bottom of Mountain Home Road and embark on a thrilling ascent with breathtaking views. Our favorite of the 10 handsomely appointed guest rooms is the Cascade Suite, which features a river-rock gas fireplace, a hand-crafted peeled-pine king-size bed, plush robes, and a lovely Jacuzzi tub. For the ultimate getaway, such as an anniversary celebration, rent one of two custom-built pine cabins, each boasting wondrous mountain views, plenty of privacy, a hand-carved king-size bed, a private deck, a spa tub set in river rocks, and a fireplace. And, for couples who can tear themselves away from the indoor playground each suite provides, just outside the door is a wondrous mountain haven. Winter rates include transportation to and from the lodge, all meals, and unlimited use of recreational equipment (snowshoes, sleds, and cross-country skis). Evenings are cozy, with hors d'oeuvres and wine served next to the stone fireplace. *$$–$$$$; DIS, MC, V; checks OK; www.mthome.com.*

Run of the River Inn and Refuge / ✿✿✿✿

9308 E Leavenworth Rd, Leavenworth; 509/548-7171
Rustic charm meets luxurious amenities at Run of the River. The inn is surrounded by a bird refuge, which is also home to deer, coyote, bear, and elk. If the suites weren't so well appointed, it'd be easy to say the inn catered

mainly to outdoorsy types, with so much surrounding hiking, biking, skiing, and other sporting options in the area. But, those interested in less-strenuous romantic activities could easily enjoy an entire weekend without leaving their suite. Each includes a river-rock fireplace, private deck, satellite TV, and two-person Jacuzzi. One unique, charming touch is the antique typewriters in each room, for composing romantic missives. The new, breathtaking Ravenwood Lodge is a majestic log mansion (with space for two parties) with all the romantic touches one could possibly dream up. This would be an obvious choice were it not for the high price, and the fact that none of the "regular" suites leave anything to be desired at all. *$$$–$$$$; DIS, MC, V; checks OK; www.runoftheriver.com.*

Solstice Spa and Suites / ✪✪✪

925 Commercial St, Leavenworth; 509/548-7515
Just reading through the multitude of options on the spa menu sets the course for a weekend of relaxations. Weary lovebirds can indulge in rejuvenating treatments like the Dead Sea Mineral and Hot Stone Foot Massage or a Cascade Couple's Massage Package, before retiring to one of the three well-appointed guest rooms, each with a hydrotherapy tub and a fireplace. We recommend the Snowgrass Mountain Suite, which has a king bed, as does the Augusta Mountain Suite. Breakfast in the morning is a continental affair, as the focus of this establishment is on their bliss-worthy (as well as kiss-worthy) spa treatments. *$$$–$$$$; AE, MC, V; checks OK; www.solsticespa.net.*

Romantic Restaurants

The Alley Café / ✪✪✪

214 8th St (at the Alley), Leavenworth; 509/548-6109
A nice change of pace from the German restaurants that abound in Leavenworth, this charming establishment provides two intimate dining rooms in which to hide away. Both dining areas are filled with chic details, including chandeliers and wine-colored carpets. The menu consists of Italian mainstays, such as ravioli and lasagne, but the house specialty, Chicken Jerusalem—topped with a creamy hollandaise and artichoke hearts—is a unique, decadent choice. Although we don't anticipate a dramatic overhaul, a new menu is in the works. *$$; AE, MC, V; checks OK; dinner every day; beer and wine; reservations recommended; www.thealleycafe.com.*

Dragonfly Bistro & Lounge / ✪✪✪✦

633A Front St, Leavenworth; 509/548-7600
For those who like their date nights with a little more spice—both figuratively and literally—this fusion of Japanese, Chinese, Thai, Vietnamese, and American cuisine is an exciting alternative to the many Bavarian choices in town. Innovative menu options include Kobe beef sliders, lavender duck, and

Dragonfries—french fries topped with crème fraîche and a drizzle of white truffle oil. Couples who like to get extraclose by dancing the evening away will be thrilled—on weekends, the restaurant is set up with a DJ who spins music after 10pm. Sip on sake or a blueberry-ginger Mojito and get your groove on. *$$$; AE, DIS, MC, V; no checks; dinner every day (closed Wed); full bar; reservations recommended; www.dragonflyleavenworth.com.*

Mountain Home Lodge / ❂❂❂❂

8201 Mountain Home Rd, Leavenworth; 509/548-7077 or 800/414-2378
The motto here is "1,000 feet closer to heaven," and we couldn't agree more. Make reservations in advance if you plan on trekking the 2-mile journey from downtown. (In winter, the lodge is only accessible to nonguest diners via the innkeepers' snowmobile—exciting!) Soft lighting, white tablecloths, and soothing music set the mood, as do expansive panoramas of the Cascades. Just one entrée is prepared each evening (such as apple-wood-smoked breast of duck with marionberry compote), but you'll always have a nice choice of wines. With the menu decisions made for you, you'll be free to gaze out at the spectacular view—and at each other. *$$$; DIS, MC, V; checks OK; breakfast, lunch, dinner every day; beer and wine; reservations required for nonlodge guests; www.mthome.com/dining.html.*

Visconti's Ristorante Italiano / ❂

636 Front St, Leavenworth; 509/548-1213
With an extensive menu, there's something here for everyone, so long as that "something" is Italian. With a wine list befitting an upscale wine bar, you can partake in pretty much any varietal found in Italy or Washington. Sure, there are crayons on the table—not generally what you'd hope to see on a romantic evening out (unless you're an aspiring Picasso), but ambient restaurants aren't plentiful in Leavenworth. So, request a table on the third floor and enjoy a view of the village. Halfway into an order of roasted Manila clams and a bottle of Chianti, you may well be singing "that's amore!" If you venture to nearby Wenatchee, the restaurant has a location there too (1737 N Wenatchee Ave; 509/662-5013). *$$; AE, DIS, MC, V; checks OK; lunch, dinner every day; beer and wine; reservations recommended; www.viscontis.com.*

Mount Rainier

Romantic Highlights

At 14,411 feet, Mount Rainier is the grand dame standing tall over the Pacific Northwest landscape. While there's some fine lodging outside of the park in Ashford, the appeal of a romantic voyage to Rainier comes in exploring the mountain itself, not in the accommodation options. Majestic views, glorious hikes, and time away from everything but each other all make this region a place everyone should visit at least once in a lifetime. Entertainment is centered around **Mount Rainier National Park** (360/569-2211; www.nps.gov/mora; $15 entry fee per vehicle, $5 entry fee per bicycle). During winter, check with park services about road closures before heading off to the area.

In the park, 300 miles of backcountry and self-guiding nature trails lead to ancient forests, dozens of massive glaciers, waterfalls, and alpine meadows. For those interested in less-active pursuits, rest assured: the drives are almost as spectacular as the hikes, such as the one to **Paradise** (just before Paradise, you'll find the Henry M. Jackson Memorial Visitor Center), located 19 miles inside the southwest entrance of the park.

Those aiming to summit Rainier would be best served with a different guide-book, but couples wanting to get as close as possible without any of the requisite climbing gear can visit **Sunrise**, open only in the summer. At 6,400 feet, it's the closest you can get to Rainier's apex without being a mountain climber.

In wintertime, the surrounding area is a wonderland for ski-bum pairs looking to work some slope time into their amorous vacation. One of the best ski areas in the entire state can be found at **Crystal Mountain Ski Resort** (off Hwy 410 just west of Chinook Pass, on northeast edge of Mount Rainier National Park; 360/663-2265; www.skicrystal.com). Located southeast of Enumclaw, Crystal features runs for beginners and experts, plus fine backcountry skiing.

Access & Information

Most people travel to Mount Rainier National Park by car. From Interstate 5 near Tacoma, Highways 7 and 706 connect the main Nisqually entrance, which is open year-round, to Paradise. Highway 706 goes right into the park. From Enumclaw to the north or Yakima to the east, you can take Highway 410 into the park; from both the southeast and southwest, Highway 12 inter-sects with Highway 123 to take you into the park.

Inside the park, Chinook and Cayuse passes are closed in winter; you can take the loop trip or the road to Sunrise in late May through October. The road from Longmire to Paradise remains open during daylight hours in win-ter; carry tire chains and a shovel, and check current road and weather condi-tions by calling the 24-hour information service (360/569-2211; www.wsdot. wa.gov/traffic/passes). Of the five entrance stations (fee is $15 per automobile or $5 per person on foot, bicycle, or motorcycle), the three most popular are described here; the northwest entrances (Carbon River and Mowich Lake) offer few visitor facilities and have unpaved roads.

For more information, contact **Mount Rainier National Park** (360/569-2211; www.nps.gov/mora). You can also request a map and brochure with points of interest from the **Mount Rainier Visitor Association** (Star Route–Tahoma Woods, Ashford; 360/569-0910 or 877/617-9950; www.mt-rainier.com).

Romantic Lodgings

Alexander's Country Inn / ◐◖

37515 SR 706 E, Ashford; 360/569-2300
This quaint Victorian inn, built in 1912, is only a mile from the Nisqually entrance to Mount Rainier National Park. Guests at Alexander's will enjoy a full country breakfast, and box lunches are provided on request, helping to fuel energetic couples eager to explore the mountain. The unique stained-glass windows in the 12 guest rooms provide character, but the dim lighting unfortunately also gives the rooms somewhat of a gloomy feel. And since many of the rooms suffer from thin walls, be sure to book one of the two suites in the tower, or one of the separate guest houses, which all feel much more private than the others. Despite these drawbacks, adventurous couples interested in spending more of their time checking out the area's many natural wonders than being cooped up in a room will relish the inn's proximity to the national park. *$$–$$$; MC, V; no checks; www.alexanderscountryinn.com.*

Almost Paradise Lodging / ●●●◖

201 Osborn Rd, Ashford; 360/569-2540
For couples who believe privacy equals paradise, these well-equipped cabins provide everything one could hope for in a secluded and rustic romantic retreat. Each cabin features a gas fireplace, barbecue, queen bed, breakfast basket delivered in the morning, and private outdoor Jacuzzi, where lovebirds can get cozy in a quiet, wooded setting. With its unique open layout, our favorite of the three locations on the main property is the Paradise Guest House. But, for unsurpassed isolation, check into the charming Woodland Cabin, about five minutes away. You won't receive the breakfast basket at this outpost, but there is a full kitchen and gas barbecue, so bring along all the groceries and create your own magical feast. *$$–$$$; DIS, MC, V; checks OK; www.almostparadiselodging.com.*

Deep Forest Cabins at Mount Rainier / ●●●

33823 SR 706E, Ashford; 360/569-2054
The main property has been in the owners' family for decades, and it shows in the care given to equipping the three main cabins and the two newer cabins nearby. All five will offer a tranquil home base as you head out for adventure on or around Mount Rainier. In the evenings, culinary couples will enjoy preparing dinners in the full kitchen or on the gas barbecue, which is probably a more appealing—and more romantic—dinner option than what is available in the immediate area's restaurants. All five cabins have private outdoor hot tubs for late-night soaking under the stars, and four cabins have fireplaces. While the amenities are fantastic at all five cabins, we recommend the authentic Mountain Home Log Cabin, built more than 50 years ago. *$$$; MC, V; checks OK; www.deepforestcabins.com.*

Three Days of Romance in the Central Cascades

Day One: In the warmer months, start out in **Leavenworth** with a smoked-salmon scramble for breakfast at **The Renaissance Café** (217 8th St; 509/548-6725). Then, for a day of wine tasting, hire a car and driver from either **Leavenworth Enchanted Tours** (877/868-7720) or **Leavenworth Winery Tours** (509/548-7433). While your driver is sure to have some recommendations, we suggest starting in Peshastin at the **Icicle Ridge Winery** (8977 North Rd; 509/548-7019), where you might be lucky enough to sample Asian Pear Wine before moving on to **Wedge Mountain Winery** (9534 Saunders Rd, Peshastin; 509-548/7068), which specializes in Bordeaux-style blends. Continue to **La Toscana Winery** in Cashmere (9020 Foster Rd; 509/548-5448) to taste its goods before snuggling into the car for the short ride back to Leavenworth. Grab some take-out food at **Village Mercantile** (920 Hwy 2; 509/548-7714), which is much more than a gas station (really!), or at **Willis Sausage Haus und Euro Markt** (Alpenhoff Mall, 217 9th St; 509/548-0681) in town. If you're so inclined, take the leisurely hike at **Waterfront Park** (from intersection of 8th St and Commercial St, follow Commercial St down a steep hill, trail is on your right), where birders often head to observe the abundant wildlife. Enjoy Leavenworth's best German dinner at **Café Mozart** (829 Front St; 509/548-0600) before heading back for

Jasmer's at Mount Rainier / ❸❸❸

30005 SR 706E, Ashford; 360/569-2682
Jasmer's consists of one main property with 3 somewhat standard yet cozy and affordable guest suites, and another 12 private cabins scattered throughout Ashford. Most are within a 5-mile drive of the park entrance, providing an unbeatable setting for couples seeking a woodsy, romantic getaway. Almost every individual cabin has its own private outdoor hot tub and barbecue, and all but one have full kitchens. The best of the best is Creekside, a two-bedroom cottage with a king bed, massive deck, and covered hot tub that overlooks a burbling rivulet. Cabins are individually decorated, so some are more up-to-date and charming than others. All have TVs and DVD players, but reception is not easy to come by in the area, so don't forget to bring along your favorite flicks. *$$$; MC, V; no checks; www.jasmers.com.*

a luxurious stay at **Run of the River Inn and Refuge**.

Day Two: Spend the day strolling in and out of Leavenworth's charming shops. Make sure to visit **A Matter of Taste** (647 Front St; 509/548-6949) for gourmet specialty foods, **Schocolat** (843 Front St, Ste D; 509/548-7274), for Belgian truffles, and the **Bavarian Soap & Candle Factory** (217 8th St; 509/548-9000). Grab a crepe at **Pavz Crepery** (833 Front St; 509/548-2103) for lunch, and, if you didn't quite get your fill yesterday, sample some more wines at **Bavarian Cellars** (208 9th St; 509/548-7717). Or, if you and your sweetheart prefer, head to **Solstice Spa & Suites** for an afternoon of rejuvenating treatments. For an evening meal, check out Leavenworth's most cosmopolitan location, **Dragonfly Bistro & Lounge**, for dinner and late-night grooving in a hip atmosphere. Return to Run of the River for the evening and enjoy a soak in the deluxe river-rock Jacuzzi before falling asleep.

Day Three: Enjoy breakfast before heading out on the long, but extremely pretty, drive to **Mount Rainier National Park**. Check the Web site for the best route based on the time of year and current road conditions (www.nps.gov/mora) and get an early start as the drive is longer than three hours. Once you arrive, visit **Paradise** or **Longmire** and marvel at one of the most gorgeous natural vistas you've likely ever seen. Leave the park and head for dinner at the **Highlander Steakhouse** (30319 SR 706E, Ashford; 360/569-2953), and then turn in for the evening at **Almost Paradise Lodging** (see Romantic Lodgings).

Mountain Meadows Inn Bed and Breakfast / ✪✪❢

28912 SR 706E, Ashford; 360/569-2788
Located on 11 beautifully landscaped acres, the Mountain Meadows Inn is a traditional bed-and-breakfast designed as a place for harried couples to get away from it all. Enjoy strolling the property's half-mile nature trail and laze away wearied muscles with a soak in the cedar-grove hot tub at the end of the day. The inn is split between the main house and the guest house, each with three guest quarters. We suggest the main house, and, more specifically, the uniquely decorated Chief Seattle Room, dotted with Native American touches, a king bed, and a two-person shower. The breakfast here is out of this world and might include smoked Alaskan king salmon and herbed cream-cheese omelets, or Belgian waffles topped with fresh local berries in season. *$$–$$$; MC, V; checks OK; www.mountainmeadowsinn.com.*

National Park Inn at Longmire / ◐⬧

Mount Rainier National Park; 360/569-2275
One of the two lodging establishments within Mount Rainier National Park, the National Park Inn lacks the outstanding views of its counterpart (Paradise Inn, 360/569-2275), but is easier to recommend as it has far nicer accommodations. That being said, this 25-room establishment serves as a fairly standard bed-and-breakfast in winter, when it offers a complimentary breakfast, and as a standard hotel during the summer. Certain details up the kissability factor considerably, like an oversize stone fireplace in the lounge, log furniture in the guest rooms, and a terrific woodsy setting at 2,700 feet—which may be reason enough to choose this inn for your getaway. *$$–$$$; AE, DC, DIS, MC, V; no checks; www.guestservices.com/rainier.*

Stormking Spa at Mt. Rainier / ⬧⬧⬧

37311 SR 706E, Ashford; 360/569-2964
This trio of cabins about a mile from the entrance to Mount Rainier National Park is a luxurious option, especially compared with the bare-bones, rustic alternatives nearby. Each cabin includes a private outdoor hot tub—which is precisely what most visitors crave after an exciting day hiking or climbing the mountain. We recommend the distinctive 16-sided Raven and Wolf cabins (shaped like yurts); each has a mystical central skylight that bathes the interior with a warm glow. Take note: The Raven is slightly farther from the noise of the road. A continental breakfast featuring items like muffins and croissants is placed in your refrigerator, to be enjoyed at your leisure. The spa offers all of the standard treatments you'd expect, along with a few unique ones, such as the Moroccan-silk clay wrap. Overall, this is a wonderfully romantic option for couples who want to do Rainier without having to sacrifice their favorite creature comforts. *$$$; MC, V; no checks; www.stormkingspa.com.*

Romantic Restaurants

Alexander's Restaurant / ◐◐

37515 SR 706E (Alexander's Country Inn), Ashford; 360/569-2300
While no one comes to Mount Rainier for fine dining, Alexander's has been satiating climbers, hikers, and other vacationers for more than 30 years. Stained-glass windows and a large wood-burning fireplace create a quaint, inviting atmosphere, making Alexander's one of the best options near Mount Rainier. Nothing on the menu aims to reinvent the wheel, but seafood dishes, such as the steelhead trout (plucked from the restaurant's pond), are done well here. For less expensive options, try something off the à la carte menu, like the halibut burger or fettuccine primavera. And make sure to sample the spectacular blackberry pie, preferably à la mode. *$$$; MC, V; no checks; lunch, dinner Fri–Sun (Nov–May), breakfast, lunch, dinner every day (June–Oct); beer and wine; reservations recommended; www.alexanderscountryinn.com.*

♡ Washington Wine Country

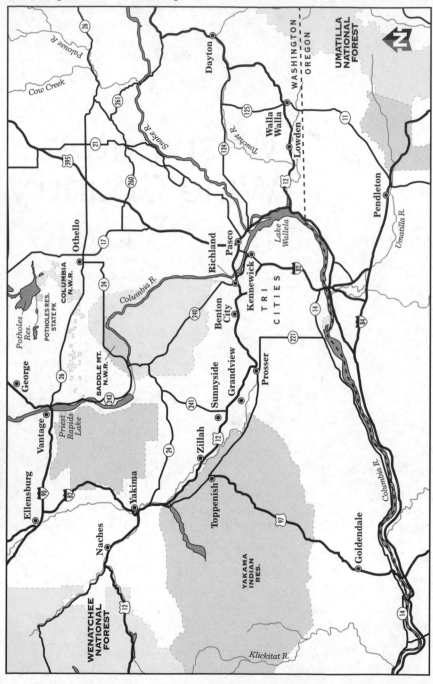

*A kiss can be a comma, a question mark, or an
exclamation point. That's basic spelling that every
woman ought to know.*

—Mistinguett

Washington
Wine Country

Wine, through the ages, has been a symbol of celebration—whether it's the clink of a glass for a day well done or a celebratory occasion, maybe a first date or an engagement. Nothing says *romantic* like a glass of wine, and, therefore, Washington offers a lot of romance.

More than 500 wineries speckle the hillsides and mountains of Washington's wine country, many of which are world-class producers with tasting rooms open year-round. With the global wine phenomena, Eastern Washington has become a bit of a mecca with its winemaker celebs; and Washington ranks second to California as the largest wine-producing state in the nation.

The state's vineyards enjoy hot, arid growing days and cool desert nights perfect for growing wine grapes. Washington wines offer something for every taste, from Merlot, Cabernet Sauvignon, and Syrah to Chardonnay, Riesling, Sauvignon Blanc, and many others. The state is particularly known for its esteemed Bordeaux blends.

A weekend is too little time to visit—even briefly—all the wineries in the region, much less to relax and spend quality one-on-one time. Yakima—about 145 miles from Seattle—is the preeminent city of central Washington as well as the seat of county government. It offers some pleasant hideaways despite its pronounced urban sprawl. The Tri-Cities—Richland, Pasco, and Kennewick—is a 3½-hour drive from Seattle. Both offer new options in lodgings and restaurants, and renowned wineries within reach. The riches of Walla Walla, with its charming historic downtown, tree-lined streets, and surprising number of excellent restaurants and inns, make it worth the drive. Walla Walla offers a unique wine adventure—the charm of a small town coupled with the sophistication of an interesting city.

It's possible to experience both places in one trip, if you've got a little extra time and don't mind doing a lot of driving. During the scorching summers, the temperature often soars upward of 100 degrees F, and since most people explore this region by car, air-conditioning is a must. For the ideal romantic getaway, we recommend visiting in spring or fall, though watch calendars for special-event weekends that bring hordes of tourists to participating wineries. Normally, area winemakers are happy to have visitors and enjoy discussing their wines, but during these busy times the overall experience can be compromised. For the quietest and most idyllic retreat, plan in advance to avoid the crowds.

Yakima Valley, Red Mountain & Walla Walla

Romantic Highlights

Yakima Valley winegrowers like to point out that their vineyards share the same latitude as the renowned wine regions of France. The city of Yakima, however, could never be confused with anywhere in the French countryside. But as they say in wine country, "Kiss French, drink local!" Once you get beyond the strip malls and freeway exits, you'll find some wonderful wineries in pretty settings. The stretch of countryside from Selah to Benton City reveals mile after scenic mile of lush orchards, cultivated fields, green-aisled hop yards, and vineyards set off by rolling hills and a network of rivers and canals. **Sagelands Vineyard** (71 Gangle Rd, Wapato; 509/877-2112; www.sagelandswinery.com; 10am–5pm every day), though large, has pockets for romance and is visible from the highway; **Silver Lake at Roza Hills** (1500 Vintage Rd, Zillah; 509/829-6235; www.silverlakewinery.com; every day), **Hyatt Vineyards** (2020 Gilbert Rd, Zillah; 509/829-6333; 11am–5pm every day in summer, 11am–4:30pm in winter; www.hyattvineyards.com), and **Sheridan Vineyards** (2980 Gilbert Rd, Zillah; 509/829-3205; www.sheridan vineyards.com; Fri–Sun) offer grassy grounds for a picnic and a smooch.

Continuing east to the Tri-Cities, find **Chandler's Reach** and **Desert Wind** among others, peppering the highway's edge. **Red Mountain** is close by and home to such award-winning wineries as **Hedges Family Estate** (see Romantic Wineries), **Fidelitas, Canon Del Sol, Col Solare**, and **Terra Blanca.**

Farther east, Walla Walla—the gem of wine country—is filled with lush parks, shady boulevards, chic restaurants, and wine bars. Spring, when clouds of blossoms give the valley an ethereal beauty, is an especially lovely time to visit wineries; summer brings soaring temperatures and dry winds, and autumn ushers in the wine crush and cooler weather. Plan your trip right, and you'll return home with a few bottles (or cases) of wine and countless happy memories of your wine-country getaway.

Numerous Web sites make great trip-planning resources. Contact the **Washington Wine Commission** (206/667-9463; www.washingtonwine.org) to get their wine-country brochure. As well, each area has a visitors center and a wine alliance, which are incredibly helpful. Contact them ahead of time to request maps and guides to the respective areas. Some of the larger producers have vast tasting rooms and even vaster parking lots—but beyond this you'll find impressive grounds full of wonderful picnic spots. Other wineries are tiny, charming, and nestled along quiet back roads lined with vineyards. The idea here is that you can tailor your wine tour to suit your desires: your days can be as busy, or as leisurely, as you please. No matter where you journey, a wine-country picnic is a must, and many local accommodations (see Romantic Lodgings) specialize in supplying provisions. A word to the wise: If you are planning a long day of wine tasting, choose a designated driver or book with a wine-tour company that provides transportation. For the most romantic option, plan a luxurious day of exploring by limo. Try **Four Star Limousines** (509/521-7849; www.fourstarlimos. com) out of Kennewick, or in Yakima, **Moonlit Ride Limousine** (509/575-6846; www.moonlitride.com).

When you're ready to take a break from the wineries, explore the quaint cobblestone streets of Yakima's **Front Street Historical District**, which invites a hand-in-hand stroll and window-shopping. If you stay into the evening, step into **Café Melange** (see Romantic Restaurants) for an Italian dinner. Or, try the **Barrel House** (22 N 1st St; 509/453-3769), a cozy, inviting pub housed in a beautifully restored turn-of-the-20th-century building.

Traveling east takes you into true farm country, including the small towns of Prosser, Sunnyside, and Grandview. If it's lunchtime, consider the **Dykstra House Restaurant** (114 Birch Ave, Grandview; 509/882-2082). In this 1914 home, decorated with lace curtains and tchotchkes, you can enjoy wholesome sandwiches, homemade soups, and great desserts. In Prosser, the **Vintner's Inn** at the venerable **Hinzerling Winery** (1520 Sheridan Ave; 509/786-2163 or 800/727-6702; www. hinzerling.com) is housed in a 1907 Victorian-style house and offers quaint rooms with private baths upstairs. Twenty-six miles south of Prosser toward the mighty Columbia River awaits the largest winery in the state, **Columbia Crest** (Hwy 221, Columbia Crest Dr, Patterson; 509/875-2061 or 888/309-9463; www.columbiacrest.com; 10am–4:30pm every day).

A bit farther east of Prosser around Benton City (which is decidedly pastoral, not urban) is the Red Mountain appellation, established in 2001. This is one of Washington's hottest wine regions, so be sure to stop at the wineries here, particularly **Terra Blanca** and **Hedges Family Estate** (see Romantic Wineries).

Though slim on lodging options (for lovers on a budget, the **Quality Inn** is perfectly reasonable and offers continental breakfast; 7901 Quinault Ave, Kennewick; 509/735-6100), there are several enticing Tri-Cities dining stops, including **Monterosso** (1026 Lee Blvd, Richland; 509/946-4525), which is housed in a cozy 1947 vintage train dining car. The restaurant was named for a favorite city in Northern Italy and translates to mean "red mountain." **Tagaris Winery and Taverna, Bookwalter Winery,** and **Desert Wind Winery** each have tasting rooms and dining (see Romantic Restaurants) offering wonderful wines and cuisine. Or enjoy views of the Columbia River and fresh Northwest seafood at the new **Anthony's** in Richland (see Romantic Restaurants).

About 130 miles east of Yakima, Walla Walla is a wonderful example of just how romantic a small town in the wine country can be. Beautiful, original

Wine Country Adventure: Walla Walla to Waitsburg

Head east toward the sun on Highway 12 for about 30 miles until you reach Waitsburg. "It takes a lot of beer to make good wine," as the wine-makers say. Whip into the **Laht Neppur Brewing Company** (444 Preston Ave, Waitsburg; 509/337-6261; www.lahtneppur.com; every day) for some beer tasting. Chiefton brewer Court Ruppenthal makes premium hand-crafted beer—on the premises. Peanuts-on-the-floor-casual, sit in or out, drink a beer, have a snack—then it's back in the car for another 6 miles east to the **Monteillet Fromagerie** (109 W Ward Rd, Dayton; 509/382-1917).

Keep your eyes peeled—no road kissing on this quest, because a simple blink could cause you to miss the little iron goat sign—and then all could be lost.

But once you find this treasure, you will be happy you did. The tasting room is patterned after a villa in Provence with rich stone and dried flow-ers. Hospitable hosts Pierre-Louis and Joan Monteillet pair local wines with their handmade artisan cheeses made from goat's and sheep's milk. Speaking of goats and sheep, get up close and personal with these fine farm friends who roam happily. Then get up close and personal with the one you love as you roam the beautiful grounds. The fromagerie is open

architecture lines the restored little downtown, where you can find wine-tasting rooms, charming restaurants, small shops, and galleries. The community is strong on the arts, and the **Walla Walla Symphony** (509/529-8020; www.wwsymphony. com) happens to be the oldest symphony orchestra west of the Mississippi. Perfor-mances are held in Cordiner Hall (345 Boyer Ave), on the grounds of the private Whitman College (509/527-5176), which anchors the town. The lovely campus is an idyllic spot for romantic strolls on warm summer evenings, when few students are about. Pioneer Park is another lovely stop with its very kissable rose gardens and gazebo.

The history of this valley, a stopping point for the Lewis and Clark Expedition in 1805, might intrigue you. An excellent interpretive center at the **Whitman Mis-sion National Historic Site** (7 miles west of Walla Walla along Hwy 12; 509/529-2761) sketches the dramatic story of the original mission, which was settled by Marcus Whitman.

It's easy to fill an entire weekend just tasting the vintages produced in this award-winning wine region. Resembling the "Starbucks effect," downtown is infused with tasting rooms at every turn: the **Waterbrook** (31 E Main St; 509/522-1262), **Dama Wines** (45 E Main St; 509/525-2299; www.damawines.com), **Sleight of Hand** (16 N 2nd Ave; 509/525-3661), and **Spring Valley Vineyards** (7 S 4th for tours on Saturdays and Sundays from 1 to 6pm and weekdays by appointment.

Head west, now, toward Waitsburg, for some delectable southern comfort at the **WhoopemUp Hollow Café** (120 Main St; 509/337-9000; www. whoopemuphollowcafe.com; reservations recommended). This is the place where you seriously want to consider the adage "Life is short, eat dessert first." With a world-renowned pastry chef, not only are the desserts beautiful, they are also an experience to eat. We recommend the Beyond Banana Split that's some kind of combination of chocolate and banana and bread pudding and ice cream. It goes way, way, way beyond the banana splits we grew up with. A nap might sound appealing about now, but in fact, there's another stop to make. The **Jimgermanbar** (119 Main St; 509/337-6001; www.jimgermanbar.com) serves handcrafted libations, Etruscan snacks, *tapas*, and *pixtos*.

Head back to Walla Walla and make your drinking day complete with a nightcap in the magnificent lobby of the **Marcus Whitman Hotel** (6 W Rose St; 509/525-2200 or 866/826-9422; www.marcuswhitmanhotel. com). Elegant dark wood with towering ceilings make this last stop an eloquent place to relax and unwind, gaze into each other's eyes, and toast to indulgence.

Ave; 509/525-1506; www.springvalleyvineyard.com; Thurs–Mon). But wine isn't the only thing happening in Walla Walla. On summer weekends, stroll through the Farmers Market on Fourth Avenue and Main Street with booths offering local produce, artisan jewelry and crafts, and homemade Mexican food (which is great fuel before wine tasting). Be sure to stop by the **Monteillet Fromagerie** booth offering artisan cheeses handcrafted from goat's and sheep's milk. Another "must stop" is **Ice-Burg Drive-In** (616 W Birch St; 509/529-1793), known for serving up one of Washington's best burgers. After a day of imbibing, a burger, fries, and shake are as satisfying as a filet mignon. Is it the relish? Other dining options include **26 brix** (see Romantic Restaurants), **Creektown Café**, **Whitehouse-Crawford Restaurant**, and hot newcomer **Saffron Mediterranean Kitchen**. You can try award-winning wine at a plethora of wineries, including **Woodward Canyon Winery** (11920 W Hwy 12, Lowden; 509/525-4129; every day), **Reininger Winery** (5858 W Highway 12; 509/522-1994; www.reiningerwinery.com; every day), and **aMaurice** (178 Vineyard Ln; 509/522-5444; www.amaurice.com; Sat or by appointment).

Access & Information

Most people visiting central and southeast Washington do so by car. Even if you fly here, you'll want to have a car for exploring. Numerous highways lead through often sparsely populated country to this dry, sunny corner of the state. Water is an important in-the-car beverage for most road trips, but through wine country, it is essential. In summer, bring sun block and a light sweater (for overactive air-conditioners and cool evenings); in winter, a turtleneck and a warm, windproof jacket should keep you toasty.

Interstate 90 is the most practical route to take from the Seattle area; it connects at Ellensburg with Interstate 82, which leads through the Yakima Valley to the Tri-Cities at the confluence of the Yakima, Snake, and Columbia rivers. From there, Walla Walla is an easy trip via I-82 and Highway 12. From Portland, Interstate 84—or the two-lane Highway 14 on the Washington side—leads to Eastern Washington. If you're heading to Ellensburg or Yakima, turn north on Highway 97. If your destination is the Tri-Cities, take Interstate 82/Highway 395. Note: The Tri-Cities includes Kennewick, Richland, and Pasco, and freeway signs usually name one of those cities only instead of the region's nickname. **Horizon Air** (800/547-9308; www.horizonair.com) serves the small airports in Walla Walla and Yakima; many other airlines fly into the larger Tri-Cities Airport (3601 N 20th Ave, Pasco; 509/547-6352); most major car-rental companies also operate here.

A map highlighting Yakima wineries is available from the **Yakima Valley Winery Association** (800/258-7270; www.yakimavalleywine.com). For general information on planning a trip to Walla Walla, contact **Tourism Walla Walla** (29 E Sumac St; 877/998-4748; www.wwchamber.com); be sure to request the winery brochure from the **Walla Walla Valley Wine Alliance** (509/526-3117; www.wallawallawine.com), which offers a handy map of the area. Additionally, the **Washington Wine Commission** (206/667-9463; www.washingtonwine.org) offers a comprehensive booklet with an overview of wineries throughout the state. And a new Web site that covers the Walla Walla Valley wine industry (www.wallawallawinenews.com) is a great overall resource. You can always pick up maps and brochures at most hotels, B&Bs, restaurants, wineries, and other locations in the region.

Romantic Wineries

Basel Cellars Estate Winery / ◐◐◐◐

2901 Old Milton Hwy, Walla Walla; 509/525-2112 or 888/259-9463
Entering the gates of the grand estate looming in the distance evokes a magical moment of enchantment. As you ascend through the winding vineyards, the grandeur of the Northwestern-style log-cabin chateau becomes apparent. Eighty-seven acres of gated property offer sweeping panoramic views, and the impressive grounds are vast with lush, secret pockets to catch a kiss. The gazebo is known to be among the best places to kiss in wine country. Under the red umbrellas on the winery's patio is another pleasant place to share a glass of wine and a little footsie under the table. The estate is available for rental to wine-club members and can accommodate small to large

weddings. *10am–4pm every day; private tastings available by appointment; www.baselcellars.com.* &

Bonair Winery & Vineyards / ◐◐◖

500 S Bonair Rd, Zillah; 509/829-6027
This bright yellow French Riviera–style winery in Rattlesnake Hills recently opened a new tasting room and is said to "accommodate lovers." The most romantic spot is a bench near the koi pond. The grassy area is shaded by bamboo, which borders the canal on the other side. The grounds are a lovely place for a picnic, a glass of wine, or a marriage proposal, if you're so inclined. Wine goddess Shirley Puryear is full of fun, amorous stories and might even be coaxed into telling about the bamboo room . . . mmm-hmm. The winery can accommodate weddings up to 75 guests. During tasting hours, Bonair Bistro serves *tapas* and other delights. *10am–5pm every day (Sat–Sun only Jan–Feb); www.bonairwine.com.* &

Dunham Cellars / ◐◐◖

150 E Boeing Ave, Walla Walla; 509/529-4685
Housed in a WWII airplane hangar near the Walla Walla airport, Dunham Cellars is a simple, welcoming gathering place. The grounds are landscaped, perfect for a stroll or picnic, and there's plenty of canine love to go around with the three iconic Dunham dogs. The tasting room abuts the larger part of the newly renovated hangar. High ceilings create an open, airy feel, while comfy sitting areas carved out of the vast space make it cozy and inviting. Cuddle up with a glass of wine, a loaf of homemade bread, and salami or cheese available at the winery; or admire winemaker and artist Eric Dunham's original art. For a secret place to kiss, ask to see the doghouse. *11am–4pm every day; www.dunhamcellars.com.* &

Hedges Family Wine Estate / ◐◐◐

53511 N Sunset Rd, Benton City; 509/430-3155
A hedge of lavender on Sunset Road guides you to this French-influenced estate. Meander through row upon row of vines, until you arrive at an elegantly appointed chateau. The winery's tasting room is adorned with rich dark wood, Gothic entryways, and ornamental pillars. The relaxed grandeur of the sitting area, its stunning white baroque fireplace mantle, and the grand piano welcomes visitors to sit down and enjoy a glass or two. Or lay a blanket on the lawn in front of the fountain while you sip the latest vintage and absorb the rolling mounds of Horse Heaven Hills in the distance. There's no shortage of romantic spots—whether you're wandering through the grounds and the vineyards or exploring the organic gardens past the 5-foot-tall rooster statue, roaming and kissing is encouraged. A fee for tasting is charged then refunded with purchase. *Noon–4pm Sat–Sun or by appointment (Mar–Nov); www.hedgesfamilyestate.com.* &

Kiona Vineyards & Winery / ⬡⬡◖

44612 N Sunset Rd, Benton City; 509/588-6716
Perched above its vineyard, Kiona is a modern steel structure with frontier-style architecture. The showcase veranda presents sweeping views of Rattle Snake Mountain and Mount Adams. Enjoy a glass of wine on the terrace or an intimate moment on the leather sofa by the fireplace. The sun streams through the skylight windows while the pyramid structure in the center of the winery floor holds a window to its soul. From above you can see the barrels and know that what's happening inside them is lively and breathing and working to produce the next vintage. *Noon–5pm every day; www. kionawine.com.* &

L'Ecole No 41 / ⬡⬡⬡

41 Lowden School Rd, Lowden; 509/525-0940
Schools aren't typically a spot for romance, but when you step inside this historic schoolhouse, located on the northern edge of Walla Walla, you may change your mind. With high ceilings, built-in bookshelves, and original windows and wood floors, the beautifully designed tasting room makes an excellent place to sample the spectacular L'Ecole No 41 wines. The tasting bar is made of slate, so you can take notes with chalk as you sip the famously rich Merlot or delicate Semillon; or skip the tasting notes, and write each other love notes instead. The grassy grounds are perfect for a picnic or a snooze on the lawn after an epic day of tasting. *10am–5pm every day; www. lecole.com.* &

Terra Blanca Winery & Estate Vineyard / ⬡⬡⬡⬡

34715 N DeMoss Rd, Benton City; 509/588-6082
The secret grottos, gardens, wine caves, and sloping grounds make Terra Blanca ripe for romance. Enter a slice of Italy in our own backyard. The cobblestone path and wisteria overhangs lead to a Tuscan-style winery. Enjoy the wines inside the spacious tasting room or find an intimate moment in the courtyard or by the pond. The wine caves give a special flavor to old-world romance, and Terra Blanca was among the first wineries to build wine caves for barrel storage. Check the Web site for cave tours and concert lineups at the winery's amphitheater. *11am–6pm every day; small fee for reserve tastings; www.terrablanca.com.* &

Three Rivers Winery / ⬡⬡◖

5641 W Hwy 12, Walla Walla; 509/526-9463
Excellent wines and festive outdoor summer concerts draw couples to this expansive winery located 6 miles west of downtown Walla Walla across from Reininger Winery. Though it is a bit more gigantic than romantic, Three Rivers offers a variety of wine to choose from. You can taste everything from Merlot, Syrah, and Sangiovese to late-harvest Gewürztraminer. Or, swirl

and sip the award-winning Meritage red wine by the cozy fireplace or on the sunny deck. You can tour the vineyards, barrel rooms, and cellar facilities; browse the gift shop; or play the winery's three short holes of golf. *10am–6pm every day; www.threeriverswinery.com.* &

Va Piano Vineyards / ❂❂❂

1793 JB George Road, Walla Walla; 509/529-0900
Tuscan-influenced Va Piano sits nestled against 20 acres of vineyards. If you plan ahead, winemaker Justin is happy to place your order and pick up a Euro-style picnic from downtown grocery Salumieri Cesario (509/529-5620) for you to enjoy at the winery. Any of the Va Piano reds will go nicely with the fare. Pick a private spot on the lawn or a picnic table and enjoy a glorious day in the vineyards. *11am–5pm Fri–Sun, Tues–Thurs by appointment; www. vapianovineyards.com.* &

Romantic Lodgings

A Touch of Europe B&B / ❂❂❂

220 N 16th Ave, Yakima; 509/454-9775 or 888/438-7073
Fresh flowers and French chocolates greet guests in their rooms at this historic Victorian B&B located in the center of Yakima. A Touch of Europe offers guests a romantic reprieve from life's hustle and bustle. Adorned with family heirlooms and antiques, the Gold Room includes a private bath and offers elegant coziness with a gas fireplace, a down comforter, and plush robes. The Mahogany Room encapsulates old Europe with its rich dark wood, English wallpaper, and turn-of-the-20th-century antiques. The private bath is located next door to the room. Jim and Erika Cenci (who is a professionally trained chef) create extraordinary breakfasts served by candlelight and stunning multicourse dinners (see Romantic Restaurants). Request Erika's gourmet lunch basket to make sure your romantic wine-country picnic food lives up to the fine wines. *$$; AE, MC, V; checks OK; www.winesnw.com/toucheuropeb&b.htm.*

Bookwalter Winery / ❂❂❂

894 Tulip Ln, Richland; 509/627-5000 or 877/667-8300
Bookwalter is an intimate lounge-style sanctuary. The Tasting Room is connected by a corridor to the smaller, cozier lounge, which is adjoined to the Garden Room. This outdoor living room is full of comfy furniture and encircled by more than 100 species of roses. Walk the paths through the gardens, where you can find a little more privacy among the coves of flowers. The Tasting Room features tall cocktail tables while the connected lounge presents comfortable sofas and oversize chairs. Red velvet drapes the windows against rich Tuscan-shaded walls. The menu includes artisan cheese samplers, small plates, light fare, meats, and desserts. Tasting Room hours

Wine Country Adventure:
Yakima Wine Horseback Tour

A great way to see wine country is on horseback, and if your idea of roughing it includes gourmet breakfasts and plush robes, you've come to the right place.

Cherrywood Bed, Breakfast, and Barn (see Romantic Lodgings) sits nestled among vineyards, orchards, and farms. Guests can choose from either of the two rooms in the house, which share a bath; one of the three rustic white-canvas teepees; or one of the cozy, retro trailers. Each of the teepees and trailers has its own private porta-potty.

Arrive the night before the big ride to the greetings of gracious hosts Pepper and Terry Fewel and settle into your room. If you're lucky enough to be staying in a teepee during a full moon, request to have the top opened so you can gaze at the countless stars from under the duvet.

The next morning, awake to a hearty breakfast, perhaps pancakes, seasonal fruit, and coffee. Visiting wineries by horseback is truly unique, and beginning around 11am, Pepper and guides from Chinook Outfitters in Naches will show you the lay of the land and get you comfortable in the saddle. It's an all-day affair in all weather, so be sure to pack accordingly. Rain gear and boots are recommended, though the area gets a minimal amount of annual rainfall.

Ride through the orchards and vineyards and watch the ever-changing sunlight dance upon the colorful canvas of fields and valleys. Guides will take you to a handful of wineries, including Sheridan Vineyard, Two Mountain Vineyards, Wineglass Cellars, and various others. Pepper brings all kinds of snacks and bottled water for guests during the ride. Terry drives his truck along to collect the bottles or cases you purchase.

At the end of the day, you'll arrive back home to tables set with white linens and silver. Get cleaned up and relax for awhile, before you dive into a Dutch-oven feast of prime rib, peach cobbler, and all the fixin's in between. (They can also accommodate vegetarian requests.) After dinner Cowboy Paul serenades you around the campfire with some good ole cowboy songs and recites authentic cowboy poetry. After a long day of riding and eating and drinking and singing and drinking . . . retire to your teepee.

are 10am–6pm, then live music takes the stage 4–5 nights a week. Check the Web site for details on current lineups. *$–$$; AE, DIS, MC, V; checks OK; www.bookwalterwines.com.* &

Cherrywood Bed, Breakfast, and Barn / ◐◐◖

3271 Roza Dr, Zillah; 509/829-3500
For rustic romance, proprietors Pepper and Terry Fewel offer an alternative for adventure-seeking couples. Perched overlooking the vineyards and five wineries, three simple white-canvas teepees command a unique, rough-and-tumble presence. Each has hardwood or cement flooring, a queen bed, soft robes, and down comforters. Rustic is the key word: each has its own porta-potty with a shared outdoor sink and shower housed in a private teepee. Inside the farmhouse, down comforters and white robes are found in both the Victorian Room, adorned with family heirlooms, and the Western Room, complete with a 4-foot-high log-post bed and TV with cable. The rooms share a bath. Guests are treated to a homemade breakfast. *$$–$$$; MC, V; checks OK; www.cherrywoodbbandb.com.*

Cozy Rose Inn Bed And Breakfast / ◐◐◐◖

1220 Forsell Rd, Grandview; 800/575-8381
This cozy country retreat is nestled into a landscape of orchards, ponds, waterfalls, and vineyards. Five suites housed in separate structures with private entrances range from cozy to plush. Each has a fireplace, a large jetted tub and shower, a satellite TV, wi-fi, and fresh flowers. We recommend the two suites on the upper floor. Suite Surrender, decorated in Italian style, boasts views of the ocean of vineyards. A large Jacuzzi tub and shower big enough for four is sure to start some good, clean fun. Guests in the Villa Vista Suite enjoy French-influenced decor, a canopy bed, and a rooftop deck. Breakfast is delivered to each room. Dinner is also available upon request and is based on inn occupancy. The trail to the family vineyard calls for a romantic stroll for two. Don't overlook the llamas: they like to give kisses too. *$$–$$$; MC, V; checks OK; www.cozyroseinn.com.*

Desert Wind Winery / ◐◐◐◖

2258 Wine Country Rd, Prosser; 509/786-7727 or 866/921-7277
You can see this large, adobe-style working winery and inn perched just off the highway and you'd be remiss not to drop in. Southwestern-inspired, with a Northwest flair, Desert Wind offers four luxurious guest suites with private, spacious baths, plasma TVs, wi-fi, and gas kiva fireplaces. An on-site masseuse is happy to arrange for an in-room massage. We recommend the Sacagawea Room with its whirlpool tub for two and rain shower. Each suite has its own balcony with views of the Yakima River, Horse Heaven Hills, and gorgeous sunsets. Breakfast baskets full of fresh scones, pastries, and coffee are served to each room. Lunch and dinner are served at La Mesa (see Romantic Restaurants). *$$$$; AE, DIS, MC, V; checks OK; www.desertwind winery.com.* ⅋

Fat Duck Inn / ❂❂❂

527 Catherine St, Walla Walla; 509/526-3825 or 888/526-8718
The Fat Duck Inn, a lovely historic Craftsman set on a tree-lined street near Whitman College and close to downtown, offers four spacious, well-appointed guest suites with private baths abundant with romance. The inn's shared spaces are ripe for love, and owners Alexa Palmer and chef Charles Maddrey suspect a lot of smooching happens on the private patio where wine is served in summer from 5 to 6pm. The couple also opens the dining room for a seasonal, four-course prix-fixe dinner ($55) at 7pm. Guests should reserve in advance, and dinner is open to nonguests as well. In the morning, enjoy a continental breakfast that can be taken to the patio or back to the room. Pet friendly, the Fat Duck Inn also accommodates small weddings, events up to 25 people, and offsite catering. *$$–$$$; AE, MC, V; no checks; www. fatduckinn.com.*

The Inn at Abeja / ❂❂❂❂

2014 Mill Creek Rd, Walla Walla; 509/522-1234
This inn is among the most luxurious and romantic retreats in all of wine country. The three cottages and two suites have been taken from their practical uses—chicken house, carriage house, haylofts—and transformed into tastefully playful accommodations. Among the most romantic is the two-story Summer Kitchen Cottage, with a deck overlooking the vineyards, a sky-lit bath with a claw-foot tub, and a full kitchen and living room. For pure privacy, we recommend the Locust Suite, which boasts an impressive Northwest decor of Montana slate floors, overstuffed leather furniture, cozy gas-fired stove, and granite-tiled kitchen. The charming remodeled barn on the property, complete with fireplace and leather couches, is a common area, and hearty gourmet breakfasts are served here. This 100-year-old 22-acre farmstead, which doubles as a working winery, is plump with places to kiss. In fact, ask innkeeper Tom Olander to show you to the secret and best place to kiss in all of wine country. *$$$$; MC, V; checks OK; closed Jan–Feb; www. abeja.net.*

Inn at Blackberry Creek / ❂❂❂

1126 Pleasant St, Walla Walla; 509/522-5233 or 877/522-5233
At this pleasant inn, located amid a quiet neighborhood just down from Pioneer Park and Whitman College, the simple sounds of the trickling nearby creek provide a relaxing calm. The three rooms are flawlessly decorated and feature king-size beds, private baths, thick robes, and mini fridges stocked with complimentary bottled water and soda. Each room has wi-fi, a DVD player, and an electric fireplace. Owner Barbara Knudson is an expert baker, and mornings bring freshly made croissants, coconut-yogurt coffee cake, or apple-nut muffins; these treats, along with fresh fruit and a main breakfast dish, are served in the dining room. For a more leisurely option, order a

breakfast tray and enjoy it in bed; or, in nice weather, adjourn to the beautiful garden for a morning picnic. *$$–$$$; AE, DC, MC, V; checks OK; www. innatblackberrycreek.com.*

Walla Walla Inns & Vineyard Suite / ❂❂❂
Vineyard Suite / ❂❂❂

214 E Main St, Walla Walla; 509/301-1811 or 877/301-1181
254 Wheat Ridge Ln, Walla Walla; 509/301-1811 or 877/301-1181
Located in a downtown renovated building, these six sophisticated suites combine small-town love with luxurious, urban-style living. Most of the suites feels like a chic, spacious apartment, with a separate bedroom, a fireplace, a stocked kitchen with complimentary treats and a bottle of wine, washer and dryer, a large Jacuzzi tub, and DSL connections. High ceilings with fans and unique skylights complement the modern decor. Very quiet, very private . . . very romantic. The Vineyard Suite, located about 3 miles east of the airport, offers vast views of the vineyards and colorful Blue Mountains. Share a glass of wine on the patio or grill a perfect dinner for two. Similar to the downtown suites, this single cottage features a fireplace, stocked kitchen, swimming pool, and hot tub. Rick and Debbie Johnson are gracious hosts who respect guests' desire for solitude. *$$–$$$$; AE, MC, V; no checks; www. wallawallainns.com.*

Romantic Restaurants

A Touch of Europe B&B / ❂❂❂❂

220 N 16th Ave, Yakima; 509/454-9775 or 888/438-7073
With clear intention and local organic ingredients, Chef Erika Cenci creates an adventure in European cuisine for up to 20 guests every evening. You need not be a guest at the B&B to enjoy the multicourse gourmet dinners, however, dinner is by reservation only, and calling early definitely pays off. Dinner is served in the formal dining room on a stunningly elegant table and by candlelight. For the utmost privacy, reserve the adjacent parlor, which can be shut off from the other guests in the dining room. Guests bring their own wine to accompany dinner (no corkage fee); if you'd like to work around that very special bottle, the chef is happy to custom design your meal to go with the wine, provided you call in advance. No jeans or tennis shoes. *$$–$$$; AE, MC, V; checks OK; dinner every day; no alcohol; reservations required; www.winesnw.com/toucheuropeb&b.htm.*

Anthony's HomePort Columbia Point / ❂❂❂

550 Columbia Point Dr, Richland; 509/946-3474
Anthony's overlooks Columbia Point Marina just off the Columbia River. Watch the sun melt away as you relax on the outdoor patio. And when the desert night turns cool, snuggle closer next to the patio's fireplace or share a

blanket provided by the restaurant. Built in typical Northwest style, the dining room boasts exposed wood beams and several fireplaces. All of the tables offer marina views, but ask for a window seat or sit underneath the arches for a little more privacy. After dinner take a romantic stroll along the Columbia River in nearby Howard Amon Park. *$$–$$$; AE, MC, V; checks OK; brunch Sun, lunch Mon–Sat, dinner every day; full bar; reservations recommended; www.anthonys.com.*

Café Melange / ◗❰

7 N Front St, Yakima; 509/453-0571
This tiny cafe offers an inviting ambience in the North Front Street Historic District. The cafe has been in the same family for decades; the delicious Italian recipes all made from scratch and the classic red and white decor haven't changed much since the early days. The expanded wine list features more than 100 Washington State wines. Romantically speaking, the modest, plant-adorned interior does not really measure up to the high quality of the meals, although the small linen-draped tables are pleasantly decorated with candles and flowers. It's the superb food here that will arouse your every passion. *$; AE, MC, V; checks OK; lunch, dinner Mon–Sat; beer and wine; reservations recommended; www.cafemelangeyakima.com.*

Gasperetti's Restaurant / ◗◗

1013 N 1st St, Yakima; 509/248-0628
Consistently voted the most romantic restaurant in town by local diners, Gasperetti's is an Italian hideaway complete with linen tablecloths, fresh flowers, intimate lighting, and delicious food. Though it's located on a busy street lined with motels and tattoo parlors, don't be deterred. Inside, the two dining rooms display distinct personalities; one boasts comfortable banquettes and a lively ambience (we like this one best), while the quieter garden room features pretty frescoed walls. In both rooms, tables are set with silver and crystal, and service is friendly and professional. Local produce provides much of the inspiration; and the award-winning wine list offers a good selection from Washington, California, and Italy. *$$; AE, DIS, MC, V; checks OK; lunch Tues–Fri, dinner Tues–Sat; full bar; reservations recommended; www. gasperettisrestaurant.com.*

La Mesa at Desert Wind Winery / ◗◗◗

2258 Wine Country Rd, Prosser; 509/786-7727 or 866/921-7277
La Mesa sits opposite the Desert Wind tasting room and gift shop inside a Southwestern-ized warehouse with a Northwest flair. The demonstration kitchen offers guests an open view to the fresh and local delectables being prepared. Chef Gene Soto serves seasonal specialties and designs a menu that changes quarterly. On the lighter side, choose a cheese plate or grilled flatbread pizza, perfectly paired with Desert Wind wines. For heartier

Best Places to Get a Picnic To Go

Yakima

Essencia Artisan Bakery & Chocolaterie (4 N 3rd St; 509/575-5570; www.essenciabakery.com)

Marketplace Deli (304 E Yakima Ave; 509/457-7170)

901 Pasta (910 Summitview Ave, Ste 7A; 509/457-4949)

Pasta Express & Espresso (1304 N 1st St; 509/248-2577)

The Sack (3607 W Nob Hill Blvd; 509/469-9744; www.lunchatthesack. com)

Walla Walla

Fat Duck Inn (527 Catherine St; 509/526-3825 or 888/526-8718; www. fatduckinn.com)

Luscious by Nature (33 S Colville St; 509/522-0424; www.lusciousww. com)

Merchants Deli (21 E Main St; 509/525-0900; www.merchantsdeli.com)

Salumiere Cesario (20 N 2nd Ave; 509/529-5620; www.salumiere cesario.com)

cravings, choose from the ground-chuck burger, pork rack, or perfected sirloin. Thursday through Saturday from 5 to 6pm La Mesa offers Fives after Five: $5 small plates and wine by the glass. Desert Wind offers large event spaces and accommodates weddings. Tasting room is open 10am–5pm every day (May–Sept), 11am–5pm (Oct–Apr). *$$$–$$$$; AE, DIS, MC, V; checks OK; lunch Thurs–Sat, dinner Thurs–Sat, brunch Sun 10am–2pm; beer and wine; reservations recommended; www.desertwindwinery.com.* &

Patit Creek Restaurant / ✪✪✪✪

725 E Dayton Ave, Dayton; 509/382-2625
When it comes to romance, Patit Creek soars off the charts. If you are looking for an intimate moment in a charming little town to enjoy after a day of winery hopping, stop your search here. Just 30 minutes east of Walla Walla in the town of Dayton lies one of the most highly rated restaurants this side of the mountains. By the way, when we say intimate, we mean *small* as well as romantic: the restaurant, housed in a 1920s service station, has only 10 tables. The focus is French classic cuisine with a wine list strong on Walla Walla selections. All ingredients are incredibly fresh, and the huckleberry pie for dessert is a must. Make reservations at least two weeks in advance. *$$; MC, V; local checks only; lunch Wed–Fri, dinner Wed–Sat; beer and wine; reservations recommended.*

Saffron Mediterranean Kitchen / ○○€

125 W Alder St; Walla Walla; 509/525-2112
Here, quiet romance is replaced with raucous passion—found in the food, in the wine, and in the atmosphere. Inspired by a trip to Spain (and you know how passionate the Spanish can be), husband and wife team Island and chef Chris Ainsworth, formerly of Todd English's Fish Club in Seattle, deliver fresh, fabulous cuisine. Entrée quantities are small, but order to share so you can taste the many delights offered on the menu. The high-energy vibe is contagious and the message you leave with is: if you give love, that's what you get. *$$–$$$; MC, V; local checks only; dinner Tues–Sun; beer and wine; reservations recommended; www.saffronmediterraneankitchen.com.* &

Tagaris Winery and Taverna / ○○€

844 Tulip Ln, Richland; 509/628-0020
Greek-influenced Tagaris offers romance paired with good food and wine. The dining room and wine bar are a mix of warm colors and hard elements (metals and concrete). Dinner favorites include Goat Cheese Tortelli paired with Chardonnay, and Apple-Wood Grilled Misty Isle Beef paired with Cabernet Sauvignon. The Ooey Gooey Chocolate Bomb and the Caramel Apple Flatbread are must-haves. During summer (May–Sept), the spacious patio opens, featuring a 33-foot fountain—a wonderful reprieve from warm temperatures, not to mention a cool place to steal a kiss. The patio offers casual dining and live music. Tagaris Winery is an estate winery producing both reds and whites. *$$–$$$; AE, MC, V; no checks; lunch, dinner Mon–Sat, tasting room 11am–5pm every day; full bar; www.tagariswines.com.* &

26 brix / ○○○€

207 W Main St, Walla Walla; 509/526-4075
Known to inspire marriage proposals, including that of the restaurant's chef/owner Mike Davis, 26 brix offers classical romance in an urban-chic setting. The restored 1899 hotel-turned-restaurant exudes cool elegance with its white linens draping the tables, highly contrasted against the exposed brick walls. Chef Mike tailors selections to the season, from lunch and dinner to *tapas* in the bar to breakfast on Sundays. Request table 40, as it's known to be lucky for love. The bar heats up in the evening and attracts the "beautiful people" of this hip small town. A separate private dining room can seat up to 28 people, and Chef Mike is available to work with you on a personalized menu. *$$–$$$; AE, MC, V; local checks only; breakfast Sun, dinner Mon–Tues, Fri–Sat; full bar; reservations recommended; www.twentysixbrix.com.*

Whitehouse-Crawford Restaurant / ❂❂❂

55 W Cherry St, Walla Walla; 509/525-2222
Housed in a beautifully restored turn-of-the-20th-century planing mill, with high ceilings, blue velvet chairs, and white-linen tablecloths, Whitehouse-Crawford is akin to Portland's industrial chic. This urban warehouse has a vast dining room, which can get a little noisy, and the tables for two are rather close together. Chef Jamie Guerin, formerly of Seattle's acclaimed Campagne restaurant, creates Northwest cuisine that is simple, fresh, and unpretentious, with an emphasis on seasonal ingredients. The luscious desserts include a classic crème brûlée and an award-winning twice-baked chocolate cake—a marriage of dense cake and chocolate soufflé. *$$$$; AE, MC, V; checks OK; dinner Wed–Sun; full bar; reservations recommended; www.whitehouse crawford.com.*

♡ Vancouver & Environs

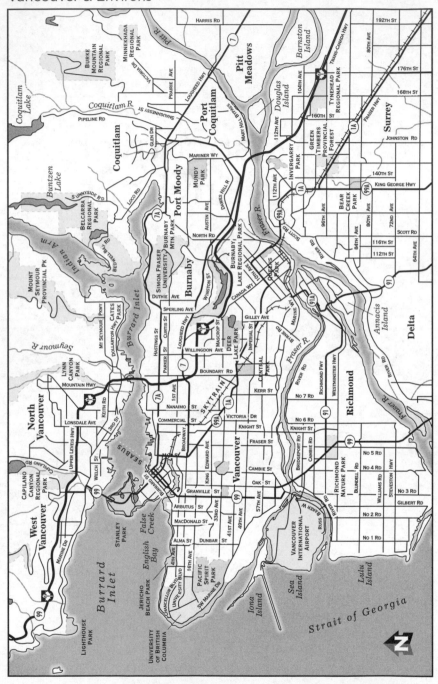

A kiss that speaks volumes is seldom a first edition.
—Clare Whiting

Vancouver & Environs

Surrounded by water on three sides with stunning mountain vistas, lush city parks, and limitless cultural offerings, the Vancouver region is considered one of the world's most livable areas. The best way to experience everything Vancouver has to offer is on foot. It's the combination of the allure of city life and the accessibility of a small town that makes Vancouver appealing for a romantic getaway.

It's an exciting time to be a Vancouverite, and likewise, to visit Canada's emerald gem. As the city prepares to cohost (with nearby Whistler) the 2010 Winter Olympics, renovation projects abound. The budget for venue construction and repair has already risen above $500 million, which equals a lot of work now, but an even more cutting-edge city when all is said and done. Adding to the city's buzz, Vancouver is the home of countless movie shoots (including *The Fantastic Four* and *X-Men* movies) and is often dubbed "Hollywood North."

Attracting residents and visitors from around the world, Vancouver offers every imaginable leisure activity. Whether it's upscale shopping, world-class dining, or exploring beautiful beaches, parks, or botanical gardens, it's hard to get bored in Vancouver. And the music scene is alive and kickin' with great live venues.

A modern-day melting pot with endless food options, Vancouver's beloved Chinatown is a terrific stop for a taste of Vancouver's renowned diversity. Vancouver's Chinatown is the second largest in North America, so there's plenty of interesting markets full of fresh ingredients and colorful tapestries. Spend an hour or a full day exploring the sights, culture, and history of this exotic retreat.

For most visitors, a trip to Vancouver would be incomplete without navigating Robson Street or sampling the culinary delights of Granville Island and the trendy West End shops. But, if you want to step into the shoes of Vancouver's hip cognoscenti, spend an evening hopping between the restaurants and bars in the revitalized Yaletown neighborhood.

Just across the Lions Gate Bridge, residential North Vancouver boasts its own appealing cultural options. And Surrey, the largest city in the area (outside of

Vancouver), is a golfer's paradise. Home to a major PGA event, there are an astounding 16 courses to choose from if your pleasure is driving side-by-side.

And, yes, Vancouver does get its share of rain, particularly from October to April. But, as Pacific Northwest residents contend, the rain will only put a damper on romance if you let it.

Vancouver

Romantic Highlights

A city of contrasts, Vancouver is a beguiling destination for those who want to experience *all* that the area has to offer. With an abundance of natural beauty, upscale shopping, and fine dining, the biggest challenge will be fitting it all in.

To see a different side of **Robson Street**, stroll the famous lane in the evening, stopping for a drink at the revolving **Cloud Nine** in the Empire Landmark Hotel (1400 Robson St; 604/662-8328) for a 360-degree view of Vancouver. Another sophisticated stop is the **Gerard Lounge** (845 Burrard St; 800/543-4300) in the Sutton Place Hotel, well known for its expansive wine list and martinis.

Couples with a mutual sweet tooth can make sure to visit another Sutton Place establishment, **Fleuri Restaurant** (845 Burrard St; 604/642-2900), for the 20-item Chocolate Buffet, served on Thursdays, Fridays, and Saturdays.

Art lovers can catch whatever is being exhibited at the **Vancouver Art Gallery** (750 Hornby St; 604/662-4719), as it often attracts work by the great masters. Another distinctive cultural attraction, **Theater Under the Stars,** is one of Vancouver's largest musical companies presenting two performances during the summer at Malkin Bowl in **Stanley Park** (2099 Bech Ave, Vancouver; 604/734-1917; www.tuts.ca). Bring a blanket and a picnic dinner from **Robson Public Market** (1610 Robson St; 604/682-2733; www.robsonpublicmarket.com).

Be sure to check out the wares at the numerous boutiques and galleries that reign in cutting-edge **Yaletown**, where hipsters and high-techies coexist in multimillion-dollar renovated warehouses. For a nightcap, try the ultrachic **Cactus Club Café** (357 Davie St; 604/685-8070).

Formerly in disrepair, the historic **Gastown** neighborhood has undergone vast redevelopment in the last few years. Make sure to have a Vancouverite steer you away from the neighborhood's seedy edges and toward the delightful **Brioche Restaurant and Bakery** (401 W Cordova St; 604/682-4037), and other highlights of a neighborhood undergoing vast redevelopment.

If you're visiting between May and September, check out the unusual sites and scents of Chinatown's **night market** (100–200 blocks of Keefer St between Gore, Main, and Columbia sts) on Friday, Saturday, and Sunday nights. Stalls and tables line the streets loaded with bargain-priced merchandise like CDs, watches, umbrellas, trinkets, toys, novelties, herbs, and food. Think "Saturday market meets flea market meets the Orient." The hustle and bustle of the market

Top Five Romantic Shopping Spots

Bare Basics Lingerie Boutique, 4431 W 10th Ave, Vancouver; 604/224-3777

Diane's Lingerie & Loungewear Ltd, 2950 Granville St, Vancouver; 604/738-5121

Scarlet, 460 Granville St, Vancouver; 604/605-1601

Thomas Haas Fine Chocolates & Patisserie, 998 Harbourside Dr, North Vancouver; 604/924-1847

Escents Aromatherapy, 2579 W Broadway, Vancouver; 604/736-7761

commences at 6:30pm and ends at 11pm. It's a perfect place to get a quick snack before heading for a sit-down dinner.

To round out a proper Vancouver visit, don't miss **Granville Island, Kitsilano,** and the **East Side**—each neighborhood offering a unique flavor of the city.

Access & Information

Vancouver International Airport (604/207-7077; www.yvr.ca) is a major international airport, with daily flights to all the continents. The modern, spacious, and well-designed airport is located 9 miles (15 km) south of downtown on Sea Island.

Two major highways connect greater Vancouver to the rest of British Columbia, other parts of Canada, and the United States. Highway 99, the main highway connecting Vancouver to Seattle and the rest of Washington State, leads south from the city across the fertile delta at the mouth of the Fraser River and connects with Interstate 5. It's about a three-hour drive between Vancouver and Seattle, crossing the international boundary at Blaine, Washington. The border crossing can add considerably to your travel time, particularly on weekends or during popular summer travel periods; your best bet is to travel at nonpeak times and to allow for possible traffic. Highway 99 also connects Vancouver to the ski resort town of Whistler, about a two-hour drive north of the city. Highway 1, the Trans-Canada Highway, winds through the Lower Mainland, up the Fraser River Valley, and east across Canada. If you drive, watch for rush-hour traffic between 7 and 9am on weekday mornings and 3:30 and 6:30pm in the evenings. For regular updates on highway conditions in the Vancouver area and across the province, call 604/299-9000, ext. 7623; information is also available online through the **British Columbia Ministry of Transportation** (www.th.gov.bc.ca; click on "Road Reports").

For more information on activities, whether climbing Grouse Mountain or shopping downtown, contact the **Vancouver Tourist Information Centre** (200 Burrard St, Plaza Level; 604/683-2000; tourismvancouver.com). Keep in mind that airfares, hotel rates, and admission fees are often lower from

Vancouver's Secret Places

Although Vancouver's main attractions like Stanley Park and Robson Street are fabulous ways to wile away the day with someone you love, the city abounds in unusual hidden gems just awaiting discovery. Here are several worthwhile destinations off Vancouver's well-beaten path:

One of the city's most beguiling attractions is the **Dr. Sun Yat-Sen Classical Chinese Gardens** (578 Carrall St; 604/662-3207), an oasis hidden in the heart of Chinatown. An authentic traditional Chinese garden, and the first of its kind outside of Asia, the garden employs a harmony among four elements: rock, water, plants, and architecture. Come here together to enjoy one of the most peaceful parts of the city.

For another unusual slice of nature, head to the **Bloedel Floral Conservatory** (Queen Elizabeth Park, between Ontario and Cambie sts; 604/257-8584). Under the large dome lives a tropical paradise with more than 500 plants from around the globe and over 100 birds who freely circle inside. Lovers of wildlife, be sure to keep your eyes peeled for a glimpse of one of the red macaws or the pink cockatoo named Charlie.

For the truly epicurious, a trip to Vancouver must include a visit to **La Casa Gelato** (1033 Venables St; 604/251-3211). Using the Italian "no

November through February, if you're undeterred by rain. In late January and early February, Tourism Vancouver promotes **Dine Out Vancouver**, with $15, $25, and $35 three-course dinners at the city's top restaurants.

Romantic Lodgings

Barclay House / ❂❂❂

1351 Barclay St, Vancouver; 604/605-1351 or 800/971-1351
In contrast to the old-fashioned, flowery decor found at many of the city's B&Bs, Barclay House truly distinguishes itself with an attractive blend of traditional and modern elements and custom furnishings by international designers. The refined yet altogether modern sitting room looks like it's straight out of the pages of a contemporary design magazine. An appealing mix of accents like a carved wood–mantled fireplace, brushed velvet side chairs, en vogue transparent polycarbonate lamps, and a winged leather sofa invite guests to lounge and relax. Each thoughtfully designed room has a different theme. (We prefer the light, airy Beach Room.) Barclay House offers chilled champagne upon arrival, freshly baked cookies, and a delicious hot breakfast, which is why it's quickly becoming one of Vancouver's most popular B&Bs. *$$–$$$; AE, MC, V; no checks; www.barclayhouse.com.*

air" method of gelato making, the mad culinary scientists at La Casa Gelato add at least 10 delightful—and often downright bizarre—gelato flavors to their repertoire each year. With more than 200 rotating flavors to choose from, highlights include pear and gorgonzola, garlic, and asparagus.

For an exotic indulgence, stop by **Miraj Hammam Spa** (1495 W 6th Ave; 604/733-5151) for a traditional Turkish steam bath and massage. A *hammam* treatment in a mist-and-steam chamber sets the mood while an esthetician exfoliates your skin with Moroccan black soap. Afterward, lay side-by-side for massages and facial treatments. This unique old-world treatment is sure to transport lovers to a state of unadulterated bliss.

And, while most visitors are so thrilled at the variety of activities Vancouver has to offer they don't venture past the city limits, lovers who choose to visit **Boundary Bay Regional Park** (about 20 miles from Vancouver; 604/224-5739) in Tsawwassen will be glad they did. Boundary Bay is internationally recognized as an important bird-watching area and is home to Centennial Beach, a local favorite. Home of the marker noting the 49th parallel, this is where you can swim back and forth across the U.S./Canada sea border.

English Bay Inn / ❷❷❹

1968 Comox St, Vancouver; 604/683-8002 or 866/683-8002
Chances are good that once you settle in, you won't want to leave this English Tudor hotel located in the heart of Vancouver's West End. What really sets this inn apart from the others is its prime location, a mere block away from Stanley Park. Appealing touches include complimentary sherry and port, sumptuous Ralph Lauren linens, and a full breakfast that typically features eggs and homemade scones. The best suite is room 5, a bilevel hideaway with a fireplace, jetted tub, and loft bedroom with skylight. *$$$–$$$$; AE, DC, DIS, MC, V; no checks; www.englishbayinn.com.*

The Fairmont Waterfront / ❷❷❷

900 Canada Place Wy, Vancouver; 604/691-1991 or 800/441-1414
Located in an enviable position overlooking Vancouver Harbour, the Fairmont Waterfront boasts many rooms with jaw-dropping views of Burrard Inlet, where floatplanes and cruise ships come and go, and mountains loom large in the distance. The grand, light-filled lobby with lavish flower arrangements hints at the opulence found throughout. All rooms feature marble bathrooms, top-of-the-line beds, and original artwork. For the ultimate in pampering, splurge on a Fairmont Gold Club room: as you enjoy the

private concierge, complimentary breakfast, and late-afternoon hors d'oeuvres, you'll quickly grow accustomed to feeling like royalty. *$$$$; AE, DC, DIS, MC, V; no checks; www.fairmont.com/waterfront.* ♿

Four Seasons Hotel Vancouver / ❂❂❂

791 W Georgia St, Vancouver; 604/689-9333 or 800/332-3442
Overlook the building's drab exterior: once you enter the hotel's expansive lobby, you'll be transported into the refined luxury and world-class service that is signature Four Seasons. After checking into one of the 376 guest rooms and snuggling into a world-famous down-dressed bed, you'll forget that you're in the heart of Vancouver with countless dining and entertainment options just steps away. To escape the big-city hustle, guests needn't travel farther than the fourth floor: an impressive sundeck surrounds Vancouver's only half-indoor, half-outdoor pool, making it a surprising and irresistible spot to laze away a warm day. *$$$$; AE, DC, DIS, MC, V; no checks; www. fourseasons.com/vancouver.* ♿

Hotel Le Soleil / ❂❂❂

567 Hornby St, Vancouver; 604/632-3000 or 877/632-3030
For lovebirds who prefer the personalized service of a boutique hotel, Hotel Le Soleil shines like a beacon amid the high-rises and cookie-cutter monoliths nearby. The high-ceilinged lobby is a study in gilded opulence, while the red and gold suites—although petite—are delightfully decorated in the hotel's signature solar theme, featuring silk-brocade accents. Le Soleil's high-end bath products and super-comfy luxurious beds are especially welcoming at the end of a long day. *$$$$; AE, DC, MC, V; no checks; www.hotellesoleil.com.* ♿

"O Canada" House / ❂❂❂

1114 Barclay St, Vancouver; 604/688-0555
This lovingly maintained 1897 Victorian home is where the national anthem, "O Canada," was written in 1909. Set in the charming West End neighborhood, the house exudes all the grace and comfort one would expect in such a refined and storied setting. Old-world details include a traditional front parlor and a wraparound porch overlooking an English-style garden. All seven guest suites are tastefully appointed; for an incomparable stay, book either the Penthouse Suite or the Cottage with fireplace and private patio. Guests can help themselves to the well-stocked complimentary pantry, open 24 hours, for late-night snacks like muffins, scones, soda, or juice. *$$$–$$$$; MC, V; no checks; www.ocanadahouse.com.*

Opus Hotel / ❂❂❂❂

322 Davie St, Vancouver; 604/642-6787 or 866/642-6787
Couples in-the-know forego the staid, traditional Vancouver luxury hotels in favor of the flamboyant, sexy Opus. Located in the heart of hip Yaletown,

the ultramodern hotel doesn't take itself too seriously. Each guest room's bold design takes inspiration from the works of local artists, displayed in every room. "Modern & Minimalist" red rooms possess strong, masculine lines; "Artful & Eclectic" green rooms showcase funky, irreverent decor. Fun-loving romantics with modern sensibilities will certainly flip for this spectacular hotel. *$$$$; AE, DC, DIS, MC, V; no checks; www.opushotel.com.* ♿

Pan Pacific Hotel / ✿✿

300-999 Canada Pl, Vancouver; 604/662-8111 or 800/937-1515 (U.S.), 800/663-1515 (Canada)

The impersonal, generic atmosphere of this Pan Pacific feels better suited for businesspeople than for couples splurging on a romantic getaway. But practical couples may still prefer this unbeatable central location, on the waterfront and close to Robson Street, to anything off the beaten path. The most expensive rooms overlook the water and offer hypnotizing vistas of Stanley Park, the Lions Gate Bridge, and the North Shore mountains. With live jazz in the atrium lobby, a heated outdoor pool, and three on-site restaurants, there's plenty to keep visitors entertained. Note, however, with countless guests at any given time, the staff often seems stretched beyond a reasonable capacity. *$$$$; AE, DC, MC, V; no checks; www.panpacific.com/vancouver/overview.html.* ♿

River Run Cottages / ✿✿✿

4551 River Rd W, Ladner; 604/946-7778

This romantic B&B nestled in a community of houseboats in historic Ladner, 30 minutes from Vancouver, feels like such a getaway that Vancouverites themselves often escape here. In the Waterlily floating cottage, guests relax on a deck overlooking the North Shore mountains and Vancouver Island while watching for bald eagles and jumping salmon. The Waterlily cottage looks like an old English sailing ship; the bed is tucked in a sleeping locker accessed by a boat ladder. (It's unique and cozy—maybe a bit cramped.) Each of the three onshore cottages enjoys a private entrance and a fireplace. If you're in the mood to go completely over the top, reserve the Romance Package, which includes a catered three-course candlelit dinner, served in the privacy of your cottage. *$$$; MC, V; checks OK; www.riverruncottages.com.*

Thistledown House / ✿✿✿½

3910 Capilano Rd, North Vancouver; 604/986-7173

Set amid a half acre of lush lawns and gardens, yet only minutes from the city center's fine dining and shopping, this white 1920s Craftsman-style home is a vision of peace and tranquility. All of the guest rooms are worthy of a special getaway, but we prefer the Under the Apple Tree suite. With a king-size bed, fireplace, private patio, and jetted-air tub for two, there's little left for

Three Days of Romance in Vancouver

Spend a long weekend in Vancouver and you'll find that a city of over 2 million people offers just as many opportunities for *amore* as more bucolic and serene settings.

Day One: Arrive in the morning and head straight to **Caffe Artigiano** (1101 W Pender St; 604/685-5333) for what may be Vancouver's best coffee. Then, rent a bicycle built for two from **Spokes Bicycle Rentals** (1798 W Georgia St; 604/688-5141) and marvel at the scenery as you pedal through Stanley Park. For a more leisurely morning, link arms and window-shop around neighboring English Bay, stopping in shops that catch your fancy. For a reliable, excellent lunch, grab a bite at the **Raincity Grill** (1193 Denman St; 604/685-7337). And save your appetite for **Mondo Gelato** (1094 Denman St; 604/647-6638), offering flavors like chocolate orange, cream puff, and Hawaiian papaya. In the afternoon, take in the action on bustling **Robson Street**, Vancouver's most famous avenue. Sip a late-afternoon drink on the terrace at Vancouver Art Gallery's **Gallery Patio Café** (750 Hornby St; 604/688-2233), then hop a cab to Yaletown. After perusing cutting-edge stores, nosh on sushi at the bar of **Blue Water Café** before retiring for the evening to the **Opus Hotel**, where you'll stay in a room specially selected to fit your mood.

Day Two: Enjoy a delicious breakfast like poached eggs or a savory crepe right inside the Opus Hotel at **Elixir** (604/642-0557). Then, take the short **Aquabus** (604/689-5858; www.theaquabus.com) ride across to **Granville Island**, where an emporium of food vendors and artisans await. Art lovers, photography buffs, and foodies should check out the attractive,

couples to desire. Breakfast is always a grand four-course affair, and afternoon tea includes European pastries, chocolates, fresh-fruit flan, and sherry. $$$–$$$$; MC, V; checks OK; *www.thistle-down.com.* &

Wedgewood Hotel / ✿✿✿❻

845 Hornby St, Vancouver; 604/689-7777
Offering old-world charm and scrupulous attention to detail, the Wedgewood is indisputably Vancouver's most esteemed hotel. From the warm and personal service to the renowned Bacchus Restaurant (see Romantic Restaurants), this is everything a small luxury hotel should be—and then some. All of the finely appointed guest rooms feature balconies, genuine antiques, and Italian-marble bathrooms with separate showers and soaking tubs. Since this is an immensely popular spot for visiting honeymooners and celebrities, it's essential to plan ahead to reserve one of the 83 rooms. If money is no object,

glossy titles available at **Blackberry Books** (1663 Duranleau St; 604/685-6188). Granville Island's **Public Market** will delight you with the bounty available. On a cold day, head straight to the **Stock Market** (1689 Johnson St, Vancouver; 604/687-2433) to share the famous red-snapper chowder. Then, take a cab to Kitsilano, one of Vancouver's most visually interesting neighborhoods. Stroll through the **Van Dusen Botanical Gardens** (5251 Oak St; 604/878-9274), or laze away an hour or two at Kitsilano's popular beach. During the summer, take in a performance of **Bard on the Beach** in Vanier Park (north foot of Chestnut St; 604/257-8400). Before heading back to the Opus Hotel, finish the evening with a meal you will not soon forget at **Lumiere**.

Day Three: On your third day, travel across the Lions Gate Bridge to North Vancouver. Authentic Dutch pancakes help start the day off right at **De Dutch Pannekoek House** (657 W 3rd St; 604/988-7658). For a knee-buckling thrill, squeeze each other's hands while you cross the swaying planks of the **Capilano Suspension Bridge** (3735 Capilano Rd; 604/985-7474), which teeters below your feet. Truly active couples may consider conquering the **Grouse Grind**, the famously rigorous climb up Grouse Mountain. At the top, sit on the patio, enjoying a drink and the view. After such active pursuits, weary couples should go straight to **North Vancouver's Spa Utopia** (160-889 Harbourside Dr; 604/980-3977) for out-of-this-world his-and-hers treatments. After the break, enjoy dinner at **The Salmon House on the Hill**, which boasts an enviable view of the city across the inlet. For a peaceful respite in North Vancouver, finish your weekend with an intimate night at **Thistledown House**.

the opulent penthouse suites are truly breathtaking. *$$$$; AE, DC, DIS, MC, V; no checks; www.wedgewoodhotel.com.* &

Romantic Restaurants

Bacchus Restaurant / ◕◕◕◕

845 Hornby St (Wedgewood Hotel), Vancouver; 604/608-5319
Consistently rated Vancouver's most romantic restaurant, the dimly lit Bacchus is furnished with leather chairs and plush velvet banquettes, with enough private niches to offer couples the intimacy they desire. The nightly cocktail hour here is one of the city's liveliest, with a pianist tapping out everything from soft rock to lounge standards. And, offerings like the tuna tartare, roasted veal tenderloin, and an expansive wine list prove that Bacchus is more than just a pretty face. *$$$$; AE, DC, MC, V; no checks;*

breakfast, lunch, dinner every day, brunch Sat–Sun; full bar; reservations recommended; www.wedgewoodhotel.com. &

Bin 941 Tapas Parlour / ❶❶❶
Bin 942 Tapas Parlour / ❶❶❶

941 Davie St, Vancouver; 604/683-1246
1521 W Broadway, Vancouver; 604/734-9421
Two of the trendiest eateries in the city, these sister spots offer unique international "tapatizers" and savvy wine lists. While you're likely to sit as close to someone at the next table as to your own date, the club music and high energy will guarantee a fun, if not intimate, experience. True mussel enthusiasts will delight in the innovative varieties available nightly. *$$; MC, V; no checks; dinner every day; beer and wine; no reservations; www.bin941.com.*

Bishop's / ❶❶❶❶

2183 W 4th Ave, Vancouver; 604/738-2025
You know things are getting serious if your date reserves a table upstairs at this highly acclaimed, intimate 40-seat restaurant located in the trendy Kitsilano district. Welsh native John Bishop uses local and organic ingredients to provide the backbone of a menu that changes weekly. Bishop says he lets the ingredients tell him what to cook: with inspired dishes such as grilled Copper River sockeye salmon, prepared with a potato-onion latke and rhubarb compote, they're obviously steering him in the right direction. *$$$$; AE, MC, V; no checks; dinner every day; full bar; reservations recommended; www.bishopsonline.com.*

Blue Water Café / ❶❶❶❶

1095 Hamilton St, Vancouver; 604/688-8078
While you wait for a table at this Yaletown brick-and-beam hot spot, order a sushi roll (among the best in town) and sip one of Blue Water's innovative signature drinks. While we recommend the Marley, a spicy concoction infused with allspice-flavored simple syrup, all of the cocktails are delightful. For dinner, request a banquette, perfect for cozying up when the mood inevitably strikes. If you're not up for heavy entrées like beef tenderloin or Kobe-style beef short ribs, the sushi options make a fantastic, lighter alternative. *$$$$; AE, MC, V; no checks; dinner every day; full bar; reservations recommended; www.bluewatercafe.net.* &

C / ❶❶❶

1600 Howe St, Vancouver; 604/681-1164
C offers exotic seafood in Zen-like surroundings with an unbeatable view across False Creek to Granville Island. You'll find cutting-edge dishes with dramatic flavors and stunning presentations. For a more complete sampling of C's exquisite cuisine, try the six-course tasting menu, which features

Stroll through Stanley Park

You could spend an entire day exploring Stanley Park, one of the largest urban parks in North America, and yet barely scratch the surface of all it offers. To fully appreciate the park's beauty and magnitude, take the time to walk, bike, or in-line skate along one of the many trails. Or, if you prefer to stay in your car, drive along the perimeter, via Stanley Park Drive. And, unless you plan to splurge on lunch at the pricey Fish House restaurant, don't forget to pack a picnic spread from **Urban Fare** (177 Davie St, Vancouver; 604/975-7550), located in Yaletown, to enjoy one of Stanley Park's hidden nooks. Take in the mountain, water, and city vistas while strolling the park's 6-mile circuit. End your day at **Third Beach**, a lovely spot for a sunset smooch. If walking the park is not an option, hire either a horse-drawn carriage from **Stanley Park Horse-Drawn Tours** (604/681-5115; www.stanleypark.com) or a chauffeured Model-A Ford from **Early Motion Tours** (604-687-5088).

seasonal bounty like Dungeness crab risotto, and macerated strawberries for dessert. In the summer, the patio is the place to spend an entire afternoon lingering over lunch with your special someone. *$$$$; AE, MC, V; no checks; lunch Mon–Fri (summer), dinner every day; full bar; reservations recommended; www.crestaurant.com.* &

CRU / ❂❂❂

1459 W Broadway, Vancouver; 604/677-4111
This modern, casually elegant restaurant is long and thin with high-backed banquettes and low, sexy lighting. In France, the term "cru" suggests a property worthy of special reference. Cru has more than proven it can live up to its name. In fact, the restaurant boasts the best duck confit in town—crackling skin outside and a hint of vinegar perfectly balances the rich meaty flavor inside. For dessert, splurge on a seasonal treat, such as the irresistible coconut-rhubarb *panna cotta. $$$; AE, MC, V; no checks; dinner every day; full bar; reservations recommended; www.cru.ca.* &

Il Giardino di Umberto / ❂❂❂

1382 Hornby St, Vancouver; 604/669-2422
For a memorable romantic meal, snag a table on the popular garden patio and enjoy the Tuscan-inspired menu by Umberto Menghi, one of Canada's best-known restaurateurs. Menghi reinvents traditional pasta and game dishes in a lighter, more contemporary style. Expect swift, polished service and a solid wine list. And, the tiramisu here is Vancouver's best. *$$$–$$$$; AE, DC, MC,*

V; no checks; lunch Mon–Fri, dinner Mon–Sat; full bar; reservations recommended; www.umberto.com.

La Terrazza / ❷❷❷

1088 Cambie St, Vancouver; 604/899-4449
This Yaletown dining room—with its soft lighting, dark painted interior, and lush drapes—could serve as the set for a postmodern performance of *Romeo and Juliet*. La Terrazza lives up to its name: in warm weather, French doors open onto a large terrace, which adds an alfresco atmosphere to the inside tables. The cuisine is inventive, modern Northern Italian. While the restaurant prides itself on its extensive wine list, the freshly made ravioli is also one of the highlights. *$$$; AE, MC, V; no checks; dinner every day; full bar; reservations recommended; www.laterrazza.ca.* ᴋ

Lumière / ❷❷❷❷
DB Bistro / UNRATED

2551 W Broadway, Vancouver; 604/739-8185
These two restaurants are the culinary stars of Vancouver's West Side. Under new ownership, Lumière is formal with crystal stemware and fine linens. Here, couples can bask in an eclectic blend of European sophistication and modern French cuisine that speaks a language all its own. Next door a new version of New York's DB Bistro Moderne is anticipated to open in late 2008. With world-renowned Chef Daniel Boulud running things, Lumière will continue to be a one of Canada's finest restaurants, and one that is uniquely suited to Vancouver's style, energy, and tastes. DB Bistro Moderne will undoubtedly be a contemporary interpretation of a classic French bistro—offering creative cuisine in a casual and accessible setting with a focus on great seasonal ingredients. *$$$$; AE, DC, MC, V; checks OK; dinner Tues–Sun; full bar; reservations recommended; www.lumiere.ca.* ᴋ

Parkside / ❷❷❷❷

1906 Haro St, Vancouver; 604/683-6912
This is where local chefs impress their dates and kissable spots abound in this sophisticated sanctuary beneath the historic Buchanan Hotel in Vancouver's West End. Whether you're seated on the garden courtyard patio, at the dark oak bar, or at Table 10—one of the most romantic spots in the city (a private room for two)—you'll find the intimate setting comfortable and inviting, if not downright sexy. Chef Andrey Durbach offers fresh seasonal cuisine with Mediterranean influence and French flair. You can order à la carte or select three courses for $65. Choose from an extensive old-world wine list. Then, mix and match a three- or four-course meal of "classically grounded cooking." Menu highlights include roasted lamb *en persillade* and *fromage frais* mousse with fresh strawberries and brown-sugar sauce. *$$$$;*

Top Five Splurge Spas

Absolute Spa, 1015 Burrard St, Vancouver; 604/684-2775

Spa Utopia, 160-889 Harbourside Dr, North Vancouver; 604/980-3977

Sanctuary Spa, 325 Howe St, Ste 501, Vancouver; 604/688-4769

Skoah, 1011 Hamilton St, Vancouver; 604/642-0200

Vida Wellness Spa, 845 Burrard St (Sutton Place Hotel), Vancouver; 604/682-8410

MC, V; no checks; dinner Wed–Sun; full bar; reservations recommended; www.parksiderestaurant.ca. &

Quattro on Fourth / ❂❂❂

2611 W 4th Ave, Vancouver; 604/734-4444
The accommodating staff at this comfortable Italian restaurant in the heart of Kitsilano makes sure that dining here is a treat in any season. In winter, the restaurant emanates mystery and romance with candlelight, crimson-washed walls, and the glow from rustic wrought-iron chandeliers. In summer, guests dine alfresco on the garden patio under the twinkling lights. With dishes like the *Filetto Etrusca*, an exquisite beef tenderloin, it's no wonder Quattro on Fourth has always been the darling of local food critics. *$$$$; AE, DC, MC, V; no checks; dinner every day; full bar; reservations required (weekends); www.quattrorestaurants.com.* &

Tojo's / ❂❂❂❂

133 W Broadway, Vancouver; 604/872-8050
Sushi lovers line up for a seat at this renowned restaurant, whose acclaim draws visiting celebs and local fanatics alike. For the true Tojo's experience, take a place at the *omakase* bar, and let chef-owner Hidekazu Tojo (respect-fully known as Tojo-san) or one of his disciples dazzle your palate with a selection of dishes they choose for you. Menus at the *omakase* bar are strictly verboten, but tailored to your dietary restrictions, likes and dislikes, and budget. Isn't it romantic to leave your dining destiny in the skilled hands of a master? *$$$$; AE, MC, V; no checks; dinner Mon–Sat; full bar; reservations required; www.tojos.com.* &

Vij's / ❂❂❂❂

1480 W 11th St, Vancouver; 604/736-6664
Bombay native Vikram Vij's imaginative home-cooked Indian fare is a sen-sual delight. Courtesy and simplicity rule, as Vij himself waits carefully on all who arrive, greeting you with a glass of chai before discussing his

seasonal menu, which changes every three months. The decor is minimalist and casual; coal-black walls and East Indian ornaments allow the food to take center stage. Don't pass on the standout appetizer, small samosas filled with ricotta. For your entrée, you can almost always count on the aromatic curry. *$$$; AE, MC, V; no checks; dinner every day; beer and wine; no reservations; www.vijs.ca.* &

West / ⬡⬡⬡⬡

2881 Granville St, Vancouver; 604/738-8938
This South Granville eatery makes a perfect special-occasion destination, with its beautifully designed dining room and ceiling-high "wall of wine," which sets the stage for an unforgettable dining experience. The sophisticated, contemporary restaurant offers three seasonal multicourse tasting menus and a three-course prix-fixe menu (available before 6pm)—a great option when heading to an evening show at nearby Stanley Theatre. *$$–$$$; AE, MC, V; no checks; lunch Mon–Fri, dinner every day; full bar; reservations recommended; www.westrestaurant.com.* &

♡ Lower
Mainland
British
Columbia

Lower Mainland British Columbia

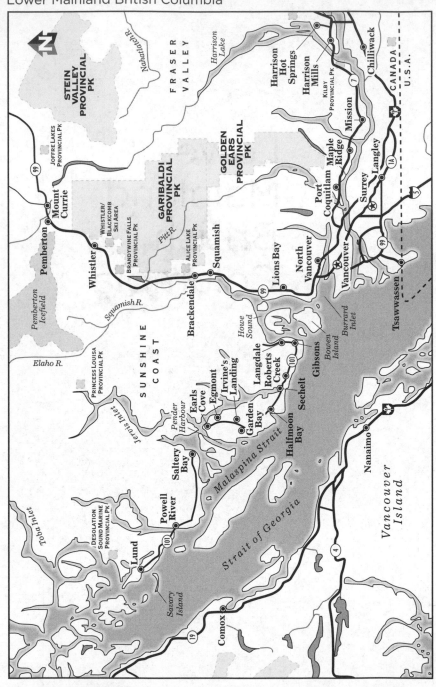

*Kissing is like drinking salted water: you drink and
your thirst increases.*

—Chinese Proverb

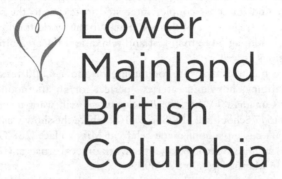 # Lower Mainland British Columbia

Visitors flock to lower mainland British Columbia, encompassing Whistler, the Fraser River Valley, and the Sunshine Coast, for its unsurpassed beauty and outdoor adventures. A quiet destination is the breathtaking Sunshine Coast, which often boasts more than 2,000 hours of sunlight in a year, meaning bright days far outnumber gloomy ones. The area benefits from a rain shadow cast by the Vancouver Island mountains, resulting in some of the best weather in the entire Pacific Northwest. Nearly 90 miles long from end to end, the Sunshine Coast offers plenty of hiking, boating, and beachcombing for outdoorsy couples, and many quaint little municipalities, each with its own array of bed-and-breakfasts. At the northernmost tip, the tiny town of Lund marks the end of the world's longest highway, the Pan-American—known as Highway 1 and 101 in parts of the United States and Canada—it starts in Chile and stretches 9,312 miles.

Whistler is a world-class destination, no matter the time of year. With countless fine-dining options, renowned spas, and warm-weather outdoor activities—like golfing and hiking—couples will never be at a loss for how to spend their time while vacationing in the village.

With the 2010 Olympics around the corner, the resort's star continues to rise. Book hotels far in advance and prepare for minimum-stay requirements during the busy summer months and the entire winter.

Despite continuous roadwork (in preparation for the Olympics), the route from Vancouver to Whistler, the Sea to Sky Highway, is considered one of North America's most stunning drives. Don't allow yourself to get too distracted by the stunning vistas—the curves of the road demand constant attention. Depending on the traffic, expect about a two-hour drive from Vancouver.

Sunshine Coast

Romantic Highlights

Possibly because it can only be accessed by ferry from Horseshoe Bay in Vancouver, the Sunshine Coast region is still something of a secret—regular visitors in-the-know probably like it that way. The laid-back atmosphere and breathtaking scenery at every turn make the region the perfect spot for couples to reconnect in relative solitude. Uncrowded hiking, biking, and boating are among the region's biggest draws. And for those couples interested in taking to the seas, Jacques Cousteau called the region one of the best places in the world for diving. But, for lovers who seek nothing more than rest and relaxation, the area offers plenty of low-key diversions as well.

Gibsons is a quaint waterfront community of about 4,000 residents with a handful of charming shops and eateries—perfect for an afternoon stroll. Fans of the longest Canadian TV hit *The Beachcombers* will want to grab lunch at **Molly's Reach** (647 School Rd; 604/886-9710), where the show was filmed. Also in Gibsons, don't pass up a homemade gelato at **Mike's Place** (268 Gower Pt Rd; 604/886-5320) and be sure to check out the work of local artists at **Gibsons Landing Gallery** (436 Marine Dr; 604/886-0099).

Heading north, stop to walk along the beach at mellow **Roberts Creek,** keeping your eyes peeled for bald eagles circling overhead. Enjoy a tasty organic meal at **The Gumboot Restaurant** (1041 Roberts Creek Rd; 604/885-4216) or order one of the oversize pastries at **The Gumboot Bakery Café** next door (1053 Roberts Creek Rd; 604/885-4218).

If there's a "main hub" to the Sunshine Coast, it's Sechelt, where you can settle in for a movie at the single-screen **Raven's Cry Theatre** (5559 Sunshine Coast Hwy; 604/885-4597). For one of the best casual meals in the area, in nearby Wilson Creek, check out local favorite **Georgia Strait Café** (4349 Sunshine Coast Hwy; 604/885-1997) where you'll find innovative sandwiches and tasty desserts.

And, if you find yourselves feeling ambitious enough to take the second ferry to the upper Sunshine Coast, treat yourself to a boat or hiking tour from **Terracentric Coastal Adventures** (604/483-7900).

Access & Information

To reach the Sunshine Coast, catch a ferry at Horseshoe Bay in West Vancouver. **BC Ferries** (888/223-3779; www.bcferries.bc.ca) operates eight daily trips each way between Horseshoe Bay and Langdale on the Sechelt Peninsula. Once in Langdale, Highway 101 runs the length of the lower Sunshine Coast to Earl's Cove in Egmont, 50 miles (80 km) north. To reach the upper Sunshine Coast, take the hour-long ferry ride from Earl's Cove to Saltery Bay in Powell River. From there, pick up Highway 101 again for access to the more secluded, but visually stunning, upper Sunshine Coast.

Romantic Lodgings

A Place by the Sea Bed & Breakfast and Spa / ❶❶❶

5810 Marine Wy, Sechelt; 604/885-2745 or 866/885-2746
Although the front of this bed-and-breakfast appears rather uninspiring upon arrival, don't be dismayed. Once you walk around to the back and take in the jaw-dropping panoramic view of Porpoise Bay, you'll understand why this establishment has been considered a true jewel in the Sunshine Coast since it opened in 2002. Although we prefer the rustic charm of the Captain's Cove, all three of the suites are well appointed, with two-person jetted tubs and gas fireplaces. At dusk, sit on one of the massive decks to watch the sunlight fade away, or bring a blanket down to the resort's small sandy beach, start a campfire, and cuddle under the stars. The charming owners are more than happy to set up boat cruises and fishing charters for guests. *$$$$; MC, V; no checks; closed 1 week in Dec; www.aplacebythesea.com.*

Bonniebrook Lodge / ❶❶❸

1532 Ocean Beach Esplanade, Gibsons; 604/886-2887 or 877/290-9916
Not too far from the quaint town of Gibsons, and close to the Langdale ferry docks, this is an excellent choice if arriving late in the day. In this cheerful yellow home built in the 1920s several different types of rooms are available, but you'll find ultimate privacy in one of the two spacious penthouses. By night, head to the private beach across the street to make a bonfire, or take a long soak in your room's luxurious two-person jetted tub. After falling asleep to the whisper of Chaster Creek, you'll awaken feeling refreshed. Enjoy the homemade breakfast, which is delivered to your door, on the small private patio overlooking the ocean. After a satisfying meal, follow the beach to quiet Chaster Park. *$$$; AE, MC, V; no checks; www.bonniebrook.com.*

Country Cottage Bed and Breakfast / ❶❶❶❸

1183 Roberts Creek Rd, Roberts Creek; 604/885-7448
Charming owners Loragene and Philip Gaulin are the perfect hosts for a stay in the Sunshine Coast, allowing you complete privacy until you have a specific question to be answered or need to be fulfilled. At the lovely 2-acre farm, the two suites are set off from the main house, ensuring total seclusion. Although the homey Rose Cottage has its own charm, we prefer the rustic Cedar Lodge, dubbed a "tree house for grown-ups." With its comfy loft bed, wood-burning fireplace, full kitchen, and books and games tucked away throughout, you might only be tempted to leave to stock up on groceries. At this bucolic paradise, distractions of the outside world are quickly forgotten, making it an ideal getaway for couples in dire need of uninterrupted R & R. Plus, while other places claim to be pet friendly, this is the region's best place for couples traveling with furry friends. *$$; no credit cards; checks OK; www. countrycottagebb.ca.*

Sunshine Coast Secret

About 4 miles off the shore of Lund on the upper Sunshine Coast lies a little-known natural aberration called Savary Island. Unlike the rocky yellow-sand beaches that line the rest of the Sunshine Coast, Savary Island is almost completely ringed by a fine, pale white-sand beach, similar to what you'd find in the tropics. In fact, locals have dubbed Savary Island Hawaii of the North. On the island's north side, where the tides meet in the Strait of Georgia, it is believed that the water temperature is the warmest north of Mexico.

Lovers ought to make a full day and night out of a Savary Island visit. With the island's limited provisions, stock up before you go at the **Safeway** in Powell River (7040 Barnet St; 604/485-7614) or **Lund Grocery** (1436 Hwy 101; 604/414-0471). Once you arrive, there are just a few restaurants and the **Savary Island General Store** (2801 Vancouver Blvd; 604/483-2210). And as the Web site for the general store and **Riggers Restaurant** states, hours may be "12 to whenever . . . 3 to whenever," or otherwise, which is part of the island's isolated charm.

Hop on the **Lund Water Taxi** (at the wharf; 604/483-9749), which heads to and from Savary Island twice daily. Reservations are strongly

Desolation Sound Resort / ●●●

2694 Dawson Rd, Powell River; 604/483-3592 or 800/399-3592
Find unforgettable adventure—including kayaking, boating, and hiking—as well as romance at Desolation Resort. The quiet at this large resort is broken only by the lapping of waves, the cry of the loons, and the squawks of ravens overhead. The 10 uniquely designed chalets overlook the pristine waterfront of Okeover Arm. The rustic cabins are simple, but the beds are inviting. Wide verandas offer sweeping views, and cabins 1, 2, 6, and 7 have outdoor hot tubs. No food is available at the resort, so be sure to bring all the provisions you'll need to cook up delicious meals in your chalet's full kitchen. Rent one of the resort's kayaks or canoes and set out to enjoy the unspoiled wilderness surrounding the area. *$$$–$$$$; MC, V; no checks; closed Nov or Jan; www.desolationresort.com.*

Halfmoon Bay Cabin / ●●●

8617 Redrooffs Rd, Halfmoon Bay; 604/885-0764 or 866/333-2468
Set on a forested hill overlooking the water, this private log cabin is an ideal retreat for couples seeking a weekend of luxurious seclusion. Large and well appointed, the cabin is spacious enough for four people to stay comfortably, but is a delightful splurge for two. On the sprawling sundeck, enjoy the rare

recommended; reserve at least a week in advance in summer. Experienced kayakers can travel to the island on their own by paddling south from Lund along the peninsula's shoreline to the closest point to Savary Island, then heading due west for 30 minutes. Although walking is a wonderful way to experience the island, bicycles are also available from **Savary Island Bike Rentals** (604/414-4079). It should be noted that there are no cars, and electricity on the island comes only from the private generators of residents and businesses. The 100 or so full-time residents (which can swell to 2,000 in summer) have generally opposed anything that could disrupt this truly unique geological haven. (First Nations people are thought to have been on Savary Island 4,000 years ago; there are few places on earth that have been inhabited for this long with so little development.)

Spread out a blanket and enjoy a kiss and picnic on the delightful beach. Gazing out at the water, it's not hard to imagine a simpler time, free from the distractions of the modern world. There are no campgrounds on Savary Island, so you might want to arrange a cottage rental (www.savary.ca/savary_services.html). If not, book a room (in advance) at the kiss-worthy **Savary Lodge B&B** on the Front Row (604/483-9481) or **Hemingway Cottage** at Indian Point (604/483-3637).

delight of an outdoor shower, or grill up a dinner on the barbecue before turning in to nuzzle in front of the living room's wood-burning fireplace. With a beachside cabana at the bottom of the hill, you'll likely want to spend your days sunning and swimming along the cabin's quiet stretch of waterfront. For a truly unforgettable evening, hire local chef Alan Barnes to prepare a gourmet feast beachside. *$$$; MC, V; no checks; www.halfmoonbaycabin.com.*

Rosewood Country House / ○○○◐

575 Pine St, Gibsons; 604/886-4714 or 604/886-0903
As you pull into the driveway, you'll immediately sense this property's handsome grace. Ponds and lush gardens peppered with the vibrant colors of flowers, fruits, and herbs—each tended to by genial owner Susan Tonne Berryman—surround the Craftsman-style home. With only two suites to choose from, the guest experience is intimate, and no detail is overlooked: guests enjoy complimentary massage oils, candles, terry robes, and renowned gourmet breakfasts. After having dinner in town, spend time in the game room playing darts or pool, on a table that dates to 1865. Many of the distinctive decorative and functional items found throughout the house, including the precious china, were passed down through generations of the owner's family. *$$$; AE, V; local checks only; closed Nov–Feb (except Valentine's Day); www.rosewoodcountryhouse.com.* &

Sunshine Coast Resort Hotel & Marina / ◗◖◗◖

12695 Sunshine Coast Hwy, Madeira Park; 604/883-9177
Built on a snug cove, the resort overlooks Pender Harbor's small marina, a common gateway to beautiful Desolation Sound and the Princess Louisa Inlet. For luxurious amenities you won't get in the other rooms, book one of the new two-bedroom cottages. Built in 2007, each one retains the rustic character of the resort, yet comes with high-tech amenities, such as the you've-gotta-see-it-to-believe-it aromatherapy bath and shower that are remote control operated. For a simpler pleasure, hold hands and take an early morning walk down to the cove and gaze at the glassy waters. If you're there before the marina stirs, you'll likely hear nothing more than the occasional call of birds. Don't forget to pack groceries, though, because there's no restaurant on-site. *$$–$$$$; AE, MC, V; no checks; www.sunshinecoastresort.com.*

The Tuwanek Hotel / ◗◖◗◖◗◖

7545 Islet Pl, Sechelt; 604/885-2040 or 800/665-2311
With theme suites such as Casablanca and the African Queen, the Tuwanek Hotel is not campy old-Hollywood, as might be expected. Instead, the design is a contemporary twist on old-world glamour, with thematic details—such as hints of animal print in the African Queen suite—subtly employed throughout. The suites, along with the Beach Cottage, blend luxurious amenities, such as a "Cloud Bed"—a Serta Luxury bed with a feather bed on top—outfitted with Egyptian linens, with a charmingly distinctive atmosphere. Downstairs, a game room, snack bar, barbecue, and private movie theater help make this waterfront destination a unique place to put fun back into romance. *$$$; AE, DC, DIS, MC, V; no checks; www.tuwanekhotel.com.*

West Coast Wilderness Lodge / ◗◖◗◖

3649 Maple Road, Egmont; 604/883-3667 or 877/988-3838
To commune with nature and with each other, it's worth the drive to the top of the lower Sunshine Coast to find this tucked-away treasure. The large post-and-beam lodge overlooks inlets dotted with verdant islands. Since the rooms are very simply appointed, make sure to book one with an ocean view, which is stunning through the floor-to-ceiling windows. Adventuresome romantics will be in their element as kayaking, canoeing, rock climbing, mountain biking, and hiking, as well as boat tours, are all available. The place to kiss here is the main lodge's spacious wraparound deck, which boasts one of British Columbia's best sunset views. *$$–$$$; AE, MC, V; no checks; www.wcwl.com.*

Wildflowers B&B / ◗◖◗◖◗◖

5813 Brooks Rd, Halfmoon Bay; 604/885-7346 or 877/885-2003
This forested haven boasts sun-dappled lawns, luxuriant gardens, and waterfowl basking in the man-made lagoon. The two spacious, elegant cottages stand apart from the owner's hilltop home. Both cottages have fireplaces,

king-size canopy beds, soaking tubs, and small kitchens (note that the Iris has a particularly sexy bathroom). A feeling of total privacy pervades the place, whether you're relaxing in a wicker lounge and listening to birdsong or soaking in the hot tub beside the lagoon. While you may wonder about choosing this forested, tucked-away haven in an area famous for its ocean views, the choice is more than justified. *$$; MC, V; no checks; www.wild flowers-bb.com.*

Romantic Restaurants

The Blue Heron Inn / ❂❂❸

5521 Delta Rd, Sechelt; 604/885-3847 or 800/818-8977
Although this old standby desperately needs a floor-to-ceiling remodel, diners still flock here for its unbeatable view of Sechelt Inlet. After almost 20 years as the destination restaurant on the Sunshine Coast, the Blue Heron Inn still serves up tried-and-true favorites. Try one of the fresh seafood dishes available nightly or favorites like the bouillabaisse or the rack of lamb. Although the owner won't accept requests for specific tables, it can't hurt to ask for one by the fireplace in the winter. *$$$$; MC, V; local checks only; dinner Wed–Sun; full bar; reservations recommended; blueheron@universe.com.* &

Daphne's Restaurant / ❂❂❸

5530 Wharf St, Sechelt; 604/885-2008
When searching for a quick, satisfying meal in downtown Sechelt, look no further than Daphne's, a true gem serving authentic Greek food. After a day of outdoor pursuits, sometimes a simple, casual meal is all one really craves before a good night's sleep. And, although there's nothing patently romantic about the decor, the spanakopita and other Greek specialties are enough to make any hungry soul swoon. *$$; AE, MC, V; no checks; lunch, dinner Tues–Sun; full bar; reservations recommended; daphnerestaurant@hotmail.com.* &

Laughing Oyster / ❂❂❂

10052 Malaspina Rd, Powell River; 604/483-9775
Couples will be charmed by both the food and the spectacular views at this premier dining destination. The waterfront restaurant's split levels ensure everyone has a good view of Oeuvre Arm, particularly from the large patio. Enjoyed by tourists and locals alike, the casual ambience and generous portions make this spot a regional favorite. In fact, even those who aren't oyster fans rave about the flavor of these oysters, fresh from the restaurant's dock. Plus, the small but thoughtfully chosen wine list is reasonably priced. On dark and stormy evenings, choose a corner table beside the fireplace. *$$$; MC, V; no checks; lunch, dinner every day (summer), Wed–Sun (winter); full bar; reservations recommended; www.laughingoyster.ca.* &

Magellan's Tapas on the Bay / ○○○◐

5764 Wharf Rd, Sechelt; 604/740-0904
Opened in 2007, this is unquestionably the rising star among Sunshine Coast dinner spots. With a sophisticated menu more akin to Vancouver or Whistler establishments, Magellan's offers a contemporary dining option for those craving cuisine with cosmopolitan flair. The hallmark of the menu is the chef's imaginative combination of ingredients, creatively displayed in the mouth-watering selection of oysters. The restaurant's magnificent circular bar is an excellent spot to rub knees, nibble on tapas, and enjoy a glass of wine. Lucky diners at Magellan's might catch a glimpse of a bald eagle out the window—they're known to soar above the waters just outside. *$$–$$$; AE, MC, V; no checks; dinner Wed–Sun; full bar; reservations recommended.* &

Ruby Lake Italian Trattoria / ○○

Ruby Lake (Ruby Lake Resort), Madeira Park; 604/883-2269
If there was a motto fit for Ruby Lake Italian Trattoria, it would be "Real Italian food by real Italians." As soon as you walk through the door, owners Giorgio and Aldo Cogrossi welcome you as one of the family. Gregarious host Giorgio flits about the restaurant, making sure guests are satisfied with brother Aldo's home-style specialties, such as bruschetta, spaghetti bolognese, and *bistecca alla griglia*. Most of the vegetables and herbs served are grown in the restaurant's garden, and the wine list offers plenty of appealing, afford-able options. *$$$; MC, V; no checks; dinner every day (summer), Thurs–Sun (winter); full bar; reservations recommended; www.rubylakeresort.com.*

Whistler

Romantic Highlights

Just north of Vancouver, off the spectacular Sea to Sky Highway, Whistler is made up of three main communities: **Whistler Village** (the main hub), **Upper Village** (at the base of Blackcomb Mountain), and **Creekside** (a short drive to the south). Upon arrival, get oriented by enjoying the short walk between the Whistler and Blackcomb mountain bases. Just before reaching Upper Village, be sure to stop for a kiss on the Fitzsimmons Trail's covered bridge, which crosses a gurgling mountain creek.

For a chance to experience the mountain before the crowds hit the slopes, hop on the Whistler Village gondola at 7:15am to enjoy the hearty Fresh Tracks breakfast at the **Roundhouse Lodge** (866/218-9690). After eating, enjoy a run or two before the mountain opens up to the masses. If you're slow to wake, fill up on one of the huge, scrumptious pastries at **Hot Buns Bakery** (4232 Village Stroll; 604/932-6883), located in the heart of the village.

When you're not skiing or hiking, grab your partner's hand and go for drinks on one of the popular patios at **Citta' Bistro** (4217 Village Stroll; 604/932-4177),

Top Five Romantic Spots to Enjoy Après Ski

Mallard Bar, 4599 Chateau Blvd, Whistler; 800/441-1414

Fifty Two 80 Bistro and Bar, 4591 Blackcomb Wy, Whistler; 604/935-3400

Bearfoot Bistro, 4121 Village Green, Whistler; 604/932-3433

Cinnamon Bear Grille, 4050 Whistler Wy, Whistler; 604/966-5060

FireRock Lounge, 4090 Whistler Wy, Whistler; 604/905-5000

La Brasserie des Artistes (4232 Village Stroll; 604/932-3569), or Garibaldi Lift Co. Bar & Grill (at the base of the Whistler Village gondola; 604/905-2220), where live music creates a fun, if not intimate, après-ski atmosphere.

Maybe there's nothing romantic about a good burger, but there's something poetic about a great one. For the best burger in Whistler, head to popular Splitz Grill (4369 Main St; 604/938-9300). Or, for a meal as big as your love, build your own stir-fry from an impressive display of meats, veggies, and sauces at Mongolie Grill (201-4295 Blackcomb Wy; 604/938-9416).

Access & Information

From Vancouver, it's a 90-minute drive up the scenic Sea to Sky Highway (Hwy 99) from West Vancouver through Squamish to Whistler. (Follow Hwy 1 west until just before Horseshoe Bay, then take the Squamish–Whistler exit to Hwy 99 north.) If you're coming from the BC Ferry terminal at Tsawwassen, Highway 17 provides the link to Highway 99. A word to the wise: On the drive, please don't allow yourself to get distracted by your partner or the breathtaking views—the curves of the road demand constant attention. If you decide you don't want to miss a single second of spectacular scenery, take the three-hour bus journey with Perimeter Transportation (604/905-0041) or Greyhound Canada (800/661-8747) and snuggle up to enjoy the view. Whistler Air (604/932-6615 or 888/806-2299; www.whistlerair.ca) offers a 30-minute floatplane service between Vancouver and Whistler twice daily from June 1 to September 30.

Border crossings (and customs) link Washington State and the lower mainland at four locations. The busiest crossings are at Blaine, Washington, where Interstate 5 links with Highway 99 at the Peace Arch, and at Douglas, where British Columbia's Highway 15 begins. The others are located just south of Aldergrove, British Columbia, and at Huntingdon-Sumas just south of Abbotsford, British Columbia. After September 11, 2001, security at the borders was significantly tightened: allow two to five hours to make the crossing at peak hours and be sure to carry a passport as proof of citizenship.

Three Days of Romance in Whistler

Day One: Wake up early on your first day in Whistler and grab a casual breakfast at **Portobello Market & Fresh Bakery** in the **Fairmont Chateau Whistler Resort**. Then, take the Excalibur gondola to the top of Blackcomb Mountain and spend several hours skiing or snowboarding. Having worked up an appetite, hold hands under the table during lunch at the **Crystal Hut** (4545 Blackcomb Wy; 604/932-3434), which is renowned for its spectacular views and Belgian waffles. Ski for a few more hours, then make your way down to your hotel for a short rest before dinner. Couples seeking the ultimate splurge should stay at the **Four Seasons Resort Whistler**, while those looking for better value will be thrilled with the **Whistler Pinnacle Hotel**. After freshening up, head to **Bearfoot Bistro Champagne Bar** to toast a magical weekend with some bubbly (and a dozen oysters). Afterward, walk to dinner at Whistler's finest restaurant, **Araxi**. End the day by cozying up in your room.

Day Two: Start your day with breakfast at **The Wild Wood Bistro & Bar** (4500 Northlands Blvd; 604/935-4077) in the Whistler Racket Club. Snuggle into a seat next to the huge fireplace and order the local favorite, banana bread French toast. Then, to experience Whistler's scenery from a different perspective, embark on a half-day cross-country-skiing trip. Rent your equipment and buy tickets from the **Lost Lake Cross**

The nearest major airport is **Vancouver International Airport** (9 miles/15 km south of downtown on Sea Island, Richmond; 604/207-7077; www.yvr.ca).

The **Whistler Chamber of Commerce** (604/932-5528) and **Tourism Whistler** (604/932-4222; www.mywhistler.com) can provide up-to-date information about activities, accommodations, and the array of annual festivals that spill onto the mountains and the villages' cobbled streets.

Romantic Lodgings

Adara Whistler Hotel / ●●❶

4122 Village Green, Whistler; 604/905-4009 or 866/502-3272
The undeniably sexy combination of modern design and a retro ski-lodge vibe makes Adara *the* place where couples in-the-know stay in Whistler. The lobby, which feels more like a funky lounge than a waiting area, is as sleek as it is quirky—with two curved burnt-orange pleather-lined sofas, an oversize stone fireplace, and Adara's playful take on mounted antlers. Thankfully, the hotel's 41 rooms are no less chic than its entrance, and couples who seek stylish, modern digs will be pleased with the guest rooms' designer furniture,

Country Connection (at the trailhead next to the ticket booth in Lost Lake Park; 604/905-0071) and set out into the wilderness on one of the many intersecting trails. Return to the village to enjoy a beer and to rest your tired feet on the heated patio at **Citta' Bistro** (4217 Village Stroll; 604/932-4177). Then, take the afternoon easy, strolling the diverse shops of the village or watching an early afternoon movie at **Village 8 Cinemas** (100-4295 Blackcomb Wy; 604/932-5815). Afterward, relax by the grand fireplace at the Fairmont's famous **Mallard Lounge**, where you can enjoy live music and a drink called Sullivan's Best (trust us, Sullivan was right). Finish your day with dinner at **Quattro in the Whistler Pinnacle Hotel**. Then head up to your room to try your in-room jetted tub.

Day Three: On your third day, slow down a bit—you've earned it. Start with a light pastry and fresh coffee at **Blenz** (101-4388 Main St; 604/932-2374). Then, enjoy a couple's massage in the spa at the **Four Seasons**. After unwinding, grab lunch at **Crêpe Montagne** (116-4368 Main St; 604/905-4444). After your meal, explore the village by foot, picking up sweet goodies along the way. As a predinner treat, share luscious chocolates from the **Rocky Mountain Chocolate Factory** (4190 Springs Ln; 604/932-4100). For dinner, canoodle at sexy **Elements Urban Tapas Parlour**. At the end of the evening, retreat back to the Pinnacle to nibble on the rest of your chocolates before turning out the lights.

rainforest showerheads, and bright white linens. But, it should be noted, without a restaurant, bar, or fitness center on premises, Adara's amenities don't quite live up to what's available at other hotels that charge similar rates. *$$$$; AE, MC, V; no checks; www.adarahotel.com.* ♿

Durlacher Hof Alpine Country Inn / ♡♡♨

7055 Nester's Rd, Whistler; 604/932-1924 or 877/932-1924
For those who are tired of feeling anonymous at large hotels, book a room at Erika and Peter Durlacher's delightful inn. Modeled after farmhouses found in the European Alps, the inn's every detail has been painstakingly chosen to reflect the owners' proud Austrian heritage. After slipping off your shoes and stepping into the European slippers they provide, sit beside the lounge area's authentic *kachelofen* (an old-fashioned farmhouse fireplace), nibble on homemade pastries, and sip on mulled wine before turning in for a restful sleep. Two guest suites are particularly inviting, with Romeo-and-Juliet balconies, jetted tubs, and cushioned reading alcoves. In the morning, enjoy one of Erika's lavish breakfasts, which have reached legendary status in Whistler.

Lacking the technological gadgetry of large hotels, the Durlacher is an ideal place to reconnect sans distraction. *$$$–$$$$; MC, V; local checks only; www. durlacherhof.com.* &

Fairmont Chateau Whistler Resort / ◐◐◐

4599 Chateau Blvd, Whistler; 604/938-8000 or 800/441-1414
Holding court at the foot of Blackcomb Mountain, the regal Chateau Whistler is often considered the crown jewel of Whistler luxury accommodations. With 550 rooms, the hotel may not feel intimate, but thankfully, personalized service remains paramount. Ski equipment valets, a holistic full-service spa, and a world-class golf course are just a few of the hotel's countless amenities. After returning from the slopes, head to the Mallard Lounge inside to enjoy live music and a drink—we recommend the Sullivan's Best, a latte spiked with Kahlúa and Godet Belgian White Chocolate Liqueur. For the best seats in the house, be sure to snag a place next to the mammoth fireplace, or outside beside a fire pit. As for the guest rooms, splurge and book one at the Fairmont Gold level. With fireplaces, private check-in, and upgraded rooms, the extra cost is worth every penny. *$$$$; AE, DC, DIS, MC, V; checks OK; www.fairmont.com/whistler.* &

Four Seasons Resort Whistler / ◐◐◐◐

4591 Blackcomb Wy, Whistler; 604/935-3400 or 888/935-2460
If money is no object, this is *the* place to stay in Whistler for the ultimate romantic getaway. The warm, sophisticated lobby—with its blend of sumptuous furniture, a wood-burning stone fireplace, and stunning original art—feels like a luxe ski lodge at its best, equally comfortable and breathtaking. The hotel's 242 rooms carry on the luxurious rustic feel with gas fireplaces, balconies, and spectacular views from practically every window. The hotel offers a plethora of extra services, including a full-service ski concierge, an exquisite spa, private yoga or Pilates classes, and even babysitting. For thoughtful service and top-of-the-line amenities in a stunning setting, the Four Seasons is the unrivaled king of Whistler hotels. *$$$$; AE, DC, DIS, MC, V; no checks; www.fourseasons.com/whistler.* &

Pan Pacific Whistler Village Centre / ◐◐◐◖

4299 Blackcomb Wy, Whistler; 604/966-5500 or 888/966-5575
Ideally situated in the heart of Whistler Village, and just a moment's walk from the gondolas, Pan Pacific Whistler Village Centre is a great choice for couples who seek comfort and convenience. Opened in 2005, this luxe all-suite hotel features just 87 contemporary rooms—each includes a kitchenette, a gas fireplace, and most likely, a spectacular view. For the ultimate in relaxation, be sure to grab your sweetheart's hand and take a dip in one of the two outdoor hot tubs or the saltwater lap pool—all boast fantastic views of

the mountains. Other irresistible perks include a lavish complimentary buffet breakfast and ski storage at the Whistler Mountain gondola base. *$$$$; AE, MC, V; no checks; www.panpacific.com/whistlervillagecentre.* &

Sundial Boutique Hotel / ❶❶❶❶

4340 Sundial Crescent, Whistler; 604/932-2321 or 800/661-2321
For the complete Sundial Boutique experience, reserve a suite with private hot tub and fireplace, then phone the concierge a few days ahead and order groceries and champagne, arrive at the hotel, and snuggle in the comforts of your room. Details in slate, granite, and fir shout Whistler, from floor to ceiling and all the way up to the rooftop, which offers a hot tub and stupendous views. Each spacious room has a large gourmet kitchen, heated slate bathroom floor, warm earth tones, and luxurious furnishings. *$$$$; AE, MC, V; no checks; www.sundialhotel.com.* &

Whistler Pinnacle Hotel / ❶❶❶❶

4319 Main St, Whistler; 604/938-3218
Although the decor is not as opulent as Whistler's other luxury hotels, this 84-suite resort stands out from the crowd because of its genuinely warm and attentive staff and well-appointed rooms. Thoughtfully designed to cater to a couple's every whim, every suite includes a two-person jetted tub, a large seated shower, a gas fireplace, a full kitchen, a king-size bed, a balcony, and air-conditioning (an often-overlooked perk until the summer). For truly special occasions, solicit help from the friendly staff: upon your arrival, they'll happily provide welcome baskets overflowing with local delicacies, chilled chocolate-covered strawberries, a rose petal–strewn room . . . or practically anything else you fancy. If a hotel set in the heart of Whistler can ever be considered a hidden treasure, this is it. *$$ $$$$; AE, MC, V; no checks; www. whistlerpinnacle.com.* &

The Westin Resort and Spa / ❶❶❶

4090 Whistler Wy, Whistler; 604/905-5000 or 888/634-5577
The Westin's luxury all-suite hotel aims to sweep lovers off their feet—and straight into bed. All of the suites feature the hotel's signature all-white Heavenly Bed with pillow-top mattress and down comforter. Although the suite decor isn't particularly inspired, amenities including an upscale kitchen, a gas fireplace, and a soaking tub leave little to be desired. The resort is just steps from the Whistler gondola, and at the end of the day, fatigued couples will appreciate the short walk to Avello Spa, on the resort's premises, where they can choose from more than 75 blissful treatments. *$$$$; AE, DC, DIS, MC, V; no checks; www.westinwhistler.com.* &

Blackcomb Horse-drawn Sleigh Rides

When your limbs are weary from snowbound pursuits, you'll be ready for a relaxing way to enjoy the region's wintry wonderland. We heartily recommend enchanting **Blackcomb Horse-drawn Sleigh Rides** (604/932-7631; www.blackcombssleighrides.com). Sip on hot chocolate and snuggle under the complimentary blankets as Percheron draft horses whisk you through Nicklaus North Golf Course or around scenic Blackcomb Mountain. For a truly unforgettable experience, splurge on the package that includes a four-course gourmet fondue dinner at the **Den Restaurant & Grill** (Nicklaus North Golf Course, 800/446-5322; www.golfbc.com), which boasts a stunning view of Green Lake.

Romantic Restaurants

Araxi / ✪✪✪✪

4222 Whistler Village Square, Whistler; 604/932-4540
Whatever you do, save an evening for a romantic dinner at Araxi, one of Whistler's culinary cornerstones. It's located in the middle of action central—Whistler Village Square—with sought-after patio dining during the summer. The menu is tailor-made for lovers, featuring two- and three-tier seafood towers and several varieties of oysters (the listing reads like a mini course in Oysters 101, describing where each oyster comes from and its unique flavor). The finale to an unforgettable meal, desserts include a molten chocolate cake and an inspired selection of ice creams and sorbets. Oenophiles, take note, the restaurant has won many awards for its impressive wine selection. *$$$$; AE, MC, V; no checks; lunch every day (summer), dinner every day (closed for 3 weeks in May or Oct); full bar; reservations recommended; www. araxi.com.* &

Bearfoot Bistro Champagne Restaurant / ✪✪✪

4121 Village Green, Whistler; 604/932-3433
Undeterred by exorbitant prices, serious-minded foodies book a reservation up to a year in advance for the opportunity to dine at the Bearfoot Bistro. To discover the restaurant's charms at more affordable prices, the adjacent Champagne Bar is the perfect spot for a nightcap or for a sampling of the restaurant's unique twist on *tapas*, including creative interpretations of yellowfin tuna tartare, sashimi, and pork belly salad. The early evening oyster special is especially appealing. An added draw is the ice river that tops the stunning bar, where hidden fiber optics provide a magical light show, flooding your bubbly (chosen from a 75-page "wine bible") with an electric

rainbow. *$$$$; AE, MC, V; no checks; dinner every day; full bar; reservations required; www.bearfootbistro.com.* &

Caramba! / ❂❂❹

12-4314 Main St, Whistler; 604/938-1879
The fun, boisterous, Mediterranean-influenced Caramba! is just right for lovers looking for good food, quick service, and an informal atmosphere. The high-energy staff deals out big, soul-satisfying portions of down-home pasta (try the spaghetti and meatballs), pizza, and roasts. The open kitchen, earthy hues, and alder wood–burning pizza ovens lend a warm feel to the room. Drinks are reasonably priced, and, if you prefer a night in, they can whip up a takeout meal in about 15 minutes. *$$; AE, MC, V; no checks; lunch, dinner every day (summer), lunch, dinner Fri–Sun (winter); full bar; reservations recommended; www.caramba-restaurante.com.* &

Ciao-Thyme Bistro / ❂❂❹

1-4573 Chateau Blvd, Whistler; 604/932-7051
With a creative menu that relies heavily on local and organic ingredients, tiny Ciao-Thyme draws flocks of residents and tourists alike to its delicious food at reasonable prices. Although dinner is available at the laidback eatery, the breakfast and lunch menus are among the most appealing in town. For breakfast, try the omelet peppered with spicy chorizo and market vegetables, or granola made from sun-dried fruits and nuts. And, at lunch, look no further than the sockeye salmon sandwich. When weather permits, ask for a table on the enchanting outdoor patio. *$–$$$; AE, DC, MC, V; no checks; breakfast, lunch, dinner every day; full bar; reservations recommended; www. ciaothymebistro.com.* &

Edgewater Lodge Dining Room / ❂❂❂

8020 Alpine Wy, Whistler; 604/932-0686 or 866/870-9065
Head to Edgewater, located on idyllic Green Lake, just before dusk to experience the region's most striking view—the sunset-tinged panorama of the glassy lakefront and its surrounding mountains. A few miles north of Whistler's main drag, this is truly the region's hidden gem, making it the ideal spot for lovers who wish to enjoy an intimate meal far from the maddening crowd. Featuring a traditional menu, the restaurant's signature dishes are venison and a salmon surf and turf. *$$$; AE, MC, V; no checks; dinner every day (summer), Wed–Sun (rest of year); full bar; reservations recommended; www.edgewater-lodge.com.* &

Elements Urban Tapas Parlour / ❂❂❂

102B-4359 Main St, Whistler; 604/932-5569
The dining room is noisy and elbow room is scarce; however, this restaurant has become Whistler's go-to spot for dates since opening in 2005. Listed as

"small bites," each mouth-watering dish is big enough to share . . . although a struggle for every last delectable bite might ensue. For a memorable starter, try the tuna tartare stacked on wonton crisps and topped with avocado relish. The dining experience is a rare combination of both style and substance, and sharing *tapas* in a tiny yet alluring room provides a perfect excuse to lean in and get a little bit closer to the one you love. *$$; AE, MC, V; no checks; breakfast, lunch, dinner every day; full bar; no reservations; www.wildwood restaurants.ca/htm/pbistro.html.* &

Fifty Two 80 Bistro and Bar at Four Seasons Resort / ⬣⬣⬣❰

4591 Blackcomb Wy, Whistler; 604/935-3400
The bistro and bar (named after the number of vertical feet from the top of Blackcomb Mountain to the village below) in the Four Seasons Resort (see Romantic Lodgings) are warm and welcoming, with high-back chairs in the bistro and leather club chairs at the bar. A magnificent circular mosaic fireplace and silver ceiling are playful touches to the otherwise restrained decor. On warmer days, dine on the outdoor terrace with its wood-burning fireplace. Thankfully, the food is as appealing as the surroundings; everything thoroughly satisfies. Plus, the extensive wine list features many excellent choices from British Columbia wineries. *$$$$; AE, DC, MC, V; no checks; breakfast, lunch, dinner every day; full bar; reservations recommended; www. fourseasons.com/whistler/dining.html.* &

La Rua Restaurante / ⬣⬣⬣

4557 Blackcomb Wy, Whistler; 604/932-5011
With its warm crimson dining room and large mural depicting an evening of revelry, La Rua sets the stage for its rich, bold food. Although its name is Spanish, highlights of the innovative menu successfully blend cuisine from around the world with traditional Northwest ingredients. BC sablefish, marinated in ginger and soy sauce and served with soba noodles, is one such menu item to consider, while more unusual dishes include arctic caribou and Quebec foie gras. The outdoor patio is perfect on balmy nights, but quiet romantics beware—when this high-energy spot gets crowded inside, it also gets noisy. *$$$; AE, MC, V; no checks; dinner every day; full bar; reservations recommended; www.larua-restaurante.com.* &

Monk's Grill / ⬣⬣❰

4555 Blackcomb Wy, Whistler; 604/932-9677
With two heated patios and a coveted location at the base of Blackcomb Mountain, it's no surprise that Monk's is a popular après-ski destination. Cuddle on one of the leather couches in the lounge, order a house cocktail (try the Julius Caesar or the Jade), and sit back and admire the unrivaled mountainside view. Or, for couples who enjoy good-natured competition, the stylish black felt pool table is a perfect outlet. For a more formal affair,

Monk's also has a traditional dining room that serves Canadian AAA prime rib, steaks, and fresh local seafood. *$$$$; AE, DC, MC, V; no checks; lunch, dinner every day (July–April), lunch Sat–Sun, dinner Wed–Sun (May–June); full bar; reservations recommended; www.monksgrill.com.*

Quattro at Whistler / ❂❂❂❂

4319 Main St (Whistler Pinnacle Hotel), Whistler; 604/905-4844
Enjoying good food in good company, with a steady flow of wine and conversation and a commitment to living with *abbondanza* (Italian for "the passion and poetry of life")—what better way to enjoy a romantic evening in Whistler? Although everything on the menu is out-of-this-world, the Spaghetti Quattro is especially beloved. Adventurous couples who are in the mood to indulge should consider ordering *L'Abbuffata*, the chef's famous five-course Roman feast. Finish with a glass of *vin santo*—with biscotti for dipping. *$$$$; AE, MC, V; no checks; dinner every day (high season), dinner Tues–Sat (low season); full bar; reservations recommended; www.quattrorestaurants.com.* ⬧

RimRock Café / ❂❂❂

2117 Whistler Rd (Highland Lodge), Whistler; 604/932-5565 or 877/932-5589
In the winter, call ahead and reserve a table for two by the stone fireplace at this cozy retreat nestled in the Highland Lodge near Creekside. Abuzz with a hip local crowd, the romantic RimRock is widely deemed Whistler's premier destination for seafood. Start with any of the oyster selections—Rockefeller is a favorite—before enjoying an entrée such as the RimRock Trio an irresistible medley of pan-fried black cod, rare ahi tuna, and grilled prawns. In summer, book a table on the back patio and dine amid the fresh herbs in the chef's garden. *$$$$; AE, MC, V; no checks; dinner every day; full bar; reservations recommended; www.rimrockwhistler.com.*

Trattoria di Umberto / ❂❂❂

4417 Sundial Pl (Mountainside Lodge), Whistler; 604/932-5858
Located inside the Mountainside Lodge, this Italian eatery's two dining rooms are separated by a massive open kitchen, lending to the restaurant's boisterous, and often noisy, atmosphere. The rustic Italian decor adds to Umberto's beguiling atmosphere, but when all is said and done, the restaurant has a devoted fan base due to its phenomenal preparation of traditional Italian dishes. Favorite menu items include a hearty minestrone soup and the Tuscan-style half roasted chicken. For couples seeking unforgettable food in a warm and sexy setting, "the Trat" is as good as it gets. *$$$$; AE, DC, MC, V; no checks; lunch, dinner every day; full bar; reservations recommended; www.umberto.com/truck.htm.* ⬧

♡ Victoria & Vancouver Island

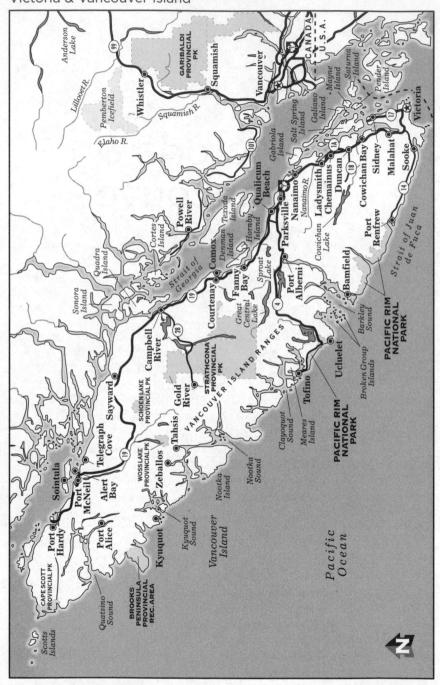

A kiss is a lovely trick designed by nature to stop
speech when words become superfluous.
—Ingrid Bergman

 Victoria & Vancouver Island

This enormous northern island is best known for the charming city of Victoria, although the rugged beaches, pristine forests, and mountain range spanning its nearly 300-mile length are equally compelling. Lavish gardens, elegant tearooms, old-world architecture, and international visitors define highly civilized Victoria, the "more English than the English" capital of British Columbia. Less than an hour's drive from Victoria is exquisite scenery along the southwestern coast near Sooke, and the Cowichan Valley and Saanich Peninsula wineries and farms. Far more remote Tofino and Ucluelet beckon couples with wild, northern beauty.

The Pacific Ocean's influence gives this area the mildest weather in Canada, allowing sublime romantic getaways year-round. Expect lovely summers and cool, mild winters with great storm-watching opportunities along the western coast. In peak season (May through August), crowds are thickest, prices are highest, and tourist services are best. The shoulder months of April and September are ideal for quieter, reduced-rate travel and relatively good weather (some hotel rates do not drop until mid-October), and winter rates are often quite low, a time when many tourism proprietors also take vacations.

Given ferry traveling times, the island's size (almost as big as England!), and the isolation of its smaller towns, any sojourn here should last at least the weekend, preferably longer. Those staying in downtown Victoria can leave the car at home; however, those exploring more remote areas might bring or rent a vehicle. Drivers should reserve ferry times (especially in summer) and come prepared with maps, as roads are not always clearly marked. For more information, contact **Tourism Vancouver Island** (250/754-3500; www.islands.bc.ca) or **Tourism Victoria** (250/953-2033 or 800/663-3883; www.tourismvictoria.com). Note: This section's costs are figured in Canadian funds and correspond with the pricing chart at the front of the book.

Victoria

Romantic Highlights

The famous Fairmont Empress Hotel, stately Parliament buildings, gorgeous Butchart Gardens, lovely parks and museums, cozy restaurants, and Edwardian-style shops—all nestled on a thriving harbor with the snowcapped Olympic Mountains in the distance—make Victoria a romantic haven that attracts visitors by the millions. Hundreds of lodgings in Victoria describe themselves as romantic, so if you select a place not recommended here, do your research: second-rate rooms can sometimes lurk even in hotels with the most storied reputations, and Web sites are no substitution for actual visits.

Victoria is a wonderfully walkable city, and if you stay within a 10-block radius of Government Street, everything you'll want to see and do is easily accessible. **Victoria Harbour Ferries** (250/708-0201; www.harbourferry.com) offers tours of local waterways in adorable 12-passenger ferries. Lovers of the great outdoors can take whale-watching tours on a nimble 40-foot boat with longtime fisherman and naturalist Captain Ron King of **Seaking Adventures** (250/381-4173; www.seaking.ca; Apr–Oct, weather and whales permitting): chances of orca sightings are best May through September. Or schedule an outing with **Blackfish Wilderness Expeditions** (250/216-2389; www.blackfishwilderness.com), which offers options ranging from guided kayak or giant cedar–canoe tours to camping trips on an uninhabited island. Then there's the timeless appeal of traveling by horse-drawn carriage; catch **Victoria Carriage Tours** (250/383-2207 or 877/663-2207; www.victoriacarriage.com) or others at the corner of Belleville and Menzies streets.

If wooing your beloved is on your agenda, we recommend an age-old tactic: chocolate and wine. At **Roger's Chocolates** (913 Government St; 250/384-7021), the handmade chocolates are made fresh daily according to recipes created over a century ago. Nearby at **Artisan Wine Shop** (1007 Government St; 250/384-9994; www.artisanwineshop.ca), enjoy a taste or two of the best offerings from mainland British Columbia's Okanagan Valley and gather some clues about local wine tasting as well.

Beyond edible delights, the shopping in Victoria is divine. Look for English and Irish goods along Government Street, where you will also find the stately **Munro's Books** (1108 Government St; 250/382-2464) and the exotic **Silk Road Aromatherapy & Tea Company & Spa** (1624 Government St; 250/704-2688). Explore the charming shops along Trounce Alley, and then duck into the romantic **Tapa Bar** (620 Trounce Alley; 250/383-0013) for lunch or late-afternoon sangria. **Re-Bar Modern Food** (50 Bastion Square; 250/361-9223), with its wholesome meals and fresh juices, is a local favorite, and **Pescatores** (614 Humboldt St; 250/385-4512) is renowned for its delicious seafood and House Fondue for Two.

Easily accessible both close to downtown Victoria and within an hour of the city are many lush natural areas and manicured gardens (see "Manicured and Wild Beauty"). Above all in Victoria, embrace the charming tradition of a leisurely afternoon tea; we see lots of romantic potential in long afternoons of conversation and decadent treats.

Access & Information

Ferry service is the most common method of traveling to Victoria and Vancouver Island. From Seattle, the **Victoria Clipper** (206/448-5000 in Seattle, 250/382-8100 in Victoria, or 800/888-2535 elsewhere; www.victoriaclipper. com) zips to downtown Victoria via a high-speed, passenger-only catamaran (sailing time: 2–3 hours). From Anacortes, Washington, **Washington State Ferries** (206/464-6400 or 888/808-7977; www.wsdot.wa.gov/ferries) offers one or two trips daily via the scenic San Juan Islands to Sidney, British Columbia, 17 miles (27 km) north of Victoria by Highway 17 (sailing time: 2–3 hours). From Port Angeles, Washington (Olympic Peninsula), **Black Ball Transport** (360/457-4491 in Port Angeles, or 250/386-2202 in Victoria; www.ferrytovictoria.com) operates the MV *Coho* car-and-passenger ferry to downtown Victoria across the Strait of Juan de Fuca on two to four sailings daily (sailing time: 1½ hours). The **Victoria Express** (360/452-8088 or 250/361-9144, www.victoriaexpress.com) is an additional ferry option transporting from Port Angeles to Victoria.

From Bellingham, Washington, **Victoria San Juan Cruises** (360/738-8099 or 800/443-4552; www.whales.com) offers a special passenger-only cruise, including whale watching and a salmon dinner, to Victoria's Inner Harbour between mid-May and early October (sailing time: 3 hours). From Tsawwassen, British Columbia, **BC Ferries** (information: 250/386-3431, or 888/223-3779 in BC; car reservations: 604/444-2890, or 888/724-5223 in BC; www.bcferries.com) runs car ferries from the British Columbia mainland (Tsawwassen terminal) into Swartz Bay, 20 miles (32 km) north of Victoria. On some sailings, staterooms are also available for an extra $25 (sailing time: 1½ hours). Important note: When traveling with a vehicle, especially during summer, it is best to reserve your space on the ferry for a small additional fee, generally under $20 each way. Check the ferry service for reservations and to ensure that you arrive at the appropriate time for boarding. Waits can be long (and frustrating) if you neglect this!

The fastest way to travel, of course, is by air, straight to Victoria's Inner Harbour. **Kenmore Air** (425/486-1257 or 800/543-9595; www.kenmoreair. com) makes regular daily floatplane flights from downtown Seattle. From Sea-Tac International Airport, **Horizon Air** (800/547-9308; www.horizonair. com) flies into Victoria International Airport (1640 Electra Blvd; 250/953-7500), 15 miles (25 km) north of the city. From downtown Vancouver and Vancouver International Airport, **Helijet International** (800/665-4354; www. helijet.com) can get you to Victoria by helicopter. **Harbour Air Seaplanes** (604/274-1277 or 800/665-0212; www.harbour-air.com) carries passengers from Vancouver Harbour to Victoria Harbour; from Vancouver International Airport, fly **Air Canada** (888/247-2262; www.aircanada.ca).

Manicured and Wild Beauty

The lush parks of Victoria make for wonderful romantic strolls. Close to downtown, the city's beloved **Beacon Hill Park** (311 Vancouver St; 250/361-0600; www.beaconhillpark.ca) boasts 184 acres of manicured gardens interspersed with natural forest and meadows, all beautiful spots to steal a kiss. At the rightfully renowned **Butchart Gardens** (800 Benvenuto Ave; 250/652-5256 or 866/652-4422; www.butchart gardens.com), 13 miles (21 km) north, chances are good it'll be a little too crowded to kiss—but 55 acres of astonishing elysian gardens will leave you breathless. Highlights include the Rose, Japanese, and Italian gardens; afternoon tea; Saturday night fireworks in July and August; and festive Christmas light displays. To discover a lesser-known gem, visit the historic Japanese **Abkhazi Garden** (10-minute drive or bus ride from downtown; 250/598-8096; www.conservancy.bc.ca/abkhazi; 11am–5pm every day Mar–Sept, by appointment other times), known as "the garden that love built." **Victorian Garden Tours** (250/380-2797; www.victorian gardentours.com; reservations required) offers individually tailored small-group guided walks through some of Victoria's most beautiful public and private gardens at their peak. Transportation is provided, and a traditional English tea can be arranged.

Up island, more beautiful gardens abound, ranging from traditional and formal to tropical, woodland, and edible. You will find luscious, edible

Once you arrive, stop by the centrally located **Tourism Victoria Visitor Info Centre** (812 Wharf St; 250/953-2033; www.tourismvictoria.com) for maps and information about tours and services in Victoria and surrounding areas. For accommodations reservations, contact **Tourism Victoria** (800/663-3883; www.tourismvictoria.com) or **Hello BC** (888/435-5622; www.hellobc. com). Victoria's bus system, operated by **BC Transit** (250/382-6161; www. bctransit.com), can take you anywhere in the city; call for information about bus routes. If you are not a resident of Canada, you might qualify for reimbursement of the goods and services tax (GST) charged on some purchases. Most lodgings provide the required forms and information explaining how you can submit your receipts for reimbursement.

Romantic Wineries

While Victoria has traditionally been a tourist destination, food and wine lovers are discovering the immense (and delicious) potential of the island's Cowichan Valley (45 minutes from downtown Victoria) and pastoral Saanich Peninsula (30 minutes from downtown Victoria). A short hop on the **Mill Bay**

gardens on the grounds of **Sooke Harbour House** (see Romantic Lodgings), and a big range of botanical, woodland, and herb gardens up the interior eastern coast of the island. Consult a helpful garden-trail guide (www.vancouverislandgardentrail.com) for specific information.

You can also find natural peace and quiet at **Mount Douglas Park** (5 miles/8 km north of town off Hwy 17; exit to Cordova Bay Rd and follow it south to the park). This 500-acre rain forest on the ocean's edge is miraculously quiet and serene; take a picnic down the beach trails to the winding shoreline or climb the 700-foot (213-m) summit for a 360-degree view of Victoria, the ocean, and the mountains of Washington State. If a wildly scenic afternoon drive sounds romantic, take the **Malahat** (Trans-Canada Hwy/Hwy 1, from Victoria to Mill Bay), for one of the prettiest routes on the island. Lush Douglas-fir forests hug the narrow-lane highway taking you past **Goldstream Provincial Park** (3400 Trans-Canada Hwy/Hwy 1; 250/478-9414; www.goldstreampark.com), where hundreds of bald eagles gather to feed on salmon between mid-December and February. At the summit, northbound pullouts offer breathtaking views over Saanich Inlet and the surrounding undeveloped hills. You can enjoy the view while lunching on the deck of the **Malahat Mountain Inn** (265 Trans-Canada Hwy/Hwy 1; 250/478-1944; www.malahatmountaininn.com) before wine and produce tasting your way through the **Cowichan Valley** (see Romantic Wineries).

Ferry (250/386-3431; www.bcferries.com) links the valley and peninsula and creates a romantic circle tour from Victoria. With both regions less than an hour north, it is possible to enjoy an afternoon wine tour and return to Victoria for dinner. If you drive, the area is well marked, and a touring map is readily available (www.wineislands.ca); however, nothing beats **Crush Wine Tours** (250/888-5748 or 877/888-5748; www.crushwinetours.com), whose owner, Marlisa Hollands, guides you on relaxed, educational treks to some of the best wineries and farms.

Cherry Point Vineyards / ❂❂❂

840 Cherry Point Rd, Cobble Hill; 250/743-1272
You will be charmed upon entering this First Nations' Cowichan Tribe winery, famous for its blackberry dessert wine and Solera-aged blackberry vintage. Grapes grown here at the vineyard, located in the midst of old-growth forest and cooled by its location near the water, include the island's predominant Ortega, Pinot Gris, and Pinot Noir. After your tasting, head to the bistro overlooking the vineyards and enjoy traditionally prepared smoked or

tempura-battered salmon and many other local specialties. The vineyard hosts jazz concerts all summer long. *No checks; every day (tasting room), every day Apr–Dec (bistro); www.cherrypointvineyards.com.* &

Glenterra Vineyards / ✪✪✪

3897 Cobble Hill Rd, Cobble Hill; 250/743-2330
In addition to Glenterra's delicious wines (try the delicate estate Pinot Noir and the amazing Vivace and Brio blends), their small cafe, Thistles, offers diners vineyard, mountain, and forest views from indoor tables and outdoor patio seats. Enjoy locally harvested salads, excellent wine pairings, and creatively prepared food at this hidden gem. *No checks; 11–5pm Thurs–Mon, dinner Fri–Sun May–Oct, Fri–Mon Oct–April; www.glenterravineyards.com.* &

Merridale Estate Cidery / ✪✪✪✪

1230 Merridale Rd, Cobble Hill; 250/743-4293 or 800/998-9908
The setting of this premier artisan cidery will enchant you even before you enter the building. A self-guided tour takes you through the property's orchard where you can learn about the cider-making process. Taste a dramatic range of ciders, as well as the fermenting Calvados brandy; then cozy in for your own orchard picnic or enjoy the delicious culinary treats at on-site La Pommeraie Bistro overlooking the beautifully landscaped grounds. Summer Sunday evenings bring back-porch dining, live music, and pizza cooked in the wood-fired brick oven. *No checks; 9am–5:30pm every day May–Oct (call for seasonal hours); www.merridalecider.com.* &

Zanatta Winery / ✪✪✪✪

5039 Marshall Rd, Duncan; 250/748-2338
Specializing in Italian-style sparkling wines, a Zanatta wine tasting is definitely a call for celebration. Enjoy the range of bubblies then dive into Zanatta's Taglio Rosso and 100 percent estate Pinot Nero in their busy, informative tasting room. With its comfortable 1903 farmhouse vibe, wraparound veranda, and bocce court, this winery/restaurant definitely encourages visitors to linger. In fact, stick around for a fabulous dining experience at on-site Vinoteca. *No checks; 12pm–4:30pm Wed–Sun April–Dec; www.zanatta.ca.* &

Romantic Lodgings

Abbeymoore Manor Bed & Breakfast Inn / ✪✪✪

1470 Rockland Ave, Victoria; 250/370-1470 or 888/801-1811
This 1912 Rockland mansion, a 20-minute walk from Inner Harbour, is one of Victoria's most relaxed and friendly bed-and-breakfasts with beautiful guest spaces on the veranda and in the cozy fireplace parlor. Room options abound with lower-level one-bedroom suites, five charming (phone- and TV-free) adults-only rooms above the main floor, and the private and self-sufficient (full kitchen) Penthouse Suite, where the treetop view from bed is

blissful. Our favorite is the Master Bedroom, with its king bed, sitting area, bathtub, and entrance to a spacious upstairs veranda (shared with the Iris Room, but separated by planters). In all rooms, count on luxurious touches including fine linens, terry robes, flowers, chocolates, and wonderful snacks. Hosts book in-room spa services, tours, and dining and happily surprise guests with extra touches for special events. A multicourse breakfast, often featuring their wonderful red Thai curry prawn omelet, is served in the light-filled sunroom or on the terrace. *$$$; MC, V; no checks; www.abbey moore.com.* ♿

Abigail's Hotel / ⬢⬢⬢⬣

906 McClure St, Victoria; 250/388-5363 or 800/561-6565
Abigail's prides itself on romantic touches in the original 17 rooms of this four-story 1930s Tudor building and 6 newer, spacious rooms in the neighboring replica. In the original building, our favorites are the two original top-floor Honeymoon Suites (no elevator, so if climbing up three flights of stairs sounds unromantic, don't book these); in the new building, we like the Coach House rooms, historically designed with modern amenities. All of the Coach House rooms enjoy oversized jetted tubs, wood-burning fireplaces, and delicious king beds; room C1 has a balcony. (Light sleepers might request a room away from busy Quadra Street.) Afternoon drinks and hors d'oeuvres and a three-course breakfast are served daily downstairs, though you can request breakfast in bed for a small fee. To ensure that your stay is enjoyable, the staff offers additional services for no (or reasonable) charge. Feeling inspired? Book an all-inclusive Elopement Package or a service at Pearl, the in-house luxury spa. *$$$$; AE, MC, V; no checks; www.abigailshotel.com.*

The Aerie Resort & Spa / ⬢⬢⬢⬣

600 Ebedora Ln, Malahat; 250/743-7115 or 800/518-1933
A beautiful half-hour drive from Victoria leads to this grandiose faux-Mediterranean villa complex with spectacular views of the distant Olympic Mountains, tree-covered hills, and peaceful fjords below. While the famously opulent interior may overwhelm those with simpler tastes, choose among the 35 rooms and suites to find one that fits your style; most offer tubs for two, private decks, and fireplaces. Romantics seeking the ultimate in luxury, privacy, and scenery may opt for one of the six suites in the separate two-story Villa Cielo, enjoying terraced gardens, a reproduction of Michelangelo's *David*, and expansive views of Finlayson Arm and distant mountains. Guests have access to the resort's facilities, including three kiss-worthy spots: an outdoor hot tub with a view, a beautiful glass-enclosed pool, and a luxurious spa. A complimentary full breakfast is served in the elegant dining room overlooking the inspiring mountain scenery. Lunch and dinner are also available to both guests and nonguests. *$$$$; AE, DC, MC, V; no checks; www. aerie.bc.ca.*

Three Days of Victoria Romance

Day One: Victoria is filled with traditionally romantic sensibilities; spend your first day taking in the city's downtown sights on a horse-drawn carriage for two before traveling to and wandering the **Butchart** or **Abkazi Gardens** and nibbling at one of the garden's wonderful tea services. If you still have time and energy, enjoy a few nearby Saanich Peninsula wineries, including **Winchester Cellars** (6170 Old West Saanich Rd; 250/544-8217; www.winchestercellars.com). When you arrive at the **Fairholme Manor**, the comfortable suites will make it difficult to pull yourself away for the dinner you already reserved at the historic, beautifully restored **Empress Dining Room**. After your meal, wander the impressive building and stop by the Empress Hotel's exotic **Bengal Lounge** for a nightcap before an evening back at the manor lulls you into blissful slumber (or something like that).

Day Two: After a delicious gourmet breakfast at the **Fairholme Manor**, arrange for Marlisa Hollands, owner of **Crush Wine Tours**, to guide you to some of the Cowichan Valley's most enchanting wineries. With her directional savvy, as well as her excellent wine background and knowledge of local food and wine artisans, the two of you are free to sit back and enjoy the introduction to Vancouver Island's wine country. When you return to Victoria, check into **Villa Marco Polo Inn** and rejuvenate for the evening with a prearranged in-house massage for two before your dinner reservations at the tiny French **L'Ecole**. Return to the villa and enjoy your sumptuous room.

Day Three: Upon departing Villa Marco Polo Inn, take the 30-minute drive up the western coast to Sooke. In summer, enjoy the wilderness your way—whether that's hiking, biking, kayaking, or taking a zip-line adventure—and by all means stop by **Smokin' Tuna Cafe** for lunch. Before or after checking into the memorable **Sooke Harbour House**, stroll arm-in-arm along Whiffen Spit, an excellent walk near the hotel, as you anticipate your evening's meal at the **Sooke Harbour House Restaurant**—take the plunge and allow your server to pair your meal with the perfect wines.

Amore by the Sea
Bed and Breakfast Inn and Seaside Spa / ✿✿✿✦

246 Delgada Rd, Victoria; 250/474-5505

The unabashed goal of the innkeepers at Amore by the Sea is to provide a pampering, memorable experience for guests at this oceanfront property on 1½ acres of Victoria's west shore, about a 20 minute drive from downtown. With three ocean-view suites, luxurious amenities, private beach access, and an on-site spa using sumptuous local products, they definitely provide the atmosphere. Enjoy sun- and moonrises as well as views of the cove and city lights from any of the guest suites, in addition to electric fireplaces and Jacuzzi or hydrotherapy tubs. For its two fireplaces, double spa shower, hydrotherapy tub, and heated floors and towel bars, we recommend Sea Star, though the views from the tub and bed of Sea Spray and the balcony of Seascape are also wonderful. Complimentary slippers, guest sketchbooks, binoculars, Roger's Chocolates, morning yoga, and delicious breakfasts are welcome touches. Before you leave a staff member will photograph you and your amore, with the stunning ocean as your backdrop, and then e-mail the photo to you. *$$$–$$$$; MC, V; no checks; www.amorebythesea.com.*

Andersen House Bed & Breakfast / ✪✪✪

301 Kingston St, Victoria; 250/388-4565 or 877/264-9988
Upon entering this 1891 Queen Anne Victorian, with its high ceilings, hardwood floors, African masks, and Cubist-influenced artwork, you know that the Andersen House is run by artists. Each guest room is distinctively appointed with antiques, hand-knotted Persian tribal rugs, stained-glass windows, and contemporary art; all have private entrances and offer romantic touches such as robes, champagne flutes, and CD players. Our favorite is the sunny Casablanca Room, where you can soak window-side in the oversize air-jet tub, open French doors to your private deck for magnificent views of the Olympics, or descend the curved staircase to the lush garden. The cozy ground-level Garden Studio is another great choice. The backyard garden offers the property's best places to kiss—dappled sunlight streams through tree branches onto a graceful brick patio, and evenings bring secluded fireside romance. Breakfast, a gourmet feast, is served in the dramatic dining room. Best of all, this gem is located right downtown. *$$$–$$$$; MC, V; no checks; www.andersenhouse.com.*

Beaconsfield Inn / ✪✪✪

998 Humboldt St, Victoria; 250/384-4044 or 888/884-4044
The innkeepers carefully maintain the traditional old-world elegance of this beautifully restored Edwardian manor a few blocks from the downtown core. Passing from the well-manicured gardens and plant-filled sunroom to the mahogany walls and roaring fireplace of the main entrance, you'll feel immediately at home, especially with afternoon tea, sherry, and snacks served in the impressive library. All nine rooms have gorgeous antiques, fine linens, and down comforters, and several have spa-quality bathtubs and fireplaces. Three walls of original leaded stained–glass windows frame the main-floor rosy-toned Parlor Room, which also boats a fireplace and Jacuzzi tub. Upstairs, the sumptuous Emily Carr Suite offers a lovers' oasis with a beautiful navy-blue bed alcove, two-person Jacuzzi tub set before the wood-burning fireplace, and crystal chandelier lighting a two-person shower. The friendly hosts are

professional, unobtrusive, and readily available. A full breakfast is served in the intimate dining room or adjacent sunroom. *$$$–$$$$; AE, MC, V; no checks; www.beaconsfieldinn.com.*

Brentwood Bay Lodge & Spa / ❂❂❂❂

849 Verdier Ave, Brentwood Bay; 250/544-2079 or 888/544-2079
This modern cedar-sided resort provides a relaxing, pleasure-filled getaway among the Saanich Peninsula's wineries, organic farms, and sheltered coves, 20 minutes from downtown Victoria. Windows and private balconies in all 33 rooms overlook the marina and forested hills; for more privacy and less noise, request rooms away from the restaurant and pool. The decor is hip West Coast: serene sage-green colors, gas fireplaces, handcrafted king-size beds, sunset tubs or jetted showers, and an outdoor pool and hot tub overlooking the bay. Splurge in the resort's spa with the decadent couples room for massages, mud wraps, and a private rain-forest shower for two. Bask in this serene vibe or enjoy the opportunity to take an eco-cruiser, a water taxi, or a kayak paddle to nearby Butchart Gardens. Enjoy your sparkling local wine greeting, and keep things cozy by opting for breakfast in bed. The Brentwood Seagrille and Pub (see Romantic Restaurants) beckons couples with its stellar views and stand-out cuisine. *$$$$; AE, MC, V; no checks; www.brentwood baylodge.com.* &

Fairholme Manor / ❂❂❂❂

638 Rockland Pl, Victoria; 250/598-3240 or 877/511-3322
Prepare for romantic indulgence and beautiful surroundings in this exquisitely restored 1885 Italianate mansion set on a parklike acre in historic, close-in Rockland. Excellent planning by proprietors Sylvia and Ross Main has resulted in individual appeal and kiss-inducing amenities in every tasteful, spacious room, although we certainly have our favorites. The Olympic Grand Suite features a double soaking tub, a luxurious king-size sleigh bed, a sparkling chandelier, robin's egg–blue ceilings, an immaculate white sofa facing a wood-burning fireplace, and a deck providing sweeping views of snow-capped peaks, dazzling water, and lush gardens. Other sublimely romantic spots are the glamorous Fairholme Grand Suite, the lovely Rose Suite with a kitchen, and the garden view and cozy cottage feel of the Tuscan Suite. All rooms offer 14-foot ceilings, original artwork, fireplaces, mini fridges, coffeemakers, robes, abundant fresh flowers, imported chocolates, floating candles, and in-room spa services to indulge you. The next morning, the charming dining room alone may lure you down for a multi-course breakfast featuring menu items from Sylvia's recently published *Fabulous Fairholme* cookbook. *$$$–$$$$; AE, MC, V; no checks; www.fairholmemanor.com.*

Fairmont Empress Hotel / ●●●●

721 Government St, Victoria; 250/384-8111 or 800/441-1414
Palatial and utterly elegant as it passes its 2008 century mark, the Empress
Hotel is to Victoria what Big Ben is to London and the Eiffel Tower is to
Paris; and it certainly draws the same crowds. Among the Empress's domin-
ions are the opulent Palm Court, with its magnificent stained-glass ceiling;
the grandly formal Empress Room (see Romantic Restaurants); the famous
and newly restored Tea Lobby; and the unique Bengal Lounge, a British
Colonial–inspired room that's perhaps the best place in Victoria to sip a
martini and enjoy weekend Curry or Death-by-Chocolate buffets. In the
perfectly tended rose gardens, potential kissing spots await discovery among
the magnolia trees and flower-covered trellises. High-season rates can be
steep for an overnight stay, but your time will be memorable, particularly
if you splurge on a Harborview Deluxe or Signature room, with stunning
views and unique Empress elements like a round bed tucked into a turret.
Fairmont and Deluxe rooms are expensive, small, and lacking views, but at
least they get you in the 477-room landmark. Reserving the Fairmont Gold
package will provide you a pampering boutique-hotel experience, and both
guests and nonguests may book conventional and alternative treatments in
the hotel's Willow Stream Spa. With this much romance under one roof,
the Empress is a favorite spot for elopements, anniversary celebrations, and
second honeymoons. *$$$$; AE, DC, DIS, MC, V; no checks; www.fairmont.
com/empress.* &

Humboldt House / ●●●

867 Humboldt St, Victoria; 250/383-0152 or 888/383-0327
This skinny Victorian home, located next to St. Ann's Academy, specializes in
romance with greetings of sparkling wine and house-made truffles, in-room
breakfasts, and extra service packages. All rooms are spacious and appeal to
different tastes; however, for privacy, quiet, and better views, we recommend
top-floor rooms away from the street. For dramatic color schemes, try the
Mikado and Oriental rooms or the British Colonial theme of street-facing
Edward's Room. Our favorite is the green-vaulted Gazebo Room with pretty
views and cozy seating. The Celebration Room is a frilly dream come true
with lit arches, angels, a glittering chandelier, and a lace-canopied bed. All
rooms have wood-burning fireplaces, CD players, and most have elevated
Jacuzzi tubs; however, some might find washing arrangements tricky with
only handheld showerheads available in the in-room Jacuzzi. Privacy reigns
supreme here in your own romantic universe, especially when breakfast is
delivered through the room's two-way butler's pantry. *$$$$; AE, MC, V; no
checks; www.humboldthouse.com.*

Villa Marco Polo Inn / ⬡⬡⬡⬡

1524 Shasta Pl, Victoria; 250/370-1524 or 877/601-1524
Villa Marco Polo is a feast for the senses—magnificent rooms, stunning villa-style grounds, and romantic boons like fine linens, flowers, and silver-domed chocolate turndowns. This tastefully restored 1923 Rockland Italian Renaissance–style mansion offers formal beauty and a relaxed adult atmosphere. All five luxurious, soundproof rooms enjoy sublime ambience, but we have three romantic favorites. The second-floor Zanzibar Suite boasts a lovely fireplace, a king bed, a romantically lit bathing haven with double soaking pedestal tub and shower, and French doors to a balcony with mountain, water, and garden views. Equally grand, the Persia Suite offers a lovers' bonus of view seats in a double-jetted tub, Persian rug and tapestries, and a king-size canopy bed. The smaller main-floor Silk Road Room enjoys a barrel vault ceiling and hand-painted angel murals. Roses, champagne, massages, and concierge services are easily arrranged here. Mornings bring four-course gourmet breakfasts in the elegant dining room, private garden room, or terrace. *$$$$; MC, V; no checks; www.villamarcopolo.com.*

Romantic Restaurants

Brasserie L'Ecole / ⬡⬡⬡

1715 Government St, Victoria; 250/475-6260
Those of the "bread, wine, and thou" school of romance will delight in this cozy 13-table French restaurant tucked in between two Chinatown grocery stores. Chef/owner Sean Brennan and sommelier/owner Marc Morrison have transformed this former schoolhouse into a nostalgic brasserie, complete with sensuous pomegranate walls, vintage fir floors, lofty ceilings, linens, and candlelight everywhere. Ask for the front nook or the hideaway in back, or—in summer—opt for one of two tables in the tiny, greenery-filled courtyard. Local, organic meat and produce are featured in Brennan's hearty, unpretentious French-country cooking. The menu changes daily but always showcases a mastery of French classics. Everything on the extensive (predominantly French) wine list is available by the glass. *$$$; MC, V; no checks; dinner Tues–Sat; full bar; reservations recommended; www.lecole.ca.* ♿

Brentwood Seagrille and Pub / ⬡⬡⬡⬡

849 Verdier Ave (Brentwood Bay Lodge & Spa),
Brentwood Bay; 250/544-2079 or 888/544-2079
The Brentwood Seagrille and Pub—the Brentwood Bay Lodge & Spa's (see Romantic Lodgings) showcase restaurant—evokes a cool, almost urban, edge with two-story-high sea-view windows, art-covered walls, and an open kitchen with a wood-fired grill. The locally sourced menu showcases the best of Vancouver Island's bounty, including local island cheeses, meats, and produce. Fish options, including sablefish or salmon, are sure to be outstanding

with beautifully presented vegetables as costars, and well-known pastry chef Bruno Feldeisen creates seasonal desserts so addictive you may need an order to go. For casual meals, try the resort's marine pub or the bakery/deli/coffee bar, where you can fill your picnic basket or purchase decadent pastries. An on-site wine shop, carrying hard-to-find local vintages, reminds us that, yes, these folks have thought of everything. *$$$$; AE, MC, V; checks OK; breakfast, lunch every day, dinner Wed–Sun; full bar; reservations recommended; www.brentwoodbaylodge.com.* &

Cafe Brio / ❀❀❀

944 Fort St, Victoria; 250/383-0009 or 866/270-5461
The ornately gated patio and sun-kissed yellow entrance beckons diners, and the interior, though loud and dimly lit, welcomes guests to this charming Italian restaurant with cozy pine booths, earthy colors, and neo-Renaissance decor. Fortunately the food, though pricey, is consistently, blissfully delicious with daily menu changes adapting to supply from local organic farms. The wine list is well chosen, with a good selection of West Coast wines and minimal markups. Decadent desserts are made in-house: try the pear *tarte Tatin*, or the rich dark-chocolate timbale. *$$$–$$$$; AE, MC, V; no checks; dinner every day; full bar; reservations recommended; www.cafe-brio.com.* &

Camille's / ❀❀❀❀

45 Bastion Square, Victoria; 250/381-3433
Camille's is Victoria's most seductive haunt, and upon entering this irresistible lower-level restaurant, you'll see why. Two eclectically decorated, partitioned dining rooms provide many cozy nooks for private dining booths, but for romantic purposes we especially like tables 2, 3, 8a, and 12. With five master chefs including chef/owner David Mincey, the kitchen nimbly adapts its menu weekly and, as an option, prepares a five-course chef's tasting meal paired with perfect wines. The internationally inspired, seasonally changing menu emphasizes fresh fish and local meat and produce; game is a particular specialty, as is the witty, informative wine list. *$$$–$$$$; MC, V; no checks; dinner Tues–Sun (call for seasonal closures); full bar; reservations recommended; www.camillesrestaurant.com.*

The Empress Room / ❀❀❀❀

721 Government St (Fairmont Empress Hotel), Victoria; 250/384-8111 or 800/441-1414
Whether you're sitting harborside or fireside, the surroundings of the formal, exquisite Empress Room are sure to inspire memorable kisses. Beautiful china, ornately carved box-beam ceilings, and light glistening through extensive wine racks will set the stage for romance as you enjoy a selection of delicious, classically prepared entrées, decadent desserts, and mouth-watering artisan cheeses, all, of course, with a local, organic focus. Let your expert

server recommend wine for your selections so that you can drink in every moment. *$$$$; AE, DC, DIS, MC, V; no checks; breakfast, lunch, dinner every day; full bar; reservations recommended; www.fairmont.comempress.* &

Il Terrazzo Ristorante / ◐◐◐

555 Johnson St, Victoria; 250/361-0028
Inside this beautiful Italian restaurant in busy Inner Harbour, the tables can feel cramped and the room bustling, but the romantic charm will ultimately win you over. Exposed-brick walls and archways, wrought-iron candelabras, and hardwood floors create an intimate, casual ambience, and the light-infused covered terrace with six outdoor fireplaces and abundant flowers is a blissful spot to linger (weekends only, Oct–Apr). Excellent Northern Italian cuisine—including *funghi arrosto*, risotto with clams and Italian sausage, osso buco, and fresh, local fish—is served by knowledgeable, friendly waitstaff. An award-winning wine list showcases a range of fine Italian and new-world wines. *$$$; AE, DC, MC, V; no checks; lunch Mon–Sat (Mon–Fri in winter), dinner every day; full bar; reservations recommended; www.ilterrazzo.com.*

Matisse / ◐◐◐◖

512 Yates St, Victoria; 250/480-0883
A profusion of flowers, candlelight, and sensuous Edith Piaf lyrics will greet you as you enter this delightful French restaurant, which regularly inspires engagements and other declarations of love. Enjoy executive chef Peter Heptonstall's four-course prix-fixe menu or select from signature options of lobster bisque or escargot, and entrées such as classically prepared lamb, duck, beef, and seafood. Gregarious owner and maître d' John Phillips will ensure that the two of you have a memorable, delicious experience. Whatever your selections, save your appetite for dessert—if the silky crème brûlée with its delicate handmade butterfly within a net of spun sugar doesn't enchant you, nothing will! *$$$$; MC, V; no checks; dinner Wed–Sun; full bar; reservations recommended; www.restaurantmatisse.com.*

The Mint / ◐◐◐

1414 Douglas St, Victoria; 250/386-6468
With Tibetan and Nepalese dishes and a sometimes-loud atmosphere, the Mint is not your typical romantic choice; however, the low-lit ambience, exotic food, and intimate seating of this basement restaurant are a winning combination—all at a very reasonable price. Select from creative, minty cocktails or the adventuresome wine and beer lists before settling into momos, naan curry pizzas, and other appetizers. Main dish specialties include lamb, mango, or butter chicken curry, each with distinctive seasoning and heat (which the vanilla-bean ice cream with ground pistachios will certainly sooth). Want extra privacy? Request table 35, known to locals as the "rockstar table," and romance the night away. *$$$; AE, MC, V; no checks; dinner every day (call for seasonal closures); full bar; reservations recommended.*

Paprika Bistro / ●●●❶

2524 Estevan Ave, Victoria; 250/592-7424
The sophisticated, modern aesthetic of this excellent Oak Bay restaurant offers a change of pace from the more ornate, formal downtown scene and is a local, sometimes noisy, favorite. Four tiny dining rooms, including an intimate six-seat wine room, are cozy, candlelit, and adorned with lovely artwork. The chef draws from his Hungarian heritage and training in classic French cooking, and main courses and house-made charcuterie tempt with an array of fresh, local seafood as well as venison, rabbit, and duck. All selections on the creative, worldly wine list are available by the glass. The owners recently opened a small-plates wine bar, Stage (1307 Gladstone Ave; 250/388-4222), providing the perfect opportunity to snuggle up to wonderful food and wine. *$$$; AE, MC, V; no checks; dinner Mon–Sat; full bar; reservations recommended; www.paprika-bistro.com.*

Sooke

Romantic Highlights

Located a half hour west of bustling Victoria, Sooke is a friendly little town with a surrounding area renowned for its natural splendor. Along with pristine coastline and serene views, it offers romantic solitude and some sublime accommodations for couples. The entire coast between Sooke and Port Renfrew, farther west, is filled with excellent parks with trails leading down to ocean beaches. Quiet time together and outdoor exploration will be highlights of any stay in this region. If you drive from Victoria, stop to see the magnificent **Hatley Castle**, formerly owned by the Dunsmuir family, at Royal Roads University (2005 Sooke Rd, Victoria; 250/391-2511 or 250/391-2600, ext. 4456; www.hatleycastle.com). The exquisite grounds are open daily, dawn to dusk, and guided tours are available.

Sooke takes its name from the T'Sou-ke people, the first inhabitants of the area. Once identified with its logging and fishing industries, Sooke's economy now relies far more on tourism, with visitors from all over the world exploring the area's kiss-worthy beaches and incredible hiking trails. Summer is a popular time to visit, but the shoulder seasons are ideal for enjoying the slow, small-town pace and moderate climate without the crowds. There is a growing restaurant scene, and romantic lodgings abound. Sooke is also home to a thriving art community and one of the largest juried fine-arts shows in British Columbia, which draws approximately 10,000 people each August. You can see art year-round at the **Blue Raven Gallery** (1971 Kaltasin Rd; 250/881-0528; www.blueravengallery.com), the **Sooke Fine Art Gallery** (6703A W Coast Rd; 250/642-6411; www.sketching. com), or the **Sooke Harbour House** (see Romantic Lodgings and Romantic Restaurants). For local crafts and organic vegetables, on Saturdays stop by the **Sooke Country Market** (at Otter Point Rd and Sooke Rd; 250/642-7528; May–Sept). It might not be highly romantic, but hearty diner fare and an authentic local

Sooke Adventure: Pacific Ocean Wanderings

The area between Sooke and Port Renfrew along the Pacific Ocean teems with beautiful views and many memorable places to cozy up with your sweetie. Enjoy a walk made for nature lovers, bird lovers, and lovers in general along **Whiffen Spit**, a narrow point that stretches far out into the water. From here, the sublime dining room at Sooke Harbour House (see Romantic Restaurants) is only footsteps away. For a longer hike, an ideal destination is the 3,512 acres of wilderness in **East Sooke Regional Park** (from Sooke, follow Hwy 14 toward Victoria, go right on Gillespie Rd, then right on E Sooke Rd to reach the park entrances at Anderson Cove Rd and Pike Rd; go left to reach the Aylard Farm entrance; www.sooke outdoors.com/eastsookepark). Here, trails winding through pristine forest and beautiful beaches offer phenomenal views.

Aylard Farm is an easy excursion and an excellent place to have a romantic picnic, or—if you go between May and September—don't miss the opportunity for a wonderful lunch (or Friday evening meal) at **Smokin' Tuna Cafe** (2412 Becher Bay Rd, Sooke; 250/642-3816), an amazing marina restaurant serving Hot Tuna Smoked Tarts, Cortes Mussels and Clams, and other seafood delights from an unlikely location in a fishing trailer park. **Anderson Cove** and **Pike Road** are also spots from which to enjoy more vigorous hikes and sweeping or tide-pool views. For a cool dip on a hot day, check out the natural swimming holes at **Sooke Potholes Provincial Park** (3 miles/5 km north of Sooke at the end of Sooke River Rd).

If you have time for a morning or afternoon excursion, visit the beautiful shoreline stretches known as **French Beach** (13 miles/21 km west of Sooke on Hwy 14) and **China Beach** (23 miles/37 km west of Sooke on Hwy 14, past the small town of Jordan River). Both are rugged, romantic spots where you can ramble through secluded groves of trees and explore spacious beaches dotted with tide pools (check a tide table for low tide). If you are in the mood for more vigorous exploration, a 45-minute forested hike leads from the China Beach parking lot to **Mystic Beach**, where shallow caves, a waterfall, and dramatic sandstone cliffs await.

experience can be found in the booths of the '50s-era **Mom's Cafe** (2036 Shields Rd; 250/642-3314). Or try the traditional pub fare at the historic **17 Mile House** (5126 Sooke Rd; 250/642-5942).

Sooke is famous for whale watching, and orcas are visible in local waters between May and October. The grace and agility of these giant mammals is amazing. **Sooke Coastal Explorations** (6971 W Coast Rd/Hwy 14; 250/642-2343; www.sookewhalewatching.com; closed Nov–Apr) or **West Coast Wildlife**

Adventures (Sooke Harbour Resort and Marina, 6971 W Coast Rd; 250/880-1024 or 888/880-1024; www.westcoastwhales.ca) are both highly recommended for their expertise and impressive sighting records. No matter how many times you encounter these larger-than-life creatures, a sighting makes for a singularly romantic experience. For another way to get closer to wildlife and scenery, look no further than **Rush Adventures** (5449 Sooke Rd; 250/642-2159; www.rush-adventures.com) for half-, full-, or multiday kayak tours and lessons.

The Galloping Goose Trail runs from Victoria through Sooke and past many amazing natural areas. If you are feeling adventurous, take your bicycles on the ferry, enjoy Victoria, and bike to Sooke. Or, for those less adventurous, simply walk into **Sooke Cycle** (6707 W Sooke Rd; 250/642-3123; www.sookebikes.com) and select the perfect ride for a leisurely pedal through town or along the trail.

Sooke is also the proud home to **Zipwest** (5128 Sooke Rd; 250/642-1933; www.zipwest.ca), offering an especially exhilarating view of the area's wildlife and scenery with eight zip-line cables and two suspension bridges across 100 acres of coastal temperate rain forest.

Access & Information

Sooke is located approximately 30 to 40 minutes by car (depending on traffic) west of Victoria on Highway 14. If you are coming from the Swartz Bay Ferry Terminal, follow the Patricia Bay Highway toward Victoria and turn at the McKenzie exit. This will take you to Highway 1. Proceed on Highway 1 to the Sooke-Colwood exit, take the exit, and follow Highway 14. For more information, check out the Sooke community Web site (www.sookenet.com) or contact the **Sooke Visitor Info Centre** (2070 Phillips Rd; 250/642-6351 or 866/888-4748; www.sooke.museum.bc.ca), located in the same building as the Sooke Region Museum.

Romantic Lodgings

Cooper's Cove Guesthouse / ✪✪✪

5301 Sooke Rd, Sooke; 250/642-5727 or 877/642-5727
This waterfront bed-and-breakfast provides guests with a culinary retreat extraordinaire. Chef/owner Angelo Prosperi-Porta offers unique packages such as the Chef's Table, a five-course interactive dinner where he shares professional techniques as he prepares sumptuous Italian-influenced cuisine. The romance here extends well beyond the kitchen and colorful gardens to the four secluded, soundproof rooms with private water-view decks or balconies, fireplaces, fridges, and luxurious bedding, robes, and slippers. Flowers, chocolate truffles, and sherry greet you upon arrival. Our romantic favorite is the Blue Heron Room for its private entrance and hot tub on a secluded ocean-view deck. Below the house, another hot tub perches on a lovely glass-screened deck. In the morning, Angelo himself prepares delicious and

beautifully presented breakfast feasts, which guests enjoy at intimate breakfast tables. *$$$; MC, V; no checks; closed Jan; www.cooperscove.com.*

Hartmann House / ◉◉◉◉

5262 Sooke Rd, Sooke; 250/642-3761
With lit paths leading you through a resplendent English cottage garden, this handcrafted, cedar-sided home sets the stage for your own private romance beginning with separate garden entrances to two large, self-contained suites full of enjoyable treats: a whirlpool tub for two, a handmade wooden shower stall, a double-sided fireplace, a kitchenette, a TV and stereo, wide-plank fir floors, and fluffy robes. Expect warm welcomes with fruit, cheese, champagne, and chocolates, and then enter into quiet seclusion. The slightly larger Honeymoon Suite was built around a four-poster "barley-twist" king-size canopied bed, hand-carved from western red cedar. (It's one of the most romantic beds we've ever seen!) Carefully selected decor and gorgeous woodwork lend elegance to this open, light-filled room. The Hydrangea Suite is similarly luxurious, with a sleigh bed and French doors leading to a secluded garden patio. In the morning, a decadent breakfast is subtly delivered to your room. *$$$; MC, V; no checks; www.hartmannhouse.bc.ca.*

Markham House / ◉◉◉

1853 Connie Rd, Sooke; 250/642-7542 or 888/256-6888
This Tudor home, tucked away on a gorgeous 10-acre estate, offers an intimate getaway on the outskirts of Sooke. The flower-filled grounds are a pleasure to explore with croquet or bocce, a putting green, private gazebo with hot tub, and patio overlooking a trout pond. The full breakfast, as well as afternoon tea and pastries, is served on the patio or in the nearby breakfast room, and chocolates and turndown service are much-appreciated touches. Of the three guest rooms on the second floor, our choice—the spacious Garden Suite—has beautiful window views, an inviting double Jacuzzi tub, an electric fireplace, and a king-size bed. A trail from the house leads to our favorite, the Honeysuckle Cottage, a cozy, beautiful, and self-sufficient place to nest in glorious privacy. Revel in your own deck-side private hot tub and have a basket of breakfast goodies delivered to the cottage door. *$$–$$$; AE, DC, DIS, JCB, MC, V; checks OK; www.markhamhouse.com.*

Point No Point Resort / ◉◉◉◉

10829 W Coast Rd, Sooke; 250/646-2020
The pure, rugged beauty of Point No Point, set on a mile of waterfront and 40 acres of untamed wilderness, has offered a sublime retreat from civilization since the 1950s. Today, 24 renovated cabins, all with kitchens, bathrooms, wood-burning fireplaces, and breathtaking water views, cater to those preferring natural beauty over phones and televisions. Sixteen enjoy private deck hot tubs—a truly memorable place to kiss. The Blue Jay and the Otter, two

sides of a spacious luxury duplex cabin, have 18-foot-high view windows, marble soaking tubs, and two-person showers. Other romantic choices are the Eagle and the Orca, two stand-alone log cabins with private outdoor hot tubs and the best views. Trails lead down to an inlet and three gorgeous sandy beaches—yet more fantastic kissing spots. Meals are not included in your stay; however, the dining room serves a highly rated lunch, afternoon tea, and dinner (see Romantic Restaurants). *$$$; MC, V; checks OK; www. pointnopointresort.com.*

Richview House / ◑◑◑◑

7031 Richview Dr, Sooke; 250/642-5520 or 866/276-2480
Handwoven wall hangings and beautiful handmade wooden furniture reflect the low-tech, naturalist simplicity of this waterfront getaway. Located just steps from Sooke Harbour House and Whiffen Spit, the home offers unobstructed views of the Olympics and the water. Come ready to leave the world behind—each of the three rooms has a private entrance, a fireplace or woodstove, a deep soaking tub on a secluded deck, and a panoramic view of the Strait of Juan de Fuca. In the downstairs Garden Spa Room's handcrafted bathroom, a two-headed shower doubles as a marble steam bath with essential oils—downright therapeutic! (Note: Light sleepers may hear noise coming from above.) The two upstairs rooms feature skylights, radiant-heat floors, and wood-burning fireplaces made of beach stone and slate. As the morning fog subsides to make way for the sun, enjoy baked grapefruit, caramelized sweet rolls, and breakfast soufflé with sautéed pears in the bright dining room or in your own room. *$$$; MC, V; checks OK; www.bnbsooke.com.*

Sooke Harbour House / ◑◑◑◑

1528 Whiffen Spit Rd, Sooke; 250/642-3421 or 800/889-9688
A fantastic water's-edge setting, abundant elegance, and Northwest artistry make Sooke Harbour House a sublime, albeit quite expensive, getaway with international acclaim. The 28 individually decorated rooms, which feature captivating views of Sooke Bay, the Strait of Juan de Fuca, and the Olympic Mountains, include thoughtful luxuries like Northwest artistic themes, wood-burning fireplaces, local artwork, fine linens, comfortable sitting areas, vaulted ceilings, beautiful furnishings, wet bars, balconies or patios, and a variety of soaking or jetted-tub options. A lavish complimentary breakfast is delivered to your door, and from May to October (and off-season weekends) a picnic lunch is also included with your stay. As an added indulgence, you can book an in-room spa service. From luxurious extras—such as fresh-cut flowers, plush robes, and decanters of fine port—to the spectacular waterfront setting, the amenities make this spot one of British Columbia's best kissing destinations. *$$$$; AE, DC, MC, V; checks OK; call for weekday closures Dec–Feb; www.sookeharbourhouse.com.* &

Romantic Restaurants

Fuse Waterfront Grill / ◐◐◖

5449 Sooke Rd, Sooke; 250/642-0011
Recently opened Fuse is a wonderful addition filling a Sooke dining gap. With a beautiful patio and interior space looking out to sailboats at Cooper's Cove, the restaurant combines creative food, a small but good wine list, solid beer offerings, and very reasonable prices. Savor entrées focusing on meats and local seafood with Sooke trout, halibut, and shellfish green curry, and select from a range of delicious side vegetables including Moroccan yams, braised greens, mashed potatoes, wild rice, or organic salad. As the sun retreats, your waiter will deliver a snuggly blanket and a huge, decadent pot of chocolate fondue for the two of you to share on the patio. *$$–$$$; AE, MC, V; local checks only; lunch, dinner every day (call for winter closures); full bar; reservations recommended; www.fusewaterfrontgrill.com.*

Markus' Wharfside Restaurant / ◐◐◐◖

1831 Maple Ave S, Sooke; 250/642-3596
This little fisherman's cottage overlooking Sooke Harbour has been transformed into a simple, art-filled Mediterranean restaurant; with just nine tables, the feel is intimate but not crowded. Every table has a water and mountain view, but our favorite space is the fireplace room for its cozy hearth and picture window. European-trained chef Markus Wieland applies his considerable talents to the great bounty of wild seafood and organic produce available locally. Starters include Tuscan seafood soup and baked goat cheese with roasted garlic. For a main course, try a local fish or the tempting daily risotto special and enjoy this intimate experience. *$$$; MC, V; no checks; dinner Tues–Sat (call for winter closures); full bar; reservations recommended; www.markuswharfsiderestaurant.com.* &

Point No Point Resort / ◐◐◐◖

10829 West Coast Rd, Sooke; 250/646-2020
The sunny and sometimes stormy water and mountain views are simply breathtaking from the window-filled dining room at this remote resort. Binoculars are placed at every table in anticipation of the frequent eagle and whale sightings, but the true excitement comes when your food arrives. Creatively prepared lunchtime offerings include creamy seafood chowder, daily pasta dishes, and a smoked-tuna salad like none you've ever tasted. Nighttime brings a lush, candlelit atmosphere with even more elegant and delicious local dishes and desserts. *$$$; MC, V; checks OK; lunch every day, dinner Wed–Sun (closed January); full bar; reservations recommended; www. pointnopointresort.com.* &

Sooke Harbour House / ◐◐◐◐

1528 Whiffen Spit Rd, Sooke; 250/642-3421 or 800/889-9688
Sooke Harbour House (see Romantic Lodgings) lives up to its stellar reputation for a memorable romantic and culinary experience. Owners Frédérique and Sinclair Philip and their team of chefs have garnered international attention for their dedication to the freshest local ingredients combined with a good deal of energy and flashes of innovation. The nightly menu reads like an exotic novel, and glamorous dishes adorned with colorful, edible blossoms and herbs from the inn's own organic gardens complement what dedicated island farmers, fishermen, and the wilderness provide. Thrill seekers can book ahead for the Gastronomic Adventure and enjoy a flight of seven to nine chef-selected courses with wine paired to induce swooning. You'll pay dearly for this memorable meal, but it's worth all the attention to detail. *$$$$; AE, DC, MC, V; checks OK; dinner every day (call for seasonal closures); full bar; reservations required; www.sookeharbourhouse.com.* ♿

Tofino

Romantic Highlights

Getting to this remote, rugged stretch of coast is half the fun, and once you arrive, the wild, unruly, romantic appeal of the region will capture your hearts. During the high season—July and August—the best accommodations are usually booked many months in advance, though August is affectionately known by locals as "Fogust." However, if you plan ahead, warm and sunny days will be your reward. With gorgeous weather and fewer crowds, September is an ideal time to visit. In winter, the two of you can curl up and watch the legendary storms lash the coast. Traveling to Tofino by car makes for a beautiful journey along Highway 4, which crosses Vancouver Island and winds by rivers, lakes, and soaring snow-covered peaks (from Victoria, the trip takes about five hours). Be sure to plan for a stop at **MacMillan Provincial Park** (20 miles/32 km west of Parksville on Hwy 4), with its sky-high old-growth forest of Douglas firs and 800-year-old cedars. Nature trails lined with magnificent trees draped in moss invite you to commune with nature (and each other).

Highway 4 is passable year-round, but try to avoid making the drive at night, as the scenery is not to be missed—and neither are the road's many winding curves. The road splits at the highway's end, with one fork heading north to Tofino, the other south to Ucluelet. Both towns, which began as fishing villages, pride themselves on their natural beauty and wilderness and are known as whale-watching destinations; in March and April, an estimated 20,000 gray whales make their annual migration past these shores. The more-frequented of the two destinations is Tofino, mainly because of its impressive number of wonderfully romantic accommodations. Ucluelet offers fewer amenities, but you'll nonetheless find a growing cluster of craft shops and galleries, excellent beach access, and stunning coastal rain-forest walks along the Wild Pacific Trail. And even if you're staying in Tofino, it's worth the 30-minute drive to the chic **Boat Basin Restaurant** (see Romantic Restaurants) in Ucluelet, set within the upscale **Tauca Lea Resort & Spa** (see Romantic Lodgings). For more casual, hearty posthike meals, don't miss clam chowder at the **Matterson House** (1682 Peninsula Rd, Ucluelet; 250/726-2200; breakfast, lunch, dinner every day).

Most of Tofino's incredible getaways are within a stone's throw of the beach's infinite romantic possibilities: cuddle up and enjoy the pounding surf, hike through the trees along the shore, or head into the chilly water for a salty frolic. In **Pacific Rim National Park Reserve** (250/726-4212), you'll quickly discover why the aptly named Long Beach—all 11 sandy miles (19 km) of it—epitomizes many people's idea of the remote, rugged northern Pacific. The best way to explore it is by hiking the beach, headlands, and woodland trails; stop by the visitor center just inside the park entrance for a free hiker's guide. You can also ask for tips on whale watching and where to see the permanent colonies of basking sea lions. Before you set off, pick up a boxed lunch in town at **Breakers Delicatessen** (4-131 1st St, Tofino; 250/725-2558), or a breakfast sandwich to go from **Caffé Vincenté** (441 Campbell St; 250/725-2599), which offers the best all-day breakfast deal. Additionally, offerings include Belgian waffles, the Big Wave smoked salmon breakfast sandwich, and daily quiche.

Excellent beach walks can also be had on **Chesterman Beach,** the longest beach outside the park, located 3 miles (5 km) south. Watch the many surfers trying to catch waves, or take the plunge yourselves with lessons at the popular **Inner Rhythm Surf Camp** (250/726-2211 or 877/393-7873; www.innerrhythm.net). This reliable outfitter also supplies wetsuits, booties, gloves, and boards, so you can get out there and share salty kisses in the rolling breakers.

For a quieter excursion, spend an afternoon exploring Tofino's small shops and cafes. The mood in this town, tucked between the surf-pounded oceanfront and calm inner inlet, is unpretentious and amiable. You might stroll through galleries like the longhouse of the **Eagle Aerie Gallery** (350 Campbell St; 250/725-3235 or 800/663-0669) or **House of Himwitsa** (300 Main St; 250/725-2017 or 800/899-1947) to see First Nations masks, jewelry, and gifts. The **Lounge Collection** (430 Campbell St; 250/725-3334), an eclectic exhibition of local artists, has been voted Tofino's favorite gallery. For refreshment, join locals for organic coffee and baked treats at the **Common Loaf Bake Shop** (180 1st St; 250/725-3915), enjoy sashimi with a view at **Tough City Sushi** (350 Main St; 250/725-2021), or try lunch or dinner at **Schooner on Second** (331 Campbell St; 250/725-3444). This historic central Tofino restaurant—part red clapboard building, part old schooner—offers great fresh seafood (try the Dungeness crab fresh off the boat). Tofino's clubby hot spot is **Shelter** (601 Campbell St; 250/725-3353), a hip seafood restaurant at the edge of the village known for its cocktails. South of town, stroll through the indigenous plants at the 12-acre **Tofino Botanical Gardens** (1084 Pacific Rim Hwy; 250/725-1220).

Five Best Places to Pick up Picnic Provisions in Tofino

Ambrosia Bakery (Davison Plaza, 1636 Peninsula, Ucluelet; 250/726-7143): Old-world breakfasts, homemade sweets, soups, and specialty sandwiches.

Caffé Vincenté (441 Campbell St, Tofino; 250/725-2599): Coffee, espresso, and baked goods.

Common Loaf Bake Shop (180 1st St, Tofino; 250/725-3915): A wholefoods bake and coffee shop.

Gray Whale Ice Cream & Deli (1950 Peninsula, Ucluelet; 250/726-2113): Gourmet subs, sandwiches, pastries, box lunches.

Jupiter Juicery & Bake Shop (241 Main St, Tofino; 250/725-4226): Fresh juices, blends, and smoothies; espresso, lunches to go, baked goods.

When it comes to romance, Clayoquot Sound's famous **Hot Springs Cove** should be on your agenda. Here, a short walk through an ancient cedar rain forest brings you to a succession of five calming geothermal pools fed by a trickling waterfall. A number of boat and floatplane companies supply transportation. **Remote Passages Marine Excursions** (250/725-3330 or 800/666-9833; www.remotepassages.com; Mar–Oct) offers the Hot Springs Explorer day trip with marine stops that may include a sea cave and a seabird nesting island, and plenty of chances to spot whales and other wildlife en route. This outfitter also offers sea-kayaking and bear-watching excursions, as well as whale watching, one of Tofino's main attractions. (There are numerous charter companies, so it's easy to arrange trips once you arrive.) Maybe seeing a spout of water explode from the ocean surface, followed by a giant, arching black profile, provides the excitement; or maybe it's simply getting out on the open water; whatever the reason, a sighting of these miraculous creatures is best shared with someone special. Although the peak of the gray whale northern migration season is March and April, these magnificent mammals are present near the coastline from March to October. Humpbacks can be seen between June and September, and transient orcas, as well as sea otters, sea lions, and other marine life, may be spotted anytime.

If you'd rather be on the water yourselves, paddle with **Remote Passages Sea Kayaking** (located in the red boathouse at the bottom of Wharf St; 250/725-3330 or 800/666-9833; www.remotepassages.com) or the **Tofino Sea Kayaking Company** (320 Main St; 250/725-4222 or 800/863-4664; www.tofino-kayaking.com), which offers kayak rentals and guided tours with experienced naturalists. For the ultimate bird's-eye view, explore the region's remote corners on the floatplanes of **Tofino Air Lines** (250/725-4454; 866/486-3247; www.tofinoair.ca).

Access & Information

Travelers arrive at Tofino primarily by car, via the winding mountainous route of Highway 4 (five hours from Victoria). From Vancouver, take the ferry from Horseshoe Bay to Nanaimo. Drive north on the Island Highway (Hwy 19) to the Parksville bypass. Turn west, onto Highway 4, to cross the island (from this point, it takes approximately 2½ hours). Continue on Highway 4, past the Ucluelet junction, north to Tofino. **Regency Express** (604/278-1608 or 800/228-6608; www.regencyexpress.com) flies to Tofino from Vancouver Airport's South Terminal. It's a good idea to rent a car here (try Budget, 250/725-2060). The **Pacific Rim Whale Festival** (mid-Mar–early Apr) hosts events in Tofino and in Ucluelet; contact the **Tofino Visitors Info Centre** (250/725-3414; www.tofinobc.org) for details.

Romantic Lodgings

A Snug Harbour Inn / ❶❶❶❶

460 Marine Dr, Ucluelet; 250/726-2686 or 888/936-5222
Perched on the edge of an 85-foot cliff above the Pacific, this bed-and-breakfast offers stunning views of the rocky shoreline and outlying islets where harbor seals, whales, and eagles play. Terraced decks, incredible views, plenty of windows, large rooms, and gorgeous bathrooms are all assets of this luxurious retreat. A pathway called the "stairway from the stars" leads to a private pebbly beach below. On the main deck, a big hot tub under the stars makes a grand place to kiss. Of the six guest accommodations, four are exquisite waterfront rooms appointed with fireplaces, unique furnishings, private decks with spectacular ocean views, and lavish private bathrooms with jetted tubs. For romance, we recommend the Sawadee or the Lighthouse rooms. The Sawadee Room, frequented by honeymooners, has captivating ocean views, a two-tiered deck, and a king-size bed. Soak in the double-jetted tub set next to the two-sided beach-stone fireplace. Our favorite, the dramatic Lighthouse Room, winds up three levels; the bedroom has the best views from all sides through portholes and picture windows. Morning brings the scent of a delicious three-course breakfast, which you can enjoy at a big harvest table or in the privacy of your room. You can add special romantic touches to your stay, like Dom Perignon or in-room massage. *$$$–$$$$; MC, V; no checks; www.awesomeview.com.* ♿

Brimar Bed & Breakfast / ❶❶❶

1375 Thornberg Crescent, Tofino; 250/725-3410 or 800/714-9373
Located just steps from spectacular Chesterman Beach, the kiss-worthy aspects become immediately apparent. The tree-lined gravel drive leads to this elegant New England–style home with light-filled interiors. Three tastefully decorated guest rooms have ocean views and private baths. The bright and airy honeymoon suite, known as the Loft, is the only room on the top floor,

Wild Pleasures of the Northwest Coast

A visit to the northeastern side of Vancouver Island (1½ hours from Victoria) is also sure to bring out the wild side of your relationship with its stunning natural beauty, 270-degree ocean views and old-growth forests in a 185-acre adult rustic retreat offered at the historic **Yellowpoint Lodge** (3700 Yellow Point Rd, Ladysmith; 250/245-7422; www.yellowpointlodge. com). This is grown-up camp for people who like being near the ocean, swimming in a saltwater pool, kayaking, walking wooded trails, biking, and dining family-style in a lodge. While its philosophy and approach clearly lean to the communal (and rustic, depending upon your cabin choice), the remote Cliff Cabins as well as many nooks, crannies, swings, benches, and walks will provide you plenty of space for private connections.

You may not want to leave the spectacular beauty surrounding the lodge; however, the nearby **Crow and Gate Pub** (2313 Yellow Point Rd, Ladysmith; 250/722-3731; www.crowandgatepub.com; lunch, dinner every day) is a local legend with a traditional English vibe, and the **Barton-Leier Gallery and Garden** (3140 Decourcey Rd, Ladysmith; 250/722-7140; www.bartonandleiergallery.com; Thurs–Sun Apr–Nov) will tantalize you with beautiful art, giftware, and a whimsical garden open for exploration. A visit to **Hazelwood Herb Farm** (13576 Adshead Rd, Ladysmith; 250/245-8007; www.hazelwoodherbfarm.com; every day Apr–Sept and Dec. Fri–Sun Oct–Nov), surrounded by an educational and exquisitely maintained herb garden, will provide you both all sorts of sensory, culinary, and healing herbal delights at very reasonable prices. Enjoy a blissful escape to the wild.

and thus extremely private. Charming features include a wrought-iron queen-size bed, lovely pale green walls, a wood-burning stove, a glassed-in shower, and a spacious claw-foot tub set beneath a skylight. The Sunset, on the floor below, features a spacious bathroom, a king-size bed, and a TV in an armoire. The smallest room, the Moonrise, has lovely views but less charm, and the private bath across the hall contains a shower but no bathtub. (For romance on a budget, it's not a bad option.) The elaborate breakfast is served family-style downstairs, and everything—from the homemade breads and granola to the asparagus-cheese torte and crispy waffles with mixed berries—is excellent. After this indulgence, you can stroll right onto the beach without even putting on your shoes. *$$$; MC, V; checks OK; www.brimarbb.com.*

Cable Cove Inn / ●●●

201 Main St, Tofino; 250/725-4236 or 800/663-6449
Tucked at the edge of Tofino's town center, this cozy retreat is an excellent bet when you have romance on your minds. Don't be fooled by the unpretentious exterior of this building: the guest suites are luxurious, and the private decks have magnificent views past the wharves to Meares Island and out to the open sea. Marble Jacuzzi tubs and glass showers for two are distinct attractions in most rooms; two have standard bathrooms but private hot tubs on their decks. The inn's seven unique rooms, accented with Indian silks, all overlook Cable Cove. In addition to its private outdoor hot tub, Suite 6 also has a cozy reading nook on the second level. The Driftwood Suite, set back from the inn, features a handcrafted driftwood queen-size canopy bed, skylights, a gas fireplace, and French doors that open to a private deck and hot tub. Every evening, one couple can reserve the waterfront cabin for an intimate dinner. Your personal chef combines West Coast ingredients with Asian spice, creating an exotic dining experience. In addition, the Ashram Spa offers a variety of Oriental treatments. Although this inn has the privacy and professionalism of a hotel, the innkeepers live right next door and see to personal touches. A continental breakfast is available for an added charge. *$$$; AE, MC, V; no checks; www.cablecoveinn.com.* &

Clayoquot Wilderness Resorts & Spa / ●●●●

Quait Bay; 250/726-8235 or 888/333-5405
This luxurious wilderness eco-resort in remote Clayoquot Sound is accessible only by boat or floatplane. Built on raised cedar platforms that form a boardwalk, the Wilderness Outpost is made up of luxurious canvas tents on the banks of the Bedwell River. In these spacious, safari-style tents—outfitted with Oriental rugs, remote-controlled woodstoves, handmade furniture, and private decks—you can enjoy fresh seafood and fine wine on china and crystal. By day, explore on horseback, mountain bike, canoe, or kayak; we spotted a magnificent black bear here during our visit; it's partly due to such sightings that all outdoor activities are done with guides or in groups. While this detracts from your privacy, it does provide more safety. By night, relax at the Healing Grounds Spa in one of the three wood-fired hot tubs or saunas, have a massage in one of the spa tents, and enjoy the deep silence. Come evening, guests dine on truly outstanding Pacific Northwest cuisine at a long table by the huge stone fireplaces in the Cookhouse, in the outdoor seating areas with plush furniture and fire pits, or at an intimate table for two in your tent. Two all-inclusive packages, Eco-Adventure or Spa, have specific check-in and check-out days. Book for three, four, or seven nights, and hike pristine coastline, ride horses in the outback, relax in cedar hot tubs, or do all of the above. Cost includes airfare from Vancouver, meals, alcoholic beverages, and activities and/or massage. *$$$$; AE, MC, V; no checks; packages for 3, 4, or 7 nights only; closed Nov–Apr; www.wildretreat.com.*

Eagle Nook Wilderness Resort & Spa / ◐◐◐◖

Barkley Sound; 250/723-1000 or 800/760-2777
No roads lead to the wilderness oasis of Eagle Nook, and that's what makes it special. Set on a private 70-acre peninsula on the edge of a marine reserve, this adults-only, phone- and TV-free getaway caters to outdoor-loving couples who revel in luxury after a day of kayaking, fishing, beachcombing, or exploring the coast by helicopter. Every package includes a cruise to see harbor seals, cormorants, bald eagles, and possibly whales in the surrounding watery wilderness; if the weather's nice the guide will drop each couple off at their own deserted beach for a romantic picnic lunch. (The romance package includes a cruise just for the two of you.) Upon return, guests dine on beautifully prepared West Coast or Continental meals at tables for two set before floor-to-ceiling ocean-view windows. The 23 lodge rooms are all large and comfortable with private bathrooms, ocean views, fluffy duvets, and feather pillows. There's also a hot tub, cedar hut sauna, and two-room spa on-site. Our choice for a romantic getaway is one of the two secluded one-bedroom cabins next to the main lodge, where water-view decks, king-size beds, wood stoves, and kitchenettes assure comfort and privacy. Breakfast, or even dinner, can be delivered to your room or cabin, though you won't want to miss dining at the lodge. *$$$$; AE, MC, V; no checks; closed Oct–May; www.eaglenook.com.*

Long Beach Lodge Resort / ◐◐◐◖

1441 Pacific Rim Hwy, Tofino; 250/725-2442 or 877/844-7873
Nestled in towering trees with spectacular views of the ocean and just steps from a seemingly endless stretch of sand, this beautiful cedar-shingled resort on the beach at Cox Bay, a great surf spot, has already stolen many hearts. With 40 rooms, you get all the five-star amenities in a completely informal, relaxed setting—minus the stiffness of fancy resorts. The great room, which was recently made exclusive to guests, defines the lodge's naturalist decor with its dramatic granite fireplace, floor-to-ceiling windows, and a "woven wall" of fir that extends into the dining room. Guest rooms feature luxurious beds made up with fine linens and slate-tiled bathrooms with soaking tubs and walk-in showers. Rooms 309 and 310, both Penthouse Suites, each boast panoramic views from the bedroom, living room, and double soaker tub in the bathroom. One cabin is fully wheelchair accessible, though the main lodge is not. *$$$$; AE, MC, V; no checks; www.longbeachlodgeresort.com.*

Middle Beach Lodge / ◐◐◐

400 MacKenzie Beach Rd, Tofino; 250/725-2900 or 866/725-2900
The private, romantic Middle Beach Lodge and its more recently constructed counterpart sit perched above the roaring Pacific. The simple, rustic guest rooms in each of the two main lodges show refined touches, including natural-fiber curtains, handcarved chairs, and tastefully unique artwork—

such as the antique wooden oars that adorn some walls. The Lodge at the Beach is kept romantic and quiet with an adults-only policy; rates here are surprisingly reasonable; and many of the 26 cozy, phone- and TV-free rooms feature full oceanfront views and private balconies. The newer, pricier Lodge at the Headlands supplies plenty of ambience, especially in the ocean-facing Headland Suites: 30 and 31 come with the best views and are popular among the just-married types, with gas fireplaces, soaking tubs, TV/VCRs, king-size beds, and private decks where you can feel the salt spray on your lips. The lodge serves a continental breakfast of home-baked goods and jams. Weekends and high season bring fresh-fish barbecues served in the dining room. *$$–$$$$; AE, MC, V; no checks; www.middlebeach.com.* ⅙

Tauca Lea Resort & Spa / ❶❶❶

1971 Harbour Dr, Ucluelet; 250/726-4625 or 800/979-9303
Tucked away on a private island in Ucluelet Inlet, this cluster of blue-stained cedar condos, complete with a spa and a restaurant, has all the makings of a secluded getaway. Although this ecologically managed resort attracts families and active outdoor types, it's also a perfect place for couples to curl up together in front of the fire and watch the coast's famous storms lash at the windows. There's little need to leave your suite: each of the spacious one- and two-bedroom units is serenely decorated in an airy, West Coast style, with leather armchairs or sofas and furniture handcrafted from cedar milled on the property. Each has a fully equipped kitchen, a private balcony, a gas fireplace, and gorgeous views of the harbor or the sheltered inlet. Bathrooms have deep soaking tubs, and about half of the units have outdoor two-person air-jetted tubs on their balconies. A continental breakfast is served in the resort's Boat Basin restaurant (see Romantic Restaurants); it can be delivered to your suite for an extra fee. You may also want to indulge in a pampering treatment at the serene rain forest–themed spa. Try the aromatherapy massage or the rain forest bath for two in a private grotto of slate and cedar. *$$$–$$$$; AE, DC, MC, V; no checks; www.taucalearesort.com.*

Wickaninnish Inn / ❶❶❶❶

Osprey Ln at Chesterman Beach, Tofino; 250/725-3100 or 800/333-4604
This exquisite property is set on a rocky cape that juts out from the western tip of Chesterman Beach; and from the moment you pass beneath the grand cedar-beamed entrance and step into the inviting lobby, where floor-to-ceiling windows offer breathtaking views of the ocean, you will know you've come to the right place. The artful environment includes architectural details by master carver Henry Nolla, handmade driftwood chairs, and furniture custom crafted from recycled old-growth fir. This theme extends to the 75 guest rooms and suites, which all feature ocean and beach views, a fireplace, and a thoughtfully placed private balcony; many have double soaking tubs set before ocean-view windows. Known for pioneering the concept of winter

storm watching, this inn is one of the few places on Vancouver Island booked year-round. The newer Wickaninnish-on-the-Beach, located just steps away from the original lodge, has 30 spacious rooms and suites with luxurious amenities similar to the rooms in the original building. The top-floor Canopy Suite, with four picture windows and shower and tub for two, is among the most romantic, and most expensive, places to stay in the province. The Cedar Sanctuary is a completely private couple's spa cabin built on the tip of a rocky promontory, where you can both enjoy a massage treatment available from the full-service Ancient Cedars Spa. The crowning glory is the on-site Pointe Restaurant (see Romantic Restaurants). *$$$$; AE, DC, MC, V; no checks; www.wickinn.com.* &

Romantic Restaurants

Boat Basin Restaurant / ◐◐◐

1971 Harbour Drive, Ucluelet; 250/726-4644
Tauca Lea Resort & Spa's stellar restaurant is a chic, modern space with an open kitchen, plenty of cedar, striking First Nations art, and romantic candlelight. The wall of windows looks out on expansive views. Chef Richard Norwood offers fresh seafood right off the boat, and using local ingredients creates delightful regional fare. The seasonally changing menu tempts with options from stone-oven pizza to gorgeously presented seafood, rack of lamb, or beef filets. Entrées that incorporate the signature sweet chili-ginger sauce are a special delight. The wine list, naturally, leans toward Northwest varietals. In winter, reserve ahead for a window seat with a view; in summer, a table on the deck is sublime. *$$ $$$; AE, DC, MC, V; no checks; dinner every day; full bar; reservations recommended; www.taucalearesort.com.*

The Pointe Restaurant / ◐◐◐◐

Osprey Ln at Chesterman Beach (Wickaninnish Inn), Tofino; 250/725-3106 or 800/333-4604
Memories of your romantic dinner at the Pointe in the Wickaninnish Inn (see Romantic Lodgings) are ones you will cherish forever. Step inside the dining room and marvel at the natural cedar posts and beams in the soaring 20-foot ceiling. The restaurant is perched over a rocky headland, and waves crash just outside the 240-degree panoramic windows; during winter storms, the dramatic surf can even splash up against the glass. The dining room is quiet and your table feels like your personal island. To top it all off, service is attentive without being pretentious. Chef Tim Cuff gives the Pacific Northwest cuisine a fresh outlook. The menu focuses on land and local waters—everything from Tea-Smoked Wenzel Duck Breast or Seared Caribou Loin and Mushroom Crepinette to Fennel-Crusted Ahi Tuna or Wickaninnish Potlatch. Go big but expect to pay for it. You will be amply rewarded. *$$$$; AE, DC, MC, V; no checks; breakfast, lunch, dinner every day; full bar; reservations recommended; www.wickinn.com.*

RainCoast Café / ●●●

120 4th St, Tofino; 250/725-2215
At this cafe run by husband-wife team Larry Nicolay and Lisa Henderson, tables are adorned with candles, and a relaxed ambience sets the stage for romance. The menu offers a mix of small and large plates. Try the slow-roasted lamb shank in a north Indian almond sauce or the seared and braised organic duck breast in a blackberry-liqueur pan sauce. You may want to sample one of the tempting small plates such as oysters on the half shell or Salt Spring Island mussels. With its laid-back charm and Pacific Rim sophistication, this is one of the best restaurants in Tofino and the perfect prelude to a kiss. *$$$; AE, MC, V; no checks; dinner every day; beer and wine; reservations recommended; www.raincoastcafe.com.* ♿

SOBO / ●●◐

311 Neill St, Tofino; 250/725-2341
SOBO moved to a new location in downtown Tofino from its rustic start in a bohemian truck. The restaurant offers West Coast–minimalist ambience—with bistro candlelight slightly impeded by the bright cafeteria-style kitchen lights. Take note: There's nothing cafeteria-style about this gem; neither in the food quality nor in the entrée prices. Some tables are more romantic than others, but there's no question: the food is fantastic. Signature staples include seasonal soups and smoked-salmon chowder, roasted beet and Okanagan goat cheese salad, a killer fish taco, forest mushroom–risotto bullets, cedar-planked wild salmon, and handmade *pappardelle* pasta with duck confit. Desserts? Oh, just go for it with the Flourless Chocolate Bomb or the specialty Key lime pie. Top off the meal with a wonderful glass of local muscat, port, or scotch. *$$–$$$; AE, DIS, MC, V; local checks only; breakfast, lunch every day, dinner Fri–Sun; beer and wine; reservations recommended; www.sobo.ca.*

♥ Southern
Gulf Islands

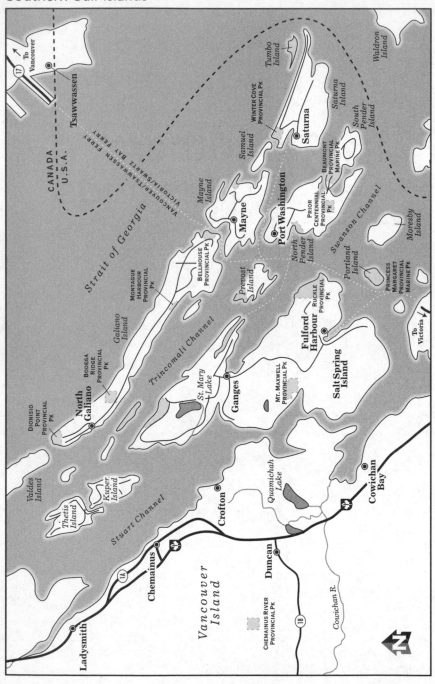

Southern Gulf Islands

As usual with most lovers in the city, they were troubled by the lack of that essential need of love—a meeting place.

—Thomas Wolfe

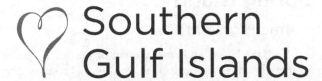# Southern Gulf Islands

Hundreds of forested isles, whose populations vary from zero to several thousand, make up the Southern Gulf Islands, located between Vancouver Island and mainland British Columbia. Scattered like a heavenly constellation in the blue ocean, all of them are havens of transcendent splendor and solitude. Choices of islands are many, but for intimate getaways we recommend Salt Spring, Mayne, Galiano, Pender, and Saturna. All are accessible via the ferry terminal at Swartz Bay outside Victoria, or from Tsawwassen outside Vancouver. If you're visiting in summer, book your ferry passage and accommodations ahead of time. Depending on your island destination, you can arrange to arrive by floatplane.

Once you land, you'll find that natural beauty and recreational opportunities abound. Located in the rain shadow of Vancouver Island's mountains, the Gulf Islands are considerably less rainy than Vancouver (but you can never be too safe in winter). The islands, which are mostly inhabited by artisans, retirees, and small-scale organic farmers, can feel quite remote, and some lack even a bank machine or a well-stocked store, so plan accordingly. The widest selection of inns, eateries, shopping, and services are found on Salt Spring and Galiano islands.

If you are planning to visit more than one island during your trip, we can't emphasize enough the importance of contacting BC Ferries (250/386-3431 or 888/223-3779; www.bcferries.com) for schedules and reservations. Island hopping is not as easy as you would think, with some ferries offering only limited transportation at odd hours designed to cater to local interisland commuting. It's possible to get stranded on one of the smaller islands overnight if you don't pay close attention to return sailing times (some days there are no ferries at all). We recommend bringing along a healthy sense of adventure and a store of patience when relying on ferry transportation between the islands. If you plan to bring a car from the mainland, we also recommend making a reservation, especially in the peak summer months; there is (so far) no extra charge for reservations on Gulf Island routes. Island hoppers may also want to check out BC Ferries' SailPass, which offers multiple crossings for a set fare. On summer weekends, it can be less stressful and less expensive to leave the car at home; most inns and B&Bs offer ferry pickup. Bring a bike or rent one; the islands (with the exception of busy Salt Spring) are wonderful (if hilly) for cycling. It's also easier to island hop without a car: during July and August, Gulf Islands Water Taxi (250/537-2510; www. saltspring.com/watertaxi) runs foot passengers from Mayne and Galiano to Salt Spring on a first-come, first-served basis.

Salt Spring Island

Romantic Highlights

Salt Spring Island, the largest and most vibrant of the Southern Gulf Islands, is home to a variety of artists, farmers, chefs, retirees, and romantic dreamers. The seaside village of Ganges is the main center for a variety of arts, restaurants, and unique shops. Dotted with pastoral farms and artisan studios, the island is packed with sublime places to stay. The beautiful summer weather draws crowds, so we recommend calling the properties you hope to visit well ahead of time for both reservations and specific directions. Shoulder seasons of spring and fall bring crisp weather and quieter retreats; the island's delightful Fall Fair makes September an ideal month to visit.

One of the highest highlights is the breathtaking panorama from the top of **Mount Maxwell** (7 miles/11 km southwest of Ganges via the Fulford-Ganges Rd and Cranberry Rd). Endless views are just the beginning of what you'll experience at the end of the (very) bumpy gravel road that takes you to the top. Scenery this magnificent and inspiring is hard to describe—suffice to say, we think your kisses will be very eloquent. To the north are the snow-covered mountains of the Canadian Rockies; to the south stands the glacial peak of Mount Baker; all around are the forested islands and the sparkling, crystalline waters of the Strait of Georgia. For a romantic seaside walk, nothing beats **Ruckle Provincial Park** (10 minutes from the Fulford Harbour ferry dock, turn right on to Beaver Point Rd).

The seaside village of **Ganges** merits an afternoon of strolling; it offers plenty of cozy waterfront restaurants, charming cafes, and boutiques that carry the work of local artists and artisans. For a casual lunch, you can cozy up under the spreading plum tree at the funky, outdoor **Treehouse Café** (106 Purvis Ln; 250/537-5379), where live music fills the air every summer evening, or enjoy a *ciabatta* sandwich and French-pressed coffee on the marina-side deck at **Auntie Pesto's Café & Delicatessen** (Grace Pt Square; 250/537-4181). Two slightly pricier downtown spots offer seafood, casual fare, and waterfront patios: the serene **Calvin's Bistro** (133 Lower Ganges Rd; 250/538-5551; www.calvinsbistro.com), where both Swiss and Thai classics appear on the evening menu, and the busy, sometimes superbusy, **Oystercatcher** (Harbour Bldg; 250/537-5041; www.oystercatcher.ca)—downstairs, visit the traditional English pub complete with fireplace. For a quintessential local experience, along with water views and great food (and no children),

Our Five Favorite Beaches on Salt Spring Island

Southey Point Trail, a.k.a. Jack Foster Trail (West) This trail's entrance is partially hidden at Southey Point Road and Sunset Drive, but locate the trail marker (a small orange diamond on a tree) a few meters up Southey Point Road on the right. Hike along the moderately difficult trail that winds through a pretty and enchanting forest down to a gravel and sand beach on Trincomali Channel across from Wallace Island.

Fernwood Point This is one of the island's best beaches at low summer tides, with lots of sea life to see. Tread carefully: these are the only *live* sand-dollar beds on the island—under the dock, to the left of the dock, and to the right.

Long Harbour/Welbury Bay Park Explore this steep, rocky beach at both Long Harbour and Welbury Bay. At the south end of the 4-acre park, there's a small, pretty low-bank beach.

Beddis Beach Walk on a beautiful, white crushed-shell ocean beach next to very cold water. This is one of the island's most popular beaches—a cool spot on a hot afternoon.

Ruckle Park The shore of Ruckle Park is great for walking, smooching, beachcombing, and smooching, with a small cove north of the picnic area great for swimming and smooching.

check out **Moby's Marine Pub** (124 Upper Ganges Rd; 250/537-5559), an island mainstay for the last several decades. It's across the harbour, about a half mile by road northeast of Ganges; a foot passenger ferry, delightfully dubbed the Queen of DeNile, can whisk you there in the summertime. If you're touring the island, plan a lunch stop at the **Raven Street Market Café** (321 Fernwood Rd; 250/537-2273). Some of the island's best, and best-value, meals appear from the wood-fired oven at this little grocery-store-cum-cafe, hidden away at the island's northern tip.

If you're a couple who loves the arts, plan to be here on the weekend so you can visit the **Salt Spring Island Saturday Market** (Centennial Park, Ganges; 250/537-4448; www.saltspringmarket.com; 8:30am–3:30pm Apr–Oct rain or shine). Go early to avoid the crowds and explore the internationally acclaimed arts and crafts that await you in every stall: handcrafted jewelry, unique pottery, hand-smoothed wooden bowls, delicious artisan cheeses, organic treats, and more. We're certain you'll find a special memento here that you will treasure for years to come. Taking the entirely self-guided **Studio Tour** (free map available at Ganges Info Centre; 250/537-5252; www.saltspring.com/studiotour) is another way to discover more than 35 artisans on the island. The main tour season is May through September, though many of the studios are open year-round. On this bona fide cultural adventure, touring the studios often takes you along some of the island's lovely, remote back roads, where the views and island tranquility may even inspire you to create art yourselves—or at least an artful kiss.

Winemaking is a relatively new art form on Salt Spring, with two wineries starting production in recent years. At **Garry Oaks Winery** (1880 Fulford-Ganges Rd, Salt Spring Island; 250/653-4687; www.garryoakswine.com; noon–5pm every day May–Oct), be sure to check out the meditative labyrinth on-site. At the charming **Salt Spring Vineyards** (off Fulford-Ganges Rd, 151 Lee Rd, Salt Spring Island; 250/653-9463; www.saltspringvineyards.com; June–Sept; check Web site for tasting-room hours) you can taste wines or stay in the romantic on-site B&B (see Romantic Lodgings). **Moonstruck Organic Cheese Co.** (1306 Beddis Rd, Salt Spring Island; 250/537-4987; www.moonstruckcheese.com) offers organic cow's milk cheese, and you can meet the Jersey cows in person at the farm; or pick up handmade goat's and sheep's milk cheese at **Salt Spring Island Cheese** (285 Reynolds Rd, Salt Spring; 250/653-2300). More wine, plus cheese, chocolate, and other sensual delights are the quarry on an **Island Gourmet Safari** (Salt Spring Island; 250/537-4118; www.islandgourmetsafaris.com). A guide takes small groups, or private pairs, to visit some of the island's most intriguing farms, wineries, breweries, studios, and more.

Access & Information

BC Ferries (250/386-3431 or 888/223-3779; www.bcferries.com) offers service to Salt Spring Island from the Tsawwassen ferry terminal, on the mainland, 22 miles (35 km) south of Vancouver. Tsawwassen is located near the U.S./Canada border and is only about a two-hour drive from Seattle when there is no traffic at the border crossing; with traffic, the trip can take considerably longer. From Vancouver Island, two BC Ferries routes serve Salt Spring Island. From Victoria, ferries leave Swartz Bay and land 35 minutes later at Salt Spring's Fulford Harbour. North of Victoria, the mill town of Crofton offers a short ferry trip to Salt Spring's Vesuvius Bay, on the island's northwest side.

An alternative route to Salt Spring Island for travelers coming from the United States is to take **Washington State Ferries** (206/464-6400 or 888/808-7977; www.wsdot.wa.gov/ferries) from Anacortes to Sidney, British Columbia; then make the short drive to the ferry terminal at Swartz Bay, and then transfer to BC Ferries for the 35-minute ride to Salt Spring's Fulford Harbour. Although this route involves two ferry lineups and can end up taking an entire day, it does make for a memorable and scenic trip.

You can also arrange to arrive by floatplane. **Harbour Air Seaplanes** (604/274-1277 or 800/665-0212; www.harbour-air.com) offers regular service from Coal Harbour in downtown Vancouver to Salt Spring and South Pender islands, and from Vancouver Airport's south terminal to Salt Spring, South Pender, Mayne, Galiano, and Saturna islands (a two-passenger minimum applies on some flights). **Kenmore Air** (425/486-1257 or 866/435-9524;

www.kenmoreair.com) makes scheduled flights from Seattle to Salt Spring between January and September; charters are available the rest of the year. SEAir (800/44SEAIR; www.seairseaplanes.com) and Salt Spring Air (800/537-9880; www.saltspringair.com) also offer flights from Vancouver Airport to Ganges Harbour.

Determined romantics can visit car-free with a judicious use of the new **bus service** (www.busonline.ca), taxis, bike rentals, pick-up services offered by most B&Bs, and the **Ganges Faerie Mini Shuttle** (250/537-6758; www. gangesfaerie.com), which runs foot passengers between the ferry terminals and the town of Ganges. Be sure to confirm these services are still available before flying in or walking on to the ferry, though, as taxi and shuttle companies tend to come and go with the seasons. Cyclists take note: The roads are beautiful, but winding, narrow, and hilly.

For more information, contact the **Salt Spring Island Visitor Info Centre** (121 Lower Ganges Rd, Ganges; 250/537-5252 or 866/216-2936; www. saltspringtoday.com; 11am–3pm every day). Also, **Tourism Vancouver Island** (335 Wesley St, Ste 203, Nanaimo; 250/754-3500; www.islands.bc.ca) can give you information on touring the Gulf Islands.

Romantic Lodgings

Cloud 9 Oceanview Bed and Breakfast / ❂❂❂❸

238 Sun Eagle Dr, Salt Spring Island; 250/537-2776 or 877/722-8233
Expansive views of Galiano Island, Mount Baker, and towering Black Tusk to the north make you feel as though you've arrived on cloud nine, indeed. This tastefully modern, romantic retreat couldn't be more aptly named. Fresh flowers grace each room, and chocolate and champagne await your arrival. The most romantic choices are the Celeste and Orion suites with luxuriously appointed furnishings and private entrances. Expansive picture windows take in the scenery (but you won't see any neighbors) and French doors lead to private patios where unobstructed views of water and islands will take your breath away. For extra privacy and extra space, the Coach House is your best bet, though the view isn't quite as extraordinary. In the evening, gaze at the stars from the hot tub, practically perched on the cliff's edge. Breakfast can be served in the main house, in your room, or on your private patio, and might include decadent dishes like pecan-filled baked pears on yogurt with a raspberry or blackberry drizzle or ginger-vanilla broiled grapefruit. *$$$; MC, V; no checks; www.cloud9oceanview.com.*

Cranberry Ridge Cottages Suites / ❂❂❸

175 Suffolk Rd, Salt Spring Island; 250/537-2214 or 888/537-4854
Romance is plentiful at the newly relocated Cranberry Ridge Cottages Suites where three new spacious cottages are settled on the edge of St. Mary Lake. Each cottage enjoys expansive water views and all that surrounds this outdoor

Island Wineries

For wine lovers in the Southern Gulf Islands, Salt Spring offers two winery choices. **Garry Oakes** (1880 Fulford-Ganges Rd; 250/653-4687; www.garryoakeswine.com; noon–5pm weekends May–June, every day July–Aug) is located on a terraced 10-acre vineyard carved out of the south-facing gravel slopes overlooking the Burgoyne Valley. Marcel Mercier and Elaine Kozak planted 7 acres of vines and rehabilitated century-old apple, pear, cherry, and plum orchards. Mercier grows and produces Pinot Noir, Pinot Gris, Gewürtztraminer, Zweigelt, and Leon Millot, while grapes used for the Bordeaux blend, Fetish, are sourced from the Okanagan. Find yourself walking hand-in-hand through the magical on-site labyrinth, or spread a blanket on the grass, and share a glass.

Farther down Fulford-Ganges Road, off Lee Road, **Saltspring Island Vineyards** (151 Lee Road, Salt Spring Island; 250/652-9463; www.saltspringvineyards.com; year-round, check Web site for tasting-room hours) is full of flourishing romance. The winery grows and produces Pinot Blanc, Pinot Noir, a sparkling blend of Pinot Noir and Chardonnay, Millotage made

paradise, from its working ranch with roaming chickens, horses, llamas, and sheep to its forest full of alder, cedar, and hemlock trees with walking trails—perfect for meandering hand-in-hand on a quiet, contemplative stroll. Guests can borrow a rowboat or canoe (on-site) and float or fish on the lake. Both the Morning Glory and Hollyhock cottage suites have wood-burning stoves or fireplaces; large, fully outfitted kitchens; and dining and living rooms with TV/DVD players. The master bedrooms have king-size beds, and the spacious bathrooms have large Jacuzzi tubs. The Honeysuckle Cottage is the smaller of the three, with a queen-size feather bed. All have cozy living areas perfect for relaxing indoors. $$$; MC, V; no checks; www.cranberryridge.com.

Hastings House / ❂❂❂

160 Upper Ganges Rd, Salt Spring Island; 250/537-2362 or 800/661-9255
Rich in history and located on the water's edge of the Ganges Harbour, this peaceful country resort blends 22 acres of gardens, meadows, and forest with comfort and casual elegance. Luxury accommodations range from modest to premier suites housed in restored historic buildings and simpler, though no less elegant, private cottages. Each room features a fireplace, cozy duvets on queen- and king-size beds, fluffy robes, over-size towels, and elegant toiletries; many have private balconies and deep soaking tubs. Our favorite, the picturesque country-chic Post cottage, looks out to the sea through French doors. In the morning at your door, a wake-up basket greets you, filled with fresh pastries and coffee or tea. Guests enjoy afternoon treats and an honor bar

from Leon Millot, as well as blackberry port. Sip a glass of the signature Millotage while listening to summer sounds of live music. Or share a picnic at one of the tables under the colorful umbrellas near the lower pond. By far, the sweetest escape is the gazebo adorned with grapevines, a candle-lit chandelier, and a wood fireplace.

On the other islands, **Morning Bay Vineyard & Estate Winery** (6621 Harbour Hill Dr, North Pender Island; 250/629-8351; www.morningbay.ca; 10am–5pm Wed–Sun) produces Pinot Noir, Merlot, Cabernet Sauvignon, Sauvignon Blanc, Gewürztraminer, and Riesling. Get lost in the ocean-front vineyards or garden and take in the sweeping water views. **Saturna Island Family Estate Winery** (8 Quarry Rd, Saturna Island; 250/539-5139 or 877/918-3388; www.saturnavineyards.com; check Web site for tasting-room hours) is one of the region's largest estate wineries and vineyards, producing Pinot Gris, Chardonnay, Gewürztraminer, Pinot Noir, and Merlot. Tours are offered daily followed by complimentary tastings. The tasting room/bistro is open for lunch May through October and is a great place to relax and bask in the charm of this magical place.

in Snug, the intimate guest lounge accessible 24 hours a day; exquisite meals are served in the Hastings House restaurant (see Romantic Restaurants). The on-site spa offers a range of services. *$$$$; AE, MC, V; no checks; closed mid-Nov–mid-Mar; www.hastingshouse.com.*

Salt Spring Vineyards Bed and Breakfast / ●●●◐

151 Lee Rd, Salt Spring Island; 250/653-9463
Salt Spring Vineyards, created by romantic retreat aficionados Jan and Bill Harkley, combines the luxuries of romance with the seductive setting of a working winery. In the spacious Winery Room, located above the tasting room adjacent to the main house (note that the tasting room opens to visitors at noon), you'll enjoy spectacular views of the terraced vineyard and fir-covered valley from the room and its Juliet balcony. In the colorful bathroom, there's a slipper-shaped soaking tub and a showerhead set directly in the ceiling (no curtains here; the whole room becomes your shower). In the main house, the smaller Vineyard Room has a jetted two-person tub and French doors leading to a large, private outdoor deck. Guests also have access to the outdoor jetted tub, set underneath a flower-covered trellis, which overlooks the vineyard. Both rooms offer tasteful country-style decor, neatly stowed microwaves and fridges, and cozy sitting areas where your breakfast is delivered in the morning; you can enjoy it here or out on your private deck or balcony. *$$; MC, V; checks OK; www.saltspringvineyards.com.*

Sky Valley Inn Bed & Breakfast / ❂❂❂

421 Sky Valley Rd, Salt Spring Island; 250/537-9800
At this centrally located Salt Spring B&B, you'll feel as if you've been transported to a villa in the South of France; here you can spend your days lounging by the pool, lingering over coffee and home-baked goods, or dallying among dahlias and sunflowers in the garden. Guests are greeted by fresh-cut flowers, a complimentary decanter of sherry, plush cotton robes, and handmade soaps. Each of the three pretty French country–style rooms has a private bath, a feather bed, and a private entrance opening onto an ivy-draped courtyard and the inn's heated outdoor pool. The spacious Ivy Master Suite is our romantic choice, with its gas fireplace, vaulted ceiling, and mahogany four-poster king-size bed. Best of all, it has views from both sides, with access to the courtyard and to a deck. The deck, with its jaw-dropping views across the Gulf Islands to the mountains of the mainland, is accessible to all guests, but chances are you'll have it to yourselves. The Wisteria Room and Garden Room are smaller, though still spacious and charming. Guests gather in the view-laden dining room for a lavish breakfast featuring homemade jams, and organic herbs and fruit from the garden. *$$$; MC, V; checks OK; www. skyvalleyinn.com.*

Romantic Restaurants

Artist's Bistro / ❂❂❂

Grace Pt Square, Salt Spring Island; 250/537-1701
Tucked in a corner of Grace Point Square in downtown Ganges, Artist's Bistro offers an intimate fine-dining experience. Known for its selection of seafood, entrées include the West Coast Seafood Hot Pot, an assortment of fresh seafood in a coconut-tomato broth spiced with lemongrass and chili peppers, and oven-baked walnut-crusted halibut fillet topped with a sweet and tangy red-onion marmalade. For lovers of meat and pasta, try the lamb osso buco, traditional wiener schnitzel, Boeuf à la "Bistro," or fettuccine *frutti di mare. $$$; MC, V; no checks; dinner Thurs–Mon; full bar; reservations recommended; www.artistsbistro.com.* &

Hastings House / ❂❂❂❂

160 Upper Ganges Rd, Ganges; 250/537-2362 or 800/661-9255
Rated one of the best restaurants in BC, Hastings House offers refined, romantic fine dining. For a very formal evening out, the atmospheric dining room at this exclusive English country–style retreat is a sublime choice. Located in the stately Manor House, an enormous Inglenook fireplace warms the living room where cocktails are served before dinner. In the dining area, a large stone fireplace, upholstered chairs, candlelight, and white linens provide understated luxury. In warm weather, tables on the enclosed veranda with spectacular views of Ganges Harbour are ideal for a summer supper. Though

prices are lofty, the food is nothing short of magnificent. The daily menu features items à la carte or as a multicourse chef's menu. Northwest cuisine relies on fresh local ingredients (many from the inn's gardens). Salt Spring Island lamb is a guest favorite. Recognized with a Wine Spectator Award of Excellence, the well-rounded wine list features a good selection of BC and island varietals. *$$$$; AE, MC, V; no checks; dinner every day (closed mid-Nov–mid-Mar); full bar; reservations required; www.hastingshouse.com.* &

Restaurant House Piccolo / ❶❶❶❶

108 Hereford Ave, Ganges; 250/537-1844
Located in old Ganges, chef/owner Piccolo Lyytikainen, a member of the prestigious Chaîne des Rôtisseurs, specializes in upscale European cuisine. Once you've sampled House Piccolo's delicious food and charming ambience, you'll see why this intimate restaurant is one of the region's finest. Set in a tiny heritage house, House Piccolo achieves romance without formality. Just nine tables, covered in ivory and blue linens, are scattered throughout two connecting dining rooms, each appointed with copper kettles, antique dishes, and pretty watercolors. In summer, another six tables appear on the patio. Main dishes include seafood, charbroiled filet of beef with gorgonzola sauce, roasted Muscovy duck breast, and Salt Spring Island lamb. Chocolate lovers should not miss the decadent, baked-to-order warm chocolate timbale. The excellent wine list, with its extensive selection of both European and Vancouver Island varietals, has been judged among the best in the world by *Wine Spectator* magazine. *$$$$; MC, V; local checks only; dinner every day; full bar; reservations recommended; www.housepiccolo.com.*

Mayne, Galiano, Pender & Saturna Islands

Romantic Highlights

Among the beautiful Southern Gulf Islands, Mayne, Galiano, Pender, and Saturna islands each have their own unique romantic appeal. Mayne Island, the smallest of the group, offers serenity, the highly romantic Oceanwood Country Inn, and quiet seclusion. Galiano, which boasts many protected parks and spectacular hikes, is an excellent choice for outdoorsy couples. Pender is actually two islands—North Pender and South Pender—linked by a short bridge. On green and rural South Pender, you can explore Mount Norman, part of the Gulf Islands National Park Reserve, and treat your honey to a night at Poets Cove Resort and Spa, the archipelago's only full-service luxury resort. The most remote island, Saturna, is blessed with plenty of parkland and is home to the well-loved Saturna Island Family Estate Winery. Whether you visit just one or all four, traveling through these exquisite islands could be defined as romance itself.

On **Mayne Island**, the tiny village of **Miners Bay** offers a small museum, a Saturday farmers market, and a handful of shops. You can browse the stacks at quiet **Miners Bay Books** (478 Village Bay Rd; 250/539-3112), stock up on supplies at the small grocery stores, or visit the **Sunny Mayne Bakery Café** (472 Village Bay Rd; 250/539-2323), offering caramel macchiato and other scrumptious delights. In summer, call ahead and they'll pack your lunch.

With picnic in hand, you're ready to explore the island's beautiful trails. For vigorous exercise, hike up **Mount Parke** to reach Mayne's highest point; the trail winds uphill for about an hour beneath leafy foliage before reaching a bluff with views of ferries crossing Active Pass. This lovely spot makes an excellent place to lay a blanket and share your picnic.

Afterward, you can stop for a snack at the **Wild Fennel** (574 Fernhill Rd; 250/539-5987) near the park entrance; be sure to check out the two arts and crafts galleries next to the cafe. For a more leisurely stroll, visit **Marine Heritage Park** (off Bennett Bay Rd). A wide quarter-mile trail leads to **Campbell Point**, where you might spot purple starfish and exotic jellyfish in the tide pools and, if you're lucky, see otters and seals hard at play.

If all you want to do is roll out of bed and then roll out the picnic, drive to **Georgina Point Heritage Park** (9am–dusk every day). Lush grass surrounds the spectacular 1885 landmark lighthouse, and the wooden gazebo is a popular spot for weddings. Another romantic spot is the **Japanese Garden** at Dinner Bay Park, built by local volunteers to commemorate the island's early Japanese settlers. This pretty acre has a peaceful, contemplative air. And it's located slightly more than half a mile (1 km) south of the Village Bay ferry terminal.

For a romantic half- or full-day trip on a crewed 33-foot sailboat (lunch included), contact **Island Charters** (250/539-5040). Or, if you prefer, do the paddling yourself with **Mayne Island Kayaking & Bike Rentals** (Miners Bay; 250/539-2463 or 877/535-2424; www.kayakmayneisland.com), or **Blue Vista Resort** for cottage accommodations, sea kayaking, or cycling (250/539-2463 or 877/535-2424; www.bluevistaresort.com). Both outfits offer kayaking instruction and tours; they also rent mountain bikes. A cycling tour of the island takes about five hours; there are some steep hills, but the small size and minimal traffic make Mayne a good bet for cyclists.

After your outdoor fun, relax on the deck of the historic **Springwater Lodge** (400 Fernhill Rd; 250/539-5521; www.springwaterlodge.com) in Miners Bay, which has been in continuous operation since 1892. The interior is well worn and the pub fare is standard, but the views from the deck at sunset are spellbinding.

Considering it's the closest of the Southern Gulf Islands to Vancouver (1 hour via the Tsawwassen ferry), **Galiano Island** feels surprisingly wild. Renowned for its protected land and well-maintained parks, this is an excellent place to enjoy pristine island beauty in natural surroundings. The jewel in this island crown is the eminently kiss-worthy **Montague Harbour** (5 miles/8 km west of ferry dock at Sturdies Bay) on the island's west side, a lovely, sheltered bay with glorious sunset views, beaches, camping areas, and picnic tables. For an artful afternoon, take a self-guided tour of island art studios, using the locally available map and watching for the numbered signs along the road. Or go by land or by sea and rent a moped or motorboat at **Toadies Roadies** (300 Sticks Allison Rd; 877/303-3456; www.galianoadventures.com). No matter which activities tempt you, our highest recommendation is the island's romantic, secluded walks.

All the hikes we recommend on Galiano are easy to find with the help of a local map, readily available when you arrive on the island. For the most spectacular views, hike up **Mount Galiano** (trailhead off Phillimore Point Rd). The hour-long climb gets steep in some places, but trust us, it's worth it. Kisses will be in order as you stand beneath the rare Garry oak trees at the summit and enjoy spectacular views of Navy Channel. Hike the trail along Bodega Ridge and you'll find **Lovers Leap View Point**—aptly named, we think, since the views over Trincomali Channel to Salt Spring Island are enough to make anyone jump into the arms of their love. If a long walk sounds like too much, you can still enjoy exquisite views by visiting **Bluffs Park** with a beach blanket and delicious lunch in tow. For picnic provisions, shop for specialty foods and organic goods at **Daystar Market** (Georgeson Bay Rd; 250/539-2505); you'll find pastries, espresso, and a full lunch menu at the adjacent vegetarian-friendly cafe. Otherwise, you can find both hearty pub food and local color at the **Hummingbird Pub** (Sturdies Bay and Georgeson Bay rds; 250/539-5472), fresh-baked breads and pastries at the **Trincomali Bakery, Deli & Bistro** (2540 Sturdies Bay Rd; 250/539-2004), or a funky diner atmosphere and live entertainment at the **Grand Central Emporium** (2470 Sturdies Bay Rd; 250/539-9885; www.grandcentral.ca).

North and South Pender islands are rich in beaches. **Mortimer Spit** (at the western tip of South Pender) and **Gowlland Point Beach** (at end of Gowlland Point Rd on South Pender) are among 30 public ocean-access points on the two islands. To take advantage of the fabled Gulf Island view scape, the trails on **Mount Norman** (accessible from Ainslie Rd or Canal Rd on South Pender), part of the Gulf Islands National Park Reserve, are steep but rewarding. Another popular trail follows the canal over to **Beaumont Marine Park** with its white shell beaches and arbutus headland. The gentle terrain of South Pender is particularly appealing for cyclists; rent bikes at **Otter Bay Marina** (2311 MacKinnon Rd; 250/629-3579) on North Pender. Your best bets for kiss-worthy dining are both at South Pender's **Poets Cove Resort and Spa** (see Romantic Restaurants). Choose from elegant West Coast cuisine at **Aurora Restaurant** or high-end casual fare at **Syrens Lounge**. For wine tasting, visit **Morning Bay Vineyard & Estate Winery** (6621 Harbour Hill Dr; 250/629-8351; www.morningbay.ca), offering a variety of wines including Pinot Noir, Merlot, Cabernet Sauvignon, Pinot Gris, and Riesling.

Remote and hard to get to, Saturna Island offers the ultimate get-away-from-it-all experience. One of the largest of the Southern Gulf Islands, Saturna is also the least populated. Crowds are simply not part of the picture here—nor are banks, cash machines, or drug stores, so come prepared. Most of the island is now part of the **Gulf Islands National Park Reserve**, so outdoor options abound. Embark on a floating adventure with **Saturna Sea Kayaking** (250/539-5553;

www.saturnaseakayaking.com). Or bring bikes and explore the sometimes steep and unpaved roads; on Saturna Island, bikers rarely run into traffic. For beach walking, you couldn't ask for more than the pristine shoreline of **Winter Cove Park** (near the junction of Winter Cove Rd and East Point Rd). Civilization has made it to the island in the form of the delightful **Saturna Island Family Estate Vineyards** (8 Quarry Trail; 250/539-3521 or 877/918-3388; www.saturnavineyards.com; every day May–Oct, by appointment the rest of the year), producing Pinot Gris, Chardonnay, Gewürztraminer, Pinot Noir, and Merlot. Located on the island's southern shore, it has a charming tasting room, wine shop, and bistro. The bistro terrace (lunch every day May–Oct), with its Mediterranean-influenced fare and ocean and vineyard views, is a prime spot for a romantic lunch. For dinner, the most romantic option is the restaurant at the **Saturna Lodge** (see Romantic Lodgings). Otherwise, dining options are limited.

While the **Lighthouse Pub** (102 East Pt Rd; 250/539-5725; lunch, dinner every day) will do in a pinch, it's not exactly romantic. Another option is the wholesome fare served at **Saturna's Café** (101 Narvaez Bay Rd; 250/539-2936; breakfast, lunch Wed–Sun May–Oct, and Wed, Fri–Sun Nov–Apr; dinner Wed–Sat May–Oct and Wed, Fri–Sat Nov–Apr) tucked inside the general store.

Access & Information

BC Ferries (250/386-3431 or 888/223-3779; www.bcferries.com) offers daily trips to the islands. Mayne (ferry terminal at Village Bay), Galiano (ferry terminal at Sturdies Bay), and Pender (ferry terminal at Otter Bay) can be accessed from the Tsawwassen ferry terminal on the mainland, 22 miles (35 km) south of Vancouver. Tsawwassen is located near the U.S./Canada border and is only about a two-hour drive from Seattle when there is no traffic at the border crossing; with traffic, the trip can take considerably longer. Advance reservations are recommended (and can be made at no additional charge) when traveling between the British Columbia mainland and the Southern Gulf Islands. From Tsawwassen, access to remote Saturna (ferry terminal at Lyall Harbour) is via a transfer at Mayne Island. From Vancouver Island, BC Ferries serves all four islands from the Swartz Bay ferry terminal, located north of Victoria.

Tourism Vancouver Island (335 Wesley St, Ste 203, Nanaimo; 250/754-3500; www.islands.bc.ca) offers information on touring the Gulf Islands. For more information on Galiano, you can also contact the **Galiano Chamber of Commerce Travel Info Centre** (250/539-2233 or 866/539-2233; www.galianoisland.com). You can view maps of Mayne Island and find other helpful information at the **Mayne Island Chamber of Commerce** Web site (www.mayneislandchamber.ca). The **Pender Island Visitor Info Centre** (250/629-6541; www.penderisland.info) has information about Pender. The Saturna Island tourism Web site (www.saturnatourism.com) offers helpful information. Island hopping is possible, but ferry schedules are complex and sailing times do not always match up well. One alternative for passenger-only interisland travel is the **Gulf Islands Water Taxi** (250/537-2510; www.salt spring.com/watertaxi). On summer weekends, it can be less stressful and less expensive to leave the car at home; most inns and B&Bs offer ferry pickup. Bring your own bike or rent one; the islands (with the exception of busy Salt Spring) are wonderful (if hilly) for cycling.

Romantic Lodgings

Galiano Inn and Spa / ✿✿✿✿

134 Madrona Dr, Galiano Island; 250/539-3388 or 877/530-3939
While Galiano Island has always been a beautiful spot, this boutique hotel and spa has transformed itself into a sublime romantic destination. Surrounded by flower gardens and perched at the edge of the water, the inn is filled with warm decor that evokes the Mediterranean. All 10 spacious rooms feature wood-burning fireplaces, sitting areas, private balconies or patios with exquisite waterfront views, luxurious down comforters, and Italian-tiled bathrooms with Jacuzzis or soaking tubs. Amenities throughout include minibars, CD/DVD players, robes, and coffee and tea makers. You'll enjoy the lovely views of Active Pass and Mount Baker from your room, as well as from the dining room, where the complimentary breakfast is served. Supreme relaxation awaits at the on-site Madrona del Mar spa, where you can enjoy a couples massage in an ocean-side cabana, or soak your cares away in a sea-mineral flotation bath. Other delights include a luxurious blackberry "vinotherapy" massage using the elements of the fruit and goodness of the grapes for their relaxation properties, followed by a bottle of blackberry port and blackberry chocolates, or the Blueberry Bliss experience, where a smoothie—made from blueberries, milk, and honey—is rubbed over your body. During summer guests enjoy yoga and meditation in the garden, and alfresco lunches at the Oceanfront Patio Grill; dinner is a romantic affair at the elegant restaurant Atrevida (see Romantic Restaurants). *$$$$; MC, V; checks OK for deposit; closed Dec–Mar; www.galianoinn.com.*

Oceanwood Country Inn / ✿✿✿✿

630 Dinner Bay Rd, Mayne Island; 250/539-5074
Enveloped by lush gardens, towering trees, and a sweeping view of Navy Channel, this large Tudor home offers 12 magnificent guest rooms, extremely cozy and inviting common areas, and an elegant restaurant with superlative views. Most rooms have water views; eight have private decks and fireplaces as well as whirlpool or deep soaking tubs. The Lavender Room is one of our favorites. It boasts two plushly carpeted levels, a queen-size four-poster bed with handsome fabric, a deep soaking tub facing a wood-burning fireplace and window, and a private deck overlooking the water. The largest room is the top-floor Wisteria Room: it has all the amenities, including a soaking tub on its private deck, but the massive square footage lacks some coziness. If

weather permits, soak in the outdoor hot tub or wander through the herb and flower gardens. The elegant downstairs dining room (see Romantic Restaurants) serves breakfast to guests only and dinner by reservation. Our earnest recommendation is that you pack your bags this minute and take advantage of what this first-class inn has to offer. At press time this property was for sale. *$$$–$$$$; MC, V; Canadian checks only; closed Nov–mid-Mar; www. oceanwood.com.*

Poets Cove Resort & Spa / ❂❂❂❂

9801 Spalding Rd, South Pender Island; 250/629-2100 or 888/512-7638
This pretty, wooded cove near the Gulf Islands National Park Reserve has long been the locals' favorite spot to propose. Though one of the largest developments on the Gulf Islands, Poets Cove Resort has what it takes to inspire. The lodge's 22 guest rooms all have ocean and sunset views, gas fireplaces, king-size or twin-size beds, comfy duvets, and large private balconies. In each bathroom, heated tiles warm the floors and the shuttered soaker tub allows you to take in the sea view while you bathe. The two- and three-bedroom Arts and Crafts–style cottages, on the hillside above the lodge, are beautifully finished with vaulted ceilings, wood-burning fireplaces, and sweeping water views from large heated decks; some have private hot tubs. The nautical-themed main lodge is home to Aurora Restaurant (see Romantic Restaurants), the chic Syrens Lounge (only open weekends during winter months), and the serene Susurrus Spa, where a lit waterfall tumbles over a steam grotto. Also on-site, a marine center for resort guests and visiting boaters has an outdoor pool, a hot tub, a fitness center, tennis courts, and a market with gourmet provisions. Getting to Poets Cove can be an adventure in itself, whether you take a seaplane directly to the pier, hop a water taxi from Sidney on Vancouver Island, or bring your car on BC Ferries. If you do drive, call for directions. This hideaway is, quite genuinely, hidden away. *$$$$; AE, MC, V; checks OK; www.poetscove.com.* &

Saturna Lodge / ❂❂

130 Payne Rd, Saturna Island; 250/539-2254 or 888/539-8800
Just a few kilometers from the vineyards, Saturna Lodge combines casual Northwest style with French simplicity. Overlooking Boot Cove, the lodge offers easy access to the ferry dock and houses Saturna's only spot for a kiss-worthy evening meal. Six guest rooms with wine-inspired names are equipped with simple pleasures and views of either the cove or surrounding farmland. The cozy Tokay room boasts sloping ceilings, country wallpaper, and the best view in the house. Sunny Aligot, reminiscent of vintages from the golden coast of Burgundy, features a four-poster queen-size bed and an old-fashioned claw-foot tub with commode sink in its private bath. After a full day of island exploring (the lodge has bikes on hand if you're in an energetic mood), relax in the hot tub overlooking the gardens. Mornings begin

with a complimentary full breakfast for two, served in the restaurant or on the patio. The Dejavu Seafood & Steakhouse menu is designed around fresh, local ingredients and changes daily; prime rib is featured on Sundays. The property is open year-round, though the restaurant is open for dinner regularly Memorial Day through November. *$$–$$$; MC, V; Canadian checks only; www.saturna.ca.*

Romantic Restaurants

Atrevida / ●●●●

134 Madrona Dr (Galiano Inn and Spa), Galiano Island; 250/539-3388 or 877/530-3939
Every seat in this glass-enclosed restaurant offers spectacular water views and memorable romantic ambience. A seasonally changing menu features West Coast cuisine using locally raised, often organic, fish, meat, and produce, and vegetarians are well served with creative entrées. With so few fine-dining options on the island, this combination is a considerable draw. The wine list offers a good selection of British Columbia wines. In the summer months, an outdoor patio doubles as the inn's casual lunch spot, Oceanside Patio Grill, so when the sun shines you can enjoy an alfresco lunch on the water. *$$$$; MC, V; no checks; lunch, dinner every day (Memorial Day–Sept), dinner on weekends during low season (closed Dec–March); full bar; reservations recommended; www.galianoinn.com.*

Aurora Restaurant at Poets Cove Resort & Spa / ●●●●

9801 Spalding Rd, South Pender Island; 250/629-2100 or 888/512-7638
The evening seascape, over yachts at harbor and the wooded hills across the inlet, is enough to set a romantic mood, but it doesn't stop there. Book a window seat or a table on the terrace for a front-row view of the cove's glorious sunset. Inside, the lighting is soft, service is friendly and efficient, and the big room feels calm, despite the open kitchen. In winter, when the sun sets long before dinnertime, you might forgo the window seat for one of the intimate curved banquettes by the fireplace. Choose from à la carte dishes featuring West Coast seafood and their signature Gulf Island lamb. The wine list is limited but interesting, ranging from local and affordable to outrageously splashy. Desserts, including ice cream, are all made in-house. One of the luscious desserts nicely rounds out a sensuous meal. For lunch, or for a casual dinner, the resort's Syrens Lounge offers burgers, pasta, fish-and-chips, and sea views in a chic, postmodern pub. *$$$–$$$$; AE, MC, V; checks OK; breakfast, dinner every day (Aurora Restaurant), lunch, dinner every day, some closures in winter (Syrens Lounge); full bar; reservations recommended; www. poetscove.com. &*

Oceanwood Country Inn / ●●●●

630 Dinner Bay Rd, Mayne Island; 250/539-5074
Fresh ingredients, beautiful food presentation, and stunning views of the terraced gardens and the glittering Navy Channel capture the finest aspects of the island experience. Housed on the ground level of the impeccable Oceanwood Country Inn (see Romantic Lodgings), the warm, intimate dining room features pale yellow walls and decor in a cozy fern-pattern fabric. Tastefully chosen background music sets the mood, and an attractive bar gleams in the corner. Service is exemplary, and the food is extraordinary from start to finish. The daily four-course menus are good examples of regional fare, making the most of such fresh, local products as wild salmon and island-raised lamb. The restaurant's wine list features excellent vintages from British Columbia. At press time this property was for sale. *$$$$; MC, V; Canadian checks only; dinner every day (closed Nov–Mar); full bar; reservations required; www. oceanwood.com.*

Wild Fennel / ●●●

574 Fernhill Rd, Mayne Island; 250/539-5987
Owned by a trio of locals, Wild Fennel is a small and intimate bistro-style gem with great food that makes up for any missing ambience. The menu, which changes weekly, features local and organic fare with a global twist. Chef Steve Alkema is developing a heavy following for his Dungeness Crab Cakes, Steve's Wicked Bison Burger (with chili-spiked sweet-onion chutney and goat-cheese aioli), Free-range Chicken Breast Amaretto (with sour cherry, almond, and Amaretto cream), and, of course, the famous Chocolate Pudding Cake. The wine list, with only British Columbia wines, features private-estate wineries like Pentage, Joie, Nichol, or Kettle Valley. The interesting hot and cold cocktail list leans toward martinis; we recommend the Queenie Martini or the Wild Fennel Martini. Co-owner Peter Weis's whimsical sculpted paintings, which literally come up off the canvas, are another popular feature. *$$; MC, V; no checks; lunch, dinner Wed–Sun (closed January); full bar; no reservations; wildfennel@shaw.ca.*

♡ Okanagan Valley

Okanagan Valley

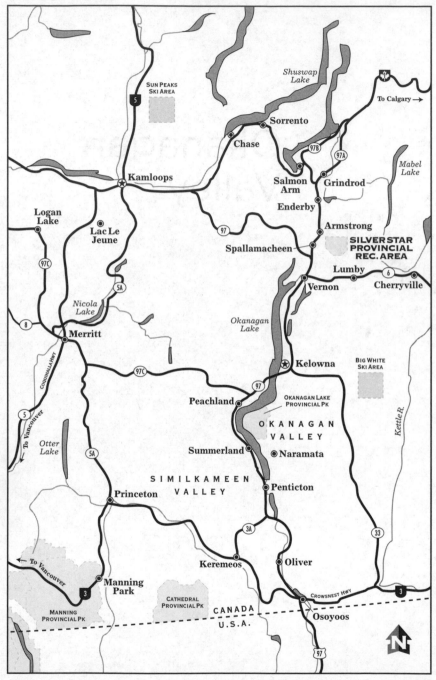

Give me a kisse, and to that kisse a score; / Then to
that twenty, adde a hundred more; / A thousand to
that hundred; so kisse on, / To make that thousand
up a million; / Treble that million, and when that is
done, / Let's kisse afresh, as when we first begun.
—Robert Herrick

Okanagan Valley

For decades, the Okanagan Valley has been British Columbia's playground. Known in the province as the Interior, the Okanagan is about a four hours' drive east of Vancouver.

The Okanagan Valley stretches about 100 miles from the border town of Osoyoos in the south to Vernon in the north. This deep and wondrous valley was carved out by glaciers over the millennia, leaving behind jaw-dropping natural beauty.

For many years, the cities of Osoyoos, Oliver, Penticton, and Kelowna have played host to families looking to escape from the rainy lower mainland to the sunny Okanagan for weekends. Many of the low-end, kitschy motels still line Lakeshore Drive on the southern end of Okanagan Lake.

But thanks to the burgeoning wine industry, the Okanagan is rapidly changing into a higher-end destination, with more hotels, resorts, restaurants, B&Bs, galleries, wine bars, and, of course, wineries. This transformation has occurred primarily in the past decade, so many Pacific Northwesterners still are discovering this little corner of paradise.

Starting from the southern end of the valley, the first 30 miles over the U.S./Canada border comprise the only desert in Canada. In fact, this "pocket desert" is a natural extension of the great Sonoran Desert, which stretches through the western United States and includes Eastern Oregon, Eastern Washington, and this tiny section of British Columbia. This area, known as the south Okanagan, is where the greatest density of vineyards are planted, especially on the east side of the valley just across the border.

By the time you reach the town of Okanagan Falls—don't blink or you'll miss it—you are out of the desert and starting to get into cooler areas. You also see your first lake. Skaha Lake runs from Okanagan Falls to Penticton; then mighty Okanagan Lake stretches another 100 miles north. These lakes help make the Okanagan such an inspiring and romantic getaway. The lakes actually moderate temperatures year-round, benefiting wineries, as well as resorts, restaurants, and B&Bs, which get you as close to the water as possible.

Penticton is the second-largest city in the Okanagan, but it isn't all that big. The downtown is evolving into a more hip destination, though a great little coffeehouse recently was converted to a Starbucks, which some say has taken away from the town's charm. Another 40 minutes north is Kelowna, the largest city in the Okanagan and the center of industry and tourism. The valley's largest resorts are here, as are its finest restaurants. Continuing north, Vernon is primarily a retirement community and, thus, is a quiet destination.

Okanagan Valley

Romantic Highlights

The Okanagan helps put the "beautiful" in British Columbia. The ambience of the entire region elicits romance, and a leisurely trip up and down this valley can turn into an unforgettable getaway. You have two obvious choices for where to launch your journey: Penticton or Kelowna. Each has its unique charms.

Kelowna's size and prominence in the valley mean it has more choices for hotels, restaurants, and amenities. The downtown area can be downright funky and fun to stroll through and people watch. The closer you get to the lake, the more romantic it becomes. The **Wine Museum** (1304 Ellis St; 250/763-0433; www.kelownamuseum.com) is a good starting point just north of the main downtown area. It is inside the historic Laurel Packinghouse and also is home to the equally fascinating Orchard Museum. The Wine Museum provides some background on the Okanagan's winemaking history, and it also has plenty of brochures on things to do in the valley. However, its primary purpose is as a wine shop.

Kelowna has a dozen wineries in the general vicinity. The most fascinating is south of downtown on the east side of the lake. **Summerhill Pyramid Winery** (4870 Chute Lake Rd; 250/764-8000; www.summerhill.bc.ca) is owned by Steve Cipes, a man who made his fortune in New York real estate, then moved to the interior of British Columbia to make wine in a pyramid. That's right, a scale replica of the Cheops Pyramid in Egypt. Cipes says the pyramid ages his wines differently. Here at the on-premise bistro, with its stunning view of the lake, you can enjoy a delicious meal made with regional ingredients. Afterward, tour the pyramid and learn about its alluring power. It is, quite easily, the most unusual wine-touring experience in the Pacific Northwest.

Across the floating bridge are three wineries worth visiting: **Quails' Gate Estate Winery** (3303 Boucherie Rd, Kelowna; 250/769-4451; www.quailsgate.com) and its Old Vines restaurant; **Mission Hill Family Estate** (1730 Mission Hill Rd, Westbank; 250/768-7611; www.missionhillwinery.com) and its stunning architecture; and **Little Straw Vineyards** (2815 Ourtoland Rd, Kelowna; 250/769-0404; www.littlestraw.bc.ca), home of the world's first ice wine made with the obscure grape auxerrois.

If you want to tour throughout the Okanagan Valley, **Penticton** is most centrally located between Kelowna and the U.S. border. Penticton is less than an hour south of Kelowna, and the entire drive is along or above the west side of Okanagan Lake. You'll travel through the towns of Peachland and Summerland, which have wineries and quaint eateries. But Penticton is the primary goal. This city at the southern end of the Okanagan Lake is still a bit rough-and-tumble and has that '50s feel to it. Yet Penticton is growing up, thanks to the thriving wine industry.

The **Naramata Bench** is emerging as a real hot spot for wineries and now is home to a classy resort, several B&Bs, and nice restaurants. The Bench is, with little doubt, the most romantic stretch in the Okanagan. It is loaded with orchards, vineyards, and breathtaking vistas of Okanagan Lake. The winding Naramata Road will take 20–30 minutes to drive. And no, it doesn't go all the way back to Kelowna—unless you have an all-terrain vehicle and a lot of time.

Back in Penticton, you can walk along Lakeshore Drive or the beach that runs parallel to it. This is quite a busy area, but enjoyable nonetheless. A pier near the Lakeside Resort extends into the lake and is wonderful for an easy stroll at sunset. If you plan to stay at the **Lakeside Resort** (21 Lakeshore Drive W; 250/493-8221; www.pentictonlakesideresort.com), request a lakeside room. Otherwise, you may be stuck looking south toward downtown.

While driving in the Okanagan is easy, consider pampering yourself with **Okanagan Wine Country Tours** (1310 Water St, Kelowna; 250/868-9463; www. okwinetours.com). It's not only perfect for wine touring, but it also offers day trips, overnight stays, skiing packages, floatplane tours, and garden tours. **Okanagan Cultural Corridor** (www.okanaganculturalcorridor.com) is a guide to arts, museums, wineries, agricultural sites, and performing arts in the Okanagan. It includes basic and in-depth information, calendars of events, and guided and self-guided itineraries.

Access & Information

Getting to the Okanagan Valley is simple enough. If you live in Vancouver, head east on the **Hope Princeton Highway** (Highway 3) if you want to end up near Penticton or the **Coquihalla Highway** (Highway 5) if you want to end up closer to Kelowna (the latter is a toll road). From Seattle, you can either drive north (on Interstate 5) across the border to the lower mainland or go over the Cascades through Wenatchee on Highway 2, then up through the border town of Oroville via Highway 97.

If you plan to fly to the Okanagan, the Kelowna Airport is served by **Air Canada** (888/247-2262; www.aircanada.com), **Horizon Air** (800/252-7522; www.alaskaair.com), **WestJet** (800/538-5695; www.westjet.com), **Central Mountain Air** (888/865-8585; www.flycma.com), and **Northwestern Air** (877/872-2216; www.nwal.ca).

Driving in the Okanagan is a snap. **Highway 97** (the same highway that crosses over from Washington) goes all the way through the valley. Thus, it is quite difficult to get lost, though there are many side roads for little adventures.

You will find plenty of romantic interludes throughout the Okanagan just by wandering around. Is there anything more sensual than biting into a ripe peach from a roadside stand and having the juice roll down your chin? How about hanging out along Okanagan Lake, watching for the elusive sea monster, Ogopogo? If you prefer a bit more structure, contact the **Thompson Okanagan Tourism Association** (2280-D Leckie Rd, Kelowna; 250/860-5999; www.totabc.com).

Romantic Wineries

Gray Monk Estate Winery / ◑◑◖

1055 Camp Rd, Okanagan Centre; 250/766-3168 or 800/663-4205
The Heiss family was one of the early Okanagan pioneers, planting vineyards in the 1970s and opening its winery in 1982. There are no monks around. In fact, the winery is named for the grape variety Pinot Gris, known as "gray monk" due to its grayish color when ripe. Gray Monk is one of the Okanagan's largest wineries, and its tasting room north of Kelowna stands above Okanagan Lake with a commanding view. Second-generation winemaker George Heiss Jr. produces a wide variety of wines, none more famous than the Latitude Fifty series. These quaffable and inexpensive blends are named for the latitude on which Gray Monk sits. With its tasting room and outside seating, Gray Monk makes plenty of room for visitors; and the Grapevine Restaurant, with stunning vistas of the central Okanagan Valley, serves delicious lunches made with regional ingredients—accompanied by Gray Monk wines, of course. *10am–5pm every day (Apr–Oct), 9am–9pm (July–Aug), 11am–5pm Mon–Sat and noon–4pm Sun (Nov–Mar); Grapevine Restaurant open for lunch at 11:30am every day (Mar–Oct); www.graymonk.com.*

Hawthorne Mountain Vineyards / ◑◑◑◖

Green Lake Rd, Okanagan Falls; 250/497-8267
Take the winding road to the top of the hill near Okanagan Falls and you will come across a view unlike any other in the Okanagan—and that's saying something. Hawthorne Mountain Vineyard is known for its wines, but the view of the valley from the deck of the winery tasting room is also a major highlight. Be sure to pack a picnic so you can sit on the deck and take it all in. The winery is known for its white wines, especially its Gewürztraminer, Pinot Gris, Riesling, and ice wine. The property was settled in the early 1900s as a ranch owned by the Hawthorne brothers. Eventually, it was sold to Hugh Fraser, who built a home and became known for his lavish social gatherings and love for animals. He even established a cemetery for his dogs, with headstones for his favorites. In honor of Fraser, Hawthorne Mountain Vineyards launched the whimsical See Ya Later Ranch label, complete with a

dog sporting angel wings and halo. The wines are fun, especially the Ehren-felser ice wine. *9am–5pm every day; www.hmvineyard.com.*

Mission Hill Family Estate / ❶❶❶❶

1730 Mission Hill Rd, Westbank; 250/768-6448
Say what you will about the gorgeous wineries in Napa Valley, but until you've been to Mission Hill near Kelowna, you have not really witnessed architectural beauty. Owner Anthony Von Mandl is the visionary behind Mission Hill. In the late '90s he started turning a nice tourist destination into a place with "wow" factor. Von Mandl funded much of the Mission Hill project with proceeds from his other operation: Mike's Hard Lemonade. The wines are better than average for the Okanagan, but the real draw is the elegant tasting room and the famous bell tower, which is 12 stories tall and holds four bronze bells crafted in France. When those bells ring, you can hear them for miles. In fact, you can see Mission Hill for miles, as it resembles a European hill town. A visit to Mission Hill is not to be missed, and the Terrace restaurant—open seasonally—provides a respite for the weary and hungry wine traveler. *10am–5pm every day; www.missionhillwinery.com.*

Nk'Mip Cellars / ❶❶❶

1400 Rancher Creek Rd, Osoyoos; 250/495-2985 or 800/665-2667
The border town of Osoyoos is best known for retirees who enjoy the lake set-ting. It's rarely thought of as a tourist destination. But thanks to Vincor (the largest producer and marketer of wine and related products in Canada) and the Osoyoos Indian band, that is changing. Nk'Mip (pronounced "in-KA-meep") Cellars is North America's first Aboriginal-owned winery. The winery building is architecturally similar to those found in the American Southwest, especially in New Mexico, and the tasting room is nothing short of elegant. The wines are all award winners, particularly the luscious ice wine. The win-ery and the nearby Nk'Mip Desert & Heritage Centre (www.nkmipdesert. com) pay tribute to the First Peoples who still live here and work the land (including many of the south Okanagan's most important vineyards, which are planted on tribal territory). For a truly unique experience, stay at the nearby Spirit Ridge Vineyard Resort & Spa and play golf at the Sonora Dunes Golf Course. *9am–5pm every day (summer), 9am–7pm every day (July–Aug), 10am–4pm every day (Nov–May); www.nkmipcellars.com.*

Red Rooster Winery / ❶❶

891 Naramata Rd, Penticton; 250/492-2424
A quaint little family winery that opened in the late '90s has evolved into a major tourism destination on the main road of the Naramata Bench north of Penticton. The spacious tasting room, large fountain, and striking view of Okanagan Lake's southern end draws visitors, while the often good and occasionally great wines keep them coming back. Admire original artwork

Top Five Okanagan Ice Wines

We can talk all day long about the various wines of the Okanagan Valley. Yes, the white wines are glorious in their bright acidity and purity of fruit. Indeed, the reds are coming along beautifully, competing with the top reds from Washington and, dare we say, California.

But the Okanagan wine everyone talks about—and will continue to embrace—is ice wine. This luscious dessert wine is the nectar of the gods. Ice wine brings the bacon to the table. It is the bomb. It will bring you to British Columbia, and it will bring you back—over and over again.

Ice wine is very difficult to make: Grapes are left on the vine well after October's harvest, often into November and December—and occasionally into January or February. Temperatures in the vineyard must reach at least minus-8 degrees C (about 17 degrees F). When it gets cold enough for a long enough period, the marble-hard grapes are harvested, usually in the middle of the night. They are crushed to obtain the thick, sugary syrup inside, then fermented for several months. The result is a low-alcohol, extremely sweet wine.

The key to great ice wine is balance. Good acidity will keep the sweetness from overwhelming the wine drinker's palate. Imbalanced acid will cause ice wine to taste more like maple syrup.

There is nothing like a chilled ice wine to bring up the temperature with your true love. Here are five of the best in the Okanagan Valley, the original home for ice wine in North America.

while you sip Pinot Gris or Chardonnay ice wine. For $300 per year, you can join the Adopt-a-Row Club, which gets you a case of wine annually, a tasting-room discount, and your name on a sign in the vineyard. *10am–6pm every day (Apr–Oct), 11am–5pm every day (Nov–Mar); www.redrooster winery.com.*

Tinhorn Creek Vineyards / ❍❍❍

32830 Tinhorn Creek Rd, Oliver; 250/498-3743 or 888/484-6467
Tinhorn Creek Vineyards is a love story. One of the first wineries you will encounter if you cross the border at Osoyoos, it is a striking building high up the west side of the hills along a stretch of highway known as the Golden Mile. Kenn and Sandra Oldfield started the winery. He was from Ontario and she grew up in Sonoma. They met while taking winemaking classes at the University of California at Davis, fell in love, got married, and decided to get into the wine business. Since then, the winery has won one award after another. The Oldfields are very particular about the environment and support

Jackson-Triggs Vintners Sparkling Riesling ice wine Frankly, Jackson-Triggs wines could fill this list (and more), but this is the finest of the bunch. It's an extremely rare sparkling ice wine, the only one of its kind made in Western Canada. The carbon dioxide lifts the aromas and flavors from the beginning through the amazing finish.

Sumac Ridge Estate Winery Gewürztraminer ice wine This grape is one of the most difficult with which to make a dessert wine because it tends to be naturally low in acidity. Yet every year Sumac Ridge manages to craft a bright, spicy Gewürztraminer ice wine. It highlights aromas and flavors of sweet spices, such as cloves, cinnamon, and cardamom.

Gehringer Brothers Estate Winery Cabernet Franc ice wine Few ice wines are red, but this one from one of the province's top producers is a stunner, from the rich red color through the delicious flavors of Rainier cherries and ripe raspberries.

Nk'Mip Cellars Qwam Qwmt Riesling ice wine This aboriginal-owned winery near the border town of Osoyoos crafts one of the province's finest ice wines. It uses Riesling, which is the finest variety for dessert wines. This version typically smells of orange blossoms and fresh Key limes, followed by flavors of ripe, rich fruit.

Hawthorne Mountain Vineyards See Ya Later Ranch Ehrenfelser ice wine You haven't heard of Ehrenfelser? Probably because it's such a rare grape outside of Germany. In British Columbia, it's great for making ice wines because it's naturally higher in acidity and offers plenty of orchard fruit aromas and flavors.

efforts to preserve the natural beauty of the Okanagan Valley. Of special note are the Merlot, the Gewürztraminer, and the Kerner dessert wine. *10 am–5pm every day; www.tinhorn.com.*

Romantic Lodgings

Burrowing Owl Estate Winery Guesthouse / ✪✪✪

100 Burrowing Owl Pl, Oliver; 250/498-0620 or 877/498-0620
Brand new in 2007 is the guesthouse at Burrowing Owl Estate Winery and surrounding vineyards. What could be more romantic than luxurious rooms nestled in among some of the finest vines in Canada? Amenities include a swimming pool, a hot tub, dining, and even a penthouse suite with a gourmet kitchen. In addition to Burrowing Owl's award-winning wines, a dozen other wineries are a few minutes away. The highly regarded Sonora Room is Burrowing Owl's on-site restaurant and is open for lunch and dinner with both indoor and outdoor dining. *$$$; AE, DIS, MC, V; no checks; www.bovwine.ca.*

Grand Okanagan Lakefront
Resort and Conference Centre / ●●●

1310 Water St, Kelowna; 250/763-4500 or 800/465-4651
The Grand lives up to its name as the finest hotel in the Okanagan. It's on the lake and just a few minutes' walk from several restaurants. You are treated like royalty from the moment you enter the lobby. When making reservations, request the newer North Tower. And for a special treat, consider the Grand Honeymoon package, which includes one night's stay, sparkling wine, fresh flowers, and breakfast for two in bed. Want to really stay in exquisite luxury? Check out the Royal Private Residence Club, 70 fully furnished villas with gourmet kitchens, lavish living rooms, jetted tubs—perfect for romance no matter which room you choose. *$$$; AE, DC, DIS, MC, V; no checks; www. grandokanagan.com.* &

Hotel Eldorado / ●●●

500 Cook Rd, Kelowna; 250/763-7500
Built in 1926 by an Austrian countess, this large property has undergone many changes, site relocations, and restoration overhauls. Today the original hotel blends old-word charm and antiques with new-world comfort and convenience. The Eldorado Arms is a newer wing with more luxurious accommodations: it houses 30 guest rooms and 6 suites with amazing amenities. Boasting casual elegance, this modern setup features cork flooring, custom woodwork, fluffy duvets, DVD players, and 8-foot floor-to-ceiling windows overlooking Okanagan Lake. We recommend one of the Lakeview Luxury Suites, which are spacious and include jetted Jacuzzi tubs perched high for a view of the lake, fireplaces, and kitchenettes. Full spa treatments are a few steps away, as is the lakeside dining room. An on-site liquor store features regional and imported wines, cold beer, and a variety of spirits. *$$$; AE, DC, MC, V; no checks; www.eldoradokelowna.com.* &

Manteo Resort Waterfront Hotel and Villas / ●●●

3762 Lakeshore Rd, Kelowna; 250/860-1031 or 800/445-5255
If any hotel can rival the Grand Okanagan, it's the Manteo Resort. This 102-room waterfront hotel might well remind you of the Italian Riviera with its rich Mediterranean colors and gorgeous vistas. It features full-size suites as well as separate villas. Each comfortable, well-appointed suite has a private balcony where you can end the day sipping a glass of wine and admiring the rosy-hued sunset. For complete privacy, consider one of the much larger two-story villas adjacent to the hotel and merely steps from Okanagan Lake. Everything is well thought out, and luxury is the motto here. *$$$$; AE, DC, MC, V; no checks; www.manteo.com.* &

Naramata Heritage Inn & Spa / ⬡⬡❖

3625 1st St, Naramata; 250/496-6808
This 100-year-old hotel has been lovingly restored along the eastern bank of Okanagan Lake on the Naramata Bench. It was built in 1908 by John Robinson, a pioneer of the fruit industry that thrives today on the bench. He built this as a hotel, and it later served as a private girls' school and the Robinson family home. Today, it offers 12 comfortable rooms, a restaurant, a spa, and a wine bar. The low-key wine bar, open to travelers who are not staying at the inn, features a wood-fired stone oven that turns out perfect flat breads and pizzas. Besides wine touring, there's not much to do in Naramata, so it's just the right destination for those who want to focus on natural beauty—and each other. *$$$; MC, V; no checks; www.naramatainn.com.* ♿

Otella's Wine Country Inn / ⬡⬡⬡❖

42 Altura Rd, Kelowna; 250/763-4922 or 888/858-8596
In the hills just above downtown Kelowna is an experience not to be missed. Proprietors Otto Schwab and Ella van Dinther emigrated from Europe, where he was an accomplished chef in Germany, Luxembourg, and Switzerland, as well as Nova Scotia, Alberta, and Victoria, BC. The accommodations are above average for a B&B—the real attraction is Otto's breakfast. He stays up late into the night preparing a meal that features fresh local ingredients and herbs from his garden. He especially loves introducing guests to edible flowers (which he grows organically, of course). These are lovely people, and the meal may be one of your favorite memories of the Okanagan. *$$$; MC, V; travelers checks only; www.otellas.com.*

Paradise Cove Guest House / ⬡⬡

3129 Hayman Rd, Naramata; 250/496-5896
Nestled in orchards and vineyards on the Naramata Bench, Paradise Cove is a charming and quaint getaway for couples. The view of Okanagan Lake cannot be overstated, nor can the hospitality of the owners. From here, you are minutes away from a dozen wineries and within hailing distance of hiking, swimming, biking, skiing, and eating. Looking for more seclusion? Try the Paradise Cove Cottage, a stand-alone getaway in "downtown" Naramata. *$$; MC, V; no checks; www.paradisecove.ca.*

Romantic Restaurants

Bouchons Bistro / ⬡⬡⬡❖

105-1180 Sunset Dr, Kelowna; 250/763-6595
In its brief history, Bouchons has quickly become one of the finest dining experiences in Kelowna. Conveniently located in the downtown district, this bistro is just a few minutes' walk from the Grand Okanagan. At Bouchons, it's all about being French: the menu features pâté and foie gras, as well as

duck, cassoulet, rabbit, steak tartare, and tenderloin. As lovers of French cuisine would expect, the sauces are divine. The bowl of *pommes frites* is regionally famous. While a good portion of the wine list is French, there is a nod to the regional wine industry in between the Chablis, Champagne, Côte Rôtie, Bordeaux, and Burgundy. For dessert, choose from pastries, soufflés, crème brûlée, or, of course, a classic cheese plate. For something truly special to top an evening try the Grand Marnier tasting flight. *$$$; MC, V; no checks; dinner every day; closed Feb 15–Mar 15; reservations recommended; www. bouchonsbistro.com.* &

Cantaloupe Annie's / ❂❂❂

34845 Main St, Oliver; 250/498-2955
Looking for the fixings to prepare a lovely and romantic picnic? This little-known gem in the south Okanagan town of Oliver is perfect. Deli meats, cheeses, crackers, artisan breads, and condiments will fill your basket. The ice creams will keep you coming back. You can also order lunch in the tea room, which offers live entertainment most Saturdays and seasonal outdoor dining. All you need after a visit to Cantaloupe Annie's is a lovely picnic spot and a willing companion. *$; MC, V; no checks; breakfast, lunch Mon–Sun (May–Sept); full bar; reservations recommended; www.cantaloupeannies.com.* &

Cellar Door Bistro / ❂❂❂❸

17403 Highway 97 (Sumac Ridge Estate Winery), Summerland; 250/494-0451
A perfect interlude in a day of wine tasting is a meal at the Cellar Door Bistro, which is inside Sumac Ridge Estate Winery along the highway between Penticton and Kelowna. After tasting through the award-winning wines of Sumac Ridge, take in a meal that defines Okanagan Valley cuisine. It focuses on fresh regional ingredients that often are downright inspiring. While everything on the menu is delicious, the soups, ice creams, and sorbets are extra special. The wine list includes those from Sumac Ridge and its sister wineries (Hawthorne, Jackson-Triggs, Inniskillin, and Nk'Mip), as well as dozens of other wineries in the valley. The ambience is elegant and yet never stuffy. *$$; AE, DIS, MC, V; no checks; lunch, dinner every day (closed Jan–Feb); beer and wine; reservations recommended; www.sumacridge.com.* &

Fresco / ❂❂❂❂

1560 Water St, Kelowna; 250/868-8805
It would be difficult to imagine a finer dining experience anywhere in the Pacific Northwest. Owners Audrey Surrao and Rod Butters focus on Northwest cuisine using local ingredients. Chef Butters's style is simple yet sophisticated, regional yet refined. Fresco, in Kelowna's downtown cultural district, is distinctive with its brick walls and open kitchen that allows diners a peek behind the curtain. All of this might sound like dozens of other

establishments around here, but what sets Fresco apart is its impeccable service and attention to detail, especially when accommodating the many proposals and romantic celebrations that occur here. The wine list is fiercely regional, with a tip of the hat to more famous areas for port and Madeira. If you seek but one excuse to travel to the Okanagan Valley, let it be Fresco. *$$$; AE, MC, V; no checks; dinner Tues–Sat (closed Jan); full bar; reservations recommended; www.frescorestaurant.net.* &

Harvest Dining Room / ❷❷❷

2725 KLO Rd (Harvest Golf Club), Kelowna;
250/862-3177 or 800/257-8577
This is not your typical 19th hole. Yes, you can get a pitcher of beer and a burger at the Harvest Grille, but for an amazing eating experience, try the Harvest Dining Room at this award-winning golf course in east Kelowna. The menu tends toward seasonal ingredients that help shape the distinctly Northwest cuisine. Seafood from the BC coast will share the table with Okanagan cheeses. Diners will have to choose between wild BC salmon with an orange verjuice reduction and herb-roasted lamb chops with quince jus, among the many entrées. Whether you've just finished 18 holes or simply want to enjoy an intimate meal with a special someone, the Harvest Dining Room is a delightful surprise. *$$$; AE, DC, MC, V; no checks; lunch, dinner every day; full bar; reservations recommended; www.harvestgolf.com.* &

Old Vines Patio / ❷❷❷

3303 Boucherie Rd (Quails' Gate Estate Winery), Kelowna;
250/769-4451 or 800/420-9463
Restaurants are opening in wineries throughout the Okanagan Valley, a trend not seen at this level elsewhere on the West Coast (not even in Napa!). A great example is the Old Vines Patio at Quails' Gate Estate Winery. Located on the west side of the lake (don't be fooled by the Kelowna address—this isn't anywhere near downtown), the restaurant is quintessentially Northwest. Choose Dungeness crab cakes with Okanagan apples or grilled Fraser Valley quail for starters, then move on to halibut from the Queen Charlotte Islands or even wild arctic caribou for a main course. The views of the vineyard and lake are as divine as the food. *$$$; AE, MC, V; no checks; brunch Sun, lunch, dinner every day; beer and wine; reservations recommended; www.quailsgate.com.* &

Theo's / ❷❷❷

687 Main St, Penticton; 250/492-4019
The warm hospitality of the Theodosakis family has made this restaurant a local institution for more than 25 years. Step inside and you'll feel transported to a Mediterranean hideaway with exquisite Greek-inspired food. On cold winter nights, the seats around the capacious fireplace are in high demand, and in any season you'll enjoy an intimate courtyard ambience filled with

beautiful art and antique tapestries. The extensive menu features consistently good Greek specialties, such as *dolmathes avgolemono*: tender grape leaves filled with herb-laced rice and ground beef and baked with a traditional Greek lemon sauce; and lamb shoulder, baked in the oven on a tray of Greek oregano branches and flavored with garlic, lemon, and an Okanagan white wine–and–mustard sauce. For dessert, seek out the sinfully good *bougatsa*, a creamy custard wrapped in phyllo pastry and topped with whipped cream, crushed nuts, and cinnamon. The impressive list of regional wines reflects the owners' passionate support of the booming local wine scene. Cushion-smothered benches in the lounge area and by the fireplace are irresistible for lingering by candlelight with an after-dinner ouzo. The chef himself may wander by and toast you with *"stin egia mas"* (to your health!). *$$; AE, MC, V; no checks; lunch, dinner every day; full bar; reservations recommended; www. eatsquid.com.* &

Toasted Oak Wine Bar & Grill / ●●●◖

34881 97th St, Oliver; 250/498-4867 or 888/880-9463
Unless you ask, you might never guess this fairly new establishment along the highway through the town of Oliver used to be the fire station. In fact, walk in and sit down in the main dining room and within minutes you might forget you're in the Okanagan and think you're actually tucked into a restaurant off the square in Healdsburg, California. The focus here is wine, which includes more than 350 selections from the Okanagan Valley, all available by the glass or bottle. Like what you're drinking? Then walk across the hall to the adjacent wine shop—also run by the Toasted Oak—and buy it at regular retail price to enjoy later. For an intimate evening, ask to be seated in the Vintage Cellar, a room for up to four in the wine cellar. The menu focuses on regional ingredients in season; choose from tantalizing entrées like seared tuna or spicy chorizo penne. *$$; AE, MC, V; no checks; lunch, dinner every day; full bar; reservations recommended; www.winecountry-canada.com.* &

Waterfront Wines / ●●●

103–1180 Sunset Dr, Kelowna; 250/979-1222
If you like funky chic, Waterfront Wines in Kelowna is for you. This establishment is a combination wine shop, restaurant, and bar. Stop in for a bottle of wine to take with you and maybe slow down long enough to sample the cheese plate or a bowl of olives. If you decide to linger awhile, order several small plates, including scallops, prawns, and calamari, or dive right into the big plates of beef, chicken, pork, lamb, or seafood. And the wine list? It's loaded with regional favorites and international discoveries classified as Blondes (white wines), Red Heads (red wines), and Airheads (sparkling). Additionally, the single-malt list is nothing short of impressive. *$$–$$$; AE, MC, V; no checks; dinner every day; full bar; reservations recommended; www. waterfrontwines.com.* &

Wedding Index

Oregon

Portland & Environs

Columbia River Gorge & Mount Hood

Willamette Valley

Oregon Coast

Southern Oregon

Central Oregon

Washington

Seattle & Environs

Index

Establishments by Lip Rating

◆ ◆ ◆ ◆

A Snug Harbour Inn
Abendblume Pension
Araxi
Ariana
Aurora Restaurant at
Poets Cove Resort &
Spa
Bacchus Restaurant
Basel Cellars Estate
Winery
Bishop's
Brightwood Guest House
Camille's
Canlis Restaurant
Carson Ridge Private
Luxury Cabins
Chauntecleer House,
Dove House, and
Potting Shed Cottages
Chez Shea and Shea's
Lounge
Chrysalis Inn and Spa
Clayoquot Wilderness
Resorts & Spa
Cliff House and Seacliff
Cottage
Coast House
Columbia Gorge Hotel
Columbia River Court
Dining Room
Country Willows Bed and
Breakfast Inn
David Hill Winery
El Gaucho
Elk Cove Vineyards
Empress Room, The
Fairhaven Vacation
Rentals
Fairholme Manor
Fairmont Empress Hotel
FivePine Lodge

Four Seasons Resort
Whistler
Fresco
Galiano Inn and Spa
Genoa
Hartmann House
Hastings House
Heathman Hotel, The
Heathman Restaurant
and Bar, The
Herbfarm Restaurant,
The
Highland Inn Bed &
Breakfast
Hotel 1000
Hotel Bellwether
Ibiza Dinner Club
Il Bistro
Illahee Manor
Inn at Abeja, The
Inn on Orcas Island
Joel Palmer House
Lara House Lodge
Lost Mountain Lodge
Lumière
Merridale Estate Cidery
Mission Hill Family
Estate
Ocean House Bed and
Breakfast
Oceanwood Country Inn
Opus Hotel
Paley's Place
Patit Creek Restaurant
Poets Cove Resort & Spa
Pointe Restaurant, The
Quattro at Whistler
Restaurant House Piccolo
Richview House
Run of the River Inn and
Refuge
Sakura Ridge
Salish Lodge & Spa
Samish Point by the Bay

Sandlake Country Inn
Sapphire Hotel
SeaQuest Inn Bed and
Breakfast
Shoalwater, The
Skagit Bay Hideaway
Sooke Harbour House
Spring Bay Inn
Springbrook Hazelnut
Farm Bed & Breakfast
Stephanie Inn
Sun Mountain Lodge
Sunriver Resort's River
Lodges
Terra Blanca Winery &
Estate Vineyard
Tojo's
Tu Tu' Tun Lodge
Villa Marco Polo Inn
West
Whistler Pinnacle Hotel
Wickaninnish Inn
Willows Lodge

◆ ◆ ◆ ◖

A Touch of Europe B&B
Abigail's Hotel
Aerie Resort & Spa, The
All Seasons River Inn
Almost Paradise Lodging
Amore by the Sea Bed
and Breakfast Inn and
Seaside Spa
Amuse Restaurant
Anchorage Inn, The
Ashland Creek Inn
Assaggio Ristorante
Atrevida
Avalon Hotel and Spa
Barolo Ristorante
Bay House
Bellevue Club Hotel
Blacksmith, The

437

Blue Water Café
BOKA Kitchen + Bar
Bouchons Bistro
Brentwood Bay Lodge
	& Spa
Brentwood Seagrille and
	Pub
Cabins on the Point
Cafe Juanita
Campbell House Inn
Castagna
Celilo Restaurant
Cellar Door Bistro
Chateaulin Restaurant
Chinaberry Hill
Cloud 9 Oceanview Bed
	and Breakfast
Colette's Bed and
	Breakfast
Country Cottage Bed and
	Breakfast
Cozy Rose Inn Bed and
	Breakfast
Desert Wind Winery
Dining Room, The
Dragonfly Bistro &
	Lounge
Duck Soup Inn
Eagle Nook Wilderness
	Resort & Spa
El Gaucho
Fairmont Olympic Hotel
Fifty Two 80 Bistro and
	Bar at Four Seasons
	Resort
Four Seasons Hotel
Four Swallows, The
Friday Harbor House
Georgian, The
Hawthorne Mountain
	Vineyards
Hotel Andra
Hotel deLuxe
Hotel Elliott
Il Fiasco
Inn at Langley, The
Inn at the Gorge

Jen's Garden
King Estate Winery
Lakecliff
Le Gourmand and
	Sambar
Long Beach Lodge Resort
Lopez Farm Cottages and
	Tent Camping
Magellan's Tapas on the
	Bay
Markus' Wharfside
	Restaurant
Matisse
Metolius River Resort
Mint
Morgan Hill Retreat
Morgan Hill View Loft
Mountain Home Lodge
Mt. Ashland Inn
Mt. Hood Hamlet Bed
	and Breakfast
Ocean Lodge
Olympic View Bed and
	Breakfast
Otella's Wine Country
	Inn
Pan Pacific Whistler
	Village Centre
Paprika Bistro
Parkside
Peerless Hotel, The
Pine Ridge Inn
Point No Point Resort
Portland's White House
Ravenscroft Inn Bed and
	Breakfast
River Ridge at Mount
	Bachelor Village Resort
Rosewood Country
	House
Salmon River Inn
Salt Spring Vineyards Bed
	and Breakfast
Shelburne Inn, The
Skamania Lodge
Staccato at the Firehall
Sundial Boutique Hotel

T's Restaurant
Tango Restaurant &
	Lounge
Thistledown House
Thornewood Castle Inn
	and Gardens
3 Doors Down Café
Toasted Oak Wine Bar
	& Grill
Tuwanek Hotel, The
26 brix
Via Tribunali
Vij's
Villa Bed and Breakfast,
	The
Wedgewood Hotel
Whale Cove Inn
Wild Coho, The
Wildflowers B&B
Willcox House
Woodland Retreat Bed
	and Breakfast
Youngberg Hill Vineyards
	& Inn
Zanatta Winery

A Cowslip's Belle Bed &
	Breakfast
A Midsummer's Dream
A Place by the Sea Bed &
	Breakfast and Spa
Abbeymoore Manor Bed
	& Breakfast Inn
Adam's Place
Alderbrook Resort & Spa
Alexis Hotel
Alice Bay Bed &
	Breakfast
Alley Café, The
Aloha Beachside Bed and
	Breakfast
Andaluca
Andersen House Bed &
	Breakfast
Andina Restaurant

Anne Amie
Anthony's HomePort
    Columbia Point
April's at Nye Beach
Aquariva
Arch Cape House
Arctic Club Hotel
Artist's Bistro
A Touch of Europe B&B
Barclay House
Bavarian Lodge
Bay Cafe, The
Bayside Cottages
Beaconsfield Inn
Bearfoot Bistro
    Champagne Restaurant
Benson Hotel, The
Bin 941 Tapas Parlour
Bin 942 Tapas Parlour
Black Rabbit Restaurant
Black Walnut Inn
Bluefish Bistro
Boat Basin Restaurant
Bonneville Hot Springs
    Resort & Spa
Boreas Bed & Breakfast
    Inn
Brasserie L'Ecole
Burrowing Owl Estate
    Winery Guesthouse
Bybee's Historic Inn
C
Cable Cove Inn
Cafe Brio
Café Langley
Camano Island Inn
Cannon Beach Property
    Management, Inc.
Cantaloupe Annie's
Capers
Cascade Dining Room
Caswell's on the Bay
    Bed & Breakfast Inn
Channel House
Chanterelle
Cherry Point Vineyards

China Beach Retreat
Ciao Vito
Cliff House
Cooper's Cove
    Guesthouse
Cork
Cottage at Home by the
    Sea, The
Country Cottage of
    Langley
Cricketwood Country
    Bed & Breakfast
CRU
Crush
Dahlia Lounge
Deep Forest Cabins at
    Mount Rainier
Desolation Sound Resort
DeVoe Mansion Bed and
    Breakfast
Domaine Madeleine
Domaine Serene
DreamGiver's Inn, The
Eagles Nest Inn
Edenwild Inn
Edgewater Lodge Dining
    Room
Elements Urban Tapas
    Parlour
Enchanted River Inn
Excelsior Inn
Fairmont Chateau
    Whistlezr Resort
Fairmont Waterfront, The
Fat Duck Inn
Flats Tapas Bar
Four Seasons Hotel
    Vancouver
Fratelli
Freestone Inn and Early
    Winters Cabins
Friday's Historic Inn
Fu Kun Wu @ Thaiku
Gilbert Inn
Glenterra Vineyards

Grand Okanagan
    Lakefront Resort and
    Conference Centre
Green Turtle, The
Greenlake Guesthouse
Guest House Log
    Cottages
Halfmoon Bay Cabin
Harborside Bistro
Harvest Dining Room
Hastings House
Heathman Hotel, The
Heceta Head Lighthouse
    Bed & Breakfast
Hedges Family Wine
    Estate
Heron Inn and Watergrass
    Day Spa, The
Higgins
Honey Moon Cabin on
    Marrowstone Island, The
Hotel Deca
Hotel Eldorado
Hotel Le Soleil
Hotel Monaco
Hotel Vintage Park
Hotel Vintage Plaza
Humboldt House
Hunt Club and Fireside
    Room, The
Husum Highlands Bed &
    Breakfast
Il Giardino di Umberto
Il Terrazzo Ristorante
Inn at Cannon Beach
Inn at El Gaucho, The
Inn at Ship Bay
    Restaurant
Inn at Spanish Head
Inn at the Market
Jacksonville Inn
James House, The
Jasmer's at Mount Rainier
Kerstin's
L'Ecole No 41

La Mesa at Desert Wind
Winery
La Rua Restaurante
La Terrazza
Laughing Oyster
Lovely Hula Hands
Mannino's Restaurant
Manteo Resort
Waterfront Hotel
and Villas
Marché
Markham House
McMenamins Old St.
Francis School Hotel
Michael's Divine Dining
Middle Beach Lodge
Mint, The
Molly Ward Gardens
Mona's Bistro and
Lounge
Monet
Morical House Garden
Inn
Morton's Bistro
Northwest
Nell Thorn Restaurant
and Pub
Newmans at 988
Nk'Mip Cellars
Noble Rot
"O Canada" House
Old Vines Patio
Oyster Bar on Chuckanut
Drive, The
Painted Lady Restaurant,
The
Pan Pacific Hotel
Pheasant Valley Orchards
Pink Door, The
Place Pigalle
Ponti Seafood Grill
Prima Bistro
Quattro on Fourth
Queen City Grill
RainCoast Café
Red Hills Provincial
Dining

RimRock Café
River Run Cottages
Roche Harbor Resort
Rogue River Lodge
Rosario's Mansion Dining
Room
Rover's
Sanctuary, The
Sandy Salmon Bed and
Breakfast Lodge
Saratoga Inn
Scanlon's
Selah Inn Bed &
Breakfast
Semiahmoo Resort
Silver Bay Resort Inn
Silver Grille Café &
Wines
Sixth Street Bistro & Loft
Sky Valley Inn Bed &
Breakfast
SkyCity at the Needle
Solstice Spa and Suites
Sorrento Hotel
Star Bar
Steps Wine Bar & Cafe
Stormking Spa at Mt.
Rainier
Stumbling Goat Bistro
Sybaris
Tauca Lea Resort & Spa
Theo's
Three Rivers
Timberline Lodge
Tinhorn Creek Vineyards
Toro Bravo
Touvelle House
Trattoria di Umberto
Trumpeter Inn Bed &
Breakfast
Turtleback Farm Inn
28
Va Piano Vineyards
Veil
Veritable Quandary
Villa Columbia
Vineyard Suite

Walla Walla Inns &
Vineyard Suite
Waterfront Wines
Westin Resort and Spa,
The
Whitehouse-Crawford
Restaurant
Wild Abandon Restaurant
and the Red Velvet
Lounge
Wild Ginger
Wild Iris Inn, The
Willows Inn, The
Winchester Inn
Winchester Inn
Restaurant
Wolf Creek Bar and Grill
Woodmark Hotel
Yummy Wine Bar &
Bistro

Abbey Road Farm
Abruzzo Italian Grill
Adara Whistler Hotel
Anthony's Homeport
Artists Studio Loft Bed
and Breakfast
Astoria Inn Bed and
Breakfast
Autumn Leaves Bed and
Breakfast
Backdoor Kitchen
Barking Frog
Beàto
Bella Italia
Big Red Barn
Bistro
Bleu Bistro
Blue Fjord Cabins
Blue Heron Inn, The
Blue Moon Beach House
Blue Plum Inn
Blue Spruce Bed &
Breakfast

Bonair Winery &
Vineyards
Bonniebrook Lodge
Bookwalter Winery
Brian's Pourhouse
Brimar Bed & Breakfast
Brookside Inn
Café Campagne
Cafe Nola
Caramba!
C'est La Vie Inn
C'est Si Bon
Chambered Nautilus Bed
and Breakfast Inn
Cherrywood Bed,
Breakfast, and Barn
Ciao-Thyme Bistro
Clementine's Bed and
Breakfast
Coolidge House
Cranberry Ridge Cottages
Suites
Cuvée Restaurant
Daphne's Restaurant
Dunham Cellars
Durlacher Hof Alpine
Country Inn
Eagle Harbor Inn, The
Eagle Rock Lodge
Eagle's View Bed and
Breakfast
Edgewater, The
Edwin K Bed and
Breakfast, The
Elan Guest Suites
Elements San Juan Islands
Hotel and Spa
11th Avenue Inn
English Bay Inn
Erath Vineyards
Excelsior Inn Ristorante
Italiano
Fairhaven Village Inn
Flery Manor Bed &
Breakfast
42nd Street Café, The
Fuse Waterfront Grill

Garden Path Suites
Gogi's Restaurant
Gray Monk Estate
Winery
Hanson Country Inn
Harrison House Suites
Heron and Beaver Pub,
The
Hill House Bed and
Breakfast
Hillside House Bed and
Breakfast
Hotel Max
Hotel Pension Anna
Il Giardino Cucina
Italiana
Il Piatto
Il Terrazzo Carmine
Inn at Blackberry Creek
Inn at Manzanita, The
Inn at Ship Bay
Island Tyme Bed and
Breakfast
JP's
Kiona Vineyards &
Winery
La Rambla
Lake Crescent Lodge
Lark
Lion and the Rose
Victorian Bed &
Breakfast
Lions Gate Inn Bed and
Breakfast
Lonesome Cove Resort
MacKaye Harbor Inn
Mattey House
Merenda
Monk's Grill
MorMor Bistro & Bar
Mosier House Bed and
Breakfast
Mountain Meadows Inn
Bed and Breakfast
Naramata Heritage Inn
& Spa

Old Consulate Inn—
F. W. Hastings House
Old Parkdale Inn
Oliver's Twist
Otter's Pond Bed and
Breakfast of Orcas
Island
Over the Moon Café
Peerless Restaurant, The
Purple Café and Wine Bar
Red Agave
Rosario Resort & Spa
Rose River Inn Bed &
Breakfast
Rosebriar Hotel
Saffron Mediterranean
Kitchen
Saffron Salmons
Salisbury House
Schmidt Family Vineyards
SOBO
Sostanza Trattoria
Stonehedge Gardens
Sunshine Coast Resort
Hotel & Marina
Tagaris Winery and
Taverna
Three Rivers Winery
Tina's Restaurant
Trattoria Giuseppe
Trellis
Tucker House
Volterra
W Seattle Hotel
Weasku Inn
West Coast Wilderness
Lodge
Wild Fennel
Wine Country Farm

Alder Wood Bistro
Alexander's Restaurant
Arrowleaf Bistro
Ashland Springs Hotel
Baked Alaska

Bay Cottage
Betty Macdonald Farm
Bistro Maison
Café Lucky Noodle
Café Soriah
Campbell's Resort
Castle Key Restaurant
and Lounge
Cedar Creek
Chevy Chase Beach
Cabins
Chez Gaudy
CRS Winery and Bistro
Fathoms Restaurant &
Bar
Gasperetti's Restaurant
Gunderson's Cannery
Café
Harrison House Bed &
Breakfast
Iovino's
Iris Hill Winery
J. James Restaurant
Kalaloch Lodge
La Conner Channel
Lodge
Lake Quinault Lodge
Lanza's Ristorante
Le Bistro
Lighthouse Bed and
Breakfast
Matt's in the Market
Mazama Country Inn

McKeown's and French
Hen Wine & Cheese Co.
Milano's Restaurant and
Deli
New Sammy's Cowboy
Bistro
Orcas Hotel
Pan Pacific Hotel
Paradise Cove Guest
House
Portofino
Quimby's
Red Rooster Winery
Rendezvous Grill and Tap
Room, The
Rex Hill Vineyards
Rhododendron Café
River's Edge Resort
Ruby Lake Italian
Trattoria
Saturna Lodge
Sea Star Restaurant and
Raw Bar
Spinner's Seafood, Steak
& Chop House
Steamboat Inn
Toga's
Torii Mor Winery
Valley View Winery
Village Market & Deli
Vita's Wildly Delicious
Water Street Inn
Wild Rose Bistro
Yarrow Bay Grill

Alexander's Country Inn
Café Melange
Fins Coastal Cuisine
Fountain Café
Holly Hill House
Lake Quinault Lodge
Lake Quinault Resort
National Park Inn at
Longmire
Place Bar & Grill, The
Resort at the Mountain,
The
River's Edge
Roseanna's Cafe
Union Creek Resort

Bilbo's Festivo
BJ's Garden Gate
Cafe Olga
Miller Tree Inn
Visconti's Ristorante
Italiano

UNRATED

Christina's
DB Bistro

The Best Places to Kiss in the Northwest Report Form

Based on my personal experience, I wish to nominate the following restaurant, place of lodging, shop, nightclub, sight, or other as a "Best Place"; or confirm/correct/disagree with the current review.

_____

_____

_____

(Please include address and telephone number of establishment, if convenient.)

REPORT

Please describe food, service, style, comfort, value, date of visit, and other aspects of your experience; continue on another piece of paper if necessary.

_____

_____

_____

_____

_____

_____

_____

_____

_____

_____

_____

I am not associated, directly or indirectly, with the management or ownership of this establishment.

SIGNED _____

ADDRESS _____

_____

_____

PHONE _____ **DATE** _____

Please address to _The Best Places to Kiss in the Northwest_ and send to:
SASQUATCH BOOKS
119 SOUTH MAIN STREET, SUITE 400
SEATTLE, WA 98104
Feel free to email feedback as well: **BPFEEDBACK@SASQUATCHBOOKS.COM**